ANCIENT GREEK ALIVE

THIRD EDITION

ANCIENT GREEK ALIVE

PAULA SAFFIRE AND CATHERINE FREIS

THE UNIVERSITY OF NORTH CAROLINA PRESS

CHAPEL HILL AND LONDON

Second revised edition copyright © 1992 by Paula Reiner.

Published by The Aldine Press, Ltd.

The paper in this book meets the guidelines for permanence and durability
of the Committee on Production Guidelines for Book Longevity of the
Council on Library Resources.

Library of Congress Cataloging-in-Publication Data

Saffire, Paula, 1943– Ancient Greek alive / Paula Saffire and Catherine Freis.
—3rd ed.   p. cm.   Includes index.   ISBN 978-0-8078-4800-5 (pbk.: alk. paper)
1. Greek language—Grammar—Problems, exercises, etc.
2. Greek language—Readers.   I. Freis, Catherine.   II. Title.
PA258.S2 1999   488.2´421—DC21—98-46276 CIP
11 10 09 08   7 6 5 4

THIS BOOK IS DEDICATED TO
GOOD STORYTELLERS EVERYWHERE.

CONTENTS

Sections (Cultural Essays in Bold; Organizational Chapters in Capitals)		Readings (Story Titles in Italics; Boldface indicates Greek Original)

Sections
(Cultural Essays in Bold;
  Organizational Chapters in Capitals)
		Readings
		(Story Titles in Italics;
		  Boldface indicates Greek Original)

Sections (Cultural Essays in Bold; Organizational Chapters in Capitals)		Readings (Story Titles in Italics; Boldface indicates Greek Original)

xii

Sections (Cultural Essays in Bold; Organizational Chapters in Capitals)		Readings (Story Titles in Italics; Boldface indicates Greek Original)

ACKNOWLEDGEMENTS xiii

Manuscripts with Sheikh Nasrudin stories go back to the thirteenth century C.E. For a good selection of Sheikh Nasrudin stories, the reader may consult especially *Tales of the Hodja* by Charles Downing or "The Subtleties of Mullah Nasrudin" in *The Sufis* by Idries Shah. Nasrudin stories belong to an oral tradition that is alive, constantly being revised and enlarged. Many collections of Nasrudin stories are available in Turkey today.

For permission to use "The Helping Hand" (originally "The Tax Collector"), taken from *The Subtleties of the Inimitable Mulla Nasrudin*, I thank Idries Shah.

For other stories, I thank the following storytellers and publishers:

Chinua Achebe, author of *Things Fall Apart*, copyright © 1957, from which "Mosquito's Buzz" and "Turtlewings" were adapted; used with permission of William Heinemann, Ltd.

Kwadwo Anokwa, author of "Who is Poor?," copyright © 1992; used with permission of the author.

Harold Courlander with Ezekiel A. Eshugbayi, *Olode the Hunter*, copyright © 1968, from which "Never Enough" (originally "Ijapa Cries for His Horse") and "The Oath" (originally "Ijapa and Yanrinbo Swear an Oath") were adapted; used with permission of the author.

Mirra Ginsburg, translator and editor of *The Kaha Bird: Tales from the Steppes of Central Asia*, copyright © 1971, from which "An Old Man's Advice" (originally "The Golden Bowl") was adapted; used with permission of the author.

Blanche Serwer, *Let's Steal the Moon*; illustrated by Trina Schart Hyman, text copyright © 1970 by Blanche L. Serwer, illustrations copyright © 1970 by Trina Schart Hyman, from which "Did the Tailor Have a Nightmare?" was adapted; used with permission of Little, Brown, and Company.

Virginia Tashjian, *Three Apples Fell from Heaven*, copyright © 1971, from which "The Gift of Gold" and "The Lazy Man" were adapted; used with permission of the author.

Vicki Kondelik, former Greek student, author of "Your Handwriting Is Bad," written in 1990; used with permission of the author.

Some stories are told without the citation of an author. Either these stories are known worldwide ("The Blind Men and the Elephant" and Nasrudin stories) or I was unable to track down the author ("Who is Wiser?" and "How to Weigh an Elephant").

For the text of Δέδυκε μὲν ἀ σελάννα, see "Δέδυκε μὲν ἀ σελάννα: The Pleiades in Mid-Heaven," by Paula Reiner and David Kovacs, *Mnemosyne* (1993).

For the excerpt from Sophocles' *Oedipus Tyrannos*, the following notice is required: Excerpt from "Oedipus Rex" from SOPHOCLES: THE OEDIPUS CYCLE, AN ENGLISH VERSION by Dudley Fitts and Robert Fitzgerald, copyright © 1949 by Harcourt Brace & Company and renewed 1977 by Cornelia Fitts and Robert Fitzgerald, reprinted by permission of the publisher. CAUTION: All rights, including professional, amateur, motion picture, recitation, lecturing, public reading, radio broadcasting, and television are strictly reserved. Inquiries on all rights should be addressed to Harcourt Brace & Company, Paralegal Group, 6th Floor, 6277 Sea Harbor Drive, Orlando, FL. 32821.

I salute the labor and learning that went into Smyth's *Greek Grammar* and Watkins's dictionary of Indo-European roots in back of the *American Heritage Dictionary* (1971); they were my constant companions as I prepared this book.

Heartfelt thanks go to my parents, Sylvia and Joseph Grossman, for starting me on the road to competence, and to Jean Pearson Schoales for teaching me ancient Greek.

Paula Saffire

Figure 1. Scene from an Athenian school, with pupils receiving instruction in music, writing, and poetry. Line drawing of half of a fifth century Attic kylix by Duris.

SOME WORDS TO STUDENTS

This book was inspired by an experience I had in my eighth month of graduate school: I "clicked in." For the first time in my life reading Greek seemed natural: I did it without the sense of mentally decoding. Of course I still needed to look up words and struggle over hard sentences. But there were some sentences I could read automatically, as I read in my own language.

The reason this happened was that I was reading Greek, happily, about eight hours a day, because of Harvard's most powerful teaching tool, the Reading List. (Read all of Aeschylus, all of Sophocles, all of Homer, seven by Euripides, and so on.) I had begun taking Greek because I fell in love with Plato and wanted to read him in the original, but in the end I fell in love with almost everything I read in ancient Greek.

Years later I began teaching Greek myself. I taught with sentences and paradigms, the way I had been taught by the most inspiring teacher of my life, Jean Pearson Schoales. But soon I decided I wanted to give my students more of a sense of ease, the sort of ease I had when I "clicked in." How? The only way was to provide lots of easy Greek. My aim was that there should be a sense of naturalness, that students would be relaxed reading ancient Greek, and feel more as if they were sitting down with a letter from a friend than taking a math exam.

Since there was almost nothing easy in original ancient Greek, readings would have to be made up. What should I use? Being a purist I was unwilling to water down or otherwise distort Greek material. I admired the Greek texts for their beauty and vigor, and did not want to tamper in the least. What then? I went to the children's library--my children were young then and I was reading stories aloud to them--and ransacked the shelves, picking out any stories I thought were funny, intriguing, or both. These I translated into ancient Greek.

At the time I picked the Sheikh Nasrudin stories because I thought they were intensely amusing-- as I hope you will. Only later, hearing a talk by a meditation teacher from India telling stories for enlightenment, did I realize that Sheikh Nasrudin was a Sufi teaching figure! As for the other stories, they are at least interesting. I hope you will be propelled forward as you read, wanting to know more, as I still am when revising.

So much for explanation. All that is left is my good wish: May you learn with joy.
This was my purpose in writing the book.

Paula Saffire
Butler University, 1999

Figure 1. Scene from an Athenian school, with pupils receiving instruction in music, reading, and poetry. Line drawing of half of a fifth century Attic kylix by Duris.

SOME WORDS TO TEACHERS

Ancient Greek Alive has been used since 1972. It offers you, as a teacher, a textbook that is a great student favorite and fun to teach, imparting a solid and thorough mastery of introductory Greek.

The book approaches the learning of Greek traditionally. Students are expected to master and generate paradigms, explicate grammar and syntax, and translate from Greek to English and (occasionally) from English to Greek.

At the same time the book has some unusual features that enhance student learning. In particular, it assumes that you are willing to use ancient Greek conversation for the first two weeks of class. This will take some boldness on your part, which will be amply rewarded by student enthusiasm.

We present below the features of the book. We would be glad to talk to you (or write or e-mail) should you wish further discussion.

Hearing and Speaking

Students find the conversational method the most natural and least intimidating way to begin ancient Greek, and they always remember what they learned through speaking. You may wish to continue with conversation beyond the first nine classes (although, except for occasional moments, we do not). Our students always regret when we drop conversation, and far into the second semester they tell us they wish we were still speaking Greek.

In the first nine days of the course students learn ancient Greek through conversation, a story, a poem that they memorize, and a skit that they read and perform many times.

Having students converse first and then read what they have already heard (and possibly spoken) allows them to work on the skill of converting sign to sound without at the same time figuring out new meanings. Sudents are reassured by their first readings and become confident and competent at reading Greek aloud.

The oral approach allows students to learn a large vocabulary in a short time without strain. This means they can be reading passages of some complexity early in the course without the burden of copious glosses.

Most importantly, the dialogues of the unit introduce students to material that will be covered more systematically in the rest of the year: gender, case, declension, mood, tense, aspect, -ω verbs, contract verbs, -μι verbs, and deponents, as well as accents, enclitics, and even meter. Because students have already encountered these features of Greek in speaking and reading, they are well prepared to learn them systematically during the remainder of the course.

Some student comments:

> *Everything I learned by speaking I remember.*

> *It's a wonderful technique, to learn so much in the first two weeks and then spend the rest of the time discovering all the things you already sort-of know. It was very scary, coming in every day and having to pay such close attention and learning with our ears. I'm not an auditory person, and I felt panicked, but it was worth it in the end. It made everything that was to come later seem less threatening and overwhelming.*

> *It's comforting to see that nothing will sneak up on you. When approaching a new chapter you can honestly say that you've seen the material, even if only in one word.*

Scripts for classroom conversation are provided. They give a "skeleton" for conversation and make it easy for teachers who have never attempted to "speak" Greek to do so; the format and the responses are already written. As you become more comfortable, you may wish to expand upon the scripts. (For a sample of expansion, see "Embroidery in Conversation," pp. 269-271.)

We recommend that you write transliterations as necessary on the board from the first day on, using any system that suits you. On the third day you will teach the alphabet and can begin writing in Greek script.

Some students find auditory learning difficult. They need to be told that they are acquiring important skills and that the work of the course will soon be primarily visual. If you are inclined to make tapes of the scripts, students enjoy practicing with them.

It is possible to use *Ancient Greek Alive* without conversation by teaching the alphabet first and then reading all scripts with your students. But we hope that you will try the method we have outlined above. Although neither of us was taught Greek in this fashion, we both find it easy and worth doing because of the high level of student enthusiasm and learning.

Grammar and Syntax

Once students complete the first conversational section, the lessons that follow present the forms and concepts of classical Greek. The presentation is meant to be clear, logical, subtle, and thorough.

The book falls into two nearly equal parts. The first part teaches all important noun, pronoun and adjective systems, ending with a comprehensive review chapter. Students have a sense of closure and mastery that sets them up well for the rest of the course.

The second part presents the Greek verb system. It has been said that the structure of the Greek verb is a great achievement of intellectual order, like the *Divine Comedy* or Newton's *Principia*. This book makes great effort to insure that students grasp that structure. As each new piece of the paradigm is given, it is shown embedded in the system of what has already been learned. In this way old material is constantly being reviewed as new material is learned. You can see how intensely systematic the verb presentation is by glancing at the format of the verb chapters and the schemata (pp. 154, 166, 173, and 200).

From the very beginning (even in the oral introduction) attention is paid to verb aspect versus tense. That attention is never dropped. Only after students are fully comfortable with the ⁻ω verb do they go on to learn the full pattern of contract and ⁻μι verbs in a systematic way. Because their control of the ⁻ω verb is secure, they can more easily absorb what differs.

Exercises

Contained within each chapter are short exercises that immediately follow the presentation of new materials. These lead students to learn by small, ordered steps, mastering one bit of information before they go on to the next. A chapter will typically introduce new forms, give a short exercise on the forms, provide further information, and then give an exercise that asks them to use that information, focusing on features that are likely to be problematic.

Exercises are supplied for every new item. These may be done during class or assigned for homework. We have included more than you might want to use so that you can choose according to your preference.

Stories

Ancient Greek Alive has an abundance of stories composed in ancient Greek for the sake of teaching Greek grammar. (As far as we know, it was the first ancient Greek textbook in the United States to use this method, in 1972 as *Beginning Ancient Greek* by Paula Reiner.) The search for stories, drawn from world folklore traditions, was described in "Words to Students." Stories were selected for their charm, interest, and humor. The result is a set of stories that students love, remember, and even retell to their children. This is because the stories have dramatic shape and are complete as small units, drawing the students to work eagerly through them. Their folkloric form allows a natural repetition, which helps students learn even difficult vocabulary and constructions. Students sometimes laugh out loud in class at a story.

The stories are easy in the beginning. As time goes on they become harder, but gradually, so that students are never overwhelmed. The last three stories (spread over many chapters) are quite challenging. In fact, when students finally come to lengthy passages in the original Greek, they are relieved to find that the first, the Hippocratic Oath, is syntactically easier than these stories. They are ready to make the transition to the Greek authors.

The Thesauros

Ancient Greek Alive contains copious short passages of original Greek. These are found in the Thesauros or "Treasure House," a section of the book which has selections from the New Testament, Heraclitus, Xenophanes, Diogenes, various sayings by the famous and not-so-famous, and a group of lively Greek epitaphs and thoughts about death. Almost every chapter has some reading from the Thesauros for inspiration and a change of pace.

The Thesauros readings have been gathered in a separate section of the book to allow for elasticity in timing. You may do them in the order indicated, or you might skip some readings and catch up later, as time allows. Bold print indicates the relevant grammatical points. Students will need your help in doing the Thesauros readings. Hearing the words "Open your Thesauros" should be a happy occasion for you and your students, which means you should not test on Thesauros passages. (And most will be too difficult to assign for homework.)

Vocabulary

Students acquire a substantial vocabulary--over 600 words. The conversational opening of the course primes them to pick up Greek vocabulary with greater ease than other methods. And they encounter familiar words over and over again in the stories.

Vocabulary is introduced in the reading passages so that students read a word before learning it, rather than the other way around. Thus students are learning the method they will be using in their subsequent reading courses.

To help students master the vocabulary and to underline the importance of this work, there are major vocabulary reviews that organize all new words by category.

Memorization of Poems

Students are asked to memorize sections of poems from the lyric poets. These highlight important grammatical items. The Anacreontic "It is difficult to love." introduces them to articular infinitives. After learning the opening of Sappho 31, they find οἱ μέν, οἱ δέ clauses natural. We ourselves still remember all the poetry we learned in first-year Greek. And students have told us that it is wonderful to be able to recite and discuss these poems if someone should ask them why they are learning Greek. (All the poetry can be found at a glance on p. 168.)

Cultural Essays

Short essays, all keyed to something the students have read, are found at intervals throughout the book. They are not meant to provide a full overview of Greek culture, but rather they present a series of openings to engage students with some important ideas and to draw them into further Greek studies. Some themes are Greek medicine, lyric poetry, the pre-Socratic philosophers of Ionia, a comparison of Nasrudin and Socrates, and Greek turtle tales. By the end of the year students who have worked through the essays, along with the map and chronological outline, will have some sense of the flow of Greek culture from the Bronze to the Hellenistic Age.

Terminology and Method

The book attempts to present material in accordance with the way that students learn best. That is why, in a book with fifty-four lessons, we have also included ten organizational chapters including four vocabulary reviews and two verb overviews. We know that only by consolidating information at intervals do students truly learn a language.

Throughout the textbook, we are willing to change customary teaching patterns if students will learn better. For example, we teach uncontracted forms first because our experience is that contracting makes better sense to students when they are acquainted with uncontracted forms. Similarly, the declension order is nominative followed by accusative because nominative and accusative forms are often the same or similar and it is easier for students to learn them if they see them together.

The following is a list of some of the principles of our approach.

Anticipate the system. Grammatical concepts and forms should be used if possible *before they are introduced systematically*. This is the key behind the oral introduction. For instance, students can remember that -ως makes an adverb far better by using ἀληθῶς repeatedly before they actually learn how to form adverbs. Students "experience," as it were, the new form, so that systematically learning it later is much easier. This principle is deliberately applied throughout the book. For example, ἔθηκε will be given as an isolated vocabulary item in a story before it is embedded in a system. Or the concept of the indirect question will be given for a single term (πότερον versus ὁπότερον) before it is applied to a whole chart's worth of words.

Be gradual and repeat important information. Difficult concepts and systems are introduced gradually. For instance, αὐτόν is introduced first as a pronoun. In later chapters, the pronoun use is reintroduced and αὐτός as *same* is added. In a still later chapter, the emphatic use of αὐτός as *himself* is presented. At this time, and again in the vocabulary for a story, and yet again later in a vocabulary review, students are reminded of the three uses of αὐτός.

Encourage punting. We encourage students to practice making educated guesses. Throughout the textbook students are asked to "punt," that is to guess at something unknown based on patterns that they have already encountered. Thus, students are constantly being prepared for the work of second-year Greek.

Make use of translationese. We feel it is more important for first-year students to try to convey the structure of the Greek than to translate into graceful English. We have developed an artificial language called "translationese." Students are asked, for example, to translate ὅδε as "this here" versus οὗτος as "this." They are asked to differentiate aspect, to use "was Xing" or "used to X" for the imperfect indicative and "X'd" for the aorist.

The point of translationese is twofold: (1) it demands that students be precise and (2) it enables students to telegraph their recognition of verb forms. It is far faster and more pleasant to say "*I will have X'd my*" than to say "future perfect middle, first person singular." We believe that this is an important tool for helping students truly get a "feel" for ancient Greek. Rather than being hampered by this demand for precision, students enjoy it. They "get" the idea that language is not a one-to-one substitution of vocabulary items but a different way of perceiving the world.

Use self-evident terminology. Important grammatical terms are taught. But we try to stay away from terms which are not self-evident. For example, we speak of the "*next-to-last*" syllable and not the *penultima*, the "*if-clause*" and not the *protasis*. We always give the traditional term so students will not be at a loss if they encounter these terms later.

Timing and the Final Readings

The book takes about two semesters to complete, with judicious cuts. If there is not time to complete the last four lessons (in which the irregular -μι verbs are given, along with some original Greek selections), students will end the year knowing the regular verb paradigm as well as the forms of δείκνυμι. They can pick up the other -μι forms the following year.

The readings for the final lessons are in the original Greek, for you to use if you wish. We chose the Hippocratic Oath because it provokes a host of interesting questions about medicine and ethics. We chose Hecuba's lament from Euripides' *Trojan Women* because students are intrigued by its contemporary relevance. We end with Sophocles' dialogue between Oedipus and Teiresias because no translation conveys its pith and speed--something which students will realize even after a single year of Greek.

Contributions

This new edition has been thoroughly revised, with the following additions: copious exercises throughout the chapters; a chapter and multiple assignments on parsing; a graduated series of schemata on the Greek verb; two major review chapters; and cultural essays, which help students to incorporate the readings and the study of Greek into a broader perspective.

In this edition of *Ancient Greek Alive* Catherine Freis composed the cultural essays and most of the exercises, while Paula Saffire wrote the lessons, composed the stories, and collected the readings in the Thesauros.

A number of people have helped to make the book what it is today:

> Joel Farber gave many useful suggestions for the 1991 edition.
> Tim Long gave encouragement and corrections for the current edition.
> Lew Bateman welcomed it at the University of North Carolina Press.
> Pam Upton of the University of North Carolina Press helped shape its format.

The new edition has been greatly improved by David Kovacs, who, with his eagle eye, detected errors great and small.

We hope you, too, will help improve the book by sending corrections and suggestions.

Finally, we can never thank our students enough, for their patience, zest, and good cheer.

At Butler University special thanks go to: Bert Steiner, for helpful advice and consenting to have his office occupied (invaded is more like it) by Paula Saffire; to David Waite for the map and other drawings; to all the people who helped with computer problems; and to first-year students Alison Beard, Bobbi Jo Goss, and Spike Wilson, who suffered through the revision process, sometimes trying out three versions of the same chapter.

At Millsaps College special thanks go to: Janice Holman and Richard Freis, as well as Winston Barham, Tom Summerford, and Ashley Sulser.

Dedication

We confess: we have tried to write a book with charm. We did this out of love for the great Greek authors. We lay this book on their collective lap. We hope they smile, finding it a key worthy to unlock their texts.

And to you, too, we offer this book. We hope that it will increase the ease and enhance the joy of your teaching.

Paula Saffire, Butler University, 1999
Catherine Freis, Millsaps College, 1999

CHRONOLOGY OF AUTHORS AND EVENTS

Bronze Age Greece
2000-1400	Bronze Age Minoan civilization on Crete
1500-1200	Bronze Age Mycenaean civilization

Iron Age Greece
1200-800	Gradual rebuilding after the collapse of Mycenae

Archaic Greece
800-700	Homeric epic poems, the *Iliad* and the *Odyssey*, composed Alphabet introduced Olympic games instituted (786) Geometric pottery
700-600	Rise of lyric poetry: Archilochus, Sappho, Alcaeus, Mimnermus Solon, Athenian statesman and poet Xenophanes, Ionian philosopher Corinthian Pottery; Archaic Sculpture
600-500	Aesop, *Fables* Anacreon and Anacreontic poetry Heraclitus, Ionian philosopher

Classical Greece
500-400	Democracy in Athens Persian Wars (490 and 480): Greece repels Persia Parthenon begun (447) Pelopponesian Wars (431-404): Sparta defeats Athens Aeschylus (ca. 524-456), tragedian Sophocles (ca. 496-406), tragedian Euripides (ca. 485-406), tragedian Aristophanes (ca. 447-386), comedian Socrates (469-399), philosopher Sophists: Gorgias, Protagoras Hippocrates, (ca. 469-399), physician Herodotus, (ca. 484-425), historian Thucydides, (ca. 460-400), historian
400-323	Plato (ca. 439-347), philosopher Diogenes (ca. 400-325), Cynic philosopher Aristotle (ca. 384-322), philosopher Phillip of Macedon (ca. 382-336) Alexander the Great of Macedon (356-323)

Hellenistic Greece
0-100 C. E.	New Testament written

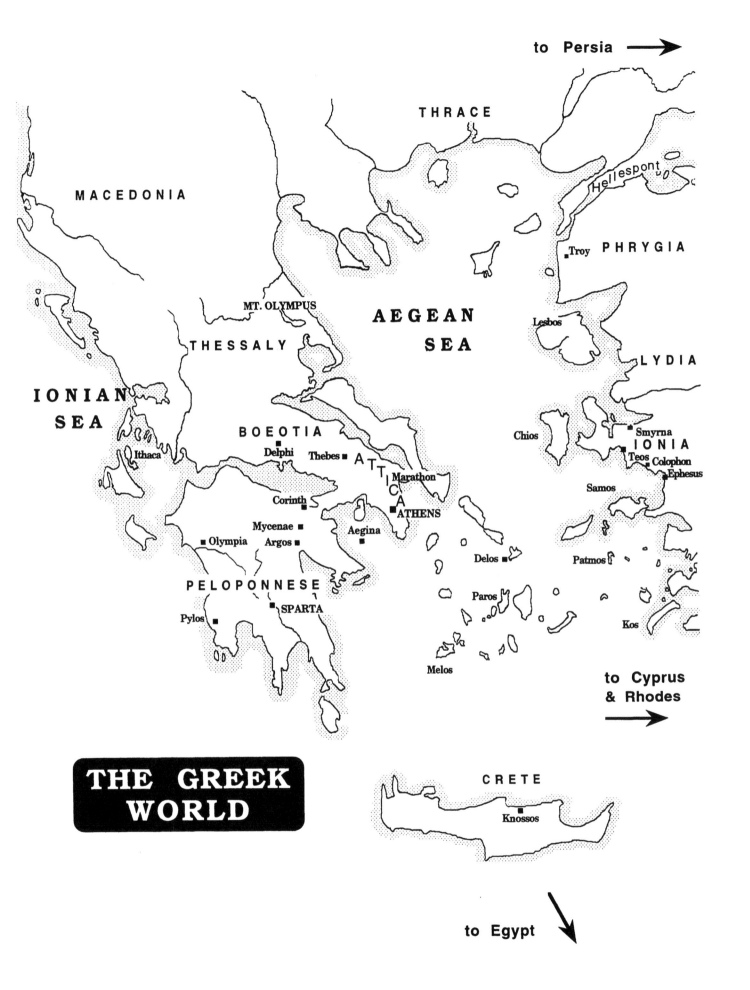

to Persia →

THRACE

Hellespont

MACEDONIA

Troy PHRYGIA

MT. OLYMPUS

AEGEAN
SEA

Lesbos

THESSALY

LYDIA

IONIAN
SEA

BOEOTIA

Chios

Smyrna

Ithaca

Delphi

Thebes A T T I C A
Marathon

Corinth

Aegina

ATHENS

Samos

Teos Colophon
Ephesus

Mycenae

Olympia Argos

Delos

Patmos

PELOPONNESE

Paros

Kos

Pylos

SPARTA

Melos

to Cyprus
& Rhodes
→

THE GREEK
WORLD

CRETE

Knossos

to Egypt ↓

--χαίρετε, ὦ φίλοι

--χαῖρε, ὦ φίλε

--χαῖρε, ὦ φίλη

--χαίρετε, ὦ φίλοι.
--χαῖρε, ὦ φίλε. χαῖρε, ὦ φίλη.

--γιγνώσκομεν ἀλλήλους;

   ⟨πάντες ἅμα⟩ *all together*
   ⟨αὖθις⟩ *again*

--οὐ γιγνώσκομεν ἀλλήλους.
--γιγνώσκωμεν ἀλλήλους.

> γιγνώσκομεν
> γιγνώσκωμεν

Endings are important. Listen for them.

--τὸ ὄνομά μου ---- ἐστιν.
--τί ἐστι τὸ ὄνομά σου; λέγε μοι· τί ἐστι τὸ ὄνομά σου;

   ⟨εὖγε⟩ *good! well done!*

--τί ἐστι τὸ ὄνομα αὐτοῦ; λέγε μοι.
--τί ἐστι τὸ ὄνομα αὐτῆς; λέγε μοι. λέγε ἡμῖν.

--οἶσθα;
--οὐκ οἶδα.

> οὐ γιγνώσκομεν
> οὐκ οἶδα

--ἐρώταε· "ὦ φίλε, τί ἐστι τὸ ὄνομά σου;"

This is a day for getting acquainted. By asking and answering in Greek, learn the names of your partners in this enterprise of learning ancient Greek.

The ancient Greek you are learning is called Attic Greek. It is the Greek that would have been spoken in Athens in the fifth century B.C.

Homework: Meet or telephone a classmate and have a conversation in ancient Greek, or teach someone who does not know Greek what you learned today.

*To teachers: See Words to Teachers on the use of scripts, particularly on the importance of transliterating Greek sounds during the first few classes. Students are not expected to read scripts beforehand, though they will read them after class starting on the fourth day. Boxes contain important information for rapid review. Usually you will use a script a day. Exception: the lesson on the Greek alphabet may take two days.

--γιγνώσκω σε. (To another student) καὶ γιγνώσκω σε. (To another) καὶ
γιγνώσκω σε. ὦ φίλε, γιγνώσκεις με; --Ah (with a sigh to the class),
ὁ --- γιγνώσκει με. --καὶ σύ, ὦ φίλη, γιγνώσκεις με; --Ah, ἡ ---
γιγνώσκει με.

--ὁράω σε. (To another student) καὶ ὁράω σε. (To another) καὶ ὁράω σε.
ὁράεις με; --Ah, (to class) ὁ --- ὁράει με. --καὶ σύ, ὁράεις με; --Ah (to
class) ἡ --- ὁράει με.

--καὶ σύ, ὁράεις αὐτόν; ὁράεις αὐτήν; λέγε μοι· ὁράεις αὐτήν;

--ὦ φίλη (drawing a turtle on the board), ὁράεις τὴν χελώνην; ὁράεις αὐτήν;
λέγε ἡμῖν. ὁράεις αὐτήν; καὶ γιγνώσκεις αὐτήν; λέγε ἡμῖν.

--ὦ φίλε, ὁράεις με; (Hiding face behind a paper) καὶ νῦν ὁράεις με; οὐχί.
νῦν οὐχ ὁράεις με.

--καὶ σύ, ὦ φίλη, ὁράεις τὴν χελώνην; καὶ σύ, ὦ φίλε, ὁράεις αὐτήν;
Ah, (to class) ἡ --- καὶ ὁ --- ὁράουσι τὴν χελώνην. ὁράουσιν αὐτήν.

--ὦ φίλε, γιγνώσκεις αὐτόν; τί ἐστι τὸ ὄνομα αὐτοῦ; --καὶ σύ,
γιγνώσκεις αὐτόν; καὶ ὁ --- καὶ ἡ --- γιγνώσκουσιν αὐτόν.

οὐ γιγνώσκω οὐκ οἶδα οὐχ ὁράω	γιγνώσκουσι τὴν χελώνην γιγνώσκουσιν αὐτήν	Α καὶ Β καὶ Α καὶ Β

--ὦ φίλε, ἔχω ὄνομα.   <Demonstrate ἔχω >
                         ἔχω γλῶτταν, ἔχω χεῖρα, ἔχω βιβλίον

--ἔχω ὄνομα. καὶ σύ, ἔχεις ὄνομα; τί ἐστι τὸ ὄνομά σου;
--τὸ ὄνομά μου --- ἐστιν. --τί ἐστι τὸ ὄνομά σου;

--καὶ ὁ --- ἔχει ὄνομα; νὴ τὸν Δία ἔχει ὄνομα. --καὶ ἡ --- ἔχει ὄνομα;
--νὴ τὴν κύνα ἔχει ὄνομα. --καὶ ἡ --- καὶ ὁ --- ἔχουσιν ὄνομα.

νὴ τὸν Δία	*by Zeus*
νὴ τὴν κύνα	*by the dog*

I	ἔχω	γιγνώσκω		ὁράω
You	ἔχεις	γιγνώσκεις		ὁράεις
He, she, it	ἔχει	γιγνώσκει		ὁράει
They	ἔχουσι(ν)	γιγνώσκουσι(ν)		ὁράουσι(ν)

Homework: Learn the three ways of negating: οὐ, οὐκ, οὐχ. How do you say these sentences in Greek?

I know the turtle.	You have the turtle.	(S)he sees the turtle.
I don't know the turtle.	You don't have the turtle.	They don't see the turtle.

--ὦ φίλη, ἐρώταε αὐτὸν ἐρώτημα. καὶ ἐρώταε αὐτὴν ἐρώτημα. ἄλλο ἐρώτημα. καὶ ἄλλο ἐρώτημα. (To class) πολλὰ ἐρωτήματα ἐρωτάει.

--ὦ φίλε, λέγε μοι τὸ ὄνομα αὐτῆς. καὶ λέγε μοι τὸ ὄνομα αὐτοῦ. καὶ ἄλλο ὄνομα. (To class) πολλὰ ὀνόματα λέγει.

ἐρώτημα ἐρωτήματα	ὄνομα ὀνόματα	Accent can't be further than 3 syllables back.

--ὦ φίλε (writing **α** on the board), ὁράεις τοῦτο; τί ἐστι τοῦτο; τοῦτο ἔστι γράμμα. καὶ τὸ γράμμα ἔχει ὄνομα; τί ὄνομα ἔχει τοῦτο τὸ γράμμα; ἔχει τὸ ὄνομα ἄλφα.

--καὶ ὁράεις (writing **β** on the board) τοῦτο τὸ γράμμα; τοῦτο ἔστιν ἄλλο γράμμα. τί ὄνομα ἔχει τοῦτο τὸ γράμμα; τοῦτο τὸ γράμμα ἔχει τὸ ὄνομα βῆτα.

γράμμα	*a letter*	τοῦτο	*this*
τὸ γράμμα	*the letter*	τοῦτο τὸ γράμμα	*this letter*

--καὶ τίς γιγνώσκει τοῦτο τὸ γράμμα; ⟨γ⟩ καὶ τίς γιγνώσκει τοῦτο τὸ γράμμα; ⟨δ⟩ (to class) πολλὰ γράμματα γιγνώσκει. ἀληθῶς (*truly*), πολλὰ γράμματα γιγνώσκει.

--ὦ φίλη, γιγνώσκεις πολλὰ γράμματα; ἀληθῶς γιγνώσκεις πάντα τὰ γράμματα; τίς γιγνώσκει πάντα τὰ γράμματα;

τίς	*who?*	πολλὰ γράμματα	*many letters*
τί	*what?*	πάντα γράμματα	*all letters*
		πάντα τὰ γράμματα	*all the letters*

--καὶ νῦν, ὦ φίλε (writing rest of alphabet), τί ποιέω; γράφω γράμματα. γράφω πολλὰ γράμματα. γράφω πάντα τὰ γράμματα.

ἐρωτάω ἐρώτημα	inner object
γράφω γράμμα	cf. *I sing a song*

--ἐγώ (pointing to self) ἐθέλω γράφειν τὰ γράμματα. --καὶ σύ, ὦ φίλη, ἐθέλεις γράφειν τὰ γράμματα; ἀληθῶς; ἀληθῶς ἐθέλεις γράφειν τὰ γράμματα; --καὶ σύ, ὦ φίλε, ἐθέλεις γράφειν τὰ γράμματα; πάντα τὰ γράμματα; εὖγε. γράφωμεν πάντα τὰ γράμματα.

γράφω τὰ γράμματα ἐθέλω γράφειν τὰ γράμματα

--καὶ νῦν λέγωμεν τὰ γράμματα. λέγωμεν πάντα τὰ γράμματα.

α β γ δ ε ζ η θ ι κ λ μ ν ξ ο π
ρ σ (ς) τ υ φ χ ψ ω   Note ' and '

Capitals: Α Β Γ Δ Ε Ζ Η Θ Ι Κ Λ Μ Ν Ξ Ο Π

Ρ Σ Τ Υ Φ Χ Ψ Ω

Names of the letters: *alpha, beta, gamma, delta, epsilon, zeta, eta, theta, iota, kappa, lambda, mu, nu, xi, omicron, pi, rho, sigma, tau, upsilon, phi, chi, psi, omega.*

Small letters were not used by the ancient Greeks. (They were developed by scribes in medieval times.) They are used because they are easier to read than capital letters. They are shown with lines so you can learn what part of a letter fills the central space and what goes above or below.

There is a letter digamma (ϝ) that dropped out of the Greek alphabet. It was pronounced "w" and, like *vav* of the Hebrew alphabet, was the sixth letter. We can tell that some words had a *w* sound, although the Greek names give no indication. For example, οἶνος was ϝοῖνος--*wine* in English. By the time the ϝ dropped out of the alphabet, the numbering system was already fixed. So that even after there was no longer a letter ϝ , that sign was used for #6, and ζ, although it was the 6th letter now, was used for # 7 and so on.

σ is given the special sign ς at the end of a word.

' indicates an *h* sound or "rough breathing" and ' indicates the lack of an *h* sound or "smooth breathing." (You can consider the marks as *h* and *non-h*.)

Originally both the *epsilon* sound and the *eta* sound were represented by ε, and η was used for the *h* sound--as you might guess by the capital letter (H). But at some point the Greeks decided to use the letter η for the *eta* sound and needed to indicate the *h* sound in another way. (It would be best if modern editors dispensed with the non-h sign altogether, as an eye-saving measure. After all, we depart in other ways from ancient Greek practice, when we have found improvements, printing Greek with small letters and a space between words. Future editors take note!)

Every word that begins with a single vowel, a diphthong (vowel combination pronounced as a single sound), or an ρ will have a rough or smooth breathing mark. The mark goes over the second vowel of a diphthong and does not affect alphabetical order.

ἐστι – is   οὐ – not   ῥόδος – rose

There are three marks indicating pitch:

(´) acute--pitch up
(^) circumflex--pitch up and back down
(`) grave--slight rise in pitch
(or no change at all, as some scholars believe)

If you look over the scripts you will find the rough or smooth breathing marks in combination with other marks showing pitch, which will be explained on p. 12. A breathing mark is written to the left of an acute (´) or grave (`) and under a circumflex (^).

λέγετε ἅμα τὸ ὄνομα ὃ οἶδα.   *Say all together the name which I know.*

	Name of Letter		Pronunciation
α	alpha	ἄλφα	*hot* (when short), *far* (held longer)
β	beta	βῆτα	*back*
γ	gamma	γάμμα	*go* (*going* before γ, κ, χ, ξ)
δ	delta	δέλτα	*dig*
ε	epsilon (literally *bare e*)	ἒ ψιλόν	*let*
ζ	zeta	ζῆτα	zd as in *wisdom* or dz as in *adze* (evidence goes both ways)
η	eta	ἦτα	*gate*
θ	theta	θῆτα	*thank* (or *at home*, see p. 6)
ι	iota	ἰῶτα	*big* (when short), *beet* (when long)
κ	kappa	κάππα	*skin*
λ	lambda	λάμβδα	*let*
μ	mu	μῦ	*met*
ν	nu	νῦ	*net*
ξ	xi	ξῖ	*axe*
ο	omicron (literally *little* o)	ὂ μικρόν	*potential* (not emphasized, but not a schwa)
π	pi	πῖ	*spy*
ρ	rho	ῥῶ	*ring* (or trilled)
σ, ς	sigma	σῖγμα	*sing*
τ	tau	ταῦ	*sting*
υ	upsilon (literally *bare u*)	ὖ ψιλόν	French *lune* (held short or long)
φ	phi	φῖ	*fill* (or *up hill*, see p. 6)
χ	chi	χῖ	Scottish *loch* (or *back home*, p. 6)
ψ	psi	ψῖ	*upset*
ω	o-mega (literally *big* o)	ὦ μέγα	*awe*

Vowels

Greek may be considered to have five basic vowel sounds, as English does. A vowel is long or short depending on the time it takes to pronounce it. Greek α, ι, and υ are used for both long and short sounds. Epsilon and omicron are always short (as their names indicate), while eta and omega are always long (as the name omega indicates). So there are short α, ε, ι, ο, υ and long α, η, ι, ω, υ.

There are varying schools of thought on how to pronounce these vowels. (The differences are mainly over the *eta* and *omega* sounds.) What matters for speaking is that all vowel sounds be distinct and that *eta* and *omega* be recognizably long.

▶ Exercise α: Read aloud:

1. σῶμα σῆμα. 2. νῦν γιγνώσκω τὸ ὄνομα. 3. πολλὰ ἐρωτήματα λέγω. 4. ἔχε βιβλίον.

Diphthongs

Diphthongs are vowels pronounced together. These important combinations may occur:

αι	aisle	ει	weigh, gate	οι	noise
αυ	sauerkraut	ευ	(slurred ε-υ)	ου	group
		ηυ	(slurred η-υ)		

▶ Exercise β: Read aloud:

1. οἱ φίλοι οὐ φιλοῦσι ταῦτα τὰ τραύματα.   4. χαίρεις, ὦ φίλε.
2. αἱ φίλαι οὐ φιλοῦσι ταῦτα τὰ τραύματα.   5. εὑρίσκει τοὺς παῖδας;
3. ὁ δεύτερος φίλος οὐ βούλεται λέγειν.   6. γιγνώσκουσιν ἀλλήλους.

Aspiration

In ancient Greek, as in Hindi (and Chinese) today, pairs of sounds could be distinguished according to whether or not there was breath "blown in" with them. These are the pairs:

unbreathed	breathed
κ	χ
π	φ
τ	θ

In English we normally give extra breath to initial t, p, k but not when they come after another consonant. Compare top and stop, pin and spin, Kate and skate. (Say these words with your hand in front of your mouth, or with a mirror. You will find a difference in breath.) In order to pronounce the Greek pairs as the Greeks did, we would have to add extra breath to every χ, φ, and θ and take away extra breath from every initial κ, π, and τ. This is too difficult for most English speakers, especially the taking away; and when done incorrectly it makes the Greek sounds hard to differentiate. Therefore, we choose to be faithful to the spirit rather than the letter, in recommending pronunciations that are clear and unambiguous (and related to modern Greek pronunciation) but not authentic: χ as in *loch*, φ as in *fill*, θ as in *thank*. The alternative is to pronounce the unaspirated member of the pair totally without breath and the aspirated member as in *back home*, *up hill*, or *at home*.

ἔργα
(homework)
~Learn the alphabet by heart.
~Write the alphabet in small letters 5 times, in capitals once.
~Write the following words in *alpha-bet*ical order:

ποίημα   ὄνομα   ξανθός   Ὠκεανός   θεός
χαῖρε   ὁράω   χαλεπόν   γιγνώσκω   ἀναγιγνώσκω

~Translate this sentence. Look words up in the dictionary at the back of the book.

πᾶς ξένος φέρει ἀργύριον.

GREEK WRITING AND LITERACY

Figure 1. A flute player, identified on this Corinthian (ca. 700 B.C.E.) vase as Polyterpos, accompanies a group of young dancers led by the leaping Pyrrhias. Courtesy of the American School of Classical Studies at Athens.

The Phoenicians with Cadmus brought arts and letters to the Greeks, since as I think the Greeks did not have them before but the Phoenicians were first to use them. With the passage of time they changed the form as well as the sound of the letters …rightly calling them Phoenician after those who had introduced them into Greece.
Herodotus v.58

The alphabet that you are now learning is one of the great inventions of human history. Modern scholars, as well as ancient sources, acknowledge that the Greek alphabet was adapted from the alphabet of an eastern Mediterranean people, the Phoenicians. Their alphabet, consisting of only twenty-two consonantal signs, was a sharp improvement over former systems of writing that represented syllables rather than individual sounds. Such systems, because of their multiplicity, required a professional class of scribes. The economy of the Phoenician alphabet, however, made reading and writing an easily mastered skill.

The Phoenician letters developed out of pictographs and represented objects whose initial sound gave the value of the letter. For instance, *aleph* means ox and *beth* means house in Hebrew, a Semitic language related to Phoenician. When the Greeks began to use the Phoenician alphabet, they kept many of the names, even though the names, such as *alpha* and *beta*, have no meaning in Greek.

The Greeks not only borrowed the Phoenician alphabet, they also improved it. The key Greek contribution was the use of letters to represent vowel sounds. Phoenician, like Hebrew, did not have letters for vowels (*aleph* in Semitic languages is not a vowel) but used a system of dots above and below their letters to indicate vowels. Thus, the Greek alphabet was the first alphabet to reproduce fully the sound of every spoken word.

This alphabet, the basis of our own (with slight modifications by the Romans), was not the first form of writing in Greece. Several different scripts have been found in Bronze Age Minoan and Mycenaean Greece and one, Linear B, has even been deciphered as an early form of Greek. But for about 400 years, after the collapse of the Mycenaean civilization in 1200 B.C.E., writing seems to have been forgotten.

Scholars are not sure when the Phoenician alphabet was first introduced into Greece or when the Greek adaptations were made, but by the mid-eighth century (about 740 B.C.E.) the Greek alphabet was in place. Eighth century Greece exploded with cultural energy: the powerful and intricate art of Geometric pottery, the epic poetry of the *Iliad* and the *Odyssey*, and the institution of the Olympic games all coincided with the introduction of the Greek alphabet.

At first, Greek writing was multidirectional and could be written top to bottom or bottom to top, or left to right or right to left. One such multidirectional form of writing in Greece is called *boustrophedon* ("as the ox plows"), when horizontal was left to right in one line and then turned, like an ox plowing a field, right to left in the next, continuing to turn direction with each new line. Figure 1 shows *boustrophedon* writing in vertical rather than horizontal turns. Sometimes, early Greek writing was entirely right to left, the direction that Phoenician and Hebrew letters eventually adopted. Soon, however, Greek writing became fixed with a horizontal script in a left to right direction.

The standardization of writing was followed by a widespread literacy that was encouraged by Greek city-states. Reading and writing were taught in schools and, from the evidence on a number of Greek vases, girls seem to have been literate (Figure 2). Schools were usually in private homes, gymnasia, hired halls, or the open air. Education, of course, consisted of more than writing and reading: mathematics, music (including dancing), and sports were also part of the curriculum.

Figure 2. A girl carrying her writing tablets and stylus pen is led, perhaps to school. Attic cup (ca. 460 B.C.E.), Metropolitan Museum of Art, Rogers Fund 1906. (06.1021.167)

--ὦ φίλη (writing **α** on the blackboard), τί ποιέω;   --γράφω γράμμα.
γιγνώσκεις τοῦτο τὸ γράμμα;   γιγνώσκεις τοῦτο;

--καὶ νῦν, ὦ φίλε, (writing alphabet) τί ποιέω;   --γράφω γράμματα.
γιγνώσκεις ταῦτα τὰ γράμματα;   γιγνώσκεις ταῦτα;

τὸ γράμμα	τοῦτο τὸ γράμμα	τοῦτο
τὰ γράμματα	ταῦτα τὰ γράμματα	ταῦτα

γράφω γράμματα μικρά. ὦ φίλη, γιγνώσκεις τὰ γράμματα
τὰ μικρά; λέγε ἡμῖν· γιγνώσκεις τὰ μικρὰ γράμματα;

--καὶ νῦν ἀναγιγνώσκω τὰ γράμματα. (Reading alpha, beta, etc.)
ἀναγιγνώσκω πάντα τὰ γράμματα τὰ μικρά. καὶ σύ, ὦ φίλε,
ἐθέλεις ἀναγιγνώσκειν τὰ γράμματα;

τὰ μικρὰ γράμματα	Both mean:	γιγνώσκω	*know*
τὰ γράμματα τὰ μικρά	*the small letters*	ἀναγιγνώσκω	*read*

--ἐγώ (pointing to self) ἐθέλω ἀναγιγνώσκειν τὰ γράμματα. καὶ σύ, ἐθέλεις
ἀναγιγνώσκειν τὰ γράμματα; ἀληθῶς ἐθέλεις ἀναγιγνώσκειν
τὰ γράμματα; εὖγε. ἀναγιγνώσκωμεν τὰ γράμματα. πάντες ἅμα.

--καὶ σύ, ὦ φίλη, ἔχεις γράφειν τὰ μικρὰ γράμματα; ἔχεις γράφειν
πάντα τὰ γράμματα τὰ μικρά; λέγε ἡμῖν.

ἔχω βιβλίον	*I have a book.*
ἔχω γράφειν	*I am able / have the ability to write.*

--καὶ σύ, ὦ φίλη, ἔχεις ἀναγιγνώσκειν ταῦτα τὰ γράμματα;
βούλεαι ἀναγιγνώσκειν τὰ γράμματα; ἐγὼ βούλομαι. καὶ σύ;
--Ah, (to class) ἡ --- βούλεται ἀναγιγνώσκειν ταῦτα τὰ γράμματα.

--καὶ σύ, ὦ φίλε, βούλεαι ἀναγιγνώσκειν ταῦτα;   Ah, (to class) ὁ ---
βούλεται ἀναγιγνώσκειν τὰ γράμματα.   καὶ ἡ --- καὶ ὁ ---
βούλονται ἀναγιγνώσκειν τὰ γράμματα.

ἐθέλω	βούλομαι	Learn both verb patterns.
ἐθέλεις	βούλεαι	
ἐθέλει	βούλεται	βούλομαι has more force. It is a full-fledged *I want.*
		ἐθέλω is weaker, more like *I am willing.*
ἐθέλουσι(ν)	βούλονται	(The original "you want" form was βούλεσαι.)

--καὶ νῦν, ὦ φίλοι, ἀναγιγνώσκωμεν ἐκ τοῦ βιβλίου.

(Turn to p. 1 of textbook. Students take turns reading.)

--ὦ φίλε (pointing to page one of book), ὁράεις γράμματα μικρά; --ὁράεις πολλὰ γράμματα μικρά; πάντα τὰ γράμματα μικρά ἐστιν; ναί, πάντα τὰ γράμματα μικρά ἐστιν. πάντα τὰ γράμματά ἐστι μικρά.

Actually the Greeks did not use small letters at all. They used only the letters we call capitals. Small letters were developed as cursive in ninth century Europe. They are used now because they are easier to read. For the same reason, we use word division, although the Greeks did not. (Another practice that would make reading easier would be to drop all smooth breathing signs.)

--καὶ σύ, ὦ φίλε (writing **?** on board), ὁράεις τοῦτο; οἱ Ἕλληνες (pointing to **?**) γράφουσι τοῦτο; οὐ γράφουσι τοῦτο.

The Greeks used the symbol **;** for questions, not our question mark. They did not have quotation marks (which are used for clarity in our stories in made-up Greek). Where we use a colon, the Greeks used a raised dot.

The Greek period and comma have the same form as our own.

ἔργα ~Read aloud the scripts of days # 1 - 4. (Do you have any questions? Keep reading and rereading until you can understand these pages perfectly.)

~Write the alphabet once in small and large letters.

~Rewrite the following passage, substituting forms of βούλομαι for forms of ἐθέλω (which are shown in bold print):

ἐθέλω γράφειν τὰ γράμματα. καὶ σύ, **ἐθέλεις** γράφειν τὰ γράμματα; ἡ χελώνη οὐκ **ἐθέλει** γράφειν τὰ γράμματα. ὁ --- καὶ ἡ --- **ἐθέλουσι** γιγνώσκειν τὸ ὄνομά μου.

~Write the poem that is in the box at the top of the following page.

Script # 5

◆
indicates
genuine ancient Greek

> χαλεπὸν τὸ μὴ φιλῆσαι·
> χαλεπὸν δὲ καὶ φιλῆσαι·
> χαλεπώτερον δὲ πάντων
> ἀποτυγχάνειν φιλοῦντα.

--χαίρετε, ὦ φίλοι. τοῦτο τί ἐστι; τοῦτο ἔστι ποίημα. --ἐγὼ (pointing to self)
ἐθέλω μανθάνειν τὸ ποίημα. --καὶ σύ, ὦ φίλε, ἐθέλεις μανθάνειν
τὸ ποίημα; λέγε ἡμῖν· ἀληθῶς ἐθέλεις μανθάνειν τὸ ποίημα;

--καὶ σύ, ὦ φίλη, βούλεαι μανθάνειν τοῦτο τὸ ποίημα; βούλεαι ἢ ἐθέλεις
μανθάνειν τὸ ποίημα;

Α καὶ Β	*A and B*
Α ἢ Β	*A or B*

--καὶ σύ, ὦ φίλε, γιγνώσκεις τὰ γράμματα; γιγνώσκεις πάντα τὰ
γράμματα; --καὶ βούλεαι ἀναγιγνώσκειν τὸ ποίημα; --εἰ βούλεαι
ἀναγιγνώσκειν τὸ ποίημα, χρὴ γιγνώσκειν τὰ γράμματα; ναί,
χρή σε γιγνώσκειν τὰ γράμματα.

βούλομαι μανθάνειν	*I want to learn*
χρή με μανθάνειν	*It is necessary for me to learn*

--καὶ νῦν, ὦ φίλε, βούλεαι ἀναγιγνώσκειν τὸ ποίημα; εὖγε. καὶ σύ;
--εὖγε. ὁ --- καὶ ἡ --- βούλονται ἀναγιγνώσκειν τὸ ποίημα.
ἀναγιγνώσκωμεν τὸ ποίημα. λέγωμεν τὸ ποίημα. πάντες ἅμα.
(The poem is read, several times.)

--τοῦτο τὸ ποίημα μακρόν (making a gesture of "long") ἐστιν; τί λέγεις;
λέγεις ὅτι τὸ ποίημα μακρόν ἐστιν; λέγω ὅτι τὸ ποίημα οὐκ ἔστι
μακρόν. ἔστι μικρόν.

λέγω ὅτι	*I say that...*
οἶδα ὅτι	*I know that...*

--ὦ φίλη, φιλέεις τοῦτο τὸ ποίημα; ἀληθῶς φιλέεις τοῦτο τὸ ποίημα;
καὶ φιλέεις μανθάνειν τὰ ποιήματα; φιλέεις ἀναγιγνώσκειν
τὰ ποιήματα;

τὰ ποιήματα	*the poems* (the particular set)
	poems (in general)

--ὦ φίλε, τοῦτο τὸ ποίημα χαλεπόν ἐστιν; οὐκ ἔστι χαλεπόν. τοῦτο
τὸ ποίημα ῥᾴδιόν ἐστιν; ἔστι ῥᾴδιον. τί ἐστι χαλεπόν; τὸ φιλῆσαι
χαλεπόν; καὶ τὸ μὴ φιλῆσαι; τί ἐστι χαλεπώτερον πάντων;

To understand how the poem works, you need to know the following:

Pitch marks

English is a stress language: certain syllables must be pronounced louder than others. The Greek of fifth century Athens was a pitch language: certain syllables had to have a change in pitch. A system of marks was eventually worked out to indicate pitch, as shown above. You may wish to try to speak with pitch change. Otherwise, give extra stress (loudness) to an accented syllable.

Syllable Division

Greek words have as many syllables as there are vowels or diphthongs. A single consonant is pronounced with the vowel that follows it. A pair of consonants is normally split. The sentence ὦ φίλοι, γιγνώσκομεν ταῦτα τὰ ἔργα would normally be divided as shown below.

ὦ / φί / λοι , / γιγ/ νώσ / κο / μεν / ταῦ / τα / τὰ / ἔρ / γα;

Certain combinations of consonants can stay together and begin the following syllable. This is an option for the combination of a mute (κ,γ,χ; π,β,φ; τ,δ,θ) + liquid or nasal (λ, μ, ν, ρ) or of a sigma (σ) + any consonant .

γιγ / νώσ / κο / μεν or γι /γνώ / σκο / μεν

Poetic Meter

Greek poetry is recognizable as poetry by a pattern of long and short syllables (not by rhymes or a stress pattern). In other words, the Greek ear was sensitive to how long it takes to pronounce a syllable. The meter for our poem, called Anacreontic after the poet Anacreon, is:

short short long short long short long long   ⏑⏑ — ⏑ — ⏑ — —

Short syllable: ends with a short vowel--ᾰ, ε, ῐ, ο, ῠ
Long syllable: has a long vowel--ᾱ, η, ῑ, ω, ῡ
                         has a diphthong-αι, ει, οι, αυ, ευ, ου, etc.
                         ends with a consonant
                         ends a line of poetry

The combination of mute + liquid gives a poet options on length. For example, πέτρος (rock) can begin with a short syllable (πέ - τρος) or a long one (πέτ - ρος).

Note: ζ, ξ, and ψ are really a pair of consonants: δ + σ, κ + σ, π + σ. So the second syllable of τράπεζα (*table*) is poetically long, though ε is a short vowel. The first syllable of ὁ ξένος (ὁ κ/σένος) is long in poetry.

Punctuation

Note punctutation. If there are complete sentences all contributing toward the expression of a complex thought, there will be a half-stop (a raised period) between them and a full stop (period) at the end. Otherwise the Greeks used commas as we do and a semicolon for our question mark. (In our made-up Greek, a period is used at the end of a sentence.)

Connectives

In good Greek when many sentences are used to develop a theme, they are usually connected by a linking word, no matter how slight.

δέ is the most common linking word. It has even less force than *and* or *but*.

ἔργα   ~Read today's script aloud and make sure you understand all of it.
               ~Write the poem two more times. Learn the poem by heart.
               ~Optional: Analyze the meter. Why are the long syllables long?

Script # 6

--ὦ φίλη, ἔμαθες τὸ ποίημα; ἐγὼ ἔμαθον τὸ ποίημα. καὶ σύ, ἔμαθες
τὸ ποίημα; λέγε μοι τὸ ποίημα. εὖγε. ἡ --- ἔμαθε τὸ ποίημα.

--ὦ φίλε, ἡδὺ ἦν μανθάνειν τὸ ποίημα; καὶ χαλεπὸν ἦν μαθεῖν τὸ ποίημα;
χαλεπόν ἐστι μανθάνειν τὰ ποιήματα; ἀληθῶς;

μανθάνω	*I learn*	ἔμαθον	*I learned*
μανθάνεις	*you learn*	ἔμαθες	*you learned*
μανθάνει	*he, she, it learns*	ἔμαθε(ν)	*he, she, it learned*
μανθάνειν	*to learn* (to be in the process of learning, to keep learning)	μαθεῖν	*to learn* (once)

ἦν - *was*

❱ **Exercise:** Translate. (λαμβάνω/ἔλαβον are related as μανθάνω/ἔμαθον. λαμβάνω = *I take, receive, get*.)
ἔλαβον βιβλίον. καὶ σύ, ἔλαβες βιβλίον; ἡ χελώνη οὐκ ἔλαβε βιβλίον. οὐκ ἐθέλει λαβεῖν βιβλίον.

--καὶ νῦν τί ποιέω (writing poem on blackboard); --ναί. γράφω τὸ ποίημα.
λέγει ὅτι γράφω τὸ ποίημα. καὶ νῦν, λέγε μοι τοῦτο τὸ ποίημα.
λέγωμεν τὸ ποίημα, πάντες ἅμα.

--καὶ νῦν ἔχω μῦθον, μῦθον μικρὸν καὶ μῶρον (silly). ἔχω μῦθον
περὶ τῶν γραμμάτων. ὦ φίλε, βούλεαι ἀκούειν (gesturing with hand to ear)
τὸν μῦθον; εὖγε. ἀναγιγνώσκωμεν τὸν μῦθον.

The Alphabet Grows

(Vocabulary to be provided by teacher as needed)

ποιητής τις φιλέει τὰ γράμματα. διὰ τί φιλέει τὰ γράμματα; διότι
ποιέει τὰ ποιήματα ἐκ τῶν γραμμάτων. καὶ ὁ ποιητὴς ποιέει δεῖπνον,
δεῖπνον μέγα. καὶ καλέει ἐπὶ τὸ δεῖπνον πάντα τὰ γράμματα. τίνα
γράμματα καλέει; καλέει τὸ ἄλφα καὶ τὸ βῆτα καὶ τὸ γάμμα καὶ τὰ λοιπά.
(καλέει ὁ ποιητὴς τὸ ζῆτα; τὸ ζῆτα οὐ καλέει. οὐδὲ τὸ ξῖ οὐδὲ τὸ ψῖ
καλέει ὁ ποιητής. διὰ τί ὁ ποιητὴς οὐ καλέει ταῦτα τὰ γράμματα;
μανθάνετε, ὦ φίλοι. ἀναγιγνώσκετε τὸν μῦθον.)

ἐπὶ τῷ δείπνῳ πάντα τὰ γράμματα ἐσθίουσι πολλὰ καὶ πίνουσι πολλά.
πίνουσιν οἶνον. καὶ ἡ σίγμα (**σ**), ὅτε πίνει, μεθύει. καὶ ὅτε μεθύει, ὧδε
ποιέει· (**ς**).* καὶ πάντα τὰ γράμματα, ὅτε ὁράουσι τοῦτο, βούλονται
γαμέειν τὴν σίγμα. καὶ ἔστι μάχη, μάχη μεγάλη. καὶ τέλος ἔστι νίκη.
τίνα γράμματα ἔχουσι τὴν νίκην; τίνα γράμματα γαμέουσι τὴν σίγμα;

---

* *She does thus.* In other words, she wiggles her hips. Sexist though it be, this story is not for all that unGreek.
Cf. Hesiod's *Works and Days* 373 ✦ Μὴ δὲ γυνή σε νόον πυγοστόλος ἐξαπατάτω.

Greek sounds are classified as in the chart below. The simple answer to our story is that δ marries σ to make ζ, κ to make ξ, and π to make ψ. _____

Actually it is more complicated than that. All labial mutes (π, β, φ, consonants made with the lips) combine with σ to make ψ, and all palatals (κ, γ, χ, made with the palate) to make ξ. Note: dental mutes (τ, δ, θ, made with the teeth) drop before σ. An σ + δ combination makes ζ.

Vowels	Liquids & Nasals	Sibilant		Mutes	(Stops)		Combinations
				Voiceless	Voiced	Aspirate (h)	
α ε η ι ο υ ω	λ ρ μ ν (γ before a palatal)	σ (ς)	Labial (lips)	π	β	φ	labial + σ --> ψ
			Palatal (palate)	κ	γ	χ	palatal + σ --> ξ
			Dental (teeth)	τ	δ	θ	(Dental drops before σ)
							σ + δ --> ζ

Indo-European

Indo-European is a language postulated as the ancestor of many related languages. (A partial list is given below.) Its original speakers may have lived somewhere near the Black Sea. In historical times Indo-European languages have spread by force of arms (to Africa and the Americas). If the same was true in prehistoric times, as is likely, speakers of early Indo-European tongues must have been competent fighters. For people are willing to lay down their lives rather than give up their language. (Consider recent resistance by Basques and Tamils to Indo-European encroachment.)

INDO   EUROPEAN

PERSIAN	GREEK
SANSKRIT	LATIN
	CELTIC
	GERMANIC
	SLAVIC

LATIN — Italian, French, Spanish, Portuguese, Rumanian

CELTIC — Irish, Welsh

GERMANIC — German, English, Dutch, Norwegian, Swedish, Danish

SLAVIC — Russian, Ukranian, Czech, Slovak, Polish

We can trace Indo-European roots by comparing the words which have descended from them in the various Indo-European languages spoken today. These roots have been used to construct the history of the various groups: what kind of institutions they had, what kind of lands they went through, and so on.

It seems that the speakers of Indo-European split up before they had a chance to see the sea together. For some descendant languages have words in common for sea and fish, but there are none to match in Sanskrit or Persian. While the Indo-European speakers were together they knew weaving and they yoked animals. We can tell that they had a god in common. Addressed as Ζεῦ πάτερ (Father Zeus) in Greek, he was *Jupiter* in Latin, and *dyaus pitṛ* in Sanskrit--all three meaning *Father Sky*.

In the word μεθύω the Greeks keep up the memory of a brew, probably made from honey, drunk by their ancestors, which we call *mead*. There is an Indo-European root: **medhu,* which --> μεθυ- in Greek, *madhu* in Sanskrit, and *mead* in English. To be sure, the Greeks now became drunk on wine (οἶνος), made from grapes. But words have a way of preserving ancient memories.

Derivatives and Cognates

There are several ways a word in English can be connected with a word in Greek:

(a) It can be **derived.** That is, the word may be deliberately taken from Greek . This is commonly done, as in *pharmacology* or *iatrogenic*. When an English word is **derived** from Greek it resembles the Greek closely. For example, *erg* looks very much like ἔργον.

☙☙ **(The logo ☙ will be used whenever a point is being made about English.)** Many English words are **derived** from Latin or French (which is based on Latin). Since Latin words closely resemble their Greek cognates, an English word derived from Latin will look like a Greek word. *Octopod* (eight-footed) is derived from Greek (hence has the Greek *pod* = foot), *pedestrian* from Latin (hence has the Latin *ped* = foot).

(b) It can be **cognate.** This means it has the same Indo-European root as the Greek word but has come down on our (Germanic) side of the family. When this has happened, there are usually so many changes that the word looks very different from its Greek relative. *Work* has this relation to ἔργον.

In this book a one-way arrow shows **derivation,** and a two-way arrow shows the **cognate** relationship. So, for example:

ἔργον <--> *work*   ἔργον --> *erg*
μεθυ- <--> *mead*   μεθυ- --> *amethyst* (the stone having been considered a charm against
                                                       drunkenness, from α = non, as in amoral, agnostic + μεθύω = be drunk)

☙☙ One interesting difference between the Latin/Greek group and the Germanic group is that what is *c/k* in the one is *h* in the other. Think of Canis Major, for example--from the Latin *canis* = dog. The Greek is κύων (as in νὴ τὴν κύνα). English **derivatives** of the *canis /κύων* family are *canine* and *cynic*. An English **cognate** is *hound*, from the German *hund*.

Or think of *cor* = heart in Latin. We see *cor* in English in such **derived** words as *cordial* or *record* (from the Latin *recordor*, since the Romans regarded the heart as the seat of memory). The Greek is καρδία, from which we **derive** *cardiac*. But what is the **cognate** in English? Simply *heart*.

☙☙ English words come from two main sources: our own Germanic heritage and the Greek/Latin family including French. The really useful words--the words we use about day-to-day experience, words we could not do without--are usually from our Germanic heritage. And notice that whenever there is a choice of words--*labor* or *work, cordial* or *hearty, amity* or *friendship, verity* or *truth*--the Germanic words call forth a stronger response, while the borrowed words seem more formal or remote.

ἔργα   ~Reread today's script and make sure you understand it.
            ~Read "The Alphabet Grows" (p. 13) aloud and silently until you understand every word.

            ~Look at the Greek-English dictionary words beginning with *gamma* and *phi*. Write all the
                derivatives you can think of, at least twelve. Derivatives will resemble the Greek closely
                in look and meaning. Remember: a Greek upsilon often shows up as the letter **y** in English.
                (Can you think of any **cognates**?)

Script # 7

--ὦ φίλε, γιγνώσκεις τὸ ποίημα; ἐθέλεις λέγειν τὸ ποίημα; βούλη λέγειν
τὸ ποίημα; ἐγὼ (pointing to self) βούλομαι λέγειν τὸ ποίημα. Καὶ σύ,
βούλῃ;

In earlier times *you want* (singular) was βούλεσαι. At a certain point, the Greeks stopped pronouncing an *s* sound
between vowels--have you ever heard someone say "*wa'n't*" for "*wasn't*"?--and used the form βούλεαι, which we
have been using. Eventually the ε and α were slurred together, to make η. (This process is called **contraction**.)

In fifth century Athens the "you singular" form would have been written **βουληι**. Eventually the iota stopped
being pronounced (around 200 B.C.E.) and was omitted. To mark that it was once there, scribes used an iota
subscript (under the vowel). When you see an iota subscript, pronounce the iota unless your teacher directs
otherwise.

Originally εσαι	Later --> ε⁻αι	Latest --> ῃ
βούλομαι	βούλομαι	βούλομαι
βούλεσαι	βούλεαι	βούλῃ
βούλεται	βούλεται	βούλεται

--Καὶ νῦν, δίδωμί σοι τὴν χεῖρα (extending hand). καὶ σύ, δός μοι τὴν χεῖρα.
τί ποιέεις; πάντες ἅμα· "δίδωμί σοι τὴν χεῖρα."

--καὶ νῦν, ὦ φίλη, δὸς αὐτῷ τὴν χεῖρα. τί ποιέεις; λέγε αὐτῷ.
--νῦν δὸς αὐτῇ τὴν χεῖρα. τί ποιέεις; λέγε αὐτῇ.

--ὦ φίλε, δὸς αὐτῷ τὴν χεῖρα. Ah, (to class) δίδωσι τὴν χεῖρα. δίδωσιν
αὐτῷ τὴν χεῖρα. καὶ νῦν δὸς αὐτῇ τὴν χεῖρα. τί ποιέει; δίδωσι
τὴν χεῖρα αὐτῇ. δίδωσιν αὐτῇ τὴν χεῖρα.

--καὶ νῦν δείκνυμί σοι τὴν γλῶτταν (showing tongue). καὶ σύ, δείκνυ μοι
τὴν γλῶτταν. τί ποιέεις; δείκνυς μοι τὴν γλῶτταν. καὶ νῦν δείκνυ
αὐτῷ τὴν γλῶτταν. τί ποιέει; δείκνυσιν αὐτῷ τὴν γλῶτταν.

--καὶ νῦν, ὦ φίλε, ἐθέλεις διδόναι μοι τὴν χεῖρα; βούλη διδόναι τὴν χεῖρα;
βούλη διδόναι τὴν χεῖρα αὐτῇ; βούλη δεικνύναι τὴν γλῶτταν αὐτῷ;

λαμβάνω	δείκνυμι	δίδωμι
λαμβάνεις	δείκνυς	δίδως
λαμβάνει	δείκνυσι(ν)	δίδωσι(ν)
λαμβάνειν	δεικνύναι	διδόναι

--καὶ νῦν, πάντες ἀνίστασθε. (Everyone stands up.) καὶ σύ, δὸς αὐτῇ
τὴν χεῖρα, καὶ σύ, δὸς αὐτῷ τὴν χεῖρα, καὶ σύ, δὸς αὐτῇ τὴν χεῖρα.
Καὶ σύ, κ.τ.λ.

--καὶ νῦν ἔστι δρᾶμα, δρᾶμα μικρόν. ἀναγιγνώσκωμεν τὸ δρᾶμα.

THE DOCTOR COMES*

ὁ ἰατρὸς ἔρχεται

παῖς·   ὦ μῆτερ, μῆτερ, νοσέω.

μήτηρ·   τί ἐστιν, ὦ παῖ; νοσέεις;

παῖς·   ναί. νοσέω. ἀληθῶς νοσέω. κάμνω, κάμνω. χρή με κεῖσθαι.

        [κεῖται.] Ah, κεῖμαι.

μήτηρ·   χρή με καλέειν τὸν ἰατρόν. [καλέει.]

        ἰατρέ, ἰατρέ. ὁ παῖς μου* νοσέει. κάμνει. κεῖται νῦν.

ἰατρός·   ἔρχομαι, ἔρχομαι.

παῖς·   τίς ἔρχεται;

μήτηρ·   ὁ ἰατρὸς ἔρχεται.

παῖς·   οὐ βούλομαι τοῦτο. οὐ νοσέω. οὐ κάμνω. [ἀνίσταται.]

        ἰδοῦ. οὐ κεῖμαι. ἀνίσταμαι.

μήτηρ·   φεῦ, φεῦ. φοβέῃ τὸν ἰατρόν;

παῖς·   ναί, φοβέομαι τὸν ἰατρόν. οἱ ἰατροί εἰσι κακοί.

μήτηρ·   οἱ ἰατροὶ οὐ κακοί εἰσιν. ἀγαθοί εἰσιν. οὐ χρή σε

        φοβέεσθαι τὸν ἰατρόν. νῦν νοσέεις. χρή σε κεῖσθαι.

        [καλέει αὖθις ἡ μήτηρ τὸν ἰατρόν.]

        ἰατρέ, ἰατρέ.

ἰατρός·   ἔρχομαι, ἔρχομαι. [ἔρχεται.]

        φεῦ. τί ἐστιν, ὦ παῖ; λέγε ἡμῖν.

παῖς·   οὐδέν ἐστιν. οὐ νοσέω. ἀληθῶς.

μήτηρ·   ναί, νοσέει. νὴ τὸν Δία, νοσέει. ἀλλά σε φοβέεται.

        κάμνει καὶ νοσέει. οἴμοι, οἴμοι.

*For vocabulary see p. 19.

Change ὁ παῖς in the skit to ἡ παῖς when the Child is played by a female.

ἰατρός·   μὴ δάκρυε. πόσον χρόνον νοσέει ὁ παῖς;*

μήτηρ·   οὐκ οἶδα. χρή σε ἐρωτάειν αὐτόν.*

ἰατρός·   ὦ παῖ, πόσον χρόνον νοσέεις; λέγε ἡμῖν.

παῖς·   οὐ νοσέω.

ἰατρός·   γιγνώσκεις με;

παῖς·   οὐ γιγνώσκω σε.

ἰατρός·   ὁράεις τοῦτο; [δείκνυσι τὴν χεῖρα.]

παῖς·   οὐχ ὁράω.

ἰατρός·   ἀκούεις τοῦτο; [κρούει (claps) τὰς χεῖρας.]

παῖς·   οὐκ ἀκούω. ἀκούω οὐδέν.

ἰατρός·   φεῦ, φεῦ. δείκνυ μοι τὴν γλῶτταν.

          [δείκνυσιν ὁ παῖς* τὴν γλῶτταν.]

          φεῦ, φεῦ. ἡ γλῶττά σου οὐχ ὑγιεινή ἐστιν.

          νῦν δείκνυ μοι τοὺς ὀφθαλμούς.

          [δείκνυσιν ὁ παῖς* τοὺς ὀφθαλμούς.]

          φεῦ. οἱ ὀφθαλμοί σου οὐχ ὑγιεινοί εἰσιν.

          [λέγει τῇ μητρί.]

          ὁ παῖς σου* νοσέει. δὸς αὐτῷ* τοῦτο τὸ φάρμακον.

          [δίδωσι τῇ μητρὶ φάρμακον.]

          καὶ νῦν δός μοι ἀργύριον.

          [ἡ μήτηρ δίδωσι τῷ ἰατρῷ ἀργύριον.]

          νῦν εἶμι. χαίρετε, ὦ φίλοι.

---

* When the Child is played by a female, change ὁ παῖς to ἡ παῖς.
  Also change αὐτόν to αὐτήν and αὐτῷ to αὐτῇ.

ἔργα   ~Read the Vocabulary and Notes on the following page.
        ~Read "The Doctor Comes" (pp. 17-18) aloud several times, until you understand it all,
            including stage directions. Be prepared to act the parts in class tomorrow.
        ~Notice the accent difference: δὸς αὐτῷ versus δός μοι. Can you think of why?

ὁ ἰατρός - doctor   --> iatrogenic,
                       pediatrics, geriatrics, psychiatric

ἔρχομαι - come (or go)

ὁ παῖς - child   --> pediatrics, pedagogue

ἡ μήτηρ <--> mother

νοσέω - be sick

κάμνω - be sick or weary

χρή - it is necessary

κεῖμαι - lie down   --> cemetery (via Latin),
                       a lying-down place

κεῖσθαι - If χρή takes an infinitive (*to X*),
          what must κεῖσθαι be?

┌───┐
│ The general principle is: **PUNT.***   │
│ Not everything is learned systematically │
│ to begin with. Sometimes you will   │
│ punt first, and learn the system later. │
└───┘

καλέω - call

ἀνίσταμαι - stand up
    στα of Greek ἵσταμαι = *sta* of stand

ἰδού - see for yourself! see! behold!

φεῦ - tsk!

φοβέομαι - I am afraid, I fear   --> phobia

κακός - bad

ἐστι, εἰσί(ν) - is, are   (ἐστι <--> is)

ἀγαθός - good   --> Agatha

οὐδέν - nothing

ἀλλά - but

οἴμοι - alas

μή ‾ don't (negative used in a command)

δακρύω - weep, shed tears

πόσος - how much?

ὁ χρόνος - time   --> chronic, chronology

οἶδα - I know
    οἶδα
    οἶσθα
    οἶδε(ν)

γιγνώσκω - know, recognize, be familiar
          with a person or thing or situation,
          vs. οἶδα = know a fact

ὑγιεινός - healthy   --> hygiene

ὁ ὀφθαλμός - eye --> ophthalmologist

τὸ φάρμακον - drug   --> pharmacy

τὸ ἀργύριον - money, literally a small
                piece of silver
    (from ὁ ἄργυρος = silver
      --> argent (in heraldry), Argentina)

εἶμι - go (or come) (with future force,
              used as future of ἔρχομαι)
    ✍✍ Cf. our usage: *I am going to the
                      beach tomorrow.*

Note: There is also εἰμι = *I am* , a different
                            verb entirely.

---

* In this book *punt* is used to mean, *Make an educated guess.* Do not wait until you've learned the system.
What you already know in combination with intuition just might give you the meaning. Take a chance! The
three meanings of *punt* are (a) pole a boat, (b) drop a football and kick it before it hits ground, and (c) gamble in
roulette, betting against the bank. Learning Greek does seem a bit like all of these!

GREEK MEDICINE

In mythology, the healing arts are taught to all the great heroes by the centaur Chiron. Achilles, Jason (whose name even means "healer"), Asclepius, and Heracles were among his pupils. Accordingly, in the *Iliad*, Homer tells of two hero-physicians, Machaon and Podalirios, the Aesclepiadae ("the sons of Aesclepius"). When Machaon is wounded, his rescue is urged because, "A physician is a man worth many men in knowing how to cut out arrows and in applying gentle remedies" (11.514-5). Achilles in the same poem is a friend of Machaon and is well versed in the healing arts. Following this tradition, Achilles is depicted on the vase in Figure 1 bandaging the wounds of his friend, Patroclus. There must have been a long and respected tradition of healing in archaic Greece that was particularly associated with hero-warriors, focused on the ability to tend to wounds and the knowledge of herbal drugs.

Figure 1. Achilles bandages Patroclus. Line drawing of an Attic cup (ca. 490 B.C.E.).

One name in the classical era stands out as the innovator of the scientific approach to medicine: Hippocrates. Later in this course, you will have a chance to read in Greek the oath ascribed to him that set standards (and still does) for medical ethics. Hippocrates was born on the island of Kos, only a short distance away from the Ionian coast and the centers of Ionian philosophy. His dates (ca. 460-388) seem to make him a close contemporary of Socrates (469-399).

Even though more than seventy works are ascribed to him, it is not likely that Hippocrates really is their author. What we can tell is that he and his followers applied the rationality of the Ionian philosophers to the study of medicine.

Hippocratic medicine is characterized by its insistence on the search for natural causes of diseases rather than supernatural explanations, for full and careful diagnoses based on precise observations, and for holistic treatments consisting not only of drugs but also of attention to diet and emotional well-being. Renae Dubos has said, "Modern medicine is but a series of commentaries and elaborations on the Hippocratic writings…" (*Man Adapting,* 323).

As a physician Hippocrates was called an Asclepiad, a son of Asclepius. The term signified that he was a member of a healing family or guild whose patron was the healing hero-god, Asclepius. After Hippocrates' death a famous Asclepieion, a temple sanctuary devoted to Asclepius and the healing arts, was founded on Kos. For almost a thousand years, until 554 C.E. when an earthquake devastated the island, people from all over the Mediterranean world came to this site for treatment and medical training.

There were more than two hundred other Asclepieions in the ancient world. Like the famous spas in Europe, some of which are actually situated on the sites of former Asclepieions, these sanctuaries were in beautiful and healthful surroundings, had fine architecture, and combined medical treatment with the pleasures of a resort. No sanctuary is more famous that the one in Epidaurus, which had not only healing facilities but temples, gymnasia, baths, shops, as well as a theatre, music hall, and stadium. The Asclepieion in Athens, situated almost directly beneath the Parthenon, adjoins the Theatre of Dionysus, where the dramas of Sophocles and Euripides were first performed.

Although there were physicians at these sanctuaries who treated their patients in a scientific manner, there were also priests who practiced a form of religious healing – a sometimes effective form as the numerous votive offerings and inscriptions tell us. Those whom traditional medicine had not helped would turn to the priests of Asclepius, in much the same way as pilgrims go to Lourdes or to faith healers today.

Such patients would be treated by incubation, a form of healing with dreams. Within the dream, the god would act as a divine physician to the patient, treating the illness, performing surgery, and giving drugs. Here is one such cure:

> Ambrosia of Athens, blind of one eye. She came as a suppliant to the god. As she walked about in the temple she laughed at some of the cures as incredible and impossible, that the lame and the blind should be healed by merely seeing a dream. In her sleep she had a vision. It seemed to her that the god stood by her and said that he would cure her, but that in payment he would ask her to dedicate to the temple a silver pig as a memorial of her ignorance. After saying this, he cut the diseased eyeball and poured in some drug. When the day came she walked out sound. (Edelstein, *Asclepius*, volume I, case 4).

Figure 2. Asclepius heals a dreaming patient with Hygieia ("Health"), his daughter, in attendance. To the left are the members of the sleeper's family. These humans are smaller in scale than the divinities on the right side. Relief (5th-4th century B.C.E.), Piraeus Museum.

--ὦ φίλη (drawing a turtle on the blackboard), ὁράεις τοῦτο; τοῦτο τί ἐστιν;
ἔστι χελώνη. ὁράεις τὴν χελώνην; καὶ σύ, ὦ φίλε, ὁράεις τὴν χελώνην;
καὶ ἡ --- καὶ ὁ --- ὁράουσι τὴν χελώνην.

--καὶ νῦν, ὦ φίλε, ἔχω φωνήν. (Demonstrate by singing a note.) καὶ σύ,
ἔχεις φωνήν; ἀκούεις τὴν φωνήν μου; καὶ νῦν (whispering) ἀκούεις
τὴν φωνήν μου, ἡ χελώνη ἔχει φωνήν, ἡ χελώνη ἔχει ὄνομα,

--καὶ ὁράεις τοῦτο, ὦ φίλη (showing tongue); τοῦτο τί ἐστιν; ἔστι γλῶττα.
ἔστιν ἡ γλῶττά μου. καὶ σύ, ὦ φίλη, ἔχεις γλῶτταν. δείκνυ μοι τὴν
γλῶτταν.

--ὦ φίλε, γλῶτταν ἔχει ἡ χελώνη; ἡ χελώνη ἔχει γλῶτταν; καὶ ὁράεις
τὴν γλῶτταν αὐτῆς; γλῶτταν ἔχει ἡ χελώνη ἀλλὰ τὴν γλῶτταν
οὐχ ὁράεις.

ἡ χελώνη	ἡ φωνή	ἡ γλῶττα
τὴν χελώνην	τὴν φωνήν	τὴν γλῶτταν

--καὶ νῦν, ὦ φίλε, τί ποιέεις; μανθάνεις γλῶτταν; ναί, μανθάνεις
τὴν γλῶτταν τὴν Ἑλληνικήν. μανθάνεις τὴν Ἑλληνικὴν γλῶτταν.

τὴν Ἑλληνικὴν γλῶτταν
τὴν γλῶτταν τὴν Ἑλληνικήν

Both mean: *the Greek language,*
the Greek tongue

--ὦ φίλε, ὅτε ἡ μήτηρ καλέει, ἔρχομαι. καὶ σύ, ὅτε ἡ μήτηρ καλέει,
ἔρχῃ; χρή σε ἔρχεσθαι; --καὶ σύ, ὦ φίλη, ἔρχῃ ἐπὶ τὰ δεῖπνα;
φιλέεις ἔρχεσθαι ἐπὶ τὰ δεῖπνα; χρή σε ἔρχεσθαι ἐπὶ τὰ δεῖπνα;

--καὶ σύ, ὦ φίλε, φοβέῃ τὸν ἰατρόν; ἐγὼ φοβέομαι τὸν ἰατρόν.
καὶ σύ, φοβέῃ τὸν ἰατρόν; βούλῃ φοβέεσθαι τὸν ἰατρόν;

ἐθέλω	βούλομαι	φοβέομαι
ἐθέλεις	βούλῃ	φοβέῃ
ἐθέλει	βούλεται	φοβέεται
ἐθέλουσι(ν)	βούλονται	φοβέονται
ἐθέλειν	βούλεσθαι	φοβέεσθαι

--ὦ φίλη, γιγνώσκεις τὸ δρᾶμα; καὶ σύ, τὸ δρᾶμα γιγνώσκεις;
εὖγε. ἀναγιγνώσκωμεν τὸ δρᾶμα.

"The Doctor Comes" is played, several times.

--ὦ φίλε, τί ἐστι τοῦτο; τοῦτο ἔστι βιβλίον. ὁρᾷς τὸ βιβλίον;
 ἐγὼ ὁρῶ τοῦτο τὸ βιβλίον, καὶ σὺ ὁρᾷς; καὶ νῦν (hiding the book)
 ὁρᾷς τὸ βιβλίον; τὸ βιβλίον οὐχ ὁρᾷς.

Do you hear the difference? Before, we were saying ὁράω and ὁράεις. Now we are saying ὁρῶ and ὁρᾷς.

The Greeks sometimes ran their vowel sounds together, as we saw with βούλη (p. 16). Two vowel sounds will be slurred or **contracted** into one sound. There are verbs that have a full set of contracted forms. These are called **contract verbs**. They may be -έω (ε contract) or -άω (α contract) verbs.

For the sake of seeing the original system (endings -ω, -εις, -ει, etc.) we began by using uncontracted sounds. From now on, we shall use the contracted forms, which were spoken and written in Athens during the fifth century B.C.E.

It is best simply to memorize the patterns below. If you want to know the rules behind contraction, you may look ahead on pp. 126 and129. You will notice that whenever there was an acute accent on a contracting α or ε, the resulting accent is a circumflex:

	-έω	Verbs
I	φιλέ-ω	φιλῶ
you (sing)	φιλέ-εις	φιλεῖς
he, she, it	φιλέ-ει	φιλεῖ
they	φιλέ-ουσι(ν)	φιλοῦσι(ν)
infinitive	φιλέ-ειν	φιλεῖν

	-άω	Verbs
ὁρά-ω	ὁρῶ
ὁρά-εις	ὁρᾷς
ὁρά-ει	ὁρᾷ
ὁρά-ουσι(ν)	ὁρῶσι(ν)
ὁρά-ε(ι)ν	ὁρᾶν*

	-έομαι	Verbs
φοβέ-ομαι	φοβοῦμαι
φοβέ-η	φοβῆ
φοβέ-εται	φοβεῖται
φοβέ-ονται	φοβοῦνται
φοβέ-εσθαι	φοβεῖσθαι

*Note that there is no iota in the infinitive. (This is because the ending was originally -εν.)

Note: A full set of forms has six persons (including *we* and *you* plural). You will learn the full set much later. For now you are learning enough forms to enable you to read interesting stories right away.

ἔργα   ~Read over today's script and make sure you understand it.
 ~Copy "The Doctor Comes" in neat handwriting, changing all uncontracted forms
  to the contracted ones. (Apply patterns above.)
 ~Practice saying all three parts aloud with the contracted forms.

Script # 9

--ὦ φίλε, νοσεῖς νῦν; λέγε ἡμῖν. νοσεῖς; Ah, (to class) λέγει ὅτι οὐ νοσεῖ.
  --(To a student who looks tired) καὶ σύ, κάμνεις νῦν; λέγε ἡμῖν, κάμνεις;
  --ναί, κάμνεις. οἶδα ὅτι κάμνεις.

--καὶ σύ, ὦ φίλη, φιλεῖς τὸν ἰατρόν; ἀληθῶς; λέγεις ὅτι ἀληθῶς φιλεῖς τὸν
  ἰατρόν; --καὶ ὅτε νοσεῖς, καλεῖς τὸν ἰατρόν; ὅτε νοσεῖς, ἡ μήτηρ σου
  καλεῖ τὸν ἰατρόν;

--τὸ δρᾶμα μακρόν ἐστιν; τὸ δρᾶμα χαλεπόν ἐστιν ἢ ῥᾴδιον; ἐν τῷ
  δράματι (in the play) ὁ παῖς φοβεῖται τὸν ἰατρόν; ναί, ὁ παῖς φοβεῖται
  τὸν ἰατρόν. καὶ σύ, φοβῇ τὸν ἰατρόν; ἐγὼ φοβοῦμαι τὸν ἰατρόν.
  καὶ σύ, φοβῇ τὸν ἰατρόν; φοβῇ τὴν χελώνην;

--καὶ σύ, ὦ φίλε, δός μοι βιβλίον. τί ποιεῖς; δίδως μοι βιβλίον.
  καὶ τί ποιῶ; λαμβάνω τὸ βιβλίον. ὦ φίλε, δὸς αὐτῇ τὸ βιβλίον.
  τί ποιεῖς; λέγε ἡμῖν· τί ποιεῖς; δίδως αὐτῇ τὸ βιβλίον; --καὶ σύ, τί
  ποιεῖς; λαμβάνεις τὸ βιβλίον; λέγε ἡμῖν.

--καὶ νῦν, πάντες ἀνίστασθε. (Everyone stand up.) καὶ σύ, δὸς αὐτῇ
  τὸ βιβλίον, καὶ σύ, δὸς αὐτῷ τὸ βιβλίον. τί ποιεῖς; λέγε· τί ποιεῖς.

(Everyone exchanges books, saying whichever is appropriate: "δίδωμί σοι τὸ βιβλίον"
or "λαμβάνω τὸ βιβλίον.")

--νῦν ἀναγιγνώσκωμεν αὖθις τὸ δρᾶμα.

"The Doctor Comes" is read from the homework copies, with contracted forms.

--νῦν ἀναγιγνώσκωμεν πάντα τὰ ὀνόματα (words). μανθάνωμεν πάντα
  τὰ ὀνόματα τὰ Ἑλληνικά. (Go over vocabulary on following page.)

ἔργα   ~Read today's script out loud. Make sure you understand it all.
           ~Learn all words in the Vocabulary Review. Learn the three verb patterns.

Learning Nouns

Nouns fall into groups. The **A-Group** has an *a* sound in its endings, the **O-Group** an *o* sound. The **Third Group** follows yet another pattern.

When you learn a noun you learn its **nominative singular** form. The nominative form is the form a noun takes when it is the **subject** of a verb. In the sentence ἡ χελώνη ἔχει φωνήν (*the turtle has a voice*) χελώνη is in the nominative form but φωνήν is not. Dictionaries list nouns and adjectives by their nominative singular form.

When you learn a noun you learn its **article** (ὁ, ἡ, τό) . The article tells you whether a noun is masculine, feminine, or neuter. All Greek nouns have **gender**. Usually gender will not violate expectations: father is masculine, mother feminine. But it can happen: little child is neuter-- τὸ παιδίον. As for what we consider other "things," often these had masculine or feminine gender in Greek--for examples, voice (fem.), tongue (fem.), and story (masc.).

Whenever we use a pronoun in Greek in place of a noun, we must respect the gender: *"Where is the little child--do you see it?"* *"That voice is beautiful--do you hear her?"* This is something you may be familiar with from studying other foreign languages. It is called **agreement**.

NOUNS (Three Groups)

A-GROUP
ἡ γλῶττα
ἡ μάχη
ἡ νίκη
ἡ φωνή
ἡ χελώνη
ὁ ποιητής

O-GROUP
ὁ ἰατρός
ὁ μῦθος
ὁ οἶνος
ὁ ὀφθαλμός
ὁ χρόνος

τὸ ἀργύριον
τὸ βιβλίον
τὸ δεῖπνον
τὸ φάρμακον
τὸ ἔργον

THIRD GROUP
ἡ μήτηρ
ὁ/ἡ παῖς
ἡ χείρ

τὸ γράμμα
τὸ δρᾶμα
τὸ ἐρώτημα
τὸ ὄνομα
τὸ ποίημα

ADJECTIVES (Additional forms will be learned later)

ἀγαθός	κακός
ῥᾴδιος	χαλεπός
μακρός	μικρός
ὑγιεινός	λοιπός
πόσος	ἄλλος
μέγας	
πολλά	πάντα

PRONOUNS

ἐγώ, με, μου, μοι   ἡμῖν
σύ, σε, σου, σοι

--, αὐτόν, αὐτοῦ, αὐτῷ
--, αὐτήν, αὐτῆς, αὐτῇ

τίς, τί   τοῦτο, ταῦτα

VERBS (Three Patterns)

ἀκούω	*I hear*
ἀκούεις	*You* (s) *hear*
ἀκούει	*He, she, it hears*
ἀκούουσι(ν)	*They hear*
ἀκούειν	*To hear*

ἀκούω
γιγνώσκω
  ἀναγιγνώσκω
γράφω
δακρύω
ἐθέλω
ἐσθίω
ἔχω
κάμνω
λαμβάνω
λέγω
μανθάνω
μεθύω
πίνω
χαίρω (Commands: χαῖρε, χαίρετε)
ἐρωτάω
ὁράω

γαμέω
καλέω   (*call* or *invite*)
νοσέω
ποιέω   (*make* or *do*)
φιλέω

βούλομαι	*I*
βούλη	*You* (s)
βούλεται	*He, she, it*
βούλονται	*They*
βούλεσθαι	*To --*

βούλομαι
ἔρχομαι

φοβέομαι

δείκνυμι	*I*
δείκνυς	*You* (s)
δείκνυσι(ν)	*He, she, it*
[to be learned later]	*They*
δεικνύναι	*To --*

δείκνυμι   (command δείκνυ)
δίδωμι   (command δός)

εἰμι	*I am*
εἶ	*You are*
ἐστι(ν)	*He, she it is*
εἰσι(ν)	*They are*

εἶμι	*I come, go* [with future sense]
εἶ	*You come, go*
εἶσι(ν)	*He, she, it comes, goes*

κεῖμαι
ἀνίσταμαι

ALSO

ἰδού	*See for yourself! See!*
χρή	*It is necessary*
οἶδα	*I know*
οἶσθα	*You know*
οἶδε(ν)	*He, she, it knows*

CONJUNCTIONS

Α καί Β	καί Α καί Β
Α ἤ Β	
ἀλλά	ὅτε
εἰ	ὅτι
δέ	διότι

OTHER [adverbs, interjections, prepositions]

οὐ, οὐκ, οὐχ	ἐπί
οὐδέ	ἐκ
μή	διά
ναί, οὐχί	διὰ τί
οἴμοι, φεῦ	νῦν
νή τὸν Δία,	αὖθις
νή τὴν κύνα	τέλος (*finally*)
	ἀληθῶς
πάντες ἅμα	ὧδε

Lesson 1. The A-Group; Cases

THE A-GROUP: ἡ ἀδελφή and ἡ γλῶττα

Use in sentence	Case	Forms		Feminine A-Endings	Forms		Fem. short a-Endings
	Singular						
the sister (subject)	nominative	ἡ	ἀδελφή	η	ἡ	γλῶττα	ᾰ
the sister (object)	accusative	τήν	ἀδελφήν	ην	τήν	γλῶτταν	ᾰν
of the sister	genitive	τῆς	ἀδελφῆς	ης	τῆς	γλώττης	ης
to / for the sister	dative	τῇ	ἀδελφῇ	ῃ	τῇ	γλώττῃ	ῃ
	Plural						
the sisters (subject)	nominative	αἱ	ἀδελφαί	αι	αἱ	γλῶτται	αι
the sisters (object)	accusative	τὰς	ἀδελφάς	ᾱς	τὰς	γλώττας	ᾱς
of the sisters	genitive	τῶν	ἀδελφῶν	ῶν	τῶν	γλωττῶν	ῶν
to / for the sisters	dative	ταῖς	ἀδελφαῖς	αις	ταῖς	γλώτταις	αις

These are paradigms for the **A-Group**. A **paradigm** is a complete set of forms that gives you the pattern that other forms will follow.

NORMAL A-GROUP NOUNS

Most nouns in the A-Group follow the pattern of ἡ ἀδελφή and are feminine.

These nouns have forms ending with an *a* sound--except for the genitive plural, where the *a* sound has been swallowed up in the long *o* sound. Accent rules will be explained later. But notice that the genitive plural of A-group nouns always has a circumflex on the final syllable.

The α of the accusative plural is long: τὰς ἀδελφᾱς, τὰς γλώττᾱς.

📖📖 Note that an English noun has far fewer forms than a Greek noun (four in writing, two in sound): *sister* (singular), *sister's*, (genitive singular), *sisters* (plural), *sisters'* (genitive plural).

❯ **Exercise α:** Say the forms of ἡ ἀδελφή in the order shown. Write the forms until you have learned them. **(These instructions are to be understood whenever new forms are introduced. Always stop to say and write the forms.)**

SHORT -α NOUNS

The usual A-group nominative ends in η. But some A-group nouns, such as ἡ γλῶττα, have a nominative and accusative singular with short α. Otherwise there is no difference in endings.

VOCATIVE AND DUAL

You see only four cases above. The fifth is the vocative case, used for calling someone or something. Although we say ἡ μήτηρ ἔρχεται, when we want to call mother we say ὦ μῆτερ, as in "The Doctor Comes." Since the vocative is easy to spot--often preceded by ὦ and set off by commas--and its form is often the same as that of the nominative, we shall concentrate on the other four cases.

There is also a set of dual forms that we shall not learn. These are special forms used optionally when there are two of a person or thing rather than many. The dual is rarely used and is usually easy to recognize.   (For vocatives and duals, see paradigms, p. 240.)

CASES

A case indicates the function of a noun, pronoun, or adjective in a sentence. We will be learning four cases for Greek nouns. **Nominative** is the case for a noun that is the **subject** of a verb, **accusative** for a noun that is the **direct object.**

🙨 English used to have four cases, and German still does. Pronouns best preserve them. Consider *he, him, his; she, her, her/hers; who, whom, whose* (nom., acc., gen.). English cases seem to be on the wane. The word *who* is often used in place of *whom*.

When reading Greek always look at the cases to understand a sentence. **Get into the habit of looking at word endings.** Do not try to guess the meaning of a sentence by word order. Do not try to think up likely meanings based on vocabulary.

The following are the names of the four Greek cases and a main use of each. We shall learn other uses soon:

Nominative	**subject** *of verb*	*The sister comes.*
Accusative	**direct object** *of verb*	*I see the sister.*
Genitive	**possessive**	*I see the house of the sister. / I see the sister's house.*
Dative	**indirect object** *of verb*	*I give a letter to the sister. / I give the sister a letter.*

Notice how three cases link a noun to a verb. But the fourth, genitive, usually links a noun to a noun. Notice also that English sometimes uses a tip-off *of* for the genitive or *to* for the dative, but you cannot count on it. Always consider the *function* of the word in its sentence when deciding what Greek form to use.

▶ **Exercise β:** Name the function of the underlined words (*subject, direct object, possessive, indirect object*). Name the Greek case that would be used. Translate the underlined words into Greek.

1. I see <u>the sisters'</u> house.
2. I give <u>the sisters</u> food.
3. I send a letter <u>to the sisters</u>.
4. <u>The sister</u> is coming.
5. <u>The sisters</u> are laughing.
6. I see <u>the sisters</u>.
7. The house <u>of the sisters</u> is big.
8. Do you see <u>the sisters</u>?
9. <u>The sister's</u> turtle is sick.
10. The turtle <u>of the sister</u> is sick.
11. They like <u>the sister</u>.
12. I send <u>the sister</u> a letter.

WORD ORDER

In Greek word order is flexible because function is known from form rather than position. The three elements ἡ ἀδελφή (*the sister* - nominative), ὁρᾷ (*sees*), and χελώνην (*a turtle* - accusative) can go in any order. (Position seems to show a difference in emphasis, the first word or phrase having the greatest emphasis.)

ἡ ἀδελφὴ ὁρᾷ χελώνην.	*The sister sees a turtle.*
ἡ ἀδελφὴ χελώνην ὁρᾷ.	(Answers question: what about my sister?)
ὁρᾷ ἡ ἀδελφὴ χελώνην.	*The sister sees a turtle.*
ὁρᾷ χελώνην ἡ ἀδελφή.	(Answers question: What is my sister doing?)
χελώνην ὁρᾷ ἡ ἀδελφή.	*My sister sees a turtle:*
χελώνην ἡ ἀδελφὴ ὁρᾷ.	(Answers question: What does my sister see?)

🙨 To say that the sister sees a turtle in English we must place *the sister* before *sees* and *sees* before *a turtle*.

▶ **Exercise γ:** Read and translate. What is the case of each underlined word? Why was that case used?
τὸ ὄνομα τῆς <u>ἀδελφῆς</u> μου <u>Νίκη</u> ἐστιν. τὴν <u>ἀδελφὴν</u> φιλῶ καὶ δίδωμι <u>αὐτῇ</u> χελώνας. τὰς <u>χελώνας</u> τῆς <u>Νίκης</u> οὐ φιλῶ . λέγω τῇ <u>Νίκῃ</u> ὅτι <u>φωνὴν</u> οὐκ ἔχουσιν αἱ <u>χελῶναι</u> <u>αὐτῆς</u> διότι <u>γλῶτταν</u> οὐκ ἔχουσιν.

ἔργα
~Write paradigms for ἡ φωνή and ἡ γλῶττα three times. Memorize.
~Read "Nasrudin and the Letter." Practice reading it aloud until you can read it smoothly while being aware of what it means.
~Learn the vocabulary for "Nasrudin and the Letter." (This instruction is to be understood with every story. Always learn the vocabulary and the grammatical notes, especially whatever is in a box.)

NASRUDIN AND THE LETTER

ἄνθρωπός τις βούλεται πέμπειν ἐπιστολὴν ταῖς ἀδελφαῖς   1*
ταῖς ἐν τῇ Βάγδαδ. ἀλλὰ οὐκ ἐπίσταται γράφειν   **2**
τὰ γράμματα. αἰτεῖ οὖν Νασρέδδινον τὸν Σοφὸν γράφειν   **3**
τὴν ἐπιστολήν. ὁ δὲ Νασρέδδινος λέγει αὐτῷ· "ὦ φίλε,
οὐκ ἐθέλω γράφειν τὴν ἐπιστολήν. οὐ γάρ ἐστί μοι σχολὴ   **5**
πορεύεσθαι εἰς τὴν Βάγδαδ."

ὁ δὲ ἄνθρωπος λέγει "ἀλλὰ οὐκ αἰτῶ σε πορεύεσθαι εἰς τὴν
Βάγδαδ. αἰτῶ σε μόνον ἐπιστολὴν γράφειν ταῖς ἀδελφαῖς   **8**
μου."

"οἶδα" ἀποκρίνεται ὁ Σοφός· "ἀλλὰ ἡ γραφή μου (handwriting)
κακή ἐστι καὶ ἀνάγκη ἂν εἴη μοι (it would be necessary for me)
πορεύεσθαι εἰς τὴν Βάγδαδ καὶ ἀναγιγνώσκειν αὐταῖς τὴν   12 ~
ἐπιστολήν."

ὁ ἄνθρωπος - person, man, human being   --> anthropology

1

> ### ἄνθρωπός τις   *a certain person, a certain man*
> Notice how accented τίς at the beginning of a sentence asks a question.
> But unaccented τις coming after a word makes that word indefinite.
>
> ἄνθρωπος = *a man*   ἄνθρωπός τις = *some man, a certain man.*

πέμπω - send   --> pomp
ἡ ἐπιστολή - letter   --> epistle

> 📖📖 Learning Greek makes us aware of how often we use the same word in
> English for what are clearly different concepts in another language, for example,
> *letter* (γράμμα and ἐπιστολή) or *know* (οἶδα and γιγνώσκω). Soon we shall
> learn *ask* (ἐρωτάω and αἰτέω).

ἡ ἀδελφή - sister
ἐν ⟨--⟩ in + dative. (Some prepositions require one particular case, others more
        than one. ἐν occurs only with the dative.)

1-2

> ### ταῖς ἀδελφαῖς ταῖς ἐν τῇ Βάγδαδ
> The prepositional phrase ἐν τῇ Βάγδαδ is used here as an adjective. (You can
> tell by its position, after the article.) Translate: *to his sisters* (the ones) *in Baghdad.*
>
> Normally, without the article, a prepositional phrase goes with the verb:
>   πορεύομαι ἐν τῇ Βάγδαδ. *I travel in Baghdad.*

ἐπίσταμαι - know how, understand (literally, *stand on*). 📖 📖 Why do we
       *stand **under*** when we know (*understand*) something, while the Greeks *stand **on***?
       The root στα- ⟨--⟩ stand. (Cf. ἀνίσταμαι - I stand up.)
3   αἰτέω - request, ask (ἐρωτάω is "ask a question." See 📖📖 above.)

---

* Lines are numbered for easier reference. Bold print in numbering means look below for a grammatical note.
   Vocabulary needs determine which lines are numbered. If no vocabulary is needed, every sixth line is numbered.
   A squiggle (~) indicates a question in the notes for students to answer.

3   οὖν - so, therefore (postpositive)

3

> ## Postpositives
>
> Some Greek words, including δέ and οὖν, must come second rather than first in their sentence. They are called **postpositive**, which means *put after*.

3

> ## Conjunctions
>
> Unless a sentence begins a wholly new unit of thought, it will be connected to the previous sentence by some linking word. (✍✍ English easily omits linking words.)
>
> We know δέ from our poem. This is the briefest all-purpose linking word-- *and* or *but*, whatever the context needs. It is the most common word for linking sentences.
>
> We also know καί (*and*), which links equivalents. Now we have learned ἀλλά (*but*), which links equivalents but in an oppositional way: A. *But B.* This shows that B is not what one would expect given A.
>
> οὖν (*therefore*) makes an inference. A. *So B.*

σοφός - wise   --> sophomore, sophisticated

5   γάρ - for (a postpositive conjunction that gives the reason for the preceding statement)
        ✍✍ The word *for* in English has two different uses: (a) as a preposition: *It is hard for me*, with the phrase *for me* is equivalent to a Greek dative, and (b) as a conjunction: *I took the food. For I was hungry.* γάρ is used as a **conjunction only**.

5

> ## Dative of Possession
>
> ἐπιστολή ἐστι τῇ ἀδελφῇ.   *The sister has a letter.*
>   Literally, *A letter is* [= belongs] *to the sister.*
>
> ἐπιστολή ἐστί μοι.   *I have a letter.*
>   Literally, *A letter is* (= belongs] *to me.*
>
> ἐπιστολή οὐκ ἔστι μοι,   *I don't have a letter.*
>   Literally, *A letter is not* [= does not belong] *to me.*

ἡ σχολή - leisure   --> school, scholar (because going to school was what people chose to do in their free time) (Cf. Diogenes' witty definition of ἔρως: ✦ τὴν ἀσχολίαν τῶν σχολαζόντων.)

    Notice that our word "time" combines a number of concepts that were separate for the Greeks: (1) χρόνος = clock-time, (2) σχολή = free time, (3) καιρός = right time, opportune moment, (4) ὥρα = season, and (5) αἰών = lifetime or eternity.

πορεύομαι - travel, journey
εἰς - into + accusative

8   μόνον - only   --> monologue, etc.
       ἀποκρίνομαι - reply

12~   Punt αὐταῖς! If αὐτῇ means *to her*, what must αὐταῖς mean?

Lesson 2. The O-Group; Neuter Plural Subject + Singular Verb; The Article

THE O-GROUP

We come now to the O-Group. Compare the endings of ὁ ἀδελφός and ἡ ἀδελφή. You will find them similar except that in the one an *o* sound is dominant, in the other an *a* sound.

	Feminine A- Endings	ὁ ἀδελφός *brother*		Masculine O- Endings	τὸ βιβλίον *book*		Neuter O- Endings
Singular							
nom.	η	ὁ	ἀδελφός	ος	τὸ	βιβλίον	ον
acc.	ην	τὸν	ἀδελφόν	ον	τὸ	βιβλίον	ον
gen.	ης	τοῦ	ἀδελφοῦ	ου	τοῦ	βιβλίου	ου
dat.	ῃ	τῷ	ἀδελφῷ	ῳ	τῷ	βιβλίῳ	ῳ
Plural							
nom.	αι	οἱ	ἀδελφοί	οι	τὰ	βιβλία	α
acc.	ας	τοὺς	ἀδελφούς	ους	τὰ	βιβλία	α
gen.	ῶν	τῶν	ἀδελφῶν	ων	τῶν	βιβλίων	ων
dat.	αις	τοῖς	ἀδελφοῖς	οις	τοῖς	βιβλίοις	οις

A linguistic change makes it hard to see just how similar the accusative plural endings are. Originally the forms were * ἀδελφανς and * ἀνθρωπονς. But the combination of vowel + ν + σ was unstable in ancient Greek. Usually the ν sound disappeared and the vowel underwent some change. In this case:

$$\text{-ανς --) ᾱς} \qquad \text{-ονς --) ους}$$

τὸ βιβλίον is a neuter O-group noun. Such nouns match the masculine in the genitive and dative endings. **All neuter nouns** have the **same nominative** and **accusative** forms, in the singular and plural. Compare:

ἡ ἀδελφή	ὁ ἀδελφός	**τὸ βιβλίον**		*she*	*he*	*it*
τὴν ἀδελφήν	τὸν ἀδελφόν	**τὸ βιβλίον**		*her*	*him*	*it*

▶ **Exercise α:** Translate the underlined words into Greek:

1. They love <u>the brothers</u>.
2. They love <u>the brothers'</u> horses.
3. Give <u>the brother</u> your letter.
4. <u>Brothers</u> should be friends.
5. I do this <u>for the brothers</u>.
6. I don't know the name <u>of the book</u>.
7. <u>The books</u> are here.
8. A poet loves <u>books</u>.
9. He is reading (a) <u>book</u>.
10. Do you see (any) <u>books</u>?

▶ **Exercise β:** Read and translate the following story. Explain the cases of the words in bold print.

ὁ ἰατρός μου φιλεῖ ἀναγιγνώσκειν τὰ **βιβλία**. καὶ ἐν τοῖς **βιβλίοις** εἰσι μῦθοι. ὁ ἰατρός λέγει μύθους τοῖς **ἀνθρώποις**. οἱ **ἄνθρωποι** φιλοῦσι καὶ τὸν **ἰατρὸν** καὶ τοὺς **μύθους** αὐτοῦ. καὶ λέγουσιν οἱ **ἄνθρωποι** ὅτι οἱ **μῦθοι** τοῦ **ἰατροῦ** ἀληθῶς τὰ **φάρμακα** αὐτοῦ εἰσιν.

NEUTER PLURAL SUBJECT + SINGULAR VERB

Normally a singular subject takes a singular verb, a plural subject a plural verb. (This is *agreement*.) But it is a convention in ancient Greek that a **neuter plural subject** takes a **singular verb**. (A plural verb was kept in the Alphabet Story, p. 11, because of the personification.)

τὰ βιβλία **ἐστὶν** ἐνταῦθα. *The books are here.* Literally, *The books is here.*

▶ **Exercise γ:** Translate the following:

1. τὰ βιβλία ἐστὶν ἀγαθά.
2. οἱ ἄνθρωποι εἰσιν ἀγαθοί.
3. τὰ μικρὰ ποιήματα χαλεπά ἐστιν.
4. The poems are difficult.
5. The books are small.
6. The difficult books are good.

THE ARTICLE (ὁ, ἡ, τό)

	Masc.	Fem.	Neuter
	ὁ	ἡ	τό
	τόν	τήν	τό
	τοῦ	τῆς	τοῦ
	τῷ	τῇ	τῷ
	οἱ	αἱ	τά
	τούς	τάς	τά
	τῶν	τῶν	τῶν
	τοῖς	ταῖς	τοῖς

The Greek article corresponds, though not exactly, to our English *the*. Its main use is to **identify a particular one or ones**: ὁ μῦθος - *the story*   οἱ μῦθοι - *the stories*

Usually the first time something is mentioned there will be no article. But once it is identified, the article will be used ever after. ἰατρὸς ἔχει χελώνην. ἡ δὲ χελώνη νοσεῖ. καὶ ὁ ἰατρὸς λέγει τῇ χελώνῃ...

👁👁 It is exactly the same for English, as you can see from the translation of the above: *A doctor has a turtle. And the turtle is sick. And the doctor says to the turtle...*

What follows are four uses of the Greek article (all of which we have seen already). 👁👁 English uses *the* for the first, but not for the others. NOTE: Whenever English has *the*, Greek has the article. But when Greek has the article, English may not have *the*.

Four Uses of the Greek Article

(1) To **identify** a particular one or ones: ἡ φωνή *the voice*   αἱ φωναί *the voices*

(2) With a **possessive**, understood or expressed:
ὁρῶ τὴν χεῖρα σου.   *I see your hand.*
δός μοι τὴν χεῖρα.   *Give me your hand.*
   Literally, *Give me the hand* (*of you*, understood).
(This is really use # 1. 👁👁 It is only English that makes it seem a special case.)

(3) With **abstracts** and **general classes**:
τί ἐστιν ἡ εὐδαιμονία;   *What is happiness?* Literally, *What is the* (idea of) *happiness?*
οἱ ἰατροί εἰσι κακοί.   *Doctors are bad.* Literally, *The* (class of) *doctors are bad.*

✦ ὁ ἄνθρωπος φύσει πολιτικὸν ζῷον.
   Man is by nature a political (*i.e., polis-dwelling*) *animal.*   Aristotle

(4) With **proper names**: τὸν Σωκράτην γιγνώσκω.   *I know Socrates.*
   Literally, *I know the* (person) *Socrates.*

👁👁 When no article comes before a Greek noun, English has *a* or *an* (sing.) and, optionally, *some* (pl.):
   ὁρῶ χελώνην   *I see a turtle.* (i.e., one turtle or another).
   ὁρῶ χελώνας   *I see turtles / I see (some) turtles.*

👁👁 While Greek uses a generalizing *the*, English generalizes with *a, an,* or *the* in the singular and with nothing in the plural.

▶ **Exercise δ:** 1. Reread "Nasrudin and the Letter" on p. 28. Find an example of each of the four uses of the article listed above. 2. Read and translate the following. How is each article (underlined) used?

τὸ ὄνομα τοῦ ἀδελφοῦ μου Φίλιππός ἐστιν. φιλῶ τὸν ἀδελφὸν ἀλλὰ οὐ φιλῶ τὴν χελώνην αὐτοῦ. λέγω τῷ Φιλίππῳ ὅτι αἱ χελῶναι οὐκ ἔχουσι φωνὴν διότι οὐκ ἔχουσι γλῶτταν.

ἔργα   ~Write the paradigms of ὁ ἀδελφός and τὸ βιβλίον three times. Memorize.
   ~Read and translate "Nasrudin Eats with His Fingers." Learn the vocabulary.

νόμος ἐστὶ τοῖς ἀνθρώποις τοῖς Τυρκικοῖς (Turkish) ἐσθίειν
τὸν σῖτον δύο δακτύλοις, τῷ τε πρώτῳ καὶ τῷ δευτέρῳ.   **2**
ἀλλὰ ἡμέρᾳ τινὶ Νασρέδδινος ὁ Σοφὸς ὡς μάλιστα πεινῇ.   **3**
καὶ τοῖς πέντε (five) δακτύλοις τὸν σῖτον ἐσθίει. καὶ φίλος τις
τοῦ Σοφοῦ, ὁρῶν τοῦτο, ἐρωτᾷ· "τί ἐσθίεις πέντε (five)   **5**
δακτύλοις;" ὁ δὲ Σοφὸς ἀποκρίνεται "διότι οὐκ ἔχω ἕξ (six)."

ὁ νόμος - tradition, custom, law --> autonomous, astronomy, Deuteronomy
ἐστί μοι - functions like our *I have* (ἐστι with Dative of Possession)
         Cf. οὐκ ἔστι μοι σχολή in "Nasrudin & the Letter," p. 24.
ὁ σῖτος - food (usually grain as opposed to meat)   --> parasite

2   δύο <--> two   --> dyad, duet, deuce
ὁ δάκτυλος - finger   --> dactylic hexameter, the rhythm of Homer,
                  so called because the basic unit was long-short-short,
                  like the segments of our index finger   --> pterodactyl

2

| **Dative of Instrument** |
| δύο δακτύλοις *with two fingers*. |

2

| **τε καί = *both and*** |
| τε is a signal that there will be a linking. We have seen καὶ A καὶ B = *both A and B*. **A τε καί** B works the same way only with less emphasis. It seems less heavy, more elegant. τε is postpositive. If τε is joining two nouns, it can follow either the noun + article combination or the article alone. It is possible to say either |
| τῷ **τε** πρώτῳ **καὶ** τῷ δευτέρῳ δακτύλῳ OR |
| τῷ πρώτῳ **τε καὶ** τῷ δευτέρῳ δακτύλῳ. |

πρῶτος <--> first   --> prototype, etc.
δεύτερος - second   --> Deuteronomy
3   ἡ ἡμέρα - day   --> ephemeral

3

| **Dative of Time When** |
| ἡμέρᾳ τινί   *one day, on a certain day* |

3   ὡς μάλιστα - as much as can be   (Translate: *is as hungry as can be*)
πεινάω - be hungry   (irregular forms: πεινῶ, πεινῇς, πεινῇ)
ὁ φίλος - friend   --> philosophy, philanthropist, etc.
5   ὁρῶν - seeing (participle)

5

| **Participle** |
| Drop -ω from the end of any verb of the ἀκούω pattern, add -ων, and you have a participle. Translate with *-ing*. |
| δακρύων ἔρχεται. *Weeping, he comes.* |
| ἀκούων τοῦτο ἔρχεται. *Hearing this, he comes.* |

τί - what? or, as here, why?

33

Lesson 3. Accents

This chapter deals with the principles behind Greek accents. In order to write ancient Greek in the traditional way, you will have to be able to answer these two questions: (1) Which syllable gets the accent? (2) Which accent does it get?

For the purpose of accent **syllable length** is determined by the **length of the vowel or diphthong.** You can tell that ε and ο are short, η and ω are long. Greek α, ι, or υ may represent long or short vowel sounds. Vowel combinations (diphthongs) such as ει, αυ, etc. are normally long (but see item # 5 below).

WHICH SYLLABLE GETS THE ACCENT?

All accents must be on one of three syllables: the *last*, the *next-to-last*, or what we will call the *third-back* (i.e., the syllable before the next-to-last). If these names seem awkward, use the traditional ones: *ultima* (Latin for *last*), *penult* (Latin for *almost the last*) and *antepenult* (Latin for *before the penult*).

The length of the **last** syllable determines how far back an accent can go.

(1) **Noun accents are persistent.** They want to stay on the syllable they were on in the nominative singular.

(2) Apparent exception: the genitive plural of A-Group **nouns** is always ‾**ῶν**.
   (This is because the ending was originally -άσων.)

(3) **Verb accents are recessive.** In a personal verb form (with endings for *I, we, you, he/she/it, they*), the accent will go back as far as it can.

(4) **Only when the last syllable is short can the accent be on the third-back syllable.** When the last syllable is long, the accent cannot go further back than the next-to-last syllable.

   This rule explains why it is ὁ ἄνθρωπος but τοῦ ἀνθρώπου. Although the accent "wants" (according to item # 2) to stay on the syllable ἀν because noun accents are persistent, it cannot because the final syllable is long.

(5) For the purpose of accent, **final ‾οι and ‾αι count as short.**

   Note: For determining **accent**, final ‾αι and ‾οι count as short. So, as far as **accent** is concerned ἄνθρωποι has a short last syllable, ἀνθρώποις a long. As far as **poetic meter** goes, the last syllables in both ἄνθρωποι and ἀνθρώποις take a long time and can be counted long. Some scholars use the terms *long* and *short* for determining pitch accent, *heavy* and *light* for scanning length in poetry.

▶ **Exercise α:** Underline the vowel that will get the accent, according to the rules above.
   Remember that the accent goes on the second letter of a diphthong.
   When reading these forms aloud in class, pronounce the accented syllable aloud.

NOUNS

1. τῶν μαχων   (nom. ἡ μάχη)
2. τὸν σιτον   (nom. ὁ σῖτος)
3. τοῦ φαρμακου   (nom. τὸ φάρμακον)
4. τὴν θαλατταν   (nom. ἡ θάλαττα)
5. τοῖς μωροις   (nom. ὁ μῶρος)
6. τῇ χελωνῃ   (nom. ἡ χελώνη)
7. αἱ χελωναι   (nom. ἡ χελώνη)

VERBS

1. χαιρε
2. συμβουλευουσι
3. ἐθελεις
4. παρελιπες
5. ἐπαιδευσατε
6. παιδευομαι
7. παιδευση
8. ἐλθετω
9. ἐξελθοιεν
10. ἐλθοιμην
11. ἐμανθανον
12. μανθανωμεν
13. μαθωμεν
14. χαιρετε

WHICH ACCENT DOES THE SYLLABLE GET?

(6)   An accent on the **third-back** syllable is **always acute**.

ὁ ἄνθρωπος   τὸ φάρμακον

(7a)   An accent on the **next-to-last** syllable is **circumflex** in a **long-short combination**
       (that is, when the next-to-last syllable is long and the last syllable is short.)

αἱ χελῶναι the turtles   ὁ μῶρος the fool   τὰ δῶρα the gifts

(7b)   and **acute** in all other situations.

ταῖς χελώναις   τῷ φίλῳ (short ι)   τῶν φαρμάκων

Can you tell whether the α in χελώνας is long or short? What about the υ in μῦθος? Why is there a circumflex in χαλεπὸν τὸ μὴ φιλῆσαι? Is the last syllable poetically short or long? (See item # 4 above.)

(8)   If the accent is on the **last** syllable, the pattern depends on the paradigm. For every **A- or O-Group** noun or adjective accented on the last syllable, the pattern down the paradigm is: **straight, straight, circumflex, circumflex**.

▶ **Exercise β:** Go back to the syllables you underlined in **exercise α** and put in the accents.

▶ **Exercise γ:** Look at the following noun patterns. What accent rules do you need to explain the forms?

sister	*turtle*	*tongue*	*story*	*gift*	*sea*	*person*	*drug, medicine*
ἀδελφή	χελώνη	γλῶττα	μῦθος	δῶρον	θάλαττα	ἄνθρωπος	φάρμακον
ἀδελφήν	χελώνην	γλῶτταν	μῦθον	δῶρον	θάλατταν	ἄνθρωπον	φάρμακον
ἀδελφῆς	χελώνης	γλώττης	μύθου	δώρου	θαλάττης	ἀνθρώπου	φαρμάκου
αδελφῇ	χελώνῃ	γλώττῃ	μύθῳ	δώρῳ	θαλάττῃ	ἀνθρώπῳ	φαρμάκῳ
ἀδελφαί	χελῶναι	γλῶτται	μῦθοι	δῶρα	θάλατται	ἄνθρωποι	φάρμακα
ἀδελφάς	χελώνας	γλώττας	μύθους	δῶρα	θαλάττας	ἀνθρώπους	φάρμακα
ἀδελφῶν	χελωνῶν	γλωττῶν	μύθων	δώρων	θαλαττῶν	ἀνθρώπων	φαρμάκων
ἀδελφαῖς	χελώναις	γλώτταις	μύθοις	δώροις	θαλάτταις	ἀνθρώποις	φαρμάκοις

GRAVE OR ACUTE ACCENT ON LAST SYLLABLE

Item # 8 above explains the accent on words *in a paradigm*. For words *in a sentence*, you need to know the following:

(9a)   A **straight accent** on the **last syllable** is **grave** before another accented word.
       Graves are found only on final syllables. (On these syllables graves are far more common than acutes. Consider the poem, χαλεπὸν τὸ μὴ φιλῆσαι, p. 11.)

(9b)   A **straight accent** on the **last syllable** is **acute before punctuation or before an enclitic.**   τὸν ἰατρὸν ὁρῶ.   But   ὁρῶ τὸν ἰατρόν.
                                                                        τὸν ἰατρόν μου ὁρῶ.

An **enclitic** is an accentless word, such as μου or ἐστι, which attaches itself ("leans in") closely to the word that comes before it. The rules for enclitics are complicated and will be given later.

(Some words have no accent but are not enclitic. They are called **proclitic** because they are felt to "lean forward" and form a unit with the word that follows. They have no effect on accents. The words ὁ, ἡ, οἱ, αἱ, οὐ, ἐκ, ἐν, and εἰς are proclitics.)

▶ **Exercise δ:** Write the proper straight accent on the final syllables of φωνή and ἐπιστολή:

1. ἀκούω τὴν <u>φωνην</u>.
2. ἀκούω τὴν <u>φωνην</u> αὐτῆς.
3. μεγάλη ἐστὶν ἡ <u>φωνη</u> μου.
4. γράφω <u>ἐπιστολην</u>.
5. ὅτε τῇ ἀδελφῇ μου γράφω <u>ἐπιστολην</u>, πέμπει μοι δῶρα.
6. ὅτε γράφω <u>ἐπιστολην</u> τῇ ἀδελφῇ μου, πέμπει μοι δῶρα.

SUMMARY

If the accent falls on the **third syllable back**	If the accent falls on the **next-to-last syllable**	If the accent falls on the **last syllable**
´ Acute Can fall on third syllable back only when last syllable is short	⌢ Circumflex when last syllable is short and next-to-last is long ´ Acute in all other circumstances	⌢ Circumflex depending on paradigm / only on a long syllable ´ Acute depending on paradigm OR when word is followed by an enclitic or by punctuation ` Grave for an accent which would have been acute, except that the word is followed immediately by an accented word

▶ **Exercise ε:** Explain each accent according to the chart above:

αἱ ἀδελφαί μου οὐ γιγνώσκουσι τοὺς ἀνθρώπους τοὺς σοφούς.

Classwork or ἔργα: Accent the following words. Write the numbers of whichever rules apply.

(1) Noun accents persistent.
(2) -ῶν for gen. pl of A-group nouns.
(3) Verb accents recessive.
(4a) Accent cannot be on third-back if last syllable is long.
(4b) Accent can be on third-back if last syllable is short.

(5) Final -οι and -αι are short (for purposes of accent).
(6) Accent on the third-back is always acute.
(7a) **Circumflex** on next-to-last in a **long-short** combination.
(7b) Acute on next-to-last in any situation other than a long-short combination.
(8) The pattern is ´ ´ ⌢ ⌢ if the accent is on the last syllable of an A- or O-Group noun.

1. τῶν μαχων   (nom. μάχη)
2. τὸν σιτον   (nom. σῖτος)
3. τοῦ φαρμακου   (nom. φάρμᾰκον)
4. τὴν θαλατταν   (nom. θάλαττα)
5. τοῖς μωροις   (nom μῶρος)
6. τῇ χελωνῃ   (nom. χελώνη)
7. αἱ χελωναι   (nom. χελώνη)
8. βαινετω   *Let him/her/it go!*

9. βαινοιεν   *If only they would go*
10. βαινοιμην ἄν   *I might go*
11. βαινε   *Go! (you sing)*
12. βαινετε   *Go! (you pl.)*
13. ἐμανθανον   *I was learning*
14. μανθανωμεν   *Let us be learning!*
15. μανθανομεν   *We are learning*
16. μαθωμεν   *Let us learn (once)!*

ἔργα   ~Translate. Use dative of possession for # 1-2. (See box on p. 29 and story p. 32.)

1. The people have a custom.   3. Turtles eat with (their) tongues.
2. My sister has a custom.   4. The wise man does not eat with (his) fingers.

~Write a short story and translate it.
~Read and translate the following story, written by a student in her third week of Greek:

"Your Handwriting Is Bad"*

ἄνθρωπός τις ἔχει χελώνην. φιλεῖ τὴν χελώνην. βούλεται γράφειν ἐπιστολὴν τῇ χελώνῃ. ἡ δὲ χελώνη οὐκ ἀναγιγνώσκει τὴν ἐπιστολήν. ἡ χελώνη δίδωσι τὴν ἐπιστολὴν τῷ ἀνθρώπῳ καὶ λέγει· "ἡ γραφή σου κακή ἐστιν." ὁ ἄνθρωπος δίδωσι τὴν ἐπιστολὴν τῇ ἀδελφῇ αὐτοῦ καὶ λέγει· "ἡ χελώνη μου οὐ βούλεται ἀναγιγνώσκειν τὴν ἐπιστολήν μου. ἡ γὰρ γραφή μου κακή ἐστιν." ἡ ἀδελφὴ λέγει· "ἡ γραφή σου οὐ κακή ἐστιν. οὐκ οἶσθα ὅτι αἱ χελῶναι οὐκ ἀναγιγνώσκουσιν;"

(Challenge: imagine the ending is **οὐκ ἔχουσιν ἀναγιγνώσκειν.**)

*Story by Vicki Kondelik; used with permission of the author.

Lesson 4. αὐτός as Pronoun; ὁ αὐτός as "Same"; Accent Review

FORMS OF αὐτός

	Masculine	Feminine	Neuter
nom.	αὐτός	αὐτή	**αὐτό**
acc.	αὐτόν	αὐτήν	**αὐτό**
gen.	αὐτοῦ	αὐτῆς	αὐτοῦ
dat.	αὐτῷ	αὐτῇ	αὐτῷ
nom.	αὐτοί	αὐταί	αὐτά
acc.	αὐτούς	αὐτάς	αὐτά
gen.	αὐτῶν	αὐτῶν	αὐτῶν
dat.	αὐτοῖς	αὐταῖς	αὐτοῖς

αὐτός has A- and O-Group forms. It follows the pattern of the article (ὁ, ἡ, τό) in that the neuter nom./acc. ends in -ο rather than ⁻ον.

αὐτός AS PRONOUN

When used alone, forms of αὐτός replace a noun, as **him, her, it, them**, etc. This is the most common use of the word: as a pronoun. αὐτός, αὐτή, αὐτό is **never used as a pronoun in the nominative**. There is no need. For a Greek, the word φιλεῖ already says, *he / she / it likes*. Why add another word?

You will notice that forms of αὐτός used as an unemphatic pronoun (*him, her, it, they, them*) never come first in a sentence.

	Masculine		Feminine		Neuter	
nom.	--	--	--	--	--	--
acc.	αὐτόν	*him*	αὐτήν	*her*	αὐτό	*it*
gen.	αὐτοῦ	*his, of him*	αὐτῆς	*her, of her*	αὐτοῦ	*its, of it*
dat.	αὐτῷ	*to / for him*	αὐτῇ	*to / for her*	αὐτῷ	*to / for it*
nom.	--	--	--	--	--	--
acc.	αὐτούς	*them*	αὐτάς	*them*	αὐτά	*them*
gen.	αὐτῶν	*their, of them*	αὐτῶν	*their, of them* (f.)	αὐτῶν	*their, of them*
dat.	αὐτοῖς	*to / for them*	αὐταῖς	*to / for them* (f.)	αὐτοῖς	*to / for them*

▶ **Exercise α: Translate the following:**

1. ὁρῶ αὐτόν.
2. ὁρῶ αὐτήν.
3. ὁρῶ αὐτό.
4. τὰ βιβλία αὐτῶν ἔχω.
5. δῶρα αὐτοῖς δίδωμι.
6. δῶρα αὐταῖς ἐστιν.
7. φιλῶ αὐτούς.
8. φιλῶ αὐτάς.
9. φιλῶ αὐτά.
10. τὴν χελώνην αὐτῆς ὁρῶ.
11. χελώνη ἐστὶν αὐτῇ.
12. χελώνην αὐτῶν ὁρῶ.

ὁ αὐτός AS "THE SAME"

Immediately following the article, αὐτός means "*same.*"

Note: As *the same* ὁ αὐτός is used in all grammatical cases, including the nominative.

	Both mean:	Compare (p. 9):	
ὁ αὐτὸς ἄνθρωπος		τὰ μικρὰ γράμματα	
ὁ ἄνθρωπος ὁ αὐτός	*the same person*	τὰ γράμματα τὰ μικρά	

▶ Exercise β: What clues distinguish the use of αὐτός as a pronoun or as "same"?

The following sentences use αὐτός as a pronoun. (It is used without an article.) Translate:

1. πίνουσιν αὐτό.
2. ὁρῶ αὐτόν.
3. γαμῶ αὐτήν.
4. φιλεῖς αὐτούς.
5. δείκνυμι αὐτὸ αὐτοῖς.
6. πέμπω αὐτὴν αὐταῖς.
7. πέμπω τὰ δῶρα αὐτῶν.

In the following phrases αὐτός means "same." Translate. (Note position of article.)

8. ὁ αὐτὸς ποιητής
9. αἱ αὐταὶ ἀδελφαί
10. οἱ αὐτοὶ νόμοι
11. οἱ νόμοι οἱ αὐτοί
12 τὰ φάρμακα τὰ αὐτά
13. ἡ αὐτὴ ἐπιστολή

Translate the following, being careful to watch for the use of the article.

14. πέμπω αὐτῇ τὴν ἐπιστολήν.
15. πέμπω τὴν αὐτὴν ἐπιστολήν.
16. ὁρῶ αὐτῶν τὴν ἐπιστολήν.
17. ἐσθίω τὸν σῖτον αὐτοῦ.
18. ἐσθίω τὸν αὐτὸν σῖτον.
19. λέγω τὸ αὐτὸ αὐτῷ.
20. ὁ αὐτὸς ἄνθρωπος ἔρχεται.
21. τὸν ἄνθρωπον τὸν αὐτὸν ὁρῶ.

ACCENT REVIEW

Review the material on accents on pp. 33-35.

It is best simply to notice which forms in a paradigm have **short endings** (outlined below). These are the only forms where you can expect to find either

     (a) an **acute** accent on the **third syllable back,** or
     (b) a **circumflex** on the **next-to-last** syllable.

Remember: The next-to-last syllable must be long, followed by a short last syllable, to receive the circumflex.

	μάχη *battle*	χελώνη *turtle*	γλῶττα *tongue*	μῦθος *story*	φάρμακον *drug*
nom.	μάχη	χελώνη	**γλῶττα**	**μῦθος**	**φάρμακον**
acc.	μάχην	χελώνην	**γλῶτταν**	**μῦθον**	**φάρμακον**
gen.	μάχης	χελώνης	γλώττης	μύθου	φαρμάκου
dat.	μάχῃ	χελώνῃ	γλώττῃ	μύθῳ	φαρμάκῳ
nom.	μάχαι	**χελῶναι**	**γλῶτται**	**μῦθοι**	**φάρμακα**
acc.	μάχας	χελώνας	γλώττας	μύθους	**φάρμακα**
gen.	μαχῶν	χελωνῶν	γλωττῶν	μύθων	φαρμάκων
dat.	μάχαις	χελώναις	γλώτταις	μύθοις	φαρμάκοις

▶ Exercise γ: For each of the bold forms above explain the accent used.

Give the accusative and genitive singular for each:

1. ὁ πρῶτος
2. ὁ δάκτυλος
3. ἡ πεῖνα *hunger*

Give the nominative and accusative plural for each:

4. ὁ πρῶτος
5. ὁ δάκτυλος
6. ἡ πεῖνα *hunger*

7. τὸ δεῖπνον
8. ὁ σῖτος
9. ἡ σελήνη *moon*
10. τὸ φάρμακον

4. Each underlined word has an accent on the last syllable. Write the proper accent:
     ὁρῶ <u>τον</u> <u>ἀγαθον</u> <u>ἰατρον</u>, ἀλλὰ οὐχ ὁρῶ <u>τον</u> <u>ἰατρον</u> <u>τον</u> <u>κακον</u>.

Classwork: ✦✦Read Heraclitus # 1-4, Thesauros p. 224. The logo ✦✦ indicates Thesauros.
     θησαυρός is Greek for *treasure* or *treasure house.* All selections in the Thesauros are in genuine ancient or Koine Greek. (There may be some changes in dialect.)

ἔργα   ~Read and translate "Looking for the Ring." Learn the vocabulary.
     ~Make up three sentences of your own using αὐτός as "same" and as a pronoun. Write them in English as well as Greek. Try to use some of the new vocabulary.

δακτύλιον (ring) πίπτει ἀπὸ τοῦ δακτύλου τοῦ Σοφοῦ ὅτε
ἐν τῇ οἰκίᾳ ἐστίν. ὁ δὲ Σοφὸς ἔρχεται εἰς τοὺς ἀγροὺς καὶ
ζητεῖ αὐτό. φίλος τις ὁρῶν τοῦτο ἐρωτᾷ αὐτὸν ἐρώτημα·   3
"ὦ φίλε, τί ποιεῖς; " ὁ δὲ Σοφὸς οὐδὲν λέγει. ἀλλὰ ζητεῖ.
ὁ δὲ φίλος ἐρωτᾷ αὐτὸν τὸ αὐτὸ ἐρώτημα· "ὦ φίλε, τί
ποιεῖς; " ὁ δὲ Νασρέδδινος ἀποκρίνεται αὐτῷ "ζητῶ τὸ
δακτύλιόν μου (ring). ἔπεσε (it fell) γὰρ ἀπὸ τοῦ δακτύλου
μου ὅτε ἐν τῇ οἰκίᾳ ἦν."   0

ὁ δὲ φίλος ἐρωτᾷ αὐτόν· "ἀλλ' ὦ Νασρέδδινε, εἰ ἐν τῇ   9
οἰκίᾳ σου τὸ δακτύλιον (ring) ἦν ὅτε ἔπεσεν (it fell),
τί ἐν τοῖς ἀγροῖς ζητεῖς αὐτό;" ἀποκρίνεται ὁ Σοφός
"διότι ἐν μὲν τῇ οἰκίᾳ μου ἔστι σκοτία, ἐν δὲ τοῖς ἀγροῖς   12
ἔστι τὸ φῶς τὸ μέγα τοῦ ἡλίου."

πίπτω - fall (aorist ἔπεσον = *I fell*)
ἀπό - from, away from + gen.
ἡ οἰκία - home, house (cf. οἶκος = home --> economy, ecology)
ὁ ἀγρός - field   <--> acre   --> agriculture (via Latin)
ζητέω - look for, seek, search
αὐτό - it

3

> ## Verbs with Two Accusatives
>
> Some verbs can take two accusatives, such as ἐρωτάω = ask, with accusative
> of thing asked and person;   or αἰτέω = request, with accusative of thing
> requested and person
>
> ἐρωτῶ σε τοῦτο.   *I ask you this.*
> αἰτῶ σε τοῦτο.   *I request this of you.*

ὁ αὐτός, ἡ αὐτή, τὸ αὐτό - the same
8   ἦν - *I was.* (Also = *he, she, it was.* See line 10.)

9

> ## Elision: ἀλλ' ὦ Νασρέδδινε
>
> When one word ends with a short vowel and the next begins with a vowel,
> the end vowel may be dropped. This is called **elision**. An apostrophe
> shows where the vowel had been (✍ as in the English *don't*).

ἦν - *he, she, it was* (Also *I was.* See line 8 above.)

12

> ## μέν / δέ
>
> Notice the **μέν / δέ** here. Always think of a pair of scales when you see
> μέν / δέ. These words bring to you two thoughts that are seen as somehow
> balancing each other. The δέ is simply the old connecting word we have
> already seen. And μέν is an early signal
> (postpositive) that a δέ is coming.
>
> Translate: μέν *on the one hand*
>   δέ   *on the other*

ἔστι(ν) - *exists, there exists* (always accented on first syllable)
ἡ σκοτία - darkness
τὸ φῶς - light   --> phosphorus
ὁ ἥλιος - sun   --> heliocentric

THE WISDOM OF NASRUDIN AND SOCRATES

Throughout this course, you will be reading a number of stories in which Nasrudin, the wise one, is the central figure. Nasrudin is a folklore figure familiar all throughout the Middle East and in those parts of Europe which have had extensive cultural contacts with Islam – Spain, the Balkans, southern Russia, and modern Greece.

Although more than five hundred stories about Nasrudin have been collected, no one really knows who he is, or where he comes from, or whether he even existed. This timeless legendary figure is celebrated in stories that are still being told. In them, Nasrudin emerges as the paradoxical figure of the wise fool.

Figure 1. Nasrudin on his donkey. (Line drawing by Constance Pierce)

The pattern of the stories follows the mythical archetype of the trickster figure. Tricksters are found in all cultures. Bugs Bunny and Brer Rabbit may be familiar to you from American culture, but Hermes and Prometheus in Greek myth also may be defined as tricksters. Tricksters are generally marked by their cleverness (which includes artistic skills) and by their defiance of ordinary rules and conventions. They are figures difficult to classify because at times they may be seen as beneficent, at other times as destructive. They can be culture heroes or culture destroyers, and human, animal, or divine. While one of their salient features is their cunning, they are just as often seen as naive fools or buffoons caught in their own misfired trickery.

Nasrudin tales generally focus either on his cleverness or his foolishness. In both roles, Nasrudin's simplicity, refusal to be led astray by the trappings of society, and inversion of the ordinary are marks of wisdom: he forces you to see the world with fresh eyes. As such, they are stories that are pondered and studied as part of the teachings of the Sufis. Sufism is a mystical Islamic sect in which direct experience of God is the goal. As a Sufi teaching figure, Nasrudin leads the Sufi disciple to mystical enlightenment by helping cut away overly rational approaches to the divine and severing dependence on familiar ways of apprehending reality.

One of the most well-known stories about Nasrudin is "Looking for the Ring," in which Nasrudin searches for a lost ring, not in the house where it was dropped but outside in the sunlight because there is more light there. In Sufi commentaries this story, which could simply be enjoyed for its humor, is used to highlight the absurdity of those who search for enlightenment in places where it is not to be found.

What appears to be naive foolishness can also be construed as a realization that ordinary ways of thinking can hinder enlightenment. In one story, depicted in Figure 1, Nasrudin is asked by his students, who are following him to a mosque, why he rides his donkey backwards. Nasrudin answers this in the only possible way: if he rides his donkey in the forward position, he would either have his back to his pupils and be disrespectful of them or his pupils would have their backs to him and be disrespectful to him. As a Sufi teacher, Nasrudin clarifies here that he is willing to violate the ordinary conventions and even appear to be ridiculous in order that he lead the way for his pupils (down a path he no longer needs to see because he has already been there).

Greek mythology and legend do not have a comparable teaching figure. But Socrates (469 -399 B.C.E.), like other famous teachers whose aim is to help us reenvision reality, displays some of the traits of the trickster and the wise fool. Yet, his methods are not the same as Nasrudin's. He does not wish to bypass logic, but to clarify how to think more clearly and definitively. And unlike Nasrudin, Socrates is a real person about whom we know a great deal because of the works of two of his pupils, Plato and Xenophon, even though Socrates never wrote a word himself.

Socrates, as one who succeeds the Ionian philosophers and is contemporary with the Sophists, turns philosophy to a new focus: how we are to tend to our souls and improve them. To do so, he uses a technique of question and answer (called *elenchus*) to examine fundamental assumptions and definitions and thereby to determine, with logic and reason, whether they are true. He claims that he has nothing to teach except *a method of inquiry*. Therefore, he can call himself a "midwife," who only helps the pupils give birth to their own understanding.

The first step is to see how little we truly know. Accordingly, Socrates ironically refuses any claim to wisdom: his only superiority, he says, is that he knows that he doesn't know. Yet, his skill at argumentation is so great that Euthyphro accused him of being like his ancestor Daedalus, a legendary trickster. Daedalus' skill at sculpting was such that he could make statues walk about, just as Socrates seems to Euthyphro to make the arguments move. Alcibiades in Plato's *Symposium* further identifies Socrates, because of his pug nose and thick lips, with other trickster figures whom Socrates physically resembles: Silens and satyrs, half-animal, half-human figures of cleverness and artistic skill. Alcibiades in particular likens Socrates to Silens sold in shops which open up to reveal the images of the gods inside. He states: "If anyone would be willing to listen to Socrates' words, they would completely seem ridiculous (*geloioi*) at first…and a person who was inexperienced and unthoughtful might laugh at his words…but anyone looking at them when they are opened out and getting inside them, will find first that they are the only ones which make sense, then that they are most divine and containing the finest images of virtue. "

Socrates' "works in words" so charm his hearers that they are like the enchanting music of the satyr Marysas. But they are all for an ultimately very serious purpose: to help us examine the premises by which we live. Both Socrates and Nasrudin invite us, by their very playfulness, to greater depth and understanding.

Figure 2. Statuette of Socrates, Agora Museum. Courtesy of the American School of Classical Studies at Athens: Agora Excavations.

Lesson 5. Use of Cases; Double Negatives; Articular Infinitive

USE OF CASES

As you can see from our stories, the four cases have other uses besides the ones we have just mentioned. Why does ἐν take the dative and εἰς the accusative? Why does τοῖς δακτύλοις mean "*with two fingers*" and ἡμέρᾳ τινί "*on a certain day*"? None of this is arbitrary. All the uses stem from the basic ideas that the cases express. Let us look at these ideas.

If we disregard the vocative, we can go back to an earlier stage of the Greek language where each noun had seven cases. This was a legacy from Indo-European. Latin kept five of the cases and Greek four. If the cases were dropped, the functions were not. The remaining cases simply absorbed the functions of the those that were dropped.

> Indo-European
> nominative - subject matter
> accusative - extent of impact
> genitive - part of whole
> dative - indirect impact
> instrumental - means, instrument
> locative - location in space or time
> ablative - separation

In Greek the ablative case was dropped and the genitive took over its function.

The instrumental and locative cases were dropped and the dative took over their functions.

Nominative -- names or describes the subject

ὁ Ιατρὸς ἔρχεται.	*The doctor is coming.*	(noun, subject of verb)
ὁ ἀγαθὸς Ιατρὸς ἔρχεται.	*The good doctor is coming.*	(adjective, with subject noun)
ὁ ἀδελφός μου Ιατρός ἐστιν.	*My brother is a doctor.*	(predicate noun)
ὁ ἀδελφός μου ἀγαθός ἐστιν.	*My brother is good.*	(predicate adjective)

Accusative -- total impact: direct object, extent of time and space, end of motion

(1) **Direct object**: the person or thing on which the impact is felt

παίει με.	*He hits me.*	(direct object)
παίει τὴν χεῖρά μου.	*He hits my hand.*	(direct object)
παίει με τὴν χεῖρα.	*He hits me in the hand.*	(direct object + accusative of part affected, used in poetry, especially in Homer)

(2) **Extent of time and space**

νοσεῖς πέντε ἡμέρας.	*You have been sick for five days.*	(accusative of duration, extent of time)
τρέχει πέντε στάδια.	*He is running five stades.* (A stade = c. 1/9 mile.)	(acc. of extent of space)
τρέχει κατὰ τὴν ὁδόν.	*He is running down (the length of) the road.*	(accusative with preposition; expresses extent of space)

(3) **End of motion**

ἔρχεται πρὸς τὴν σκηνήν.	*She is coming toward the tent.*
ἔρχεται εἰς τὴν σκηνήν.	*She is coming into the tent.*

▶ **Exercise α:** If the following sentences were in Greek what would be the case of the underlined words?
(Note: An adjective always has the case of the noun it modifies.)

The <u>doctor</u> came into <u>town</u>. He stayed <u>three months</u>. I saw <u>him</u>. He was <u>tall</u> and <u>bald</u>. A <u>woman</u> went toward <u>him</u>. That <u>woman</u> was my <u>aunt</u>. She hit <u>him</u> <u>on the cheek</u>.

Genitive -- partitive, possession, separation, comparison, hanging noun to noun

---

Early in our language learning we find that we cannot say "a piece cake"--there must be an *of* to connect. Similarly in Greek you cannot hang one noun onto another--unless you put one of them in the genitive. The genitive "hangs" a noun onto a noun, a verb, or a preposition. It expresses many notions. These notions are often expressed in English by *of, from,* and *than*.

(1) **Partitive**: part of whole -- noun + noun   or   noun + verb

μέρος τοῦ οἴνου	*a portion of the wine*
πίνω τοῦ οἴνου.	*I drink (of) the wine.*

(2) **Possession** -- noun + noun

τὸ ὄνομα τοῦ ἰατροῦ οἶδα.	Both mean: *I know the doctor's name / the name of the doctor.*
τὸ τοῦ ἰατροῦ ὄνομα οἶδα.	Note: A genitive may be used in the position of an adjective.

(3) **Separation** -- noun + verb   or   noun + preposition   or   noun + adjective

παύεται μάχης.	*He ceases from battle.*
ἔρχεται ἐκ τῆς σκηνῆς.	*He is coming out of the tent.*
ἐνδεὴς οἴνου ἐστίν.	*He is in need of wine.*

(4) **Comparison** -- a special use of the genitive that involves the basic idea of separation, since one person or thing goes beyond (is separate from) others

comparative adjective or adverb + noun

τὸ σιγᾶν ἐστι χαλεπώτερον **πάντων**.	*To be silent is harder **than all things**.*
σοφώτερος **τοῦ ἰατροῦ** ἐστιν.	*He is wiser **than the doctor**.*
σοφώτερον **τοῦ ἰατροῦ** λέγει.	*He speaks more wisely **than the doctor**.*

(5) **Joker** -- These are all the ways a noun may hang on another noun. It seems impossible to classify all the ways, though grammarians have tried. (Genitive of value, of material, of origin, of quality, and so on.) ✍ The "joker" use includes the myriad relationships expressed by the word *of* in English--*a man of learning, a thing of value, a taste of honey, a feeling of pain.*

πορεία πέντε **ἡμερῶν**	*a journey of five days*

▶ **Exercise β**: Say which idea is behind the Greek genitives in bold print:

1. πάντα τῶν **γραμμάτων**
2. μικρότερος **τοῦ ἰατροῦ**
3. τὰ ποιήματα τῶν **ἀνθρώπων**
4. ἐκ τοῦ **βιβλίου**
5. ἄνευ τῆς **ἀδελφῆς** (ἄνευ = without)
6. δακτύλιον (ring) **ἀργύρου** (ἄργυρος = silver)
7. χαλεπώτερον **τοῦ μύθου**
8. ἡ τῆς **χελώνης** γλῶττα

Dative -- Indirect object, possession, means, manner, circumstance

---

Many prepositions convey the ideas behind the dative case: *to, for, with, in, at, on.*

(1) **Indirect object** - the person for whom something is done or to whom something is given or for whom something is the case (often expressed by *to* or *for* in English).

πέμπω αὐτῷ ἐπιστολήν.	*I send **him** a letter / I send a letter **to him**.*
δίδωμι αὐτῇ δῶρον.	*I give **her** a gift / I give a gift **to her**.*

(2) **Dative of Possession**

ἔστι μοι σκηνή	*I have a tent.* Literally, *There is* [= belongs] ***to me** a tent.*

(3) Dative of Means, Manner, Instrument - (old instrumental)   answers the question *how?*

often expressed by the prepositions *with* or *by* in English

τοῖς δακτύλοις ἐσθίω.   *I eat **with** my fingers.*
σιγῇ ἐσθίω.   *I eat **in** silence.*
δώροις αὐτοὺς πείθω.   *I persuade them **by means of** gifts.*

(4) Dative of Place Where, Time When, Circumstance (old locative)

(answers *where?* or *when?*)   usually with a preposition in English: *in, on, at,* etc.

often with a preposition in Greek

The dative is static and tells where (*at, in, on*),
while the genitive shows motion away (*from, out of*)
and the accusative motion to (*to, toward, into*).

ἐν τῇ σκηνῇ ἐστιν.   *She is **in** the tent.*
ταύτῃ τῇ ἡμέρᾳ ἔρχεται.   *She comes **on** this day.*
τῷ δώρῳ χαίρω.   *I rejoice **in** the gift.*
αὐτῇ / ἐπ' αὐτῇ ὀργίζομαι   *I am angry **at** her.*

▶ **Exercise γ:** The following passage was written by a famous nineteenth century reteller of Greek and Norse myth, Thomas Bullfinch. For each word in bold, give the case you would expect the word to have in Greek and the reason why it would be in that case.

```
Laius, king of Thebes, was warned by an oracle that there was danger to his throne
and life if his new-born son should be suffered to grow up.  He therefore committed
the child to the care of a herdsman with orders to destroy him; but the herdsman,
moved with pity, yet not daring entirely to disobey, tied up the child... Many years
afterwards Laius being on his way to Delphi, accompanied only by one attendant, met
in a narrow road a young man also driving in a chariot.  On his refusal to leave the
way at their command the attendant killed one of his horses, and the stranger,
filled with rage, slew both Laius and his attendant.  The young man was Oedipus,
who thus unknowingly became the slayer of his own father.
```

DOUBLE NEGATIVES

Double (and triple) negatives are good Greek:

οὐχ ὁρᾷ οὐδέν.   *He does not see anything.*   Literally, *He does not see nothing.*
οὐ λέγω οὐδὲν οὐδενί.   *I don't say anything to anyone.*   Literally, *I don't say nothing to no one.*

ARTICULAR INFINITIVE

An infinitive is a neuter singular noun made from a verb. It can be given an article and used in any of the cases.

τὸ γράφειν χαλεπόν ἐστιν.   *To write is difficult / Writing [the act of writing] is difficult.*
ἀντὶ τοῦ γράφειν λέγεις.   *Instead of writing you speak.*
χαίρουσι τῷ ἐσθίειν.   *They rejoice in eating [in the act of eating].*

✍✍ Important Note: Be careful when translating from English to Greek; always look at function and not just form. English uses **-ing words** three ways.

Verb	λέγεις.	*You speak / You are speaking.*
Participle	λέγων δακρύεις.	*While speaking you cry.*
Infinitive	τὸ λέγειν ῥᾴδιόν ἐστιν.	*Speaking [the act of speaking] is easy.*

▶ **Exercise δ:** Which form (verb, participle, or infinitive) would translate the underlined word(s) into Greek?
1. The art of singing is difficult.   2. Singing a song, he left.   3. She is singing.   4. Is singing pleasant?

▶ **Exercise ε:** Translate: 1. τὸ μανθάνειν ῥᾴδιόν ἐστιν.   3. χαίρουσι τῷ πίνειν οἶνον.
2. ὁρῶν τὴν μάχην δακρύω.   4. ἡ τέχνη (art, skill) τοῦ γράφειν χαλεπή.

ἔργα   ~Read and translate "Nasrudin Gives Figs." Learn the Vocabulary.

ὁ βασιλεὺς τῶν Μογγόλων (Mongols) ἔρχεται ἡμέρᾳ τινὶ
εἰς τὴν πόλιν τοῦ Σοφοῦ. καὶ ὁ Σοφὸς βούλεται αὐτῷ
δῶρον διδόναι. λαμβάνει οὖν πολλὰ μῆλα ἐκ τῆς οἰκίας καὶ   3
ἔρχεται φέρων τὰ μῆλα πρὸς τὰς σκηνὰς τοῦ βασιλέως.
ἐν δὲ τῇ ὁδῷ ἐντυγχάνει (happens on, meets up with) φίλῳ. ὁ δὲ
φίλος λέγει αὐτῷ · "μὴ φέρε μῆλα, φέρε σῦκα (figs)."   6
κατέρχεται οὖν ὁ Νασρέδδινος εἰς τὴν οἰκίαν καὶ σῦκα
(figs) λαμβάνει ἀντὶ τῶν μήλων. καὶ ἔρχεται αὖθις τὰ σῦκα
φέρων πρὸς τὰς σκηνὰς τοῦ βασιλέως. καὶ ὅτε ἔρχεται
εἰς τὴν σκηνὴν οὗ καθίζεται ὁ βασιλεύς, λέγει αὐτῷ· "ὦ   10
βασιλεῦ, δίδωμί σοι τοῦτο τὸ δῶρον. ἔστι σοι νῦν πολλὰ
σῦκα." καὶ δίδωσιν αὐτῷ τὰ σῦκα.

ὁ δὲ βασιλεύς, τὰ σῦκα (figs) μισῶν, οὐ χαίρει τῷ δώρῳ.
οὐ χαίρει οὐδαμῶς τῷ λαμβάνειν σῦκα. ἀλλ' ὀργίζεται.
ὀργίζεται ὡς μάλιστα. καὶ λέγει τοῖς στρατιώταις βάλλειν   15
τὸν Σοφὸν τοῖς σύκοις. τοῦτο δὲ ποιοῦσιν οἱ στρατιῶται.
ὁ δὲ Σοφὸς λέγει· "ὁ θεός ἐπαινείσθω (God be praised)."

ὁ δὲ βασιλεύς, τοῦτο ἀκούων, ἐρωτᾷ· "τί ἐπαινεῖς (do you
praise) τὸν θεὸν ὅτε ἄνθρωποί σε σύκοις (figs) βάλλουσιν;"   19
ὁ δὲ λέγει· "οὐ χαλεπὸν τὸ ἀποκρίνεσθαι· τὸν θεὸν ἐπαινῶ
(I praise) διότι σῦκα ἤνεγκον (I brought) ἀντὶ μήλων. τὰ μὲν
γὰρ μῆλα μεγάλα (big) ἐστιν, τὰ δὲ σῦκα οὔ.

ὁ βασιλεύς - king
ἡ πόλις - city -->   metropolis, political (Note εἰς τὴν πόλιν which, corrupted, -->
                                                      Istanbul.)
3   τὸ δῶρον - gift
τὸ μῆλον - apple   --> melon
ἐκ + gen. - out of   --> ecstasy, eclipse, eccentric
φέρω - bear, carry, bring   <--> bear   --> metaphor, phosphorus
πρός + acc. - to, toward
ἡ σκηνή - tent   --> scene   Cf. σκηνὴ πᾶς ὁ βίος - All life's a stage.
ἡ ὁδός - road, way   --> method, odometer

6
┌───┐
│   μή |
│ οὐ is the negative for facts. μή is the negative in other contexts. │
│   χαλεπὸν τὸ μὴ φιλῆσαι   *It is difficult not to love.* (With infinitive) │
│   μὴ δάκρυε   *Don't cry.* (With command) │
└───┘

κατέρχομαι - go back, return
ἀντί + genitive - instead of   --> antidote, etc.
10   οὗ - where
καθίζομαι - sit down, sit   <--> sit. (The ζ of ἵζω represents σ + δ. Cf. Latin *sedeo* --> sedentary)
μισέω - hate   --> misanthrope, misogyny
οὐδαμῶς - nohow.
ὀργίζομαι - be angry

15   λέγω - tell, say, speak; tell, command + dat. + infinitive
       (a) λέγω τὸ ὄνομα. *I tell / say / speak the name.* (b) λέγω ὅτι νοσεῖ. *I say that he is sick.*
       (c) λέγω αὐτῷ πέμπειν δῶρα. *I tell / command him to send gifts.*
ὁ στρατιώτης - soldier

15,19   βάλλω - throw; hit by throwing, pelt   --> ballistics (via Latin)
       (a) βάλλω σῦκα - *I throw figs.* (b) βάλλω αὐτόν - *I hit him (by throwing) / I pelt him*
ὁ θεός - god   --> theology, atheist, Theodore

Lesson 6. Masculine A-Group Agent Nouns; Feminine Nouns with ᾱ after ε, ι, ρ; Feminine O-Group Nouns

	ὁ -της (Masc. A-Group) ὁ στρατιώτης *soldier*	Long α after ε,ι,ρ (Fem. A-Group) ἡ οἰκία *house*	ἡ -ος (Fem. O-Group) ἡ ὁδός *road*
Singular			
nom.	ὁ στρατιώτης	ἡ οἰκίᾱ	ἡ ὁδός
acc.	τὸν στρατιώτην	τὴν οἰκίᾱν	τὴν ὁδόν
gen.	τοῦ στρατιώτου	τῆς οἰκίᾱς	τῆς ὁδοῦ
dat.	τῷ στρατιώτῃ	τῇ οἰκίᾳ	τῇ ὁδῷ
Plural			
nom.	οἱ στρατιῶται	αἱ οἰκίαι	αἱ ὁδοί
acc.	τοὺς στρατιώτας	τὰς οἰκίας	τὰς ὁδούς
gen.	τῶν στρατιωτῶν	τῶν οἰκιῶν	τῶν ὁδῶν
dat.	τοῖς στρατιώταις	ταῖς οἰκίαις	ταῖς ὁδοῖς

Besides the short-alpha nouns like γλῶττα, there are two other types of nouns in the A-Group whose endings vary somewhat from the norm.

MASCULINE A-GROUP AGENT NOUN

The masculine agent noun ends in -της. This ending shows that someone is an agent or doer. (It corresponds to our -*er*, as in writ*er*, photograph*er*, etc.) The endings are as expected except for the nominative and genitive singular.

FEMININE NOUNS WITH ᾱ AFTER ε, ι, ρ

It seems that the Athenians did not pronounce an η sound after an ε, ι, or ρ, but rather a long alpha. This makes a difference only in the singular.

θεά *goddess*   ἡμέρα *day*   οἰκία *house*

O-GROUP FEMININES

In the O-Group there are no variations in the endings. There are, however, a small number of **feminine** nouns that have the normal O-group endings.

ἡ πάρθενος *the maiden*   ἡ δρόσος *the dew*   ἡ νόσος *the sickness*

▶ **Exercise α:**

I. Using what you know about accents, write the paradigm for:

1. ὁ ποιητής (the poet)
2. ἡ θεά (the goddess)
3. ἡ νόσος (the sickness)

II. Write the correct form of the article for the following:

4. οἰκίᾳ
5. στρατιώτης
6. ὁδοί
7. στρατιώτου
8. ὁδοῦ
9. στρατιώταις
10. οἰκίας (2 ways)

III. Make the following phrases plural:

11. τῷ στρατιώτῃ
12. τῆς οἰκίας
13. τὴν ὁδόν
14. τὸν στρατιώτην
15. ἡ ὁδός

Classwork: ✦✦ Read **New Testament** # 1, Thesauros p. 221

ἔργα ~Write each one of the paradigms three times. Memorize.
~Review the vocabulary and forms of Lessons 1-6. Then write a dialogue using as many new vocabulary words as possible. Be prepared to speak this dialogue with a partner in class.

Lesson 7. O-A-O Adjectives; Agreement; Alpha Privative;
Two-ending Adjectives; Adjective with Noun Understood

O-A-O ADJECTIVES

πρῶτος, πρώτη, πρῶτον *first*

	Masculine	Feminine	Neuter		
nom.	πρῶτος	πρώτη	πρῶτον	ἀγαθός,ή,όν	*good*
acc.	πρῶτον	πρώτην	πρῶτον	κακός,ή,όν	*bad*
gen.	πρώτου	πρώτης	πρώτου	σοφός,ή,όν	*wise*
dat.	πρώτῳ	πρώτῃ	πρώτῳ	Ἑλληνικός,ή,όν	*Greek*
				ὑγιεινός,ή,όν	*healthy*
nom.	πρῶτοι	πρῶται	πρῶτα	χαλεπός,ή,όν	*difficult*
acc.	πρώτους	πρώτας	πρῶτα	πρῶτος,η,ον	*first*
gen.	πρώτων	πρώτων	πρώτων	καλός,ή,όν	*beautiful*
dat.	πρώτοις	πρώταις	πρώτοις	λοιπός,ή,όν	*remaining*

Most adjectives follow the O-A-O pattern given above. They have masculine and neuter forms in
the O-Group and feminine forms in the A-Group. Adjectives follow the normal patterns
described earlier except that feminine A-Group adjectives do **not** necessarily have a circumflex
on the genitive plural ending, as do feminine A-Group nouns.

The masculine nominative singular sets the pattern for accent. Note accent on
ἕτοιμαι, fem. nom. plural of the adjective ἕτοιμος, ἑτοίμη, ἕτοιμον = *ready*.

AGREEMENT

If a noun is masculine plural accusative, the adjective modifying it will be, too. This is called
agreement. The **gender, number, and case** will always match, though the endings may
not look the same.

φοβοῦμαι **τοὺς κακοὺς ἰατρούς**.	*I fear **bad** doctors.*
ποιητὴν σοφὸν ὁρῶ.	*I see a **wise** poet.*
γλῶτταν ὑγιεινὴν ὁρῶ.	*I see a **healthy** tongue.*
ποίημα χαλεπὸν μανθάνω.	*I learn a **difficult** poem.*

▶ Exercise α: Complete the following, using adjectives shown in the list above. Make sure they match the
noun they modify in case, number, and gender.

ὁ (bad) _____ βασιλεὺς τῶν (remaining) _____ Μογγόλων ἔρχεται. ὁ δὲ Σοφὸς ἐθέλει αὐτῷ δῶρον
(good) _____ διδόναι. λαμβάνει οὖν πολλὰ καὶ (healthy) _____ μῆλα ἐκ τῆς οἰκίας καὶ φέρει αὐτὰ
πρὸς τὰς (beautiful) _____ σκηνὰς τῆς (wise) _____ ἀδελφῆς τοῦ (bad) _____ βασιλέως.

▶ Exercise β: Translate the following phrases:
1. of the Greek house 2. for the wise soldiers 3. the healthy tongue (subject) 4. the difficult roads (direct object)

ALPHA PRIVATIVE

An alpha (**ἀ / ἀν** before vowels) at the beginning of an adjective can negate meaning.
This is called **alpha privative**.

ὁ/ἡ θεός	*god*	-->	**ἄθεος**, ον *godless*	*atheist* in English
τὸ αἷμα	*blood*	-->	**ἄναιμος**, ον *bloodless*	*anemic*

There are alpha privatives in nouns and verbs as well.

αἰσθάνομαι	*perceive*	-->	ἡ ἀναισθησία	lack of perception	*anaesthesia*
μνάομαι	*remember*	-->	ἡ ἀμνησία	lack of memory	*amnesia*
μνημονεύω	*mention, call to mind*	-->	ἀμνημονέω	leave unmentioned, unremembered	--> *amnesty*

✍✍ Many English derivatives have an alpha privative: *amoral, agnostic, amnesty, analgesic, anarchy,* etc.

TWO-ENDING ADJECTIVES

Some adjectives are called **two-ending adjectives.** These have only O-Group endings.

ἄδικος,ον *unjust* (ἀ *without*, δίκη *justice*)

	M/F	N
nom.	ἄδικος	ἄδικον
acc.	ἄδικον	ἄδικον
gen.	ἀδίκου	ἀδίκου
dat.	ἀδίκῳ	ἀδίκῳ
nom.	ἄδικοι	ἄδικα
acc.	ἀδίκους	ἄδικα
gen.	ἀδίκων	ἀδίκων
dat.	ἀδίκοις	ἀδίκοις

ὁρῶ τὰς ἀδίκους ἀδελφάς.
I see the unjust sisters.

ἀθάνατος ἡ ψυχή.
The soul is deathless.

NOTE: In any sentence ἐστι
may be omitted

Most, but not all, of these adjectives are compounds made with an alpha privative. They have a recessive accent.

ἄλογος, ον	*irrational*	(without λόγος = *reason*)
ἄτιμος, ον	*dishonored*	(without τιμή = *honor*)
ἀθάνατος, ον	*deathless*	(without θάνατος = *death*)

▶ **Exercise γ:** Translate the following phrases:
1. by an unjust deed   2. of an unjust battle   3. the unjust poets (subject)   4. the unjust poet (object)

ADJECTIVE WITH NOUN UNDERSTOOD

The article (ὁ, ἡ, τό) + an adjective (or a prepositional phrase used as an adjective) can be used with a noun understood.

ἡ σοφή ἀναγιγνώσκει.	*The wise one* (woman) *reads / is reading.*
οἱ σοφοὶ διώκουσι τὴν ἀρετήν.	*The wise* (persons) *pursue excellence.*
μανθάνεις τὰ ἰατρικά.	*You are learning medical (material)* (skills, information, etc.).
ἡ ἐν τῇ ὁδῷ νοσεῖ.	*The one* (feminine) *in the road is sick.*
τὰ ἐν τῇ οἰκίᾳ ὁρῶ.	*I see the (things) in the house.*

Only context can show whether a general class is meant. For example, ἡ σοφή ἀναγιγνώσκει could mean, "*The wise woman* (in general) *reads*" OR "*The wise woman* (already mentioned) *is reading.*"

🙠 English uses *the* + adjective to generalize **only in the plural**, not in the singular: "*The brave are free,*" but not "*The brave is free.*" Greek uses the article to generalize in the singular or plural.

τό with a **neuter singular adjective** often gives us an **abstract.** τὸ ἀγαθόν may signify *the good*, i.e. *goodness*, rather than a particular good thing.

τί ἐστι τὸ δίκαιον;	*What is justice / the just?*
τὸ ἀγαθόν ζητῶ.	*I seek goodness / I seek the good.* OR, if context justifies,
	I seek the good thing (already mentioned).

▶ **Exercise δ:** Write the following in Greek. Omit nouns when possible (as indicated by parentheses).

1. The wise love good (things).
2. The wise love goodness.
3. I see the bad (woman).
4. The wise (man) does not love evil (= the bad).
5. The (people) in the house are crying.
6. Bad (things) happen to good (people). (τυγχάνω = happen to + dat.)

Classwork: ✦✦ Read: **New Testament # 2**, Thesauros p. 221.
   Pair up and read dialogues (from homework). Make corrections.

ἔργα   ~Write the paradigm for σοφός. Memorize.
   ~Read and translate "Feeding the Cloak." Learn the vocabulary.

FEEDING THE CLOAK

ἄνθρωπός τις μάλα πλούσιος καλεῖ τὸν Σοφὸν ἐπὶ δεῖπνον. 1
καὶ ἔρχεται ὁ Νασρέδδινος φορῶν ἱμάτιον ὃ (which) φορεῖ
καθ' ἑκάστην ἡμέραν--ἱμάτιον καὶ παλαιὸν καὶ φαῦλον. 3
ἐπὶ δὲ τῷ δείπνῳ ὁ πλούσιος οὐ διαλέγεται (converse with)
αὐτῷ οὐδὲ δίδωσιν αὐτῷ σῖτον.   τέλος δὲ ἔξεισιν ὁ 5
Νασρέδδινος καὶ ἄλλο ἐνδύεται (puts on) ἱμάτιον--ἱμάτιον
νέον καὶ καλόν. καὶ κατέρχεται αὐτὸ φορῶν.

νῦν δὲ ὅτε εἰσέρχεται ὁ Σοφὸς λέγει αὐτῷ ὁ πλούσιος·
"ὦ φίλε, ἐθέλεις καθίζεσθαι ἐπὶ θρόνου;"   καὶ καθίζεται 9
παρὰ τῷ Νασρεδδίνῳ ὁ πλούσιος καὶ δίδωσιν αὐτῷ σῖτον.
ὁ δὲ ἀνίσταται καὶ λέγει " ἄδικός εἰμι εἰ τὸν σῖτον ἐσθίω."
καὶ τὸ ἱμάτιον ἐκδύεται (takes off) καὶ αὐτὸ τίθησι (he puts)
ἐπὶ τοῦ θρόνου. προσποιεῖται (pretends) δὲ αὐτῷ διδόναι
σῖτον   ὁ δέ, τοῦτο ὁρῶν, ἐρωτᾷ· "ὦ φίλε, διὰ τί τοῦτο 14
ποιεῖς;" ὁ δὲ Σοφὸς ἀποκρίνεται "διότι δῆλόν ἐστιν ὅτι τῷ
ἱματίῳ σῖτον ἐδίδους (you were giving), οὐ τῷ ἀνθρώπῳ."

μάλα - very
πλούσιος, ον - rich   (ὁ πλοῦτος = wealth --> Pluto, plutocracy)

1,4,9 ἐπί takes three cases: ἐπί + **acc.** = **to**   (ἐπὶ δεῖπνον *to dinner*)   --> epitaph,
                    ἐπί + **gen.** = **on**   (ἐπὶ θρόνου *on a chair*)   epidermis,
                    ἐπί + **dat.** = **at**   (ἐπὶ δείπνῳ *at dinner*)   Episcopal, etc.

φορέω - wear (a frequentative from φέρω-- carry around a lot, i.e. wear)
τὸ ἱμάτιον - cloak, piece of clothing

3 καθ' = κατά (κατά drops its α before a vowel and the τ --> θ.   See p. 38 on elision.)
κατά + acc. - down along, in the course of
ἕκαστος,η,ον - each
παλαιός,ά,όν - old (from πάλιν) --> paleontology, paleolithic, paleography
φαῦλος,η,ον - crummy, second rate

5 οὐδέ - nor (= οὐ + καί)
ἔξειμι = ἐξ + εἶμι come or go out   (ἐκ --> ἐξ before vowels --> exodus)
ἄλλος,η,ο - other (note the special neuter ending, like that of αὐτό) --> allergy, allopathic
νέος,α,ον <--> new --> neo-, as in neoclassical, neonate
καλός,ή,όν - beautiful --> calligraphy, callisthenics
εἰσέρχομαι - come in (εἰς + ἔρχομαι)

9 ὁ θρόνος - chair --> throne
παρά + dative - at the side of
ἄδικος,ον - unjust (α + δίκη *justice*)

14

> ### ὁ δέ = *and he, but he*
> Sometimes in Greek one finds the article (ὁ, ἡ, τό) plus δέ at the beginning of a
> sentence with no noun or modifier to complete the article. This happens in narrative,
> most often with the masculine singular ὁ δέ. The ὁ δέ usually refers to a new
> subject, different from the subject of the previous sentence. Translate as follows:
> *and he* [new he], OR *but he* [new he]. οἱ δέ, ἡ δέ, αἱ δέ, τὸ δέ, and τὰ δέ may be used this way.
>
> δῶρα δίδωσιν ὁ βασιλεὺς τῷ φίλῳ· **ὁ δὲ** λαμβάνει αὐτά.
>   *The king gives gifts to his friend **And he** (the friend) takes them.*
>
> δῶρα δίδωσιν ὁ βασιλεὺς τοῖς φίλοις· **οἱ δ'** οὐ λαμβάνουσιν αὐτά.
>   *The king gives gifts to his friends. **But they** (the friends) do not take them.*

διά + acc. - on account of   (διότι = διά + ὅτι)
δῆλος,η,ον - clear   --> psychedelic

Lesson 8. Bound versus Unbound Position;
Emphatic αὐτός (Unbound); Intensive καί

BOUND POSITION

ὁ σοφὸς ἄνθρωπος	Both mean:
ὁ ἄνθρωπος ὁ σοφός	*the wise man*

This is called *bound* position (also *attributive* position). The article (ὁ, ἡ, τό) makes a tight unit, binding the adjective to the noun. The function is to identify a particular one or ones. Which man? *The wise man.*   ✍✍ English has only one binding position, while Greek has two.

You can use a genitive or a prepositional phrase in bound position in Greek, since they identify a particular one or ones.

ἡ τῆς ἀδελφῆς χελώνη	Both mean:
ἡ χελώνη ἡ τῆς ἀδελφῆς	*my sister's turtle / the turtle of my sister*

αἱ ἐν τῇ Βάγδαδ ἀδελφαί	Both mean:
αἱ ἀδελφαὶ αἱ ἐν τῇ Βάγδαδ	*my sisters in Baghdad*

UNBOUND POSITION

ὁ ἄνθρωπος σοφός	Both mean:
σοφὸς ὁ ἄνθρωπος	*The man is wise.*

This is called *unbound* position (also *predicate* position). The adjective makes an assertion about the noun rather than serving to identify it.

Since ἐστι can always be omitted in Greek, it is **position alone** that tells you that the above are whole sentences.

The genitive can be in bound or unbound position. Either way, it identifies:

ἡ τῆς ἀδελφῆς χελώνη	Both mean:
ἡ χελώνη τῆς ἀδελφῆς	*my sister's turtle*

ALSO POSSIBLE:

τῆς ἀδελφῆς ἡ χελώνη	(used to emphasize the genitive)
ἡ χελώνη ἡ τῆς ἀδελφῆς	(possible, but rare)

A prepositional phrase in unbound position usually goes with the verb:

αἱ ἀδελφαὶ ἐν τῇ Βάγδαδ οἰκοῦσιν.   *My sisters live in Baghdad.*

This answers the question "where do they dwell?," not "which sisters?" ✍✍ Compare the difference in English between *The man is stopping in the road* and *The man in the road is stopping.*

▶ **Exercise α:** Translate the following sentences and phrases. Pay attention to the position of the adjective:

1. ὁ ἄνθρωπος μῶρος
2. μῶρος ὁ ἄνθρωπος
3. ὁ μῶρος ἄνθρωπος
4. ἡ ὁδὸς ἡ τοῦ βασιλέως
5. ἡ τοῦ βασιλέως ὁδός
6. οἱ ἰατροὶ καλοί
7. τὸ ποίημα χαλεπόν
8. τὸ ποίημα τὸ χαλεπόν
9. χαλεπὸν τὸ ποίημα

EMPHATIC αὐτός (IN UNBOUND POSITION)

We have seen αὐτός used alone (except in the nominative) as a pronoun (*him, her, it*). We have seen ὁ αὐτός meaning *the same*. We come now to the third and last use of αὐτός:

himself, herself, itself, themselves (emphatic).

Emphatic αὐτός,ή,ό emphasizes an expressed or implied noun or pronoun. It never functions by itself but only to underline something else that is understood in a sentence.

τὸν ἰατρὸν αὐτὸν ὁρῶ.	Both mean:
αὐτὸν τὸν ἰατρὸν ὁρῶ.	*I see the doctor himself.*

Whenever you see a **nominative** form of αὐτός **without an article**, it is **emphatic**. It is unbound, and goes with the (unexpressed) subject of the verb.

αὐτοὶ ἔρχονται.	*They themselves are coming.*
γράφει αὐτή.	*She herself is writing.*

Note: αὐτός may be emphatic, it is never reflexive. The English words *himself, herself, itself, themselves* have two different uses: *She came **herself**.* (Emphatic. Greek uses forms of αὐτός.) *She cut **herself**.* (Reflexive. Greek uses a different word.)

With αὐτός position is all-important.

> (1) **Alone**, not modifying anything: **as pronoun**
> **(*him, her, it, them*, etc.)**
> ὁρῶ αὐτόν.   *I see him.*
>
> (2) In **bound** position, with article: *the same*
> ὁ αὐτὸς παῖς ἔρχεται.   *The same child is coming.*
> τὸν παῖδα τὸν αὐτὸν ὁρῶ.   *I see the same child.*
>
> (3) In **unbound** position: **emphatic** (*himself, herself*, etc.)
> ὁ παῖς αὐτὸς ἔρχεται.   *The child himself is coming.*
> αὐτὸν τὸν παῖδα ὁρῶ.   *I see the child himself.*
> ἔρχεται αὐτός.   *He himself is coming.*

▶ **Exercise β:** Translate. Label the uses of αὐτός in the following sentences according to the box above:

1. τὸν αὐτὸν μῦθον ἀναγιγνώσκει.
2. τὴν ἀδελφὴν αὐτὴν ὁρῶ.
3. ὁ ἀδελφὸς αὐτῆς ἔρχεται.
4. λαμβάνω αὐτό.
5. αὐτὴ ἔρχεται.
6. αὐτοὶ αὐτὴν φιλοῦσιν.
7. τὰ αὐτὰ βιβλία ἀναγιγνώσκεις.
8. αὐτοὶ τὸν αὐτὸν οἶνον πίνουσιν.
9. λαμβάνει τὰ βιβλία αὐτῶν αὐτός.

INTENSIVE καί

We have seen καί used as a conjunction, *and*. This is its most common use: joining word to word, phrase to phrase, or sentence to sentence: **A καὶ B.**

καί is an adverb when it puts emphasis on a single word, phrase, or clause: **καὶ A.** Translate as *too, also,* or *even.*

λέγω ὅτι **καὶ** οἱ σοφοὶ μεθύουσιν.   *I say that **even** the wise get drunk.*

χαλεπὸν τὸ φιλεῖν. ἀλλὰ **καὶ** τὸ μὴ φιλεῖν χαλεπόν. *Loving is hard. But not loving is hard, too.*
         But not loving also is hard.

Classwork: ✦✦ Read **New Testament** # 3, Thesauros p. 221.
          Consider this passage and Heraclitus 1-4. Are the underlying assumptions the same?

ἔργα   ~Read and translate "The Name Dropper." Learn the vocabulary.

ἡμέρᾳ τινὶ ἔρχεται ὁ Νασρέδδινος εἰς τὴν τοῦ βασιλέως
σκηνήν. καὶ τὸν βασιλέα ὁρᾷ καὶ αὐτοῦ ἀκούει. καὶ ὅτε
κατέρχεται ὁ Σοφὸς εἰς τὴν πόλιν, πάντες (all) τῶν
ἀνθρώπων βούλονται μαθεῖν τί ἐγένετο (happened).   4~

"ὦ φίλοι" λέγει αὐτοῖς ὁ Σοφός· "αὐτὸν τὸν βασιλέα εἶδον."
οἱ δὲ ἄνθρωποι λέγουσι "παπαῖ (wow), ὦ Νασρέδδινε,
νομίζομεν τοῦτο εἶναι θαυμάσιον (wonderful)." ὁ δὲ Σοφὸς
λέγει· "οὐ μόνον τὸν βασιλέα εἶδον ἀλλὰ καὶ εἶπέ τί μοι   8
αὐτός." καὶ αὖθις λέγουσιν οἱ ἄνθρωποι "παπαῖ (wow), ὦ
Νασρέδδινε, νομίζομεν τοῦτο εἶναι θαυμάσιον (wonderful)."

εἷς (one) δὲ αὐτῶν ἐρωτᾷ· "τί εἶπέ σοι ὁ βασιλεύς;"
ὁ δὲ Νασρέδδινος οὐ λέγει οὐδέν. μετὰ δὲ χρόνον μικρὸν   12
ἐρωτᾷ ὁ ἄνθρωπος τὸ αὐτὸ ἐρώτημα· ὁ δὲ οὐ λέγει
οὐδέν. ὁ δ' ἄνθρωπος αὖθις τὸ αὐτὸ ἐρωτᾷ. τέλος δὲ
ὁ Σοφὸς ἀποκρίνεται· "ἀλλ' εἰ χρή σε εἰδέναι (σε εἰδέναι =
for you to know), εἶπέ μοι ὁ βασιλεὺς τὰ αὐτὰ ἃ (which) λέγει
ἄλλοις ἀνθρώποις. εἶπέ μοι· ἴθι ἐκποδών."   17

ἀκούω + gen. of person. NOTE: The sound one hears is in the accusative, but the person
in the genitive. Could this be a partitive genitive, as Smyth assumes in *Greek Grammar*--as
if we embrace only part of a person by hearing, but all by seeing?

4~ Why μαθεῖν rather than μανθάνειν? (See p. 13.)

αὐτός, αὐτή, αὐτό -

(a) alone - *him, her, it*	not in nominative
(b) bound - *the same*	all cases
(c) unbound - *himself, herself*, etc. (emphatic)	all cases / used alone in nom.

εἶδον - *I saw* (aorist of ὁράω)
νομίζω - consider (For the form νομίζομεν, see p. 1)
εἶναι - *to be* (infinitive of εἰμί)

8 οὐ μόνον ... ἀλλὰ καί - not only ... but also (καί is intensive)
εἶπε(ν) - *he, she, it said* (aorist of λέγω)
εἶπέ τί μοι. *He said something to me.*

8

Enclitics: εἶπέ τί μοι

Sometimes a normal accented word that comes before an enclitic is given
an extra accent. This explains εἶπέ in lines 8, 11, and 16. (More detailed
enclitic rules will be given on p. 90.)

A one-syllabled enclitic followed by an enclitic will be given an accent.
This explains why τι = *something* is here accented as if it were τί = *what* ?

This practice--to make an indefinite τι (*something*) sound like a question-asking τί (*what?*)
simply because it is followed by an enclitic--seems counterintuitive, and some dispute the rule.
(See W. S. Barrett in Appendix II to his edition of Euripides' *Hippolytus*.)

---

12 μετά + acc. - after

17 ἴθι - go! (command of εἶμι = go) The stem of εἶμι is ι, while -θι is a command ending.
ἐκποδών - "out of the way" (literally "out of the feet")
          ped-, pod- foot, as in pedestrian (via Latin), podiatrist (via Greek)
ἴθι ἐκποδών = *Get out of the way!*

Lesson 9. ε,ι,ρ Adjectives; Indirect Discourse; ὁ μέν / ὁ δέ

ε,ι,ρ ADJECTIVES

The long α after ε,ι,ρ pattern holds for adjectives as well as nouns:

ῥᾴδιος,α,ον *easy*

	M	F	N		
nom.	ῥᾴδιος	ῥᾳδία	ῥᾴδιον		
acc.	ῥᾴδιον	ῥᾳδίαν	ῥᾴδιον	νέος,α,ον	*new, young*
gen.	ῥᾳδίου	ῥᾳδίας	ῥᾳδίου		
dat.	ῥᾳδίῳ	ῥᾳδίᾳ	ῥᾳδίῳ	πλούσιος,α,ον	*wealthy*
nom.	ῥᾴδιοι	ῥᾴδιαι	ῥᾴδια	μικρός,ά,όν	*small*
acc.	ῥᾳδίους	ῥᾳδίας	ῥᾴδια	μακρός,ά,όν	*long*
gen.	ῥᾳδίων	ῥᾳδίων	ῥᾳδίων	μῶρος,α,ον	*foolish*
dat.	ῥᾳδίοις	ῥᾳδίαις	ῥᾳδίοις		

This is a very common pattern, since the endings -ιος, -ειος, and -ρος are often used to make adjectives from nouns:

πλούσιος, α, ον	*wealthy*	(from πλοῦτος = *wealth*)
ἀνθρώπειος, α, ον	*human*	(from ἄνθρωπος = *human being*)
πονηρός, ά όν	*wicked*	(from πόνος = *toil*)

Notice the accent on ῥᾴδιαι, the fem. nominative plural. (For explanation, see p. 46 on ἕτοιμαι.)

▶ **Exercise α:** Fill in the blanks with the correct forms of ῥᾴδιος,α,ον. Be careful to use the correct accents.

1. τὰ _____ βιβλία   2. ἡ _____ νίκη   3. οἱ _____ νόμοι   4. τῇ _____ ὁδῷ   5. τὴν _____ μάχην

▶ **Exercise β:** Translate:

1. of the young sister   2. of the young sisters   3. in a small tent   4. a small turtle (acc.)   5. for a new soldier

INDIRECT DISCOURSE: ὅτι or ACCUSATIVE + INFINITIVE

When something is reported as being said, perceived, thought, etc., this is called *indirect discourse*. The simplest way to report indirectly is by the use of ὅτι. Also an infinitive construction may be used. What was the subject of the verb in a direct statement becomes the subject of the infinitive in indirect discourse. The construction is usually accusative + infinitive.

Direct:	"ἡ χελώνη ἐσθίει."	*"The turtle is eating."*
Indirect:	λέγω ὅτι ἡ χελώνη ἐσθίει.	*I say that the turtle is eating.*
	λέγω τὴν χελώνην ἐσθίειν.	*I say (that) the turtle is eating.*
		Literally, *I say the turtle to be eating.*

There is agreement in indirect discourse. If the subject of an infinitive is accusative, then any adjectives or nouns referring to it will be accusative also:

| λέγω τὴν χελώνην εἶναι καλήν. | *I say (that) the turtle is beautiful.* |
| λέγω τὸν ἄνθρωπον εἶναι ποιητήν. | *I say (that) the man is a poet.* |

Some verbs, such as λέγω, take either ὅτι or the infinitive. Others are restricted, using only one or the other. ✍ Similarly in English: *To say* takes only a *that* construction, whereas *to believe* takes *that* OR an infinitive: *I say that she is wise*, vs. *I believe that she is wise* OR *I believe her to be wise*.

▶ **Exercise γ :** Translate the following. What were the original statements in Greek?

1. λέγεις τὸν Σοφὸν μῆλα φέρειν.
2. λέγουσι τὸν ἥλιον εἶναι μικρόν.
3. λέγω τοὺς θεοὺς εἶναι ἀγαθούς.
4. λέγωμεν τοὺς θεοὺς χαίρειν.

ὁ μέν, ὁ δέ / ἡ μέν, ἡ δέ / ETC.

When μέν and δέ are used with the article alone, use the translation *the one / the other* (or *one man, one woman, one thing / another*) for the singular and *some / others* (or *some men, women, things / others*) for the plural. The ὁ μέν / ὁ δέ construction works for **all cases and genders.**

ὁ **μὲν** ὕδωρ φιλεῖ πίνειν, ὁ **δὲ** οἶνον.	*One (man) likes to drink water, another wine.*
τὰς **μὲν** νομίζω σοφὰς εἶναι, τὰς **δὲ** οὔ.	*Some (women) I consider wise, others not.*

Note: Originally the article functioned as a pronoun, "he," "she," "it," etc. Eventually it became used as "the." The ὁ δέ and the ὁ μέν, ὁ δέ construction are remnants, with the earlier use as pronoun still operating.

Greek makes magnificent use of all of its various μέν/δέ balances. Nothing in English matches this construction for brevity and elegance.

> Herodotus states that no one is so foolish as to prefer war (ὁ πόλεμος) to peace (ἡ εἰρήνη).
> In normal Attic Greek he might have continued this way: ἐν γὰρ τῇ **μὲν** οἱ παῖδες τοὺς πατέρας θάπτουσι, ἐν τῷ **δὲ** οἱ πατέρες τοὺς παῖδας. θάπτω = *bury*

▶ **Exercise δ:** Fill in the missing words, using either a ὁ μέν/ὁ δέ or a ὁ δέ construction. (For ὁ δέ see p. 48.)

1. One woman laughs, another cries. ____ γελᾷ, ____ δακρύει.
2. To some I give gifts, to others I don't. ____ δῶρα δίδωμι, ____ οὔ.
3. You give gifts to your friend, and she takes them. δῶρα δίδως τῇ φιλῇ. ____ λαμβάνει αὐτά.
4. You give gifts to your friend, but he does not take them. δῶρα δίδως τῷ φίλῳ. ____ οὐ λαμβάνει αὐτά.

Classwork: ✦✦ Read **Heraclitus # 5**, Thesauros p. 224.
　　　　　　　Learn the poem below, by Sappho.

Sappho is said to have been the first Greek poet to make love her main theme. Her songs were a delight to the ancients, and, though so few survive, still give delight. It is as if each fragment still possesses a fragrance. As an ancient comment on Sappho's poems goes: "Few, but roses."

Sappho's dialect, Aeolic, differed from Attic Greek in many ways. There was no *h* sound, and nouns had a recessive accent. (To see how different the two dialects are, consider the Attic version, shown to the right.)

✦

> οἱ μὲν ἱππήων στρότον οἱ δὲ πέσδων
>
> οἱ δὲ νάων φαῖσ' ἐπὶ γᾶν μέλαιναν
>
> ἔμμεναι κάλλιστον· ἔγω δὲ κῆν' ὄτ-
> 　　　τω τις ἔραται.

(Words that differ are underlined.)

οἱ μὲν ἱππέων στρατόν, οἱ δὲ πεζῶν
οἱ δὲ νεῶν φασιν ἐπὶ γῆν μέλαιναν
εἶναι κάλλιστον· ἐγὼ δὲ ἐκεῖνο ὅ-
τ̲ο̲υ̲ τις ἔραται.

ἔργα 　　~Write the lines of the poem twice. Learn them by heart.
　　　　　~Write the following in Greek, using a μέν/δέ, ὁ μέν/ὁ δέ, or ὁ δέ construction
　　　　　　whenever possible. (For these constructions see pp. 38, 48, and 53.)

1. Some are eating; others are drinking.
2. The soldiers are sick; the doctors are not.
3. Some like stories; others like poems.
4. I write a letter to the doctor. But he does not read (it).
5. To the poets I show my stories; to the soldiers I do not.
6. The poems of some are easy; (the poems) of others (are) difficult.
7. I send apples to the sisters. But they do not eat (them).

*For using pitch accent to recite, sing, or chant Greek poetry, see/hear *The Sound of Greek* by W. B. Stanford, Berkeley, 1967, with accompanying record; *The Pronunciation and Reading of Ancient Greek* by Stephen G. Daitz, second edition 1984, audiotape distributed by Audio-Forum, Guilford, CT; *Singing Greek Poetry*, videotape by Paula Reiner, 1989, distributed by Instructional Resource Center, University of Georgia.

Lesson 10. Μέγας and πολύς; Uses of ἐστι; Participle with -όμενος

μέγας, μεγάλη, μέγα *big, great, large*   πολύς, πολλή, πολύ *much,* (in plural) *many*

	M	F	N		M	F	N
nom.	**μέγας**	μεγάλη	**μέγα**		**πολύς**	πολλή	**πολύ**
acc.	**μέγαν**	μεγάλην	**μέγα**		**πολύν**	πολλήν	**πολύ**
gen.	μεγάλου	μεγάλης	μεγάλου		πολλοῦ	πολλῆς	πολλοῦ
dat.	μεγάλῳ	μεγάλῃ	μεγάλῳ		πολλῳ	πολλῃ	πολλῳ
nom.	μεγάλοι	μεγάλαι	μεγάλα		πολλοί	πολλαί	πολλά
acc.	μεγάλους	μεγάλας	μεγάλα		πολλούς	πολλάς	πολλά
gen.	μεγάλων	μεγάλων	μεγάλων		πολλῶν	πολλῶν	πολλῶν
dat.	μεγάλοις	μεγάλαις	μεγάλοις		πολλοῖς	πολλαῖς	πολλοῖς

◆ μέγα βιβλίον μέγα κακόν.   A saying attributed to Callimachus

◆ καιρός ἐστιν ἐν ᾧ χρόνος οὐ πολύς.   A remark about καιρός = *the "anvil moment"* from the Hippocratic corpus

μέγας, μεγάλη, μέγα and πολύς, πολλή, πολύ follow the expected O-A-O pattern except for the forms in bold print, which must be memorized, and the accent on μεγάλοι and μεγάλα.

▶ Exercise α: Translate the following:

1. He is big.
2. of the big man/person
3. of the big houses
4. I see the great man.
5. I see much money.
6. I see many (things).
7. of much time   (time = ὁ χρόνος)
8. The majority (= the many) are listening. (ἀκούω)

USES OF ἐστι

(1)	**Linking Verb** Links subject with an equivalent noun or with a descriptive adjective, noun, or phrase. Can be omitted.	A ἐστι B.	*A is B.* (the weakest sense)
(2)	**With Dative of Possession** Links nom. with dative of possessor. Can be omitted.	σχολή ἐστιν αὐτῇ.	*She has leisure.* Literally, *Leisure is* [= belongs] *to her.*
(3)	**Existence.** Asserts. No predicate at all. Accented on the first syllable.	ἔστι X. X ἔστιν.	*There is an X / X exists.*
(4)	**Possibility** Subject is infinitive. Accented on the first syllable.	ἔστιν ὁρᾶν.	*It is possible to see.* Literally, *To see exists.* (An application of use # 3)

▶ Exercise β: Translate. Label the uses of ἐστι in the following sentences according to the list above:

1 ἀγαθόν ἐστιν.
2. τὸ ἀγαθὸν ἔστιν.
3. ἔστιν ἀκούειν τὸν μῦθον;
4. ἡ σκηνὴ κακή ἐστιν.
5. γράφειν τὰ ποιήματα οὐκ ἔστιν.
6 τῷ ἰατρῷ σχολή ἐστιν.

PARTICIPLE WITH -όμενος

For a verb of the βούλομαι type, you make a participle by dropping the -ομαι and adding -όμενος, η, ον.

βούλομαι *I want*   βουλόμενος, βουλομένη, βουλόμενον *wanting*

A participle is an adjective made from a verb. When used to give a circumstance, it is not in adjective position. When used to identify, it is in adjective position.

πορευόμενος πολλὰ ὁρᾷ.   *Traveling he sees many things.*

τὸν ποιητὴν τὸν **πορευόμενον** ὁρῶ   BOTH MEAN:
τὸν **πορευόμενον** ποιητὴν ὁρῶ.   *I see the traveling poet.*

Classwork: Game: **"Coming into Baghdad"**

A male student says: ἐρχόμενος εἰς τὴν Βάγδαδ εἶδον--
A female student says: ἐρχομένη εἰς τὴν Βάγδαδ εἶδον--

This is a variant of "Grandmother's Trunk," a memory game. The first student says, "Coming into Bagdhad I saw" and ends the sentence with an adjective and noun. For example: ἐρχομένη εἰς τὴν Βάγδαδ εἶδον σκηνὴν φαύλην. The second student repeats the first adjective-noun pair and adds one of his or her own. For example: ἐρχόμενος εἰς τὴν Βάγδαδ εἶδον σκηνὴν φαύλην καὶ σῖτον πολύν. And so on, until someone cannot remember the list, and it starts over again. Use the following words:

A-GROUP NOUNS	O-GROUP NOUNS	ADJECTIVES
ἡ ἀδελφή	ὁ ἄνθρωπος	ἀγαθός,ή,όν
ἡ ἐπιστολή	ὁ δάκτυλος	δῆλος,η,ον
ἡ νίκη	ὁ θησαυρός	Ἑλληνικός,ή,όν
ἡ σκηνή	ὁ θρόνος	κακός,ή,όν
ἡ σχολή	ὁ ἰατρός	σοφός,ή,όν
ἡ φωνή	ὁ μῦθος	ὑγιεινός,ή,όν
ἡ χελώνη	ὁ νόμος	φαῦλος,η,ον
	ὁ οἶνος	χαλεπός,ή,όν
ἡ ἡμέρα	ὁ ὀφθαλμός	
ἡ οἰκία	ὁ σῖτος	νέος,α,ον
	ὁ φίλος	παλαιός,ά,όν
	ὁ χρόνος	πλούσιος,α,ον
ὁ ποιητής		ῥάδιος,α,ον
ὁ στρατιώτης	τὸ βιβλίον	μικρός,ά,όν
	τὸ δεῖπνον	μακρός,ά,όν
	τὸ δῶρον	μῶρος,α,ον
	τὸ ἱμάτιον	
	τὸ μῆλον	ἄδικος,ον (unjust)
	τὸ φάρμακον	
		μέγας, μεγάλη, μέγα
	ἡ ὁδός	πολύς, πολλή, πολύ

ἔργα   Write these sentences in Greek:

1. The wise doctors see the small turtles.
2. The road is both long and difficult.
3. The wise are sick, but the foolish are healthy. (Use μέν, δέ.)
4. The unjust sisters have many gifts. (Use dative of possession.)
5. The poems of the traveling doctor are difficult.
6. The good poet writes short (μικρός,ά,όν) poems; the bad (poet) long. (Use μέν, δέ.)

Lesson 11: Comparatives and Superlatives; Genitive of Comparison or Same Case with ἤ; ὡς or ὅτι + Superlative

COMPARATIVE AND SUPERLATIVE

In Greek, as in English, an adjective has three degrees: positive, comparative, and superlative. ✍✍ In English one normally adds *-er* or *-est*, as in *wise, wiser, wisest*.

The common way to make a comparative in Greek is to take the stem (χαλεπ-, ὑγιειν-; just drop the -ος) and add:

-ότερος,α,ον	after a long syllable	ὑγιεινότερος	*healthier, more healthy*
-ώτερος,α,ον	after a short syllable	σοφώτερος	*wiser, more wise*

The point is to avoid four short syllables in a row.
Note that the -ερ in Greek is like our *-er* in English: *faster, better*, etc.

The common way to make a superlative is to take the stem and add:

-ότατος,η,ον	after a long syllable	ὑγιεινότατος	*healthiest, most healthy*
-ώτατος,η,ον	after a short syllable	σοφώτατος	*wisest, most wise*

The class to which a superlative belongs is in the genitive.
ὁ Σωκράτης σοφώτατος πάντων ἀνθρώπων. *Socrates is wisest of all men.*

▶ **Exercise α:** Form the nominative singular of the comparative and superlative for σοφός and ὑγιεινός.

▶ **Exercise β:**   1. παλαιότερος νόμος   3. τὰ νεώτερα βιβλία   5. τῇ δηλοτέρᾳ φωνῇ
  Translate: 2. τὸ παλαιότατον τῶν ἱματίων   4. τῇ δηλοτάτῃ φωνῇ   6. τῇ χαλεπωτάτῃ ὁδῷ

GENITIVE OF COMPARISON OR SAME CASE WITH ἤ

The standard of comparison (that to which someone or something is being compared) can be expressed in the genitive or by using the same case + ἤ:

νομίζω αὐτὴν σοφωτέραν εἶναι **τοῦ ἀδελφοῦ**.   Both mean:

νομίζω αὐτὴν σοφωτέραν εἶναι **ἤ** τὸν ἀδελφόν.   *I consider her wiser **than her brother**.*

The basic idea is separation, since one person or thing goes beyond (is separate or different from) others.
We have already seen a genitive of comparison in our Anacreontic poem: **χαλεπώτερον δὲ πάντων** ...

▶ **Exercise γ:** Translate the following. Express the same meaning in a sentence using a gen. of comparison.

1. ὁ στρατιώτης πλουσιώτερος ἢ ὁ ποιητής.   2. τὸν στρατιώτην νομίζω νεώτερον εἶναι ἢ τὸν ποιητήν.

ὡς OR ὅτι + SUPERLATIVE   (STRENGTHENED SUPERLATIVE)

To translate ὡς or ὅτι + superlative, use *as ... as can be, as ... as possible, exceedingly*. Strictly speaking, there is no real comparison being made. ✍✍ Compare the statement, "*You are most polite.*"

ἔστιν ὡς ῥᾳδιώτατον.   Both mean:

ἔστιν ὅτι ῥᾳδιώτατον.   *It is as easy as can be / exceedingly easy / as easy as possible.*

Classwork: ◆◆ Read Heraclitus #6 - 9, Thesauros p. 224.

ἔργα   ~Translate into Greek: 1. She is wiser than her sister. (2 ways)
2. I consider her to be wiser than her sister. (2 ways)
3. He is as rich as can be.
4. He is the richest of the doctors.
5. I do not give gifts to the most foolish doctors.
~Read and translate "Sun or Moon?" and "A Lamp for Others." Learn the vocabulary.

οἱ φίλοι τοῦ Νασρεδδίνου νομίζουσιν αὐτὸν εἶναι ἢ τὸν
σοφώτατον ἢ τὸν μωρότατον ἀνθρώπων. καὶ ἐρωτῶσιν
ἀλλήλους· "πότερός ἐστιν--σοφώτερος πάντων ἄλλων ἢ
μωρότερος;" διότι δὲ βούλονται μαθεῖν ὁπότερός ἐστιν,   4
ἀεὶ ἐρωτῶσιν αὐτὸν ἐρωτήματα ὡς χαλεπώτατα.

ἡμέρᾳ τινὶ φίλος ἐρωτᾷ τὸν Σοφόν· "ὦ φίλε, σοφὸς εἶ (you
are). λέγε ἡμῖν· πότερός ἐστι χρησιμώτερος, ὁ ἥλιος ἢ ἡ
σελήνη; " ὁ δὲ ἀποκρίνεται ὧδε· "ἐρωτᾷς με ὁπότερός ἐστι   8
χρησιμώτερος; νομίζω τὴν σελήνην χρησιμωτέραν εἶναι
τοῦ ἡλίου."

ὁ δὲ φίλος ἐρωτᾷ· "διὰ τί τὴν σελήνην χρησιμωτέραν
εἶναι ἢ τὸν ἥλιον νομίζεις;" ὁ δὲ ἀποκρίνεται ὧδε· "διότι   12
ὁ μὲν ἐν τῇ ἡμέρᾳ λάμπει (shines), ὅτε φῶς ἔστιν, ἡ δὲ
ἐν τῇ νυκτί, ὅτε σκοτία ἔστι καὶ ἔνδεια (need) μεγάλη   14
τοῦ φωτός."

ἤ ... ἤ - either ... or
μῶρος,α,ον - moronic, foolish, (as noun) a fool   --> moron
πότερος,α,ον - which [of 2]?   (used in direct questions)
4   ὁπότερος,α,ον - which(ever) [of 2]?   (used in indirect questions)

---

4 | **Direct versus Indirect questions**
Greek uses different forms for direct and indirect questions (☜ unlike English).

| πότερος νοσεῖ; | *Which one* [of 2] *is sick?* | (Direct question) |
| ἐρωτᾷς ὁπότερος νοσεῖ. | *You ask which(ever) one* [of 2] *is sick.* | (Indirect question) |

ἀεί - always
χρήσιμος,η,ον - useful
8   ἡ σελήνη - moon
ὧδε - in this (the following) way, as follows
12   ἤ - than (in comparison)
τὸ φῶς, gen. φωτός - light   --> photon, photography
14   ἡ νύξ, gen. νυκτός   <--> night   (cf. nocturnal)

A LAMP FOR OTHERS

Νασρέδδινος:	δύναμαι ὁρᾶν ἐν τῇ σκοτίᾳ.	
Φίλος:	ἀλλὰ τί φέρεις λύχνον (lamp) ἐν τῇ νυκτί;	
Νασρέδδινος:	ὥστε τοὺς ἄλλους μὴ προσπίπτειν μοι.	**3**

δύναμαι - I am able   --> dynamo, dynamic, dynamite

---

3 | **ὥστε + Infinitive**

ὥστε + infinitive shows probable or intended result. Translate *so as to* ....
When there is a new subject for the infinitive, translate *so as for X to* ...

| γράφω ὥστε μανθάνειν. | *I write so as to learn.* | [I write; I learn.] |
| γράφω ὥστε αὐτὸν μανθάνειν. | *I write so as for him to learn.* | [I write; he learns.] |

προσπίπτω - fall onto, collide with + dative   (πρός + πίπτω)

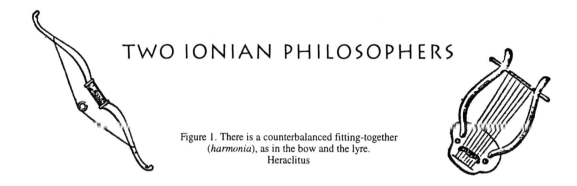

TWO IONIAN PHILOSOPHERS

Figure 1. There is a counterbalanced fitting-together
(*harmonia*), as in the bow and the lyre.
Heraclitus

The political unit in ancient Greece was not the nation but the independent, self-ruling city, the *polis*. Such Greek-speaking cities were scattered not only through what we now call Greece but in southern Italy, on islands in the Adriatic and Aegean seas, and along the coast of Asia Minor. It was in the cities of Asia Minor, crossroads for commerce and therefore for many cultures, that the great intellectual revolutions that led to the Greek classical period of the fifth and fourth centuries began.

The first of these revolutions is embodied in the two epic poems of Homer, the *Iliad*, the story of the wrath of the young warrior Achilles and its tragic consequences, and the *Odyssey*, the story of the ten-year struggle of Odysseus to return home after the war in Troy. Herodotus, a Greek historian, says that Homer and Hesiod gave the Greeks their gods. He means that Homer crystallized for succeeding generations the image of the human-figured but undying gods who dwelt on Mt. Olympus.

The Homeric poems were probably composed in the eighth century B.C.E. and their influence was pervasive. But through the sixth century a sequence of thinkers, first in Asia Minor in a region called Ionia and then in other Greek cities, revised aspects of the Homeric picture of the world. In doing so they laid the foundation for a study of the order of nature (*physis*, from which comes "physics") and for philosophy. You will read selections from two of these fascinating and challenging thinkers: Xenophanes and Heraclitus.

Xenophanes, a poet who was born in Colophon about 570 B.C.E., challenged the view of the gods established by his predecessor, Homer. Homer pictured the gods as shaped like human beings and, worse, as sometimes misbehaving like human beings, stealing, committing adultery, and deceiving one another. For Xenophanes, this undignified picture of the gods was the result of a common human error: every people pictures the gods in their own image. Even animals, he says, if they pictured gods, would doubtless picture them as animals!

Xenophanes asserts that we can say only a few things about the divinity, including what God is not like. God is one, and not like human beings in shape or thinking. Therefore, God has no particular organs of perception; but nevertheless, we can say that God thinks and is in some sense aware. Nor does God change or move; but by divine thought and will God moves all other things.

In the next generation, Heraclitus builds upon Xenophanes' idea of a god who is the ruling principle of an orderly world. Heraclitus was born in Ephesus and reached maturity around 500 B.C.E., and was therefore a contemporary of Aeschylus the tragedian. He writes riddling statements that, like the paradoxes of Socrates and the parables of Jesus, challenge our ordinary sense of the way things are and invite us to resee the world in a deeper way.

Heraclitus first emphasizes that everything in the world changes continuously, often taking on opposite qualities: "cool things grow warm, the warm becomes cool; the moist dries, the parched becomes moist." Most people respond to this "war," this "strife," this "rubbish heap" – as Heraclitus calls the jumble of different qualities that flow by in our ordinary experience – by accepting some as beautiful or good and rejecting others as ugly or bad. For them the world is discordant.

But Heraclitus recognizes something else beyond this: hints in the world that these opposing things have a hidden fitting-together (*harmonia*) or rational order (*logos*). "If you listen not to me," he says, "but to the *logos*, it is wise to agree that all things are one." God judges from the viewpoint of this hidden fitting-together in which all things are necessary and work together as one: "To God all things are beautiful and good and just; human beings distinguish some things as just and some as unjust." The wise man or woman catches glimpses of God's perspective by thought; but most of us, like dreamers, hold on to a partial view and do not waken into the whole of reality. Heraclitus tries again and again to make us recognize in the flow and jostle of different and opposite things the expression of this underlying harmony and complementarity: to see the world as <u>both</u> many and one, a paradox, a *concordant discord*.

Both Xenophanes and Heraclitus influenced the work of Plato and Aristotle. Plato incorporates Xenophanes' critique of the Homeric gods; and God as the unmoved mover of Xenophanes is seen again in Aristotle. Heraclitus' insistence on *logos* is seen not only in Plato but also in the New Testament, particularly in John's fourth Gospel, which opens, "In the beginning was the word (*logos*)."

Figure 2. Reconstruction of the Temple of Artemis at Ephesus (ca. 560 B.C.E.). Heraclitus is said to have deposited his works in this temple as offerings to Artemis. An inscription tells us that the king of Lydia, Croesus, famous for the extent of his wealth, contributed to the cost of this magnificent Ionic temple. The temple is indicative of the wealth and sophistication of the Ionian cities in which Ionian philosophy flourished. (©Ernst Wasmuth, Verlage Tübingen)

VOCABULARY REVIEW, pp. 1-59

ARTICLE

ὁ, ἡ, τό

NOUNS

ἡ --- ἡ

ἡ ἀδελφή
ἡ ἐπιστολή
ἡ μάχη
ἡ νίκη
ἡ σελήνη
ἡ σκηνή
ἡ σχολή
ἡ φωνή
ἡ χελώνη

Long α after ε,ι,ρ

ἡ ἡμέρα
ἡ οἰκία
ἡ σκοτία

α

ἡ γλῶττα

ὁ --- της

ὁ ποιητής
ὁ στρατιώτης

ὁ --- ος

ὁ ἀγρός
ὁ ἄνθρωπος
ὁ δάκτυλος
ὁ ἥλιος
ὁ θεός
ὁ θησαυρός
ὁ θρόνος
ὁ ἰατρός
ὁ μῦθος
ὁ νόμος
ὁ οἶνος
ὁ ὀφθαλμός
ὁ σῖτος
ὁ φίλος
ὁ χρόνος

τό --- ον

τὸ βιβλίον
τὸ δεῖπνον
τὸ δῶρον
τὸ ἔργον
τὸ ἱμάτιον
τὸ μῆλον
τὸ φάρμακον

ἡ --- ος

ἡ ὁδός

Third Group

ἡ μήτηρ
ἡ νύξ
ἡ πόλις
ὁ/ἡ παῖς
ὁ βασιλεύς

τὸ φῶς

τὸ γράμμα
τὸ δρᾶμα
τὸ ἐρώτημα
τὸ ὄνομα
τὸ ποίημα

PRONOUNS

ἐγώ (emphatic)
   με, μου, μοι
σύ (emphatic)
   σε, σου, σοι

αὐτόν, αὐτήν, αὐτό
   (*him, her, it* - prounoun)

ὁ αὐτός Α./ ὁ Α ὁ αὐτός
   the same (adj.)

αὐτὸς ὁ Α / ὁ Α αὐτός
   himself, herself, itself (emphatic)

τοῦτο, ταῦτα
ἄλλος, η, ο
ἀλλήλους

ADJECTIVES

ἀγαθός,ή,όν
δεύτερος,α,ον
δῆλος,η,ον
ἕκαστος,η,ον
Ἑλληνικός,ή,όν
κακός,η,ον
καλός,ή,όν
λοιπός,ή,όν
μακρός,ά,όν
μικρός,ά,όν
μῶρος,α,ον
παλαιός,ά,όν
πλούσιος,α,ον
πρῶτος,η,ον
χρήσιμος,η,ον
  (or χρήσιμος,ον)
ῥᾴδιος,α,ον
σοφός,ή,όν
ὑγιεινός,ή,όν
φαῦλος,η,ον
  (or φαῦλος,ον)
φίλος,η,ον
χαλεπός,ή,όν

ἄδικος,ον

μέγας,μεγάλη,μέγα
πολύς,πολλή,πολύ

Also:
πάντα
δύο
οὐδέν

ADVERBS

ἀεί	ἅμα
νῦν	αὖθις
ὧδε	μόνον
	οὐ μόνον...ἀλλὰ καί

ὡς μάλιστα
ὡς and ὅτι + superlative
  e.g ὡς σοφώτατος
ἀληθῶς
οὐδαμῶς
τέλος (noun used as adverb)

VERBS

ἀκούω	βούλομαι
ἀκούεις	βούλῃ
ἀκούει	βούλεται
ἀκούουσι(ν)	βούλονται
inf. ἀκούειν	inf. βούλεσθαι
part. ἀκούων, -ουσα, -ον	part. βουλόμενος, η, ον

ἀκούω	ἀποκρίνομαι
βάλλω	βούλομαι
γιγνώσκω	ἔρχομαι
ἀναγιγνώσκω	εἰσέρχομαι
γράφω	κατέρχομαι
δακρύω	καθίζομαι
ἐθέλω	
ἐσθίω	ὀργίζομαι
ἔχω	πορεύομαι
κάμνω	φοβέομαι
λαμβάνω	
λέγω	
μανθάνω	δύναμαι
μεθύω	ἵσταμαι *stand*
νομίζω + acc.+ inf.	ἀνίσταμαι
πέμπω	ἐπίσταμαι
πίνω	κεῖμαι
πίπτω	
προσπίπτω	
τυγχάνω (*hit the mark, succeed*)	
ἀποτυγχάνω	
φέρω	
χαίρω	

	δείκνυμι
	δείκνυς
	δείκνυσι(ν)
	inf. δεικνύναι

αἰτέω	δείκνυμι
γαμέω	δίδωμι
ζητέω	
καλέω	εἰμί *I am*
μισέω	εἶναι *to be* (inf. of εἰμί)
νοσέω	
ποιέω	εἶμι *I go / will go*
φιλέω	ἴθι *go!* (command)
φορέω	ἔξειμι *I go out / will go out*

ἐρωτάω + 2 acc.	Also
πεινάω	
ὁράω	εἶδον *I saw* (aorist of ὁράω)
Note command: ἰδού	εἶπον *I said* (aorist of λέγω)
	οἶδα *I know*
	χρή *it is necessary*
	(= an old noun , necessity,
	no longer declined)

CONNECTORS

A καὶ B
καὶ A καὶ B
καὶ A
ἤ *or, than*
ἤ A ἤ B *either /or*
δέ (postpositive)
οὐδέ *nor, not*
ὁ δέ (p. 48)
μέν / δέ (both postpositive)
ὁ μέν / ὁ δέ
ὥστε + inf. *so as to*
ὥστε + acc. + inf. *so as for X to*
ἀλλά
γάρ (postpositive)
οὖν (postpositive)
ὅτι
διότι
ὅτε
οὗ

PREPOSITIONS

διά + acc.
κατά + acc.
πρός + acc.
μετά + acc.
ἀντί + gen.
ἀπό + gen.
ἐν + dat.
παρά + dat.
εἰς + acc. (sometimes ἐς)
ἐκ + gen. (ἐξ before vowel)
ἐπί + acc., dat., gen.

QUESTION-ASKERS, INDEFINITES

τίς, τί,
τις, τι
πόσος,η,ον
πότερος,α,ον
ὁπότερος,α,ον

OTHER

οὐ, οὐκ, οὐχ
μή
οὐχί *no*   ναί *yes*
φεῦ   οἴμοι
εὖγε   ὦ
νή   νὴ τὸν Δία
  νὴ τὴν κύνα
ἐκποδών

Lesson 12. Relative Pronoun ὅς, ἥ, ὅ; Subordination

ὅς, ἥ, ὅ *who, which, etc.*

	M	F	N	M	F	N
nom.	ὅς	ἥ	ὅ	*who, which*	*who, which*	*which*
acc.	ὅν	ἥν	ὅ	*whom, which*	*whom, which*	*which*
gen.	οὗ	ἧς	οὗ	*whose, of whom*	*whose, of whom*	*of which*
dat.	ᾧ	ᾗ	ᾧ	*to / for whom*	*to / for whom*	*to / for which*
nom.	οἵ	αἵ	ἅ	*who*	*who*	*which*
acc.	οὕς	ἅς	ἅ	*whom*	*whom*	*which*
gen.	ὧν	ὧν	ὧν	*whose, of whom*	*whose, of whom*	*of which*
dat.	οἷς	αἷς	οἷς	*to / for whom*	*to / for whom*	*to / for which*

Except for the masculine singular (ὅς), the form of a relative pronoun is simply that of the article (ὁ, ἡ, τό) with an *h* sound instead of a *t* sound, always accented. **These words are small but all-important. Learn them.**

▶ Exercise α: Identify as either article or relative pronoun. Translate:

1. ὁ 2. οἵ 3. τά 4. ἅ 5. ἥ 6. ἡ 7. τούς 8. ὧν

▶ Exercise β: Give case, number, and gender (all possibilities) for the following relative pronouns:

1. οὗ 2. ἅ 3. αἷς 4. ἧς 5. ὅ 6. ᾧ 7. ὧν 8. ὅς

Using a **relative pronoun** allows you to be brief and at the same time to organize a statement, showing what is the main idea and what is additional information. You could always make short statements: *I know a man and he is a poet* or *You have a child's dog and I know the child.* But it is more elegant to say *I know a man **who** is a poet* or *I know the child **whose** dog you have.*

The relative pronoun always refers to a noun. The noun to which it refers is called its *antecedent*, in Latin *coming before*. Logically the antecedent *does* come before its relative pronoun--in that one would not use a relative if the antecedent were not already in mind. But in any given sentence the antecedent may be missing (understood but not expressed) or may even come after the relative pronoun.

✦ ὅν οἱ θεοὶ φιλοῦσιν ἀποθνήσκει νέος. *(He) Whom the gods love dies young.* (Menander)

The relative pronoun introduces a verb in a new relative clause. This is why it is so important to recognize relative pronouns. If you miss them, you will not understand what the verb in the relative clause is doing in its sentence.

The relative pronoun, like any noun, has the **case**, **number, and gender.** It has the number and gender of its antecedent. Its **case** depends on how it is used in its clause.

τῶν ἀδελφῶν ἀκούω **αἵ** ἐν τῇ σκηνῇ εἰσιν.	*I hear the sisters **who** are in the tent.*
Fem. pl. *sisters* = antecedent	**Nom.** Subject. **They** are in the tent.
τοῖς δώροις χαίρω **ἅ** φέρεις μοι.	*I rejoice in the gifts **which** you bring me.*
Neut. pl. *gifts* = antecedent	**Acc.** Direct Object. You bring **them** to me.
τὴν ἀδελφὴν γιγνώσκω **ἧς** ἡ χελώνη νοσεῖ.	*I know the sister **whose** turtle is sick.*
Fem. sing. *sister* = antecedent	**Gen.** Possessive. **Her** turtle is sick.
τὸν ἰατρὸν γιγνώσκω **ᾧ** δίδως βιβλία.	*I know the doctor **to whom** you give books.*
Masc. sing. *doctor* = antecedent	**Dat.** Indirect object. You give books **to him.**

Greek has entirely different words for a question-asking pronoun and a relative pronoun (🖉🖉 unlike English).

| Who is coming? | (interrogative) | τίς ἔρχεται; |
| I know the man **who** is coming. | (relative) | τὸν ἄνθρωπον γιγνώσκω **ὅς** ἔρχεται. |

▶ **Exercise γ:** Translate the underlined words. Be able to explain your translation.

1. The sisters <u>whom</u> she saw went to town.
2. Of all the men in the world, the one <u>whom</u> you love happens to be the one <u>who</u> loves me.
3. The poet <u>whose</u> house is so beautiful gave her the gifts <u>in which</u> she rejoices.

SUBORDINATION

Take the simple sentence ὁ ἄνθρωπος γελᾷ = *The man laughs*. There are three major ways of inserting additional information:

(1) Conjunction	**ὅτε** ἐσθίει ὁ ἄνθρωπος γελᾷ.	**When** he eats, the man laughs.
(2) Participle	**ἐσθίων** ὁ ἄνθρωπος γελᾷ.	**Eating**, the man laughs.
(3) Relative Pronoun	ὁ ἄνθρωπος **ὅς** ἐσθίει γελᾷ.	The man **who** eats laughs.

Conjunctions are of two kinds: coordinating and subordinating. Coordinating conjunctions join clauses of equal importance and subordinating conjunctions join a clause of lesser to a clause of greater importance. **καί**, **ἤ** and **ἀλλά** are coordinating conjunctions. **ὅτε**, **διότι**, and **εἰ** are subordinating.

ἡ μήτηρ δίδωσι **καί** ὁ παῖς λαμβάνει.	*The mother is giving **and** the child is receiving.*
ἡ μήτηρ δίδωσιν **ἀλλά** ὁ παῖς οὐ λαμβάνει.	*The mother is giving **but** the child is not receiving.*
ὅτε ἡ μήτηρ δίδωσιν ἡ παῖς λαμβάνει.	***When** the mother is giving, the child is receiving.*
εἰ ἡ μήτηρ δίδωσιν ἡ παῖς λαμβάνει.	***If** the mother is giving, the child is receiving.*

Do you see how there is a difference in emphasis? The first set of sentences gives two facts with equal emphasis. The second asserts that the child is receiving, adding a circumstance or condition.

Participles are verbal adjectives. Like adjectives, they have case, number, and gender and go with a noun. Like verbs, they can take objects. Like relative pronouns, participles always subordinate; that is, they introduce material of lesser importance. The information they give could also be shown by the use of a subordinating conjunction and personal verb.

ὁρῶν αὐτούς, ὁ πατὴρ δακρύει.	*Seeing them, the father weeps.*
ὅτε ὁρᾷ αὐτούς, ὁ πατὴρ δακρύει.	*When he sees them the father weeps.*
πορευόμενος πολλὰ μανθάνει.	*Traveling he learns many things.*
διότι πορεύεται πολλὰ μανθάνει.	*Because he travels he learns many things.*

The Greeks were very fond of using participles to introduce large amounts of information into a sentence. Sometimes the bulk of a sentence will be a participial phrase. It is useful to bracket participial phrases, at least mentally, as you read:

[πάντα τὰ δῶρα τοῦ βασιλέως εἰς τὴν σκηνὴν φέρων] σφάλλεται.

Carrying all the gifts of the king into the tent, he trips.

Classwork: ✦✦ Read **Heraclitus # 10-12**, Thesauros pp. 224.

ἔργα ~Write the paradigm for ὅς, ἥ, ὅ three times. Memorize.
~Write these sentences in Greek:
1. The book which you are taking is small.
2. The books which you are taking are small.
3. I love the person whose voice is great.
4. The house in which you see (ὁρᾷς) many books is good.
5. I consider the house in which you see many books to be good.
6. Do you see the doctor to whom the rich man is sending many gifts?

~Read and translate "Supreme Tact." Learn the vocabulary.

ἄνθρωπός τις μάλα πλούσιος ὃς φιλεῖ τὰ βιβλία τὰ ἱερὰ
τὸν Νασρέδδινον καλεῖ ἐπὶ δεῖπνον. καὶ ὅτε ὁ Σοφὸς
ἵσταται ἐπὶ ταῖς θύραις, λέγει ὁ πλούσιος αὐτῷ τάδε·   3
"εἴσιθι, ὦ φίλε. ἐγὼ ὁ κύριος τῆς τε οἰκίας καὶ τοῦ   4~
δείπνου. καὶ φιλῶ ἀκούειν λόγους ἐκ τοῦ βιβλίου τοῦ
ἱεροῦ, λόγους οἳ ἱεροὶ καὶ ἀγαθοί εἰσιν. ἐθέλεις
ἀναγιγνώσκειν μετὰ τὸ δεῖπνον τοὺς λόγους οὓς φιλῶ
ἀκούειν; ὁ δὲ ἀποκρίνεται ὅτι μάλα ἐθέλει. καὶ   8
καθίζονται οἱ δύο ὥστε ἐσθίειν.

καὶ ἐπὶ τῷ δείπνῳ δίδωσιν ὁ κύριος τῷ Σοφῷ πάντα ἃ
νόμιμά ἐστιν ἐσθίειν πλὴν τῶν σύκων (figs). καὶ μετὰ τὸ
δεῖπνον, ὡς ὁ νόμος ἐστίν, αἰτεῖ τὸν Σοφὸν ἀναγιγνώσκειν   12
τοῦ βιβλίου τοῦ ἱεροῦ.   13~

ὁ δὲ ἀναγιγνώσκει ἐκεῖνο τὸ μέρος ἐν ᾧ ἐστὶ γεγραμμένα
(written) τάδε· "μῆλα ὁρᾷ καὶ σῦκα (figs) καὶ τῇ γῇ χαίρει   15
ὡς μάλιστα." ἀλλὰ ἀναγιγνώσκει ὁ Σοφὸς ὧδε· "μῆλα
ὁρᾷ καὶ τῇ γῇ χαίρει ὡς μάλιστα." ὁ δὲ πλούσιος, ἀκούων
τοῦτο, λέγει αὐτῷ· "ὦ φίλε, μῆλα μόνα ἀναγιγνώσκεις;   18
τῶν σύκων (figs) λανθάνῃ;" ὁ δὲ ἀποκρίνεται· "οὐκ ἐγὼ
λανθάνομαι αὐτῶν, ὦ φίλε, ἀλλὰ σύ."

ὅς, ἥ, ὅ - who, which (relative pronoun)
ἱερός, α, ον - holy, sacred   --> hierarchy, hierophant
3   ἡ θύρα <--> door   --> thyroid
    τάδε - these (the following) things. (The Greeks often referred to a quotation as a
                             neuter plural: "*these things.*")
4~   Punt εἴσιθι - You know εἰς and ἴθι. What verb must this be?
    κύριος, α, ον or κύριος, ον - in charge of, master of
       The adjective is often used as a noun: *master*, lord, (fem.) *mistress.*
       Kyrie eleison (in Greek **κύριε ἐλεῆσον**) *Lord have mercy on us*
    ὁ λόγος - an all-purpose Greek word that means word, thought, story, argument,
      rational account, reason, line of reasoning, etc. --> logic, mythology, biology
8   μάλα with verb - very much, indeed
    πάντα (as noun) - all things, everything
    νόμιμος, η, ον (also νόμιμος, ον) - customary
    πλήν + gen. - except for
12   ὡς - as
13~   Why the genitive τοῦ βιβλίου?
    ἐκεῖνος, η, ο - that (demonstrative pronoun), used in predicate position
    ἐκεῖνο τὸ μέρος - *that portion.* (Note: τὸ μέρος is a **neuter** noun ending in **-ος**.
           It is in the Third Group, which remains to be learned, not in the O-Group.)
15   ἡ γῆ - earth, land.   ἡ γῆ can be either the whole earth or a particular part or country.
        Either works in this context.   --> geology, geometry
    χαίρω + dat. - rejoice in
18   μόνος, η, ον - only, sole, alone   ὁ μόνος παῖς - the only child
                       μόνος ὁ παῖς - only the child
    λανθάνομαι + gen. - forget, be forgetful of

Lesson 13. οὗτος, ἐκεῖνος, ὅδε; Translationese

DEMONSTRATIVE PRONOUNS: οὗτος, ὅδε, ἐκεῖνος

Greek uses three demonstrative (*pointing out*) pronouns: **this**, **that**, and what can best be translated as **this here** or **this the following**. ✍ In English we have only **this** and **that**.

(The difference seems to be a matter of vividness. How do we decide whether something is *this* or *that*? A small child may call anything within arms' reach *this* and everything else *that*.)

Demonstrative pronouns can be used with a noun or in the place of a noun.

<table>
<tr><td colspan="3" align="center">οὗτος, αὕτη, τοῦτο
this, these</td><td colspan="3" align="center">ὅδε, ἥδε, τόδε
this here, this the following / these here, these the following</td></tr>
<tr><td>M</td><td>F</td><td>N</td><td>M</td><td>F</td><td>N</td></tr>
<tr><td>οὗτος</td><td>αὕτη</td><td>τοῦτο</td><td>ὅδε</td><td>ἥδε</td><td>τόδε</td></tr>
<tr><td>τοῦτον</td><td>ταύτην</td><td>τοῦτο</td><td>τόνδε</td><td>τήνδε</td><td>τόδε</td></tr>
<tr><td>τούτου</td><td>ταύτης</td><td>τούτου</td><td>τοῦδε</td><td>τῆσδε</td><td>τοῦδε</td></tr>
<tr><td>τούτῳ</td><td>ταύτῃ</td><td>τούτῳ</td><td>τῷδε</td><td>τῇδε</td><td>τῷδε</td></tr>
<tr><td>οὗτοι</td><td>αὗται</td><td>ταῦτα</td><td>οἵδε</td><td>αἵδε</td><td>τάδε</td></tr>
<tr><td>τούτους</td><td>ταύτας</td><td>ταῦτα</td><td>τούσδε</td><td>τάσδε</td><td>τάδε</td></tr>
<tr><td>τούτων</td><td>τούτων</td><td>τούτων</td><td>τῶνδε</td><td>τῶνδε</td><td>τῶνδε</td></tr>
<tr><td>τούτοις</td><td>ταύταις</td><td>τούτοις</td><td>τοῖσδε</td><td>ταῖσδε</td><td>τοῖσδε</td></tr>
</table>

<table>
<tr><td colspan="3" align="center">ἐκεῖνος, ἐκείνη, ἐκεῖνο
that, those</td></tr>
<tr><td>M</td><td>F</td><td>N</td></tr>
<tr><td>ἐκεῖνος</td><td>ἐκείνη</td><td>ἐκεῖνο</td></tr>
<tr><td>ἐκεῖνον</td><td>ἐκείνην</td><td>ἐκεῖνο</td></tr>
<tr><td>ἐκείνου</td><td>ἐκείνης</td><td>ἐκείνου</td></tr>
<tr><td>ἐκείνῳ</td><td>ἐκείνῃ</td><td>ἐκείνῳ</td></tr>
<tr><td>ἐκεῖνοι</td><td>ἐκεῖναι</td><td>ἐκεῖνα</td></tr>
<tr><td>ἐκείνους</td><td>ἐκείνας</td><td>ἐκεῖνα</td></tr>
<tr><td>ἐκείνων</td><td>ἐκείνων</td><td>ἐκείνων</td></tr>
<tr><td>ἐκείνοις</td><td>ἐκείναις</td><td>ἐκείνοις</td></tr>
</table>

The endings match those of the article: neuter nom. and acc. -ο rather than -ον.

The forms of ὅδε, ἥδε, τόδε are the forms of the article, always accented, + δε.

The stem for οὗτος, αὕτη, τοῦτο varies. The stem has **ου** when the ending has an *o* sound and **αυ** when it has an *a* sound. The stem has an **h** sound (shown in bold) when the article has an *h* sound and a *t* sound when the article has τ.

When used with a noun, Greek demonstratives always have the **unbound position**:

οὗτος ὁ ἰατρός / ὁ ἰατρὸς οὗτος   *this doctor*
ἥδε ἡ χελώνη / ἡ χελώνη ἥδε   *this here turtle*
ἐκεῖνο τὸ βιβλίον / τὸ βιβλίον ἐκεῖνο   *that book*

▶ **Exercise α:** Write the following phrases in Greek:

1. this sister (subject)
2. this victory (object)
3. on these days
4. that turtle (object)
5. of those laws
6. by that road
7. for these-here friends
8. these-the-following poems (object)
9. this-here leisure (subject)
10. of this law
11. these-here apples
12. of these stories

There are adverbs to go with οὗτος and ὅδε:

οὕτως - in this way, thus   (οὕτω before a consonant)   literally, "*thisly*"
ὧδε -   in this here way, in the following way

▶ Exercise β: Write the following in Greek:
1. They speak thus. 2. I write in the following way. 3. They cry in this way. 4. You eat in this-here way.

Translationese

Translationese is an artificial language that is extremely useful in learning Greek. Its purpose is to convey instantly, to yourself and to your teacher, that you have understood the Greek. Translationese represents the structure of the original Greek as clearly as possible. It is not elegant. You might be interested in making elegant translations (a) for the challenge of it or (b) for the sake of others who do not know Greek. But for yourself, as you learn Greek, use translationese.

νομίζω τόνδε τὸν παῖδα εἶναι μῶρον
normal English: *I think this child is foolish.*
translationese: *I consider this-here child to be foolish.*

Some principles:

Translate μέν *on the one hand* and δέ *on the other*, awkward though it may be.

Translate forms of οὗτος and ὅδε so plurals show and so that one can tell whether the Greek was οὗτος or ὅδε:

ταῦτα εἶπεν.   *He said these things* (not *this*).
τάδε εἶπεν.   *He said these here things* OR *these the following things* (not *this*).

ὧδε ἐσθίουσιν.   *They eat in this here way.*
οὕτως ἐσθίουσιν.   *They eat in this way / thus.*

Translate ὅτι as *that*. Show indirect discourse with the infinitive construction by using parentheses:

λέγω ὅτι ἐσθίουσιν.   *I say that they are eating.*
λέγω αὐτοὺς ἐσθίειν.   *I say (that) they are eating.*

There will be times when showing the Greek structure would be too awkward and no real translationese is possible--for example, with neuter plural subject and singular verb, or with dative of possession. You might want to write extra information in parentheses.

τὰ βιβλία ἐστι μικρά.   *The books are (is) small.*
βιβλίον ἐστιν αὐτῷ.   *He has a book.* Literally, *A book is* (= belongs) *to him.*

The general rule: reveal the Greek structure whenever you can.

Note: Your teacher may prefer that you use smooth English rather than translationese. In that case, keep the Greek in mind. As you write *this* for τάδε, be thinking, "neuter *plural.*"

ἔργα   ~Write the paradigms for οὗτος, ὅδε, ἐκεῖνος. Memorize.
~Read and translate "The Soup of the Soup." Learn the vocabulary.
(Do not be daunted by its length. There is a lot of repetition.)

φίλος τις τοῦ Σοφοῦ χελώνην εὑρίσκει ἐν τῇ ὁδῷ καὶ δίδωσιν αὐτὴν
τῷ Νασρεδδίνῳ. ὁ δὲ τὴν χελώνην ἕψει (boils) ἐν πολλῷ ὕδατι καὶ
ἐσθίει αὐτὴν ἐπὶ δείπνῳ. τῇ δὲ ὑστεραίᾳ ἡμέρᾳ, ὅτε ὁ Νασρέδδινος   3
μέλλει ἐσθίειν τὸν τῆς χελώνης ζωμόν (soup), ἔρχεται ὁ αὐτὸς φίλος
καὶ ἵσταται ἐπὶ τῇ θύρᾳ. "ὦ φίλε," λέγει αὐτῷ ὁ Σοφός· "οὐκ ἔστιν
οὐδὲ ὁρᾶν τὴν χελώνην, καὶ δὴ καὶ οὐκ ἔστιν ἐσθίειν αὐτῆς. ἀλλὰ   **6~**
ἔστιν ζωμός (soup). εἴσιθι, καὶ κοινωνῶμεν (= κοινωνέ-ωμεν) τούτου   7
τοῦ ζωμοῦ." ὁ δὲ φίλος εἰσέρχεται καὶ τοῦ ζωμοῦ κοινωνοῦσιν οἱ δύο.

τῇ δὲ ὑστεραίᾳ ἡμέρᾳ ὁ Νασρέδδινος τὸ λοιπὸν τοῦ ζωμοῦ ἐν πολλῷ
ὕδατι κεράννυσι (mixes) καὶ ἕψει (boils). καὶ αὖθις, ὅτε μέλλει ἐσθίειν,
ἔρχεταί τις καὶ ἵσταται ἐπὶ τῇ θύρᾳ. "τί βούλῃ;" ἐρωτᾷ ὁ Σοφός·   11
"πεινῶ καὶ μέλλω ἐσθίειν." "οἶδα" ἀποκρίνεται ὁ ἄνθρωπος· "φίλος
εἰμὶ τοῦ φίλου ἐκείνου ὃς ἤνεγκέ σοι τὴν χελώνην." τί χρὴ ποιεῖν;
οὐ βούλεται ὁ Νασρέδδινος διδόναι τοῦ ζωμοῦ (soup) τούτῳ τῷ
ἀνθρώπῳ, ἀλλὰ νόμος ἐστίν. λέγει δὲ τῷ ἀνθρώπῳ τάδε· "εἴσιθι·   15
κοινωνῶμεν (= κοινωνέ-ωμεν τοῦ ζωμοῦ."

τῇ δὲ ὑστεραίᾳ δεῖπνον οὐ ποιεῖ ὁ Σοφός. ἀλλὰ πολὺ ὕδωρ ἕψει
(boils) καὶ μένει. μετὰ δὲ μικρὸν χρόνον ἔρχεταί τις καὶ ἵσταται ἐπὶ   18
τῇ θύρᾳ. "τί βούλῃ" αὖθις ἐρωτᾷ ὁ Σοφός· "μέλλω ἐσθίειν." "οἶδα"
ἀποκρίνεται ὁ ἄνθρωπος· "φίλος εἰμὶ τοῦ φίλου τοῦ φίλου ἐκείνου ὃς
ἤνεγκέ σοι τὴν χελώνην." ὁ δὲ Σοφὸς λέγει "εἴσιθι" καὶ δίδωσιν   21
αὐτῷ τὸ ὕδωρ. "τί ἐστι τοῦτο;" ἐρωτᾷ ὁ ἄνθρωπος· "δίδως μοι μόνον
ὕδωρ;" ὁ δὲ Σοφὸς ἀποκρίνεται ὧδε· "τῷ φίλῳ τοῦ φίλου τοῦ φίλου
δίδωμι τὸν ζωμὸν τοῦ ζωμοῦ τοῦ ζωμοῦ."

εὑρίσκω - find   (aorist - ηὗρον = I found)   --> heuristic
τὸ ὕδωρ, gen. ὕδατος <--> water   --> hydro-, hydrogen
ὑστεραῖος,α,ον - next, following (often in the phrase τῇ ὑστεραίᾳ ἡμέρᾳ)
    Note: In the above phrase, ἡμέρα is often omitted, since it is easily understood.
μέλλω - be about to, intend to + infinitive

6

Intensive οὐδέ = *not even*

καί sometimes links (*and*) and sometimes is intensive (*even, also, too*). Since
οὐδέ functions as οὐ + καί, it follows that οὐδέ will have two uses, also.

οὐδέ *nor* (*not* + καί = *and*)   οὐδέ *not even* (*not* + καί = *even*)

ὁ ποιητὴς οὐ λέγει **οὐδὲ** ὁ βασιλεύς.   *The poet does not speak, **nor** the king.*
οὐδὲ ὁ βασιλεὺς λέγει.   ***Not even** the king speaks.*

δή - particle showing emphasis on word before (equivalent to underlining
    the word before); "*certainly*" or "*indeed*" overtranslate δή
καὶ δὴ καί - *and especially*
6~ Why αὐτῆς here but αὐτὴν in line 3?
7 κοινωνέω - have or do in common, partake of, share in something with
    another + genitive of thing shared + dative of person
λοιπός,ή,όν - left over, remaining
11 τις (as a pronoun) - somebody, someone
οὗτος, αὕτη, τοῦτο - this (in unbound position)
15 ὅδε, ἥδε, τόδε - this here, this the following (in unbound position).
    τάδε often = *these here words*
18 μένω - wait, remain, stay
21 ἤνεγκε(ν) - *he, she, it brought* (aorist of φέρω)

Lesson 14. The Third Group

<table>
<tr><td colspan="2" align="center">ὁ/ἡ δαίμων
spirit, divinity
Stem: δαίμον</td><td colspan="2" align="center">τὸ ὕδωρ
water
Stem: ὕδατ</td></tr>
<tr><td>nom.</td><td>ὁ /ἡ   δαίμων</td><td>τὸ   ὕδωρ</td></tr>
<tr><td>acc.</td><td>τὸν /τὴν   δαίμονα</td><td>τὸ   ὕδωρ</td></tr>
<tr><td>gen.</td><td>τοῦ /τῆς   δαίμονος</td><td>τοῦ   ὕδατος</td></tr>
<tr><td>dat.</td><td>τῷ /τῇ   δαίμονι</td><td>τῷ   ὕδατι</td></tr>
<tr><td>nom.</td><td>οἱ /αἱ   δαίμονες</td><td>τὰ   ὕδατα</td></tr>
<tr><td>acc.</td><td>τοὺς /τὰς   δαίμονας</td><td>τὰ   ὕδατα</td></tr>
<tr><td>gen.</td><td>τῶν   δαιμόνων</td><td>τῶν   ὑδάτων</td></tr>
<tr><td>dat.</td><td>τοῖς /ταῖς   δαίμοσι(ν)</td><td>τοῖς   ὕδασι(ν)</td></tr>
</table>

This group is called the **Third Group** (or sometimes the **Consonant Group**). Stems in the Third Group often end with a consonant rather than with an *a* or *o* sound. Because the nominative is ambiguous as to stem--for example, ὄρνις has the stem ὀρνιθ- while χάρις has the stem χαριτ--**it is necessary to learn the genitive as well as the nominative in order to know the stem.** (You need not bother, however, with the large number of neuters ending in -μα. The stem, as you already know, ends in ματ-- as in γράμματα, ποιήματα, ὀνόματα, etc.)

The accusative plural for M/F in the Third Group is ας, with short α. How can you tell that δαίμονας has a short a ending, while χελώνας has a long one?

The Third Group includes feminines, masculines, and neuters. The normal pattern is as follows:

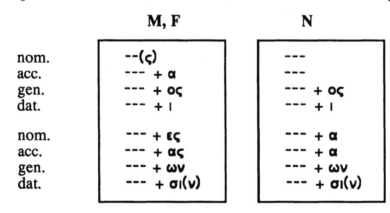

	M, F	**N**
nom.	--(ς)	---
acc.	--- + α	---
gen.	--- + ος	--- + ος
dat.	--- + ι	--- + ι
nom.	--- + ες	--- + α
acc.	--- + ας	--- + α
gen.	--- + ων	--- + ων
dat.	--- + σι(ν)	--- + σι(ν)

A Note on Third Group -α / -ας Accusative Endings

Here is an explanation of the hidden kinship between the accusative endings of the A-, O-, and Third Group, to be learned only if it helps you: In Indo-European an *n* could have a <u>vocalized</u> nasal sound in certain situations. We can imagine that it sounded something like *anh*. (Linguists show this sound by writing an *n* with a circle under it: ạ.) Originally the accusative markers of ancient Greek were simply an *n* sound for the singular and an *ns* sound for the plural. These markers were preceded by an *a* sound in the A-Group, by an *o* sound in the O-Group, but in the Third Group by no vowel at all. The *n* sound of the Third-group accusative was vocalized. (It had to be; there was no other way to pronounce it.) However, changes happened over time. We have already seen how ανς --> ᾱς and how ονς --> ους. By the time the Greeks got around to writing, the Third-group *anh* endings (with vocalic n) had begun to be pronounced simply as α or ας, and so were spelled with an alpha.

χελώνην   ἄνθρωπον   κώνωπν --> κώνωπα

χελώνανς --> χελώνᾱς   ἀνθρώπονς --> ἀνθρώπους   κώνωπνς --> κώνωπας

▶ **Exercise α:** Insert form(s) of ἀγαθός,ή,όν. (Remember: δαίμων can be masculine or feminine.)

1. _____ or _____ δαίμονα   4. _____ or _____ δαίμονος   7. _____ ὕδατος
2. _____ or _____ δαίμονες   5. _____ or _____ δαίμονας   8. _____ ὕδατα
3. _____ or _____ δαίμοσι(ν)   6. _____ or _____ δαίμονι   9. _____ ὑδάτων

COMBINATIONS WITH SIGMA

The only time there is any difficulty at all with normal Third Group nouns is when the consonant ending meets a sigma. When that happens, we find the expected combinations.

Contact with σ:

π, β, φ	+ σ	--> ψ
κ, γ, χ	+ σ	--> ξ
τ, δ, θ, ν	drop before σ	
ντ	drops before σ, causing a vowel change	

(See remarks about the Alphabet Story, pp. 13-14.)

Examples of σ-changes can be found in the following paradigms. Notice the dative plurals and some of the nominatives.

ὁ κώνωψ *mosquito* stem in π, β,φ	ἡ κύλιξ *cup* stem in κ,γ,χ	ἡ ἀσπίς *shield* stem in τ,δ,θ	ἡ χάρις *grace* stem in τ,δ,θ	ὁ γέρων *old man* stem in ντ	τὸ ποίημα *poem* stem in τ
κώνωψ	κύλιξ	ἀσπίς	χάρις	γέρων	ποίημα
κώνωπα	κύλικα	ἀσπίδα	χάριν	γέροντα	ποίημα
κώνωπος	κύλικος	ἀσπίδος	χάριτος	γέροντος	ποιήματος
κώνωπι	κύλικι	ἀσπίδι	χάριτι	γέροντι	ποιήματι
κώνωπες	κύλικες	ἀσπίδες	χάριτες	γέροντες	ποιήματα
κώνωπας	κύλικας	ἀσπίδας	χάριτας	γέροντας	ποιήματα
κωνώπων	κυλίκων	ἀσπίδων	χαρίτων	γερόντων	ποιημάτων
κώνωψι(ν)	κύλιξι(ν)	ἀσπίσι(ν)	χάρισι(ν)	γέρουσι(ν)	ποιήμασι(ν)

With the dative plural, we are seeing several stages of linguistic change. At a certain point in time, if a stem ended in ν, the ν simply dropped out before σ without resulting in any change. δαίμονσι --) δαίμοσι(ν). However, if the stem ended in -ντ, the ν ("protected" by the τ) did not drop out. Later, the τ dropped out, at a time when -ον + σ (ς) was changing to ουσ (ς), as happened with the accusative plural, θεόνς --> θεούς. and also with the dative pl: γέρονται(ν) --> γέρουσι(ν) --> γέρουσι(ν).

▶ Exercise β: Translate into Greek: ὁ γέρων (gen γέροντος) *elder, old man* τὸ σῶμα *body*
1. the elders (subject)   3. of the bodies   5. the elder (object)
2. for the elder   4. by means of the body   6. by means of the bodies

⁻ιν ACCUSATIVE SINGULAR

Some Third Group nouns whose nominatives end in ⁻ις have an accusative ending with ⁻ιν.
ἡ χάρις (*grace, favor*), τὴν χάριν. (The form is underlined in the paradigm above.)

Some ⁻ις nouns have an accusative ending with ⁻α, the expected ending.
ἡ ἀσπίς (*shield*), τὴν ἀσπίδα.

Some ⁻ις nouns have an accusative ending with either ⁻ιν or ⁻α.
ὁ/ἡ ὄρνις (*bird*), τὸν/τὴν ὄρνιθα OR ὄρνιν.

All nouns with a ⁻σις ending are feminine and have an accusative ending with ⁻ιν (as does πόλις).
ἡ γένεσις (*origin, genesis*), τὴν γένεσιν. ἡ μίμησις (*imitation*), τὴν μίμησιν

▶ Exercise γ: Write the accusative singular and dative plural of the following, using information on pp. 68-69:
1. ὁ θώραξ = breastplate, chest (gen. θώρακος)   4. ἡ χέρνιψ = purification, handwashing (gen. χέρνιβος)
2. ὁ ἄρχων = leader (gen. ἄρχοντος)   5. ὁ ἡγεμών = leader (gen. ἡγεμόνος)
3. τὸ πρᾶγμα = business (gen. πράγματος)   6. ἡ ἔρις = strife (gen. ἔριδος), like ὄρνις above.

Classwork: ✦✦ Read **Walk Through a Greek Graveyard** #1-3, Thesauros p. 227.

ἔργα   ~Write the paradigms for δαίμων and γράμμα. Memorize.
~Write the paradigms for γέρων, κύλιξ, κώνωψ, ἀσπίς.
~Read and translate "Mosquito's Buzz," an Armenian tale. Learn the vocabulary.

MOSQUITO'S BUZZ (Armenian)

δράκων (dragon, snake) ἦν τε καὶ οὐκ ἦν ποτε ἐν τοῖς
οὐρανοῖς ὃς ἐβούλετο (was wanting) ἐσθίειν τὸ γλυκύτατον   2~
τῶν ζῴων. ἀλλ' οὐκ οἶδε (p. 25) τί τὸ γλυκύτατον.
πέμπει οὖν τὸν κώνωπα (mosquito) πρὸς τὴν γῆν καὶ
κελεύει αὐτὸν γεύεσθαι (taste, have a taste of) πάντων τῶν
ζῴων καὶ ἀπαγγέλλειν τριῶν ἡμερῶν ὅ τι (which(ever))   6
ἐστι τὸ γλυκύτατον. ὁ δὲ κώνωψ πέτεται πρὸς τὴν γῆν
ὥστε αὐτὸ τοῦτο ποιεῖν.   8

καὶ πρῶτον μὲν γεύεται (tastes of) ἵππου καὶ λέγει·
"φεῦ. τοῦτο οὐ γλυκύ." ἔπειτα δὲ κυνὸς γεύεται καὶ λέγει·
"φεῦ. οὐδὲ τοῦτο γλυκύ." τέλος δὲ ἀνθρώπου γεύεται καὶ
λέγει· "τοῦτο γλυκύ. τοῦτο γλυκύτερον τῶν ἄλλων ζῴων.   12~
ἡδύ ἐστι γεύεσθαι τῶν ἀνθρώπων."

ὁ δὲ ἄνθρωπος, ταῦτα ἀκούων, τὸν δράκοντα (dragon)
φοβεῖται. διὰ δὲ τοῦτο ἀποτέμνει τῷ κώνωπι τὴν γλῶτταν.   15
ὁ δὲ κώνωψ κατέρχεται εἰς τοὺς οὐρανούς. ἀλλ' ὅτε ἐρωτᾷ
αὐτὸν ὁ δράκων τί τὸ γλυκύτατον πάντων τῶν ζῴων,
ὁ κώνωψ ἔχει ἀποκρίνεσθαι μόνον "μμμμμ."

διὰ δὲ τοῦτο, καὶ νῦν, οὐκ ἐσθίει τοὺς ἀνθρώπους
ὁ δράκων, καὶ ὁ κώνωψ (mosquito) οὐ δύναται οὐδὲν λέγειν   20
πλὴν τοῦ "μμμμμμμ."

ἦν - he, she, it was; there was (past tense of εἰμι)
ποτε - once, ever, at some time (versus πότε = when? at what time? Cf. τις versus τίς)
    "Once there was and was not..." - typical beginning of an Armenian tale
ὁ οὐρανός - sky, heaven   --> Uranus

2~ γλυκύς, γλυκεῖα, γλυκύ - sweet --> glucose   What must γλυκύτατος mean?
    τὸ ζῷον - creature, living thing
    κελεύω - bid, urge, order someone (acc. or dat.) to do something (infinitive)
    ἀγγέλλω - announce   (ἄγγελος - messenger --> angel)
    ἀπαγγέλλω - announce or report back

6

> ## Genitive of Time within Which
> τριῶν ἡμερῶν   *in three days*

    πέτομαι - fly   --> impetus (via Latin), impetuous
8   αὐτὸ τοῦτο - *this very thing*. (Since τοῦτο already identifies, αὐτό must be intensive.)
    ὁ ἵππος - horse   --> hippopotamus, Philip
    ἔπειτα - then, next (in time sequence)
    ὁ/ἡ κύων, gen. κυνός - dog <--> hound --> canine (via Latin)   (For the accent
12~ γλυκύτερον - Punt again!   on κυνός, see p. 77.)
    ἡδύς,εῖα,ύ - pleasant   --> hedonism <--> sweet
    τέμνω - cut   --> appendectomy, lobotomy, atom --> temple (via Latin)
    ἀποτέμνω - cut off

15

> ## Dative of Advantage (or Disadvantage)
>
> Notice the dative τῷ κώνωπι. This is the most general sort of dative.
> It goes with the whole sentence and tells for whose advantage or (here)
> disadvantage the action occurred. ✍ We can translate dative of advantage as *for*.
> The dative of disadvantage is almost impossible to translate. For a rare equivalent, cf.
> *"My car died on me."*

Lesson 15. Adverbs in ⁻ῶς, ⁻ως; μάλα, μᾶλλον, μάλιστα + Adjective; Comparison of Adverbs

ADVERBS ENDING IN ⁻ῶς, ⁻ως

An adverb describes the action of a verb or modifies an adjective or other adverb.

✐✐ Examples in English: *Please come soon. You are so beautiful. I see them very well.* We often make an adjective into an adverb by adding *-ly*: *You are truly beautiful. You run really quickly.*

To make an adverb out of a Greek adjective, take the stem and add ⁻ως. If the accent was on the last syllable of the adjective, the adverb will end in ⁻ῶς; otherwise in ⁻ως. There is **no declension of adverbs.**

σοφῶς	*wisely*	(from σοφός)
ῥᾳδίως	*easily*	(from ῥᾴδιος)

Note: the adverb for ἀγαθός is εὖ.
εὖ λέγεις *You speak well.*

▶ **Exercise a:** Write the following in Greek:

1. They speak badly. 2. You speak usefully. 3. I speak foolishly. 4. He speaks with difficulty. 5. She speaks well.

μάλα, μᾶλλον, μάλιστα + ADJECTIVE

μάλα, μᾶλλον, and μάλιστα are adverbs. Translate them as *very, more,* and *most* when they are used with an adjective or adverb. Adjective combinations with μᾶλλον or μάλιστα can replace regular comparatives and superlatives; they are more emphatic. Syntax is the same.

μάλα	*very*
μᾶλλον	*more*
μάλιστα	*most*

μάλα σοφός	*very wise*	
μᾶλλον σοφός	*more wise*	= σοφώτερος
μάλιστα σοφός	*most wise*	= σοφώτατος

νομίζω αὐτὴν μᾶλλον σοφὴν τοῦ ἀδελφοῦ.	*I consider her wiser than her brother.*
ὁ Σωκράτης μάλιστα σοφὸς ἀνθρώπων.	*Socrates is wisest of men.*
ὁ Σωκράτης ὅτι μάλιστα σοφός ἐστιν	*Socrates is as wise as can be.*

▶ **Exercise β:** Translate these sentences. Rewrite using μᾶλλον or μάλιστα to express the same thought.

1. χρησιμωτέρα ἐστίν. 2. ὑγιεινότατός ἐστιν. 3. ὡς χαλεπώτατά ἐστιν. 4. ἀδικώτερόν ἐστιν.

COMPARISON OF ADVERBS

To make the comparative of an adverb, use the **neuter accusative singular** of the adjective.

To make the superlative of an adverb, use the **neuter accusative plural.** (This is easy to remember. Just think of μᾶλλον and μάλιστα, which fit that pattern.)

Note: **comparative and superlative adverbs do not decline.**

λέγεις **σοφώτερον**	*You speak more wisely*
λέγεις **σοφώτατα**	*You speak most wisely*

	POSITIVE	COMPARATIVE	SUPERLATIVE
Adj.	σοφός,ή,όν	σοφώτερος,α,ον or μᾶλλον σοφός	σοφώτατος,η,ον or μάλιστα σοφός
Adv.	σοφῶς	σοφώτερον or μᾶλλον σοφῶς	σοφώτατα or μάλιστα σοφῶς

▶ **Exercise γ:** Write in Greek:

1. She reads most easily. 2. They speak most foolishly. 3. The poet learns more easily than the doctor.

ἔργα   ~Read and translate "Mosquito's Buzz" (the Nigerian version). Learn the vocabulary.

MOSQUITO'S BUZZ* (West African)

ὁ Κώνωψ (Mosquito) βούλεται γαμεῖν τὴν Ἀκοήν (Ear). καὶ
λέγει αὐτῇ· "ὦ φίλη, νομίζω σε μᾶλλον σοφὴν εἶναι τῶν
ἄλλων διότι πάντα ἀκούεις. καὶ νομίζω σε μάλιστα καλὴν
εἶναι. βούλομαί σε γαμεῖν. νῦν οὖν τόδε ἐρωτῶ· πότερον   4
τοῦτο βούλῃ καὶ σὺ ἢ οὔ;"   5

ἡ δὲ Ἀκοὴ ὧδε ἀποκρίνεται· "τὸ μωρότατον τῶν ζῴων εἶ.
οὐ μέλει μοι εἰ βούλῃ με γαμεῖν, οὐδαμῶς τοῦτο βούλομαι
ἐγώ. σὺ γὰρ εἶ ἤδη ξηρός (dried up) καὶ εὖ οἶδα ὅτι οὐκ
ἔσται σοι ζωὴ μακρά."   9

ἐπὶ τούτῳ δὲ ὁ Κώνωψ μάλα ὀργίζεται καὶ οὔποτε αἰτεῖ
αὖθις γαμεῖν αὐτήν. ἀλλὰ νῦν, ὅταν ἐθέλῃ πίνειν ζητεῖ τὴν   11
Ἀκοὴν καὶ πέτεται παρ' αὐτῇ. καὶ ὅταν πέτηται παρ'   12
αὐτῇ, ἀεὶ λέγει τὸ αὐτό· "ἔτι ζωός, ἔτι ζωός, ἔτι ζωός."

μᾶλλον - more
μάλιστα - most, exceedingly

4   πότερον (as adverb) - whether   (It is often untranslatable, used at the beginning
       of a question to indicate that a question is coming.)

5   Note accent: οὔ. οὐ, normally proclitic, receives an accent at the end of a sentence.
       μέλει μοι - *it is a concern to me* (impersonal construction), i.e., *I care, I care about*
       ἤδη - already, now
       εὖ - well (adverb of ἀγαθός)   --> eugenics, euphony, eucharist
       ἔσται - he, she, it will be   (future of ἐστι(ν))

9   ἡ ζωή - life   --> Zoe
       οὔποτε - never (from οὐ + ποτε)

11   ὅταν - whenever (made from ὅτε)

11, 12

Subjunctive

    ὅταν ἐθέλῃ   ὅταν πέτηται

The subjunctive can be formed by taking the ε or ο sound that comes toward the
end of the verb and making it long:

      -ῃ instead of -ει   -ηται instead of -εται

Subjunctives are used for general conditions.

For smooth translation of the subjunctive you might want to use "*whenever he wishes*" or
"*whenever he flies.*" For **translationese**, use "*whenever he should wish*" or "*whenever he
should fly,*" always remembering that this is <u>not</u> a moralizing *should*.
(See p. 147.)

      ὅτε ἐθέλει - *when he wishes* (on a certain occasion)
      ὅταν ἐθέλῃ - *whenever he should wish* (in general)

      ὅτε πέτεται - *when he flies* (on a certain occasion)
      ὅταν πέτηται - *whenever he should fly* (in general)

ἔτι - still, yet
ζωός,ή,όν - alive   --> zoology, protozoan   (Notice how perfect the zeta sounds are
                                     for a mosquito's buzz. This story was *made* for translation into Greek!)

PARSING

Parsing is an old-fashioned technique for learning a language. When you parse a sentence, you write each word on a separate line and then you give the "**what?**" and the "**why?**" of it. The "*what?*" of the words is their form; the "*why?*" is their function.

THE "WHAT?" IN ENGLISH

For English there are nine possibilities for the "*what*?": noun or pronoun, adjective or article, adverb, verb, preposition, conjunction, interjection. These are called *parts of speech.*

Noun - *dog, cat, liberty, refreshments*

    Pronoun - *I, you, he, she, it, we, they* ; *who, which* (relative pronouns),

                this, that (demonstrative pronouns)   (A pronoun functions as a noun.)

Adjective - *short, real, unbelievable, interesting*

    Article - *a* (indefinite), *the* (definite)   (An article can be considered a special adjective.)

Verb - *will go, has come, is running, threatens, go*

Adverb - *truly, quickly, well, soon*

Preposition - *in, at, of, by, for*

Conjunction - *and, while, because, if, although, but*

Interjection - *hey, oh, ah, hi*

Here is the "**what?**" for the words of a short English sentence: *The dog is in the road.*

The - article	*in* - preposition
dog - noun	*the* - article
is - verb	*road* - noun

▶ **Exercise a:** Give the part of speech of every word in the following sentence. It is best to add these categories to the parts of speech listed above: **participles** (*singing, having sung*), **infinitives** (*to sing, to have sung*), and the **gerund** (*singing,* used as a noun). Notice that "*in*" is a preposition used as an adverb. And in case you think τέλος, a noun used as an adverb, is strange, consider the use of "*home.*"

The obstinate dog strained at her leash until the little boy, crying tears of frustration, turned wearily and started to go home. "Hey!" called his older brother sharply. "Giving in is easy. Show her who is master."

THE "WHY?" IN ENGLISH

The "**what** " is form; the "**why?**" is function. The main verb is the anchor of a sentence or a clause. Every other word is linked, directly or indirectly, to it. Always look for the verbs first when translating.

Some functions of words in a sentence are: subject of verb, object of verb, preposition with verb, object of preposition, and so on. Here is the short sentence from above completely parsed: *The dog is in the road.*

The - article, goes with *dog*	*in* - preposition, goes with verb *is*
dog - noun, subject of verb *is*	*the* - article, goes with noun *road*
is - main verb	*road* - noun, object of preposition *in*

THE "WHAT?" IN GREEK

Noun - ἄνθρωπος, ἡμέρα, βιβλίον	Has case, number, and gender
Pronoun - (personal) ἐγώ, σύ, ἡμῖν, αὐτόν, αὐτήν, (relative) ὅς, (demonstrative) οὖτος, ἐκεῖνος	Has case, number, and gender
Adjective - μέγας, ἀγαθή, μικρόν	Has case, number, and gender
Article - ὁ, ἡ, τό	Has case, number, and gender

Verb - χαῖρε, λέγω, ἐθέλεις, ἐθέλῃ, γιγνώσκωμεν, βούλεται, πέτηται

Infinitive - χαίρειν, βούλεσθαι, διδόναι, εἶναι, μανθάνειν, μαθεῖν

Participle - λέγων, ὁρῶν, ἐθέλουσα, ἐρχόμενος   **Has case, number, and gender**

Preposition - ἐν, εἰς, ἐκ, πρός, διά, ἐπί

Conjunction - καί, ἀλλά, ὅτε, ὅτι, διότι

Adverb - ἀληθῶς, σοφῶς, ῥᾳδίως, εὖ, νῦν, αὖθις

Interjection - ὦ, φεῦ

Particle - δή (as in καὶ δὴ καί), τε (as in Α τε καὶ Β), γε (as in εὖγε)

If a word is a *noun, pronoun, adjective, article,* or *participle,* you need to give **case**, **number**, and **gender**. Then you have completely described its form.

By **verb** is meant a verb with a personal ending--for *I, you* (s.), *he/she/it, we, you* (pl.), or *they.* An **infinitive** is a verbal noun and is always understood to be neuter singular. A **participle** is a verbal adjective and has case, number, and gender. (Infinitives and participles can take direct and indirect objects just as a verb can.)

Verbs, infinitives, and participles are all made on verb **stems**. ἀκούω gives the stem for the forms ἀκούεις, ἀκούειν, and ἀκούων. (Drop the ‑ω to find the stem.) ἔμαθον gives the stem for ἔμαθες and μαθεῖν. (Drop the ‑ον.)

If a word is a **verb, infinitive,** or **participle,** it is enough for now simply to identify it as such, giving case, number, and gender for any participle. Eventually, you will give **voice** and **stem or tense** for every verb, infinitive, and participle as well as **mood** and **person** for every verb form.

Prepositions, conjunctions, adverbs, interjections, and particles never change form. Simply identify them and you are finished as far as the "**what?**" goes.

Particles exist in Greek but not in English. Perhaps the Greeks used particles because they could not express their attitudes through pitch, as we can in English. Consider the difference between *"They're smart!"* (in an affirmative, emphatic tone) and *"They're sma-art "* (in a dipping tone). The dip indicates there is a *"but"* somewhere: *"They're smart, but sometimes they can be so foolish.").* A Greek might say, σοφοὶ **δή** for the former and σοφοί **γε** for the latter.

δή can be used alone for emphasis. It indicates, "Underline the preceding word." The Greeks used δή in speech to accomplish what we might accomplish by giving extra loudness to the word before it: ὁρῶ **δή** αὐτούς.   *"I see them,"* as in   *"I see them. So stop telling me to look."*

▶ **Exercise β:** Write each word of the following sentence on a separate line and identify the **form:**

ὁ παῖς ἀληθῶς δὴ φιλεῖ τὴν μικρὰν χελώνην καὶ τίθησιν (*puts*) αὐτὴν αὖθις ἐν τῷ ἀγρῷ.

THE "WHY?" IN GREEK

Every word in a Greek sentence hangs on (i.e. is related to) some other word in the sentence except the main verb, which is the only word that can stand alone. (δακρύουσιν is a sentence. ἵπποι is not.) How do you show the function of a Greek word in its sentence?

Giving the function of a word means saying how it hangs on either the main verb or some other word that hangs on the main verb.

In general, these are the possibilities for the "**why?**" in Greek:

Noun or Pronoun	Subject of verb or agrees with subject (as noun in apposition or predicate noun) Object of verb Indirect object of verb Genitive with noun or verb Object of preposition Other: See Use of Cases at top of p. 103.
Adjective or Article	Modifies a noun (expressed or understood)
Verb	Main verb Verb in a clause (introduced by a conjunction or relative pronoun)
Infinitive	Completes a verb (*I want to sing.*) Completes an adjective (*That's hard to sing.*) Acts as a noun (*To sing is easy.*) In indirect discourse, stands for a verb with personal endings (*I consider her to sing well*, i.e., *I consider that she sings well.*) With ὥστε (so as *to sing*)
Participle	Goes with a noun or pronoun (expressed or understood), either identifying the noun or giving a circumstance
Preposition	Usually goes with a verb, infinitive, or participle. Sometimes a prepositional phrase is used as an adjective (in predicate position) to identify a noun.
Conjunction	Links words, phrases, clauses, or sentences.
Adverb	Modifies a verb, adjective, or adverb.
Interjection	Grammatically isolated. A burst of energy that stands on its own.
Particle	Particles add "flavor" to a sentence but have no grammatical function. (Conjunctions link. If words such as οὖν or γάρ are used to link one sentence to another, it is better to consider them as conjunctions, **not** particles.)

Here is a sentence that you have read in the New Testament. Can you parse it?

ἔκβαλε πρῶτον ἐκ τοῦ ὀφθαλμοῦ σοῦ τὴν δοκόν, καὶ τότε **διαβλέψεις** ἐκβαλεῖν τὸ κάρφος ἐκ τοῦ ὀφθαλμοῦ τοῦ ἀδελφοῦ σου.

ἔκβαλε - **main verb**
πρῶτον - adverb with main verb
ἐκ - preposition with main verb
τοῦ - article, gen. masc. sing. with ὀφθαλμοῦ
ὀφθαλμοῦ - noun, gen. masc. sing., object of preposition ἐκ
σοῦ - pronoun (emphatic), gen. masc. sing., with ὀφθαλμοῦ
τήν - article, acc. fem. sing. with δοκόν
δοκόν - noun, acc. fem. sing., direct object of main verb ἔκβαλε
καί - conjunction, links two verbs (ἔκβαλε & διαβλέψεις)
τότε - adverb, with διαβλέψεις

διαβλέψεις - **main verb in its clause**
          (introduced by καί)
ἐκβαλεῖν - infinitive, completes διαβλέψεις
τό - article, acc. neut. sing., with κάρφος
κάρφος - noun, acc. neut. sing., direct object of ἐκβαλεῖν
ἐκ - preposition with ἐκβαλεῖν
τοῦ - article, gen. masc. sing., with ὀφθαλμοῦ
ὀφθαλμοῦ - noun, gen. masc. sing., with preposition ἐκ
τοῦ - article, gen. masc. sing., with ἀδελφοῦ
ἀδελφοῦ - noun, gen. masc. sing., possessive with ὀφθαλμοῦ
σου - pronoun (unemphatic), gen. masc. sing., with ὀφθαλμοῦ

The Virtues and Drawbacks of Parsing

Parsing has its virtues and also its limitations. The main virtue of parsing is that it concentrates your mind. It allows you to dwell on grammar (forms) and syntax (how words are put together) in a way that nothing else can. If you are of a methodical nature it gives you satisfaction--to realize that everything has its category and function. It reveals to you exactly what you do not understand. It does not allow you to remain fuzzy. It is a "no place to hide" technique.

Example: Imagine you are translating the following sentence. δύο ἡμερῶν ἀκούσουσι μύθους. (Notice the σ on the stem in ἀκούουσι; this tips you off that the verb is future.) Does this mean *In two days they will hear stories* (time within which) or *On two days they will hear stories* (time when) or *"For two days they will hear stories"* (duration) ?

If you are fuzzy and vague, you might do some handwaving: "Oh, it's something about hearing stories and about two days." If you are careless and bold, you might guess at a translation: *"They'll hear stories for two days."* (Actually this would require an accusative of duration.) If you are parsing, you cannot evade the issue. There it is: ἡμερῶν - genitive plural feminine. Fine! You've got the form. But what is the function?

You might remember the genitive of time within which. You might hunt through the book at random. You might look up genitive in the Index and search until you find your answer. Or you might write, "I do not understand this genitive." **No matter which of these you do, you will be better off**, having either reviewed what you have learned or identified what you need to learn.

On the other hand, parsing can be frustrating. If you parse to the point where you want to scream and/or abandon Greek, you will *not* be better off. I confess, there are many words that stump me on parsing, even though I know how to translate the sentence perfectly. There are so many functions of the genitive--which one? And is the chart really complete? I don't like to classify οὐ as an adverb; it seems so different from all the others. Should I call it a negative and add another category? And on and on.

The trick with parsing is: **Use it for the learning it can give and stop when it becomes too hard.** Don't be lazy. Give every word a try. Stay with the puzzles when you have a hunch that you might solve them. But don't be compulsive. Let go when you hit a dead end. Be content to bring your questions to class. Be willing to leave some questions unanswered, being satisfied merely to have identified them as questions. Remember that this is Socratic wisdom: *to know what you do not know.*

Classwork: Parse the following sentence (from **Exercise β** above):

ὁ παῖς ἀληθῶς δὴ φιλεῖ τὴν μικρὰν χελώνην καὶ τίθησιν* αὐτὴν αὖθις ἐν τῷ ἀγρῷ.

> * τίθησι is from τίθημι = *I put*. It resembles δείκνυσιν in form.

ἔργα   ~Parse the first paragraph of Mosquito's Buzz p. 72.

Lesson 16. Third Group: One-Syllable Stems and Family Terms;
μάλα, μᾶλλον, μάλιστα with Verbs

This chapter introduces you to a number of words that you should know for rapid recognition.

ONE-SYLLABLE STEMS

ὁ/ἡ παῖς child	ὁ/ἡ κύων dog	ἡ νύξ night	τὸ πῦρ fire	τὸ οὖς ear	ὁ πούς foot	ἡ χείρ* hand
παῖς	κύων	νύξ	πῦρ	οὖς	πούς	χείρ
παῖδα	κύνα	νύκτα	πῦρ	οὖς	πόδα	χεῖρα
παιδός	κυνός	νυκτός	πυρός	ὠτός	ποδός	χειρός
παιδί	κυνί	νυκτί	πυρί	ὠτί	ποδί	χειρί
παῖδες	κύνες	νύκτες		ὦτα	πόδες	χεῖρες
παῖδας	κύνας	νύκτας		ὦτα	πόδας	χεῖρας
παίδων	κυνῶν	νυκτῶν		ὠτῶν	ποδῶν	χειρῶν
παισί(ν)	κυσί(ν)	νυξί(ν)		ὠσί(ν)	ποσί(ν)	χερσί(ν)

*Note that in prose the stem of the word for *hand* is χειρ- except in the dative plural. In poetry authors have their choice of χερ- or χειρ- for all cases.

The accent pattern for Third-Group nouns with stems of one syllable is: (a) accent on the **next-to-last** syllable of **nominative and accusative,** (b) on the **last** syllable of **genitive and dative.** (But note παίδων, the exception to the exception!)

A mnemonic (going down the declension) that may help: *left, left, right, right.*

▶ **Exercise α:** Give the stem for the following words. Using the stem, form the nominative plural.

1. ὁ παῖς   2. ἡ χείρ   3. τὸ οὖς   4. ἡ νύξ   5. ἡ κύων   6. ὁ πούς

▶ **Exercise β:** Translate the following phrases:

1. of the children   2. of night   3. for the dogs   4. with the hands   5. by foot   6. with ears   7. of the fire

FAMILY TERMS

Notice the changing pattern for the following important words:

	ὁ πατήρ father	ἡ μήτηρ mother	ὁ ἀνήρ man, husband	ἡ γυνή woman, wife
nom.	πατήρ	μήτηρ	ἀνήρ	γυνή
acc.	πατέρα	μητέρα	ἄνδρα	γυναῖκα
gen.	πατρός	μητρός	ἀνδρός	γυναικός
dat.	πατρί	μητρί	ἀνδρί	γυναικί
nom.	πατέρες	μητέρες	ἄνδρες	γυναῖκες
acc.	πατέρας	μητέρας	ἄνδρας	γυναῖκας
gen.	πατέρων	μητέρων	ἀνδρῶν	γυναικῶν
dat.	πατράσι(ν)	μητράσι(ν)	ἀνδράσι(ν)	γυναιξί(ν)
vocative	πάτερ	μῆτερ	ἄνερ	γύναι

▶ **Exercise γ:** Give the appropriate article. (Use ὦ for the vocative.)

1. γύναι   2. ἀνδράσι   3. μητρί   4. πάτερ   5. γυναικός   6. πατήρ   7. μητέρες   8. γυναιξίν   9. ἄνδρας

μάλα, μᾶλλον, μάλιστα WITH VERBS

Since **μάλα**, **μᾶλλον**, and **μάλιστα** are adverbs, they may go directly with a verb. Translate as follows:

μάλα χαίρουσιν.	*They rejoice **especially** / **very much**.*
μᾶλλον χαίρουσιν.	*They rejoice **more**.*
μάλιστα χαίρουσιν.	*They rejoice **most**.*

Also:

βούλονται χαίρειν **μᾶλλον ἢ** δακρύειν.	*They want to rejoice **rather than** weep.*
χαίρουσιν **ὡς μάλιστα**.	*They rejoice **as much as possible**.*

▶ Exercise δ: Translate the following, using material from pp. 56, 71, and 78:

1. τοῦτο τὸ ἱμάτιον ὡς μάλιστα φαῦλον.
2. τοῦτο τὸ ἱμάτιον μᾶλλον φαῦλον ἐκείνου.
3. ὁ ποιητὴς μάλιστα σοφός ἐστιν.
4. ὁ στρατιώτης σοφώτερον λέγει τοῦ ποιητοῦ.
5. μάλα δακρύουσιν.
6. ἐθέλει κεῖσθαι μᾶλλον ἢ ὀρχεῖσθαι (dance).
7. ἡ ἀδελφὴ γλυκύτατα λέγει. (see p. 70)
8. ἡ ἀδελφὴ ὡς γλυκύτατα λέγει.

Classwork: ✦✦ Read Graveyard # 4 and 13, Thesauros pp. 227, 228.

ἔργα   ~Write the paradigms for νύξ, μήτηρ, and ἀνήρ.

~Write the following sentences in Greek, which use material from many lessons.

1. I like this poem.
2. I am reading these poems.
3. I am learning this here poem.
4. The sister is wiser than the poet.
5. Wearing a new robe, I receive gifts, but wearing an old (robe), (I receive) nothing.   (Use μέν/δέ.)
6. The father of this child is as hungry as can be.   (Use πεινάω, p. 32.)
7. The mothers tell the children to share the food with each other.
   λέγω + dat. + acc. *tell* someone to do something, p. 44, line 15 (What is λέγω + acc. + inf.?)
   κοινωνέω + gen. + dat. *share* in something (gen.) with someone (dat.) (See p. 67 line 7 and note.)
8. For living creatures life is (something) good.   (Indicate *something* by gender only.)
9. The children are as wise as can be.
10. The wisest men are always the most useful.

~Read and translate the first part of "The Oath," a West African story. Learn the vocabulary.

THE OATH (Part 1)*

ἐν τῇ γῇ τῇ Ἀφρικανῇ (African), ἐν ᾗ οἰκοῦσιν ἡ χελώνη
καὶ ὁ ἀνὴρ αὐτῆς, νόμος ἐστὶν ὡς ὅταν τις καταγιγνώσκῃ
τινός, χρὴ ἐκεῖνον τὸν καταγνωσθέντα (accused) τὸν
ὅρκον τόνδε ὀμνύναι· "τεθναίην εἰ ἐχρησάμην (I made use   4
of + dat.) χερσὶ καὶ ποσὶν ὥστε ποιεῖν ἄδικα ἔργα." καὶ
ἔπειτα χρὴ αὐτὸν φάρμακον πίνειν.

καὶ ἀκούουσιν οἱ θεοὶ τὸν ὅρκον, καὶ ὧδε ποιοῦσιν· εἰ μὲν
ἀληθῶς ὄμνυσιν ὁ καταγνωσθεὶς (accused), οὐ πέμπουσι   8~
θάνατον. εἰ δὲ ψευδῶς, θάνατον πέμπουσι τῷ φαρμάκῳ.   9~
καὶ οὕτω φυλάττουσι τὸ ὅσιον.

καὶ νῦν ἀκούετε μῦθον περὶ τῆς σοφῆς χελώνης καὶ τοῦ   11~
ἀνδρὸς αὐτῆς.

οἰκέω - dwell   (cf. οἰκία)
ὁ ἀνήρ - man (male as opposed to female),   husband
ὡς - how, that
τις, τι (unaccented), gen. τινος - someone, something.
καταγιγνώσκω - make an accusation against + gen. (literally "know down on" someone)
τινος - genitive of τις
4   ὁ ὅρκος - oath   Greek saying:

✦ ἀνδρῶν δὲ φαύλων ὅρκον εἰς ὕδωρ γράφε.

ὄμνυμι - swear
τεθναίην - *May I be dead!*
ἡ χείρ, gen. χειρός - hand (dative plural χερσί(ν))   --> chiropractor
ὁ πούς, gen. ποδός - foot   (See p. 77.)   pod/ped <--> foot   --> podiatrist,
            podium, pseudopod --> pedal, pedestrian, quadruped (via Latin)
τὸ ἔργον - deed, work   <--> work   ---> erg
τὸ φάρμακον - drug, whether used as medicine or (as here) poison
8~   ἀληθής (m./f.), ἀληθές (n.) - true (declension to be learned later) (What is ἀληθῶς?)
      ὁ θάνατος - death   --> thanatology, euthanasia
9~   ψευδής, ές - false   (What is ψευδῶς?)   --> pseudo-, as in pseudonym
      περί + gen. - about (concerning)
      οὕτω(ς) - thus, so (adverb of οὗτος)
      φυλάττω - guard   --> prophylactic, anaphylactic, phylactery
      ὅσιος,α,ον and ος,ον - hallowed, sanctioned by divine law, spiritually right
11~   σοφός, ή, όν - wise, clever   (Can you guess which is meant in this story?)

Lesson 17. Third-Group Adjectives; 3-A-3 Adjectives

There is a small group of Third-Group adjectives, among them εὐδαίμων (fortunate), κακοδαίμων (unfortunate), σώφρων (sensible), ἄφρων (senseless). The accent is recessive.

εὐδαίμων, ον = *happy, fortunate*

M / F	N
εὐδαίμων	εὔδαιμον
εὐδαίμονα	εὔδαιμον
εὐδαίμονος	εὐδαίμονος
εὐδαίμονι	εὐδαίμονι
εὐδαίμονες	εὐδαίμονα
εὐδαίμονας	εὐδαίμονα
εὐδαιμόνων	εὐδαιμόνων
εὐδαίμοσι(ν)	εὐδαίμοσι(ν)

👀 Ambiguity Alert:
Note εὐδαίμονα   acc. m. / f sing.
            nom. neut. pl.
            acc. neut. pl.

▶ **Exercise α:** Give the proper form of εὐδαίμων, εὔδαιμον for the following:

1. ἡ _____ γυνή   4. τὸν _____ ἄνδρα
2. τοῖς _____ φίλοις   5. τὰ _____ βιβλία
3. τοῦ _____ ἰατροῦ

There are also adjectives that follow a 3-A-3 pattern: with masculine and neuter forms in the Third Group, feminine in the A-Group. The fem. gen. pl. of a 3-A-3 adjective ends in -ῶν. The most important word in this category is πᾶς, πᾶσα, πᾶν.

πᾶς, πᾶσα, πᾶν *every, all.*

M	F	N
πᾶς	πᾶσα	πᾶν
πάντα	πᾶσαν	πᾶν
παντός	πάσης	παντός
παντί	πάσῃ	παντί
πάντες	πᾶσαι	πάντα
πάντας	πάσας	πάντα
πάντων	πασῶν	πάντων
πᾶσι(ν)	πάσαις	πᾶσι(ν)

πᾶς ἀνήρ - every man
πάντες ἄνδρες - all men
πάντες οἱ ἄνδρες - all the men

In bound position, πᾶς makes a whole:
ἡ πᾶσα πόλις - the entire city
           the whole of the city

▶ **Exercise β:** Translate the following:
πᾶσα γυνή   ἡ πᾶσα γυνή   πᾶσαι αἱ γυναῖκες

Also important are the forms for *one* and its negative *no, not one.* The masculine nominative (οὐδείς) is often used alone with the meaning *no one* and the neuter (οὐδέν) means *nothing.*

εἷς, μία, ἕν *one*
εἷς ἀνήρ *one man*

M	F	N
εἷς	μία	ἕν
ἕνα	μίαν	ἕν
ἑνός	μιᾶς	ἑνός
ἑνί	μιᾷ	ἑνί

οὐδείς, οὐδεμία, οὐδέν *no, not one*
οὐδείς ἀνήρ *no man*   *no one, nothing*

M	F	N
οὐδείς	οὐδεμία	οὐδέν
οὐδένα	οὐδεμίαν	οὐδέν
οὐδενός	οὐδεμιᾶς	οὐδενός
οὐδενί	οὐδεμιᾷ	οὐδενί

▶ **Exercise γ:** Give the proper form of the underlined words. Use both genders when possible.

1. <u>One</u> gift is sufficient.
2. I see <u>no one</u>.
3. <u>No</u> man is an island.
4. Give me <u>one</u> victory (νίκη).
5. I see <u>no</u> mother.
6. <u>Nothing</u> is sweeter than success.
7. They speak with <u>one</u> voice (φωνή).
8. Give it <u>to no one</u>.
9. What is the price of <u>one</u> chair (θρόνος)?

Classwork: ♦♦ Read **Graveyard # 11, Heraclitus # 15-17, Thesauros, pp. 228, 225.**

ἔργα   ~Write the paradigm for εὐδαίμων, ον. Memorize. Write the paradigm for σώφρων, σῶφρον.
        ~Write the paradigms for πᾶς, πᾶσα, πᾶν, and εἷς, μία, ἕν. Memorize them.
        ~Read and translate the conclusion of "The Oath." Learn the vocabulary.

οὐ φιλοῦσιν οὔτε ἡ χελώνη οὔτε ὁ ἀνὴρ αὐτῆς χαλεπὰ
ποιεῖν καὶ δὴ καὶ οὐ φιλοῦσι γεωργεῖν. ἀλλὰ φιλοῦσιν
ἐσθίειν. καὶ ἡμέρᾳ τινὶ λέγει τῷ ἀνδρὶ ἡ χελώνη τάδε·
"ὦ φίλε, οὐκ ἔστιν ἡμῖν πολὺς σῖτος. ἀλλὰ πεινῶ ὡς
μάλιστα, καὶ ἄνευ τοῦ σίτου οὐκ ἔχω χαίρειν. ἄκουε νῦν   5
μου καὶ ποίει (= ποίε‑ε) ὃ κελεύω· πέλας (nearby) οἰκεῖ
γεωργὸς ὃς μάλα πλούσιός ἐστιν. καὶ ἐν τῇ οἰκίᾳ αὐτοῦ
ἐστι πολὺς σῖτος. ὧδε χρὴ ποιεῖν· ἐμὲ μὲν χρὴ βαίνειν   8
τοῖς ποσὶ παρὰ τὴν οἰκίαν, σὲ δὲ καθίζεσθαι ἐπὶ τῶν ὤμων
μου (shoulders) καὶ τὰς χεῖράς σου τιθέναι εἰς τὴν οἰκίαν
ὥστε κλέπτειν τὸν σῖτον."   11

τοῦτο ποιοῦσιν οἱ δύο. τῇ δὲ ὑστεραίᾳ μανθάνει
ὁ γεωργὸς ὅτι κλέπτης τις ἔκλεψε (stole) τὸν σῖτον.
καὶ καταγιγνώσκει ἢ τῆς χελώνης ἢ τοῦ ἀνδρὸς αὐτῆς.
ὁρᾷ γὰρ σήματα τῶν ποδῶν χελώνης. ἔρχεται οὖν   15
ὁ γεωργὸς παρὰ τὸν δικαστήν. "ὦ δικαστά," λέγει·
"εὖ οἶδα ὅτι ἄδικος ἡ χελώνη καὶ ἄδικος ὁ ἀνὴρ αὐτῆς.
νῦν χρὴ αὐτοὺς τὸν ὅρκον ὀμνύναι τὸν μέγαν." ὁ δὲ
δικαστὴς ἀποκρίνεται· "ἀληθῶς λέγεις." καὶ δίδωσι τῇ
χελώνῃ καὶ τῷ ἀνδρὶ τὸ φάρμακον.

καὶ πίνουσιν οἱ δύο. καὶ πρῶτον μὲν ὄμνυσιν ἡ χελώνη·   21
"τεθναίην (may I be dead) εἰ ἐχρησάμην (I made use of + dat.)
χερσὶ καὶ ποσὶν ὥστε ἄδικα ἔργα ποιεῖν." ἔπειτα δὲ τὸν
αὐτὸν ὅρκον ὄμνυσιν ὁ ἀνήρ. "τεθναίην (may I be dead) εἰ
ἐχρησάμην (I made use of) χερσὶ καὶ ποσὶν ὥστε ἄδικα
ἔργα ποιεῖν."

καὶ πάντες μένουσιν. ἀλλὰ οὐ πέμπουσιν οἱ θεοὶ θάνατον.   27
ἀληθὴς γὰρ ἦν ὁ ὅρκος. ὁ μὲν γὰρ ἀνὴρ ταῖς χερσὶν
ἐχρήσατο (made use of + dative) ὥστε ποιεῖν ἄδικα ἀλλ'
οὔποτε πόδα ἔθηκεν (put) ἐπὶ γῆς, ἡ δὲ χελώνη τοῖς ποσὶν
ἐχρήσατο (made use of + dat.), ἀλλ' οὔποτε χεῖρα ἔθηκεν
(put) εἰς τὴν οἰκίαν.

οὕτως ἡ σοφὴ χελώνη καὶ ὁ ἀνὴρ αὐτῆς σῖτον ἔκλεψαν   32
(stole) ἄνευ τοῦ θανάτου. τὸν γὰρ ὅρκον τὸν μέγαν
οὕτως ὤμοσαν (swore) ὥστε τοὺς θεοὺς θάνατον μὴ   34
πέμπειν.

οὔτε ... οὔτε - neither ... nor   (οὐ + τε)
γεωργέω - farm, cultivate,   literally work (related to ἔργον) the earth (γῆ)
5   ἄνευ + genitive - without.
    ὁ γεωργός - farmer   --> George
8   ἐμέ - emphatic form of με
    βαίνω - walk, step, go   --> basis
    σέ - emphatic, versus unemphatic σε
    τίθημι - put, place   --> thesis
11 κλέπτω - steal   --> kleptomaniac
    ὁ κλέπτης - thief
    τὸ σῆμα - sign   --> semantics
    παρά + acc. - to (the side of)
    ὁ δικαστής - judge
34-5 οὕτως ... ὥστε + infinitive = so (in such a way) ... as for

Lesson 18. Participles

PARTICIPLES

Participles of ⁻ω verbs fall into a 3-A-3 pattern.

βαίνων,ουσα,ον *stepping*

M	F	N
βαίνων	βαίνουσα	βαῖνον
βαίνοντα	βαίνουσαν	βαῖνον
βαίνοντος	βαινούσης	βαίνοντος
βαίνοντι	βαινούση	βαίνοντι
βαίνοντες	βαίνουσαι	βαίνοντα
βαίνοντας	βαινούσας	βαίνοντα
βαινόντων	βαινουσῶν	βαινόντων
βαίνουσι(ν)	βαινούσαις	**βαίνουσι(ν)**

⚘⚘ **Ambiguity Alert: βαίνουσι(ν)** is either *they step* OR *to those stepping*. Only context can show which. For every ⁻ω verb, you cannot tell a dative plural masc. / neut. participle from the "*they*" present.

✦ ποταμοῖς* τοῖς αὐτοῖς **ἐμβαίνουσιν** ἕτερα καὶ ἕτερα ὕδατα ἐπιρρεῖ.

For those stepping in the same rivers, other and yet other waters flow by.

(= Heraclitus # 4)

The masc./neuter dative plural ends in ⁻οντσι --> ονσι --> ουσι. (We have seen this already, p. 69. The Third-Group noun ὁ γέρων is actually a participle.) Note -ῶν with mandatory circumflex on feminine genitive plural.

❱ Exercise α· Translate the underlined words.

1. Stepping over the stone, the woman tripped.
2. Give it to the man stepping into the boat.
3. I see the men stepping onto the boat.
4. I know the names of the women stepping into the boat.

CONTRACT PARTICIPLES

There will be contraction in participles of ⁻έω and ⁻άω verbs. ε + ο --> ου α + ο --> ω. The participle starts as φιλέων, φιλέουσα, φιλέον. Anytime there would have been an έ or ά (accented) in the uncontracted form, the contracted form will have a circumflex. (We have seen a contracted participle in the poem on p. 11: ἀποτυγχάνειν **φιλοῦντα**.)

φιλῶν,οῦσα,οῦν = *loving*

φιλῶν	φιλοῦσα	φιλοῦν
φιλοῦντα	φιλοῦσαν	φιλοῦν
φιλοῦντος	φιλούσης	φιλοῦντος
φιλοῦντι	φιλούση	φιλοῦντι
φιλοῦντες	φιλοῦσαι	φιλοῦντα
φιλοῦντας	φιλούσας	φιλοῦντα
φιλούντων	φιλουσῶν	φιλούντων
φιλοῦσι(ν)	φιλούσαις	**φιλοῦσι(ν)**

ὁρῶν,ῶσα,ῶν = *seeing*

ὁρῶν	ὁρῶσα	ὁρῶν
ὁρῶντα	ὁρῶσαν	ὁρῶν
ὁρῶντος	ὁρώσης	ὁρῶντος
ὁρῶντι	ὁρώση	ὁρῶντι
ὁρῶντες	ὁρῶσαι	ὁρῶντα
ὁρῶντας	ὁρώσας	ὁρῶντα
ὁρώντων	ὁρωσῶν	ὁρώντων
ὁρῶσι(ν)	ὁρώσαις·	**ὁρῶσι(ν)**

❱ Exercise β: Translate the underlined words.

1. Seeing the soldiers, the women ran.
2. Send a message to the man seeing the stars.
3. He orders those men loving archery to stand up.
   (two ways, κελεύω p. 70.)
4. I love loving creatures. (τὸ ζῷον)
5. For the sons of those (women) loving the outdoors, life is sweet.

*Notice that when a preposition is added as a prefix to a verb, the verb as a whole often takes the case that the preposition would have taken: ἐμβαίνω τῷ ποταμῷ = βαίνω ἐν τῷ ποταμῷ.

BOUND PARTICIPLE

In bound position the participle identifies a particular one or ones or generalizes. (Only context shows which.) It can be used alone, with the noun understood.

ὁ τρέχων ἀνὴρ ὁ ἀδελφός μου.　　　　Both mean:

ὁ ἀνὴρ ὁ τρέχων ὁ ἀδελφός μου.　　*The man running is my brother.*　(Identifies)

ὁ τρέχων κάμνει.　　　　*The running (man) is weary.*　　(May identify or generalize)

CIRCUMSTANTIAL PARTICIPLE

In unbound position the participle gives some circumstance that applies to the main verb. This is by far the most important and most common use of the participle.

> τρέχων ἔπεσεν　　　　*Running he fell.*

▶ **Exercise γ:** Go back to **Exercise α.** Which participles are circumstantial, which identify? Which would have an article immediately before the participle?

▶ **Exercise δ:** Write these sentences in Greek. Remember: not every -*ing* word is a participle (see p. 43). Which -*ing* words are participles? Are they bound or circumstantial?

I stay home = μένω οἴκοι.　　(οἴκοι is a fossil form, an old locative of οἶκος *house, home.*)

1. <u>Staying</u> home is easy.　3. The men <u>staying</u> home are lucky.　5. She gets sick <u>staying</u> home.
2. I am <u>staying</u> home.　4. <u>Staying</u> home the women rejoice.　6. Send apples to the women <u>staying</u> home.

Circumstantial participles add information about a circumstance connected with the verb. (The noun is already fully identified.) How that circumstance is connected is usually left vague in Greek.

For translationese you can usually use **Xing** for the participle. Sometimes you may ned to choose the best interpretation according to context. And in going from English to Greek, you need to realize all the possibilities:

ἔπεσε τρέχων.　*He fell*

while running	*because he was running*
in running	*although he was running*
by running	*if he was running*
through running	*as he was running, etc.*

Sometimes, but not usually, a word is used along with the participle that indicates which interpretation to use:
ὡς *as if, on the grounds that* (gives motivating assumption)　καίπερ *even though, although*　ἅτε *since.*

πέμπε αὐτῷ σῖτον ὡς πεινῶντι.　　*Send him food on the assumption that he is hungry.*

πέμπε αὐτῷ σῖτον ἅτε πεινῶντι.　　*Send him food since he is hungry.*

μὴ πέμπε αὐτῷ σῖτον καίπερ πεινῶντι.　*Don't send him food, even though he is hungry.*

Classwork: ✦✦ Read New Testament # 4-5, Thesauros p. 222.

Classwork or ἔργα: Write the following in Greek: Identify participles as bound or circumstantial.

1. By hearing their stories she learns many things.　5. I rejoice in the ones rejoicing. (Use masc. part.)
2. While eating she writes letters.　6. I rejoice in those who rejoice. (Use relative pron.)
3. I see the crying child.　7. The loving ones send gifts.
4. I see the child crying.　8. Because of loving (part.) we send gifts.
9. Although I love my sister and consider her to be very wise (use καίπερ + participle), I do not wish to dwell in her house.

ἔργα　　　~Write the paradigm for γράφων, ουσα, ον. Memorize.
　　　　　~Read and translate the first part of a tale from Ghana, "Who Is Poor?" Learn the vocabulary.
　　　　　　Parse the fourth sentence. (καὶ δεῖπνον ποιεῖ)

WHO IS POOR?* (Part 1)

ἡμέρᾳ τινὶ ἐν τῇ γῇ τῇ Ἀφρικανῇ γυνὴ τοῦ βασιλέως
τίκτει υἱόν. ὁ δὲ βασιλεὺς χαίρει ὡς μάλιστα τῷ υἱῷ.
ἔστι γὰρ ὁ παῖς ὁ πρῶτος. καὶ δεῖπνον ποιεῖ ὁ βασιλεὺς
πάσαις ταῖς γυναιξὶ καὶ πᾶσι τοῖς οἰκοῦσιν ἐν ταύτῃ τῇ   4
γῇ. καὶ ἐπὶ τῷ δείπνῳ τάδε λέγει· "ὦ φίλοι, οἶδα ὅτι
τρισὶν οἱ ἄνθρωποι κακοδαίμονες· τῷ πολέμῳ καὶ τῇ νόσῳ
καὶ τῇ πείνῃ. ἀλλ' ἐγὼ οὐ νομίζω κακοδαίμων εἶναι.
χαίρων γὰρ τῷ νέῳ υἱῷ εὐδαίμων δὴ νομίζω εἶναι· καὶ   **8**
οὕτως εὐδαίμων εἰμι ὥστε πάντας τοὺς ἀνθρώπους, τοὺς   **9**
ἐν ταύτῃ τῇ γῇ βούλομαι ποιεῖν εὐδαίμονας. νῦν οὖν   10
πέμπω ἄγγελον οὗ τὸ ἔργον ἐστὶ τόδε· ζητεῖν ἐν πάσῃ τῇ
γῇ ὥστε εὑρεῖν πένητα καὶ ἀποφέρειν μοι. καὶ τοῦτον τὸν   12~
πένητα πλούσιον ποιήσω (I shall make)."

ἡ γυνή, gen. γυναικός - woman, wife   <--> queen   --> gynecology, misogyny
τίκτω - give birth
ὁ υἱός - son   (Cf. ΙΧΘΥΣ - Ἰησοῦς Χριστὸς Θεοῦ Υἱὸς Σωτήρ)
ὁ/ἡ παῖς, gen. παιδός - child   --> pediatrics, pedagogue

4   πᾶς, πᾶσα, πᾶν - all, every
     τρεῖς, τρία   <--> three (gen. τριῶν, dat. τρισί(ν))   --> tripartite, triple
5   κακοδαίμων,ον - unfortunate (literally, having a bad δαίμων *divinity, guiding spirit*)
     ὁ πόλεμος - war   --> polemics
     ἡ νόσος - sickness, disease
     ἡ πεῖνα - hunger, famine
8   εὐδαίμων,ον - fortunate   (literally, having a good δαίμων *divinity, guiding spirit*)

8

Cases with εἶναι

εἰμί as a linking verb links nominative to nominative. εἶναι as a linking verb in indirect discourse usually links accusative to accusative--except when the subject of εἶναι is the subject of the verb introducing the indirect discourse. Then εἶναι links a nominative (understood) to a nominative.

     νομίζω αὐτὴν σοφὴν εἶναι.   *I consider her to be wise.*
     νομίζω **σοφὴ** εἶναι.   *I consider (myself) to be wise.*

---

9   οὕτως . . . ὥστε   + verb = so (in such a way) . . . that

9

ὥστε

ὥστε + **infinitive** gives the intended or **probable result**.
ὥστε + a **verb** with personal ending gives the **actual result**.

     γράφω ὥστε μανθάνειν.   *I write so as to learn.*
     γράφω ὥστε μανθάνω.   *I write so that I learn.*

10
13

ποιέω + Two Accusatives

ποιέω is a *factitive* verb--a verb that acts on its object so as to turn it into something or give it a new characteristic. Such verbs take a direct object and an adjective or noun to complete it.

Compare our English construction: *We elected him president. We painted the house red.*

     ὁ ἄγγελος - messenger   --> angel
12~   εὑρίσκω, ηὗρον - find, found   (Why εὑρεῖν rather than εὑρίσκειν? See p.13.)
     ὁ πένης, gen. πένητος - poor man   --> penury
     ἀποφέρω - carry away; bring back, hand over to + dat.

*This story was freely adapted from a story told by Kwadwo Anokwa, © 1992; used with permission of the author.

THE NEW TESTAMENT

Figure 1. In the foreground is the cliff of the Areopagus that overlooks the Acropolis and the Parthenon. (Photo: Alison Frantz)

All of the New Testament is written in a Greek dialect called Koine. Koine (*koinos, koine, koinon,* "common") Greek developed as the common language of the *oikoumene* ("inhabited world") that came about as part of the unification of Alexander's empire after his death in 323 B.C.E. It was widely used from the third century B.C.E. to the sixth century C.E. The *oikoumene,* in which Greek was spoken, extended from India to Spain and included Italy, Asia Minor, and Egypt. The writers of the New Testament, therefore, chose to write in Greek, because they wanted their message to be accessible to everyone.

The forms of Koine Greek are very close to Attic but its syntactical structures are simpler. Luke was the only writer of the New Testament who may have been a native speaker of Greek. But two other writers of the New Testament have particular associations with Greece.

Paul made three journeys to Greece, visiting and preaching in a host of Greek cities. We know about these journeys through Luke's account of them in his *Acts of the Apostles.* In addition, we have a number of letters that Paul wrote to those whom he converted, including the Christian communities of Thessalonians, Corinthians, and Ephesians. Paul even visited the most famous city of Greece, Athens. While there, Paul preached in a synagogue and held daily debates in the *agora* ("gathering place, marketplace") with passers-by, among whom were Stoic and Epicurean philosophers. Paul was particularly familiar with Stoic doctrines since his native city, Tarsus, was the home of several Stoic philosophers: Antipater, Zeno, and Chrysippus.

Paul was even invited to make an address on the Areopagus, the site of the Athenian homicide court. The many temples and altars of the Acropolis and the *agora* are beautifully visible from this rocky promontory (Figure 1). Paul's speech appropriately begins by acknowledging that his hearers are already devoted to religious matters:

> O men of Athens, I observe how very godfearing you are in all things. As I walked around looking at your shrines, I even discovered an altar inscribed, "To an Unknown God." Now, what you reverence in ignorance, I intend to proclaim to you. (*Acts* 17:22-24)

Later in the speech, Paul quotes from Greek poets to affirm the affinity of Greek thought and his message: "In him (God) we live and move and have our being...for we too are his offspring" *(Acts*

17:28). Paul seeks to move the Athenians, through this common belief in a divine origin of the world, away from polytheism to an acceptance of one God.

Paul's speech, however, convinced only a few to join him, including Damaris, an otherwise unknown woman, and Dionysius, a member of the court of the Areopagus, who eventually went on to convert many Athenians. In present day Athens, on the feast day of Saints Peter and Paul, June 29, Athenians in large numbers gather at the Areopagus for a sunset Vesper Liturgy during which Paul's speech is read to the worshipers.

Not only in Athens but throughout modern Greece, people take pride in the sites Paul visited. One such place is Lindos on Rhodes. Here, in a small bay, now called St. Paul's Bay, the disciple is said to have found refuge from a tempest which almost sank his ship. According to the villagers, St. Paul converted them during his stay there after the storm. A small church dedicated to the Apostles marks the site. The road to this church is washed out every year, yet the women in the village manage to care for it daily, despite difficulties in reaching the church.

Another author closely tied to Greece is John the Evangelist. Although the evidence is not clear, many believe that he is the author of the fourth Gospel, three Epistles, and the Book of Revelation. You will be reading selections from the Epistles later in the course. The Greeks on the island of Patmos claim that John wrote both the fourth Gospel and the Book of Revelation while he lived there, after he had been exiled from Ephesus by the Roman authorities.

In order to pray, John would retreat to a cave that overlooked the beautiful harbor of Patmos. It was there he had his visions that he records in the Book of Revelation with the help of his disciple, Prochoros (Figure 2):

> I, John, your brother...was on the island called Patmos....On the Lord's Day, I was caught up in the Spirit and I heard behind me a great voice like the sound of a trumpet which said, Write in a book what you now see....(1. 9-11)

The Patmians credit John with their conversion to Christianity and there are many local legends of the miracles he performed. The cave is now a place of religious pilgrimage. On the hilltop above the cave, an influential and still flourishing monastery, dedicated to St. John, was erected in the eleventh century. It occupies the acropolis where a temple to Artemis formerly stood.

Figure 2: John in his cave at Patmos dictating the book of Revelation and the Fourth Gospel to his disciple Prochoros. (Line drawing of an icon)

Lesson 19. τίς, τί / τις, τι; Interrogatives and Indefinites; Adverbial Accusative; Articular Infinitive

	τίς, τί (interrogative)			**τις, τι** (indefinite)	
	who? what? (with noun) *which?*			*someone, something* (with noun) *a certain, some*	
	M / F	N		M / F	N
nom.	τίς	τί		τις	τι
acc.	τίνα	τί		τινα	τι
gen.	τίνος	τίνος		τινος	τινος
dat.	τίνι	τίνι		τινι	τινι
nom.	τίνες	τίνα		τινες	τινα
acc.	τίνας	τίνα		τινας	τινα
gen.	τίνων	τίνων		τινων	τινων
dat.	τίσι(ν)	τίσι(ν)		τισι(ν)	τισι(ν)

Interrogative **τίς, τί** in all forms will have a high pitch on the first syllable. Note: **τίς** and **τί** keep their acute even when followed by an accented word.

Used alone, the forms mean *who? what? whom? whose?*, etc. Used with a noun, they mean *which? what?* And **τί** is used by itself as an adverb meaning *why?*

τίς ἔρχεται;	*Who is coming?*
τίς γυνὴ ἔρχεται;	*Which woman is coming?*
τίνα ὁρᾷς;	*What (things) do you see?* / *Whom (m./f. sing) do you see?*
τίνα δῶρα ὁρᾷς;	*What gifts do you see?*
τί δῶρα φέρεις;	*Why do you bring gifts?*

▶ **Exercise α:** Translate:

1. τίς εἶ;
2. τίνα ὁρᾷς;
3. τίνος ἀκούεις;
4. τίς ἰατρὸς ἔρχεται;
5. τίνα ἀδελφὴν ὁρᾷς;
6. τίνι φέρεις οἶνον;
7. τίνι δῶρα πέμπουσιν;
8. τίνας ἰατροὺς φιλεῖς;
9. τίσι φέρεις οἶνον;
10. τίνι ἀνθρώπῳ δῶρα πέμπουσιν;
11. τίνες εἰσὶν αἱ γυναῖκες;
12. τίνων φίλων τὰς ἐπιστολὰς μάλιστα φιλεῖς;

▶ **Exercise β:** Translate the underlined words. If context indicates a singular or plural, use that. Otherwise give both translations. ✍✍ Notice that in English forms of *who* do not differ for masc./ fem., or singular/ plural.

1. <u>To whom</u> are you speaking?
2. <u>Whose</u> poems do you prefer?
3. <u>Who</u> was chosen?
4. <u>Who</u> were the winners?
5. <u>Whom</u> did you see?
6. <u>Why</u> do you smile?
7. <u>Who</u> smiles?
8. I like a man <u>who</u> smiles.

Indefinite **τις, τι** in all forms is bound to the word that precedes and is usually without accent. (The exception is situation #3b, p. 90 below.) The forms convey indefiniteness--*someone, something* when used alone, *a certain, some* when used with a noun. Remember: indefinite **τις, τι** comes *after* its noun, and enclitics never come first in a sentence or clause.

| βαίνει **τις** | *Someone is walking.* |
| ἀνήρ **τις** βαίνει | *Some man is walking.* |

▶ **Exercise γ:** Translate the underlined words. Be careful on word order in # 1. Be careful on # 9. *"Some"* cannot always be translated by τις, τι. (See p. 53 on ὁ μέν, ὁ δέ.)

1. Give her <u>some apples</u>.
2. <u>Some turtles</u> are small.
3. <u>Some men</u> can't swim. (Use two words.)
4. Give the wreath to <u>some poet</u>.
5. I show my poems <u>to some women</u>.
6. <u>Some women</u> can't write poems.
7. I see <u>someone</u> coming.
8. Give it <u>to someone</u> else.
9. The houses <u>of some</u> are tidy; <u>of others</u>, messy. Careful!

INTERROGATIVES AND INDEFINITES

It is a common pattern in Greek that an accented word will ask a question and the same word unaccented will be indefinite, a "shrug-word":

τίς *who?* τις *someone*	πότε *when?* ποτε *sometime, ever*	πῶς *how?* πως *somehow*	ποῦ *where?* που *somewhere* (also used colloquially = *somehow, I suppose*)

▶ **Exercise δ:** What clues distinguish an interrogative from an indefinite? Translate the following and put the proper punctuation (period or question mark) at the end.

1. ἀδελφή τις ἔρχεται
2. πῶς χαίρουσιν
3. εἰσί πότε
4. ἔρχεταί τις
5. χαίρουσι πως
6. εἰσί ποτε
7. τίς ἔρχεται
8. δός τινα
9. ποῦ οἰκεῖς
10. ἰατρούς τινας φιλῶ
11. γράμματά τινα γράφει
12. τίνας ἰατροὺς φιλεῖς
13. ποῦ γῆς οἰκεῖς
14. τίνα δίδως
15. οἰκεῖς που

ADVERBIAL ACCUSATIVE

Sometimes an accusative will be used much as an adverb would. Examples are: τέλος *finally*, τί *why?*, τι *in some way*, and μόνον *only*.

τέλος ἔρχονται.	*Finally they come.*	acc. of the noun τὸ τέλος
τί δακρύεις;	*Why are you crying?*	neuter acc. of τίς, τί
οὔ τι ὀργίζεται.	*(S)he is not in any way angry.*	neuter acc. of τις, τι
μόνον ἐσθίει ἀλλὰ οὐ πίνει.	*(S)he only eats but does not drink.*	neuter acc. of μόνος,η,ον

ARTICULAR INFINITIVE

As we saw on p. 43, the infinitive is considered neuter singular. Used with an article it is called an *articular* infinitive.

τὸ ὁρᾶν ῥᾷον τοῦ ἀκούειν.   *To see is easier than to hear.*
                                        Seeing is easier than hearing.

Phrases with articular infinitives can become quite complicated. It is important to bracket them before translating.

ἀντὶ τοῦ [τὸν πατέρα γράφειν ἐπιστολάς], ἡ μήτηρ λέγει.
         Instead of the father's writing letters, the mother speaks.

τὸ [τοὺς παῖδας μανθάνειν ποιήματα πρὶν δύνασθαι ἀναγιγνώσκειν] ἀγαθόν τι ἐστιν.
         For children to learn poems before being able to read is something good.

▶ **Exercise ε:** Translate the following sentences. Put brackets around the articular infinitive phrases.

1. νομίζουσί τινες τὸ μεθύειν χαλεπώτερον εἶναι τοῦ νοσεῖν.
2. νομίζω μῶρον τὸ τοὺς στρατιώτας μανθάνειν λέγειν τῇ γλώττῃ τῇ Ἑλληνικῇ.
3. λέγει πολλὰ περὶ τοῦ οἰκεῖν ἐν τῇ γῇ τῇ Ἀφρικανῇ σὺν ταῖς ἀδελφαῖς. (περί + gen. = *concerning, about*)
                                           (σύν dat. = *with*)

Classwork: ✦✦ Read **New Testament # 6** and **Famous Sayings # 1**, Thesauros pp. 222 and 232.

ἔργα   ~Read and translate Part 2 of "Who is Poor?" Learn the vocabulary.
            ~Parse the first two sentences of the messenger's first speech. ("εἶμι. ἀλλ' ὦ βασιλεῦ ... εἰσιν")

ὁ δὲ ἄγγελος λέγει τῷ βασιλεῖ· "εἶμι. ἀλλ', ὦ βασιλεῦ,
πάντες οἱ ἐν ταύτῃ τῇ γῇ οἰκοῦντες **εὐδαίμονές** **εἰσιν**.
ἡ γὰρ γῆ ἡ Ἀφρικανὴ εὔκαρπος (fertile) καὶ οἱ ἄνθρωποι
ἰσχυροὶ καὶ ὑγιεινοί. ποῦ γῆς **ἔστι** πένης;" ὁ δὲ βασιλεὺς 4
ἀποκρίνεται· "οὐκ οἶδα ποῦ γῆς ἐστιν, ἀλλὰ πένητα **χρή**
σε εὑρεῖν καὶ **ἀποφέρειν** **μοι**."

ὁ δὲ ἄγγελος ζητεῖ πολλὰς ἡμέρας. καὶ τέλος εὑρίσκει
ἄνδρα καθιζόμενον ἐπὶ πυρί, ἄνδρα ᾧ **οὐκ** **ἔστιν** οὔτε 8
οἰκία οὔτε θρόνος οὔτε ἱμάτιον. καὶ χαίρει ὁ ἄγγελος
ὁρῶν αὐτόν. νομίζει γὰρ εὑρεῖν (to have found) ὃ ζητεῖ-- 10
ἄνδρα πένητα. 11

ὁ δὲ ἀνὴρ ἐρωτᾷ· "ὦ φίλε, τί ἔρχῃ; τί βούλῃ;" ὁ δὲ
ἄγγελος ὧδε ἀποκρίνεται· "ἔρχομαι ζητῶν **πένητά**
τινα. τὸ εὑρεῖν ἄνδρα πένητα ἐν ταύτῃ τῇ γῇ **οὐκ** **ἔστι** 14
ῥᾴδιον. τέλος δύναμαι εὑρεῖν ἄνδρα πένητα." ὁ δὲ ἀνὴρ
λέγει· "ἄπιθι. οὐ γὰρ **πένης** **εἰμί**. καίπερ οὐδὲν ἔχων, 16
οὐκ **εἰμι** πένης." ὁ δὲ ἄγγελος τίθησι τὸν ἄνδρα ἐπὶ τῶν
ὤμων (shoulders) καὶ ἀποφέρει τῷ βασιλεῖ.

ὁ δὲ βασιλεὺς τὸν ἄνδρα ὁρῶν λέγει αὐτῷ τάδε· "ὦ φίλε,
μεγάλη μὲν ἡ εὐδαιμονία μου, σὺ δὲ κακοδαίμων εἶ. καὶ
δῆλόν **ἐστιν** ὅτι πένης εἶ. οὐ **γάρ** **ἐστί** **σοι** οὐδὲ μία 21
οἰκία, **καί** **εἰσί** **μοι** τρεῖς. **οὐκ** **ἔστι** σοι οὐδὲ μία γυνή,
καί **εἰσί** **μοι** τρεῖς. **οὐκ** **ἔστι** σοι οὐδὲ ἓν ἱμάτιον
φαῦλον, **καί** **ἐστί** **μοι** τέτταρα νέα καὶ καλά. αὔριον
(tomorrow) ἔσται δεῖπνον μέγα. καὶ ἐπὶ τῷ δείπνῳ πάντες
δώσουσί **σοι** (will give you) δῶρα, δῶρα ὡς μέγιστα καὶ 26~
ὡς κάλλιστα. καὶ οὕτως ἔσται σοι πλουσίῳ γίγνεσθαι."

(The bold print is for the sake of the next lesson, which is on Accents.)

4   ἰσχυρός, ά, όν - strong
      ποῦ - where? (The Greeks ask *where of earth?*, while we ask *where on earth?*.)
8   τὸ πῦρ, gen. πυρός <--> fire   --> pyre, pyromaniac
10   εὑρεῖν - Translate *he considers (that) he found*. Usually an aorist infinitive shows
      aspect: εὑρεῖν = *to find* (once), as on p. 84, line 12. But here it is replacing an aorist
      verb in indirect discourse. Since no new subject of the infinitive is given the reader
      understands it is the same as the subject of the main verb. Literally, *he considers (himself)*
      to have found.
11   ἄνδρα πένητα - The Greeks sometimes used ἀνήρ redundantly.   Cf. our
                        phrase *soldier boy* or the song, "*Oh, Sinner Man*."
14   τις, τι (unaccented) - some (as adj.); someone, something (used alone, as noun)
16   ἄπιθι - ἀπό (away) + ἴθι - go (command of εἶμι)
      περ - indeed (enclitic particle, often joined to other words, as in καίπερ)
      καίπερ + participle - even though
      ἡ εὐδαιμονία - good fortune
21   εἷς, μία, ἕν - one   (forms on p. 80)
      τέτταρες, τέτταρα - four (gen. τεττάρων, dat. τέτταρσι(ν))   --> tetralogy
26~ ὡς μέγιστα καὶ ὡς κάλλιστα - Can you guess what this means? **στ** is a
      marker for the superlative (as in our *biggest, best*) of certain adjectives.
      γίγνομαι - become, be   <--> kin, kindergarten, kind, king   --> benign,
      malign, pregnant, cognate (via Latin)   --> (with initial g dropped) native,
      nature, nation)   The aorist root (**γεν** as in γένος) of this all-important verb
      is extremely productive: --> genesis, genus, general, generate

Lesson 20. Proclitics and Enclitics

There are two groups of words in Greek that usually have no accent: proclitics and enclitics.

(1) The **forward-leaning** group, called *proclitics*, are seen as being united with the word that follows. They cause no changes in accent. There are ten:

ὁ, ἡ, οἱ, αἱ,   εἰ ὡς οὐ   ἐν ἐκ (ἐξ before vowel) εἰς (ἐς)

(2) The **backward-leaning** group, called *enclitics*, are considered to form a unit with the word that precedes. This can bring about **changes in accent**. Common enclitics are:

με, μου, μοι	τε (*and*)	εἰμι, ἐστι, etc. = *I am*
σε, σου, σοι	τοι (*y'know*)	φημι, φησι, etc. = *I say*
τις, τι (all unaccented forms)	γε (*at any rate* = a shrug)	

RULES OF COMBINATION FOR ACCENTED WORDS + ENCLITICS

word	one-syllable enclitic	change on preceding word		two-syllable enclitic	change on preceding
(1)	ἄνθρωπός τις	extra acute on final syllable		ἄνθρωπός ἐστι	
(2)	γλῶττά τις	extra acute on final syllable		γλῶττά ἐστι	
(3a)	φίλος τις	[no change]	(3b)	**φίλος ἐστί**	[no change; accent on last syllable of enclitic]
(4)	φωνή τις	acute rather than grave		φωνή ἐστι	
(5)	παῖς τις	[no change]		παῖς τινος	

(1) A word with an acute on the third syllable back gets a second accent before an enclitic.   (ἄνθρωπός)

(2) A word with a circumflex on the next-to-last syllable gets a second accent before an enclitic.   (γλῶττά)

(3a) A word with an acute on the next-to-last-syllable has no change before a one-syllable enclitic.   (φίλος τις)
(3b) A word with an acute on the next-to-last-syllable has no change before a two-syllable enclitic.
   The **two-syllable enclitic** gets a straight **accent** on its final syllable.   (φίλος τινός)

(4) A word with straight accent on the last syllable has an acute (rather than a grave) before an enclitic.   (φωνή)

(5) A word with a circumflex on the last syllable has no change before an enclitic.   (παῖς)

▶ **Exercise α:** Which rule above explains the accents in each of the following combinations?

1. φάρμακόν τι	3. φαρμάκοις τισί	5. μῦθός ἐστι	7. σκηνή τε	9. θρόνος τις
2. φάρμακά τινα	4. μῦθός γε	6. σκηνή ἐστι	8. ποιητῶν τινων	10. θρόνοι τινές

ADDITIONAL RULES FOR PROCLITICS AND ENCLITICS

(6) An enclitic gets an accent when followed by another enclitic:
   ὅταν τίς τινά πως φιλεῖ - whenever someone somehow loves someone.

(7) ἐστι is accented when it means *there exists* or *it is possible.*

(8) ἐστι is also accented when it comes at the beginning of a sentence or after τοῦτο, οὐκ, μή, εἰ, ὡς, or ἀλλά. (So an accent on the first syllable is no guarantee of existential meaning.)

(9) A proclitic gets an acute accent when followed by an enclitic: εἴ με φιλεῖς *if you love me*
   οὐκ εἰμι *I am not.*   This may happen when proclitic and enclitic join in a single word:
   ὡς + τε --> ὥστε   οὐ + τε --> οὔτε

(10) An enclitic never comes first in a sentence or clause. (Nor do forms of αὐτός as unemphatic pronoun.)

Classwork: Look at the words in bold print on p. 89 and say which rule explains the enclitic combinations.

ἔργα   ~Read and translate Part 3 of "Who Is Poor?" Learn the vocabulary.
      ~Say which rule operates for each enclitic combination (shown in bold print).
      ~Write sentences using enclitic patterns # 1-5. Provide an English translation.

WHO IS POOR? (Part 3)

ὁ δὲ ἀνὴρ ἀποκρίνεται· "ταῦτα τὰ δῶρα οὐ βούλομαι
λαμβάνειν. χαλεπὸς γὰρ ὁ **βίος μου** ἀλλ' οὐ **πένης εἰμί**.
κρίνεις **σύ με** πένητα, ὦ βασιλεῦ. ἀλλὰ κατὰ τὴν ἐμὴν
κρίσιν, οὐ πένης εἰμί." ὁ δὲ βασιλεὺς λέγει· "ὦ φίλε, πῶς
λέγεις ὅτι οὐκ εἶ πένης, οὐδὲν ἔχων; οἶδα γὰρ ὅτι οὐκ   5
εἰσί σοι οὐδεμίαι γυναῖκες, οὐδεμίαι οἰκίαι, οὐδένα ἱμάτια."

τῇ δὲ ὑστεραίᾳ ἡμέρᾳ πάντες ἔρχονται ἐπὶ τὸ δεῖπνον
φέροντες δῶρα. οἱ μὲν ἱμάτιον φέρουσιν, οἱ δὲ θρόνον,
οἱ δὲ σῖτον. ὁ δὲ ἀνὴρ οὐ λαμβάνει ταῦτα τὰ δῶρα. καὶ
ἐν ᾧ πάντες ἐσθίουσι λέγει ὁ ἀνὴρ τάδε· "ὦ βασιλεῦ,   10
ἕτοιμος εἶ ὁρᾶν **πένητά τινα**; ὁ δὲ βασιλεὺς λέγει· "
ἕτοιμός εἰμι." καὶ πάντας τοὺς ἄλλους ἐρωτᾷ ὁ ἀνὴρ
τὸ αὐτὸ ἐρώτημα· "ὦ φίλοι, **ἕτοιμοί ἐστε** (are you) ὁρᾶν
πένητά τινα;" καὶ οἱ ἄνθρωποι πάντες ἀποκρίνονται ὅτι
ἕτοιμοί εἰσιν. "εὖγε" ὁ ἀνὴρ λέγει·

καὶ ἄγει (he leads) αὐτοὺς πρὸς τόπον οὗ οἱ τεθνεῶτες   16
κεῖνται ἐν τῇ γῇ. καὶ ὁρῶσιν ἄνδρα τεθνεῶτα, ὃς νόσῳ
ἀπέθανεν ἐν τῇδε τῇ ἡμέρᾳ. "ὦ βασιλεῦ," ἐρωτᾷ ὁ ἀνήρ·   18
"ὁρᾷς τοῦτον τὸν ἄνδρα, ᾧ οὐκέτι **φωνή ἐστιν**, ᾧ δὲ
οὐκέτι ζωή; ὁ θάνατος παύει πάντα τὰ ἔργα τούτου τοῦ   20
ἀνδρός." ὁ δὲ βασιλεὺς λέγει· "ὁρῶ αὐτόν. τί **ἐρωτᾷς με**
τοῦτο;" ὁ δὲ λέγει τάδε· "ὦ βασιλεῦ, νῦν ὅρα (= ὅρα-ε)
ἐμέ, ᾧ **φωνή ἐστιν** ᾗ λέγω καὶ ᾧ **ὀφθαλμοί εἰσιν** οἷς   23
ὁρῶ, καὶ χεῖρες καὶ πόδες οἷς γεωργῶ. ὑγιεινὴ ἡ
γλῶττά μου. ὑγιεινοὶ καὶ οἱ **ὀφθαλμοί μου**. καὶ αἱ
χεῖρές μου ὑγιειναὶ καὶ οἱ **πόδες μου**. λέγεις ὅτι βούλη
ὁρᾶν **πένητά τινα**; οὗτος **πένης ἐστίν**, ἀλλ' οὐκ ἐγώ.   **27**

ὁ βίος - life   --> biology
πῶς - how?
κρίνω - judge   --> critic, criticism, hypocrisy   --> (via Latin) discern
κατά + acc. - according to
ἡ κρίσις - judgment (as well as contest)
5   οὐδείς, οὐδεμία, οὐδέν - not one, no (as adjective), no one, nothing (used alone,
         as noun). Literally, *not even one* = οὐδέ + εἷς, μία, ἕν. Used in singular and plural,
         with plural forms as expected.
10   ἐν ᾧ - while (short for ἐν τῷ χρόνῳ ἐν ᾧ)
     ἕτοιμος,η,ον - ready
16   ὁ τόπος - place   --> topic, topography
     τεθνεώς, gen. τεθνεῶτος - dead   (from θνήσκω - die)
18   ἀποθνήσκω = die (more common in prose)   aorist ἀπέθανεν - *he, she, it died*
     οὐκέτι - no longer
20   παύω - stop, check, cause to stop   --> pause
23   ἐμέ = emphatic form of με. The enclitic pronouns are unemphatic. (We saw
         emphatic σοῦ versus unemphatic σου in New Testament # 1, Thesauros p. 221.)

27

> ### Omission of forms of εἰμι
> Forms of the verb εἰμι are often omitted--most commonly
> ἐστι(ν) and εἰσι(ν), but other forms as well.

Lesson 21. Third-Group Comparatives and Superlatives; Superlative as "Exceedingly"; Special Words for Pairs

Most adjectives have comparative forms ending with -ότερος,α,ον or -ώτερος,α,ον. But some have comparative forms in the Third Group. These forms are like the forms of εὐδαίμων, with some optional variants. The accent is recessive.

ἀμείνων,ον *better* (comparative of ἀγαθός)

	M / F	optional forms	N	optional forms
nom.	ἀμείνων		ἄμεινον	
acc.	ἀμείνονα	[ἀμείνω]	ἄμεινον	
gen.	ἀμείνονος		ἀμείνονος	
dat.	ἀμείνονι		ἀμείνονι	
nom.	ἀμείνονες	[ἀμείνους]	ἀμείνονα	[ἀμείνω]
acc.	ἀμείνονας	[ἀμείνους]	ἀμείνονα	[ἀμείνω]
gen.	ἀμεινόνων		ἀμεινόνων	
dat.	ἀμείνοσι(ν)		ἀμείνοσι(ν)	

⚡⚡ Ambiguity Alert: The nom. and acc. pl. for M / F are the same for the optional forms.

The forms in brackets are optional and are frequently used. These by-forms, as they are sometimes called, can cause confusion if you do not learn them. Memorize them carefully.

▶ Exercise α: Give the proper form of ἀμείνων,ον for the following nouns. Include variants.

1. ἡ ____ οἰκία
2. τὴν ____ ἡμέραν
3. τὰ ____ βιβλία
4. τοὺς ____ θρόνους
5. τὸν ____ νόμον
6. τῆς ____ μητρός
7. οἱ ____ ποιηταί
8. τοῖς ____ φαρμάκοις

Many common and important adjectives have -ων,ον comparatives and -ιστος superlatives. **Learn all the words in the box.**

POSITIVE	COMPARATIVE	SUPERLATIVE
ἀγαθός, η, ον *good*	ἀμείνων, ἄμεινον (*better, often morally*) κρείττων, κρεῖττον (*more powerful*)	ἄριστος, η, ον κράτιστος, η, ον
κακός, η, ον *bad*	κακίων, κάκιον (*worse, often morally*) χείρων, χεῖρον (*worse, often lesser in power*)	κάκιστος, η, ον χείριστος, η , ον
καλός, ή, όν *beautiful*	καλλίων, κάλλιον	κάλλιστος, η, ον
μέγας, μεγάλη, μέγα *big, great*	μείζων, μεῖζον	μέγιστος, η, ον
πολύς, πολλή, πολύ *much, many*	πλείων, πλεῖον (*more; greater in size, number, or extent*)	πλεῖστος, η, ον *most*
ῥᾴδιος, α, ον *easy*	ῥᾴων, ῥᾷον	ῥᾷστος, η, ον
ταχύς, ταχεῖα, ταχύ *fast, quick*	θάττων, θᾶττον	τάχιστος, η, ον
ἡδύς, ἡδεῖα, ἡδύ *sweet, pleasant*	ἡδίων, ἥδιον	ἥδιστος, η, ον

The syntax of these Third-Group comparatives and -σт- superlatives is as usual.

θάττων ἵππος ἢ χελώνη.　　　　　　　　*A horse is faster than a turtle.*
τοῦτο τὸ ποίημα ῥᾷστον πάντων.　　　　*This poem is easiest of all.*
ἀγαθοῦ μὲν υἱοῦ οὐδὲν ἄμεινον, κακοῦ δὲ οὐδὲν κάκιον.　　*Nothing is better than a good son;*
　　　　　　　　　　　　　　　　　　　　　　　　nothing is worse than a bad one.

▶ **Exercise β:** Translate the following:

1. οἱ ἄριστοι	4. τὸ κάλλιον	7. ἡ ταχίστη	10. τὰ πλείονα	13. τὸ κράτιστον	16. αἱ ἡδίονες
2. τὸ ῥᾷον	5. οἱ μέγιστοι	8. ὁ χείρων	11. τὰ ῥᾷστα	14. ὁ κακίων	17. ἡ μείζων
3. τὰς ἡδίους	6. τὰ κρείττω	9. οἱ θάττους	12. τὸν ἀμείνω	15. τὰ πλείω	18. τὴν καλλίω

▶ **Exercise γ:** Translate each underlined word or phrase with a single word, using the chart on p. 92.

1. Deeds undertaken with joy are the <u>easiest</u>.　　3. Do you think our victory was <u>swifter</u> and <u>greater</u> than theirs?
2. Give me <u>more</u> wine and <u>more</u> apples.　　4. Send reinforcements to the <u>best</u> and <u>most powerful</u> men.

SUPERLATIVE AS "EXCEEDINGLY"

Sometimes a superlative is used simply to indicate a high pitch of some quality. ✍✍ Compare our English *She's the greatest,* meaning *very great,* or *This is most strange,* meaning *very strange.*

πλουσιώτατός ἐστιν.	Both mean:
μάλιστα πλούσιός ἐστιν	*He is richest* OR *He is **exceedingly** rich*

▶ **Exercise δ:** Translate the sentences. (Consult chart on p. 92 for comparatives and superlatives.)

1. She is bigger than her sister. (two *than* constructions)　　3. Children are swifter (two ways) than turtles.
2. The doctors are exceedingly good. (two ways)　　4. The doctors are as good as can be.

SPECIAL WORDS FOR PAIRS

The Greeks distinguished much more carefully than we do between two of something and many. They used to have the dual, a special set of endings for two of anything--used only rarely in classical times. And they had special words for distributing and question-asking in situations of two-ness:

τίς	*which?*	πότερος	*which?* (of two)
ἄλλος	*other*	ἕτερος	*other* (of two)
ἕκαστος	*each*	ἑκάτερος	*each, either* (of two)
πάντες	*all*	ἀμφότεροι	*both*

πότερον (neuter = *which of two?*) must have originally been used to introduce a question with two possible answers. Then it came to be used generally to introduce any question:

πότερον ἐθέλεις ἐλθεῖν ἢ οὔ;　　*Do you want to come or not?*
πότερον ἐθέλεις ἐλθεῖν;　　　　*Do you want to come?*

ἕτερος occasionally = *other* (of many, not just of two). This gives better sense for Heraclitus' statement that for those stepping in the same rivers ἕτερα καὶ ἕτερα ὕδατα ἐπιρρεῖ.

ἀμφότεροι and ἑκάτερος take predicate position.

ἀμφοτέραις ταῖς χερσίν βάλλεις.　　*You throw with both your hands.*
ἐν ἑκατέρᾳ τῇ πόλει δημοκρατία ἐστίν.　　*There is democracy in each city (of two).*

Classwork: ✦✦ Read **Heraclitus #13, Graveyard #12, 27-28,** Thesauros pp. 225, 228, and 230.

ἔργα　　　~Write the paradigm for καλλίων,ον. Memorize the pattern.
　　　　　~Read and translate "Who Is Wiser?" a west African tale. Learn the vocabulary.
　　　　　~Parse the third sentence of the last paragraph. (καὶ σὺ μὲν.)

WHO IS WISER?

ἡμέρᾳ τινὶ χελώνη λεαίνῃ ἐντυγχάνει βαινούσῃ ἐν τοῖς
ἀγροῖς. καὶ ἑκατέρα αὐτῶν φορεῖ τόξον. "ὦ φίλη"
λέγει ἡ χελώνη, "ἐγὼ ἡ σοφωτάτη πάντων τῶν ζῴων
καὶ νὴ τὸν Δία σοφωτέρα σοῦ εἰμι." ἡ δὲ λέαινα τοῦτο   4
ἀκούουσα ὀργίζεται καὶ λέγει τῇ χελώνῃ "διὰ τί νομίζεις
εἶναι σοφωτέρα ἐμοῦ; τὸ γένος τῶν χελωνῶν οὐκ ἔστι   6
σοφόν." ἡ δὲ ἀποκρίνεται ὧδε· "αἱ χελῶναι ἄρισται δή.
οἶδα ὅτι ἡ σοφωτάτη εἰμί καὶ δύναμαι δεικνύναι σοι."

καὶ ἔρχονται αἱ δύο παρὰ ποταμὸν ταχύν. ἡ δὲ χελώνη   9
λέγει τῇ λεαίνῃ· "ὡς ταχὺς καὶ ὡς εὐρὺς (broad) ἐστιν
οὗτος ὁ ποταμός. νῦν προτίθημι (I propose) κρίσιν.
βάλωμεν ἑκατέρα ἡμῶν (of us) τὰ τόξα ἐν τῷ ποταμῷ.   12~
πότερον σὺ ἐθέλεις βαλεῖν πρῶτον;" ἡ δὲ λέαινα βάλλει
μεγάλῃ ῥώμῃ (force) ὥστε τὸ τόξον πίπτει ἐν μέσῳ τῷ   **14**
ποταμῷ καὶ ἀφανίζεται (disappears) ἐν τοῖς τοῦ ποταμοῦ
ὕδασιν. ἔπειτα δὲ βάλλει ἡ χελώνη οὐδεμιᾷ ῥώμῃ (force)
ὥστε τὸ τόξον πίπτει πρὸ τῶν ποδῶν.   17

καὶ ἀναλαμβάνει αὐτὸ ἡ χελώνη τάδε λέγουσα· "ὦ φίλη,
οὐ περὶ τοῦδε ἡ κρίσις ἦν--ποτέρα ἡμῶν (of us)
ἰσχυροτέρα ἐστίν--ἀλλὰ περὶ τοῦδε--ποτέρα σοφωτέρα.
καὶ σὺ μὲν μείζονι ῥώμῃ (force) ἔβαλες ὥστε οὐκέτι ἔχεις   21
τὸ τόξον σου. ἐγὼ δὲ οὐδεμιᾷ ῥώμῃ ἔβαλον ὥστε τὸ
τόξον ἔτι ἔχω. τοῦτο δείκνυσιν ὅτι ἐγὼ ἡ σοφωτέρα." ἡ
δὲ λέαινα οὐ λέγει οὐδὲν ἀλλὰ σιγᾷ. καὶ τέλος ἀμφότεραι
κατέρχονται εἰς τοὺς ἀγρούς, ἡ μὲν νομίζουσα εἶναι
σοφωτάτη πάντων τῶν ζῴων, ἡ δὲ ἑτέρα οὔ.   26

ἐντυγχάνω - meet up with + dat.
ἡ λέαινα - lioness   --> lion
ἑκάτερος,α,ον - either, each (of two)
τὸ τόξον - bow (for shooting arrows)
τὸ γένος - race, tribe, category, kind   --> generic, phylogeny   --> genus (via Latin)
ἄριστος,η,ον - best   --> aristocrat, aristocracy
ὁ ποταμός - river   --> hippopotamus
9   ταχύς,εῖα,ύ - swift, quick   --> tachometer
ὡς - how! (in exclamation)
ἡ κρίσις - contest   (from κρίνω = judge)
12~ Why βάλωμεν rather than βάλλωμεν? (ἔβαλον - aorist of βάλλω. See p. 13.)
14   μέσος,η,ον - middle

14

ἐν μέσῳ τῷ ποταμῷ

Notice the Greeks use an **adjective in predicate position** in *middle the river*
where we would use a noun + noun *in the middle of the river*.

This is a peculiarity of Greek that has to do with location. The same holds true for
ἄκρος,α, ον *topmost* and ἔσχατος,η,ον *edgemost*.

ἐπ' ἄκρων τῶν δενδρέων *on the tops of the trees* - (lit. *on topmost the trees*)
ἐπ' ἐσχάτῳ τῷ ἀγρῷ *at the edge of the field* (lit. *at edgemost the field*)

---

17   πρό + gen. - before, in front of
ἀναλαμβάνω - take up, pick up
21   μείζων, ον - greater, bigger
σιγάω - be silent
ἀμφότεροι,αι,α - both (of two)   from Greek ἀμφι --> amphitheater, amphibian
--> ambidextrous (via Latin)
26   ἕτερος,α,ον - other (of two)   --> heterodoxy, heterosexual

Lesson 22. Neuter εσ- Stem Nouns; εσ- Stem Adjectives

	τὸ γένος (neuter) *race, tribe, kind*		**τὸ μέρος** (neuter) *part, portion, share*	**τὸ τέλος** (neuter) *end, aim, fulfillment*
nom.	τὸ γένος		μέρος	τέλος
acc.	τὸ γένος	originally	μέρος	τέλος
gen.	τοῦ γένους	(= γένεσος)	μέρους	τέλους
dat.	τῷ γένει	(= γένεσι)	μέρει	τέλει
nom.	τὰ γένη	(= γένεσα)	μέρη	τέλη
acc.	τὰ γένη	(= γένεσα)	μέρη	τέλη
gen.	τῶν γενῶν	(= γένεσων)	μερῶν	τελῶν
dat.	τοῖς γένεσι(ν)	(= γένεσσι)	μέρεσι(ν)	τέλεσι(ν)

There is an important subgroup of the Third Group: neuters with nominatives ending in ⁻ος. The stem actually ends in ⁻εσ (γενεσ-, μερεσ-, τελεσ-), but the σ drops out before the endings, causing various changes.

▶ **Exercise α:** Put the correct article before the form.

1. ___ γένους 2. ___ γένη 3. ___ γένεσι 4. ___ γένος 5. ___ γένει 6. ___ γενῶν

▶ **Exercise β:**   Circle the Greek words that must be neuter ⁻εσ stem nouns.

In the first year of the war, the soldier throws many spears in battle. And with the spears he hits a certain enemy in both his legs. And the enemy tries to walk toward a nearby mountain. And a doctor sees him walking with difficulty and says, "I see limbs (that are) not healthy." ἐν τῷ πρώτῳ ἔτει τοῦ πολέμου ὁ στρατιώτης βάλλει πολλὰ βέλη ἐν μάχῃ. καὶ τοῖς βέλεσι ἐχθρόν τινα βάλλει ἀμφότερα τὰ σκέλη. ὁ δὲ ἐχθρὸς πειρᾶται βαίνειν πρὸς ὄρος πλήσιον. ἰατρὸς δὲ ὁρᾷ αὐτὸν βαίνοντα χαλεπῶς καὶ λέγει· "μέλη οὐχ ὑγιεινὰ ὁρῶ."

εσ- STEM ADJECTIVES

Adjectives in this group have the same form for nom. and acc. M / F plural. (In this they resemble the optional forms of ἀμείνων., etc.)

ἀληθής,ές   *true*

	M / F	N
nom.	ἀληθής	ἀληθές
acc.	ἀληθῆ	ἀληθές
gen.	ἀληθοῦς	ἀληθοῦς
dat.	ἀληθεῖ	ἀληθεῖ
nom.	ἀληθεῖς	ἀληθῆ
acc.	ἀληθεῖς	ἀληθῆ
gen.	ἀληθῶν	ἀληθῶν
dat.	ἀληθέσι(ν)	ἀληθέσι(ν)

👀 **Ambiguity Alert:**
Note ἀληθεῖς:
nom. + acc. M / F pl.

▶ **Exercise γ:** Translate:
1. the true doctor (acc.)
2. the true laws (acc.)
3. the true kinds (nom)
4. of the true sister

Classwork: Learn this poem, which is probably by Sappho. (For the text, see Reiner and Kovacs, cited on p. xiii.) Sappho's dialect has a recessive accent on nouns and pronouns. You can see that in νύκτος and ἔγω.

✦

Δέδυκε μὲν ἀ σελάννα
καὶ Πλείαδες μέσαι δή·
νύκτος δὲ παρέρχετ' ὤρα·
ἔγω δὲ μόνα κατεύδω.

The moon's gone down.
The Pleiades are midway.
The round of night is slipping past,
While I, alone I lie.

ἔργα   ~Learn the poem by heart.
~Write the paradigm for τὸ τέλος three times. Memorize.
~Write the paradigm for ἀληθής,ές. Be able to recognize all forms.

Lesson 23. Personal Pronouns

PERSONAL PRONOUNS   ἐγώ *I, me*, etc.   σύ *you*

	ἐγώ		σύ	
nom.	ἐγώ		σύ	
acc.	ἐμέ	με	σέ	σε
gen.	ἐμοῦ	μου	σοῦ	σου
dat.	ἐμοί	μοι	σοί	σοι
nom.	ἡμεῖς		ὑμεῖς	
acc.	ἡμᾶς		ὑμᾶς	
gen.	ἡμῶν		ὑμῶν	
dat.	ἡμῖν		ὑμῖν	

✍✍ English, of course, does not distinguish *you (sing.)* from *you (pl.)*. This makes it more ambiguous than Greek.

▶ **Exercise α:** Translate: 1. ἐμοί, μοι 2. ἡμῖν 3. ὑμῶν 4. σε 5. σύ 6. ὑμᾶς 7. ἡμεῖς

▶ **Exercise β:** Translate the underlined words.
1. Give <u>me</u> the book. 2. <u>You</u> (sing.) read; <u>I</u> don't. 3. <u>We</u>, not <u>you</u>, are the responsible parties. 4. Make <u>us</u> well.

REFLEXIVE PRONOUNS

ἐμαυτόν, ήν *myself* (reflexive)   **σεαυτόν, ην** *yourself* (reflexive)

acc.	ἐμαυτόν	ἐμαυτήν	σεαυτόν (σαυτόν)	σεαυτήν (σαυτήν)
gen.	ἐμαυτοῦ	ἐμαυτῆς	σεαυτοῦ (σαυτοῦ)	σεαυτῆς (σαυτῆς)
dat.	ἐμαυτῷ	ἐμαυτῇ	σεαυτῷ (σαυτῷ)	σεαυτῇ (σαυτῇ)
acc.	ἡμᾶς αὐτούς	ἡμᾶς αὐτάς	ὑμᾶς αὐτούς	ὑμᾶς αὐτάς
gen.	ἡμῶν αὐτῶν	ἡμῶν αὐτῶν	ὑμῶν αὐτῶν	ὑμῶν αὐτῶν
dat.	ἡμῖν αὐτοῖς	ἡμῖν αὐταῖς	ὑμῖν αὐτοῖς	ὑμῖν αὐταῖς

A reflexive pronoun refers (literally "*bends back*") to the subject of a sentence. There is, of course, no nominative. The forms σεαυτόν, etc. are often contracted to σαυτόν, etc. The reflexive pronouns for "*ourselves*," "*yourselves*" are made up of "*us*" or "*you*" + "*selves*."

The translation for the reflexive pronoun has some form of "*self*" except for the possessive genitive, which is translated *my / your / his / her / our / their own*.

✍✍ Note: English uses the same word for emphatic and reflexive pronouns.

I came **myself**	αὐτὸς ἦλθον	(emphatic)	Be careful translating.
I see **myself**	ἐμαυτὸν ὁρῶ	(reflexive)	

ἑαυτόν, ήν, ό *himself, herself, itself* (reflexive)

acc.	ἑαυτόν (αὐτόν)	ἑαυτήν (αὐτήν)	ἑαυτό (αὐτό)
gen.	ἑαυτοῦ (αὐτοῦ)	ἑαυτῆς (αὐτῆς)	ἑαυτοῦ (αὐτοῦ)
dat.	ἑαυτῷ (αὐτῷ)	ἑαυτῇ (αὐτῇ)	ἑαυτῷ (αὐτῷ)
acc.	ἑαυτούς (αὐτούς)	ἑαυτάς (αὐτάς)	ἑαυτά (αὐτά)
gen.	ἑαυτῶν (αὐτῶν)	ἑαυτῶν (αὐτῶν)	ἑαυτῶν (αὐτῶν)
dat.	ἑαυτοῖς (αὐτοῖς)	ἑαυταῖς (αὐταῖς)	ἑαυτοῖς (αὐτοῖς)

The forms ἑαυτόν etc. are often contracted to αὐτόν, etc. Be sure to check for rough breathing:

αὐτὴν ὁρᾷ *(S)he sees* **her**   versus   αὑτὴν ὁρᾷ *She sees* **herself**.

▶ **Exercise γ:** Translate the underlined words. Give all possibilities.
1. I am giving <u>myself</u> a gift.   3. We like <u>ourselves</u>.   5. You like <u>your own</u> books.   7. He came <u>himself</u>.
2. They give <u>themselves</u> gifts.   4. I have <u>my own</u> book.   6. They have <u>their own</u> books.   8. He likes <u>himself</u>.

Classwork: ✦✦ Read **Heraclitus #14** and **New Testament #7**, Thesauros pp. 225 and 222.

ἔργα   ~Write the paradigms for ἐγώ and σύ three times. Memorize.
~Read and translate the first part of "Turtle Wings," a Nigerian tale. Learn the vocabulary.

TURTLE WINGS* (Part 1)

οἱ δαίμονες οἱ ἐν τῷ οὐρανῷ ποιοῦσι δεῖπνον. καὶ ἐπὶ τὸ
δεῖπνον καλοῦσι πάντα τὰ ζῷα. ἀλλὰ τῶν ζῴων μόνοι
οἱ ὄρνιθες δύνανται ἐλθεῖν ἐπὶ τὸ δεῖπνον. ἔχουσι γὰρ
πτέρυγας ὥστε πέτεσθαι ἐν τῷ οὐρανῷ.   4

τῶν δὲ ζῴων τῶν ἐπὶ γῆς ἡ χελώνη μάλιστα πεινῇ καὶ
μάλιστα βούλεται ἐλθεῖν ἐπὶ τὸ δεῖπνον. καὶ λέγει τῷ
ἀδελφῷ τάδε· "ὦ φίλε ἀδελφέ, οἰκτείρω (I pity) ἐμαυτήν.
οἶσθα ὡς πεινῶ. μεγάλη ἡ ἐμὴ πεῖνα, οὐκ ἴση τῇ σῇ.   8
μισοῦσα δὲ τὴν πεῖναν ταύτην καὶ σίτου ἐπιθυμοῦσα, εἶμι
νῦν σὺν τοῖς ὄρνισιν ἐπὶ δεῖπνον." τοῖς δὲ ὄρνισι λέγει
τάδε ἡ χελώνη· "ὦ φίλοι, ὑμεῖς μὲν ὅμοιοι τοῖς θεοῖς· ἐγὼ
δὲ ὑμῖν οὐχ ὁμοία, διότι οὐκ ἔχω πτέρυγας ὥσπερ ὑμεῖς. 12
δός μοι ἕκαστος ὑμῶν ἓν πτερὸν ἐκ τῶν πτερύγων ὑμῶν."
τοῦτο δὲ ποιοῦσιν οἱ ὄρνιθες. καὶ ἐκ τῶν πτερῶν ποιεῖ
ἑαυτῇ πτέρυγας ἡ χελώνη αἷς πέτεται σὺν τοῖς ὄρνισιν εἰς 15
τοὺς οὐρανούς.

καὶ ἡ χελώνη, ὥσπερ οἶσθα, σοφωτάτη πάντων τῶν
ζῴων. καὶ ἐν ᾧ πέτονται λέγει τοῖς ὄρνισιν· "ὦ φίλοι,
ἔστι νόμος παλαιὸς καὶ ὅσιος, ὡς ἐπὶ δείπνῳ πάντας δεῖ   19
ὄνομα αἱρεῖσθαι νέον. ποιῶμεν (ποιέ-ωμεν) καὶ ἡμεῖς
τοῦτο."

οἱ δὲ ὄρνιθες ὁμολογοῦσιν ὅτι ἀγαθὸς ὁ νόμος καὶ
αἱροῦνται πάντες ὀνόματα νέα. τὸ δὲ ὄνομα ὃ αἱρεῖται
ἡ χελώνη ἐστὶ Πᾶσιν-ὑμῶν. οἱ δ' ὄρνιθες νομίζουσι τοῦτο
τὸ ὄνομα ἄτοπον, ἀλλ' ὁμολογοῦσι τὴν χελώνην καλεῖν τῷ 25
ὀνόματι Πᾶσιν-ὑμῶν.

ὁ/ἡ δαίμων, gen. δαίμονος - spirit, divinity   --> demon
ὁ/ἡ ὄρνις, gen. ὄρνιθος - bird   --> ornithology
ἐλθεῖν = infinitive of ἦλθον *I came*

4   ἡ πτέρυξ, gen. πτέρυγος - wing (related to πτερόν)   --> archaeopteryx
     ὁ ἀδελφός - brother   (Philadelphia)
     φίλος,η,ον - dear
     ἐμαυτόν,ήν - myself

8   ἐμός, ή,όν - my
     ἴσος,η,ον - equal, equal to + dat.   --> isometric, isosceles, isotrope
     σός,σή,σόν - your (you singular)
     ἐπιθυμέω + gen. - desire, have a desire for
     σύν + dative - with (= in company with)
     ὅμοιος,α,ον (or ὁμοῖος,α,ον) - similar, similar to + dative   --> homeopathy
          (ὁμο *same*, ὅμοιος "*samish*"   ὁμο --> homogenize, homonym, homosexual)

12   ὥσπερ - just as   (ὡς + enclitic περ)
     τὸ πτερόν - feather (often in plural = wings) <--> feather --> pterodactyl, helicopter

15   ἑαυτόν, ἑαυτήν, ἑαυτό - himself, herself, oneself

19   δεῖ - it is binding, there is need, one ought   (δεῖ has more of a sense of moral
        obligation, while χρή has more of a sense of destiny or cosmic necessity.)
     αἱρέομαι - choose
     ὁμολογέω - agree, agree to + inf. (from ὁμο + λέγω - to say the same thing)

25   ἄτοπος, ον - strange (literally "placeless")   Cf. οὐ + τόπος --> utopia

---

*This story is freely adapted from a story told in *Things Fall Apart* by Chinua Achebe, © 1957; used with permission
of William Heinemann, Ltd.

Lesson 24. ὤν, οὖσα, ὄν; Possessive Adjectives; Generalizing μή; Innner and Cognate Accusatives

ὤν, οὖσα, ὄν = "being"

nom.	ὤν	οὖσα	ὄν
acc.	ὄντα	οὖσαν	ὄν
gen.	ὄντος	οὔσης	ὄντος
dat.	ὄντι	οὔσῃ	ὄντι
nom.	ὄντες	οὖσαι	ὄντα
acc.	ὄντας	οὔσας	ὄντα
gen.	ὄντων	οὐσῶν	ὄντων
dat.	οὖσι(ν)	οὔσαις	οὖσι(ν)

Forms of the participle of εἰμί look like disembodied endings. It is important to be able to identify them. The declension is exactly the same as for βαίνων, ουσα, ον.

Note that τὸ ὄν, the neuter participle from εἰμι, refers to *being* in general, i.e., to reality. We find in Greek τῷ ὄντι *in reality* and ὄντως *really*.

▶ Exercise α: Add articles to the following forms:

1. ___ ὄντων 2. ___ ὤν 3. ___ οὔσας 4. ___ ὄντας 5. ___ or ___ ὄντα 6. ___ ὄντι 7. ___ οὖσα

▶ Exercise β: Translate the following phrases using articles and participles only:

1. in reality 3. the men being (subject) 5. for the men who are 7. the thing being (subject)
2. of the women being 4. the woman being (direct object) 6. to the thing which is 8. of the things which are

POSSESSIVE ADJECTIVES

There are four possessive adjectives in Greek. You choose which word to use according to the possessor. But case, number, and gender match those of the possessed.

ἐμός,ή,όν = μου *my*   ἡμέτερος,α,ον = ἡμῶν *our*
σός σή σόν = σου *your* (you sing.)   ὑμέτερος,α,ον = ὑμῶν *your* (you pl.)

To say *his sisters* you have only one choice in Greek--use of the pronoun: αἱ ἀδελφαὶ αὐτοῦ. To say *my sisters* you may use a pronoun (μου) or an adjective (ἐμός,ή,όν) in bound position.

αἱ ἀδελφαί μου ἔρχονται.   Both mean:
αἱ ἐμαὶ ἀδελφαὶ ἔρχονται.   *My sisters are coming.*

▶ Exercise γ: Translate the underlined 2 ways.

1. Give me your apples. (*you* sing.)   3. Show them our turtle.
2. I love my fields.   4. Show them your poems. (*you* pl.)

GENERALIZING μή

When a participle is generalizing, its negative will be μή. (We have seen this many times in the New Testament.)

ἡ οὐ πίνουσα διψήσει.   *The one (fem.) not drinking will be thirsty.*
ἡ μὴ πίνουσα διψήσει.   *Whoever (fem.) is not drinking will be thirsty.*

✦ ὁ μὴ γαμῶν ἄνθρωπος οὐκ ἔχει κακά.   Menander

▶ Exercise δ: Using participles translate the following:

1. Whoever does not love does not hate. (μισέω = hate)   2. The one who does not love his mother is our king.

INNER AND COGNATE ACCUSATIVES

A verb may have an external object (someone or something already existing that is affected by the action of the verb) or an internal object (something that comes into being as a result of the action of the verb). The internal object will be expressed as an **inner accusative**.

ὁρῶ κύνα.   *I see a dog.*   (external object)

ὁρῶ πικρὸν θέαμα.   *I see a bitter sight.*   (internal object--inner accusative)

An inner accusative may be a **cognate accusative** as well. This means that the word for the object has the **same root as the verb.**

ἐρωτῶ ἐρώτημα.   *I ask a question.* Actually: *I ask a thing asked.*

✍✍ In English we have corresponding pairings: *sing a song, fight the good fight*, etc.

Often a neuter accusative adjective will be used alone with an inner or cognate accusative understood. We might say it functions as an adverb.

πολλὰ δακρύεις.   *You weep a lot.* Literally, *You weep many* (weepings).

Classwork: ✦✦ Read **Graveyard #6-7** and **Diogenes #1-2 and 5**, Thesauros pp. 227 and 234.

ἔργα   ~Read and translate the conclusion of "Turtle Wings." Learn the vocabulary.
                 ~Parse the first sentence of the last paragraph. (διὰ δὲ ταῦτα)

οὐ πολλῷ ὕστερον ἐπὶ τῷ δείπνῳ εἰσίν. καὶ ὁρῶσι πολὺν   **1**
σῖτον. ἡ δὲ χελώνη ἐρωτᾷ τοὺς δαίμονας· "τίσιν ἐστὶν
οὗτος ὁ σῖτος;" οἱ δὲ ἀποκρίνονται· "οὗτος ὁ σῖτός ἐστι
πᾶσιν ὑμῶν." καὶ ὁρῶσα πᾶν τὸ κρέας (meat) ἐρωτᾷ ἡ
χελώνη· "τίσιν ἐστὶ τοῦτο τὸ κρέας;" οἱ δὲ ἀποκρίνονται   **5**
αὖθις ὧδε· "πᾶσιν ὑμῶν ἐστι τοῦτο."

λέγει δὲ ἡ χελώνη τοῖς ὄρνισιν· "ἐκ τούτου ἔστι μαθεῖν ὅτι
ἐμοί ἐστι ταῦτα παντα. δηλόν ὅτι οὗτος ὁ σῖτος ἐμός
ἐστίν, οὐχ ὑμέτερος. καὶ τοῦτο τὸ κρέας ἐμόν ἐστιν, οὐχ   **9**
ὑμέτερον. οἱ γὰρ δαίμονες αὐτοὶ λέγουσιν ὅτι ἐστὶ Πᾶσιν-
ὑμῶν, καὶ τοῦτο ἔστι τὸ ὄνομά μου. νῦν χρὴ ἐμὲ ἐσθίειν
πρώτην." καὶ οὕτω πεινῇ ἡ χελώνη ὥστε τὸ πᾶν ἐσθίει.

οἱ δὲ ὄρνιθες τοῦτο ὁρῶντες ὡς μάλιστα ὀργίζονται.
λέγουσι δὲ ἀλλήλοις· "κακίστη πάντων ἥδε ἡ χελώνη.   **14**
ἐσθίει γὰρ τὸν ἡμέτερον σῖτον." καὶ ἕκαστος αὐτῶν
ἀπολαμβάνει τὸ πτερὸν ὥστε τέλος ψιλή (bare) ἐστιν ἡ
χελώνη.

νῦν δὲ οὐ δύναται ἡ χελώνη πέτεσθαι πάλιν πρὸς τὴν
οἰκίαν καὶ φοβεῖται. λέγει δὲ τάδε τῇ ψιττάκῃ (parrot)·   **19**
"ὦ φίλε, χρή με πηδᾶν (jump). κέλευε τὸν ἀδελφόν μου
τιθέναι πάντα τὰ **μαλακά** (soft) ἐπὶ τῆς γῆς πρὸ τῆς
οἰκίας." ἀλλὰ καὶ ἡ ψιττάκη (parrot) ὀργίζεται αὐτῇ καὶ
ἀντὶ τῶν μαλακῶν (soft) κελεύει τὸν ἀδελφὸν πάντα τὰ   **23**
σκληρὰ (hard) τιθέναι πρὸ τῆς οἰκίας.

διὰ δὲ τοῦτο, ὅτε ἡ χελώνη πίπτει πρὸς γῆν, πίπτει ἐπὶ τὰ
σκληρὰ (hard). καὶ ῥήγνυται τὸ χελώνιον (her shell breaks)
ὥστε μέρη πολλὰ διασκεδάννυται (are scattered) ἐπὶ τῆς
γῆς. τοῦτο δ' ὁρῶν καλεῖ τὸν ἰατρὸν ὁ ἀδελφός. καὶ τὰ   **28**
μέρη τοῦ χελωνίου (shell) συντίθησιν ὁ ἰατρὸς κόλλῃ (glue).

διὰ δὲ ταῦτα ἔστι, καὶ νῦν, ὁρᾶν πάντα τὰ μέρη τοῦ τῆς
χελώνης χελωνίου (shell). ἀληθῶς, τὸ τέλος τοῦ μύθου
δείκνυσι διὰ τί ἔστιν ὁρᾶν τὰ μέρη τοῖς σοῖς ὀφθαλμοῖς.

1

Dative of Degree
πολλῷ *not later* **by much**, i.e., *not much later*

ὕστερον - later (accusative used as adverb, from adj. ὕστερος,α,ον = next, after)

9 ὑμέτερος,α,ον - your (plural)

14 κάκιστος,η,ον - worst (superlative of κακός)

ἡμέτερος, α, ον - our

ἀπολαμβάνω - take back, take away

πάλιν - back --> palindrome

19-
23 This is a story about greed, cleverness, and the dangers of relying on a translator.
By learning ancient Greek you will be able to verify translations for yourself.
(Do you know the Italian saying *Traduttori traditori? Translators, traitors.*)

28 τὸ μέρος - part, partion, share

συντίθημι - put together, from σύν + τίθημι

τὸ τέλος - the end --> teleology

TURTLE TALES

Figure 1. Apollo, holding a lyre made from a turtle shell, offers libations. White Slip Kylix (ca. 470 B.C.E.) Delphi National Museum.

The turtle is a common folkloric figure. Her shell, longevity, slow gait, and amphibious nature fascinate the tellers of legendary stories.

You have been reading a number of such tales that feature Turtle. These tales, which are African in origin, reveal Turtle as a trickster figure who sometimes triumphs because of her cleverness, as she does in "The Oath" and "Who is the Wiser?," but at other times is trapped by her cleverness, as in "Turtle Wings."

Turtle's role in world mythology is not confined to her role as a clever but sometimes foiled trickster. Like all trickster figures, Turtle is often associated with creation stories. In American Indian stories, for instance, it is Turtle who creates the world while coming up from the bottom of a lake floor. She carries with her all the potential elements of the world in the mud trapped under her fingernails. In other mythologies, her shell and its strength make Turtle the cosmic foundation of the world, since she carries the universe on her back and maintains its stability.

Turtle herself is a character in a number of Greek stories. In fact, the most famous of all writers of beast fables, Aesop, has three stories about Turtle, including the world's best-known story, "The Tortoise and the Hare."

We do not have clear factual information about Aesop, who may have been a legendary figure, even though Herodotus (2.134) tells us that he lived in the sixth century B.C.E. and was a slave on the island of Samos. By the end of the fifth century the name of Aesop was synonymous with beast fables. Indeed, Socrates himself is said to have composed poetic versions of Aesop's fables just before he died (Plato, *Phaedo*, 60D). Hesiod and Archilochus, seventh-century poets, also wrote beast fables. But it is Aesop who fixed the form that would influence all subsequent European literature.

You are familiar with many of Aesop's stories, "The Goose Who Laid the Golden Egg," "The Ant and the Grasshopper," "The Wind and the Sun," and later in the course you will read a version of an Aesop story in Greek. His stories are marked by their terseness, the plain style of the Greek prose, and the didactic morals that each story illustrates.

One of Aesop's turtle stories seems to be a variation of the story in "Who is the Wiser?" In the African story, Turtle proves her cleverness by exploiting her lack of strength. In the Greek story, "The Turtle and the Hare," Turtle wins the race because she doggedly persists while the swift hare foolishly dawdles.

Aesop's other two stories show Turtle as the overreaching greedy trickster. In Aesop's "The Turtle and the Eagle," Turtle begs the eagle to teach her to fly and insists even when Eagle tells her it is not possible. Turtle thus falls to her death. You can discern some similarities with "Turtle Wings," in which the land and sea creature attempts to master, to her harm, the air.

In "Zeus' Marriage," Turtle is the only one who does not come to the banquet celebrating Zeus's marriage to Hera. When Zeus questions her about her absence, she foolishly answers *oikos philos, oikos aristos* ("My home is dear, my home is best"). Zeus in anger decrees that she should henceforth carry her house with her forever. This just-so fable corresponds to the end of "Turtle Wings," which explains why turtle shells are segmented.

The turtle, like many trickster figures, is also associated with music: the turtle shell is the sounding board for Greek lyres. Hermes, whose role in Greek mythology is that of a trickster himself, is depicted in the *Homeric Hymn to Hermes* as the creator of the lyre from a turtle shell when he was only one day old. He later gives the lyre to Apollo as a peace offering for his theft of Apollo's cattle (Figure 1).

A legend about the death of Aeschylus, the tragic poet, seems to further connect the turtle with music and poetry. According to this legend, which seems to be a variety of Aesop's "The Turtle and the Eagle," Aeschylus was told that something thrown from the sky would kill him. Subsequently, an eagle wishing to eat a turtle needed to break her shell. The eagle dropped it on Aeschlyus' bald head, mistaking it for a rock, and thus killed the poet. The ironies of the story abound: Aeschylus the poet, who celebrates Zeus in his tragedies, is killed by an animal associated with poetry and music and by the bird most associated with Zeus.

Figure 2. "Turtles" from Aegina.   Figure 3. "Owls" from Athens.

Turtles are also famous in Greek culture as coins, called "Chelonai." The Turtle coins of Aegina were the first coins ever minted in Europe, dating from the sixth century B.C.E., and were produced for at least a century. Aegina, an island in the Saronic Gulf, was only rivaled by nearby Athens for the prevalence of her coins. On the Aeginetan coins, the turtle was an emblem for Poseidon and for the sea power of Aegina. Eventually, Aegina's power and coins were overshadowed by the "Owls" of Athens. These coins featured Athena, the deity of Athens, and her sacred bird, the owl.

REVIEW OF GRAMMAR AND SYNTAX

This should bring together all that you have learned. Review what is in this chapter. And don't forget to congratulate yourself for having learned so much Greek!

NOUN   CASES

Nominative	Accusative	Genitive	Dative
Names or describes subject of verb.	Direct object of verb (may be inner or external, may be cognate)	Genitive of possession	Indirect object
Predicate nominative	Accusative of end of motion (often with prepositions)	Partitive genitive	Dative of possession
Subject nominative in indirect discourse (box p. 84)	Accusative of extent or duration	Genitive of time within which (a kind of partitive?)	Dative of means, manner, or circumstance
	Accusative of part affected	Genitive of separation	Dative of place where or time when
	Adverbial accusative	Genitive of comparison (a kind of gen. of separation)	Dative of advantage or disadvantage
	Subject in indirect discourse	Joker (genitive of price or value, etc. etc.)	Dative of degree

NOUN   FORMS

You now know most important noun patterns. Turn to p. 237 of the Paradigm section. Be able to WRITE OUT **all of the A- and O- Group forms** as well as the declensions of **δαίμων, ποίημα,** and **γένος.** Be able to RECOGNIZE every Third Group form on the page except for πόλις and βασιλεύς (which are reserved for later in the course).

For your convenience a list of endings is provided below.

χελώνη	γλῶττα	οἰκία	πολίτης
η	α	α	ης
ην	αν	αν	ην
ης	ης	ας	ου
ῃ	ῃ	ᾳ	ῃ
αι	αι	αι	αι
ας	ας	ας	ας
ῶν	ῶν	ῶν	ῶν
αις	αις	αις	αις

μῦθος	βιβλίον
ος	ον
ον	ον
ου	ου
ῳ	ῳ
οι	α
ους	α
ων	ων
οις	οις

δαίμων [stem δαιμον-]	ποίημα [ποιηματ-]	γένος [γενες-]
(ς)	--	ος
α	--	ος
ος	ος	ους
ι	ι	ει
ες	α	η
ας	α	η
ων	ων	ῶν
σι(ν)	σι(ν)	εσι(ν)

ARTICLE: Be able to WRITE OUT the forms of ὁ, ἡ, τό.

ADJECTIVES: Be able to WRITE OUT the forms of πρῶτος,η,ον and ῥᾴδιος,α,ον.
Be able to WRITE OUT the forms of ἀμείνων, ον (including the optional forms), and of πᾶς, πᾶσα, πᾶν.
Be able to RECOGNIZE all the adjective forms on p. 238 except for ἡδύς (reserved for later).

PRONOUNS: Be able to WRITE OUT all forms of ἐγώ and σύ, singular, plural, and unemphatic forms.
Be able to WRITE OUT the forms of ὅς, ἥ, ὅ.
Be able to RECOGNIZE all the pronoun forms on p. 239 except ὅστις (reserved for later) and ἕ
(not covered in this course but included for the sake of completeness).

COMPARATIVES and SUPERLATIVES OF ADJECTIVES AND ADVERBS: This material is covered on pp. 50, 63, and 82-83. Test yourself to make sure you understand all the possibilities by translating the following:

1. I consider my sister beautiful.
2. I consider my sister very beautiful.
3. I consider my sister more beautiful. (two ways)
4. I consider my sister more beautiful than my friend. (two ways--with ἤ and with gen.)
5. I consider my sister most beautiful. (two ways)
6. I consider my sister the most beautiful of all.
7. I consider my sister as beautiful as can be.

8. My sister speaks beautifully.
9. My sister speaks very beautifully.
10. My sister speaks more beautifully. (two ways)
11. My sister speaks more beautifully than my friend. (two ways--with ἤ and with gen.)
12. My sister speaks the most beautifully.
13. My sister speaks most beautifully of all.
14. My sister speaks as beautifully as possible.

FIVE USES OF ὡς:

(1) **how** roughly equivalent to ὅτι = *that*, as when we say, "*I saw how you came late.*"	οἶδα ὡς πεινῇς.	*I know how (= that) you are hungry.*
(2) **how** in exclamation:	ὡς καλή ἐστιν.	*How beautiful she is!*
(3) **on the grounds / assumption that** (with participles)	πέμπε σῖτον αὐτῇ ὡς πεινώσῃ.	*Send her food on the grounds that she is hungry.*
(4) **as ... as possible** ὡς+superlative	ὡς καλλίστη.ἐστίν. ἴθι ὡς τάχιστα.	*She is as beautiful as can be.* *Come as quickly as possible.*
(5) **as** (relative)	ὡς ὁ νόμος ἐστιν τρέχει ὥσπερ ἵππος	*As is the custom* *He runs just as a horse* (runs) / *He runs just like a horse.*

USES OF ὥστε AND οὕτως ὥστε:

ὥστε + **infinitive** gives expected, intended, or probable result.
> *so as to* OR *so as for ___ to* when there is a new subject (in the accusative) for the infinitive.

ὥστε + **personal verb** gives actual result. *so that*
οὕτως ὥστε   *so . . . as to . . .   so . . . as for X to . . .   so . . . that*
(Translate οὕτως as *so* and ὥστε as merely *as to* or *that*. In other words, drop the *so* from the translation of ὥστε.)

οὐ VERSUS μή

Greek has two negatives. Basically οὐ is the negative for verb forms that indicate **facts**:

οὐ γράφεις. *You are not writing.*   λέγω σε οὐ γράφειν. *I say that you are not writing.*
ἀκούω σε οὐ γράφοντα. *I hear that you are not writing.*

μή is the negative for **all else**. Use μή for:

Commands	μὴ γράφε.	*Don't write!*
Infinitive of probable result:	οὕτω πεινῇ. ὥστε μὴ ἐθέλειν ζῆν. .	*She is so hungry as not to wish to live,* versus οὕτω πεινῇ ὥστε οὐκ ἐθέλει ζῆν *She is so hungry that she does not wish to live.*
Articular Infinitive	τὸ μὴ ἐσθίειν χαλεπόν.	*Not eating is difficult.*
Generalizations	ὁ μὴ γεωργῶν πεινῇ.	*Whoever doesn't farm goes hungry,* versus ὁ οὐ γεωργῶν πεινῇ *The one not farming goes hungry.*

Note: When μή is used with a circumstantial participle, that is a clue to the interpretation "if":

οὐ βούλομαι διαλέγεσθαι αὐτῇ **οὐκ** οὔσῃ σοφῇ. *I do not want to converse with her, **since** she is not wise.*
οὐ βούλομαι διαλέγεσθαι αὐτῇ **μὴ** οὔσῃ σοφῇ. *I do not want to converse with her **if** she is not wise.*

ACCENTS

The basic rules for accents are covered on pp. 33-35 and 37. Reread them to make sure you understand the rules. Enclitics and proclitics are discussed on p. 90. Can you explain all the accents in the paradigms? Can you explain the various graves and acutes you see on final syllables in stories? Can you answer the following questions? (Answers are on the next page. Don't look until you have tried to answer the questions yourself.)

1. When do you find a Greek word with two accents?
2. When do you find a final acute in mid-sentence?
3. When do you find an enclitic with an accent?
4. When do you find a proclitic with an accent?

When do you find a Greek word with two accents? When the word is in the φάρμακον or γλῶττα pattern and is followed by an enclitic. (This is the *only* time you find a Greek word with two accents.)

When do you find a final acute in mid-sentence? When it is a form of τίς, τί or when it is on the final syllable before an enclitic (whether it belongs to the original word, as in φωνή, or is additional, as in ἄνθρωπός τις or γλῶττά τις).

When do you find an enclitic with an accent? When it is followed by another enclitic or when it is a two-syllable enclitic and follows a word of the φίλος pattern.

When do you find a proclitic with an accent? When it is followed by an enclitic.

NUMBERS

CARDINALS		ORDINALS
1) εἷς, μία, ἕν	Normal Third-Group forms (See p. 80.)	1st: πρῶτος, η, ον
2) δύο	Not declined. OR you may find	2nd: δεύτερος, α, ον
3) τρεῖς, τρία	δυοῖν for the gen. and dat.	3rd: τρίτος, η, ον
4) τέτταρες, α		4th: τέταρτος, η, ον

τρεῖς, τρία (three)

M, F	N
τρεῖς	τρία
τρεῖς	τρία
τριῶν	τριῶν
τρισί(ν)	τρισί(ν)

(like pl. of ἀληθής, ές)

τέτταρες, τέτταρα (four)

M, F	N
τέτταρες	τέτταρα
τέτταρας	τέτταρα
τεττάρων	τεττάρων
τέτταρσι(ν)	τέτταρσι(ν)

(like pl. of εὐδαίμων, ον)

CHECKLIST

~~Know how to recognize and use the **relative pronoun ὅς, ἥ, ὅ.** (See pp. 62-63.)
  These may be small but they are ALL-IMPORTANT.

~~Understand the difference between question-asking τίς, τί and shrug words τις, τι.   (pp.87-88)

~~Know the three uses of **αὐτός.** (pp. 36, 50)

~~Know the uses of **ἐστί.** (p. 54)

~~Understand the use of intensive καί and intensive οὐδέ. (pp. 50, 67)

~~Know the three verb patterns in the boxes on p. 61.

~~What does **-όμενος,η,ον** tell you on the end of a verb stem? (p. 55)

~~What do these endings indicate: γιγνώσκωμεν, ὅταν ἐθέλῃ, ὅταν βούληται.   (pp. 1, 72)

~~What is **bound versus unbound** position? What are the two normal position for an adjective-noun combination (e.g. "the wise doctor")?   (p. 49) What position do οὗτος, ὅδε, and ἐκεῖνος take? (p. 65) What about μέσος? (p. 94)

~~Remember that **double negatives** are good Greek. (p. 43)

~~Remember that a **neuter plural subject** normally takes a **singular verb.** (p. 30)

▶▶ **Review Exercise:** Translate the following, which use grammar and syntax from many chapters.

1. These unjust women are not dear to me.
2. Don't order the new judges to learn foolish things.
3. The lioness, since she is very strong (use a participle), takes all things which she wants.
4. I find true happiness to be better than money; you do not. (Note: οὐ has an accent at sentence end: οὔ)
5. Birds rejoice in their wings; men in their strong hands and feet; women in their dear children.
6. Why do they live (ζῶσι) in such a way that they do not ever rejoice in better things?
7. Certain men die so as to bring happiness to all.
8. It is possible to live nobly.

106

VOCABULARY REVIEW (pp. 62-100)

NOUNS

ἡ ---η
ἡ γῆ
ἡ ζωή

α after ε,ι,ρ
ἡ εὐδαιμονία
ἡ θύρα

α
ἡ λέαινα
ἡ πεῖνα

ὁ ---της
ὁ δικαστής
ὁ κλέπτης

ὁ ---ός
ὁ ἀδελφός
ὁ ἄγγελος
ὁ βίος
ὁ γεωργός
ὁ θάνατος
ὁ ἵππος
ὁ λόγος
ὁ ὅρκος
ὁ οὐρανός
ὁ πόλεμος
ὁ ποταμός
ὁ τόπος
ὁ υἱός

ἡ ---ος
ἡ νόσος

τὸ ---ον
τὸ ζῷον
τὸ πτερόν
τὸ τόξον

Third Group

ὁ ἀνήρ,
  gen. ἀνδρός
ἡ γυνή,
  gen. γυναικός
ἡ μήτηρ,
  gen. μητρός
ὁ πατήρ,
  gen. πατρός
ὁ/ἡ δαίμων,
  gen. δαίμονος
ὁ/ἡ ὄρνις,
  gen. ὄρνιθος

ἡ πτέρυξ,
  gen. πτέρυγος
ὁ πένης,
  gen. πένητος
τὸ ὕδωρ,
  gen. ὕδατος
τὸ σῆμα

ὁ/ἡ κύων,
  gen. κυνός
ὁ/ἡ παῖς,
  gen. παιδός
ὁ πούς,
  gen. ποδός
ἡ χείρ,
  gen. χειρός
τὸ πῦρ,
  gen. πυρός

τὸ γένος
τὸ μέρος
τὸ τέλος

ἡ κρίσις *contest, judgment*

ADJECTIVES

ἕτοιμος,η,ον
ζωός,ή,όν
ἱερός,ά,όν
ἴσος,η,ον
ἰσχυρός,ά,όν
κύριος,α,ον (or ος,ον)
λοιπός,ή,όν
μέσος,η,ον
μόνος,η,ον
νέος,α,ον
νόμιμος,η,ον
ὅμοιος,α,ον (or ὁμοῖος,α,ον)
ὅσιος,α,ον (or ος,ον)
ὑστεραῖος,α,ον
φίλος,η,ον

ἄτοπος,ον

εὐδαίμων,ον
κακοδαίμων,ον

ἀληθής,ές
ψευδής,ές

γλυκύς, εῖα, ύ
ἡδύς,εῖα,ύ

τεθνεώς, gen. -ῶτος *dead*
(perfect participle, to be learned later)

SPECIAL COMPARATIVES AND SUPERLATIVES

ἀγαθός
  ἀμείνων, ἄμεινον
  ἄριστος,η,ον
ἀγαθός
  κρείττων, κρεῖττον,
  κράτιστος,η,ον

κακός,
  κακίων, κάκιον
  κάκιστος,η,ον
κακός,
  χείρων, χεῖρον
  χείριστος,η,ον

καλός,
  καλλίων, κάλλιον
  κάλλιστος,η,ον

ῥᾴδιος
  ῥᾴων, ῥᾷον,
  ῥᾷστος,η,ον

μέγας
  μείζων, μεῖζον
  μέγιστος,η,ον

πολύς
  πλείων, πλεῖον
  πλεῖστος,η,ον

ταχύς
  θάττων, θᾶττον
  τάχιστος,η,ον

ἡδύς
  ἡδίων, ἥδιον
  ἥδιστος,η,ον

ADVERB SERIES

μάλα
μᾶλλον   (μᾶλλον ἤ with verbs = *rather than*)
μάλιστα

ὅτι or ὡς μάλιστα

VERBS

ἀγγέλλω
  ἀπαγγέλλω
βαίνω
βάλλω, ἔβαλον
γιγνώσκω
  καταγιγνώσκω
εὑρίσκω, ηὗρον
θνήσκω, ἔθανον
  τεθναίην (May I die)
  ἀποθνήσκω (more common)
κελεύω
κλέπτω
κρίνω
λαμβάνω
  ἀναλαμβάνω
  ἀπολαμβάνω
μέλλω
μένω
παύω
πίπτω
τέμνω
  ἀποτέμνω
τυγχάνω
  ἐντυγχάνω
φέρω, ἤνεγκον
  ἀποφέρω
φυλάττω

γεωργέω
ἐπιθυμέω
κοινωνέω
οἰκέω
ὁμολογέω

σιγάω

ὄμνυμι
τίθημι
  συντίθημι

ἔρχομαι, ἦλθον
γίγνομαι
λανθάνομαι
πέτομαι

αἱρέομαι

εἰμί, ἦν, ἔσται
εἶμι (command: ἴθι)
  ἄπειμι
  εἴσειμι

ἵσταμαι

ALSO
μέλει (impersonal)

PRONOUNS

ἐγώ, etc.
  (ἡμεῖς)
σύ, etc.
  (ὑμεῖς)
αὐτόν, αὐτήν, αὐτό

ἐμαυτόν,ήν
σεαυτόν,ήν
  (σαυτόν,ήν)
ἑαυτόν, ήν,ό
  (αὑτόν,ήν,ό)

ὅς, ἥ, ὅ

οὗτος, αὕτη, τοῦτο
ἐκεῖνος, ἐκείνη, ἐκεῖνο
ὅδε, ἥδε, τόδε
  τάδε these the following (words)
  (used when reporting speech)

DISTRIBUTIVE ADJECTIVES

πᾶς, πᾶσα, πᾶν
  gen. παντός, πάσης, παντός

πάντα - everything

εἷς, μία, ἕν
  gen. ἑνός, μιᾶς, ἑνός

οὐδείς, οὐδεμία, οὐδέν,
  gen. οὐδενός, οὐδεμιᾶς, οὐδενός

μόνος,η,ον

ἐμός,ή,όν
σός,ή,όν
ἡμέτερος,α,ον
ὑμέτερος,α,ον

ἑκάτερος,α,ον
ἕτερος,α,ον
πότερος,α,ον
ἀμφότεροι,αι,α

PREPOSITIONS

κατά + acc.
παρά + acc.
ἄνευ + gen.
περί + gen.
πλήν + gen.
πρό + gen.
σύν + dat.

ADVERBS

αὖθις
ἔπειτα
ἔτι
οὐκέτι

εὖ

πάλιν
ὕστερον

ποῦ
πῶς
πότερον

πότε
οὔποτε

OTHER

ὡς Note five uses of ὡς:

(1) "**as**" (relative, as in ὡς νόμος
  ἐστιν *as is the custom*)
(2) "**how**" in exclamation:
  ὡς ἡδύ ἐστιν *how sweet it is!*
(3) "**how**" - as roughly equivalent
  to ὅτι = "**that**," as when we
  say, "*I saw how you came late.*"
(4) ὡς+ superlative - *as . . .
     as possible*
(5) "**on the grounds that**"
    (with participles)

περ
ὥσπερ
καίπερ

ἐν ᾧ
ὅταν

οὔτε . . . οὔτε

δή
καὶ δὴ καί

τρεῖς, τρία
τέτταρες,τέτταρα

πολλῷ (dative of degree)

δεῖ

ὤν, οὖσα, ὄν

VERB OVERVIEW: ASPECT and TENSE

You can use verbs to command (*go!*), to show possibilities (*she might leave*), to show fear (*lest she leave*), or to show purpose (*so that she may leave*). But the main function of a verb is to relate facts: *she left, she was leaving*, etc. One may report on facts in the present or past; one may make predictions about the future.

The forms of the Greek verb used to report or predict facts are in the Indicative Mood. We shall start our systematic study of the verb with this. (You will learn the full system later.)

An Indicative verb expresses **aspect** and **time**. Of these, **aspect** is fundamental. There are three aspects (continuous, aorist, and perfect) and three times (past, present, future).

THE THREE ASPECTS

(1) **Aorist**. The aorist is the simplest aspect. It shows that an action is thought of at a single point of time, usually the finish point: "*he did it*," "*she left*." You can think of the aorist as expressing what we express with a finger snap or a hand-rubbing gesture of "*well, that's over with*." Occasionally an aorist will show a beginning point rather than an end: "*he got sick*," "*I burst into tears*." But here, too, there is the expression of the same basic idea: occurrence at a single point in time, occurence thought of as a single event--as a snapshot rather than a movie.

(2) **Continuous**. In contrast to the aorist, the continuous aspect shows that an action is thought of as ongoing, in process, occupying a stretch of time: "*I am doing it*," "*they were dancing*." If an action in the past was in fact completed (e.g., they were dancing and they stopped), the past continuous does not give us this information: it tells us only that an action was going on. The continuous aspect is used also for activities that are repeated: "*I write poems*" (habitually, for an occupation), "*she used to go to school*." Again, the basic idea is to show the activity as occupying a stretch of time.

(3) **Perfect**. The perfect expresses not only that something was done in the past but also that its **effect** is still being felt. To say "*I have left*" is really to talk about a present state: "*I have left* (and therefore am gone)." If you think about English, you will see that we sometimes use our perfect form this way. "*Did you wash?*" is a question we might ask to find out what happened ten years ago. But "*have you washed?*" is a question we ask only when we want to know "*have you washed* (and are you therefore clean)?" There can be a past perfect in Greek--"*I had washed* (and therefore was clean)," and a future perfect "*I shall have washed* (and therefore shall be clean)."

THE THREE TIMES

Of course the Greek verb also expresses time. (When a verb indicates time, this is called **tense**.) For the Greeks, as for us, there are three times: **present**, **past**, and **future**. As you can see, time is irrelevant to aspect. A perfect may hold true in the present, past or future. A continuous may be going on now or in the past. An aorist is past and normally cannot be thought of as present, since the present is ongoing, part of a flow of time.

Logically we might expect a separate future for continuous and aorist. (Indeed, Russian, like English, has two such futures: *I shall go* and *I shall be going*.) But in Greek we have a special stem for future time grafted awkwardly onto a system that uses stems to show aspect:

	Continuous	Future	Aorist	Perfect
Present	*I leave, am leaving*			*I have left*
Past	*I used to leave, was leaving*		*I left*	*I had left*
Future		*I shall leave, be leaving*		*I shall have left*

Lesson 25. The Continuous Stem

λείπω   *leave*

PRESENT   *I leave, am leaving*

Singular			Plural	
I (first person)	λείπω	λείπομεν	*we* (first person)	**ʊʊ Ambiguity**
you (second person)	λείπεις	λείπετε	*you* (second person)	**Alert:** λείπετε =
he, she, it (third person)	λείπει	λείπουσι(ν)	*they* (third person)	*you are leaving* and *leave!* (command)

IMPERFECT   *I was leaving, used to leave*

I	ἔλειπον	ἐλείπομεν	*we*	
you	ἔλειπες	ἐλείπετε	*you*	*(You* [pl.] is like the Southern
he, she, it	ἔλειπε(ν)	ἔλειπον	*they*	*y'all.)*

INFINITIVE   *to leave, to be leaving*
λείπειν

PARTICIPLE   *leaving*
λείπων, λείπουσα, λεῖπον

The **stem** is that part of a verb that persists throughout a set of forms. The stem **λειπ** shows **meaning** (*leave*) and **aspect** (ongoing). (Technically, the continuous stem is λειπ-ε/ο -- that is, λειπ + a vowel that is sometimes ε and sometimes ο. This vowel is called a *thematic* or *variable* vowel.)

The accent on personal verbs is recessive: it goes back as far as it can. The accent on infinitives and participles is arbitrary and should be learned for each stem. (This makes sense since an infinitive is a noun and a participle an adjective.)

Using the continuous stem one may report about the present or the past. The **continuous past** is called the **imperfect** from Latin *im = not + perfectum = completed.*

The continuous verb may tell what is or was happening or it may tell about something that is or was repeated, continual, habitual. Only context can reveal which.

ζητῶ τὴν ἀλήθειαν.   *I am* (now) *seeking the truth.*   OR   *I* (habitually) *seek the truth.*
ἔπινον οἶνον.   *I was drinking wine.*   OR   *I used to drink wine.*

Translationese
Translate the **present** as *am / is / are Xing* or *X*.
Translate the **imperfect** as *was / were Xing* or *used to X*, never as *X'd*.
(Reserve *X'd* for the aorist.)

Inflection is a term for changes in the form of a word. **Declension** is the system of changes for nouns, pronouns, and adjectives. (The A-Group, O-Group, and Third Group are known as First Declension, Second Declension, and Third Declension.) **Conjugation** is the system of changes for verbs. You are beginning to learn the conjugation of regular Greek verbs.

▶ Exercise α: Translate the following:

1. λείπειν	3. λείπει	5. λεῖπον	7. ἔλειπον	9. λείπουσι (2 ways)
2. λείπουσα	4. λείπομεν	6. ἐλείπομεν	8. ἔλειπες	10. λείπεις

THE TIME-MARKER

A time-marker (also called an *augment*) is used in Greek to indicate past time.
The time-marker is usually ἐ coming before the stem, as seen in ἔλειπον above.

If the verb begins with a vowel, the vowel will become long to show past time. If the verb begins with an iota-diphthong, the first vowel is lengthened and the iota is subscripted.

ἀκούω, ἤκουον	
ἐθέλω, ἤθελον	Exception:
οἰκέω, ᾤκουν	ἔχω, εἶχον

The time-marker always comes immediately before the verb stem. This means there may be some changes if there is a preposition combined with the verb. Often the last short vowel of a preposition will drop off. Or the final sound of the preposition will change.

| ἀναγιγνώσκω | ἐκμανθάνω | ἀποτέμνω | συμβάλλω |
| ἀνεγίγνωσκον | ἐξεμάνθανον | ἀπέτεμνον | συνέβαλλον |

(Συμβάλλω is συν + βάλλω. An *n* sound naturally becomes an *m* sound before a *b* Try to pronounce "inport." It will most likely come out "import." The time-marker allows the original ν to be in evidence.)

The accent can never go further back than the time-marker.

| ἄπεστι | *He, she, it is away.* | | ἀπέχω | *I hold off.* |
| ἀπῆν | *He, she, it was away.* | | ἀπεῖχον | *I used to hold off.* |

▶ **Exercise β:** Form the imperfect for the following verb forms, keeping the same person and number:

Example: λείπει, ἔλειπε(ν)

1. γιγνώσκει
2. ἔχεις
3. κλέπτουσι(ν)
4. εὑρίσκω
5. ἀναλαμβάνετε
6. ἀποτέμνουσι(ν)
7. ἀκούομεν
8. συμβάλλεις

▶ **Exercise γ:** Suppose you were reading and came across the following forms. Try to figure out the "*I do*" form and look up the meaning in the dictionary at the back of the book. Can you find the words?

1. ηὗδες
2. ἐξέβαλον
3. ἀπέθνησκον
4. ἀπελαμβάνομεν
5. ἐνετύγχανον
6. ᾤκτιρετε
7. εἶχον
8. ἦρχε
9. εἰσῆγε
10. προσεῖχες

INFINITIVES AND PARTICIPLES

There is an infinitive and participle for every stem. There is **no time-marker** on any infinitive or participle since they have aspect but not tense and the time-marker shows past time. (For this reason it is more correct to speak of a *continuous* **infinitive** rather than a "*present infinitive*" and a *continuous participle* rather than a "*present participle*.")

PARSING

When you parse a sentence, for now simply say whether the verb is present, imperfect, or aorist, and give its "*I do*" form and the person. For example:

ἐμάνθανε - imperfect of μανθάνω, *he, she, it*
OR imperfect of μανθάνω, third person singular

(You will soon learn to give more information.)

Classwork or ἔργα: ~Write the following sentences in Greek. (Consult p. 43 on *-ing* words.)

1. I want to find wise messengers.
2. I am finding wise messengers.
3. Finding wise messengers is difficult.
4. Finding the beautiful horse, she was rejoicing.
5. I used to read many poems.
6. They were leaving (their) mother.

ἔργα ~Write the continuous forms for γράφω, βάλλω, and ἀναγιγνώσκω. Memorize.
~Read and translate the first part of "The Lazy Man," an Armenian story. Learn the vocabulary.
~Circle every imperfect. (There are twelve, counting ἦν twice.)

THE LAZY MAN* (Part 1)

ἦν ποτε καὶ οὐκ ἦν ἐν τῇ γῇ τῶν Ἀρμήνων (Armenians)
γυνή τις ἧς ὁ ἀνὴρ οὐκ ἤθελε πονεῖν. καὶ ἐν τῇ ὥρᾳ τοῦ   2
σπείρειν (sowing), οἱ μὲν ἄλλοι ἄνδρες ἔβαινον ἐν τοῖς
ἀγροῖς ὥστε γεωργεῖν, οὗτος δὲ μόνος ἔμενεν ἐν τῇ οἰκίᾳ.
ἡ δὲ γυνὴ ἐδάκρυε καὶ ἐκέλευεν αὐτὸν βαίνειν εἰς τοὺς
ἀγρούς καὶ πονεῖν ὥσπερ οἱ ἄλλοι. ὁ δὲ ἀνὴρ ἔλεγε
πάντα--ὅτι οὐκ ἔστιν ἰσχυρός, ὅτι νοσεῖ, ὅτι κλέπτης τις   7
ἔλαβε (took) τὰ ὄργανα (tools), ὅτι ἡ σχολὴ καλλίστη--
ὥστε μὴ ἐκβαίνειν εἰς τοὺς ἀγρούς.

ἀλλὰ ἡμέρᾳ τινὶ τὴν γυναῖκα δακρύουσαν καὶ λέγουσαν
ὡς οὐκ ἔσται αὐτοῖς οὔτε καρπὸς οὔτε χρυσὸς ᾤκτιρεν   11
ὁ ἀνήρ. καὶ σπέρματα λαβὼν (having taken) ἐν ταῖς
χερσίν, ἀπῆλθεν εἰς τοὺς ἀγρούς. ἀλλ' οὐκ ἐθέλων πονεῖν
καὶ τιθέναι τὰ σπέρματα εἰς τὴν γῆν ἀνεῖχεν ὁ ἀνὴρ τὰς
χεῖρας ὥστε τὸν ἄνεμον λαμβάνειν τὰ σπέρματα. καὶ ὧδε   15
ἐνόμιζεν· "τὸ πονεῖν λυπεῖ με. καὶ εἰ καρπὸς ἔσται διὰ τὰ
σπέρματα ἃ λαμβάνει ὁ ἄνεμος, μέγας πόνος ἔσται ἐμοὶ
τὸν καρπὸν ἀγείροντι (gathering) καὶ φέροντι εἰς τὴν
οἰκίαν." καὶ οὕτω τὸν πόνον ἐφοβεῖτο (= ἐφοβέ-ετο) ὥστε   19
ἔπεσε πρὸς γῆν ὥσπερ ἀποθνῄσκων.

ἦν ποτε καὶ οὐκ ἦν - "*Once there was and there was not*" (traditional
   beginning for Armenian stories, like our *Once upon a time*.)
2   πονέω - toil, work
    ἡ ὥρα - season   --> hour
7   νοσεῖ   He said "*I am sick* (present tense)." ✍✍ When reporting in English, but
     not in Greek, we must convert to a past tense: "*He said that he was sick.*"
    κάλλιστος,η,ον - most lovely, most beautiful, noblest
    ἔλαβον - *I took*, aorist of λαμβάνω - take (ἔλαβε - *he, she, it took*)
    ἐκβαίνω - go out, step out (ἐκ + βαίνω)
11   ὁ καρπός - fruit, harvest
    ὁ χρυσός - gold   --> chrysanthemum, chrysalis
    οἰκτίρω (also spelled οἰκτείρω) - have pity on + acc.
    τὸ σπέρμα - seed (from σπείρω = *sow*)   --> sperm
    ἀπῆλθον - *I went away*, aorist of ἀπέρχομαι
    ἀνέχω - hold up
15   ὁ ἄνεμος - wind   --> anemometer
    λυπέω - cause pain of mind or body, vex, distress
    ὁ πόνος - toil, work

19

> ### ⁻ΕΤΟ   ⁻ΟΝΤΟ
>
> You have learned ⁻εται, ⁻ονται, which are endings for the present:
>   βούλεται *he, she, it wants*   βούλονται *they want*
>
> Be alert for ⁻ετο ⁻οντο endings, which are used for the imperfect of verbs
> following the βούλομαι pattern:
>   ἐβούλετο *he, she, it was wanting*   ἐβούλοντο *they were wanting*

ἔπεσον - *I fell*, aorist of πίπτω

*This story is freely adapted from"The Lazy Man," in *Three Apples Fell from Heaven* by Virginia Tashjian, © 1982; used with permission of the author.

Lesson 26. The ε/o Aorist

	CONTINUOUS		**AORIST**	
Present	λείπω	λείπομεν	ἔλιπον	ἐλίπομεν
	λείπεις	λείπετε	ἔλιπες	ἐλίπετε
	λείπει	λείπουσι(ν)	ἔλιπε(ν)	ἔλιπον
Imperfect	ἔλειπον	ἐλείπομεν		
	ἔλειπες	ἐλείπετε		
	ἔλειπε(ν)	ἔλειπον		
Infinitive	λείπειν		λιπεῖν	
Participle	λείπων, ουσα, ον		λιπών, οὖσα, όν	

The use of an aorist stem indicates that an action is thought of as a single event: *I X'd,*
you X'd, etc. (accompanied by a finger snap to show it happened and is over). It is the **stem**
(λιπε/ο vs. λειπε/ο) that gives indication of the aspect. (To find the stem, drop off ‾ov from
the *I X'd* form.) Time-marker (ἐ) and personal endings are the same as for the Imperfect.

Translationese

When translating personal verbs, always translate the aorist as *X'd* (or, for the
negative, *did not X*). Translate the imperfect *was Xing* or *used to X*.
This way you signal immediately to others (and yourself) that you have recognized
the form. Your teacher will not need to ask "what stem?" or "what tense?"
This will save a great deal of time. And it is a habit which will keep you careful.

To translate an infinitive use *to X (once)* for the aorist infinitive versus *to X* or
to be Xing for the continuous infinitive. (In indirect discourse, where the infinitive
represents a "real" verb [with personal endings], you will translate differently.)

Use *having X'd* for the aorist participle and *Xing* to translate the continuous
participle whenever you can. This will almost always work. (Translation of a
participle in indirect discourse will be discussed later.)

▶ **Exercise α:**

How can you distinguish between the continuous and aorist forms of λείπω?
Translate the following, giving all possibilities.

1. ἔλιπεν, ἔλειπεν 2. λιπεῖν, λείπειν 3. ἐλείπετε, ἐλίπετε, λείπετε 4. λιποῦσα, λείπουσα 5. λείπουσι (2)

THE ε/o AORIST

When the stem undergoes an internal change, we have what is called an **ε/o Aorist** after the
endings (which are attached to the stem by an ε or o vowel) or a **Strong Aorist** (since the stem
change is strong). 🔊 Compare English *drive/drove, swim/swam* (strong changes) vs. *stay/stayed*. (weak
change).

Some but not all Greek verbs have ε/o or Strong Aorists. Of the verbs we have learned so far,
the following have ε/o Aorists, which should be learned:

Continuous	stem	Strong Aorist	stem	Continuous	stem	Strong Aorist	stem
μανθάνω	μανθαν-	ἔμαθον	μαθ-	εὑρίσκω	εὑρισκ-	ηὗρον	εὑρ-
λαμβάνω	λαμβαν-	ἔλαβον	λαβ-	θνήσκω	θνήσκ-	ἔθανον	θαν-
τυγχάνω	τυγχαν-	ἔτυχον	τυχ-	βάλλω	βαλλ-	ἔβαλον	βαλ-
κάμνω	καμν-	ἔκαμον	καμ-	λείπω	λειπ-	ἔλιπον	λιπ-
πίνω	πιν-	ἔπιον	πι-	πίπτω	πιπτ-	ἔπεσον	πεσ-

As you can see, the aorist stem is usually the more basic stem. The continuous stem is built on the aorist stem in various ways--by a nasal infix (ν), by σκ, by doubling, etc. Remember that the aorist stem is found by removing the -ον ending as well as the time-marker.

As with the imperfect, the time-marker of an aorist may cause changes in the preposition:
ἀποθνήσκω, ἀπέθανον.

Some important verbs have entirely new aorist stems. Learn them. (✍✍ Cf. English *go/went*.)

λέγω	---->	εἶπον	Stem:	(εἰπ)
ὁράω	---->	εἶδον		(ιδ)
φέρω	---->	ἤνεγκον		(ἐνεγκ)
ἐσθίω	---->	ἔφαγον		(φαγ)
ἔρχομαι	---->	ἦλθον		(ἐλθ)

The ε in the infinitive εἰπεῖν is not a time- marker. It is there because of an original digamma.
(stem = ϝειπ)

The aorist stem for *see* was originally ϝιδ.
The infinitive was ϝιδεῖν, related to our *video* and *vision*, via Latin. The aorist was ἔϝιδον --> εἶδον.

▶ **Exercise β:** Translate the following. Then give the imperfect form that has the same person and number.

1. ἔλαβες   2. ἔβαλον   3. ἐθάνετε   4 ἔπιες   5 ηὗρον   6 εἶπε   7. ἠνέγκομεν

▶ **Exercise γ:** Give the aorist infinitives of the verb forms in exercise β above.

THE PARTICIPLE

The participle on the strong aorist stem has the **same endings** as the continuous participle.
Stem and accent differ. (The Strong Aorist participle is accented like ὤν, οὖσα, ὄν.)

λείπων,ουσα,ον *leaving*

M	F	N
λείπων	λείπουσα	λεῖπον
λείποντα	λείπουσαν	λεῖπον
λείποντος	λειπούσης	λείποντος
λείποντι	λειπούσῃ	λείποντι
λείποντες	λείπουσαι	λείποντα
λείποντας	λειπούσας	λείποντα
λειπόντων	λειπουσῶν	λειπόντων
λείπουσι(ν)	λειπούσαις	λείπουσι(ν)

λιπών,οῦσα,όν *having left*

M	F	N
λιπών	λιποῦσα	λιπόν
λιπόντα	λιποῦσαν	λιπόν
λιπόντος	λιπούσης	λιπόντος
λιπόντι	λιπούσῃ	λιπόντι
λιπόντες	λιποῦσαι	λιπόντα
λιπόντας	λιπούσας	λιπόντα
λιπόντων	λιπουσῶν	λιπόντων
λιποῦσι(ν)	λιπούσαις	λιποῦσι(ν)

▶ **Exercise δ:** Form the aorist participle that corresponds (in case, number, gender) to the following:

1. κάμνουσα   3. πίπτοντα   5. φέρουσι   7. λέγον
2. εὑρίσκων   4. λαμβάνοντας   6. θνήσκοντι   8. πινούσης

Classwork: ✦✦ Read **Graveyard #8, 10, 14**, and **Famous Sayings #2**, Thesauros pp. 227, 228, 232.

ἔργα   ~Write the aorist forms of ἔβαλον three times. Memorize.
~Write the participle βαλών,οῦσα,όν once.
~Read and translate the conclusion of "The Lazy Man." Learn the vocabulary.

καὶ οἱ φίλοι νομίζοντες αὐτὸν εἶναι τεθνεῶτα ἤνεγκον
αὐτὸν εἰς τὸ ἱερόν (church). καὶ ἔμελλον θάπτειν αὐτὸν τῇ
ὑστεραίᾳ ἡμέρᾳ. ἀλλὰ ἡ γυνὴ οὐκ ἐνόμιζεν αὐτὸν
τεθνεῶτα εἶναι. καὶ ἐν ταύτῃ τῇ νυκτὶ εἰσῆλθεν εἰς τὸ
ἱερὸν (church) καὶ τόνδε τὸν λόγον εἶπε μεγάλῃ φωνῇ·   5
"ὦ βροτοί, ἀκούετέ μου; ἄγγελός εἰμι τοῦ Θεοῦ. παύω
τὸν τοῦ θανάτου ὕπνον. κρύπτω οὐδέν. ὅδε ἐστὶν   7
ὁ λόγος τοῦ Θεοῦ τοῦ κυρίου τῆς τε γῆς καὶ τῶν
οὐρανῶν, ὃν λέγω πᾶσι τοῖς τεθνεῶσιν· νῦν ἐν τοῖς
οὐρανοῖς ἐστε (you are). καὶ χρὴ πάντας ἐν τοῖς οὐρανοῖς
ὥσπερ ἐπὶ τῆς γῆς πονεῖν. ἐν τῷ πρώτῳ ἔτει κελεύει   11
ὑμᾶς ὁ Θεός καθαίρειν τὰς νεφέλας (clouds) τῶν οὐρανῶν
ὥστε τὸ πᾶν γίγνεσθαι καθαρόν."

ταῦτα ἀκούων οὐκ ἔχαιρεν ὁ ἀνήρ, οὐκ ἔχαιρεν οὐδαμῶς.
ἀλλὰ ἀνέστη (he stood up) καὶ κατῆλθεν εἰς τὴν οἰκίαν.
ἡ δὲ γυνὴ θᾶττον κατελθοῦσα--ἐπορεύσατο (she had   16
traveled) γὰρ ὁδῷ μικροτέρᾳ--ἦν ἤδη ἐν τῇ οἰκίᾳ. τὸν δὲ
ἄνδρα ὁρῶσα εἰσβαίνοντα, "ὦ φίλε," ἔφη, "ἐνομίζομέν σε
εἶναι τεθνεῶτα." "ναί," ἀπεκρίνατο (replied) ὁ ἀνήρ·
"τοῦτο ἐνόμιζον καὶ ἐγώ. ἀλλ' ὅτε ἔμαθον ὅτι χρὴ οὐ
μόνον τοὺς ζῶντας ἀλλὰ καὶ τοὺς τεθνεῶτας πονεῖν,   21
ἔδοξέ μοι (it seemed) κρεῖττον κατελθεῖν καὶ πονεῖν ἐπὶ   22
γῆς."

ἤνεγκον - aorist of φέρω
θάπτω - bury
ἦλθον - aorist of ἔρχομαι
5   εἶπον - aorist of λέγω
βροτός, ὁ - mortal   --> ambrosia ("*not mortal*" and therefore food for gods)ὁ
ὕπνος - sleep   --> hypnosis
7   κρύπτω - hide   --> crypt, cryptic
11   τὸ ἔτος - year   (originally ϝέτος) -> Etesian (winds) --> (via Latin) veteran
κ αθαίρω - cleanse, purify
καθαρός, ά, όν - clean, pure   --> Catharine, cathartic
16   θάττων, θᾶττον - faster (comparative of ταχύς)
εἰσβαίνω - enter (εἰς + βαίνω)
21   ζάω - live, be alive   (related to ζωός, etc.)
     *ζάω has forms with η, like πεινάω·

ζῶ	πεινῶ
ζῇς	πεινῇς
ζῇ	πεινῇ
inf. ζῆν	inf πεινῆν

22   κρείττων, κρεῖττον - better, comparative of ἀγαθός
       ἀμείνων is "better" in quality, moral worth
       κρείττων is "better" in the sense of being more powerful, or higher ranking,
              or a stronger argument, or a more compelling course of action
              (related to τὸ κράτος = *power*, as in *democracy*)

THE BRIDE OF DEATH

Every culture responds to the human need to keep alive its cherished dead in memory. In Lesson 26, you read the epitaph of a young woman named Phrasikleia. The monument set up to preserve her memory stood for a brief period, was lost for centuries, and, now rediscovered, renews her life in our memory. Phrasikleia's epitaph was discovered in 1729 in a church near Marathon in Attica. Much later, in 1972, her statue itself was unearthed less than two hundred yards away. It had been purposely buried along with a male statue, perhaps to protect it in a time of political upheaval or invasion.

During the archaic period, from 600 - 480 B.C.E., life-size marble statues of young males (called *kouroi*) or young females (called *korai*) were widely made. They were either grave markers, like the statue of Phrasikleia, or dedications to a divinity.

Modern viewers tend to think of Greek statues as bare, white marble; but Greek statues and temple decorations were originally painted. So Phrasikleia's statue was painted and adorned with metal earrings. She holds a bud, the symbol of a life about to unfold, in her right hand and on her head wears an ornate crown also decorated with buds. An elaborate necklace adorns her neck and on her arm is a bracelet. With her left hand, she demurely displays her garment: the traces of paint left on the statue indicate its intricate decorations. This is the costume and jewelry of a bride.

Figure 1. The statue of Phrasikleia and an unknown youth (perhaps her brother) as they were found by the excavator in 1972. The female statue was identified as Phrasikleia because the base of the statue fit exactly into the hollow of an inscription base. (Photo: Nikos Kontos).

Thus, both her statue and epitaph emphasize the same meaning: because Phrasikleia died young, she will be an eternal virgin, a bride of death, instead of knowing the fuller life of a married woman and mother.

During the archaic period, not only were statues erected as grave markers, but so were tall marble shafts called *stelai*, which were decorated with relief sculpture. Since grave markers in Greece and Rome were commonly erected on the sides of roads, their families could know that these visible funeral monuments would ensure a wide memory for their dead ones.

In the classical period, after work on the Parthenon was completed, sculptors looking for work turned their skill to the carving of tombstones, *stelai*, and other memorial sculpture. We are fortunate to have a number of these beautifully carved tombstones that were excavated from graveyards in Athens, especially the Kerameikos. This cemetery, situated within view of the Acropolis, was renowned for the lavishness of its monuments as well as for being the site in which Pericles' Funeral Oration was delivered.

One tombstone from the Kerameikos cemetery depicts Ampharete holding her grandchild (Figure 2). Her epitaph states: "Here I hold my daughter's child, my darling, whom once I held on my knee when we both lived and saw the sunlight; now I am dead, and hold her dead, too." Ampharete's downturned gaze meets the gaze of her grandchild, whose small hand reaches upward towards her grandmother. Tombstones, such as this one, give us a poignant glimpse into the family life of the Greeks and, in particular, the lives of women.

Figure 2. The tombstone of Ampharete. Kerameikos Museum ca. 400 B.C.E. German Archeological Institute Athens, Negative Ker. 2619.

Lesson 27. The α-Aorist (σα or λα); The Ingressive Aorist

THE α-AORIST

While many basic verbs have an ε/ο aorist, the majority have an **α-aorist**. This means there is an **α** sound in the aorist endings (except for the "*he, she, it*" ending). Traditionally this aorist has been called the Weak Aorist or First Aorist. In this book it is called the **α-aorist**, signifying that the vowel that precedes the personal ending is **α** instead of ε or ο.

THE σα-AORIST

Most α-aorists are σα-aorists. That is, the α sound is preceded by a sigma: παύω, ἔπαυσα. The **stem** of these σα-aorists is usually made from the **continuous stem** + σ. There may be combinations. For examples: πέμπω --> aorist ἔπεμψα, γράφω --> aorist ἔγραψα, πλήττω --> aorist ἔπληξα *strike*

ἔπαυσα = *I stopped*

ἔπαυσα	ἐπαύσαμεν
ἔπαυσας	ἐπαύσατε
ἔπαυσε(ν)	ἔπαυσαν

Infinitive

παῦσαι

Participle

παύσας, ασα, αν

παύσας, ασα, αν = *having stopped*

M	F	N
παύσας	παύσασα	παῦσαν
παύσαντα	παύσασαν	παῦσαν
παύσαντος	παυσάσης	παύσαντος
παύσαντι	παυσάσῃ	παύσαντι
παύσαντες	παύσασαι	παύσαντα
παύσαντας	παυσάσας	παύσαντα
παυσάντων	παυσασῶν	παυσάντων
παύσασι(ν)	παυσάσαις	παύσασι(ν)

The aorist and imperfect share many personal endings: (-ς - *you* [sing.], -μεν - *we*, ⁻τε - *you* [pl.], ⁻ν - *they*). We can think of **α** as the "theme vowel" (known formally as the thematic vowel) that connects the personal endings to the stem. (Before now we have seen ε/ο as a variable theme vowel, p. 109.)

The time-marker works the same way for the α-aorist as for the ε/ο aorist. The accent of the α-aorist infinitive is always on the next-to-last syllable. The accent on nominative participle is always on the next-to-last syllable: τὸ παιδίον κελεῦσαν *the little child having urged*

▶ Exercise α: Translate the following forms of πέμπω = *send* (which has the same pattern as παύω):

1. πέμψας	3. πέμψαι	5. ἔπεμψαν	7. ἔπεμψα	9. πεμψασῶν
2. ἔπεμψας	4. πέμψασαι	6. πέμψαν	8. ἔπεμψε	10. πεμψάντων

Almost all -**έω** and -**άω** verbs have an *I X'd* aorist form ending in -**ησα**. Some non-contract verbs also follow that pattern. These are some verbs we have learned that have a σα-aorist:

ἀκούω	ἤκουσα	πέμπω	ἔπεμψα	νοσέω	ἐνόσησα	ἐρωτάω	ἠρώτησα
δακρύω	ἐδάκρυσα	νομίζω	ἐνόμισα	οἰκέω	ᾤκησα	πεινάω	ἐπείνησα
κελεύω	ἐκέλευσα	αἰτέω	ᾔτησα	ποιέω	ἐποίησα	Note ἐθέλω	ἠθέλησα
γράφω	ἔγραψα	ζητέω	ἐζήτησα	φιλέω	ἐφίλησα	μέλλω	ἐμέλλησα
κλέπτω	ἔκλεψα	κοινωνέω	ἐκοινώνησα	φορέω	ἐφόρησα	δοκέω	ἔδοξα

▶ Exercise β: Translate each form and give the aorist infinitive.

1. ἠρωτήσαμεν 2. ᾤκησεν 3. ἔδοξα 4. ἠθέλησαν 5. ἠκούσατε 6. ᾔτησαν

You are finally able to understand completely our short but not-so-simple poem:

◆

χαλεπὸν τὸ μὴ **φιλῆσαι**·
χαλεπὸν δὲ καὶ **φιλῆσαι**·
χαλεπώτερον δὲ πάντων
ἀποτυγχάνειν φιλοῦντα

(1) Articular infinitive with μή, φιλῆσαι = aorist infinitive of φιλέω
(2) Intensive καί with articular infinitive φιλῆσαι
(3) Comparative with genitive of comparison
(4) Accusative-infinitive construction [X to do Y] with the infinitive understood as being articular, φιλοῦντα = participle of an -έω verb

THE λα-AORIST

ἤγγειλα = *I announced*   **ἀγγείλας,ασα,αν** = *having announced*

ἤγγειλα	ἠγγείλαμεν
ἤγγειλας	ἠγγείλατε
ἤγγειλε(ν)	ἤγγειλαν
inf. ἀγγεῖλαι	
part. ἀγγείλας,ασα,αν	

ἀγγείλας	ἀγγείλασα	ἀγγείλαν
ἀγγείλαντος	ἀγγειλάσης	ἀγγείλαντος
κτλ.	κτλ.	κτλ.

Aorist whose stems end in λ, μ, ν, ρ have what we call, for simplicity, a liquid or **λα-aorist**. This includes nasals (μ, ν) as well as liquids (λ, ρ) --sounds which can be held indefinitely. (Try holding these sounds.) The endings are the same as for a σα-aorist except that there is **no σ sound**. The σ has dropped out, usually (but not always) causing a vowel change in the stem.

ἀγγέλλω	ἤγγειλα	*announce*
μένω	ἔμεινα	*wait, stay, remain*
οἰκτίρω	ᾤκτιρα	*pity, have pity on*
κτείνω	ἔκτεινα	*slay, kill*
γαμέω	ἔγημα	*marry*

▶ **Exercise γ:** Translate the following.

1. ἀγγεῖλαι   2. ἀγγείλαν   3. ἤγγειλαν   4. γήμας   5. ἔκτειναν   6. ᾤκτιρας   7. οἰκτίρας

▶ **Exercise δ:** Translate the following, reasoning back and using the dictionary.

1. ᾤμωξεν   2. πλήξας   3. ἀπέκτειναν   4. ἔβλεψαν   5. θάψασιν   6. ἀνεβοήσατε   7. ἀπηγγείλατε

INGRESSIVE AORIST

Some Greek verbs express states ("I am sick," "I am silent"). For these verbs, the aorist may indicate simply that the state was entered. This is called an **ingressive** aorist from the Latin word for "enter."

ἐδάκρυσα   *I burst into tears.*   **ἐσίγησα**   *I fell silent.*
ἐνόσησα   *I got sick.*

Most ingressive aorists are of the **α-type**. But note: ἔχω, εἶχον, **ἔσχον** *I have, I had,* **I got**

▶ **Exercise ε:** Translate.

1. ἐνόσεις / ἐνόσησας τῇ πρώτῃ ἡμέρᾳ.   2. ἔσχομεν / εἴχομεν ἵππον νέον.

Classwork: ✦✦ Read: **Graveyard #5, 15-17, and 23, Thesauros pp. 227, 228, and 229** .

Classwork or ἔργα:
Translate:

1. I wish to be stopping the battle.
2. I wish to stop (once) the battle.
3. Did he marry her?
4. Having married her, he fell ill.
5. Having heard the story, she burst into tears.
6. While stopping the battle, they announced victory.
7. Having stopped the battle announced victory.
8. The ones having stopped the battle announced victory.

ἔργα
~Write aorist forms of ἔγραψα three times. Memorize.
~Read and translate "The Blind Men and the Elephant." Learn the vocabulary.
~Parse all verbs in the last paragraph. (ἀπεκρίνατο is a challenge. Do your best.)

Parsing

When parsing be as specific as you can. Give **tense** (*present, imperfect, aorist*) for a personal verb that is indicative or fact-reporting. Give **stem** (*continuous, aorist*) for all else. Examples:
ἐμάθομεν - *aorist of* μανθάνω, *we* (pl.)   ἐμάνθανες - *imperfect of* μανθάνω, *you* (sing.)
μαθεῖν - *aorist infinitive of* μανθάνω.   μανθάνῃ - *continuous subjunctive of* μανθάνω, *he, she, it*

THE BLIND MEN AND THE ELEPHANT

βασιλεὺς ἦν ποτε ὃς οὔποτε ἐγέλασεν. ἐβούλετο γελᾶν
ὥσπερ οἱ ἄλλοι ἄνθρωποι, ἀλλ' οὐδὲν αὐτῷ ἔδοξε γελοῖον.

ἡμέρᾳ τινὶ τέτταρες τυφλοὶ ἐκαθίζοντο (were sitting) παρὰ   3
τείχει τῆς οἰκίας τῆς βασιλικῆς. καὶ ἀνήρ τις ἦλθεν
ἐλέφαντα ἄγων ὃν ἔμελλε διδόναι τῷ βασιλεῖ. οἱ δὲ
τυφλοὶ ἥψαντο ταῖς χερσὶ τοῦ ἐλέφαντος, ὁ μὲν πρῶτος   6~
τῆς ῥινός (trunk), ὁ δὲ δεύτερος σκέλους, ὁ δὲ τρίτος
πλευρᾶς (side), ὁ δὲ τέταρτος τῆς οὐρᾶς (tail). καὶ   8
ἤρξαντο διαλέγεσθαι ἀλλήλοις περὶ τοῦ ἐλέφαντος.   9~

"ὦ φίλοι," εἶπεν ὁ πρῶτος· "δῆλόν ἐστιν ὅτι ὁ ἐλέφας ἐστὶ
μακρόν τι καὶ εὔκυκλον (round)." ὁ δὲ δεύτερος εἶπεν·
"πῶς δῆλον; οὐ δῆλον οὐδαμῶς. ἁπτόμενος γὰρ τοῦ
σώματος τοῦ ἐλέφαντος οἶδα ὅτι βραχὺς (short) καὶ παχύς
(thick) ἐστιν." ὁ δὲ τρίτος ἐβόησεν· "ὦ μῶροι, οὐδέτερος   14
ὑμῶν τὸ ἀληθὲς λέγει. ὁ γὰρ ἐλέφας ἐστὶ μέγα τι καὶ
εὐρύ (broad) ὥσπερ τεῖχος." ὁ δὲ τέταρτος εἶπε πᾶσι τάδε·
"ὦ ἄνδρες μωρότατοι, ἁψάμενος (punt!) τοῦ ἐλέφαντος, εὖ
οἶδα ὅτι τὸ λεπτότατον (λεπτός = delicate) πάντων ἐστίν."   18

οἱ δὲ τέτταρες ὡς μάλιστα ὠργίζοντο ἀλλήλοις. τέλος δὲ
ὁ βασιλεὺς τὸν θόρυβον (racket) ἀκούσας ἦλθεν ἐκ τῆς
οἰκίας. καὶ τοὺς τυφλοὺς ὁρῶν καθιζομένους παρὰ ταῖς
θύραις καὶ βοῶντας ἐγέλασεν. οἱ δὲ ἠρώτησαν αὐτόν·   22~
"ὦ βασιλεῦ, διὰ τί ἐγέλασας;" ὁ δὲ βασιλεὺς ὧδε
ἀπεκρίνατο· "τυφλοὶ ὄντες μάτην (in vain) ἀμφισβητεῖτε.   24~
οὐ γὰρ γιγνώσκετε ὅτι ἕκαστος ὑμῶν μέρους τῆς
ἀληθείας ἅπτεται καὶ οὐδεὶς ἔχει τὸ ὅλον."

γελάω, aorist ἐγέλασα - laugh   (Note: the aorist ends in -ασα rather than -ησα.)
δοκέω, aorist ἔδοξα - seem   --> paradox, orthodox, dogma
γελοῖος,α,ον - funny   (related to γελάω)
3   τυφλός,ή,όν - blind
τὸ τεῖχος - wall
βασιλικός, ή, όν - royal, kingly   (related to βασιλεύς)   --> basilica
ὁ ἐλέφας, gen. ἐλέφαντος <--> elephant
ἄγω, aorist ἤγαγον - lead
6~   ἅπτομαι + gen. - take hold of   What must ἥψαντο be? Punt!
τὸ σκέλος - leg   --> skeleton
τρίτος,η,ον <--> third   --> tritium
8   τέταρτος,η,ον - fourth   --> tetralogy, tetracycline   --> (via Latin) quarter
7-8   You need not learn ῥίς = *trunk* (gen. ῥινός) or οὐρά = *tail* . But what animal has a nose-horn? (horn =
κέρας). What animal, whose name has a strange spelling, has a tail (οὐρά) like a shadow (σκία) ?
9~   ἄρχομαι - begin to + infinitive, make a beginning of + gen. Punt ἤρξαντο.
διαλέγομαι - converse with + dat.   --> dialogue
τὸ σῶμα - body   --> somatic, psychosomatic
14   βοάω, aorist ἐβόησα - shout
οὐδέτερος,α,ον - neither of two (negative of ἕτερος)
22~   ἐγέλασεν in line 1 was a normal aorist. Here it may be ingressive. How to translate?
24~   Punt ἀπεκρίνατο. Put together information on pp.111 (box) and 118.
ὅλος, η,ον <--> whole   --> Catholic, holistic, holograph
ἀμφισβητέω - dispute, argue

Lesson 28. The Genitive Absolute; Special Aorists

GENITIVE ABSOLUTE

Usually a participle "hangs" on some noun that is part of the main sentence. For example:

κατελθὼν ὁ παῖς ἔχαιρεν   *Having returned, the child was rejoicing.*

But it is possible to use an **entirely new subject for the participle.**

τῆς μητρὸς κατελθούσης, ὁ παῖς ἔχαιρεν.   *His mother having returned, the child was rejoicing.*

In this situation **subject and participle** are given in the **genitive** case. The whole thought expressed by these genitives (and any words that go with them) is thus set free grammatically from the rest of the sentence and is called a **Genitive Absolute** (from the Latin *absolutus-- released, loosened, freed*). Genitive absolutes can be very long. It is important to isolate them when translating. Bracket them, at least mentally.

[τῆς παιδὸς τῆς νεωτάτης καὶ καλλίστης κατελθούσης εἰς τὴν πόλιν]
ἡ μήτηρ ἔχαιρεν. *Her youngest and most beautiful child having returned to the city, the mother was rejoicing.*

Translationese of Genitive Absolute

Having X'd normally works for an aorist participle in a genitive absolute. The English will be stilted but perfectly understandable (as in the examples above). **X**ing rarely works well for a continuous participle (except for special phrases such as "*All things being equal*").

You may have to interpret a continuous participle: *when, while, if, although, because*, etc. ("*Because his mother was returning, the child was rejoicing.*") Otherwise use "with" for all participles. This is awkward but preserves the ambiguity of the Greek: "*With his mother returning*," "*With his mother having returned.*"

▶ **Exercise α:** Translate these genitive absolute phrases, remembering always to translate the noun first.
1. ἐλθόντων τῶν παίδων   3. τῶν παίδων οὐκ ὄντων φίλων   5. τῆς γυναικὸς οὐ κελευσάσης ταῦτα
2. τῶν παίδων ἐσθιουσῶν   4. τῶν παίδων μὴ ὄντων φίλων   6. τοῦ σοφοῦ κελεύσαντος αὐτὴν μένειν

SPECIAL AORISTS

ἔβην *I went*	**ἔστην** *I stood*	**ἔγνων** *I knew*
Aorist of βαίνω	Aorist of ἵσταμαι	Aorist of γιγνώσκω

ἔβην	ἔβημεν	ἔστην	ἔστημεν	ἔγνων	ἔγνωμεν
ἔβης	ἔβητε	ἔστης	ἔστητε	ἔγνως	ἔγνωτε
ἔβη	ἔβησαν	ἔστη	ἔστησαν	ἔγνω	ἔγνωσαν
βῆναι		στῆναι		γνῶναι	
βάς, βᾶσα, βάν		στάς, στᾶσα, στάν		γνούς, γνοῦσα, γνόν	
gen. βάντος, βάσης, βάντος		gen. στάντος, στάσης, στάντος		gen. γνόντος, γνούσης, γνόντος	

What is special about the aorists above is that there is no theme vowel at all, neither ε/ο nor α. (They are called *athematic* aorists.) Their stems end in a vowel (βη/βα; στη/στα; γνω/γνο).

NOTE: ἔβη, ἔστη, and ἔγνω have no personal ending. Just as ἔλιπε = ἔ + λιπ (stem) + ε (theme vowel) + zero, so ἔβη = ἔ + βη (stem) + zero. The participle was originally stem + -ντς, ντσα, -ντ (vs. -οντς, οντσα, οντ or -αντς, αντσα, αντ in participles with theme vowels).

▶ **Exercise β:** Translate: 1. ἔστη   3. στάσαις   5. βάντες   7. ἔγνων   9. γνῶναι
                                         2. ἔστησαν   4. βῆναι   6. ἔβημεν   8. ἔγνω   10. γνούς

Classwork: ✦✦ Read **Famous Sayings #3-4, Diogenes #20, Graveyard #19, 24.**
                    Thesauros, pp. 232, 235, and 229.

ἔργα   ~Read and translate "Climbing the Stairs" and "Collecting the Fine." Learn the vocabulary.
               ~Parse the verbs in the third paragraph of "Climbing the Stairs." (When parsing identify
                  genitive absolutes: e.g., "*continuous participle acting as verb in a genitive absolute.*")

ἡ οἰκία τοῦ Νασρεδδίνου ἐστὶ τριώροφος (three-storied).
καὶ ἡμέρᾳ τινὶ ὁ Νασρέδδινος ἐκάθευδεν ἐν τῷ ἄνω μέρει   **2**
τῆς οἰκίας καταβλέπων πρὸς τὴν ὁδόν. καὶ ἄνδρα πένητα
εἶδεν αἰτοῦντα ἐν τῇ ὁδῷ. ὁ δὲ ἀνὴρ ἀναβλέψας καὶ ἰδὼν
τὸν Σοφὸν ἐκάλεσεν· "ὦ φίλε, κατάβηθι. βούλομαι γὰρ   5
λέγειν τί σοι."

ὁ δὲ Νασρέδδινος κατέβη εἰς τὸ κάτω μέρος τῆς οἰκίας.
καὶ καταβὰς ἠρώτησεν τὸν πένητα· "τί βούλῃ λέγειν μοι;"
ὁ δὲ εἶπεν αὐτῷ αἰτῶν "δός μοι ἀργύριον." ὁ δὲ Σοφὸς
οὐκ εἶπεν οὐδέν, ἀλλ' ἐσήμηνε τῷ αἰτοῦντι (= αἰτέοντι)   10
ἀναβῆναι. καὶ ἀμφοτέρων ἀναβάντων εἰς τὸ ἄνω μέρος
τῆς οἰκίας, ἀπεκρίνατο ὁ Νασρέδδινος τῷ αἰτοῦντι· "οὐχί."

ὁ δὲ πένης εἶπεν "ὦ φίλε, εἴπερ μηδὲν εἶχες διδόναι μοι,   13
διὰ τί ἐχρῆν με ἀναβῆναι;" ἀπεκρίνατο ὁ Σοφός· "ἀλλ εἰ
μηδὲν ἐν νῷ εἶχες ἄλλο ἢ αἰτεῖν με ἀργύριον διδόναι, διὰ
τί ἐχρῆν ἐμὲ καταβῆναι;"

καθεύδω, καθευδήσω, (no aorist) - sleep, lie down to sleep
  (imperfect. καθηῦδον, καθεῦδον, or ἐκάθευδον)

2
> ### ἐκάθευδε
> The time-marker normally must come directly before the verb stem. But some prefixed verbs are "felt" as a root verb and treated that way, with the time-marker coming at the beginning before the prefix. For example: ἐκαθίζετο.
>
> Sometimes both prefix and stem will be marked: ἠμφεσβήτουν *they were arguing*

ἄνω - upward. The adverb is here used as an adjective--the upper story
βλέπω , aorist ἔβλεψα - look
καταβλέπω - look down   (κατά has the basic meaning of *down*)
αἰτέω - ask, request; beg
ἀναβλέπω - look up   (ἀνά has the basic meaning of *up*)
5   καταβαίνω - go down
βῆθι - *go!* Command for Special Aorist ἔβη.
  (Cf. ✦ γνῶθι σεαυτόν *Know thyself*, the famous maxim with γνῶθι,
            command for Special Aorist ἔγνων)
10   σημαίνω, aor. ἐσήμηνε - show by a sign, signify; give a sign to do something,
            bid one to do something --> semantics, semiotics
ἀναβαίνω - go up
εἴπερ - if in fact (εἰ + περ)
13   μηδείς, μηδεμία, μηδέν - no one, nothing.

13
> ### οὐ / μή Forms
> Notice that all forms made from οὐ + some other root (οὔποτε, οὐκέτι, etc.) have corresponding μή forms (μήποτε, μηκέτι, etc.). Whenever context would demand μή as the negative (in a command, in "if" clauses, etc.), the μή forms are used.

ἐχρῆν - imperfect of χρή
ὁ νοῦς - mind, sense (a contract O-Group noun, originally νόος) --> noetic, paranoia
ἔχειν ἐν νῷ - have in mind

ἡμέρᾳ τινὶ τὸν Νασρέδδινον προβαίνοντα ἐν τῇ ὁδῷ τὰ
ὦτα ἀνήρ τις κατόπισθεν (from behind) ἔπληξεν. ὁ δὲ
Σοφὸς ἐστράφη (turned) ὥστε ὁ ἀνὴρ ἐδύνατο ὁρᾶν τὸ
πρόσωπον (face) αὐτοῦ. ὁ δὲ ἀνήρ, ὁρῶν τὸν Σοφόν, ἔφη   4
τάδε· "παραιτοῦμαι (I beg pardon). βλέπων κατόπισθεν
(from behind) ἐνόμισά σε ἄλλον ἄνδρα εἶναι ὅνπερ μισῶ."

ὁ δὲ Νασρέδδινος ὀργιζόμενος ἐκέλευσε τὸν ἄνδρα ἐλθεῖν
μεθ' ἑαυτοῦ (= μετὰ ἑαυτοῦ) πρὸς τὸν δικαστήν. ὁ δὲ
ἑκατέρου τὸν μῦθον διελθόντος εἶπεν ὡς ὁ ἀνὴρ ἠδίκησεν   9
καὶ ἐκέλευσεν αὐτὸν διδόναι τῷ Σοφῷ ἓν ἀργύριον ὡς
ζημίαν (a fine). ὁ δὲ ἀνὴρ ἔφη τάδε· "ἀλλ' ἀργύρια οὐ
φορῶ. δός μοι λαβεῖν ἓν τῶν ἀργυρίων ὧν ἐν τῇ οἰκίᾳ   12
ἔχω καὶ λαβόντι κατελθεῖν εἰς τὸ δικαστήριον (courthouse).
δοκῶ σοὶ εἶναι ἄνθρωπος ἀγαθός, ὥσπερ σὺ ἐμοί; ἔστι
πείθειν σε;" "πείθεις με" εἶπεν ὁ δικαστής· " ἴθι. ἀλλὰ
κελεύω σε κατελθεῖν ὡς τάχιστα."   16

ὁ μὲν ἀνὴρ ἐξῆλθεν, ὁ δὲ Νασρέδδινος καὶ ὁ δικαστὴς
ἔμενον. καὶ ἔμενον πολὺν χρόνον, ἀλλ' οὐ κατῆλθεν
ὁ ἀνήρ. τέλος δὲ ὁ Νασρέδδινος ἀνέστη καὶ ἀναστὰς
τὸν δικαστὴν ἔπληξε τὰ ὦτα. καὶ ἐξῆλθεν ἐκ τοῦ
δικαστηρίου (courthouse) εἰπὼν τῷ δικαστῇ· "τοῦ ἀνδρὸς
κατελθόντος, λαβὲ τὸ ἀργύριον σύ."   22

προβαίνω - step forth
τὸ οὖς, gen. ὠτός - ear
πλήττω, ἔπληξα - strike, strike a blow   --> paraplegic, apoplexy
ἔπληξεν αὐτὸν τὰ ὦτα   (See p. 32: acc. of part affected [common in Homer])

4   ἔφη - he, she, it said (aorist of φημί = *say*)   --> euphemism, aphasia,
                blasphemy, prophet --> fame, fate, ineffable, infant (via Latin)
ὅσπερ, ἥπερ, ὅπερ - the very one who
μετά + gen. - with, in company with

9   διέρχομαι - go through
ἀδικέω - be unjust, commit an injustice
τὸ ἀργύριον - small coin, piece of money; money (in general)

12   δός μοι - permit me. (δίδωμι with an infinitive has the sense of *permit*)

12

Attraction of Relative

Sometimes a relative is "attracted" to the case of its antecedent. Most often this
is an accusative, which is "attracted" to the genitive or dative case. So here:
ἓν τῶν ἀργυρίων **ὧν** ἔχω (We would expect ἅ ἔχω.)

πείθω - persuade, prevail upon
16   τάχιστος,η,ον - superlative of ταχύς
ἐξέρχομαι - come or go out (ἐξ + ἔρχομαι)
22   λαβέ (Note odd accent on last syllable. Five aorist commands are accented
                this way: εἰπέ, ἐλθέ, εὑρέ, ἰδέ, and λαβέ.)

Lesson 29: The Future

CONTINUOUS	FUTURE	AORIST
λείπω λείπομεν λείπεις λείπετε λείπει λείπουσι(ν) ἔλειπον ἐλείπομεν ἔλειπες ἐλείπετε ἔλειπε(ν) ἔλειπον	λείψω λείψομεν λείψεις λείψετε λείψει λείψουσι(ν)	ἔλιπον ἐλίπομεν ἔλιπες ἐλίπετε ἔλιπε(ν) ἔλιπον
Inf. λείπειν *to X, to be Xing*	Inf. λείψειν *to be about to X*	Inf. λιπεῖν *to X (once)*
Part. λείπων, ουσα, ον *Xing*	Part. λείψων, ουσα, ον *being about to X*	Part. λιπών, οῦσα, όν *having X'd*

Future endings are the same as present endings. Only the stems differ. This holds true for every verb whose "*I do*" form ends in -ω, whether it has an ε/ο or α-aorist. Translate personal verbs on the future stem with *will* or *shall*.

Normally the σ sound marks a future stem. **σ + ε/ο** shows **future**, σα the α-aorist:

λείπω, **λείψω**, ἔλιπον   *I leave, will leave, left*
παύω, **παύσω**, ἔπαυσα   *I stop, will stop, stopped (someone or something)*

▶ **Exercise α:**   1. λείψεις   2. λείψειν   3. λείψοντες   4. λείψουσιν   5. λιπόν
Translate: 6. παύσειν   7. παύσομεν   8. παύσων   9. παῦσαι   10. παύσασιν

σ-COMBINATIONS	The *s* sound may **combine** with the consonant of the stem according to the usual pattern. (We have already seen this in the σα-aorist.)

| π,β,φ + σ --> ψ
γράφω, **γράψω**, ἔγραψα
κλέπτω, **κλέψω**, ἔκλεψα | κ,γ,χ + σ --> ξ
ἄγω, **ἄξω**, ἤγαγον
*πλήττω, **πλήξω**, ἔπληξα | τ,δ,θ **drop before** σ
πείθω, **πείσω**, ἔπεισα |

* ττ often represents an original palatal, combining with σ to --> ξ:

-ήσω future on έω / άω **verbs**	ποιέω, **ποιήσω**, ἐποίησα φιλέω, **φιλήσω**, ἐφίλησα πεινάω, **πεινήσω**, ἐπείνησα	But: δοκέω **δόξω**, ἔδοξα

OTHER VARIATIONS	Entirely new stem λέγω, **ἐρῶ**, εἶπον φέρω, **οἴσω**, ἤνεγκον	-έω future* βάλλω, **βαλῶ**, ἔβαλον μένω, **μενῶ**, ἔμεινα	βούλομαι pattern ἀκούω, **ἀκούσομαι**, ἤκουσα

*especially after λ, μ, ν, ρ

COMBINATION of the above variations (Which?)	ὁράω, **ὄψομαι**, εἶδον	θνήσκω, **θανοῦμαι**, ἔθανον λαμβάνω, **λήψομαι**, ἔλαβον

▶ **Exercise β:** Translate:
1. he will throw   2. you (s) will make   3. they will love   4. she will leave   5. I will hear   6. it will carry

PRINCIPAL PARTS

The Greek verb has many forms, generated by a small number of stems. So far you know how to use three stems: the **continuous, future,** and **aorist.** The "*I*" forms of these seminal stems are called *principal parts*. (What we have been calling the "*I do*" form of the verb is its first principal part.)

Eventually you will learn the first three principal parts of all verbs: *I X, I will X, I X'd*. For now the first three principal parts of new verbs will be given in the vocabulary if needed. Here is a sampling of principal parts. (A full list is given on p.249-250.)

ε/ο AORISTS	σα- AORISTS	NON-THEME AORISTS
ἄγω, ἄξω, ἤγαγον	ἀκούω, ἀκούσομαι, ἤκουσα	βαίνω, βήσομαι, ἔβην
βάλλω, βαλῶ, ἔβαλον	γράφω, γράψω, ἔγραψα	γιγνώσκω, γνώσομαι, ἔγνων
εὑρίσκω, εὑρήσω, ηὗρον (or εὗρον)	δοκέω, δόξω, ἔδοξα	ἵσταμαι, στήσομαι, ἔστην stand,
θνήσκω, θανοῦμαι, ἔθανον	ἐθέλω, ἐθελήσω, ἠθέλησα	intransitive, part of the system
λαμβάνω, λήψομαι, ἔλαβον	κλέπτω, κλέψω, ἔκλεψα	of ἵστημι I stand, cause to stand
λέγω, ἐρῶ, εἶπον	νομίζω, νομιῶ, ἐνόμισα	
λείπω, λείψω, ἔλιπον	οἰμώζω, οἰμώξομαι, ᾤμωξα	
μανθάνω, μαθήσομαι, ἔμαθον	πείθω, πείσω, ἔπεισα	
ὁράω, ὄψομαι, εἶδον		
πίνω, πίομαι, ἔπιον	LIQUID α- AORISTS	
πίπτω, πεσοῦμαι, ἔπεσον	ἀγγέλλω, ἀγγελῶ, ἤγγειλα	
τυγχάνω, τεύξομαι, ἔτυχον	γαμέω, γαμῶ, ἔγημα	
φέρω, οἴσω, ἤνεγκον	ἐγείρω, ἐγερῶ, ἤγειρα	
(or ἤνεγκα)	μένω, μενῶ, ἔμεινα	

▶ **Exercise γ:** Translate, using the information above. (Use pp. 249-250 or the dictionary for #12-14.)

1. γράψειν   3. μενεῖ   5. πλήξω   7. πεινήσομεν   9. κλέψοντι   11. ὄψεται   13. ἔψονται
2. ἄξοντας   4. δόξομεν   6. οἴσεις   8. ἀκούσονται   10. θανεῖται   12. πείσετε   14. πράξουσαι

THE FUTURE INFINITIVE

The **future infinitive** is sometimes used **with certain verbs** which anticipate future time. There is no distinctive translation.

ὑπισχνέομαι - *promise*	ὑπισχνοῦμαι **γράψειν**	*I promise to write.*
ἐλπίζω - *hope*	ἐλπίζω **πέμψειν** δῶρα	*I am hoping to send gifts.*
μέλλω - *be about to, intend to*	ἔμελλον **λείψειν**	*I was about to leave.* (Consider the Southern idiom: "I was **fixing** to leave.")

THE FUTURE PARTICIPLE

The **future participle** is also used to show **purpose**. The perfect translationese, if you can bear the quaintness, is *a-Xing* as in "*Froggie went a-courting*." (Or try *about to X*.)

   ἔρχομαι **κλέψων** δῶρα.   *I come a'stealing gifts / I come about to steal gifts.*

▶ **Exercise δ:** Translate:
1. They intend to steal. 2. She comes to stop the battle. 3. I promise to write a letter. 4. He is about to steal.

Classwork: ✦✦ Read: **New Testament #8-9,** Thesauros p. 223.

ἔργα   ~Write out the future forms for λείπω three times. Memorize.
          ~Read and translate "The Helping Hand." Learn the vocabulary.
          ~Parse all verb forms in bold print. (Use the form chart above.)

ἄνθρωπός τις **ἔπεσέν** ποτε εἰς ποταμὸν ὃς οὔποτε **ἔμαθε** 1
νεῖν (to swim). καὶ ὁ ἄνθρωπος **ἐκάλεσεν**· "ἆρα οὐδεὶς
ὠφελήσει με; κακῶς πράττω. οὐκ ἔμαθον νεῖν (to swim). 3
ἀποθανοῦμαι ἐν τούτῳ τῷ ποταμῷ." καὶ πρὸς τὸν
ποταμὸν **ἔβαινον** πολλοὶ βουλόμενοι αὐτὸν **σῶσαι**. "δός
μοι τὴν χεῖρα" ἔλεγον. ἀλλ' ὁ ἄνθρωπος οὐδὲν ἐποίησεν.

τέλος δ' ὁ Νασρέδδινος ἔτυχε παρερχόμενος ζητήσων τὴν 7
κύνα. καὶ αὖθις ὁ ἄνθρωπος ἀνεβόησεν· "ὦ φίλε, μέλλεις
με **λείψειν** ἐν τούτῳ τῷ ποταμῷ;" ὁ δὲ Σοφός εἶπε τάδε· 9
"δός μοι τὴν χεῖρα καὶ ὑπισχνοῦμαι **σώσειν** σε." ἀλλὰ
ὁ ἄνθρωπος οὐκ ἐποίησεν οὐδέν. ὁ δὲ Νασρέδδινος
ἠρώτησεν· "τί ἐστι τὸ ἔργον σου;" ὁ δ' ἄνθρωπος
ἀπεκρίνατο ὅτι τελώνης (tax collector) ἐστίν.

καὶ μετὰ χρόνον εἶδον πάντες τὸν Σοφὸν ἄγοντα τὸν
ἄνθρωπον ἐκ τῶν ὑδάτων τοῦ ποταμοῦ. "πῶς **ἔτυχες**;" 15~
ἠρώτησέ τις. "ῥᾳδίως" ἀπεκρίνατο ὁ Σοφός. "τούτου τοῦ
ἀνθρώπου **εἰπόντος** ὅτι τελώνης ἐστίν, οὐκ ἐκέλευσα
αὐτῷ <u>διδόναι</u> μοι τὴν χεῖρα ἀλλὰ <u>λαβεῖν</u> τὴν χεῖρά μου.
γιγνώσκω γάρ τοι τοὺς τελώνας, ὡς οὐδὲν οὐδενὶ 19
δώσουσιν."

---

1 | **Aorist as Prior Past**

Translate ἔμαθε = **had learned**. Greek has only one past tense, the aorist, for a "once done" action.

εἶπεν ὅτι τὰ μῆλα ἔκλεψα - He said that I stole / I had stolen the apples.

🕮 In English we can distinguish between a past act ("*She called*") and a past act prior to another ("*She had called before he came*"). Greek uses the aorist for both.

ἆρα - indicates a question (perhaps with a tone of impatience or anxiety)
3 ὠφελέω - benefit, be of service to + acc.
πράττω, πράξω, ἔπραξα - do, fare, act   --> practice, practical
σῴζω, σώσω, ἔσωσα - save
7,15 τυγχάνω, τεύξομαι, ἔτυχον - happen to be + participle; meet up with + dative;
                                happen, succeed (when used alone)
παρέρχομαι - go by
ἀναβοάω - shout out (literally "shout up")
μέλλω, μελλήσω, ἐμέλλησα - intend, be about to + infinitive (usually future)
9 λείπω, λείψω, ἔλιπον - leave   --> eclipse, ellipse
ὑπισχνέομαι - promise + future infinitive
15~ ἔτυχες - see τυγχάνω above. Which meaning? (See 7 above.)
19 τοι - "you know," an enclitic particle used more often in poetry than prose to add a kind of
emphatic confidentiality, possibly = dative σοι. "*Mark you*" or "*let me tell you*"
overtranslate it.

---

19 | **Anticipated Object**

Sometimes what is going to be the subject in an indirect statement or question will be given as the object of the verb that introduces that clause. This is called *anticipation* (or *prolepsis*).

γιγνώσκω σε ὡς νοσεῖς - I know that you are sick.
                    Literally, I know you, that you are sick.

(Greek grammar is often more relaxed than English.)

δώσω - future of δίδωμι

Lesson 30. -έω Verbs

CONTINUOUS	FUTURE	AORIST
Present		
φιλῶ　φιλοῦμεν	φιλήσω　φιλήσομεν	ἐφίλησα　ἐφιλήσαμεν
φιλεῖς　φιλεῖτε	φιλήσεις　φιλήσετε	ἐφίλησας　ἐφιλήσατε
φιλεῖ　φιλοῦσι(ν)	φιλήσει　φιλήσουσι(ν)	ἐφίλησε(ν)　ἐφίλησαν
Imperfect		
ἐφίλουν　ἐφιλοῦμεν		
ἐφίλεις　ἐφιλεῖτε		
ἐφίλει　ἐφίλουν		
Infinitive	**Infinitive**	**Infinitive**
φιλεῖν	φιλήσειν	φιλῆσαι
Participle	**Participle**	**Participle**
φιλῶν, οὖσα, οὖν	φιλήσων, ουσα, ον	φιλήσας, ασα, αν

Many verbs have an -έω ending for the "*I do*" form. These are called **-έω verbs** or epsilon-contract verbs or E-contract verbs. The -έω verbs **show contraction**--a slurring together of vowel sounds--**only on the continuous stem.** These are the rules that explain the changes:

ε + ε --> ει
ε + ο --> ου
ε + any **long vowel or diphthong** --> the long vowel or diphthong (i.e., ε is absorbed).

If **accented έ** is contracted, the resulting accent is a **circumflex.** ἐφιλέ-ομεν --> ἐφιλοῦμεν
Otherwise the original accent remains unchanged. ἐφίλε-ον --> ἐφίλουν

▶ **Exercise α:** Write out all the uncontracted forms, apply the rules above, and see if they generate the paradigm.
Example: ἐ - φίλ - ε - ον -〉 ἐφίλουν

The participle is as expected. **φιλῶν, οὖσα, οὖν** = *loving*

M	F	N
φιλῶν	φιλοῦσα	φιλοῦν
φιλοῦντα	φιλοῦσαν	φιλοῦν
φιλοῦντος	φιλούσης	φιλοῦντος
φιλοῦντι	φιλούσῃ	φιλοῦντι
φιλοῦντες	φιλοῦσαι	φιλοῦντα
φιλοῦντας	φιλούσας	φιλοῦντα
φιλούντων	φιλουσῶν	φιλούντων
φιλοῦσι(ν)	φιλούσαις	**φιλοῦσι(ν)**

⚘⚘ **Ambiguity Alert:** As with uncontracted verbs, there is no difference in form between the third person active and the dative masc./neut. pl. participle:

φιλοῦσι(ν) 　*they love* or *to / for loving ones.*

We have actually learned most of the ε-combinations by learning the pattern for τὸ γένος. The stem was originally γενεσ- but the σ dropped out.

$$ε + ι \rightarrow ει \qquad τῷ γένει \qquad \leftarrow γένε⁻ι$$
$$ε + ο \rightarrow ου \qquad τοῦ γένους \qquad \leftarrow γένε⁻ος$$
$$ε + ω \rightarrow ω \qquad τῶν γενῶν \qquad \leftarrow γενέ⁻ων$$

Most -έω verbs have a **future** ending in -ήσω, and an **aorist** ending in -ησα. You can see how few of our έω verbs have irregular forms (given in bold print).

ἀδικέω	ἀδικήσω	ἠδίκησα
αἰτέω	αἰτήσω	ἤτησα
γαμέω	**γαμῶ**	**ἔγημα**
γεωργέω	γεωργήσω	ἐγεώργησα
δοκέω	**δόξω**	**ἔδοξα**
ζητέω	ζητήσω	ἐζήτησα
καλέω	**καλῶ**	**ἐκάλεσα**
κοινωνέω	κοινωνήσω	ἐκοινώνησα

μισέω	μισήσω	ἐμίσησα
νοσέω	νοσήσω	ἐνόσησα
οἰκέω	οἰκήσω	ᾤκησα
ὁμολογέω	ὁμολογήσω	ὡμολόγησα
ποιέω	ποιήσω	ἐποίησα
πονέω	πονήσω	ἐπόνησα
φιλέω	φιλήσω	ἐφίλησα
φορέω	φορήσω	ἐφόρησα

Classwork: ✦✦ Read **Diogenes #6**, Thesauros p. 234.

Classwork or ἔργα: "Earth's Treasure" (paraphrased) by Aesop.* Put the sentences in order and translate.

(1) ἔπειτα δὲ ἀπέθανεν ὁ πατήρ.

(2) "ἐν τοῖς ἀγροῖς μου ἐστι θησαυρός."

(3) "παῖδές μου," εἶπεν ὁ πατήρ· "οἱ ἄλλοι νομίζουσί με πένητα εἶναι. ἀλλὰ τῷ ὄντι (p. 98) πλούσιός εἰμι."

(4) ὁ λόγος δείκνυσιν ὅτι ὁ πόνος θησαυρός ἐστι τοῖς ἀνθρώποις.

(5) θησαυρὸν μὲν οὐχ ηὖρον, καρπὸν δὲ πολὺν ἡ γῆ αὐτοῖς ἀντέδωκεν (gave back).

(6) γέρων (old man) ἦν ποτε οὗ οἱ παῖδες οὐκ ἤθελον πονεῖν οὐδὲ γεωργεῖν.

(7) μετὰ δὲ τὸν τοῦ πατρὸς θάνατον, οἱ παῖδες ἄροτρον (plow) καὶ δικέλλας (shovels) λαβόντες τὴν γῆν διώρυξαν βουλόμενοι τὸν θησαυρὸν εὑρεῖν. (διορύττω - dig through)

(8) μέλλων δὲ ἀποθανεῖσθαι, μετεπέμψατο τοὺς παῖδας, ἐλπίζων αὐτοὺς ποιήσειν πλουσίους τῷ γεωργεῖν. (μεταπέμπομαι - *send for*) (ἐλπίζω - *hope*)

(9) "ὑμῖν τὸν θησαυρὸν εὑροῦσιν ἔσται χρυσὸς πολύς."

Classwork or ἔργα: What is the story so tersely told below? State or draw the sequence of events.
(You can see how much information the participles and relative pronouns convey.)
ὁ βρόχος - noose   αὐτάρ - but   λίπεν = ἔλιπεν   ἅπτω - fasten

✦
> Χρυσὸν ἀνὴρ εὑρὼν ἔλιπε βρόχον· αὐτὰρ ὁ χρυσὸν
> ὃν λίπεν οὐχ εὑρὼν   ἧψεν ὃν ηὖρε βρόχον.

Statyllius Flaccus

ἔργα   ~Write the continuous forms for ζητέω and οἰκέω. Memorize.
~Write the participle for ζητέω.
~Read and translate "You're Right!" Learn the vocabulary.

*The idea of scrambling and the choice of story was borrowed from *Ancient Greek* by Carl Ruck, used with permission.

YOU'RE RIGHT!

ἦν ποτε ὁ Νασρέδδινος δικαστής. ἐν δὲ νυκτί τινι τοῦ
Νασρεδδίνου καθεύδοντος ἐν τῷ ἄνω (upper) μέρει τῆς οἰκίας
ἦλθον δύο ἄνδρες οἳ ἐμίσουν ἀλλήλους καὶ οἳ ἠμφεσβήτουν
περὶ κλοπῆς ἱματίου. καὶ ἀμφότεροι τὸν Σοφὸν ἐκάλουν·   4
"κατάβηθι. κατάβηθι. ζητοῦμεν τὴν ἀλήθειαν. ζητοῦμεν τὴν
δίκην."

ὁ δὲ Νασρέδδινος καταβὰς ἠρώτησεν αὐτούς · "ὦ ἄνδρες, τί
ἔτυχεν. διὰ τί ἐκαλεῖτέ με; τί ζητεῖτε," καὶ οἱ δύο ᾔτουν τὸν
Σοφὸν λέγειν πότερος ὁ δίκαιος καὶ πότερος ὁ ἀδικῶν. καὶ   9
ἑκάτερος εἶπεν ὡς ὁ ἕτερος τὸ ἱμάτιον ἔκλεψεν. ὁ μὲν πρῶτος
τάδε εἶπεν τῷ ἑτέρῳ· "σίγα (= σιγά-ε), κλέπτης. ἀπώλεσα τὸ   11
ἱμάτιόν μου. εὖ οἶδα ὅτι κλέψας ἔβαλες αὐτὸ ἐν τῷ ἀγρῷ."
ὁ δὲ ἕτερος εἶπε τάδε· "οὐ σιγήσω. σὺ γὰρ ὁ κλέπτης. διὰ σοῦ
ἀπώλεσα τὸ ἐμὸν ἱμάτιον." ὁ δὲ Σοφὸς ᾔτησεν ἀμφοτέρους τοὺς 14
ἄνδρας λόγον τῆς κλοπῆς διδόναι.

καὶ τοῦ μὲν πρώτου τὸν λόγον ἀκούσας εἶπεν αὐτῷ "ὦ φίλε,
ἀληθῆ λέγεις." ἐβούλετο γὰρ παῦσαι τὴν μάχην. ἔπειτα δὲ τοῦ
ἑτέρου τὸν λόγον ἀκούσας εἶπε τὸ αὐτὸ καὶ αὐτῷ· "ὦ φίλε,   18
ἀληθῆ λέγεις."

ἡ δὲ γυνὴ τοῦ Σοφοῦ, ταῦτα ἀκούσασα, εἶπε τῷ ἀνδρί· "ὦ φίλε
ἄνερ, οἱ μὲν ἄλλοι καλοῦσί σε σοφόν, ἐμοὶ δὲ δοκεῖς μῶρος.
οὐχ ὁμολογῶ οὐδὲ ὁμολογήσω οὔποτε. πῶς γὰρ ἔστι δύο
ἄνδρας τὰ ἐναντία λέγοντας ἀμφοτέρους ἀληθῆ λέγειν;   23
οὐκ ἔστιν οὐδαμῶς." ὁ δὲ ἐννοούμενος εἶπε τῇ γυναικὶ τάδε·
"ὦ φίλη, ἀληθῆ λέγεις."

4   ἡ κλοπή - theft (κλέπτω)
     ἡ ἀλήθεια - truth
     ἡ δίκη - justice
9   δίκαιος,α,ον - just
11   ὄλλυμι, -ωλῶ, -ώλεσα - destroy, ruin, lose (used in poetry)
     ἀπόλλυμι - destroy utterly, lose (common in prose)

11

Compound versus Uncompounded Verbs

When you look up principal parts, you will sometimes find a hyphen in front
of certain parts. For example: βαίνω, -βήσομαι, -έβην. This shows that
while the uncompounded form is found on the continuous stem, future and aorist
forms are always prefixed--e.g., ἀναβήσομαι, κατέβην.

Some verbs occur in poetry in uncompounded form but not in prose:

θνήσκω (in poetry), ἀποθνήσκω (in prose)
ὄλλυμι (in poetry), ἀπόλλυμι (in prose)

Some verbs are never used except with a prefix· ἀμφισβητέω.

✎✎ This situation occurs in English as well. We have the compound verbs *to remember*
and *to dismember*, but no simple verb *to member*.

---

23   ἐναντίος,α,ον - opposite (ἐν + ἀντί)
     ἐννοέομαι - reflect on, consider (have in one's νοῦς)

Lesson 31. -άω Verbs; Use of πρίν; The 99% Principle

τιμάω   *I honor*
CONTINUOUS

τιμῶν,ῶσα,ῶν

Present	
τιμῶ	τιμῶμεν
τιμᾷς	τιμᾶτε
τιμᾷ	τιμῶσι(ν)

	M	F	N
	τιμῶν	τιμῶσα	τιμῶν
	τιμῶντα	τιμῶσαν	τιμῶν
	τιμῶντος	τιμώσης	τιμῶντος
	τιμῶντι	τιμώσῃ	τιμῶντι
	τιμῶντες	τιμῶσαι	τιμῶντα
	τιμῶντας	τιμώσας	τιμῶντα
	τιμῶντων	τιμωσῶν	τιμῶντων
	τιμῶσι(ν)	τιμώσαις	**τιμῶσι(ν)**

Imperfect	
ἐτίμων	ἐτιμῶμεν
ἐτίμας	ἐτιμᾶτε
ἐτίμα	ἐτίμων

Infinitive
τιμᾶν

Participle
τιμῶν,ῶσα,ῶν

Many verbs have an -άω ending for the "*I do*" form. These are called **-άω verbs** or alpha-contract verbs or A-contract verbs. The άω verbs are less common than έω verbs. These are the patterns:

α + ε --> ᾱ	α + ο --> ω
α + ει --> ᾳ	α + ου --> ω
α + η --> ᾱ	α + ω --> ω

α combined with any ε sound is long α; a combined with any o sound is ω.
Another way to say this is that an initial α "conquers" any α, ε, or η that follows.

▶ **Exercise α:** Write out all the uncontracted forms, apply the rules above, and see if they generate the paradigm.
Example: ἐ - τίμ - α - ον --> ἐτίμων

▶ **Exercise β:** Translate:
1. τιμᾷ 2. ἐτίμα 3. τιμῶσι 4. τιμῶσαι 5. ἐτίμων 6. τιμῶν 7. ἐρωτᾶτε 8. ἠρώτα 9. ὁρῶμεν 10. ὥρα

They, too, have a **future** ending in **-ήσω**, and an **aorist** with ending in - **ησα**. The following are the -άω verbs we have learned, with irregular forms in bold print.

ἐρωτάω	ἐρωτήσω	ἠρώτησα
βοάω	**βοήσομαι**	ἐβόησα
γελάω	γελάσομαι	**ἐγέλασα**
ὁράω	**ὄψομαι**	**εἶδον**
σιγάω	σιγήσω	ἐσίγησα

πεινάω*	πεινήσω	ἐπείνησα
ζάω*	ζήσω	ἔζησα

*πεινάω and ζάω are irregular in having an **eta in their continuous forms** where an alpha is expected. (See p. 114.)

▶ **Exercise γ:** Translate:
1. ζήσετε 3. ὥρας 5. ἐβοῶμεν 7. ἠρωτήσατε 9. γελάσονται (punt)
2. ἐγέλων 4. ἐπείνα 6. ἠρώτων 8. ἐρωτήσετε 10. ὄψῃ (forms on p. 124)

USE OF πρίν (*before, until*)

| πρίν + **infinitive** | *before* | (may take accusative + infinitive construction) |
| πρίν + **personal verb** | *until* | (verb introducing πρίν is usually negative) |

ἔλαβες δῶρα πρὶν ἐλθεῖν.   *You received gifts before coming.*
ἔλαβες δῶρα πρὶν ἡμᾶς ἐλθεῖν.   *You received gifts before our coming.*
οὐκ ἔλαβες δῶρα πρὶν ἤλθομεν.   *You didn't receive gifts until we came.*

▶ **Exercise δ:** Translate:

1. I learned the story before leaving (once) the city.   3. I didn't learn the story until they left the city.
2. I learned the story before their leaving (once) the city.

THE 99% PRINCIPLE

Basically the stem of a participle tells **aspect**--ongoing (or repeated) vs. completed. In fact, what is ongoing is usually (let us say, 99%) contemporary with the time of the main verb, while what is complete is almost always past.

For this reason, the **usual** translation of a continuous participle is *Xing*, of an aorist participle **having X'd**.

ζητῶν τὸ δακτύλιον ἔπεσεν.   ***Seeking** the ring, he fell.*
       (The seeking and the falling happened together.)

ζητήσας τὸ δακτύλιον ἔπεσεν.   ***Having sought** the ring, he fell.*
       (The seeking happened prior to the falling.)

However, it is possible (a small percent of the time) that what is ongoing will **not** be **contemporaneous** with the main verb and therefore is **not** to be translated *Xing*.

For example, here is a line from a poem attributed to Plato, in which Lais, an older woman who has lost her looks, dedicates her mirror to Aphrodite. She describes herself this way:

✦   ἡ τῶν ἐραστῶν ἑσμὸν ἐπὶ προθύροις Λαῒς **ἔχουσα** νέων
       *Lais, the one **who used to have** a crowd of young lovers at her door*
       (Obviously she does not currently have a crowd of lovers.)

Likewise, it is possible that an aorist participle will be about what is momentary but **not prior** to the main verb and therefore is **not** to be translated **having X'd**:
ἀναβλέψας εἶπεν. ***With an upward glance**, he spoke.* (It is not that he looked up first and
                 then spoke. Rather as he spoke, he gave a completed upward glance.)

> This is relevant to Plato's description of Socrates' last hour. Socrates, who had been condemned to death for not having the proper regard for the gods asks whether he may pour out a drop of his poison as an offering to the gods before drinking the it. He asks the man who brought the hemlock ταυρηδὸν ὑποβλέψας --*with a bull-like up-from-under glance*. It is impossible to translate this gracefully. One pictures Socrates giving a fierce, upwards glance, as a bull might. It is not likely that he gave the glance and *then* spoke. Rather he must have spoken *with* a (completed) glance.

The 99% principle is a subtlety of Greek. Be aware of it.

Classwork: ✦✦ Read **Graveyard #21** and **Diogenes #3-4**, Thesauros pp. 229 and 234.

ἔργα   ~Write the continuous forms for ἐρωτάω (including full participle)
           ~Read the first part of "Never Enough," a Nigerian story.
           ~Parse the last sentences. (οὐδεὶς γὰρ to the end.).

NEVER ENOUGH (Part 1)*

ἡμέρᾳ τινὶ ηὗρεν ἡ χελώνη ἵππον ἐν τοῖς ἀγροῖς. καὶ
κατῆλθεν εἰς τὴν ἑαυτῆς πόλιν ἐποχευομένη (riding) ἐπ'
αὐτοῦ. ἰδόντες δὲ τοῦτο πάντες οἱ ἐν τῇ πόλει ἔλεγον
ἀλλήλοις· "ὡς μεγαλοπρεπὴς (magnificent) ἡ χελώνη." καὶ
πάντες ἐτίμων αὐτήν. καὶ πᾶν τὸ ἔτος οἱ μὲν πλούσιοι   5
αὐτῶν ἐκάλουν αὐτὴν ἐπὶ δεῖπνον, οἱ δέ πένητες ἔλεγον ὡς
εὐδαίμων ἐστίν. διὰ δὲ ταῦτα ὡς μάλιστα τὸν ἵππον ἐφίλει
ἡ χελώνη καὶ οὔποτε ἀνείχετο εἶναι ἄνευ αὐτοῦ.

καὶ ἡμέρᾳ τινὶ ἐπορεύσατο ἡ χελώνη εἰς ἄλλην πόλιν. ἐκεῖ   9~
δὲ ἐκάλεσεν αὐτὴν ἀνήρ τις πλούσιος ἐπὶ δεῖπνον. μετὰ δὲ
τὸ δεῖπνον ἠρώτησεν ὁ πλούσιος· "ὦ φίλη, ἐθέλεις καθεύδειν
τῆσδε τῆς νυκτὸς ἐν τῇ οἰκίᾳ μου; σοὶ μὲν ἔστι καθεύδειν
ἐν τῇ οἰκίᾳ, τῷ δὲ ἵππῳ ἐν τῇ ἀποθήκῃ (barn)." "οὐδαμῶς"
ἀπεκρίνατο ἡ χελώνη· "ὅπου γὰρ καθεύδω ἐγώ, ἐν τούτῳ   14
τῷ τόπῳ καὶ ὁ ἵππος μου καθεύδει." ὁ δὲ πλούσιος καίπερ
νομίζων τοῦτο ἄτοπον οὐκ εἶπεν οὐδέν. καὶ ὁ ἵππος καὶ ἡ
χελώνη καθηῦδον ἐν τῷ αὐτῷ.

καὶ ταύτῃ τῇ νυκτί, ὅτε ἡ χελώνη καθηῦδεν, πρὶν πεσεῖν εἰς   18
ὕπνον, ἤκουσε τοῦ ἵππου στόνον μέγαν. καὶ δραμοῦσα
(having run) πρὸς αὐτὸν βουλομένη μαθεῖν διὰ τί στένει τὸν
ἵππον ηὗρε τεθνεῶτα. νῦν δὲ ἡ χελώνη μέγα ἔστενε καὶ
μέγα ἐβόα καὶ ᾤμωζεν· "οἴμοι, τὸν ἵππον ἀπώλεσα. οἴμοι,
οἴμοι." καὶ οὕτως ἀνεβόα ὥστε ὁ θόρυβος (racket) ἤγειρε   23
πάντας τοὺς ἄλλους τοὺς ἐν τῇ οἰκίᾳ.

ὁ δὲ δεσπότης εἰσελθὼν ἠρώτησε "τί ἐστι; διὰ τί ἐγείρεις
ἡμᾶς τούτῳ τῷ θορύβῳ (racket)." "οἴμοι" ἀνεβόησεν ἡ
χελώνη· "τεθνεὼς ὁ ἵππος μου." ὁ δὲ δεσπότης "ἀλλὰ τοῦτο"
ἔφη "οὐκ ἄτοπον. γεραιὸς γὰρ ἦν ὁ ἵππος. τί μέλει σοι;"   28
ἡ δὲ χελώνη ἀπεκρίνατο "πᾶς με ἐτίμα διὰ τοῦτον τὸν
ἵππον. καὶ εὖ οἶδα ὅτι οὐκέτι ἔσται μοι τιμή. οὐδεὶς γὰρ
τιμᾷ χελώνην μὴ ἔχουσαν ἵππον οὐδὲ καλεῖ ἐπὶ δεῖπνον.
τοῦτο κάκιον πάντων. οἴμοι. τὸν ἵππον ἀπώλεσα."

---

5   τιμάω, τιμήσω, ἐτίμησα - honor   (from ἡ τιμή = honor)
     ἀνέχομαι - endure
9~   ἐπορεύσατο - from πορεύομαι   Punt.
     ἐκεῖ - (adv.) there
14   ὅπου - wherever
18   πρίν + infinitive - before
     πίπτειν εἰς ὕπνον - Note the continuity of idiom; we say *fall* asleep, *fall into* a deep sleep.
     ὁ στόνος - groan
     στένω (no future or aorist) - groan   <--> thunder --> stentorian --> (via Latin) detonate
     οἰμώζω, οἰμώξομαι, ᾤμωξα - wail aloud, lament (literally, "say οἴμοι")
23   ἐγείρω, ἐγερῶ, ἤγειρα - wake
     ὁ δεσπότης - master --> despot
     γεραιός, ά, όν - old   (of persons, often a term of respect)   --> geriatrics
     ἡ τιμή - honor   --> timocracy, Timothy
28   ἔφη - Notice how ἔφη may break up a quotation. Look for this in the Thesauros.
     κακίων, ον - worse (comparative of κακός)

*This story is freely adapted from "Ijapa Cries for His Horse" in *Olode the Hunter*, © 1968, by Harold Courlander
with Ezekiel A. Eshugbayi; used with permission of the author.

132

DIOGENES

Students who came to hear Aristotle lecture on politics in the 320s B.C.E. would have heard what became a famous remark. "A human being is a living being whose nature is to live in a *polis*." The being who can live *apart* from a *polis*, the independent, self-ruling city, he added, is either a god or a beast.

At about this same time, a young man whom many called a god is said to have made his way to visit a homeless man who called himself a beast. "I am Alexander," said the young man, "the Great King." "And I," answered the homeless man, "am Diogenes, the Dog."

Figure 1. Alexander and Diogenes by Mauro Gandolfi. Bologna Pinacoteca Nazionale.

It is unlikely that such an encounter ever happened. But Diogenes and Alexander are appropriately paired in legend, because they set in motion changes that were to make the *polis* a secondary political structure. Alexander, before he died of fever at the age of thirty-three, conquered the lands to the east of the Mediterranean all the way to India. In so doing, he prepared the way for the *polis* to become a mere part of larger confederations and empires. And Diogenes, unlike Socrates and Plato, did not refer to himself primarily as a citizen of a *polis*, but, in a phrase he invented, a *cosmopolites*, a citizen of the universe.

Diogenes' remarks are often like philosophical jokes, whose punch lines make us look at things in a new way. Watching the temple officials lead away a fellow who stole a bowl that belonged to the temple, Diogenes responded, "The big crooks are leading away the little one." So much for the temple officials!

In his challenge to the conventional viewpoint of the listeners, Diogenes' words and actions are like the words of Socrates or the stories you have been reading about Nasrudin. But there is a difference in tone. The words of Diogenes the Dog often have, as he himself said, a "bite." Because of Diogenes' name for himself, this biting philosophy came to be called "cynicism (*kunismos*) of the dog."

Not only is the "bite" of the dog important for cynics, but also the dog's freedom from the rules that dictate the social behavior of humans. Thus Diogenes, like a dog, could live in a cistern, engage in bodily functions in public, and be indifferent to his own discomfort.

There is a certain freedom in Diogenes' independence from material possessions, passions, and the desire for power and honor. Perhaps it was because he recognizes this freedom that the great Alexander is supposed to have said, "If I were not Alexander, I would wish to be Diogenes."

Lesson 32. Contrary-to-Fact Conditions

The Constant Lover
by Sir John Suckling

Out upon it, I have lov'd
Three whole days together;
And am like to love three more,
If it hold fair weather.

Time shall moult away his wings
Ere he shall discover
In the whole wide world agen
Such a constant lover.

But a pox upon't, no praise
There is due at all to me:
Love with me ***had made*** *no stay*
Had it any been *but she.*

Had it any been *but she*
And that very face
There ***had been*** *at least ere this*
A dozen dozen in her place.

We humans like to speculate. We have a way of talking about possibilities that never became realized:

*If it **were** raining*	(understood: *but it is not*)
*I **would** be wearing boots.*	(understood: *but I am not*)
*If you **had** invited him*	(understood: *but you did not*)
*he **would have** come.*	(understood: *but he did not*)

This *if-then* sequence is called a **contrary-to-fact** or **unreal condition**.

✍✍ In an earlier stage of English we could use the past tense in both *if* and *then* clauses, as Greek does. (See Suckling's poem above.) Now we use a **past tense** in the *if* clause and a *would* in the *then* clause.

GREEK CONTRARY-TO-FACT CONDITIONS

	If clause (called *protasis*)	*Then* clause (called *apodosis*)
Present: Past:	εἰ + **imperfect** εἰ + **aorist**	**imperfect** + ἄν **aorist** + ἄν

Present contrary-to-fact (verbs are imperfect):

εἰ ἤκουες, ἐμάνθανες ἄν.   *If you **were** listening* (now), *you **would be learning*** (now).

Past contrary-to-fact (verbs are aorist):

εἰ ἤκουσας, ἔμαθες ἄν.   *If you **had** listened* (then), *you **would have** learned* (then).

NEGATIVE

The negative of an *if* clause is **μή**, of a *then* clause **οὐ**.

εἰ **μὴ** ἤκουσας, **οὐκ** ἔμαθες ἄν.   *If you had **not** listened, you would **not** have learned.*

▶ **Exercise α:** Label the conditions first, then translate. (πίνω, aor. ἔπιον, πίπτω, aor. ἔπεσον)

1. If they were drinking, they would be falling.
2. If they were not drinking, they would not be falling.
3. If they had drunk, they would have fallen.
4. If they had not drunk, they would not have fallen.
5. If they were seeking, they would be finding.
6. If they had not sought, they would not have found.

MIXED CONDITIONS

As in English, there may be mixed conditions in Greek, for example with a past "if clause" and a present "then clause."

εἰ μὴ ἤκουσας, οὐκ ἂν ἐμάνθανες   *If you had not been listened (then) you would not be learning* (now).

OMITTED "IF" CLAUSE

The *if* clause will not always be given. Therefore it is **crucial to notice ἄν with the imperfect or aorist**, because it **completely changes the meaning.**

ἦλθον.   *I came.*
ἦλθον ἄν.   *I would have come* (but did not).

▶ **Exercise β:** Translate: 1. ἐγράψαμεν. 2. ἐγράψαμεν ἄν. 3. εἰ μὴ ἡ γυνὴ ἦλθεν, ἐγράψαμεν ἄν.
4. εἰ μὴ ἦν βιβλία αὐτοῖς, οὐκ ἂν ἠθέλησαν ἀναγιγνώσκειν.

THE 99% PRINCIPLE (AGAIN)

While the imperfect in a contrary-to-fact condition usually (let us say, 99% of the time) refers to what is or is not going on in current time, there may always be that small per cent of statements in which it refers to the past. (For the 99% principle with participles, see p. 130 above.)

εἰ ἤκουες   *if you were listening* (now) OR (rarely, say 1%) *if you had been listening* (then)
ἐμάνθανες ἄν   *you would be learning* (now) OR (rarely, say 1%) *you would have been learning* (then)

In fact the imperfect will often refer to the past for verbs whose meaning necessarily involves a state or ongoing process. For example, *having* (ἔχω) is always ongoing. And εἰμι has no aorist at all, so that the imperfect must be used for any state of being in the past.

Given all the ambiguities, the following Greek statement can be translated several ways.

εἰ ἦσθα σοφός, οὐκ ἂν εἶχες κακά.   (ἦσθα = *you* (s.) *were*, imperfect of εἰμι)

If you were (now) *wise, you would not* (now) *have troubles.*
If you had been (ongoing, in past) *wise, you would not* (now) *have troubles.*
If you had been (ongoing, in past) *wise, you would not have* (in the past) *had troubles.*

(In fact it is only sense, not grammar, that prevents the fourth possibility: *"If they were now wise, they would have had (in the past) troubles"*--impossible only because time does not run backwards!)

Classwork: ✦✦ Read **Heraclitus #18-19, Xenophanes #5,** and **Graveyard# 22,** Thesauros pp. 225, 226, and 229   (This passage shows Xenophanes as the father of cultural relativism.)

Classwork or ἔργα: Translate. (See p. 124 for principal parts.) Which pairs are the same?

1. If you (sing.) were not drinking, you would not be falling.
2. If you had not been drinking, you would not be falling.
3. If you had not drunk, you would not have fallen.
4. If you had not been drinking, you would not have fallen.
5. If she were (see above) wise, she would be rich.
6. If she had been wise, she would be rich.
7. If he had books, he would know the story.
    (Use a form of ἔχω and γιγνώσκω.)
8. If he had had books, he would know the story.
9. If he had had books, he would have known the story.

ἔργα   ~Read and translate the conclusion of "Never Enough." Learn the vocabulary.
~Parse the last sentence.

ὁ δὲ δεσπότης τοῦτο ἀκούσας εἶπεν "ξένος μου εἶ, καὶ
ἐθέλω ποιεῖν πάντα ὥστε τοὺς ξένους (guests) χαίρειν.
νῦν δίδωμί σοι ἵππον καινόν." καὶ ἐκέλευσέ τινα τῶν
δούλων ἄγειν πρὸς τὴν χελώνην ἵππον καινόν.   4

καὶ ὁ κύριος τῆς οἰκίας αὖθις ἔπεσεν εἰς ὕπνον, καὶ πάντες
οἱ ἄλλοι οἱ ἐν τῇ οἰκίᾳ--πλὴν τῆς χελώνης. καὶ μετὰ
χρόνον τὸ δεύτερον ἐβόα καὶ ᾤμωζεν ὥστε πάντας
ἐγεῖραι. καὶ ὁ δεσποτὴς αὖθις ἠρώτησε τί ἐστιν. ἡ δὲ
χελώνη ἀπεκρίνατο· "οἴμοι. ἀθυμῶ. μεγάλη ἡ λύπη μου.   9
εἰ γὰρ μὴ ὁ πρῶτος ἵππος ἀπέθανεν, εἶχον ἂν νῦν δύο."

ὁ δὲ κύριος "οἰμώζεις" ἔφη "διότι οὐκ ἔχεις δύο ἵππους.
ἀλλὰ πάντα ἐθέλω ποιεῖν ὥστε τοὺς ξένους μου χαίρειν."
καὶ ταῦτα εἰπὼν ἐκέλευσεν ὁ πλούσιος τῶν δούλων τινὰ
εἰσάγειν ἔτι ἄλλον ἵππον.   14

καὶ αὖθις ἔπεσον εἰς ὕπνον πάντες οἱ ἐν τῇ οἰκίᾳ πλὴν τῆς
χελώνης. οὐ γὰρ ἐδόκουν αὐτῇ οὐδὲ δύο ἵπποι ἱκανοὶ
εἶναι. καὶ μετὰ μικρὸν χρόνον τὸ τρίτον ἀνεβόα καὶ
ᾤμωζεν. τῷ δὲ δεσπότῃ ἐρωτήσαντι τί ἐστιν εἶπεν ἡ
χελώνη· "οἴμοι. ὡς μάλιστα ἀθυμῶ. μεγάλαι αἱ λῦπαί
μου. εἰ μὴ ὁ πρῶτος ἀπέθανεν, νῦν ἂν εἶχον τρεῖς καὶ   20
ἐνόμιζον ἂν εἶναι πάντων εὐδαιμονεστάτη." ὁ δὲ δεσπότης
"ἀλλὰ οὕτως" ἔφη "νόμιζε. δίδωμι γάρ σοι ἔτι ἄλλον ἵππον.
νῦν δὲ σίγα (= σίγα-ε) ὥστε πάντας καθεύδειν."

ἀλλὰ τῇ χελώνῃ οὐκ ἐδόκουν οὐδὲ τρεῖς ἵπποι ἱκανοὶ εἶναι. 24
καὶ τὸ τέταρτον ᾤμωζεν· "εἰ μὴ ὁ πρῶτος ἀπέθανε, νῦν ἂν
εἶχον τέτταρας." νῦν δὲ ὁ δεσπότης μάλα ὀργιζόμενος
ἐκέλευσε τὸν δοῦλον τοὺς ἵππους αἱρεῖν καὶ τὴν χελώνην   27
ἐκβαλεῖν ἐκ τῆς οἰκίας. ὁ δὲ δοῦλος τοῦτο ἐποίησεν· τοὺς
ἵππους εἷλε καὶ τὴν χελώνην ἐξέβαλεν ἐκ τῆς οἰκίας.

μετὰ δὲ ταῦτα ἡ χελώνη κατῆλθεν εἰς τὴν ἑαυτῆς πόλιν
ἄνευ ἵππου. καὶ πᾶσι τοῖς ἐρωτῶσι "ποῦ ὁ ἵππος σου;" ἀεὶ
τὸ αὐτὸ ἔλεγεν· "οἴμοι. εἰ μὴ τὸ τέταρτον ᾤμωξα,   32
νῦν ἂν εἶχον τρεῖς."

ὁ ξένος - guest / host. The Greeks had a single word for either person in this
relationship. Guest-friendship, the relationship of host and guest, was a sacred tie.
          --> xenophobia (from ξένος in the sense of foreigner)
4   ὁ δοῦλος - slave
     καινός, ή, όν - new
     μετὰ χρόνον - after a while, after a time
9   ἀθυμέω - be disheartened (from ἀ + θυμός - spirit, courage   --) thyme 〈--〉 fume
     ἡ λύπη - pain, grief
14   εἰσάγω - lead in (εἰς + ἄγω)
     ἔτι - yet, still (in degree as well as time)
24   ἱκανός, ή, όν - sufficient, enough
27   αἱρέω, αἱρήσω, **εἶλον** - take, seize   --> (by a devious route) heretic
     ἐκβάλλω - throw out

Lesson 33. Indirect Discourse in Greek and English; The Gnomic Aorist

INDIRECT DISCOURSE

In indirect discourse a statement (of what someone says, thinks, observes, etc.) is given indirectly--i.e., is introduced by a verb of saying (λέγω), thinking (νομίζω), or observing (ἀκούω). There are three ways of giving the situation as reported, in indirect discourse:

(1) ὅτι or ὡς   (2) Infinitive   (3) Participle

✍ Do we sometimes use *how* in English to mean little more than *that*? -for example, in such a statement as *"You know how they came into the house and told lies to everyone."*

The way of reporting depends on the verb of thinking, saying, observing, etc. A Greek child would learn (by being corrected) that while (s)he may use λέγω with ὅτι and ὡς or with an infinitive, νομίζω always takes an infinitive and ἀκούω takes a participle. And so on.

Original statement:	"λείπουσι τὴν πόλιν."	*"They are leaving the city."*
Indirect Discourse:	λέγω ὅτι λείπουσι τὴν πόλιν.	*I say that they are leaving the city.*
	νομίζω αὐτοὺς λείπειν τὴν πόλιν	*I think [that] they are leaving the city.*
	ἀκούω αὐτοὺς λείποντας τὴν πόλιν	*I hear [that] they are leaving the city.*

❭ **Exercise α:** Translate the following, using the grammatical constructions above:
1. She says I am crying (2 ways).   2. She thinks that I am crying.   3. She hears that I am crying.

PERSON IN INDIRECT DISCOURSE

There **may** be a change of person in indirect discourse. It happens in Greek exactly as it happens in English, and it makes perfect sense. The direct statement is from the point of view of whoever is speaking, thinking, or observing. But the indirect statement is from the point of view of whoever is *reporting*. We make these changes constantly and automatically.

       Person A: *"**He's** a fool."*
       Person B: *"So! You say that **he's** a fool?"*   Third person: no change.

       Person A: *"**You're** a fool."*
       Person B: *"So! You say that **I'm** a fool?"*   Second person: change.

TENSE IN GREEK INDIRECT DISCOURSE

Indirect discourse is utterly simple in Greek. When using a personal verb (one with personal endings) with ὅτι or ὡς, use the **same tense** in indirect discourse as was in the direct statement. When using an infinitive or participle, use the **same stem**.

As was said before, the future is really a tense inserted into a system that shows aspect. The most common use of the future participle and infinitive are to represent a future indicative verb in indirect discourse.

Direct statement:	"λείψουσι τὴν πόλιν."	*"They will leave the city."*
Indirect statement:	λέγω ὅτι **λείψουσι** τὴν πόλιν.	*I say [that] they will leave the city.*
	νομίζω αὐτοὺς **λείψειν** τὴν πόλιν.	*I think [that] they will leave the city.*
	ἀκούω αὐτοὺς **λείψοντας** τὴν πόλιν.	*I hear [that] they will leave the city.*

❭ **Exercise β :** Translate the following, using the grammatical constructions above:
1. They say that we will write.   2. They think that we will write.   3. They hear that we will write.

COMPLICATIONS: TENSE IN ENGLISH INDIRECT DISCOURSE

There are further complications in English indirect discourse. In Greek, the tense (or stem) of the direct statement is used in the indirect statement. In English a change must sometimes be made.

| Direct: | "γράφει" | Indirect: | λέγεις ὅτι **γράφει**. | *You say that she is writing.* |
| | "She is writing." | | εἶπες ὅτι **γράφει**. | *You said that she was writing.* |

Not only do we change an *is* to a *was* when reporting on what was said in the past, we normally change a future *will* to a conditional *would*.

| Direct: | "γράψει." | Indirect: | λέγεις ὅτι **γράψει**. | *You say that she will write.* |
| | "She will write." | | εἶπες ὅτι **γράψει**. | *You said that she would write.* |

✍✍ English is more precise and more demanding than Greek. Suppose you report on Wednesday what she said last Saturday. Does it matter whether she said she would write the coming Tuesday or the coming Thursday? You would usually report, "She said she **would write**." When would you report, "She said she **will write**"?

| Direct: | "γράψει." | Indirect: | λέγεις ὅτι **γράψει**. | *You say that she will write.* |
| | "She will write." | | εἶπες ὅτι **γράψει**. | *You said that she will / would write.* |

There is even more complication when the aorist as prior past is taken into account. (p. 125.)

Direct:	"ἔγραψεν."	Indirect:	λέγεις ὅτι **ἔγραψεν**.	*You say that she wrote / had written.*
	"She wrote yesterday."		ἐρεῖς ὅτι **ἔγραψεν**	*You will say that she wrote / had written.*
	"She had written		εἶπες ὅτι **ἔγραψεν**	*You said that she wrote / had written.*
	(*before I called*)."			

✍✍ All this shows how time-conscious we English speakers are, and also how much information we may give without even being aware of it. There are at least four times to keep track of: (a) the time the statement was made, (b) the time the statement referred to, (c) the time the statement was reported, and (d) real time = NOW. Remember: it is English, not Greek, which is complicated.

GNOMIC AORIST

An aorist may be used in wise sayings (γνῶμαι) to express a universal truth. This is called the **gnomic aorist**. Always translate a gnomic aorist as if it were present tense.

✦ παθὼν νήπιος **ἔμαθεν**. *A fool **learns** by suffering.* Literally, *A fool **learned** having suffered.*
(proverb in *The Agamemnon* by Aeschylus)

✍✍ Compare "*Faint heart never **won** fair lady*." We use a past tense, but we really mean "*never did win, never wins, and never will win*."

Classwork: ✦✦ Read **Heraclitus #20-22**, Thesauros p. 225.

Classwork or ἔργα: Circle the direct statement behind each of the following sentences. Then translate. There may be several choices for the translation. Give as many as you can.

1. λέγω ὅτι αἱ χελῶναι οὔποτε γράψουσιν ἐπιστολάς.
2. εἶπες ὅτι οἱ ἀδελφοὶ οὔποτε γράψουσιν ἐπιστολὰς τῷ στρατιώτῃ.
3. ἐρεῖ ὅτι οἱ γεωργοὶ ἔθαπτον τὸν θησαυρόν.
4. εἶπον ὅτι οἱ γεωργοὶ οὐκ ἐποίησαν ταῦτα.
5. ἐλέγομεν ὅτι αἱ τοῦ πλουσίου ἀδελφαὶ οὐ φιλοῦσι πίνειν ὕδωρ.
6. εἴπετε ὅτι ἐθελήσετε ὁρᾶν τὴν οἰκίαν τῆς νέας ἧς τὸν ἀδελφὸν εἴδετε ἐν τοῖς ἀγροῖς γεωργοῦντα.

ἔργα   ~Translate the following sentences into Greek:
1. We were saying that the three sisters would remain in the house.
2. She says that the king did not know her.
3. You (s) said that the soldier would bring strangers into the city.
4. They said that they had not stolen the money.

~Read over Heraclitus #1-22. Find three other gnomic aorists besides the one in today's reading. Heraclitus is a mysterious author. Can you find a common thread of meaning in the readings?

Lesson 34. More on Indirect Discourse

CONSTRUCTION IN INDIRECT DISCOURSE

ὅτι, ὡς εἶπον ὅτι, ὡς or Inf. λέγω ὅτι, ὡς or Part μανθάνω	Infinitive δοκέω *think* νομίζω ἡγέομαι *consider* φημί (including ἔφη) ὄμνυμι, ὑπισχνέομαι	Participle or Infinitive ὁράω εὑρίσκω	All Three ἀγγέλλω ἀκούω αἰσθάνομαι *perceive*

Verbs of *thinking* usually take an **infinitive**, verbs of *saying* often take an **infinitive**, and verbs of *perceiving* or *finding* seem to prefer the **participle**.

▶ **Exercise α:**   Translate the underlined words, being sure to give all possibilities:

1. Are you saying (φημί) that she <u>wants</u> to go?
2. They say (λέγω) that <u>you</u> (sing.) <u>write</u> often.
3. I learned that <u>he steals</u>.
4. I swear that <u>they are bringing</u> the gifts.
5. Did you find that <u>they drink</u> wine?
6. We see that <u>you</u> (pl.) <u>are sick</u>.
7. He announced that <u>she is leaving</u>.
8. He thinks that <u>you are staying</u>.
9. Do you perceive that the children <u>are</u> really <u>learning</u>?

NEGATIVE IN INDIRECT DISCOURSE

In indirect discorse an οὐ in the direct statement is represented by an οὐ in the indirect statement. (Except in indirect discourse οὐ is rarely found before an infinitive.)

Direct statement: "**οὐκ** ἐποίησε δεῖπνον."

λέγω ὅτι **οὐκ** ἐποίησε δεῖπνον.	*I say that he did not make dinner.*
νομίζω αὐτὸν **οὐ** ποιῆσαι δεῖπνον.	*I consider [that] he did not make dinner.*
ἀκούω αὐτὸν **οὐ** ποιήσαντα δεῖπνον.	*I hear [that] he did not make dinner.*

SAME SUBJECT OF INFINTIVE OR PARTICIPLE

If the person reporting is the same as subject of the verb in the direct statement, no new subject for the infinitive will be given. Any words agreeing with the subject will be nominative.

DIRECT		INDIRECT	
ἀποθνήσκουσιν. ἀποθνήσκω.	*They are dying.* *I am dying.*	νομίζω αὐτοὺς ἀποθνήσκειν. **νομίζω ἀποθνῄσκειν.**	*I think [that] they are dying.* *I think [that] I am dying.*
σοφοί εἰσιν. σοφή εἰμι.	*They are wise.* *I am wise.*	νομίζω αὐτοὺς σοφοὺς εἶναι. **νομίζω σοφή εἶναι.**	*I think [that] they are wise.* *I think [that] I am wise.*
νοσεῖ νοσῶ.	*He is sick.* *I am sick.*	ἀγγέλλω αὐτὸν νοσοῦντα. **ἀγγέλλω νοσῶν.**	*I announce [that] he is sick.* *I announce [that] I am sick.*
σοφαί εἰσιν. σοφή εἰμι.	*They are wise.* *I am wise.*	ἀγγέλλω αὐτὰς σοφὰς οὔσας. **ἀγγέλλω σοφή εἶναι.**	*I announce [that] they are wise.* *I announce [that] I am wise.*

▶ **Exercise β:**
Translate:

1. νομίζετε οὐ νοσήσειν.
2. ἐνομίζετε οὐ νοσήσειν.
3. ἀγγέλλομεν θνῄσκοντες.
4. ἀγγέλλομεν αὐτὸν θνῄσκοντα.
5. ἀγγέλλεις τὸν υἱὸν εὑροῦσα.
6. λέγει σε οὔποτε φιλήσειν πίνειν ὕδωρ.
7. λέγει οὔποτε φιλήσειν κλέπτειν.
8. ἀγγέλλεις με τὸν υἱὸν εὑροῦσαν.

POSSIBLE AMBIGUITY IN ὅτι / ὡς CONSTRUCTION

Notice that in the ὅτι / ὡς construction there is sometimes ambiguity, in Greek as in English. For the statement λέγουσιν ὅτι ἔγραψαν, ***They say that they wrote***, only context can show whether the ones who say and the ones who wrote are the same.

ὅτι and ὡς seem to be interchangeable. (Or could ὡς be a shade more tentative?)

NO AMBIGUITY OF PERSON WITH INFINITIVE OR PARTICIPLE

Ambiguity of person may occur with the ὅτι construction but not with the infinitive or participle:

ἀγγέλλουσι ὅτι λείψουσιν.   *They announce that they* (same *they?*) *will leave.*   (Ambiguous)

ἀγγέλλουσι λείψειν.   *They announce [that] they* (same *they*) *will leave.*   (Nonambiguous)
ἀγγέλλουσι αὐτοὺς λείψειν.   *They announce [that] they* (different *they*) *will leave.*

ἀγγέλλουσι λείψοντες.   *They announce [that] they* (same *they*) *will leave.*   (Nonambiguous)
ἀγγέλλουσι αὐτοὺς λείψοντας.   *They announce [that] they* (different *they*) *will leave* .

▶ **Exercise γ:** Translate, indicating clearly whether the person in each part of the sentence is the *same*, *different*, or *ambiguous*. (αἰσθάνομαι = *perceive*)

Direct Statement: **νοσεῖ.**

1. αἰσθάνεται ὅτι νοσεῖ.
2. αἰσθάνεται νοσεῖν.
3. αἰσθάνεται αὐτὸν νοσεῖν.
4. αἰσθάνεται νοσῶν.
5. αἰσθάνεται αὐτὸν νοσοῦντα.

Direct Statement: **γράψουσι.**

6. ἤγγελον αὐτοὺς γράψειν.
7. ἤγγελον γράψοντες.
8. ἤγγελον ὅτι γράψουσιν.
9. ἤγγελον αὐτοὺς γράψοντας.
10. ἤγγελον γράψειν.

AMBIGUITY OF STEM WITH INFINITIVE OR PARTICIPLE

An infinitive or a participle in indirect discourse has the **same stem** as the personal verb had in the original statement. Since the same stem is used for a present and an imperfect, the infinitive and participle constructions does not show tense as precisely as the ὅτι / ὡς construction.

λέγω ὅτι γράφετε εὖ.   *I say that you* (pl.) *write well.*
  Nonambiguous. Original statement: εὖ γράφετε
λέγω ὅτι ἐγράφετε εὖ.   *I say that you used to write well.*
  Nonambiguous. Original statement: εὖ ἐγράφετε
νομίζω ὑμᾶς **γράφειν** εὖ.   *I think [that] you **write** / **used to write** well.*
  Ambiguous. Was original statement εὖ γράφετε or εὖ ἐγράφετε?
ἀκούω ὑμᾶς **γράφοντας** εὖ.   *I hear [that] they **write** / **used to write** well.*
  Ambiguous. Was original statement εὖ γράφετε or εὖ ἐγράφετε?

Note: If ἀκούω connotes hearing rather than learning a fact through hearing, it will take a genitive object.
For verbs of finding and discovering, only context may show whether there is indirect discourse or not:

ηὗρον αὐτὸν ἐσθίοντα.   *I found [that] he is/was eating*   OR   *I found him eating* (ambiguous)
ἀκούω αὐτὸν καλοῦντα   *I hear [that] he is/was calling*   vs.   ἀκούω αὐτοῦ καλοῦντος   *I hear him calling*

Classwork: ✦✦ Read all of **Xenophanes** (rereading Xenophanes #5), Thesauros p. 226.

Classwork or ἔργα: Translate into Greek. Use the infinitive construction in the first four sentences, and a participle in the next four.

1. I swear that I will bring the money.
2. I found that she had brought the money.
3. They thought that they (different they) would bring the money.
4. They thought that they (same they) were bringing the money.
5. She announced that she (same she) will send the apples.
6. I perceive that she sent the apples.
7. Will you announce that he is sending the apples?
8. They heard that they (different they) are sending the apples.

Challenge: Consider the statement ἤκουσα τὸν βασιλέα νοσοῦντα. Could it be translated (a) "I heard that the king is sick," (b) "I heard that the king was sick," and (c) "I heard that the king had been sick"? Yes! Explain. (Hint: If there can be an aorist as prior past, why not an imperfect?)

ἔργα   ~Read and translate "The Death of the Pot." Learn the vocabulary.
          ~Parse the last speech in the fourth paragraph. (πῶς . . . ἀπέθανεν)

ἡμέρᾳ τινὶ ὁ Σοφὸς εἰσῆλθεν εἰς τὴν οἰκίαν φίλου τινος καὶ
ἀγγεῖα μεγάλα ἰδὼν εἶπε τάδε· "ὦ φίλε, τύχῃ ἀγαθῇ ὁρῶ
τὰ σὰ ἀγγεῖα. μέλλω γὰρ ποιήσειν δεῖπνον μέγα καὶ
πάντα τὰ ἐμὰ ἀγγεῖα μικρά ἐστι. δός μοι χρῆσθαι ἑνὶ τῶν   4
σῶν ἀγγείων, καὶ ὑπισχνοῦμαι ἀποδώσειν τριῶν ἡμερῶν."
"εὖγε" εἶπεν ὁ φίλος. Καὶ ὁ Νασρέδδινος κατῆλθεν εἰς τὴν
οἰκίαν ποιήσων τὸ δεῖπνον.

μετα δὲ τρεις ἡμερας ἔστησεν ὁ Σοφος ἀγγειον μαλα   8
μικρὸν ἐν τῷ τοῦ φίλου ἀγγείῳ καὶ ἦλθεν ἀποδώσων.
ὁ δὲ φίλος, ἰδὼν ἀγγεῖον μικρὸν ἱστάμενον ἐν τῷ μεγάλῳ,
ἠρώτησεν· "ἀλλ, ὦ φίλε, τί ἔτυχεν; ἕν σοι ἀγγεῖον ἔδωκα
(I gave), καὶ νῦν δύο ὁρῶ." ὁ δὲ Σοφὸς ἤγγειλε τὸ ἀγγεῖον
τεκεῖν παῖδα. ὁ δὲ φίλος χαίρων ἐδέξατο τὰ δύο ἀγγεῖα.   13

μετὰ δὲ πολὺν χρόνον, ἦλθεν αὖθις ὁ Νασρέδδινος τὸ αὐτὸ
αἰτήσων· ἔφη μέλλειν ποιήσειν δεῖπνον μέγα καὶ χρῄζειν   15
ἀγγείου μεγάλου.   "δός μοι χρῆσθαι αὖθις τῷ ἀγγείῳ
τῷ μεγάλῳ καὶ ὑπισχνοῦμαι ἀποδώσειν τριῶν ἡμερῶν."
"εὖγε" εἶπεν ὁ φίλος. καὶ ὁ Σοφὸς ἔλαβε τὸ ἀγγεῖον.

καὶ ἡμέραι πολλαὶ παρήρχοντο. ἀλλὰ ὁ Νασρέδδινος
οὐ κατῆλθεν ἀποδώσων τὸ ἀγγεῖον. ἦλθεν οὖν ὁ φίλος   20
πρὸς τὴν τοῦ Σοφοῦ οἰκίαν. "ὦ φίλε" ἠρώτησεν· "ποῦ
τὸ ἀγγεῖον μου;" "ἀπεκρίνατο δὲ ὁ Σοφός ὧδε· "ὦ φίλε,
αἰσθάνῃ με δακρύοντα; δεῖ με δεινόν τί σοι ἀγγεῖλαι·   23
τύχῃ κακίστῃ τὸ ἀγγεῖον ἀπώλεσας. λυπεῖ με ἀγγεῖλαι
τὸ ἀγγεῖον σου ἀποθανεῖν." ὁ δὲ φίλος ἀνεβόησεν.
"πῶς; ποῖον λόγον λέγεις; ἡγῇ με μῶρον εἶναι; οὐκ ἔστιν
ἀγγεῖον ἀποθανεῖν. ' ὁ μὴ ζῶν οὐκ ἀπέθανεν.' "   27~

ὁ δὲ Σοφὸς ἀπεκρίνατο μόνον τόδε· "εἴ μοι ἐπίστευες ἐν
τῷ πρὶν τὸ ἀγγεῖον ἀγγέλλοντι τεκεῖν, χρὴ νῦν πιστεύειν
μοι τὸ ἀγγεῖον ἀγγέλλοντι ἀποθανεῖν."

     τὸ ἀγγεῖον - pot, vessel

     ἡ τύχη - fortune good or bad, chance; good fortune (τυγχάνω)

4   χράομαι, χρήσομαι (aor. ἐχρησάμην) - use, make use of + dat.
            (Has *eta*-forms: χρῶμαι, χρῇ, χρῆται, inf. χρῆσθαι)

     ἀποδίδωμι, fut. ἀποδώσω - give back

8   ἵστημι, στήσω, ἔστησα - set upright, stand something up
            (vs. ἵσταμαι - *I stand* intransitive)

13   τίκτω, τέξομαι, ἔτεκον - give birth

     δέχομαι - accept, receive

15   χρῄζω (no future or aorist) - have a lack, want, or need of + gen.

23   αἰσθάνομαι, αἰσθανοῦμαι, ἠσθόμην - perceive, perceive of + acc. or gen.
       (Often takes participle in indirect discourse) --> aesthetics, anaesthesia

     δεινός,ή,όν - awesome both in the sense of terrible and/or wonderful

     κάκιστος,η,ον - worst (superlative of κακός)

     ἡγέομαι - consider

     ποῖος,α,ον - what sort? what sort of a?

27~ ἀποθνήσκω, aorist ἀπέθανον. What sort of aorist is ἀπέθανεν?

     πιστεύω, πιστεύσω, ἐπίστευσα - trust, trust in + dative

PRINCIPAL PARTS

The Greek verb has many forms, generated by a small number of stems, which are learned as principal parts. There are six main principal parts:

I X, I shall X, I X'd, I have X'd, I have X'd my..., I was X'd

The "*I X*" form is called the *first principal part*. Verbs are listed in any dictionary by their first pricipal part. In other words, to find the meaning of ἐξέβαλεν you need to look up ἐκβάλλω.

The first three principal parts are the most important: Present, Future, and Aorist Active Indicative. Memorize them over the next four days. Later you will learn to recognize the others. Not all verbs have all six principal parts. (στένω has only the first principal part.)

ε/ο AORISTS

ἄγω, ἄξω, ἤγαγον

βάλλω, βαλῶ, ἔβαλον

εὑρίσκω, εὑρήσω, ηὗρον (or εὗρον)

ἔχω, ἕξω or σχήσω, ἔσχον

θνήσκω, θανοῦμαι, ἔθανον
 (in prose ἀποθνήσκω)

κάμνω, καμοῦμαι, ἔκαμον

λαμβάνω, λήψομαι, ἔλαβον

λείπω, λείψω, ἔλιπον

μανθάνω, μαθήσομαι, ἔμαθον

πίνω, πίομαι, ἔπιον

πίπτω, πεσοῦμαι, ἔπεσον

τέμνω, τεμῶ, ἔτεμον (or ἔταμον)

τίκτω, τέξομαι, ἔτεκον

τυγχάνω, τεύξομαι, ἔτυχον

CHANGE-OF-STEM ε/ο AORISTS

αἱρέω, αἱρήσω, εἷλον

ἔρχομαι, ἐλεύσομαι, ἦλθον

ἐσθίω, ἔδομαι, ἔφαγον

λέγω, ἐρῶ, εἶπον

ὁράω, ὄψομαι, εἶδον

φέρω, οἴσω, ἤνεγκον (or ἤνεγκα)

σα- AORISTS

ἀκούω, ἀκούσομαι, ἤκουσα

βασιλεύω, βασιλεύσω, ἐβασίλευσα

βλέπω, βλέψομαι, ἔβλεψα

βουλεύω, βουλεύσω, ἐβούλευσα

γράφω, γράψω, ἔγραψα

δακρύω, δακρύσω, ἐδάκρυσα

ἐθέλω, ἐθελήσω, ἠθέλησα

εὕδω, εὑδήσω (no aorist)   (in prose, καθεύδω)

θάπτω, θάψω, ἔθαψα

κελεύω, κελεύσω, ἐκέλευσα

κλέπτω, κλέψω, ἔκλεψα

κρύπτω, κρύψω, ἔκρυψα

μέλλω, μελλήσω, ἐμέλλησα

νομίζω, νομιῶ, ἐνόμισα

οἰμώζω, οἰμώξομαι, ᾤμωξα

παιδεύω, παιδεύσω, ἐπαίδευσα

παύω, παύσω, ἔπαυσα

πείθω, πείσω, ἔπεισα

πέμπω, πέμψω, ἔπεμψα

πιστεύω, πιστεύσω, ἐπίστευσα

πλήττω, πλήξω, ἔπληξα

πράττω, πράξω, ἔπραξα

σώζω, σώσω, ἔσωσα

φυλάττω, φυλάξω, ἐφύλαξα

IRREGULAR CONTRACT with σα- AORISTS

δοκέω, δόξω, ἔδοξα

καλέω, καλῶ, ἐκάλεσα

βοηθέω, βοηθήσομαι, ἐβοήθησα

γελάω, γελάσομαι, ἐγέλασα

σιγάω, σιγήσομαι, ἐσίγησα

λα- AORISTS

ἀγγέλλω, ἀγγελῶ, ἤγγειλα

γαμέω, γαμῶ, ἔγημα

ἐγείρω, ἐγερῶ, ἤγειρα

καθαίρω, καθαρῶ, ἐκάθηρα

κρίνω, κρινῶ, ἔκρινα

κτείνω, κτενῶ, ἔκτεινα (prose ἀποκτείνω)

μένω, μενῶ, ἔμεινα

οἰκτίρω (or οἰκτείρω), οἰκτιρῶ, ᾤκτιρα

σημαίνω, σημανῶ, ἐσήμηνα

SPECIAL AORISTS

βαίνω, βήσομαι, ἔβην

γιγνώσκω, γνώσομαι, ἔγνων

ἵσταμαι, στήστομαι, ἔστην

χαίρω, χαιρήσω, ἐχάρην

| παύω, παύσω, ἔπαυσα | | τιμάω, τιμήσω, ἐτίμησα | | φιλέω, φιλήσω, ἐφίλησα |

Most verbs with an upsilon (υ) before the ‑ω ending follow the παύω pattern and need not be learned separately. (For example, βασιλεύω, βουλεύω, δακρύω, κελεύω, and πιστεύω.)
Most Contract Verbs follow the τιμάω / φιλέω pattern and need not be learned separately.
Some verbs lack some principal parts. For example, μεθύω, στένω, and χρήζω have no future or aorist.
καθεύδω has a future but no aorist in Attic Greek.

Memorize the principal parts listed on page 141. Be prepared to write them. As you work on each segment of the principal parts, read the corresponding segment (see Roman numerals) of "How to Weigh an Elephant," a Chinese story going back to Han times (third century C.E.).

Do not be dismayed if the memorization seems tedious. It is well worth the effort and will allow you one day to read Greek secure in your knowledge of the forms.

Vocabulary is given in advance for once, so that you may have a smoother experience of reading. To know what it is like to read with full knowledge of vocabulary, learn the vocabulary lists on pp. 60-61, 106-107, and p. 145. How does it feel to read a text without looking up words?

VOCABULARY for "How to Weigh an Elephant"

I   βασιλεύω - be king, rule over + gen. (βασιλεύς)
       φοβερός,ά,όν ‑ fearful, either causing fear or experiencing fear (φόβος = fear)
   6   δέχομαι - accept, receive
       ξενικός,ή,όν - foreign (ξένος)
       περί + acc. - about (in the sense of *around*) --> perimeter
       ἔξω - outside (adv.), outside of + gen. (ἐκ, ἐξ)
       πλήν (as conjunction) - except
   11   βουλεύω, βουλεύσω, ἐβούλευσα - plan, deliberate
       ὁ νόμος here = law
   13   συμβουλεύω - plan with, i.e., give advice to + dat., counsel (σύβμουλος)
       ὁ σύμβουλος - adviser, counsellor (σύν + βουλεύω)
   22   ἡ σπουδή - haste

II   25   φημι - I say (enclitic) + accusative infinitive construction --> fame, infamy, etc.
   26   δοκέω has three meanings: (a) **seem**, (b) **think** (introducing indirect discourse), and (c) **seem best** (used in decrees, e.g., *It seemed best to the people to free the prisoners*)
       ὁ φόβος - fear --> phobia, phobic
       εἰδέναι - to know (infinitive of οἶδα)
   30   ὁ κίνδυνος ‑ danger, risk
       ἡ σιγή - silence; σιγῇ is used as an adverb - silently, in a whisper (σιγάω)
   36   ὀρθός,ή,όν - straight, correct, right --> orthodox, orthodontist
   42   τὸ μέτρον - the measure, measurement, limit --> meter, metric, odometer
       ὁ σταθμός - weight (related to ἵστημι and ἵσταμαι)
       μετρέω - measure (μέτρον)

III   51   προσέχω τὸν νοῦν - apply the mind to, pay attention to, concentrate on + dat.
       ὁ πόρος - solution, literally, a way to cross a river <--> ferry, fare, ford
             (Note: Oxford is a translation of the Greek Βόσπορος, literally, cow-crossing.)
             --> (via Latin) port, transport, export, import, important
   57   τίμιος,α,ον, also τίμιος,ον - honored, valued, valuable (ἡ τιμή)
       κτείνω, κτενῶ, ἔκτεινα ‑ kill, slay (in poetry)
       ἀποκτείνω - kill off, slay (the normal term in Attic prose)
   62   φεύγω, φεύξομαι, ἔφυγον ‑ flee --> (via Latin) fugitive
       νέος,α,ον - young (as well as new)

IV   82   ἐνταῦθα - (adv.) here
       ὁ λίθος - stone -- > lithograph, megalith
       θήσω = future of τίθημι
   93   παιδεύω, παιδεύσω, ἐπαίδευσα - educate, bring up a child (παῖς)

HOW TO WEIGH AN ELEPHANT

I   βασιλεὺς ἦν ποτε ἐν τῇ γῇ τῇ Σινικῇ (Chinese) ὃς ἀνθρώπων
ἐβασίλευεν πολλῶν ἀλλ' οὐ πάντων . καὶ οὗτος ὁ βασιλεὺς ἦν
φοβερός. οἱ δὲ ἄλλοι βασιλεῖς ἐνόμιζον αὐτὸν φοβερώτατον διότι
οἱ στρατιῶται αὐτοῦ ἦσαν ὡς πλεῖστοι καὶ ὡς ἰσχυρώτατοι.
διὰ δὲ τοῦτο πάντες οἱ βασιλεῖς ἔπεμπον αὐτῷ δῶρα. ὁ δὲ
ὡς μάλιστα ἐφίλει δέχεσθαι δῶρα ἀπὸ γῆς ξενικῆς ὥστε   6
μανθάνειν περὶ πάντων ἃ ἐπὶ τῆς γῆς ἔστι. περὶ γὰρ τὴν οἰκίαν
τὴν βασιλικὴν ἦν τεῖχος μέγα καὶ ὑψηλόν (high). ὁ δὲ βασιλεὺς
οὔποτε ἐξῆλθεν ἔξω τοῦ τείχους. καὶ οὐκ ἐξελθὼν οὐκ εἶχε
γιγνώσκειν περὶ τῶν ἐπὶ τῆς γῆς πλὴν τοῖς δώροις.

καὶ τῷ βασιλεῖ βουλεύοντι καὶ κρίνοντι περὶ ἀμφισβητήσεων   11
(disputes) καὶ ποιοῦντι νόμους πᾶσιν ὧν ἐβασίλευε συνεβούλευον
τέτταρες σύμβουλοι. καὶ τούτοις τοῖς συμβούλοις ἦν δύο ἔργα,   13
τὸ μὲν πρῶτον τῷ βασιλεῖ συμβουλεύειν ποιοῦντι νόμους, τὸ δὲ
δεύτερον ἀγγέλλειν τῷ βασιλεῖ περὶ πάντων τῶν δώρων ἃ
ἔπεμπον αὐτῷ οἱ βασιλεῖς οἱ ξενικοί.

καὶ ἡμέρᾳ τινὶ τῶν τεττάρων συμβούλων καθιζομένων παρὰ τῷ   17
τείχει τῆς οἰκίας τῆς βασιλικῆς ἀνήρ τις ἦλθεν ἐλέφαντα ἄγων
ὃν ἔπεμψε βασιλεὺς τῆς γῆς τῆς Ἰνδικῆς (of India). οἱ δὲ
σύμβουλοι ἔπεμψαν δοῦλον τῷ βασιλεῖ ἀγγελοῦντα ἄνθρωπον
ἀγάγοντα δῶρον ὡς μέγιστον ἐκ τῆς γῆς τῆς Ἰνδικῆς. ὁ δέ
βασιλεὺς ταῦτα ἀκούσας πολλῇ σπουδῇ ἦλθε βουλόμενος ἰδεῖν τὸ   22
δῶρον.

II   οἱ δὲ σύμβουλοι ἤρξαντο διαλέγεσθαι ἀλλήλοις περὶ τοῦ δώρου·
ὁ μὲν πρῶτος εἶπε τάδε· "ὦ φίλοι, τὸν βασιλέα ἡμῶν φημι τούτῳ   25
τῷ δώρῳ χαιρήσειν· δοκῶ αὐτὸν ὡς μάλιστα χαιρήσειν. ἀγαθῇ   **26**
δὴ τύχῃ ἔρχεται ὁ ἐλέφας." ὁ δὲ δεύτερος εἶπε φόβῳ μεγάλῳ·
"πῶς ἀγαθῇ τύχῃ; γιγνώσκομεν τὸν βασιλέα ὡς πάντα βούλεται
μαθεῖν, πάντα εἰδέναι. εὖ οἶδα ὅτι ἐρωτήματα ὡς χαλεπώτατα
ἐρωτῶντος αὐτοῦ, ἡμῖν ἔσται κίνδυνος ὡς μέγιστος." ὁ δὲ τρίτος   30
"σιγᾶτε" ἔφη. "ὁρῶ γὰρ τὸν βασιλέα ἐρχόμενον νῦν. οὐχ ὁρᾶτε
αὐτὸν βαίνοντα;" ὁ δὲ τέταρτος εἶπε τάδε σιγῇ ὥστε χαλεπῶς
ἤκουον τὴν φωνὴν αὐτοῦ· "ὡς δεινός ἐστιν ὁ ἡμέτερος βασιλεύς
καὶ ὡς δεινὰ τὰ ἐρωτήματα αὐτοῦ. εἰ μὲν τύχῃ ἀγαθῇ ὁ ἐλέφας
ἔρχεται, εἰ δὲ κακῇ, ταχέως εὑρήσομεν."

καὶ ὀρθῶς ἐφοβοῦντο οἱ σύμβουλοι. ὁρῶν γὰρ τὸν ἐλέφαντα   36
εἶπεν ὁ βασιλεύς· "ὡς καλός ἐστιν ὁ ἐλέφας." ἀπεκρίνατο δὲ
σύμβουλος ὁμολογούμενος· "ναί, ὦ βασιλεῦ, καλός ἐστιν ὁ ἐλέφας,
καλλίων τοῦ ἵππου." ὁ δὲ βασιλεὺς εἶπεν· "καὶ ὡς μέγας ἐστίν."
ἄλλος δὲ σύμβουλος ὡμολόγησεν· "μέγας ἔστιν, μείζων τοῦ
ἵππου." ὁ δὲ βασιλεύς ἀπεκρίνατο ὧδε· "τοῦτο καὶ μῶρος ἔχει
ὁρᾶν. βούλομαι μαθεῖν ἀκριβῶς (precisely) τάδε· πόσα τὰ μέτρα   42
τούτου τοῦ ζώου καὶ πόσος ὁ σταθμός. ποίῳ μέτρῳ μετροῦσιν οἱ
ἄνθρωποι ἐλέφαντα;"

οἱ δὲ σύμβουλοι εἶπον· "ὦ βασιλεῦ, πῶς ἔστιν εὑρεῖν τὸν σταθμὸν
τοῦ ἐλέφαντος; οὐ γὰρ ἔστι τιθέναι αὐτὸ ἐν τοῖς ταλάντοις (trays
of a scale)." ὁ δὲ εἶπεν μόνον τόδε· "ἀκούσατε· ὑμῖν μὴ τὸν
σταθμὸν τοῦ ἐλέφαντος τριῶν ἡμερῶν εὑροῦσι θάνατος ἔσται."   48

III   οἱ δὲ σύμβουλοι ταῦτα ἀκούσαντες ὡς μάλιστα ἐφοβοῦντο.
καὶ τήν τε πρώτην καὶ τὴν δευτέραν ἡμέραν οὐδὲν ἄλλο ἐποίουν
ἢ προσέχειν τὸν νοῦν τῷδε· πῶς ἔστιν εὑρεῖν τὸν σταθμὸν   51
ἐλέφαντος. καὶ οὐδένα πόρον εὑρόντες τῇ τρίτῃ ἡμέρᾳ ὡς
μάλιστα ἠθύμουν. δῆλον γὰρ ἦν αὐτοῖς ὡς τῇδε τῇ ἡμέρᾳ χρὴ
αὐτοὺς τὸ φῶς τοῦ ἡλίου λιπεῖν.

καὶ τῶν συμβούλων ἀθυμούντων καὶ λεγόντων ἀλλήλοις ὅτι οὐκ
ἔστι φυγεῖν τὸν θάνατον, εἰσῆλθε παῖς τις νέος, υἱὸς γεωργοῦ.
καὶ τάδε εἶπεν· "ὦ ἄνδρες τίμιοι, πῶς πράττετε;" ὁ δὲ σύμβουλος   57
ὁ νεώτατος ἤγγειλεν αὐτοὺς κακῶς πράττοντας καὶ τῷ παιδὶ
τάδε εἶπεν· "ὦ παῖ, τύχῃ κακῇ εἰσήγαγέ τις ἐλέφαντα τῷ βασιλεῖ
καὶ ἔδοξεν αὐτῷ ἡμᾶς ἀποκτεῖναι μὴ τὸν σταθμὸν τοῦ ἐλέφαντος
εὑρόντας. μιᾶς δὲ ἡμέρας ἐρωτήσει ἡμᾶς τὸν σταθμὸν καὶ οὐκ
ἔσται ἡμῖν τὸ τέλος θανάτου φυγεῖν."   62

ὁ δὲ παῖς ὧδε ἀπεκρίνατο· "ὦ ἄνδρες τίμιοι, οἶδα ὅτι ἐγὼ νέος εἰμὶ
καὶ ὑμεῖς ἐστε ἄνδρες σοφοὶ καὶ γεραιοί. ἀλλὰ δοκῶ πόρον εὑρεῖν
ὡς ὑμῖν ἔσται μαθεῖν τὸν τοῦ ἐλέφαντος σταθμόν. τὸν βασιλέα
λέγω οὐκ ἀποκτενεῖν ὑμᾶς."

IV   οἱ δὲ σύμβουλοι διελέγοντο ἀλλήλοις· ὁ μὲν πρῶτος ἠρώτησεν·   67
"πῶς ἔστι τοῦτο; " ὁ δὲ δεύτερος ὧδε εἶπεν· "παῖς τις νέος λέγει
εὑρεῖν ὅπερ ἡμεῖς οἱ σοφοὶ καὶ γεραιοὶ δύο ἡμέρας ζητοῦντες οὐχ
ηὕρομεν. μὴ αὐτοῦ ἀκούσωμεν." ὁ δὲ τρίτος ἔφη "οὐ μένει ἡμῖν
χρόνος. ἀλλ᾽ ἐν τῷ χρόνῳ τῷ λοιπῷ χρὴ βουλεύεσθαι περὶ τοῦ
σταθμοῦ τοῦ ἐλέφαντος." ὁ δὲ νεώτατος σύμβουλος εἶπε τὸ
τέταρτον, καὶ οὗτος σοφώτατα εἶπεν· "δύο ἡμέρας ζητοῦμεν τὸν   73
σταθμὸν τοῦ ἐλέφαντος, οὐδένα πόρον εὑρόντες. χρὴ νῦν ἡμᾶς
ἀκούειν καινόν τι." καὶ τῷ παιδὶ εἶπεν· "ὦ παῖ, λέγε ἡμῖν, τίνα
πόρον ηὗρες;"

ὁ δὲ παῖς εἶπε τάδε· "ὦ ἄνδρες ἔντιμοι, ὧδε, ὡς δοκῶ, χρὴ ὑμᾶς   77
ποιεῖν· πρῶτον μὲν εἰς πλοῖον (boat) ἀγαγεῖν τὸν ἐλέφαντα ὃ ἐν
τῷ ποταμῷ ἐστιν. καὶ τοῦτο ποιήσασι ἔσται ὑμῖν ὁρᾶν τὰ τοῦ
ποταμοῦ ὕδατα ἀναβαίνοντα ἀνὰ τὰς πλευρὰς (sides) τοῦ πλοίου
(boat). καὶ ὅποι ἂν τοῦ πλοίου (to whatever point of the boat) τὰ
ὕδατα ἀναβαίνῃ (should rise), ἐνταῦθα χρὴ ὑμᾶς γράψαι σῆμα.   82
ἔπειτα δὲ χρὴ ὑμᾶς τὸν ἐλέφαντα ἀγαγόντας ἐκ τοῦ πλοίου ἀντὶ
αὐτοῦ εἰσφέρειν λίθους εἰς τὸ πλοῖον ἕως ἂν (until) τὰ ὕδατα
ἀναβαίνῃ (should rise) ἐπὶ τὸ αὐτό. καὶ μετὰ τοῦτο, εἰ τούτους
τοὺς λίθους θήσετε ἐν τοῖς ταλάντοις (trays of a scale) ἔσται ὑμῖν
τὸν σταθμὸν τοῦ ἐλέφαντος εὑρεῖν."

οἱ δὲ σύμβουλοι ταῦτα ἀκούσαντες ὡς μάλιστα ἔχαιρον. καὶ   88
ἐποίησαν ὡς ἐκέλευσεν ὁ παῖς.

καὶ διὰ ταῦτα τῷ βασιλεῖ ἐρωτῶντι τῇ τρίτῃ ἡμέρᾳ περὶ τοῦ
σταθμοῦ τοῦ ἐλέφαντος ἐδύναντο ἀποκρίνασθαι οἱ σύμβουλοι.
καὶ οὕτως ὁ μὲν βασιλεὺς ἔμαθε τὸν τοῦ ἐλέφαντος σταθμόν, οἱ δὲ
σύμβουλοι ἔμειναν ἐν τῷ βίῳ. τὸν δὲ παῖδα οἱ σύμβουλοι αὐτοὶ   93
ἐπαίδευσαν ὥστε ἐγένετο (he became), ὅτε ἀνὴρ ἦν, οὐ γεωργὸς
ὥσπερ ὁ πατήρ, ἀλλὰ σύμβουλος τοῦ μεγάλου βασιλέως.

VOCABULARY REVIEW (pp. 108-144)

NOUNS

A-Group

ἡ δίκη
ἡ κλοπή
ἡ λύπη
ἡ τιμή
ἡ σιγή
ἡ σπουδή
ἡ τύχη

ἡ ὥρα

ἡ ἀλήθεια

ὁ δεσπότης

O-Group

ὁ ἄνεμος
ὁ βροτός
ὁ δοῦλος
ὁ καρπός
ὁ κίνδυνος
ὁ λίθος
ὁ λόγος
ὁ ξένος
ὁ πόνος
ὁ πόρος
ὁ στόνος
ὁ τόπος
ὁ ὕπνος
ὁ κύκλος
ὁ σταθμός
ὁ σύμβουλος
ὁ φόβος
ὁ χρυσός

ὁ νοῦς (= νό-ος)
  ἔχειν ἐν νῷ
  προσέχω τὸν νοῦν
τὸ ἀγγεῖον
τὸ ἀργύριον
τὸ μέτρον

Third Group

ὁ ἐλέφας,
  gen. ἐλέφαντος
τὸ οὖς, gen. ὠτός

τὸ ἔτος
τὸ σκέλος
τὸ τεῖχος

τὸ σπέρμα
τὸ σῶμα

ADJECTIVES

βασιλικός,ή,όν
γελοῖος,α,ον
γεραιός,ά,όν
δεινός, ή, όν
δίκαιος,α,ον
ἐναντίος,α,ον
ἱκανός,ή,όν
καινός,ή,όν
καθαρός,ά,όν
ξένικός,ή,όν
ὅλος,η,ον
ὀρθός,ή,όν
τίμιος,α,ον & ος,ον
τυφλός,ή,όν
φοβερός,ά,.όν

τεθνεώς,υῖα,ός

πρῶτος,η,ον
δεύτερος,α,ον
τρίτος,η,ον
τέταρτος,η,ον

ποῖος,α,ον

μηδείς,μηδεμία,
    μηδέν

οὐδέτερος,α,ον

VERBS

ἄγω
  εἰσάγω
βαίνω (imper. βῆθι)
  ἀναβαίνω
  εἰσβαίνω
  ἐκβαίνω
  καταβαίνω
  προβαίνω
βάλλω
  ἐκβάλλω
βασιλεύω
βλέπω
  ἀναβλέπω
  καταβλέπω
βουλεύω
  συμβουλεύω
ἐγείρω
εὕδω
  καθεύδω (more
     common)
ἔχω
  ἀνέχω
  προσέχω τὸν νοῦν

θάπτω
καθαίρω
κρύπτω
κτείνω
  ἀποκτείνω
λείπω
οἰκτίρω
οἰμώζω
παιδεύω
πείθω
πιστεύω
πλήττω
πράττω
στένω
σῴζω
τίκτω
φεύγω
χρῄζω

ἀδικέω
ἀθυμέω
αἱρέω
ἀμφισβητέω
βοηθέω
δοκέω – seem, think,
       seem best
λυπέω
μετρέω
πονέω
ὠφελέω

βοάω
  ἀναβοάω
γελάω
ζάω
τιμάω

δίδωμι
  ἀποδίδωμι
ἵστημι
ὄλλυμι
  ἀπόλλυμι

αἰσθάνομαι + gen.
or acc.
ἀνέχομαι
ἅπτομαι + gen.
ἄρχομαι
δέχομαι
διαλέγομαι + dat.

ἔρχομαι
  ἀπέρχομαι
  διέρχομαι
  ἐξέρχομαι
  παρέρχομαι

χράομαι + dat.

ἐννοέομαι
ἡγέομαι
ὑπισχνέομαι often + future
            infinitive

NOTE ALSO

ἐχρῆν (imperfect of χρή)
ἔφη
εἰδέναι (infinitive of οἶδα)

δοκέω: think, seem, seem best

OTHER

μηδείς, μηδεμία, μηδέν
τοι

ἤδη
μάτην

πρίν
πλήν

ὅπου
οὕτως . . . ὥστε

ἆρα
πότερον

περ
εἴπερ
ὅσπερ, ἥπερ, ὅπερ

ἐκεῖ
ἐνταῦθα

ἔξω + gen.
μετά + gen.
περί + acc.

ἔξω
ἄνω
κάτω

ἀνα- up (in compounds)
κατα- down (in compounds)

VERB OVERVIEW: MOOD

To understand the form of a Greek verb is to know how to locate it in its paradigm. Eventually you will need to keep track of the following:

3 VOICES	(Active, Middle, Passive)
4 STEMS	(Continuous, Future, Aorist, Perfect)
4 MOODS	(Indicative, Subjunctive, Optative, Imperative)
INFINITIVE and PARTICIPLE	(one for each stem)

Each of the three **voices** has a page for its paradigm. For the next set of lessons, we will concentrate only on the **active** forms of -ω **verbs.** Once you have learned the shape of the entire active page, it will be easier to go on with the other two pages of forms.

Going across each page are four **stems.** You have learned forms for three of the four: continuous, future, and aorist. You will learn the perfect soon.

Going down are the four **moods.** You have learned the **indicative mood** and some forms of the subjunctive and imperative. Soon you will learn the **subjunctive, optative,** and **imperative moods** in a systematic way.

The indicative is the fact-reporting mood. Facts necessarily happen in time. **Only in the indicative mood are there time-markers or tense.** The other moods show aspect.

The paradigm of the active forms of παύω are given below. Forms marked by an asterisk (*) have already been learned.

παύω *I stop* (someone or something)

ACTIVE VOICE

CONTINUOUS		FUTURE		AORIST		PERFECT	
INDICATIVE							
*παύω	*παύομεν	*παύσω	*παύσομεν	*ἔπαυσα	*ἐπαύσαμεν	πέπαυκα	πεπαύκαμεν
*παύεις	*παύετε	*παύσεις	*παύσετε	*ἔπαυσας	*ἐπαύσατε	πέπαυκας	πεπαύκατε
*παύει	*παύουσι(ν)	*παύσει	*παύσουσι(ν)	*ἔπαυσε(ν)	*ἔπαυσαν	πέπαυκε(ν)	πεπαύκασι(ν)
*ἔπαυον	*ἐπαύομεν					ἐπεπαύκη	ἐπεπαύκεμεν
*ἔπαυες	*ἐπαύετε					ἐπεπαύκης	ἐπεπαύκετε
*ἔπαυε(ν)	*ἔπαυον					ἐπεπαύκει(ν)	ἐπεπαύκεσαν
SUBJUNCTIVE							
παύω	*παύωμεν			παύσω	παύσωμεν	πεπαυκὼς ὦ	
παύῃς	παύητε	--		παύσῃς	παύσητε	etc.	
*παύῃ	παύωσι(ν)			παύσῃ	παύσωσι(ν)		
OPTATIVE							
παύοιμι	παύοιμεν	παύσοιμι	παύσοιμεν	παύσαιμι	παύσαιμεν	πεπαυκὼς	
παύοις	παύοιτε	παύσοις	παύσοιτε	παύσειας	παύσαιτε	εἴην	
παύοι	παύοιεν	παύσοι	παύσοιεν	παύσειε(ν)	παύσειαν	etc.	
IMPERATIVE							
*παῦε	*παύετε			παῦσον	παύσατε	πεπαυκὼς	
παυέτω	παυόντων	--		παυσάτω	παυσάντων	ἴσθι	
						etc.	
INFINITIVE							
*παύειν		*παύσειν		*παῦσαι		πεπαυκέναι	
PARTICIPLE							
*παύων, ουσα, ον		*παύσων, ουσα, ον		*παύσας, ασα, αν		πεπαυκώς, υῖα, ός	

Lesson 35. The Subjunctive

CONTINUOUS	FUTURE	ε/o AORIST	α-AORIST

INDICATIVE

CONTINUOUS	FUTURE	ε/o AORIST	α-AORIST
λείπω λείπομεν λείπεις λείπετε λείπει λείπουσι(ν) ἔλειπον ἐλείπομεν ἔλειπες ἐλείπετε ἔλειπεν ἔλειπον	λείψω λείψομεν λείψεις λείψετε λείψει λείψουσι(ν)	ἔλιπον ἐλίπομεν ἔλιπες ἐλίπετε ἔλιπε(ν) ἔλιπον	ἔπαυσα ἐπαύσαμεν ἔπαυσας ἐπαύσατε ἔπαυσε(ν) ἔπαυσαν

SUBJUNCTIVE

CONTINUOUS	FUTURE	ε/o AORIST	α-AORIST
λείπω λείπωμεν λείπῃς λείπητε λείπῃ λείπωσι(ν)	- - -	λίπω λίπωμεν λίπῃς λίπητε λίπῃ λίπωσι(ν)	παύσω παύσωμεν παύσῃς παύσητε παύσῃ παύσωσι(ν)

INFINITIVE

λείπειν	λείψειν	λιπεῖν	παῦσαι

PARTICIPLE

λείπων,ουσα,ον	λείψων,ουσα,ον	λιπών,οῦσα,όν	παύσας,ασα,αν

❦❦ **Ambiguity Alert:** λείπω: The "I" present indicative and "I" continuous subjunctive are identical.
παύσω: The "I" future indicative and the "I" aorist subjunctive are identical.

To form the subjunctive, take the appropriate stem and add the subjunctive endings. The subjunctive endings are basically those of the present, but with a lengthened ε / o vowel:

⁻ω	⁻ωμεν
⁻ῃς	⁻ητε
⁻ῃ	⁻ωσι(ν)

The time-marker (ἐ) is found **only in the indicative**, which reports facts in time. There is **no time-marker** in the subjunctive, optative, or imperative.

Since the subjunctive is never used for reporting facts, its **negative is always μή**.

The subjunctive shows **aspect** (not tense). Therefore there is no future subjunctive. (And therefore it is correct to speak of a *continuous subjunctive* rather than a *"present subjunctive."* The phrase *"aorist subjunctive"* works, since the aorist is both a stem and a tense.)

▶ **Exercise α:** Give the aorist form that corresponds with the following continuous subjunctives:
1. ἄγῃς 2. ἐθέλητε 3. νομίζωσι 4. μανθάνωμεν 5. κλέπτω 6. ἀγγέλλῃ

TRANSLATION OF SUBJUNCTIVE / TRANSLATIONESE

There is no single translation that can gracefully express all meanings of the subjunctive. The best translationese is *should X.* The subjunctive is used in various ways and, remarkably, the word *should* works (though not well) for almost all those ways. It may sound stilted and be almost misleading. Still, it is the most rapid way to signal that you have recognized a subjunctive. Though not wholly satisfying, it is chosen as the least of all evils.

To translate an isolated subjunctive use *should* in inverted order.
ἔλθωσι *"should they come"* (as in, *"Should they come, welcome them"*)

▶ **Exercise β:** Translate: 1. ἄγῃς 2. νομίζωσι 3. ἐθέλητε 4. μανθάνωμεν 5. κλέπτω 6. ἀγγέλλῃ

THE SUBJUNCTIVE: USE

The basic ideas expressed by the subjunctive are: **WILL, PURPOSE, and FEAR.** Aspect is primary with the subjunctive, not tense. Is the action ongoing (continuous) or snapshot (aorist)?

AS MAIN VERB

HORTATORY SUBJUNCTIVE	~Usually limited to "*I*" and "*we*" forms. ~Translate *let me* (as in "*Let me see...*") or *let us* (as in "*Let's go!*") (*Let me* is a way of spurring oneself on, not a command)

λαμβάνωμεν τοὺς ἵππους.   *Let's be taking the horses. Let's take (repeatedly) the horses.*
      (i.e. *We should be taking / take the horses and let's do.*)

λάβωμεν τοὺς ἵππους.   *Let's take* (once) *the horses.*
      (i.e. *We should take* (once) *the horses and let's do.*)

λάβω τοὺς ἵππους.   *Let me take* (once) *the horses.*

μὴ λάβωμεν τοὺς ἵππους.   *Let's not take* (once) *the horses.*

DELIBERATIVE SUBJUNCTIVE	~Usually limited to *I* and *we* forms. ~Translate *should I?* or *should we?*

λείπωμεν τὴν πόλιν;   ***Should we be leaving the city?***

τί λάβω;   ***What should I take*** (once)?

τί ποιῶμεν;   ***What should we be doing? What should we do*** (repeatedly)?
      What are we to do?

SUBJUNCTIVE OF PROHIBITION	~Only on **aorist stem, always negative**, mainly in "*you*" forms ~Translate as a command. "***Don't X*** (once)."

Μὴ βοήσῃς.   ***Don't shout*** (once)! (i.e., *You* (s) *should not shout* (once), so don't.)

Μὴ γελάσητε.   ***Don't laugh*** (once)! (i.e., *You* (pl) *should not laugh* (once), so don't.)

▶ **Exercise γ:**   1. βλέπωμεν.   3. ἀγγείλωμεν τάδε.   5. τί λέγωμεν;   7. μὴ πέμψωμεν τὰ βιβλία.
   Translate: 2. βλέψωμεν.   4. μὴ ποιήσητε τάδε.   6. τί ποιήσω; (2 ways)   8. μὴ βάλητε τὰ μῆλα.

AS SUBORDINATE VERB

SUBJUNCTIVE OF PURPOSE	~with ἵνα, ὡς, or ὅπως = *so that* ~Translate with *should* or *may / might*	🖙🖙 *So that* in English may express purpose (ἵνα, ὡς, ὅπως + subj.) or result (ὥστε + indicative)

τοῦτο ποιῶ ἵνα **ἔλθωσιν.**   *I do this so that **they should** [or *might*] **come** (once).*

τοῦτο ἐποίησα ἵνα **ἔλθωσιν.**   *I did this so that **they should** [or *might*] **come** (once).*

τοῦτο ποιῶ ὅπως **ἐσθίητε.**   *I do this so that **you should** (or *might*) **eat** (repeatedly).*

τοῦτο ποιῶ ὡς μὴ **ἔλθῃ.**   *I do this so that **he should** [or *might*] **not come** (once).*

SUBJUNCTIVE OF FEARING	~with μή = *lest* (negative οὐ) ~Translate with *lest* and *should* or the English subjunctive.

φοβοῦμαι μὴ **δακρύῃ.**   *I fear lest he should cry / lest he cry.* (Note: *He cry* is an English subjunctive. This usage seems to be dying out.)

φοβοῦμαι μὴ οὐκ **ἔλθωσιν.**   *I fear lest they should not come* [or *lest they not come*].

▶ **Exercise δ:**   1. φοβοῦμαι μὴ κάμνητε.   3. ἔλθωμεν ὡς ἴδωμεν τοὺς παῖδας.
   Translate: 2. ἀναγιγνώσκει ἵνα μανθάνῃ τι.   4. τοῦτο ποιῶ ὡς μὴ τὸ ἀργύριον ξένοι κλέψωσιν.

Classwork: ✦✦ Read **Famous Sayings #5** and **Diogenes #12-13**, Thesauros pp. 232 and 234-235.

ἔργα   ~Write out the paradigm forms you have learned so far for ἄγω and again for φυλάττω.
      Label all forms as shown on the chart on p. 146.
   ~Read and translate the first part of "An Old Man's Advice," a Siberian tale. Learn the vocabulary.
      Circle and parse the subjunctives. (There are eight.) Say whether the subjunctive is hortatory,
      deliberative, a subjunctive of prohibition, purpose, or fearing. Do the aspects make sense?

AN OLD MAN'S ADVICE* (Part 1)

ἦν ποτε βασιλεὺς ἐν τῇ γῇ τῶν Μογγόλων (Mongolians),
οἳ πάντες ᾤκουν ἐν σκηναῖς. τῆς δὲ γῆς ταύτης οὐκ οὔσης
ἱκανῶς καρπίμου ἔδοξε τῷ βασιλεῖ πάντας τοὺς ἀνθρώπους
εἰς γῆν νέαν πορεύεσθαι ἵνα πλείονα σῖτον εὕρωσιν--πάντας   4
πλὴν τῶν γεραιῶν. ἡ γὰρ ὁδὸς ἡ ἄγουσα πρὸς τὴν νέαν
γῆν μακρὰ ἦν καὶ χαλεπή. τῷ δὲ βασιλεῖ ἐννοουμένῳ περὶ
τούτων οὐκ ἔδοξαν ἱκανῶς ἰσχυροὶ οἱ γέροντες πορεύεσθαι
ὁδὸν τοιαύτην. ἔπεμψεν οὖν ἄγγελον ὃς τάδε ἤγγειλεν·   8
"ὦ ἄνδρες, ἀποκτείνωμεν τοὺς γέροντας."

οἱ δὲ ἀκούσαντες ἠρώτων "ἀποκτείνωμεν τοὺς τεκόντας; "
ὁ δὲ ἄγγελος εἶπεν ὅτι χρὴ ποιῆσαι τοῦτο ἵνα μὴ ἀποθάνωσι
πάντες ἐν ταύτῃ τῇ γῇ. καὶ ἔφη χρῆναι αὐτοὺς τοῦτο   12
ποιήσαντας τάς τε γυναῖκας καὶ τοὺς παῖδας συλλαβόντας
πορεύεσθαι ὡς οἰκῶσιν ἐν ἄλλῃ γῇ καρπιμωτέρᾳ καὶ ἀμείνονι.

οἱ δ' ἄνδρες ταῦτα ἀκούσαντες ὡς μάλιστα ἠθύμουν. ἐφίλουν
γὰρ πάντες τοὺς τεκόντας. ἀλλὰ τὸν βασιλέα ἐφοβοῦντο καὶ
ἔδοξεν αὐτοῖς ποιεῖν ἃ ἐκέλευσεν. εἷς δὲ μόνος αὐτῶν, ἀνὴρ
ᾧ τὸ ὄνομα ἦν Ζυρήν, ἐτόλμα ἀπειθεῖν. τὸν γὰρ πατέρα   18
τὸν γεραιὸν ὡς μάλιστα ἐτίμα καὶ ἐβούλετο σῶσαι αὐτόν.

ἀντὶ οὖν τοῦ τὸν ἑαυτοῦ πατέρα ἀποκτεῖναι ἐν σάκκῳ
μεγάλῳ ἔθηκεν αὐτὸν ὅπως φέρῃ αὐτὸν πορευόμενος. καὶ   21
τὸν σάκκον συνεῖλκε (he used to draw together) ὥστε μηδένα
δύνασθαι εἰσιδεῖν. καὶ ἐν τῇ νυκτὶ τῶν ἄλλων ἀνθρώπων
καθευδόντων ὁ Ζυρὴν κατετίθει (used to put down) τὸν σάκκον
τῆλε τῶν ἄλλων καὶ ἀνεῴγνυ ἵνα τῷ πατρὶ παρέχῃ τι ἐσθίειν   25~
τε καὶ πίνειν.

       κάρπιμος, ον - fruitful (καρπός)
4   ἵνα + subjunctive - so that
       πλείων, πλεῖον - more (comparative of πολύς) <--> full   --> pleonasm
       ὁ γέρων, οντος - old man; as adjective old (actually a participle) --> gerontology
8   τοιοῦτος, τοιαύτη, τοιοῦτο/τοιοῦτον - of such a sort (with forms of οὗτος, αὕτη,
                                         τοῦτο preceded by τοι)
       ὁ τεκών, gen. τεκόντος - father, pl. parents   (actually an aorist participle of τίκτω)
12 χρῆναι - used as infinitive of χρή
       συλλαμβάνω - gather together (συν + λαμβάνω)
18 τολμάω - have the heart, endure, dare
       ἀπειθέω - disobey   (πείθω = persuade, πείθομαι = obey)
       ὁ πατήρ, gen. πατρός <--> father --> patriarchy --> (via Latin) paternal, paternity
       ὁ σάκκος - sack (probably derived from a Semitic word for sackcloth) --> sack
21 τίθημι, θήσω, ἔθηκα - put, place   --> thesis
       ὅπως + subjunctive - so that
       εἰσοράω - look into
       τῆλε - far from + gen.   --> telephone, telescope
       οἴγνυμι, οἴξω, ᾦξα - open (more common with a prefix)
25~ ἀνοίγνυμι - open up (ἀνα + οἴγνυμι) Can you punt this? (-νυμι verbs have no
                                         theme-vowel in the present and imperfect)
       παρέχω - provide (παρά + ἔχω)

---

*This story is freely adapted from "The Golden Bowl" in *The Kaha Bird: Tales from the Steppes of Central Asia*,
translated and edited by Mirra Ginsburg, © 1971; used with permission of the author.

Lesson 36. More Uses of the Subjunctive; Forms of εἰμί

A major use of the subjunctive is in **generalizing**--*whoever* vs. *who, wherever* vs. *where,* etc. There will be an **ἄν** (*ever*) in the neighborhood, either standing alone (ὃς ἄν δακρύῃ = *whoever should cry*) or in combination (as in ὅταν *whenever* = ὅτε + ἄν or in ἐάν *if ever*) = εἰ + ἄν.

| **WITH RELATIVE PRONOUN** | (ὅς ἄν, ὅν ἄν, ᾗ ἄν, etc.) |

ὃς ἄν γαμῇ μῶρός ἐστιν.　　　*Whoever should marry* [OR *marries*] *is a fool.*
ὃς ἄν μὴ γαμῇ μῶρός ἐστιν.　*Whoever should not marry* [OR *does not marry*] *is a fool.*
ὃν ἄν ἴδῃς βασιλεὺς ἔσται.　*Whomever you should catch sight of* [OR *catch sight of*]
　　　　　　　　　　　　　　　　　　　　　　　　will be king.

μή as Negative in Generalizations

Remember: μή tips you off that there is a generalization, whether the indicative, subjunctive,
　　　　　　　　　　　　　　　　　　　　　　　　　or a participle has been used.

ὃς μὴ γαμεῖ μῶρός ἐστιν.　　　*Who does not marry is a fool.*
ὃς ἄν μὴ γαμῇ μῶρός ἐστιν.　*Whoever does / should not marry is a fool.*
ὁ μὴ γαμῶν μῶρός ἐστιν.　　　*The one not marrying is a fool.*

For a generalization with the indicative, see Socrates' famous statement of his "ignorance":

✦ ἃ μὴ οἶδα οὐδὲ οἴομαι εἰδέναι.　　*What I do not know, I also do not think I know.*

| **WITH TEMPORAL CONJUNCTIONS** | (ὅταν = ὅτε + ἄν, ἐπειδάν = ἐπειδή *when* + ἄν) |

ὅταν γράφῃ, χαίρω.　　　　　　　*Whenever she should be writing* [OR *writes*], *I rejoice.*
ἐπειδάν γράψῃ, δὸς αὐτῇ δῶρα.　*Whenever she should write (once), give her gifts.*

| **IN CONDITIONS** | with ἐάν or ἤν *if ever* (either one = εἰ + ἄν) |

PRESENT GENERAL　　ἐάν or ἤν + subj. in the *if* clause, present in the *then* clause:

　　ἐάν γεωργῆτε χαίρω　　*If ever you should farm* [OR *farm*], *I rejoice.*

FUTURE MORE VIVID　　ἐάν or ἤν + subj. in the *if* clause, future or equivalent in the *then* clause:

　　ἤν ἔλθῃ δὸς αὐτῇ δῶρα.　*If ever she should come* [OR *comes*] (once) *give her gifts.*
　　　　　　　　　　　　　　　OR *Should she come* (once), *give her gifts.*

NOTE: There will be a review of conditions on p. 172.

TRANSLATIONESE AGAIN

There is no perfectly satisfactory translation for a generalizing subjunctive. If you use the English indicative, there is no quick way to signal that you have recognized a subjunctive. If you use *should,* you signal instantly that you have recognized a subjunctive, but the English is stilted and someone might think you were using a moralizing *should,* with the meaning *ought to.* You need to keep in mind that this is <u>not</u> a moralizing *should.*

Students ask: "What should I put on the back of my subjunctive flashcards?" There is no single translation that will do for all subjunctives (or for all optatives). Rule of thumb for flashcards: Use *should* in inverted order for the subjunctive. (The order shows that it is not a moralizing *should.*)

λείπωσι(ν) - *should they be leaving*　　λίπωσι(ν) - *should they leave* (once)

▶ **Exercise γ:**　1. ὃς ἄν ἔχῃ φίλους, εὐδαίμων ἐστίν.　　4. ἤν ὁ παῖς πέσῃ, οἰμώζει ἡ μήτηρ.
　Translate:　　　2. ἐάν ποιήσῃ ταῦτα, ἀδικήσει / ἀδικεῖ.　　5. ἤν ὁ παῖς πέσῃ, οἰμώξεται ἡ μήτηρ.
　　　　　　　　　3. ἐπειδάν ἐσθίωσι, πίνουσιν.　　　　　6. ἐπειδάν φάγωσι, καλοῦσι ποιητήν.

εἰμί = I am

INDICATIVE

Present

εἰμί	ἐσμέν
εἶ	ἐστέ
ἐστί(ν)	εἰσί(ν)

Imperfect

ἦ or ἦν	ἦμεν
ἦσθα	ἦτε
ἦν	ἦσαν

SUBJUNCTIVE

ὦ	ὦμεν
ἦς	ἦτε
ἦ	ὦσι(ν)

INFINITIVE

εἶναι

PARTICIPLE

ὤν, οὖσα, ὄν

All present forms of εἰμί = *I am* are enclitic except for εἶ = "*you* (sing.) *are*." In deference to tradition the last syllable of the enclitic forms is shown with an acute accent. In fact, in only one of five combinations (see Chart p. 96) will there be an accent in the flow of written Greek.

⚹⚹ Ambiguity Alert: ἦν can be *I was* OR *he/she/it was.*

The subjunctive stem is εσ. The σ drops, leaving the ε to contract, so that the subjunctive of εἰμι looks like a set of disembodied endings.

As you might expect from the continuous nature of being, there is no aorist for the verb εἰμί

▶ **Exercise β:** Translate the following (written in large print so breathing can easily be seen):

ἦ   ἐστε   ἐστι   ἦσθα   ὄντες   οὔσης   εἶναι   ἦν   ὄν   εἰσι

▶ **Exercise γ:** Distinguish between words that resemble the forms of εἰμί and other words, translating when possible. (Each set has at least one form of the verb εἰμί.)

ὄν / ὅν   ὦ / ὤ / ῷ   ἦς / ἧς   ἡ / ἥ / ᾗ / ῇ / ἦ

Classwork: Read **Graveyard #18** and **Diogenes #7-8**, Thesauros pp. 228 and 234.

Learn the beginning of a poem in the Anacreontic meter.

◆

> Μακαρίζομέν σε, τέττιξ,
> ὅτε δενδρέων ἐπ' ἄκρων
> ὀλίγην δρόσον πεπωκὼς
> βασιλεὺς ὅπως ἀείδεις.

We deem you blessed, cricket,
When, from the tree tops,
Drunk on a little dew,
You sing like a king.

Note ἐπ' ἄκρων δενδρέων = at the tipmost trees, where we would say "at the tip, or top, of the trees." ἄκρος (tipmost) is used like μέσος. (--> acrophobia, acronym, acropolis)

ἔργα   ~Memorize the lines of the poem printed above.
~Write out the paradigm for εἰμί three times. Memorize.
~Make up five Greek sentences using *whoever*, *whenever*, and *if ever*. Include a translation.

THE PERSONAL MUSE

Figure 1. The Crowning of Sappho. Line drawing of an Attic hydria (ca. 450 B.C.E.).

Throughout this course, you will read and memorize a number of lines from Greek poetry, including selections from Homer, Archilochus, Mimnermus, Sappho, and Anacreon. Greek literature begins with the epic Homeric poems, the *Iliad* and the *Odyssey*. These two poems, composed in the eighth century B.C.E., influenced all subsequent Greek poetry. "We are all beggars at the feast of Homer," Aeschylus, the tragic poet, is reported to have said.

The narrative style of Homer, praised by Aristotle in his *Poetics*, is one of objectivity: the poet does not intrude into the narrative but lets his characters speak and act for themselves. But in the seventh and sixth centuries, a poetry developed in which the voice of the author is heard.

Archilochus (ca. 680-640 B.C.E) is the earliest such poet whose work survives. He was born on the island of Paros and seems to have been a mercenary soldier: "I am a servant of the Lord of War and I am expert in the lovely gift of the Muses." His poems indicate his versatility. He could in a few lines depict the loveliness of a woman: "She rejoiced as she held a shoot of myrtle and the beautiful flower of a rose. And her hair shaded her shoulders and her back." He could just as easily write invective: "May he gnash his teeth, lying on his stomach like a dog, powerless, at the edge of the sea breakers. I would like to see this: he wronged me, stepped with his heel on our oaths, once my true friend."

Not only does Archilochus break the Homeric narrative style by using the "I" person, but he also challenges Homeric heroic codes. He rejects, he says, great generals, full of swagger and good looks, in favor of a small bandy-legged man, "full of heart." Similarly, in a poem you will soon memorize, he is unheroically ready to abandon his shield and save his life.

Like Archilochus, Mimnermus uses Homeric diction while going beyond Homeric themes. He was born either in Colophon (the home of Xenophanes) or Smyrna, a colony of Colophon ca. 670 B.C.E.

His poems depict the pleasures of love and the difficulties of old age. Solon, an Athenian lawmaker and poet, objects to Mimnermus' praise of youthful love and fear of old age. For Solon the wisdom that comes with age is important: "I grow old, always learning many things."

The most famous poet of love is Sappho (ca. 630 B.C.E.), who was born in the island of Lesbos, an island off the coast of Asia Minor. She too acknowledges her debt to Homer, while bringing in a new perspective. You have already memorized part of her poem that begins, "Some say the fairest thing on the black earth is a host of horsemen, others say it is a host of infantry or of warships, but I say it is whatever one loves." The opening of the poem contrasts the beauty of Greek cavalries, armies, and navies - the Homeric background - with a more intimate, and yet more general, idea of what is beautiful. It is *whatever* one loves.

As proof of her generalization, Sappho uses a Homeric example: Helen, who gave up her husband, child, and parents to follow Paris to Troy. Although we do not have the full text of the poem, we know that somehow Helen's beauty reminds Sappho of the one she loves, Anactoria, whose lovely step and radiance she would prefer to see than the richly ornamented Lydian chariots and infantry.

Many other poems of Sappho's celebrate and catalog the effects of love. In one she graphically describes the physical symptoms of love as she looks upon her beloved: "No longer am I able to speak, my tongue shatters, soon a delicate fire races under my skin, my eyes are blind, my ears ring, sweat pours down over me, trembling seizes me, and I am paler than the dry grass.... "

Anacreon is remembered as a master of the drinking song. Born in Teos in Asia Minor (ca. 575 B.C.E.), he composed court poetry for the tyrant Polycrates on Samos and then for the tyrant Hippocrates in Athens. His poems treat love with sophistication and wit rather than passion: "Once again golden haired Love, hitting me with a purple ball, invites me to sport with a girl of richly colored slippers. But she, since she is from well-built Lesbos, mocks my grey hair, and gawks after another girl."

His poems were so popular that they inspired a host of imitative drinking songs, called Anacreontics, "in the style of Anacreon." You have read two of these: "It is difficult to love...," and "We deem you blessed, cricket." Both of these Anacreontics display the pointed humor suitable for drinking songs.

Figure 2. A Symposium. Line drawing.

Lesson 37. The Perfect

So far you have learned the parts of the Active verb paradigm shown in bold below. These are the most frequently used forms. If you did not learn the remaining forms, you would still be able to read much of the New Testament and many statements in Attic Greek. Before going further, stop and make sure you can write these forms out easily. Then you will be ready to go on and fill out the remainder of the Active paradigm.

ACTIVE VOICE

CONTINUOUS	FUTURE	AORIST	PERFECT
INDICATIVE			
▐▐▐	▐▐▐	▐▐▐	XXX
▐▐▐			XXX
SUBJUNCTIVE			
▐▐▐	- -	▐▐▐	+++
OPTATIVE			
XXX	XXX	XXX	+++
IMPERATIVE			
XXX	- -	XXX	+++
INFINITIVE			
▐▐▐	▐▐▐	▐▐▐	XXX
PARTICIPLE			
▐▐▐	▐▐▐	▐▐▐	XXX

▐▐▐   already learned

- -   doesn't exist

XXX   to be learned

+++   made by combination of known forms

THE PERFECT ACTIVE INDICATIVE: MEANING AND TRANSLATION

What do you not know how to express yet in Greek? "*I have X'd*" as opposed to "*I X'd*." "*I X'd*" is an aorist. "*I have X'd*" is a **perfect**.

Think of the difference between "*Did you go to Europe?*" and "*Have you been to Europe?*" The former question asks whether an event occurred in the past. The latter asks about you: "*Have you been to Europe (and therefore are you acquainted with European culture)?*" Or think of the difference between "*I drank*" and "*I have drunk.*" "*I have drunk*" indicates not only that I drank but that the effect of the drinking is still felt. (For example, "*I have drunk and so I know what that drink tastes like.*" Or "*I have drunk and so I am not thirsty.*" Or "*I have drunk and so am drunk.*") When Hippolytus wants his horses to stop dragging him to death he addresses them with a perfect passive participle as "***having been nourished in my stalls.***" The point is not that once in the past he nourished them but that they **now** feel the effects of that nourishment, for which they owe him kindness.

The perfect shows that an action took place in the past that has an effect in the present. It is really a kind of present tense. (*I have washed the horse* is almost the same as *I have a washed horse*.)

There is a past perfect, called the **pluperfect**, as well. Translate that as "*I had X'd*." Notice that not every use of *I had X'd* in English represents a Greek pluperfect. If you say, "*I had called the doctor a week before she fell ill*," that is an aorist as prior past because it is simply asserting that one past act took place before another. If you say, "*I had cleaned the house for my guests*," meaning "*I had cleaned it and therefore it was clean*," that would be a pluperfect. The pluperfect shows that an action took place in the past that continued to have an effect in the past. It is a kind of past tense. (*I had washed the horse* is almost the same as *I had a washed horse*.)

Translationese for the perfect participle is difficult. *Having X'd* is translationese for the aorist participle. "*Having stumbled, he fell.*" This asserts nothing more than that he stumbled and fell. *Having drunk, he fell*. If we mean simply that he drank (for example, a cup of water) and then fell, *having drunk* is an aorist participle. If we mean that he drank a cup of wine and was drunk--that is a perfect participle. In our Anacreontic poem πεπωκώς is a perfect participle. That is why it is better to translate it "*being drunk on*" than "*having drunk*." The best translationese for a perfect participle, clumsy as it is, is *being in a state of having X'd*.

As for the **perfect infinitive**, the best translationese, clumsy again, is: *to be in a state of having X'd*.

PERFECT (= present perfect)	
πέπαυκα	πεπαύκαμεν
πέπαυκας	πεπαύκατε
πέπαυκε(ν)	πεπαύκασι(ν)

PLUPERFECT (= past perfect)	
ἐπεπαύκη	ἐπεπαύκεμεν
ἐπεπαύκης	ἐπεπαύκετε
ἐπεπαύκει(ν)	ἐπεπαύκεσαν

INFINITIVE

πεπαυκέναι

PARTICIPLE

πεπαυκώς, υἶα, ός
gen. (m./n.) πεπωκότος

K-less PERFECT (= present perfect)	
λέλοιπα	λελοίπαμεν
λέλοιπας	λελοίπατε
λέλοιπε(ν)	λελοίπασι(ν)

PLUPERFECT (= past perfect)	
ἐλελοίπη	ἐλελοίπεμεν
ἐλελοίπης	ἐλελοίπετε
ἐλελοίπει(ν)	ἐλελοίπεσαν

INFINITIVE

λελοιπέναι

PARTICIPLE

λελοιπώς, υἶα, ός
gen. (m./n.) λελοιπότος

The perfect has its **own stem**. The normal pattern for making a perfect stem is this:

παύω, παύσω, ἔπαυσα,   πέπαυκα
σιγάω, σιγήσω, ἐσίγησα,   σέσιγηκα
ποιέω, ποιήσω, ἐποίησα,   πεποίηκα

Memorize the **perfect** endings. (If you know the word *Eureka*, you have a head start.)
Be able at least to recognize the pluperfect forms.

✦ εὕρηκα   *I have found it!*   Famous saying of Archimedes in the bathtub

▶ **Exercise α:** Take the two statements: ἵππον **λύσας**, κατῆλθον χαίρων and ἵππον **λελυκὼς**, κατῆλθον χαίρων. (λύω = *release*) What is the difference in meaning? How can you get that difference across in English? Or consider νομίζω αὐτὴν μαθεῖν τὴν Ἑλληνικὴν γλῶτταν. vs. νομίζω αὐτὴν **μεμαθηκέναι** τὴν Ἑλληνικὴν γλῶτταν. Which one implies that she still knows Greek? How do you translate?

▶ **Exercise β:**   1. πεπαύκαμεν   3. πεπαυκώς   5. πεπαυκός   7. πέπαυκεν
    Translate·   2. πεπαυκέναι   4. πεπαυκυῖαν   6. ἐπεπαύκης   8. πεπαυκότα

There are **κ-less perfects** (just as there are σ-less α-aorists). The endings are normal.

γράφω, γέγραφα   κλέπτω, **κέκλοφα**   λείπω, **λέλοιπα**,   πλήττω, **πέπληγα**,   φέρω, **ἐνήνοχα**.

▶ **Exercise γ:** Translate: 1. κεκλόφασι   2. ἐνήνοχε   3. ἐγεγράφει   4. πεπληγός   5. λελοιπέναι   6. κεκλοφότες

REDUPLICATION

The perfect is often recognizable by its **reduplication**. Actually this is just duplication of the initial stem sound, connected with an ε. If the initial sound is a vowel, it is lengthened, as in time-marking. If the initial sound has breath (χ, φ, θ), the reduplication has no breath (κ,π,τ).

For a stem beginning with **a single consonant** sound, reduplicate with the consonant sound + ε:		For most stems beginning with a **mute + liquid** (λ, μ, ν, ρ), reduplicate the mute + ὲ:	
λέλυκα	(from λύω)	γέγραφα	(from γράφω)
σέσωκα	(from σῴζω)	βέβληκα	(from βάλλω)
μεμάθηκα	(from μανθάνω)	κέκληκα	(from καλέω)
κεχάρηκα	(from χαίρω)		
πέφευγα	(from φεύγα)	exception: ἔγνωκα	(from γιγνώσκω)

If stem begins with ρ or with some **combination besides mute + liquid**, just add ἐ before the stem, doubling any ρ. NOTE: This ἐ is **not** a time-marker. It indicates reduplication.		If the stem begins with a **short vowel**, lengthen it; if stem begins with a **diphthong**, lengthen the first vowel	
ἐζήτηκα	(from ζητέω)	ἤγγελκα	(from ἀγγέλλω)
ἔφθαρκα	(from φθείρω)	ἠθέληκα	(from ἐθέλω)
ἐσπούδακα	(from σπουδάζω)	ὤρθωκα	(from ὀρθόω)
ἔρριφα	(from ῥίπτω)	ηὕρηκα	(from εὑρίσκω)

▶ **Exercise δ:** Try to look up the "*I do*" forms in the dictionary for the following perfects:

1. ἠδίκηκα 2. ἐζήτηκα 3. ἧρηκα 4. ἠθέληκα 5. πεφύλαχα 6. τέθνηκα 7. ἔγνωκα 8. ἠρώτηκα

FOURTH PRINCIPLE PART: PERFECT ACTIVE

The "*I have X'd*" form is the fourth principal part. You need not memorize this principal part. Look over the perfects below. You could "punt" most perfects if you found them in your reading. Memorize the forms you would not be able to punt. (Those with entirely new stems are underlined. Make sure to learn them.) If you ever need to know a principle part, consult pp. 249-250.)

κα-Perfect				**κ-less**	
ἀγγέλλω	ἤγγελκα	νομίζω	νενόμικα	ἄγω	ἦχα
βαίνω	βέβηκα	παύω	πέπαυκα	ἐγείρω	ἐγρήγορα
βάλλω	βέβληκα	πίνω	πέπωκα	ἔρχομαι	ἐλήλυθα
βουλεύω	βεβούλευκα	πίπτω	πέπτωκα	κλέπτω	κέκλοφα
γιγνώσκω	ἔγνωκα	πιστεύω	πέπιστευκα	κτείνω	-έκτονα*
ἐθέλω	ἠθέληκα	τέμνω	-τέτμηκα*	λαμβάνω	εἴληφα
ἐσθίω	ἐδήδοκα	σῴζω	σέσωκα	λείπω	λέλοιπα
εὑρίσκω	ηὕρηκα or	τίκτω	τέτοκα	πέμπω	πέπομφα
	εὕρηκα	τυγχάνω	τετύχηκα	πλήττω	πέπληγα
ἔχω	ἔσχηκα	χαίρω	κεχάρηκα	φέρω	ἐνήνοχα
θνῄσκω	τέθνηκα			φεύγω	πέφευγα
κάμνω	κέκμηκα	NOTE:			
λέγω	εἴρηκα	ὁράω	ἑώρακα	NOTE:	
μανθάνω	μεμάθηκα		*I have seen* AND	γίγνομαι	γέγονα (Note
μένω	μεμένηκα		οἶδα *I know*		active form.)

* A hyphen means that the perfect form is found in compound. (You will find ἀποτέτμηκα but not τέτμηκα.)

Not all verbs have perfect forms. Some verbs which have no active perfect are: βλέπω, εἰμί, εἶμι, εὕδω, κελεύω, οἴγνυμι, οἰκτίρω, οἰμώζω, θάπτω, καθαίρω, κρύπτω, μεθύω, μέλλω, σημαίνω, στένω.

▶ **Exercise ε:** Translate:

1. πεπώκα	3. εἰρηκέναι	5. τετοκυῖα	7. ἐπεπτώκει
2. ἐδηδόκατε	4. εἰλήφαμεν	6. ἐγρήγορα	8. ἐνηνοχός

Classwork: ✦✦ Read **New Testament #10, Graveyard #26, Famous Sayings #6,** and **Diogenes # 21,** Thesauros pp. 223, 230, 232, and 235.

Classwork or ἔργα: ~Translate the following, using a form on the perfect stem in each sentence:

1. Have you (pl.) stopped the battle?
2. Has he written a letter?
3. I had drunk the wine.
4. Friend, tell me the names of those (in the state of) having learned the poems.
5. To be in the state of having stolen is terrible.
6. She shows me the ones (masc.) who have kept their silence.

ἔργα ~Write the perfect forms of λέλυκα and πέπομφα. Memorize the endings of the perfect.
~Cover the first principal parts in the above list. Looking only at the perfect forms, determine the first principal part. Circle and memorize all the forms you could not recognize.
~Read and translate Part 2 of "An Old Man's Advice." Circle every perfect.

πολλὰς ἡμέρας ἐπορεύοντο οἱ Μόγγολοι (Mongolian). καὶ
τέλος ἀφίκοντο ἐπὶ τὴν θάλατταν. ὁ δὲ βασιλεύς, πρὸς τὴν
θάλατταν ἀποβλέπων, εἶδε ἐν τοῖς ὕδασι κύλικα χρυσῆν--   3
κύλικα μεγάλην καὶ καλήν. "ἑώρακα " ἔφη "πολλὰ καλὰ καὶ
πολλαῖς κύλιξι πέπωκα οἶνον. ἀλλὰ ταύτην τὴν κύλικα
νομίζω καλλίστην. τίς βέβληκεν αὐτὴν ἐν τῇ θαλάττῃ; καὶ
τίς μοι λήψεται; ἐὰν λάβῃ τις αὐτήν μοι, ἄξιον νομιῶ αὐτὸν   7
πολλῶν δώρων. σφόδρα γὰρ ἐπιθυμῶ τὴν κύλικα
κεκτῆσθαι." ὁ δὲ βασιλεὺς ἐκέλευσε κληροῦσθαι (to cast lots),   9
τὸν δὲ κληρωτὸν (chosen by lot) ἐκέλευσεν εἰσελθεῖν εἰς τὴν
θάλατταν ἵνα λαβὼν τὴν κύλικα ἀπενέγκῃ αὐτῷ.

ὁ δὲ κληρωτὸς οὐ κατῆλθεν. "ὦ ἄνδρες" ἔφη ὁ δὲ βασιλεὺς
"μὴ ἀθυμεῖτε. ἄνθρωπος εἷς τέθνηκεν. πέμψωμεν ἄλλον.   13
ἐὰν δὲ καὶ οὗτος ἀποθάνῃ, πέμψωμεν ἄλλον. ἢν δὲ καὶ
οὗτος ἀποθάνῃ, πέμψωμεν καὶ ἔτι ἄλλον." καὶ αὖθις
ἐκέλευσε κληροῦσθαι (to cast lots). εἰς δὲ τὴν θάλατταν
εἰσῆλθεν ὁ κληρωτὸς ὁ δεύτερος ζητήσων τὴν κύλικα.
ἀλλὰ τὰ αὐτὰ ἔπαθεν· ἀπέθανεν ἐν τοῖς τῆς θαλάττης   18
ὕδασιν. ὁ δὲ βασιλεύς, ὡς μάλιστα τῆς κύλικος ἐπιθυμῶν,
ἔπεμπεν ἄλλον καὶ ἔτι ἄλλον ἄνδρα εἰς τὴν θάλατταν.
ἀλλὰ ἀεὶ τὸ αὐτὸ ἔπαθον. τέλος ὁ Ζυρὴν ἦν κληρωτὸς
(chosen by lot). καὶ δοκῶν ἀποθανεῖσθαι ἦλθε πρὸς τὸν
σάκκον (sack) ὡς λέγῃ χαίρειν τῷ πατρὶ τῷ γεραιῷ.   23

ἀφικνέομαι, ἀφίξομαι, ἀφικόμην - come to, arrive (common in prose)
  (= ἀπό + ἱκνέομαι = come. The simple form ἱκνέομαι = is seen in poetry.)
3 ἡ θάλαττα - sea, ocean   (thalassemia)
ἀποβλέπω - look off, look away
ἡ κύλιξ, gen. κύλικος - cup --> chalice
χρυσοῦς, ῆ, οῦν - golden (contraction of χρυσέος, η, ον) --〉 chrysanthemum
7 ἐάν + subjunctive - if ever (from εἰ + ἄν)
ἄξιος,α,ον - worthy, worthy of + gen. or + inf.   --> axiom
σφόδρα - strongly, vehemently
9 κτάομαι - acquire;   **κέκτημαι** - *I possess* (perfect as present)

13

	τέθνηκα	*I have died, am dead*
		(perfect as present)
PERFECT	τέθνηκα	τέθναμεν
	τέθνηκας	τέθνατε
	τέθνηκε(ν)	τεθνᾶσι(ν)
INFINITIVE	τεθνάναι	
PARTICIPLE	τεθνεώς, υῖα, ός	
	gen. τεθνεῶτος,-υίας,-ῶτος	
	OR	
	τεθνηκώς,υῖα,ός,	
	gen. τεθνηκῶτος,υίας,ῶτος	

Notice **stem alternation** for the perfect of θνῄσκω· **τεθνηκ**- in the
singular, **τεθνα**- everywhere else. (The simple perfect τέθνηκα is
common in prose; for other stems ἀποθνῄσκω is normally used.)

ἢν + subjunctive - if ever (from εἰ + ἄν)
18 πάσχω, πείσομαι, ἔπαθον - undergo, suffer, experience   --> sympathy,
  ὡς + subjunctive - so that   empathy, pathetic
23 λέγω χαίρειν - say goodbye (literally, *tell someone to rejoice*)

ὅστις, ἥτις, ὅ τι AS INDEFINITE RELATIVE

The indefinite relatives *whoever, whatever* (literally, "*anyone who*," "*anything which*") are common in Greek. Learn the forms, which are a combination of ὅς and τις (enclitic), each declined.
(The neuter singular ὅ τι is printed as two words, which distinguishes it from ὅτι = "*that*" in indirect discourse.)

Make sure to learn the optional short forms, which are in parentheses. They are commonly used.

ὅστις, ἥτις, ὅ τι — *whoever, whatever, whichever*

M		F		N	
ὅστις		ἥτις		ὅ τι	
ὅντινα		ἥντινα		ὅ τι	
οὗτινος	(ὅτου)	ἧστινος		οὗτινος	(ὅτου)
ᾧτινι	(ὅτῳ)	ᾗτινι		ᾧτινι	(ὅτῳ)
οἵτινες		αἵτινες		ἅτινα	(ἅττα)
οὕστινας		ἅστινας		ἅτινα	(ἅττα)
ὧντινων	(ὅτων)	ὧντινων		ὧντινων	(ὅτων)
οἷστισι(ν)	(ὅτοις)	αἷστισι(ν)		οἷστισι(ν)	(ὅτοις)

✦ ὅ τι καλὸν φίλον αἰεί.   Euripides, *Bacchae* v. 881

▶ **Exercise α:** Translate the underlined. Give the short forms as well as the long forms when you can.

1. <u>Whoever</u> she is, she is beautiful.   2. <u>Whomever</u> (pl. fem.) you send, we will welcome.
3. <u>Whatever</u> books you see you may have.   4. Give the letter <u>to whomever</u> (pl.) you run into (ἐντυγχάνω).

ὅστις, ἥτις, ὅ τι IN INDIRECT QUESTIONS

ὅστις, ἥτις, ὅ τι can also be used in indirect questions. Using the direct interrogative seems to make the question more vivid.

Direct	Indirect		
τίς ἔρχεται;	ἐρωτᾷς τίς ἔρχεται.	*You ask who is coming.*	(Vivid)
Who is coming?	ἐρωτᾷς ὅστις ἔρχεται.	*You ask who(ever) is coming.*	(Less vivid)

▶ **Exercise β:** Translate the underlined words. Give all possibilities and include alternate forms.
1. I know <u>who</u> is coming.   2. They wonder <u>what</u> gifts she will bring.   3. You asked <u>which</u> poets she loved best.
4. He asked <u>whose</u> homes had been robbed.   5. I ask you for <u>which</u> goddesses are you picking flowers?

PERFECT AS PRESENT

Often it is the enduring effect that counts far more than the past event that produced it. Then we have a perfect that can best be translated as a present. For certain verbs the perfect is regularly used this way:

τέθνηκα	*I am dead (have died and therefore am dead)*	θνῄσκω	*die*
ἔγνωκα	*I know (have recognised and therefore know)*	γιγνώσκω	*know*
οἶδα	*I know (have seen and therefore know)*	ὁράω	*see*
ἕστηκα	*I stand (have stood and therefore am standing)*	ἵστημι	*stand*
πέποιθα	*I trust (have put my trust in and therefore trust)*	πείθω	*persuade*
πέφυκα	*I am by nature (have become and therefore am by nature)*	φύω	*grow*
	(from φύω = *to grow, be by nature*)		

If you want to be really careful in your translationese, translate these the full way:

τέθνηκα   "*I (have died and therefore) am dead*," rather than simply "*I am dead.*"

There can be a perfect as present for -ομαι verbs also.

κέκτημαι	*I own (have acquired and therefore own)*	κτάομαι	*acquire*
μέμνημαι	*I remember (have recalled and therefore remember)*	μίμνήσκω	*remind*

▶ **Exercise γ:** Translate fully: 1. πεφύκασι 3. ἐγνωκέναι 5. ἑστηκυῖαι
2. ἐπεποίθη 4. κεκτημένος 6. τεθνηκώς

οἶδα (PERFECT of ὁράω)

οἶδα *I have seen and therefore I know*

```
        PERFECT  I know
     οἶδα          ἴσμεν
     οἶσθα         ἴστε
     οἶδε(ν)       ἴσασι(ν)

        PLUPERFECT  I knew
     ᾔδη           ᾖσμεν
     ᾔδησθα        ᾖστε
     ᾔδει(ν)       ᾖσαν

     INFINITIVE    εἰδέναι

     PARTICIPLE    εἰδώς, υῖα, ός
```

The verb ὁράω has a normal -κα perfect ἑώρακα *I have seen*, based on the stem ὁρα.
It also has a perfect οἶδα, based on the stem ἰδ (from the verb that gave the aorist εἶδον).

The perfect stem shows up three ways: as οἶδ-, εἰδ-, and ἰδ-. ἰδ- is the original root behind ἴστε, ἴσασι(ν)
and, by analogy, ἴσμεν.

The original digamma can be seen in the Sanskrit *veda = I know* = cognate of Greek οἶδα. (From this comes
the term Vedas, referring to the scriptures of India.)

▶ **Exercise δ:** Translate: 1. οἶσθα 2. εἰδότες 3. ἴσασι 4. εἰδέναι 5. ἴσμεν 6. εἶδε 7. ᾔδησθα 8. εἰδότα
9. Explain the difference between ᾖσαν and ἦσαν.

Classwork: ✦✦ Read **Famous saying #7**, Thesauros p. 232.

Classwork: Learn some lines of a poem by Mimnermus.

✦

τίς δὲ βίος, τί δὲ τερπνὸν ἄτερ χρυσῆς Ἀφροδίτης; τεθναίην, ὅτε μοι μηκέτι ταῦτα μέλοι.

And what is life, what is pleasure,
without golden Aphrodite?
May I be dead when these things
are no longer a concern for me.

ἔργα   ~Memorize the lines of the poems above.
~Write out the forms of ὅστις, ἥτις, ὅ τι including optional forms twice. Memorize.
~Go back to "An Old Man's Advice" (Part 2) p. 157 and parse every verb, infinitive, and
participle in the second paragraph except κληροῦσθαι. Explain each stem.

On Parsing

From now on write Indicative or Subjunctive to show Mood. Give the most specific
information possible: tense for the Indicative, aspect for the Subjunctive. Give person, too.

Lesson 39. The Optative

Human beings spend a lot of time speculating about possibilities. In the Greek language there is a special mood for what is possible, remote, potential. This is the optative, the third of the four moods of the Greek verb. It is used in wishes ("*if only*," "*would that*"), for future possibilities ("*might*"), and for conditions ("*would*").

THE OPTATIVE: FORMS

The optative has an iota after the connecting vowel, giving optative verbs forms their characteristic οι or αι sound.

⁻οιμι	⁻οιμεν
⁻οις	⁻οιτε
⁻οι	⁻οιεν

⁻αιμι	⁻αιμεν
⁻αις / ⁻ειας	⁻αιτε
⁻αι / ⁻ειε(ν)	⁻αιεν / ⁻ειαν

Note: The aorist -αι forms are easier to remember. The optional -ει forms are more common, and so are used in the paradigm.

CONTINUOUS	FUTURE	ε/o AORIST	α-AORIST

INDICATIVE

CONTINUOUS	FUTURE	ε/o AORIST	α-AORIST
λείπω λείπομεν λείπεις λείπετε λείπει λείπουσι(ν) ἔλειπον ἐλείπομεν ἔλειπες ἐλείπετε ἔλειπεν ἔλειπον	λείψω λείψομεν λείψεις λείψετε λείψει λείψουσι(ν)	ἔλιπον ἐλίπομεν ἔλιπες ἐλίπετε ἔλιπε(ν) ἔλιπον	ἔπαυσα ἐπαύσαμεν ἔπαυσας ἐπαύσατε ἔπαυσε(ν) ἔπαυσαν

SUBJUNCTIVE

CONTINUOUS	FUTURE	ε/o AORIST	α-AORIST
λείπω λείπωμεν λείπῃς λείπητε λείπῃ λείπωσι(ν)	- - -	λίπω λίπωμεν λίπῃς λίπητε λίπῃ λίπωσι(ν)	παύσω παύσωμεν παύσῃς παύσητε παύσῃ παύσωσι(ν)

OPTATIVE

CONTINUOUS	FUTURE	ε/o AORIST	α-AORIST
λείποιμι λείποιμεν λείποις λείποιτε λείποι λείποιεν	λείψοιμι λείψοιμεν λείψοις λείψοιτε λείψοι λείψοιεν	λίποιμι λίποιμεν λίποις λίποιτε λίποι λίποιεν	παύσαιμι παύσαιμεν παύσειας παύσαιτε παύσειε(ν) παύσειαν

INFINITIVE

CONTINUOUS	FUTURE	ε/o AORIST	α-AORIST
λείπειν	λείψειν	λιπεῖν	παῦσαι

PARTICIPLE

CONTINUOUS	FUTURE	ε/o AORIST	α-AORIST
λείπων,ουσα,ον	λείψων,ουσα,ον	λιπών,οῦσα,όν	παύσας,ασα,αν

For the purpose of accent, a final οι and αι in the **optative** count as **long**. Note accent on λείποι, λείποις, παῦσαι, and παύσαις.

The difference between the continuous and aorist optative is one of aspect only--ongoing versus snapshot. (A future optative exists only because of patterns in indirect discourse, to be learned soon.)

▶ **Exercise α:**   1. λίποι   3. λείποιεν   5. λείψοιμι   7. λείποις   9. παύσειαν
   Parse the optatives: 2. παύσειεν   4. παύσοιεν   6. παύσοις   8. παύσαις   10. παύσοιτε

OPTATIVE OF WISH	Alone or with **εἴθε** or **εἰ γάρ**. The negative is μή. Translate *may, would that, if only!*

τίκτοι
εἴθε τίκτοι
εἰ γὰρ τίκτοι

All three mean the same thing:
May (s)he be giving birth / give birth (repeatedly)*!*
Would that (s)he would . . . / If only (s)he would . . .

μὴ ἔλθοι   *May he / would that he not come* (once)*! If only he would not come* (once)*!*

τεθναίην in the poem by Mimnermus is an optative of wish on a special perfect stem.

POTENTIAL OPTATIVE	With **ἄν**. The negative is οὐ. Translate *might, may, could, would.*

ἔλθοιεν ἄν.

They might / may / could come (once).
They would come (once) (with some condition understood).

οὐκ ἄν δακρύοιεν.

They might / may / could / would not be crying.

▌ **Exercise β:** Translate the following. Be sure to show aspect in your translation:

1. εἴθε λείποι.   2. λίποιμεν ἄν.   3. μὴ θάνοιεν.   4. εἰ γὰρ μανθάνοις.   5. οὐ παύσειαν ἄν τὴν μάχην.
6. May she send the gifts (once).   7. If only they would not keep stealing.   8. We might not be writing.

AS SUBORDINATE VERB

OPTATIVE IN PAST SEQUENCE	When main verb is past tense. Negative is unchanged.

After an introductory **main verb in the past tense**, a subordinate verb in the subjunctive (purpose, fear) may be switched into the **optative**, keeping the **same stem.** This is called the optative in *secondary sequence.*

τοῦτο ποιῶ ἵνα μὴ ἔλθῃ.   *I do this so that he should not come / not come* (once).

τοῦτο ἐποίησα ἵνα μὴ ἔλθῃ.   *I did this so that he should not come / not come* (once).
τοῦτο ἐποίησα ἵνα μὴ ἔλθοι.   *I did this so that he would not come* (once). [less vivid?]

OPTATIVE IN OPTATIVE SEQUENCE	When main verb is optative Negative is unchanged

After an introductory **main verb in the optative**, a subordinate verb may be switched into the **optative**, keeping the **same stem.**

(When a subordinate verb becomes optative to match an optative main verb, this is called **assimilation**.)

ἄγει φίλους οὓς οὐ γιγνώσκεις.   *She is leading friends whom you do not know.*

ἄγοι φίλους οὓς οὐ γιγνώσκεις.   Both mean:
ἄγοι φίλους οὓς οὐ γιγνώσκοις.   *May she lead / be leading friends whom you do not know.*

▌ **Exercise γ:**   Translate the following.
1. πέμψειας ταῦτα ἃ ἐθέλοιμι ὁρᾶν.   3. ἀνεγίγνωσκε ἵνα μανθάνοι τι.   5. ἐφοβεῖτο μὴ πέσοις.
2. ἦλθον ὅπως σώσειαν τοὺς παῖδας.   4. οἰμώξειαν ὅτε ἴδοι τὸν τεθνεῶτα βασιλέα.

▌ **Exercise δ:** Translate the following, using optative forms whenever possible.
1. I am reading so that I may learn (once) the story.   4. She was afraid (ἐφοβεῖτο) lest they burst into tears.
2. I was reading so that I might be learning the story.   5. May she save (once) the poet whom she sees (βλέπω).
3. She was afraid (ἐφοβεῖτο) lest they keep crying.   6. May she save (once) the poet whom she saw (βλέπω).

✦✦ Read **Graveyard #34-36, Famous Sayings #8**, and **Diogenes #14,** Thesauros pp. 231, 232, 235.

ἔργα   ~Write out the optative forms of βάλλω and βασιλεύω. Memorize.
           ~Read and translate Part 3 of "An Old Man's Advice." Learn the vocabulary.
             Circle and explain all optatives.

"ὦ πάτερ," εἶπεν ὁ Ζυρήν· "ὁ βασιλεὺς ἐκέλευσέ μ' εἰσελθεῖν
εἰς τὴν θάλατταν κύλικα χρυσῆν ζητήσοντα οὗ ἐπεθύμησεν.   2~
πάντες δὲ οἳ τοῦτο ἐποίουν κακὰ πεπόνθασιν--τεθνᾶσι γὰρ--   **3**
καὶ οἶδα ὅτι πείσομαι τὸ αὐτό. καὶ φοβοῦμαι μὴ μετὰ ταῦτα
εὑρών σε ἐν τούτῳ τῷ σάκκῳ ὁ βασιλεὺς ἀποκτείνῃ "   5~

ὁ δὲ πατὴρ εἶπεν· "ὦ ἄνδρες μῶροι, μάτην (in vain) τέθνατε;
εἴθε μὴ ἀποθάνοιεν πλείονες. εἰ γὰρ μηκέτι ἄλλον ἄνδρα   7
πέμψειεν ὁ βασιλεὺς εἰς τὴν θάλατταν, ὦ υἱέ, λάβοις ἃ
ἐθέλοις λαβεῖν· οὐδὲν ῥᾷον τούτου. ἓν χρή σ' εἰδέναι ὥστε
πράττειν σοφίᾳ. τόδε ἴσθι· ὃ ἑώρακας ἐν τῇ θαλάττῃ οὐκ   10
ἦν κύλιξ ἀλλὰ εἰκὼν (image) κύλικος ὥσπερ ἐν κατόπτρῳ
(mirror). ἀνάβλεπε νῦν πρὸς τήνδε τὴν πέτραν. ἐπ' ἄκρας
τῆς πέτρας ἐστὶν ἡ κύλιξ ἣν ὁ βασιλεὺς τοσοῦτον ἐπιθυμεῖ
κεκτῆσθαι. ταῦτα εἰδώς, λαβὲ αὐτήν.   14

ὁ δὲ Ζυρὴν ἀναβλέψας εἶπεν· "ὦ πάτερ, οὐκ ἔστιν ἀνὴρ
ὅστις ἂν ἔχοι τὴν πέτραν ἀναβῆναι. ὀρθία (too steep) γάρ
ἐστιν ἀναβῆναι." ὁ δὲ ἀπεκρίνατο· "λάβοις ἂν τὴν κύλικα
ἄνευ τοῦ τὴν πέτραν τήνδε ἀναβῆναι. μένε ὑπὸ (below) τῇ
πέτρᾳ· καὶ ὄψει πολλοὺς κύνας ἐπ' ἄκραν τὴν πέτραν
ἐρχομένους. βάλλε πέτρους ὥστε φοβεῖν (frighten) αὐτούς.   20
οἱ δὲ κύνες φεύξονται τοὺς πέτρους καὶ τὴν κύλικα
λακτιοῦσιν (will kick) ἀπὸ τῆς πέτρας. σὺ δέ, μείνας κάτω,
λάβοις ἂν αὐτὴν καὶ τῷ βασιλεῖ ἐνέγκοις ἄν."

ταῦτα ἐποίησεν ὁ Ζυρήν. τῷ δὲ βασιλεῖ ἐρωτήσαντι· "πῶς   24
ηὗρες αὐτήν;" ἀπεκρίνατο ὧδε· "ἡ κύλιξ ἦν ἐπ' ἄκρᾳ τῇ
πέτρᾳ. ὃ ἐν τῇ θαλάττῃ ὡρῶμεν ἦν εἰκὼν (image) ὥσπερ ἐν
κατόπτρῳ (mirror)." ὁ δὲ ἠρώτησεν· "τίς σοι ταῦτα ἔδειξεν;"   27
ὁ δὲ Ζυρὴν ἔφη· "οὐδεὶς ἔδειξεν· αὐτὸς δι' ἐμαυτοῦ ηὗρον."

2~   ἐπεθύμησεν - How can you translate this to show that it is an ingressive aorist?

3

> ### Conative Imperfect
>
> ἐποίουν must be translated "*were trying to do*," not "*were doing*," as the
> context shows. (The men did not succeed.) This is called a *conative* imperfect,
> from the Latin *conor = try.*

4   πάσχω, πείσομαι, ἔπαθον, πέπονθα
5~   Which is a better choice of aspect for ἀποκτείνῃ? (The form could be continouous or aorist.)
7   εἴθε, εἰ γάρ + optative - used for wishes "*if only / would that ...*"
     ῥᾴων, ῥᾷον - easier (comparative of ῥάδιος,α,ον)
10   ἡ σοφία - wisdom (from σοφός)
     ἴσθι - *Know! you* (sing.) command of οἶδα
     ἡ πέτρα - cliff
     ἄκρος, α, ον - topmost, inmost, outermost; used in predicate position to mean
          at the tip, furthest point, end (see p. 151)   --> acrophobia, Acropolis
11   τοσοῦτος, τοσαύτη, τοσοῦτο or τοσοῦτον - so large, so great;
          neuter as adverbial. acc. - so much, to such an extent
     ὅστις, ἥτις, ὅ τι - whoever, whichever (indefinite relative)
20   ὁ πέτρος = stone, rock   --> Peter, petrify
27   δείκνυμι, δείξω, ἔδειξα
     διά + gen. - through, by (of agent); as we say in English, *by myself*

Lesson 40. The Series: Asking, Shrugging, Relating and Pointing
πόλις, βασιλεύς

1. ASKING Direct Interrogative	2. SHRUG-WORD Indefinite (enclitic)	3. RELATING Relative	4. Indirect Interrogative OR Indefinite Relative	5. POINTING Demonstrative
τίς τί who? what?	τις, τι someone, something	ὅς, ἥ, ὅ who, which	ὅστις, ἥτις, ὅ τι who(ever)? what(ever)? whoever, whatever	οὗτος this ὅδε this here ἐκεῖνος that
πότε when?	ποτε sometime	ὅτε when	ὁπότε when(ever)? whenever	τότε then
πῶς how?	πως somehow	ὡς as, how	ὅπως how(ever)? as, however	οὕτως thus ὧδε thus ἐκείνως that way
ποῦ where?	που somewhere	οὗ where	ὅπου where(ever)? wherever	ἐνταῦθα here ἐκεῖ there
ποῖ to where?	ποι to somewhere	οἷ whither	ὅποι to where(ever)? to wherever	ἐνταῦθα to here ἐκεῖσε to there
πόθεν from where?	ποθεν from somewhere	ὅθεν from where	ὁπόθεν from where(ever)? from wherever	ἐντεῦθεν from here ἐκεῖθεν from there
πόσος, η, ον how much? how many?	ποσος, η, ον of some quantity	ὅσος, η, ον as much as, as many as	ὁπόσος, η, ον how(ever) much or many? however much or many	τόσος, η, ον τοσοῦτος, η, ον so much, so many
ποῖος, α, ον of what sort?	ποιος, α, ον of some sort	οἷος, α, ον of such a sort as	ὁποῖος, α, ον of what(ever) sort? of whatever sort	τοῖος, α, ον τοιοῦτος, η, ον of such sort

There is a patterned series in Greek. Notice how regular the first four columns are.

    (1) The **direct interrogative** (ASKING) word begins with π.
    (2) The **indefinite** (SHRUG) word begins with π and is **enclitic.**
    (3) The **relative** (RELATING) word begins with an *h* sound.
    (4) The **indefinite relative** or **indefinite interrogative** word begins with *ὁ* + π.
    (5) The **demonstrative** (POINTING) word sometimes begins with τ.

☜☞ The English pattern is similar but not so full as the Greek: An asking word often begins with *wh--* when? where? what? who?--while the corresponding pointing word often begins with *th--then, there, that.*

INDEFINITE RELATIVE / INDIRECT INTERROGATIVE

The words in column **(4)** can be used two ways: either as an indefinite relative, which both shrugs (2) and relates (3) at the same time OR as an indirect interrogative, which asks a question (1) but one that is embedded in another statement.

✍✍ If it seems odd that the same word should have two functions, consider English, which uses the same words for (1), (3), and (4) = indirect interrogative.

  (1) *Who came?*   **(3)** *The boy **who** came is my son.*   **(4)** *I asked **who** came.*

Translationese: You can distinguish the two functions of column (4) in translationese by using *whoever* for the indefinite relative and *who(ever)* for the indirect interrogative:

ὅστις ἦλθεν μέγας ἦν. **Whoever** *came was big.* ἐρωτᾷ ὅστις ἦλθεν. *He asks **who(ever)** came.*

A direct question uses (1) the direct interrogative. An indirect question (embedded in some other statement) uses (4) an **indirect interrogative** (as we saw earlier for ὅστις p. 158). But for vividness the **direct interrogative** (1) may be used.

πότε ἦλθεν;	*When did he come?*
ἐρωτᾷς ὁπότε ἦλθεν.	*You ask when he came / when(ever) he came.*
ἐρωτᾷς πότε ἦλθεν.	*You ask when he came / when did he come.* (Vivid)

▶ **Exercise α:** Give the function (asking, shrugging, etc.) of the underlined words. (Consult chart on p. 163.)

1. Where are we? Who are you? From where do you come? How and when did we get here? To where are you bringing us?   2. He comes from somewhere or other and he will go whenever and however he wants to.   3. How many and what sort of apples did you get? We will buy however many and whatever sort you bring us. 4. Somewhere there is a city where she will find whatever she desires. Whenever she finds it, she will go there.

▶ **Exercise β:** Translate the sentences in two ways:
1. I ask where she is going. 2. I ask how many apples you will bring. 3. I ask what kind of books they like.

πόλις, βασιλεύς

	ἡ **πόλις** *city, polis*		ὁ **βασιλεύς** *king*	
nom.	ἡ	πόλις	ὁ	βασιλεύς
acc.	τὴν	πόλιν	τὸν	βασιλέα
gen.	τῆς	πόλεως	τοῦ	βασιλέως
dat.	τῇ	πόλει	τῷ	βασιλεῖ
nom.	αἱ	πόλεις	οἱ	βασιλεῖς
acc.	τὰς	πόλεις	τοὺς	βασιλέας
gen.	τῶν	πόλεων	τῶν	βασιλέων
dat.	ταῖς	πόλεσι(ν)	τοῖς	βασιλεῦσι(ν)

Learn to recognize the forms when you see them; you need not be able to write them. There are many important words that follow the πόλις pattern.

πόλις is a Third Group ι-stem noun. There are many oddities in the πόλις pattern. Most important to notice is the -ιν accusative singular. (The genitive singular was originally πόλη-ος. A reversal occurred, with the long-short vowel pair [η-ο] changing to short-long [ε-ω]. It is because of this that the accent is on the third syllable back, even though the last syllable is long.) ✂✂ **Ambiguity Alert:** There is a single form for the nominative and accusative plural, as with ἀληθεῖς.

By putting -σις on a verb stem, one can make an abstract noun, which follows the πόλις pattern:

ἡ γένεσις	*birth*	(from γεν- of γίγνομαι = *become*)
ἡ φύσις	*nature*, etc.	(from φυ- of φύω = *grow*)
ἡ μίμησις	*imitation, mimesis*	(from μιμέομαι = *I imitate*)

βασιλεύς is a Third Group ευ-stem noun. βασιλεύς has its distinctive pattern. (The genitive was originally βασίληϝος. The ϝ dropped out, and the long-short η-ο switched to short-long ε-ω., as happened with πόλεως.)

Classwork: ✦✦   Read **Graveyard #30, Famous Sayings #9,** and **Diogenes #9,** Thesauros
pp. 230, 232-233, and 234.

ἔργα   ~Write out three times the paradigms of πόλις and βασιλεύς.
        ~Read and translate "An Old Man's Advice" (Part 4). Learn the vocabulary.
          Circle the eight words that belong on the chart on p. 163. Identify function:
            asking, shrugging, relating, indefinite relative, indirect interrogative, or pointing.

καὶ αὖθις ἐπορεύοντο οἱ ἄνθρωποι. καὶ μετὰ χρόνον εἰς τόπον
ἀφίκοντο οὗ οὐκ ἦν ὕδωρ. οἱ δὲ ἄνθρωποι πάντες καὶ πάντα
τὰ πρόβατα (herds) ἐβούλοντο πίνειν, ἀλλ' οὐδεὶς ἐδύνατο
εὑρεῖν ὕδωρ. τέλος δὲ τῇ τετάρτῃ ἡμέρᾳ ὁ Ζυρὴν ἀπορῶν ἦλθε
πρὸς τὸν σάκκον καὶ τάδε εἶπεν· "ὦ πάτερ, οὐκ ἔστιν ὕδωρ.   5
πάντες ἀποθανοῦνται ἡμερῶν οὐ πολλῶν."

ὁ δὲ πατὴρ ἠρώτησεν· "ἆρ' ἔλαθόν σε οἱ ἵπποι εἰδότες εὑρίσκειν   7
ὕδωρ; οὐκ ἐμὲ ἔλαθον. τάδε οὖν κελεύω σε ποιεῖν· ἀφιέναι
ἵππον νέον καὶ ἕπεσθαι αὐτῷ ὅποι ἂν βαίνῃ. καὶ ὅπου ἂν   9
ὀσφραίνηται (he should sniff at) τὴν γῆν ἐνταῦθα ὀρύξας ὕδωρ
εὑρήσεις." ταῦτα δὲ ποιήσας, ὁ Ζυρὴν ὕδωρ ηὗρεν.   τῷ δὲ
βασιλεῖ ἐρωτήσαντι ὅπως ὕδωρ ηὗρεν, ἀπεκρίνατο· "σήμασιν."   12

καὶ αὖθις ἐπορεύοντο. καὶ νυκτί τινι οὕτω σφόδρα ὗε (it was
raining) ὥστε ἀποσβεννύναι (quench) τὸ πῦρ αὐτῶν. ὁ δὲ
βασιλεύς, ἀναβλέπων πρὸς ὄρος πῦρ εἶδεν ἐπ' ἄκρῳ τῷ ὄρει.   15
καὶ ἔπεμψεν ἄνδρα, τάδε λέγων· " ὅστις ἂν τόδε τὸ ὄρος
ἀναβὰς ἀπενέγκῃ ἡμῖν πῦρ, δώρων ἄξιον νομιῶ." ὁ ἀνὴρ
ἀνέβη τὸ ὄρος ζητήσων τὸ πῦρ. καὶ τὸ πῦρ εὑρὼν ἔλαβε ξύλον
(log) μέγαν ἐκ τοῦ πυρὸς καὶ κατέβαινε φέρων τὸν ξύλον (log).
ἀλλ' ἐν ᾧ κατέβαινε οὕτω σφοδρὰ ὗε (it was raining) ὥστε τὸ   20
ὕδωρ τὸ πῖπτον ἀπέσβεσε (quenched) τὸ πῦρ.

πῦρ δὲ οὐκ ἀποφέροντι ὁ βασιλεὺς εἶπεν αὐτῷ τάδε· "μῶρός εἶ,
ὃς πῦρ οὐκ ἀπήνεγκες ἡμῖν." καὶ πᾶσι τοῖς ἀνδράσιν εἶπε τάδε·   23
"ὅστις ἂν πῦρ ἀπενέγκῃ δῶρα ἕξει. ἀλλὰ ὅστις ἂν πῦρ μὴ
ἀπενέγκῃ, τοῦτον ἀποκτενοῦμαι (I shall have this one killed)."   25
καὶ ἄλλον ἔπεμψε καὶ ἔτι ἄλλον, καὶ ἀεὶ τὸ αὐτὸ ἐγίγνετο.

4   ἀπορέω - be at a loss, be without a πόρος = means (of crossing a river)
7   λανθάνω, λήσω, ἔλαθον, λέληθα - escape notice + supplementary participle

7

Supplementary Participle
A circumstantial participle that goes especially closely with the verb is called a
supplementary participle. Certain verbs take a supplementary participle and
might seem incomplete without one: τυγχάνω, λανθάνω, and ἥδομαι *enjoy*

τυγχάνει ὢν σοφός.   *He **happens to be** wise.*
ἥδομαι πίνουσα οἶνον.   *I **enjoy drinking** wine.*
ἔλαθε με ἵππον κλέπτων.   *I did not notice he was stealing a horse.*
                            Literally, *He **escaped my notice** stealing a horse.*

εἰδότες - see box on p. 159
ἵημι - let forth, release, let go
ἀφίημι - send forth, send away
9   ἕπομαι, ἕψομαι, ἑσπόμην - follow + dative
     ὅποι - to wherever   (end of motion) related to ποῖ = to where?
     ὅπου - wherever   (place where)   related to ποῦ = where?
     ἐνταῦθα - here, in this place; also = to here, to this place, hither
     ὀρύττω, ὀρύξω, ὤρυξα - dig
12   ὅπως - how Notice ὅπως is used indirectly versus πῶς, used in direct questions
     τὸ πῦρ, gen. πυρός <--> fire   --> pyre, pyromaniac, pyrotechnics
15   τὸ ὄρος - mountain

23

Causal ὅς, ἥ, ὅ
The relative can have causal force, as here: not just "who" but "since you"

Lesson 41. Optative of εἰμί; Periphrastic Perfect (Subjunctive and Optative) Optative in Conditions and Indirect Discourse

OPTATIVE OF εἰμί

εἴην	εἶμεν
εἴης	εἶτε
εἴη	εἶεν

Learn these forms. They are different from the others. By learning them you will be preparing to learn contract optatives as well as some passive optative forms.

▶ **Exercise α:** Translate:
1. εἴην εὐδαίμων.
2. εἶεν ἂν τυφλοί.
3. εἴθε μὴ εἶμεν τυφλοί.
4. εἰ γὰρ εἶτε ἀγαθαί.
4. If only he might not be old!
5. They might be more useful.

PERIPHRASTIC PERFECT (SUBJUNCTIVE AND OPTATIVE)

ACTIVE VOICE

CONTINUOUS	FUTURE	AORIST	PERFECT

Why did you not learn the entire perfect column all at once? Because some forms (marked by crosses above) are made in combination and to learn them you need to know the forms of εἰμί. These forms are rare and can be punted; they are included here for the sake of completeness.

PERFECT SUBJUNCTIVE

ὦ τεθνεώς	ὦμεν τεθνεότες
ᾖς τεθνεώς	ἦτε τεθνεότες
ᾖ τεθνεώς	ὦσι(ν) τεθνεότες

PERFECT OPTATIVE

εἴην τεθνεώς	εἶμεν τεθνεότες
εἴης τεθνεώς	εἶτε τεθνεότες
εἴη τεθνεώς	εἶεν τεθνεότες

φοβεῖται μὴ τεθνυῖα ᾖ.
ἐφοβεῖτο μὴ τεθνυῖα ᾖ / εἴη.

He fears lest she should be dead = have died
He was afraid lest she should / would be dead
= have died.

The perfect subjunctive and the perfect optative are **periphrastic** (from περί "around" and φράσις "speech"). That is, they are made in a "roundabout" way--by combining already known forms--the subjunctive or optative of εἰμί + the perfect participle (nom. sing. or pl.). ✍✍ English is full of periphrastic verb forms, which makes the English verb easy to learn. In English, one learns the three principal parts (go / went / gone) and then a host of combinations that work for every single set of three: *will go, have gone, will have gone, had gone*, etc.

▶ **Exercise β:** Translate:
1. ἔπεμψα δῶρα ὑμῖν ἵνα πεποιθυῖαι εἶτέ μοι.
2. ἀναγιγνώσκει ὅπως πολλὰ εἰδὼς ᾖ.
3. φοβεῖται μὴ οἱ στρατιῶται πεπωκότες ὦσιν.
4. ἐφοβεῖτο μὴ οἱ στρατιῶται πεπωκότες εἶεν.

OPTATIVE IN CONDITIONS

PAST GENERAL CONDITION: εἰ + **optative** in the *if* clause,
imperfect indicative (or equivalent) in the *then* clause

εἰ ἔλθοιεν, ἐδάκρυες. *If they would come* (=*used to come*), *you used to cry.*

FUTURE LESS VIVID CONDITION εἰ + **optative** in the *if* clause,
optative + ἄν in the *then* clause

εἰ ἔλθοιεν, δακρύοις ἄν. *If they would come* (= *were to come*), *you would cry.*

We can call this a *would / would* condition. (It has traditionally been called a *should / would* condition.) The main verb is simply the potential optative (already learned), with the condition spelled out in the *if* clause.

The normal negative rule for conditions still holds: μή negates an *if* clause, οὐ a *then* clause.

▶ **Exercise γ:** Translate:
1. εἰ κελεύσειε ταῦτα, ἐποίουν.
2. εἰ κελεύσειε ταῦτα, ποιήσαιμι ἄν.
3. εἰ οἱ σύμβουλοι λέγοιεν, ὁ βασιλεὺς ἤκουεν.
4. εἰ λίποιμεν, ὁ δοῦλος μένοι ἄν.

OPTATIVE IN INDIRECT DISCOURSE

This is just a particular application of the optative in a past tense sequence. When the main verb of thinking, saying, or perceiving is in the **past tense**, the verb in indirect discourse may be given in the optative. The stem remains the same.

Only because of indirect discourse is there a **future optative.** Normally the optative shows aspect only, as does the subjunctive. But in indirect discourse it represents the indicative, which shows tense, and therefore has a future set of forms (shown in the box below).

NON-PAST REPORT (Present, Future, Perfect)

λέγω, ἐρῶ, εἴρηκα ὅτι λείπει
λέγω, ἐρῶ, εἴρηκα ὅτι ἔλειπεν
λέγω, ἐρῶ, εἴρηκα ὅτι **λείψει**
λέγω, ἐρῶ, εἴρηκα ὅτι ἔλιπεν
λέγω, ἐρῶ, εἴρηκα ὅτι λέλοιπεν
λέγω, ἐρῶ, εἴρηκα ὅτι ἐλέλοιπεν

PAST REPORT (Imperfect, Aorist, Pluperfect)

ἔλεγον, εἶπον, εἰρήκη ὅτι λείπει / λείποι
ἔλεγον, εἶπον, εἰρήκη ὅτι ἔλειπεν / λείποι
ἔλεγον, εἶπον, εἰρήκη ὅτι **λείψει / λείψοι**
ἔλεγον, εἶπον, εἰρήκη ὅτι ἔλιπεν / λίποι
ἔλεγον, εἶπον, εἰρήκη ὅτι λέλοιπεν / εἴη λελοιπώς
ἔλεγον, εἶπον, εἰρήκη ὅτι ἐλέλοιπεν / εἴη λελοιπώς

▶ **Exercise δ:** Change the direct statements (in bold) into indirect statements, using the verbs listed. Be sure to give all possibilities.
1. **γράψουσιν.** λέγω ὅτι, εἶπον ὅτι
2. **οἰκτίρομεν.** εἴρηκα ὅτι, εἰρήκη ὅτι
3. **ἔμαθεν.** εἰρήκη ὅτι, ἔλεγον ὅτι.
4. **πεπαύκατε.** ἔλεγον ὅτι, ἐρῶ ὅτι.

Classwork: ✦✦ Read **Diogenes #10,** Thesauros p. 234.

On the following page is a new poem by Archilochus along with all the poems we have learned so far. Review the poems and learn the new one, which will fix several points of grammar indelibly in your mind.

See ✦✦ **Famous Saying #17** for the normal Greek attitude about not dropping your weapon, Thesauros p. 233. Notice how Archilochus thumbs his nose at group values.

ἔργα   ~Write the optative of εἰμί three times. Memorize.
~Form the perfect subjunctive and optative for παύω and γράφω.
~Memorize the poem by Archilochus.

Anacreontic

χαλεπὸν τὸ μὴ φιλῆσαι·
χαλεπὸν δὲ καὶ φιλῆσαι·
χαλεπώτερον δὲ πάντων
ἀποτυγχάνειν φιλοῦντα.

Sappho

οἱ μὲν ἰππήων στρότον οἱ δὲ πέσδων
οἱ δὲ νάων φαῖσ' ἐπὶ γᾶν μέλαιναν
ἔμμεναι κάλλιστον· ἔγω δὲ κῆν' ὅτ-
                    τω τις ἔραται.

Sappho (?)

Δέδυκε μὲν ἁ σελάννα
καὶ Πλειαδες μέσαι δή·
νύκτος δὲ παρέρχετ' ὥρα·
ἔγω δὲ μόνα κατεύδω.

Anacreontic

Μακαρίζομέν σε, τέττιξ,
ὅτε δενδρέων ἐπ' ἄκρων
ὀλίγην δρόσον πεπωκὼς
βασιλεὺς ὅπως ἀείδεις.

Mimnermus

τίς δὲ βίος, τί δὲ τερπνὸν ἄτερ χρυσῆς Ἀφροδίτης;
τεθναίην, ὅτε μοι μηκέτι ταῦτα μέλοι.

Archilochus

ἀσπίδι μὲν Σαΐων τις ἀγάλλεται ἣν παρὰ θάμνῳ
ἔντος ἀμώμητον κάλλιπον οὐκ ἐθέλων.
αὐτὸν δ' ἐξεσάωσα. τί μοι μέλει ἀσπὶς ἐκείνη;
ἐρρέτω· ἐξαῦθις κτήσομαι οὐ κακίω.

Some Saian is strutting with a shield which I left behind,
Blameless weapon, near a bush--not willingly.
But I saved myself. As for that shield,
The hell with it. I'll get (another) again no worse.

τὰ ἔντεα is used in the plural for weapons, as *arms* in English. Archilochus playfully
uses the singular, *arm*!
ἔρρομαι - literally, *go wandering*
κακίω is what form?

Lesson 42. The Imperative; Imperative of εἰμί

THE ACTIVE IMPERATIVE: CONTINUOUS AND AORIST

All that remains of the Active paradigm for you to learn is the imperative--the command mood. The imperative has forms only for the second person (*you*) and third (*he, she, it* / *they*). (To make a command in the first person, the hortatory subjunctive is used.)

The imperative shows aspect, not tense. There is no future imperative. (You could say that an imperative always refers to future time, by its nature.)

CONTINUOUS IMPERATIVE

Second pers. | λεῖπε λείπετε | *Be leaving!*
Third pers. | λειπέτω λειπόντων | *Let* him / her / it be leaving!*
              | | *Let* them be leaving!*

⚹⚹ Ambiguity Alert: The *you* (pl.) continuous imperative = the *you* (pl.) present.
The *they* continuous imperative = the gen. pl. masc./neut. participle.

ε/ο AORIST IMPERATIVE

λίπε λίπετε	*Leave (once)!*
λιπέτω λιπόντων	*Let* him/her/it leave once)!*
	Let* them leave (once)!

α-AORIST IMPERATIVE

παῦσον παύσατε	*Stop (once)!*
παυσάτω παυσάντων	*Let* him/her/it stop!*
	Let* them stop! (once)

The verb accent is recessive as usual--except for the strong aorist active imperatives of five important verbs: εἰπέ, ἐλθέ, εὑρέ, ἰδέ, and λαβέ.

You have learned some imperative forms already: χαῖρε and χαίρετε on the first day of class and ἐρρέτω in the poem by Archilochus. If you can remember the phrase **Kyrie Eleison** (*Lord have mercy*, heard often in church services or music), you will always know the α-aorist imperative. (Why do you think the aorist rather than the continuous imperative of ἐλεέω = *have pity* was used?)

▶ **Exercise α:** Translate, showing aspect:

1. λίπετε
2. λειπέτω
3. λεῖπε
4. λειπόντων
5. λείπετε (2 ways)
6. λιπόντων (2 ways)
7. λίπε
8. παῦσον
9. λαβέ
10. ἰδέ
11. εὑρέτω
12. εἰπέ
13. παυσάτω
14. Let them save (once)!
15. Be sending (sing)!
16. Let him be saving.

IMPERATIVE of εἰμί

ἴσθι ἔστε	*Be!*
ἔστω ὄντων	*Let* him/her/it be!*
	Let* them be!

PERFECT PERIPHRASTIC IMPERATIVE

πεπωκὼς ἴσθι πεπωκότες ἔστε	*Be drunk!*
πεπωκὼς ἔστω πεπωκότες ὄντων	*Let* him/her/it be drunk!*
	Let* them be drunk!

You have already seen -θι endings on the following imperatives: ἴθι ἐκποδών *Get (go) out of the way!*
κατάβηθι *Come down!* ἀνάβηθι *Come up!* γνῶθι σαυτόν *Know thyself.*

▶ **Exercise β:** Translate:
1. Be (sing.)!
2. Be (pl.)!
3. Let him be!
4. Let them be!
5. γεγραφότες ὄντων.
6. τεθνεὼς ἴσθι.
7. μεμαθηκὼς ἔστω.
8. πεποιθότες ἔστε.

Classwork: ✦✦ Read **Graveyard #20** and **#40**, and **Diogenes #22**, Thesauros pp. 229, 231, and 235.

ἔργα   ~Read and translate the conclusion of "An Old Man's Advice." Learn the vocabulary.

* Keep in mind that this is translationese for a third person command (about him, her, it, or them) and <u>not</u>, as it might seem, a second person command (to you), meaning "*Allow him / her / it to go.*"

ὁ δὲ Ζυρὴν ἐλθὼν πρὸς τὸν σάκκον ἠρώτησε τὸν πατέρα ὅ τι χρὴ
ποιεῖν. ὁ δὲ ἐκέλευσεν αὐτὸν μὴ λαβεῖν ξύλον (log) μέγα ἀλλὰ
τεμεῖν τὸ ξύλον (log) εἰς πολλὰ μέρη καὶ τὰ μέρη τιθέναι ἐν ἀγγείῳ
μεγάλῳ καὶ χρῆσθαι ἐπιθήματι (lid) ὥστε τὸ ὕδωρ μὴ δύνασθαι
ἀποσβεννύναι (quench) τὸ πῦρ. εἶπε δὲ ὅτι ὅστις πράττοι ἄττα   5
κελεύοι, δύναιτο ἂν ἀπενέγκαι πῦρ τῷ βασιλεῖ. τέλος δὲ ὁ Ζυρὴν
πῦρ ἤνεγκε τῷ βασιλεῖ πάντα ποιήσας ἃ ἐκέλευσεν ὁ πατήρ.

ὁ δὲ βασιλεὺς ἠρώτησεν· "εἰπέ ἡμῖν· εἰ εἶχες πόρον λαβεῖν τὸ πῦρ,
διὰ τί οὐκ εἶπές τι ἡμῖν πρὸ τοῦδε;" ὁ δὲ ἀπεκρίνατο· "ἀλλ' οὐκ   9
εἶχον πόρον πρὸ τοῦδε." ὁ δὲ βασιλεὺς ἠρώτησεν· "πῶς δῆτα
ηὗρες πόρον; λέγε ἡμῖν ὅπως εὕρηκας τὸν πόρον." ὁ δὲ Ζυρὴν
ἔφη τὸν πατέρα εἶναι τὸν εὑρετήν. ὁ δὲ "ποῖον λόγον" ἔφη   12
"εἴρηκας; οὔποτε τοιαῦτα ἀκήκοα. οὐκ ἔστι τεθνεῶτα εἶναι
εὑρετήν." ὁ δὲ Ζυρὴν εἶπεν· "οὐ τεθνεώς ἐστιν· οὐ τέθνηκεν διότι
οὐκ ἀπέκτεινα αὐτόν· ἐν σάκκῳ αὐτὸν ἐκρυψάμην (I hid him for   15
myself)."

ὁ δὲ βασιλεὺς ταῦτα ἀκούσας ὧδε ἐνενοεῖτο· "ἀκήκοα τοιαῦτα
ὁποῖα οὐδεὶς ἄνθρωπος ἀκούοι. δεῖ με ἀποκρίνεσθαι λόγῳ ποίῳ.   18~
ἀλλὰ ποίῳ; νῦν συγγιγνώσκω ἐμαυτῷ κακῶς ποιήσαντι ὅτε
ἐκέλευσα τοὺς γέροντας ἀποκτεῖναι." τῷ δὲ Ζυρενὶ εἶπε μόνον
τόδε· "εὖ πέπραγας σωζόμενος (saving for yourself) τὸν πατέρα.   21~
οὐ χρή σε οὐκέτι κρύπτεσθαι (hide for yourself) αὐτόν. ἀλλ' ἴθι·   22
κέλευσον αὐτὸν ἐκβαίνειν ἐκ τοῦ σάκκου ἵνα πορεύηται μεθ' ἡμῶν.
ἐλθέτω ἐνταῦθα. ὄμνυμι οὐδένα πλήξειν αὐτόν. μᾶλλον δὲ
τιμήσωμεν αὐτὸν καὶ οἴσωμεν μεθ' ἡμῶν ὅπου ἂν πορευώμεθα."   25~
καὶ πᾶσι τοῖς Μογγόλοις εἶπε τάδε· "ἀγαθόν ἐστιν ἀκούειν ἄττα
ἂν συμβουλεύσωσιν οἱ γεραιοί. οὔποτε αὖθις κελεύσω οὔτε πείσω
ὑμᾶς ἀποκτεῖναι τοὺς γέροντας. τὸ γὰρ γῆρας γνώμην ἔχει."   28

καὶ μετὰ ταῦτα ἀεὶ ἐτίμα ὁ βασιλεὺς τοὺς γέροντας καὶ ἐφίλει
αὐτούς. καὶ ὁπότε οὐκ εἰδὼς εἴη τί ποιεῖν, πρῶτον μὲν τοῖς
γεραιοῖς συνεβουλεύετο, ἔπειτα δὲ τοῖς ἄλλοις.

9   πρὸ + gen.- before (in time or space)   πρὸ τοῦδε = πρὸ τοῦδε (τοῦ χρόνου)
         δῆτα = more emphatic version of δή
12   ὁ εὑρετής - finder, discoverer   (from εὑρίσκω)
12, 17   ποῖος / ποιος - what sort of a? / some sort of a
16   ἀκήκοα - Consult Principal Parts p. 249.
18~   Greek can have a wishing clause whose subject is a relative pronoun, not English.
            It is impossible to capture this construction in translation.
         συγγιγνώσκω - to be conscious of; acknowledge, confess   Literally, *to know with.*
            Notice how both Greek and Latin use the preposition *with*. **Conscience** and **consciousness** are
            from the Latin *conscire* = know (*scire*, related to *science*) with (*con*)--as if consciousness involves
            sharing knowledge **with** oneself.
21~   πέπραγα (related to the word *pragmatic*) Can you find this on p. 250?
            Note. εὖ πράττειν in Greek has two meanings, as does do well in English. It may refer
                to *doing good things* or *faring well.* The former fits the context better.
         μᾶλλον with verb - rather
28~   If πορευόμεθα = we journey, what what would πορευώμεθα be?   Punt!
27   τὸ γῆρας - old age   (related to γεραιός)
         ἡ γνώμη - wisdom   (related to γιγνώσκω)
         πότε / ὁπότε - when? / whenever, when(ever)
         συμβουλεύομαι (middle) get advice for onself, consult with + dative

ACTIVE VOICE

| CONTINUOUS | FUTURE | AORIST | PERFECT |

|---|---|---|---|

INDICATIVE

IIIII   IIIII   IIIII   IIIII

IIIII   IIIII

SUBJUNCTIVE

IIIII   - -   IIIII   + + +

OPTATIVE

IIIII   IIIII   IIIII   + + +

IMPERATIVE

IIIII   - -   IIIII   + + +

INFINITIVE

IIIII   IIIII   IIIII   IIIII

PARTICIPLE

IIIII   IIIII   IIIII   IIIII

Congratulations! You have completed the Active paradigm. Now you need to practice writing it. Learning the Active paradigm well will enable you to learn the Middle and Passive forms with far less struggle than it took to learn the Active forms. Practice writing out the entire paradigm. Know how to label all the parts yourself.

For any regular ⁻ω verb, you should be able to write the entire Active paradigm given the *I X* form. For any irregular ⁻ω verb, you should be able to write the entire Active paradigm given the first four principal parts. **Keep practicing until you can write the entire active paradigm** (excluding the pluperfect) **in less than twenty minutes.**

You may wish to learn the endings first. Then when you write the paradigm write the stem for each column (with time-marker if needed) and fill in the endings. Translationese for the Paradigm is given below.

CONTINUOUS	FUTURE	AORIST	PERFECT
INDICATIVE			
I X / I am Xing *I used to X / I was Xing*	*I will X /* *I will be Xing*	*I X'd [I had X'd]**	*I have X'd (I X) **** *I had X'd (I X'd) ****
SUBJUNCTIVE			
Should I X /Should I be Xing	- -	*Should I X (once)*	*Should I be in the state* *of having X'd*
OPTATIVE			
I would X / I would be Xing	(Ind disc.)	*I would X* *(once)*	*I would be in the state* *of having X'd*
IMPERATIVE			

X! Be Xing!
Let him /her/ it/ them
      X / be Xing!
	- -	*X (once)!*
		Let him/her/it/them X (once)
			Be in the state of having X'd!
			Let him/her/it/them be in
			    the state of having X'd!

INFINITIVE			
to X /to be Xing	*about to X*	*to X (once)***	*to be in a state of having X'd*
PARTICIPLE			
Xing	*about to X*	*having X'd*	*being in a state of having X'd*

*Aorist as prior past.

**In indirect discourse (and only in indirect discourse): *to have X'd*.   ***Perfect as present / Pluperfect as past.

REVIEW OF CONDITIONS

Greek conditions may be divided according to general versus particular, real versus contrary-to-fact (or impossible), or according to the time of the "*then*" clause. (The traditional division is given below.)

Conditions may be mixed. That is, there may be an "*if*" clause from one set with a "*then*" clause from another.

The negative of the "*if*" clause is μή, of the "*then*" clause οὐ.

"Present " means any indicative that represents present time and includes both the present and the perfect.
"Past" means any indicative that represents past time and includes the imperfect, the aorist, and the pluperfect.
"Future" means any indicative that represents future time and includes the future as well as the future perfect.

Equivalents may be used. For example, a "*whoever*" or "*whenever*" clause can be used as an "*if*" clause.
Or a subjunctive or an imperative can be used in the "*then*" clause. "*Whoever would come, she always used to offer them food.*" "*Wherever he should go, let us follow.*" "*If ever she should come, give her gifts.*"

		"IF" CLAUSE (protasis)	"THEN" CLAUSE (apodosis)
SIMPLE	PRESENT	εἰ + present	present
	PAST	εἰ + past	past
GENERAL	PRESENT	ἐάν + subjunctive	present
	PAST	εἰ + optative	imperfect
CONTRARY-TO-FACT (UNREAL)	PRESENT	εἰ + imperfect	imperfect + ἄν
	PAST	εἰ + aorist	aorist + ἄν
FUTURE	MOST VIVID	εἰ + future tense	future
	MORE VIVID	ἐάν + subjunctive	future
	LESS VIVID (WOULD/WOULD)	εἰ + optative	optative + ἄν

	What question does it answer?	TRANSLATIONESE
Simple Condition	What is he doing now if . . .? What was he doing yesterday if . . .? What did he do yesterday if . . .?	*If you are leaving him, he is suffering.* *If you were leaving him, he was suffering.* *If you left him, he suffered.*
General Condition	What does he do in general if . . .? What did he generally used to do if . . .?	*If ever you should leave him, he suffers.* *If you would leave him, he used to suffer.*
Contrary-to-Fact-Condition	What would he be doing now if . . .? What would he have done then if...?	*If you were (now) leaving him, he would be suffering.* *If you had left him, he would have suffered.*
Future Condition	What will he do if . . .?	*If you will be leaving / leave (once) him, he will suffer.* (Most vivid. Used in warning.)
	What will he do if ever . . .? What would he do if . . .?	*If ever you should leave him, he will suffer.* (More vivid.) *If you would leave him, he would be suffering/suffer (once).* (Less vivid)

▶ **Exercise α:** Translate all of the conditions above (in the Translationese column) into Greek.

     leave – λείπω, λείψω, ἔλιπον   *suffer* – πάσχω, πείσομαι, ἔπαθον

Classwork: ✦✦ Read Famous Sayings #10, Thesauros p. 233.

Classwork or ἔργα: ~Look through the ✦✦ Thesauros and find the conditional patterns in what you have read so far.

~Review ✦✦ **New Testament, #1-10.** You will know almost all the forms. Which ones do you not yet know systematically? This tells you what is left to learn.

CONTINUOUS FUTURE AORIST PERFECT

ACTIVE VOICE

INDICATIVE			
⦀	⦀	⦀	⦀
⦀			⦀
SUBJUNCTIVE			
⦀	- -	⦀	+++
OPTATIVE			
⦀	⦀	⦀	+++
IMPERATIVE			
⦀	- -	⦀	+++

INFINITIVE			
⦀	⦀	⦀	⦀
PARTICIPLE			
⦀	⦀	⦀	⦀

This is an overview of the entire paradigm of a regular Greek verb.

MIDDLE VOICE

INDICATIVE			
⦀	⦀	⦀	⦀
⦀			⦀
SUBJUNCTIVE			
⦀	- -	⦀	+++
OPTATIVE			
⦀	⦀	⦀	+++
IMPERATIVE			
⦀	- -	⦀	+++

INFINITIVE			
⦀	⦀	⦀	⦀
PARTICIPLE			
⦀	⦀	⦀	⦀

Do not despair. There is far less to learn than you think. The Middle system parallels the Active system. (And you already know at least ten middle forms.)

PASSIVE VOICE

INDICATIVE			
⦀	⦀	⦀	⦀
⦀			⦀
SUBJUNCTIVE			
⦀	- -	⦀	+++
OPTATIVE			
⦀	⦀	⦀	+++
IMPERATIVE			
⦀	- -	⦀	⦀

INFINITIVE			
⦀	⦀	⦀	⦀
PARTICIPLE			
⦀	⦀	⦀	⦀

Half the forms in the Passive system are exactly the same as in the Middle system (including the ten you know).

Note: The concepts of Middle and Passive are so important for organizing Greek verb forms that the two words will be capitalized whenever they refer to a voice or system. Also Active, Middle, and Passive will be capitalized in parsing to break up the tedium of two or three grammatical terms together.

There are three "pages" or three voices for a Greek verb: Active, Middle, Passive. Why?

Exactly the same relationship exists between Active and Passive Voice in Greek as in English. *"I am washing the cloak"* (active verb) vs. *"The cloak is being washed"* (passive verb). When a verb is passive, the subject is seen as being acted on by another agent.

To be a "True Passive," a verb must have an active form as well. For example, because a person can *see* (active) the sky, the sky can *be seen* (passive).

We do not have a Middle Voice in English. And the Middle Voice does not exist in modern Greek. Was it ever needed? Perhaps not. But it exists and must be learned. What does the Middle Voice show?

The Middle Voice shows a variety of meanings all having to do with a special relationship between subject and verb. You have been seeing middle forms all along (ἀποκρίνομαι, ἀπεκρίνατο, ἐγίγνετο), but these do not have middle meanings. (They are *deponent* and will be discussed later.)

For a verb to be a "True Middle," there must be an active form in contrast. Because I can say λούω (= *I wash*), λούομαι can be a True Middle and have a special middle meaning.

MEANINGS OF THE MIDDLE

(1) Action performed on what belongs/pertains to oneself. λούεται τὸ ἱμάτιον.
(Indirect Reflexive Middle) *She is washing her cloak.*
She is washing a cloak for herself.

We saw this Middle on p. 170, lines 15 and 21. Zyren said of his father "αὐτὸν ἐκρυψάμην" ("*I hid him for myself*") and Zyren was told "οὐ χρή σε κρύπτεσθαι αὐτὸν οὐκέτι" (*"You no longer need to hide him for yourself"*).

(2) Action performed on oneself. λούομαι.
(Direct Reflexive Middle) *I am washing myself.*

✍✍ In English, we use the verb without an object and understand it as reflexive: *I wash, dress, hide*, etc.

(3) Action performed on each other. λούονται.
(Reciprocal Middle) *They are washing each other.*

(4) Arranging or causing something to be done by another. λουόμεθα τὸ ἱμάτιον
(Causative Middle) *We are having the cloak washed.*

We saw this use of the Middle Voice on p. 165, line 25. The Mongolian king said "τοῦτον ἀποκτενοῦμαι" ("*I will have this one killed*"). Sometimes only context can show which Middle is meant: θάπτομαι τὸν παῖδα could mean (1) "*I am burying my child*" OR (4) "*I am having the child buried*." Only context can tell us which.

▶ **Exercise α:** Say whether the verb would be active, middle, or passive in Greek. If middle, which meaning?

1. I freed the horse.	4. We saved each other.	7. We will have our horses freed.	10. I love myself.
2. I freed (my) horse.	5. We saved ourselves.	8. Will you free the horses?	11. I took it.
3. I had the horse sold.	6. We were saved.	9. Have our horses been freed?	12. Thy will be done.

(5) Action with an interior aspect. New verb needed for translation

Perhaps this is simply a special case of (1) the Indirect Reflexive Middle. But there is such a degree of difference that we need to change verbs in order to translate these middle verbs.

αἱρέω - take	αἱρέομαι - choose
ἅπτω - fasten	ἅπτομαι - take hold of + gen. (fasten oneself to)
ἄρχω - begin, be first to (ahead of others)	ἄρχομαι - begin + part., make a beginning of
γαμέω - marry, take in marriage (of the man)	γαμέομαι - get married to + dat. (of the woman)
παύω - stop (something outside oneself)	παύομαι - cease + part. (stop oneself)
πείθω - persuade	πείθομαι - obey + dat. (persuade oneself)
λόγον ποιέω - compose a speech (perhaps for someone else)	λόγον ποιοῦμαι - make a speech, speak (oneself)

▶ **Exercise β:** Say whether the verb would be active or middle in Greek.

1. Stop that thief!	3. He can't persuade you.	5. I'll marry this woman	7. They began to speak.
2. Stop screaming!	4. He won't obey you.	6. I'll be married to this man.	8. They were first to speak.

Lesson 43. The Indicative Middle; Primary and Secondary Endings; Deponent Verbs

MIDDLE VOICE

λείπομαι *I leave my ...*

CONTINUOUS	FUTURE	ε/ο AORIST

INDICATIVE					
λείπομαι	λειπόμεθα	λείψομαι	λειψόμεθα	ἐλιπόμην	ἐλιπόμεθα
λείπῃ*	λείπεσθε	λείψῃ*	λείψεσθε	ἐλίπου	ἐλίπεσθε
λείπεται	λείπονται	λείψεται	λείψονται	ἐλίπετο	ἐλίποντο
ἐλειπόμην	ἐλειπόμεθα				
ἐλείπου*	ἐλείπεσθε				
ἐλείπετο	ἐλείποντο				

INFINITIVE

λείπεσθαι	λείψεσθαι	λιπέσθαι

PARTICIPLE

λειπόμενος,η,ον	λειψόμενος,η,ον	λιπόμενος,η,ον

☙☙ **Ambiguity Alert:** **λείπῃ**: The "*you*" (sing.) present indicative Middle has the same form as the "*he, she, it*" continuous subjunctive Active.

παύομαι *I stop my ...*

CONTINUOUS	FUTURE	σα- (or λα) AORIST

INDICATIVE					
παύομαι	παυόμεθα	παύσομαι	παυσόμεθα	ἐπαυσάμην	ἐπαυσάμεθα
παύῃ	παύεσθε	**παύσῃ**	παύσεσθε	ἐπαύσω	ἐπαύσασθε
παύεται	παύονται	παύσεται	παύσονται	ἐπαύσατο	ἐπαύσαντο
ἐπαυόμην	ἐπαυόμεθα				
ἐπαύου	ἐπαύεσθε				
ἐπαύετο	ἐπαύοντο				

INFINITIVE

παύεσθαι	παύσεσθαι	παύσαθαι

PARTICIPLE

παυόμενος,η,ον	παυσόμενος,η,ον	παυσάμενος,η,ον

☙☙ **Ambiguity Alert:** παύῃ: As above

παύσῃ: The "*you*" (sing.) future indicative Middle has the same form as the "*he, she, it*" σα-aorist subjunctive Active.

The Middle uses the same stems as the Active for the continuous, future, and aorist (but not the perfect). When translating a True Middle in isolation, use meaning (1), the most common meaning: *I am Xing my ...* Translate exactly as you would for the equivalent active verb (see table on p. 171), adding a possessive: "*I X'd my ...*" "*They will X their ...*" and so on.

❱ **Exercise α:** Look over the paradigm above. How does the Middle system resemble the Active system? Consider the relationship of future to present and of aorist to imperfect. What persons have the same endings in present, imperfect, future, and aorist? What is the relationship between the α-aorist and the ε/ο aorist?

❱ **Exercise β:** Translate

1. ἐπαύεσθε
2. ἐπαυσάμην
3. ἐπαύσω
4. παύσονται
5. παύσῃ (2 ways)
6. λείπῃ (2 ways)
7. λείψεται
8. λειψομένην
9. λείπεσθε (2 ways)
10. ἐλίπου

*Sometimes the *you* (sing.) Middle ending is spelled -ει: λείπει, λείψει, παύει, παύσει. This textbook uses only -ῃ.

The forms of the Middle Voice are actually very easy to learn. There are two sets of endings: *primary* and *secondary*. You will see them in their purity in the perfect Middle. Memorize the following and you will be able to "punt" almost every form of the Middle paradigm.

PRIMARY ENDINGS (used for present, future, perfect, and subjunctive)		**SECONDARY ENDINGS** (used for imperfect, aorist, pluperfect, and optative)		**INFINITIVE & PARTICIPLE**
- μαι	- μεθα	- μην	- μεθα	- σθαι
- σαι	- σθε	- σο	- σθε	- μενος,η,ον
- ται	- νται	- το	- ντο	

Primary endings are used for what is more vivid--**present, future, subjunctive**. Secondary endings are used for what is less vivid--**past and optative**. (Remember: the present includes the perfect. The past includes the imperfect, aorist, and pluperfect.)

The "theme-vowel" is as expected: (1) ε / o for present, imperfect, future and ε/o aorist and lengthened ε / o for subjunctive, (2) α for α-aorist, (3) οι or αι diphthongs in optative. The sigma of the "you" (sing.) ending remains visible only in the perfect Middle forms. Elsewhere it drops, leaving two vowels to contract, which obscures the regularity (and rhyme) of the original pattern. **Memorize all "*you*" (sing.) patterns:**

εσαι --) ῃ	εσο --) ου	ασο --) ω

▶ Exercise γ: Parse the following. Punt if necessary.

1. κελευόμεθα	4. ἐκελεύσασθε	7. ἐλίπετο	10. λίπωνται	13. λέλυνται
2. ἐκελευόμεθα	5. κελεύσησθε	8. λίποιτο	11. λείπωνται	14. ἐλέλυντο
3. κελευώμεθα	6. κελεύσαισθε	9. λιπέσθαι	12. λείπονται	15. λελύσθαι

DEPONENT VERBS

Verbs with middle or passive but no active forms are called **deponent**, from the Latin *depono* = *put down*, as if these verbs have "put down" their active forms. There is no verb βούλω, so βούλομαι is deponent. **These verbs are translated in the same way as active verbs are.** (There is no "*my . . .*," "*myself*," etc., added on.)

Middle Deponents with ε / o Aorist	**Middle Deponents with α-Aorist**
αἰσθάνομαι, αἰσθήσομαι, ᾐσθόμην *perceive* ἀφικνέομαι, ἀφίξομαι, ἀφικόμην *come, arrive* γίγνομαι, γενήσομαι, ἐγενόμην *become* ἕπομαι, ἕψομαι, ἑσπόμην *follow* πέτομαι, -πετήσομαι, -επτόμην *fly* ὑπισχνέομαι, ὑποσχήσομαι, ὑπεσχόμην *promise*	ἀποκρίνομαι, ἀποκρινοῦμαι, ἀπεκρινάμην *reply* δέχομαι, δέξομαι, ἐδεξάμην *accept, receive* διαλέγομαι, διαλέξομαι, διελεξάμην *converse with* κτάομαι, κτήσομαι, ἐκτησάμην *acquire* ὀρχέομαι, ὀρχήσομαι, ὠρχησάμην *dance*

You have already seen active verbs with deponent futures: ἀκούω/ἀκούσομαι, λαμβάνω/λήψομαι, ἀποθνῄσκω/ἀποθανοῦμαι. The change to middle forms for the future brings no change in meaning. Deponent verbs have no active forms at all (though sometimes a verb like ἔρχομαι will not be deponent in all tenses, e.g., ἦλθον and ἐλήλυθα). If you open any Greek text at random, more than half the verbs with middle forms will be deponent. True Middles are rare. Perhaps this is a clue as to why the Middle voice died out.

▶ Exercise δ: Translate. Which verb forms are True Middles, which deponents? (Principal Parts pp. 249-250)

1. βούλεται	3. ἐβάλλετο	5. αἰσθάνῃ	7. ἔρχεσθαι	9. ἡγοῦμαι
2. γράφονται	4. ἐδεχόμεθα	6. γιγνόμενος	8. βλέπεσθε	10.ἐπεμπόμην

Classwork: ◆◆ Read: Famous Sayings #11-12, Diogenes #15-16, Thesauros pp. 233 and 235.

ἔργα   ~Write the primary and secondary endings 3x. Memorize.
~Write the indicative forms, infinitives, and participles of παύω and λείπω 3x. Memorize.
~Read and translate "The Gift of Gold" (Part 1). Learn the vocabulary. (You will need to punt some forms.) All forms that have endings presented in this chapter are in bold print. Can you parse them all? If not, ask! Explain the four True Middles (verbs with active alternatives).

ἦσάν ποτε καὶ οὐκ ἦσαν ἐν τῇ γῇ τῶν Ἀρμήνων (Armenians)
ἀνήρ τις πένης καὶ ἡ γυνὴ αὐτοῦ. τούτοις δὲ οὐκ ἦν δύο
ἱμάτια ἀλλὰ ἑνὸς μόνου ἐκοινώνουν. εἰ μὲν γὰρ ὁ ἀνὴρ
βούλοιτο ἐξελθεῖν ἐκ τῆς οἰκίας ἐφόρει τὸ ἱμάτιον καὶ ἡ
γυνή, οὐκ ἔχουσα οὐδὲν φορεῖν, ἔνδον (within) ἔμενεν. εἰ δὲ   5
ἡ γυνὴ **βούλοιτο** ἐξελθεῖν τὰ ἐναντία **ἐγίγνετο**· ὁ ἀνὴρ
ἔμενεν ἔνδον τῆς γυναικὸς ἐκβαινούσης.

οἱ δὲ δύο καίπερ πένητες ὄντες οὕτως ἔχαιρον τῷ βίῳ ὥστε
νόμος ἦν αὐτοῖς ἐν ἑκάστῃ νυκτὶ ᾄδειν καὶ **ὀρχεῖσθαι** πρὶν   9
ἐν ὕπνῳ καθεύδειν· πρῶτον μὲν ὁ ἀνὴρ ᾖδε καὶ ἡ γυνὴ
ὠρχεῖτο. ἔπειτα δὲ ἡ γυνὴ ᾖδε τοῦ ἀνδρὸς **ὀρχουμένου**.
καὶ οὕτως ἐποίουν πολλὰ ἔτη.

καὶ ἐν ταύτῃ τῇ γῇ ἦρχε βασιλεὺς ὃς **βουλόμενος** εἰδέναι   13
περὶ τῶν ἀνθρώπων τῶν ἐν τῇ γῇ-- ποῖος ὁ βίος αὐτῶν,
τίνες αἱ ἡδοναὶ καὶ αἱ λῦπαι--ἐν ἑκάστῃ νυκτὶ **κρυπτόμενος**
τὸ πρόσωπον ἐν ἱματίῳ ἔβαινεν ἐν ταῖς ὁδοῖς μετὰ συμβούλου   16
ἐπισκοπῶν (observing) τοὺς ἀνθρώπους.

καὶ νυκτί τινι ὁ βασιλεὺς καὶ ὁ σύμβουλος **ἐπορεύοντο** ἐν
μέρει τῆς πόλεως ἐν ᾧ μικραί τε καὶ φαῦλαι ἦσαν αἱ οἰκίαι
καὶ πένητες οἱ ἄνθρωποι οἱ οἰκοῦντες ἐν αὐταῖς. καὶ οὐκ ἦν   20
φῶς ἐν ταῖς οἰκίαις διότι καθηῦδον ἐν ὕπνῳ πάντες οἱ
ἄνθρωποι. ἐν δὲ μιᾷ μόνῃ φῶς εἶδον καὶ φωνὴν ἤκουσαν
γυναικὸς ᾀδούσης. καὶ ἐλθόντες ἐγγὺς (near to) τῆς οἰκίας
ᾔσθοντο ἀνδρὸς **ὀρχουμένου** ἐν ᾧ ᾖδεν ἡ γυνή.

"θαυμάζω ἀκούων" εἶπεν ὁ βασιλεύς· "ὡς καλῶς ᾄδει." καὶ   25
ἐλθόντες ἐγγύτερον (nearer) ἤκουσαν τῆς γυναικὸς τάδε
ᾀδούσης· "ἀργύριον οὐ **σεσώσμεθα** οὐδὲ **κεκτήμεθα** οὐδὲν   27~
πλέον ἢ ἱμάτιον ἕν. καὶ ὕδωρ πίνομεν ἀντὶ οἴνου. ἀλλὰ
φιλούμεθα καὶ οὔποτε **παυσόμεθα** χαίροντες τῷ βίῳ."

"θαυμαστὸν ὡς οὗτοι οἱ ἄνθρωποι καίπερ πένητες ὄντες   30
χαίρουσι τῷ βίῳ" εἶπεν ὁ βασιλεύς. ὁ δὲ σύμβουλος
ἀπεκρίνατο· "οὐδὲν θαυμαστόν. παντὶ ἀνθρώπῳ ἔστι μία
νὺξ εὐδαιμονίας. ἀλλ' εἰ αὔριον κατελθόντες τὸ αὐτὸ   33
αἰσθοίμεθα, τοῦτο δόξειεν ἄν μοι θαυμαστόν τι."

9   ᾄδω, ᾄσομαι, ᾖσα - sing   (Attic contracted form for ἀείδω)

   ✦ μῆνιν ἄειδε, θεά   *Wrath, goddess, sing* . . . First three words of Homer's *Iliad*

        ὀρχέομαι - dance --> orchestra (originally a dancing place)
13   ἄρχω, ἄρξω, ἦρξα - (as active verb) - be first, be first over, rule over + gen.
16   τὸ πρόσωπον - face   (what is looked at, from πρός + the οπ of ὄψομαι)
25   θαυμάζω - wonder, marvel   --> thaumatology, thaumaturge
27~   Can you punt σεσώσμεθα? (κέκτημαι is a perfect as present, see p. 159.)
        παύομαι + supplementary participle (see box p. 165) - stop (oneself from) doing
                                            something, cease
        θαυμαστός,ή,όν - wonderful, marvelous
33   αὔριον - tomorrow

THE HUMAN CITY

Figure 1. The ruins of the Athenian *agora*. Visible on the extreme far left is the temple of Hephaistos and in the center of the photograph, beneath Mt. Lykabettos, is the reconstructed stoa of Attalos. To the far right are the Acropolis and the Areopagus. On the south slope of the Acropolis (not visible in the photograph) is the Theatre of Dionysius. (Photo: American School of Classical Studies at Athens, Agora Excavations)

Athenian democracy ("rule of the people") was a hard-won political achievement. Like all the city-states that emerged in the archaic age, Athens went through a period of instability as its forms of government changed from monarchy, to aristocracy, to tyranny (which merely means rule by an unconstitutional leader), and finally to democracy. When Athens was almost single-handedly able to repel the Persian invaders in 490 at the Battle of Marathon, and once again in 480 at the Battle of Salamis, the Athenians believed these victories proved the power of their democratic form of government.

It is difficult for us in the twentieth century to imagine just how radical the democracy at Athens was. For instance, all citizens, rather than just elected representatives, met monthly in the Assembly to debate and pass laws. Every citizen had practical experience in the governance of the city since all citizens were required to serve in rotation as administrators, jurors, judges, military personnel, and police. All citizens participated in the numerous religious festivals of the city. Indeed, all citizens (even those in jail) were required to attend the performances of the tragedies and comedies produced, performed, and written by their fellow citizens for the religious festivals in honor of Dionysius. In short, every citizen was required to be part of the fabric of the city in all of its religious, artistic, military, and political aspects. So deeply rooted was the conviction that human potential could only be realized by participation in this rich public realm that the term identifying a person who was concerned only with private affairs, an *idiotes* in Greek, eventually came to denote one who was foolish and irresponsible, an idiot.

Even the physical layout of the city reflects the conviction that the city is the place where we fulfill all the major aspects of our humanity. The Greek city is centered around a large open area, the *agora*, a public space where the activity of the city is to be carried out. This central public space was surrounded by such a mélange of temples, altars, museums, gymnasia, administration buildings, law courts, and shops that the central area of the city was the place not only of political activity in the narrow sense, but of all the other activities that nurtured the lives of the citizens in common.

It is important to note that women were not citizens and that the slave population of Athens was at least as large as the citizen population. "Freedom" therefore was reserved for only a select few. But the self-confidence of the Athenian city-state in the mid-fifth century was so great that drama, one of the institutions of the Athenian *polis*, was free enough to question many of the entrenched beliefs of the citizens it addressed.

You are now ready for the fifth of the six principal parts. The system of the Middle Voice uses the same stems as the Active voice except for the perfect, which has its own special stem:

παύω, παύσω, ἔπαυσα, πέπαυκα, πέπαυμαι = *I have stopped my...*

PERFECT *I have stopped my . . .*

πέπαυμαι	πεπαύμεθα
πέπαυσαι	πέπαυσθε
πέπαυται	πέπαυνται

PLUPERFECT *I had stopped my*

ἐπεπαύμην	ἐπεπαύμεθα
ἐπέπαυσο	ἐπέπαυσθε
ἐπέπαυτο	ἐπέπαυντο

INFINITIVE

πεπαῦσθαι

PARTICIPLE

πεπαυμένος, η, ον

The perfect Middle stem has reduplication, which works exactly as in the Active. (See p. 155.)

There is no tell-tale κ. It is usually easy to punt.

EXAMPLES

βέβλημαι	(βάλλω)	κέκλημαι	(καλέω)
γεγάμημαι	(γαμέω)	πεποίημαι	(ποιέω)

The next-to-last syllable of the infinitive is accented.

Notice the accent on the -μέν syllable of the participle. This is a tip-off for the perfect Middle.
(Seen only in forms with a short last syllable)

▶ **Exercise α:** Translate: λύω = *release*

1. λέλυνται	3. ἐλελύμην	5. λελυμένος	7. λέλυσθε
2. λελύσθαι	4. λέλυσαι	6. ἐλελύμεθα	8. λελυμένα

CONSONANT COMBINATIONS IN PERFECT MIDDLE FORMS

When a stem consonant comes into contact with an ending consonant, there may be changes. This can make a perfect Middle form difficult to recognize.

LABIALS

π, β, φ + μ --⟩ μμ
      + σ --⟩ ψ
      + τ --⟩ πτ
      + θ* --⟩ φθ

λέλειμμαι	λελείμμεθα
λέλειψαι	λέλειφθε*
λέλειπται	λελειμμένοι εἰσί(ν)
ἐλελείμμην	ἐλελείμμεθα
ἐλέλειψο	ἐλέλειφθε*
ἐλέλειπτο	λελειμμένοι ἦσαν

Inf. λελεῖφθαι*
Part. λελειμμένος, η, ον

PALATALS

κ, γ, χ, + μ --⟩ γμ
       + σ --⟩ ξ
       + τ --⟩ κτ
       + θ* --⟩ χθ

δέδειγμαι	δεδείγμεθα
δέδειξαι	δέδειχθε*
δέδεικται	δεδειγμένοι εἰσί(ν)
ἐδεδείγμην	ἐδεδείγμεθα
ἐδέδειξο	ἐδέδειχθε*
ἐδέδεικτο	δεδειγμένοι ἦσαν

Inf. δεδεῖχθαι*
Part. δεδειγμένος, η, ον

DENTALS

τ, δ, θ + μ --⟩ σμ
      + σ --⟩ σ**
      + τ --⟩ στ
      + θ* --⟩ σθ

πέπεισμαι	πεπείσμεθα
πέπεισαι	πέπεισθε*
πέπεισται	πεπεισμένοι εἰσί(ν)
ἐπεπείσμην	ἐπεπείσμεθα
ἐπέπεισο	ἐπέπεισθε
ἐπέπειστο	πεπεισμένοι ἦσαν

Inf. πεπεῖσθαι
Part. πεπεισμένος, η, ον

*A sigma drops out between two consonants.   ****A dental drops out before σ.**

Note: The Greeks did not add an ˉνται or ˉοντο ending to a perfect stem ending with a consonant. Rather they used a periphrastic form, made from the perfect participle + εἰσί(ν) or ἦσαν.

λελειμμένοι εἰσίν. *They are in the state of having left their . . .*
λελειμμένοι ἦσαν. *They were in the state of having left their . . .*

▶ **Exercise β:** Translate:

1. λελεῖφθαι	3. πεπεισμένοι εἰσίν	5. ἐδέδειχθε	7. λελειμμένη ἦν
2. λέλειψαι	4. πεπεῖσθαι	6. ἐλέλειψο	8. λελειμμένοις

You are not expected to learn all the perfect Middle stems. But you should know the patterns so that you may make an educated guess.

▶ **Exercise γ:** Guess at the meaning of the following forms. You may verify a hunch by consulting Principal Parts pp. 249-250. Remember that reduplication may occur by vowel lengthening: α/ε --> η, ο --> ω.

1. ἧγμαι	3. πεπραγμένοι ἦσαν	5. ὠργίσθαι	7. ἐπέπληξο
2. κέκλεφθε	4. ἦρξαι	6. ἐβέβληντο	8. ἡρημένοι εἰσίν

ALL FORMS of εἰμί

Now that you know about the Middle system, you will be able to understand every form of εἰμί.

εἰμί = I am

CONTINUOUS

εἰμί has enclitic forms only in the present. All present forms are enclitic except for εἶ.

It is traditional to write enclitic forms with an acute on the second syllable.

As you might expect from the continuous nature of being, there is **no aorist** for the verb εἰμί.

INDICATIVE
Present

εἰμί	ἐσμέν
εἶ	ἐστέ
ἐστί(ν)	εἰσί(ν)

Imperfect

ἦ (or ἦν)	ἦμεν
ἦσθα	ἦτε
ἦν	ἦσαν

SUBJUNCTIVE

ὦ	ὦμεν
ἦς	ἦτε
ἦ	ὦσι(ν)

OPTATIVE

εἴην	εἶμεν
εἴης	εἶτε
εἴη	εἶεν

IMPERATIVE

ἴσθι	ἔστε
ἔστω	ἔστων

INFINITIVE
εἶναι

PARTICIPLE
ὤν, οὖσα, ὄν

FUTURE

INDICATIVE

ἔσομαι	ἐσόμεθα
ἔσῃ	ἔσεσθε
ἔσται	ἔσονται

- - - -

OPTATIVE

ἐσοίμην	ἐσοίμεθα
ἔσοιο	ἔσοισθε
ἔσοιτο	ἔσοιντο

- - - -

INFINITIVE
ἔσεσθαι

PARTICIPLE
ἐσόμενος, η, ον

The deponent future is regular except that you would expect ἔσεται instead of **ἔσται**.

This is the first time you are looking at a future optative. Isn't it just what you would expect?

(Note: the s drops out in the you [sing.], so that we see ⁻οιο instead of ⁻οισο.)

▶ **Exercise δ:** Translate:

1. ἔσῃ	4. εἴη	7. ἴσθι	10. εἶεν	13. εἶτε	16. ἔστων
2. ἦ	5. ὄντος	8. ἔσται	11. ὦ	14. ἐστέ	17. ὄντων
3. ἦσαν	6. οὔσῃ	9. ἦν	12. ὤν	15. ἔστε	18. ἐλέγομεν ὅτι ἐσοίμεθα

▶ **Exercise ε:** Translate:

1. we will be	3. [I said that] you (s.) would be	5. to be	7. you (pl.) are	9. you (sing.) were
2. you (s.) are	4. would that we were	6. we will be	8. let them be	10. she will be

Classwork: ✦✦ Read: **Diogenes #17** and **Graveyard #9**, Thesauros pp. 235 and 227.

ἔργα   ~Read and translate "The Gift of Gold" (Part 2). Learn the vocabulary. Circle the verbs with middle endings. Most of them are deponent. Can you find some True Middles? Parse the verbs in bold print.

καὶ μεθ' ἡμέρας οὐ πολλὰς ὁ βασιλεὺς καὶ ὁ σύμβουλος εἰς τὸ
αὐτὸ μέρος τῆς πόλεως ἦλθον καὶ ἐν τῇ αὐτῇ οἰκίᾳ εἶδον φῶς.
καὶ προσερχόμενοι πρὸς τὴν οἰκίαν **ᾔσθοντο** τοῦ ἀνδρὸς   3
ᾄδοντος. καὶ ὅτε **ἀφίκοντο** ἐπὶ τὴν οἰκίαν τὴν γυναῖκα εἶδον
ὀρχουμένην ἐν ᾧ ᾖδεν ὁ ἀνήρ. καὶ τῶν δύο ἤκουσαν ἀλλήλοις
διαλεγομένων. "ὦ γύναι" εἶπεν ὁ ἀνήρ· "εὐδαίμονές ἐσμεν." ἡ δὲ
γυνὴ ἀπεκρίνατο· "ναί, εὐδαιμονέστεροί ἐσμεν τοῦ βασιλέως."   7

ταῦτα ἀκούσας ὁ βασιλεὺς εἶπε τῷ συμβούλῳ "νῦν ὁρᾷς ὡς τῷ
βίῳ χαίρουσιν οὗτοι οἱ ἄνθρωποι; εἰσέλθωμεν καὶ **διαλεγώμεθα**
αὐτοῖς. βούλομαι γὰρ μαθεῖν πῶς τοιαύτην εὐδαιμονίαν ἐν τῷ
βίῳ εὑρίσκουσιν ." οἱ δὲ δύο ἔκρουσαν τὴν θύραν. "τίνες **ἐστέ**;"   11
ἠρώτησεν ἡ γυνή. "δύο ἄνδρες ἐσμὲν πορευόμενοι οἳ βουλόμεθα
χρόνον μικρὸν **ἀναπαύεσθαι**." "**εἰσέλθετε**" ἐκάλεσεν ἡ γυνή.   13

καὶ αὐτοῖς εἰσερχομένοις εἶπεν· "χαίρετε, ὦ ξένοι. οὐκ ἔχομεν
σῖτον διδόναι ὑμῖν ἀλλὰ ἔχομεν ὕδωρ μάλα γλυκύ." καὶ ἤνεγκεν
ἡ γυνὴ ὕδωρ αὐτοῖς ἐν κύλιξιν. καὶ τῶν ξένων πιόντων τὸ ὕδωρ
εἵλιξε (she rolled) δύο λίθους μεγάλους λέγουσα τάδε."οὐκ ἔχομεν 17
θρόνους ἐν τῇ οἰκίᾳ, ἀλλὰ ἡδύ ἐστι καθίζεσθαι ἐπὶ τούτων τῶν
λίθων." ὁ δὲ βασιλεὺς ἠρώτησεν "ἀλλ' ὅτε **ἀφικόμεθα**, οὐκ ἦσθα
μόνη. νῦν ποῦ ἐστιν ὁ ἀνήρ;" ἡ δὲ γυνὴ ἀπεκρίνατο· "ἐν τῇ
ἑστίᾳ (hearth) κρύπτεται." "ἀλλὰ διὰ τί **κρύπτεται**;" ἠρώτησεν ὁ
βασιλεύς· "**αἴτει** (= αἴτε-ε) αὐτὸν ἐξελθεῖν."   21

ἡ δὲ γυνὴ προσῆλθε σπουδῇ πρὸς τὴν ἑστίαν (hearth) καὶ ἔδωκε 23
τῷ ἀνδρὶ τὸ ἱμάτιον. ὁ δὲ ἀνὴρ ἐξελθὼν καὶ ὁρῶν τοὺς ξένους
"χαίρετε" εἶπεν. ὁ δὲ βασιλεὺς ἠρώτησεν· "ἀλλὰ νῦν, ὦ φίλε ξένε,
ποῦ ἐστιν ἡ γυνή σου;"

ὁ δὲ ἀνὴρ **ἀπεκρίνατο** ὅτι κρύπτεται ἐν τῇ ἑστίᾳ. "διὰ τί   27
κρύπτεται;" ἠρώτησεν ὁ βασιλεύς. ὁ δὲ ἀνὴρ εἶπε τάδε·
"πένητές **ἐσμεν**, ὥσπερ ὁρᾶτε. καὶ οὐ κεκτήμεθα δύο ἱμάτια·
ὥστε χρὴ νῦν τὴν ἐμὴν γυναῖκα οὐκ ἔχουσαν ἱμάτιον φορεῖν
κρύπτεσθαι." ὁ δὲ βασιλεὺς εἶπε· "μανθάνω (understand). ἀλλὰ
λέγε μοι τόδε· εἰ οὕτως ἐν πενίᾳ (poverty) ἐστὲ ὥστε μηδὲ δύο
κεκτῆσθαι ἱμάτια πῶς ᾄδετε καὶ ὀρχεῖσθε ὥσπερ εὐδαίμονες;"   33
"ἀλλ' εὐδαίμονές ἐσμεν" ἀπεκρίνατο ὁ ἀνήρ· νομίζομεν
εὐδαιμονέστεροι εἶναι αὐτοῦ τοῦ βασιλέως. χαίρομεν γὰρ
ἀλλήλοις καὶ αὐτῷ τῷ βίῳ."

3   προσέρχομαι - come or go toward   (πρός + ἔρχομαι)
     ἀφίκοντο - from ἀφικνέομαι (The ι is long (time-marked) in the aorist indicative.)
7   εὐδαιμονέστερος, α, ον − more fortunate; εὐδαιμονέστατος, η, ον − most
       fortunate. (The comparative and superlative of ἀληθής are ἀληθέστερος and
       ἀληθέστατος. Although there is no ες on the stem of εὔδαιμων, ον, its comparative
       and superlative are made by analogy with ἀληθής and have an unexpected -εσ.)
11   κρούω - knock, knock on, clap (hands)
13   ἀναπαύομαι − take a rest, rest "*up*" (as we say)
23   ἔδωκε(ν) - he, she, it gave, aorist of δίδωμι. (Note the κ. Usually κ on an ending
       signals the perfect, but not here. The perfect of δίδωμι is **δέδωκα**, with reduplication + κ.)

Lesson 45. Middle Imperatives; Impossible Wishes;
U-Stem Nouns; U-A-U Adjectives

THE MIDDLE IMPERATIVE

Learn the imperative Middle forms. Remember ἰδοῦ from "The Doctor Comes" and that will give you the "you" (sing.) ε/ο aorist Middle command. Think of it as meaning *"See (once) for yourself!"* rather than merely *"See (once)!"*

For the α-aorist, try to remember λόγισαι. (Graveyard# 29, from λογίζομαι *reckon, calculate*).

	CONTINUOUS		ε/ο AORIST		α-AORIST	
2nd pers.	λείπου	λείπεσθε	λιποῦ	λίπεσθε	παῦσαι *	παύσασθε
3rd pers.	λειπέσθω	λειπέσθων	λιπέσθω	λιπέσθων	παυσάσθω	παυσάσθων

*Ambiguity Alert ☙ ☙ : There will be ambiguity only when the verb stem is a single syllable. If the stem is more than one syllable, there will be no ambiguity.

Learn the following patterns, which hold for all normal σα- and α- aorists:

infinitive Active	optative Active	imperative Middle
κελεῦσαι	κελεύσαι	κέλευσαι
παῦσαι	παύσαι	παῦσαι
θάψαι	θάψαι	θάψαι
αι short; accent on next-to-last	αι long; recessive accent	αι short; recessive accent

PERFECT

πεπαυμένος ἴσθι	πεπαυμένοι ἔστε
πεπαυμένος ἔστω	πεπαυμένοι ἔστων

The perfect commands are periphrastic.

Second pers. *Be in the state of having stopped your!*

Third pers. *Let him / her / it / them be in the state of having stopped his / her /its / their*

▶ **Exercise α:** Translate:

1. Keep accepting! (sing.)
2. Accept (once) (pl.)
3. Be guarding yourselves!
4. Let him be saving his . . .
5. γράφου
6. γραφόνωτων (2 ways)
7. κρύπτεσθε (2 ways)
8. κρυψάντων (2 ways)

IMPOSSIBLE WISHES

For wishes pertaining to the present or past (unattainable or impossible wishes), the Greeks used εἴθε or εἰ γάρ + past tense. The negative is μή.

εἴθε or εἰ γάρ + **imperfect** for **present impossible**:
εἴθε μὴ ἀπέθνῃσκον. *If only I were not dying!* (But I am.)

εἴθε or εἰ γάρ + **aorist** for **past impossible**:
εἰ γὰρ ἦλθον.   *If only I had come!* (But I did not.)
εἰ γὰρ μὴ ἔθαψεν τὸν παῖδα.   *If only he had not buried the child!* (But he did.)

(Note: The optative is used for wishes pertaining to the future, attainable or not: *"If only she would come!"*)

▶ **Exercise β:**
Translate:

1. If only they had not left the city!
2. If only they had not left (*their*) city! (Use Middle)
3. If only they were leaving the city!
4. If only they would leave (once) the city!
5. If only you were saving each other!
6. If only it were not dead!
7. Challenge: Translate, using the 99% principle: If only they had not been leaving the city!

U-STEM NOUNS

The Third Group includes U-stem nouns of any gender. The stem ends in υ. The genitive ends in -εως, sometimes in -υος. There are also some Third Group nouns whose nominatives end in -αυς or -ους. You need not memorize these forms, but you should be able to recognize them.

ὁ ἰχθύς *fish*	τὸ ἄστυ *town*	ἡ ναῦς *ship*	ὁ/ἡ βοῦς *cow/ox*	ὁ υἱός *son*
ἰχθύς	ἄστυ	ναῦς	βοῦς	υἱός
ἰχθύν	ἄστυ	ναῦν	βοῦν	υἱόν
ἰχθύος	ἄστεως	νεώς	βοός	υἱοῦ
ἰχθύι	ἄστει	νηΐ˙	βοΐ˙	υἱῷ
ἰχθύες	ἄστη	νῆες	βόες	υἱεῖς
ἰχθῦς	ἄστη	ναῦς	βοῦς	υἱεῖς
ἰχθύων	ἄστεων	νεῶν	βοῶν	υἱέων
ἰχθύσι(ν)	ἄστεσι(ν)	ναυσί(ν)	βουσίιν)	υἱέσι(ν)

Note: υἱός is an O-Group noun in the singular, a Third Group υ-stem noun in the plural.

▶ **Exercise γ:** Give the correct article for the following forms:

1. ____ υἱεῖς   3. ____ νηΐ˙   5. ____ ἰχθῦς   7. ____ βοΐ˙(2)   9. ____ νεώς
2. ____ βοῦς (4)   4. ____ ἄστη   6. ____ ἰχθύς   8. ____ βοός (2)   10. ____ ναῦν

U-A-U ADJECTIVES

There are U-A-U adjectives with U-stems in the masculine and neuter, such as ταχύς, εῖα, ύ. Again, you need not memorize the forms. Be able to recognize them.

ἡδύς, εῖα, ύ *pleasant*

ἡδύς	ἡδεῖα	ἡδύ
ἡδύν	ἡδεῖαν	ἡδύ
ἡδέος	ἡδείας	ἡδέος
ἡδεῖ	ἡδείᾳ	ἡδεῖ
ἡδεῖς	ἡδεῖαι	ἡδέα
ἡδεῖς	ἡδείας	ἡδέα
ἡδέων	ἡδειῶν	ἡδέων
ἡδέσι(ν)	ἡδείαις	ἡδέσι(ν)

▶ **Exercise δ:** Using the information below, match the following forms to the appropriate nouns.

1. βαρύ   A. ἐλέφαντα
2. ἡδέος   B. λόγῳ
3. ταχείας   C. σώματα
4. γλυκεῖς   D. πόνου
5. ἡδεῖ   E. νεώς
6. βαρύν   F. κάρπους
7. ταχέα   G. ἀργύριον

U-A-U comparatives and superlatives will be formed with   **-ύτερος, α, ον** and
                                                            -ύτατος, η, ον.

		BUT	
γλυκύς, εῖα, ύ	βαρύς, εῖα, ύ	ταχύς, εῖα, ύ	ἡδύς, εῖα,, ύ
γλυκύτερος, α, ον	βαρύτερος, α, ον	θάττων, θᾶττον	ἡδίων, ἥδιον
γλυκύτατος, η, ον	βαρύτατος, η, ον	τάχιστος, η, ον	ἥδιστος, η, ον
sweet, sweeter, sweetest	*heavy, heavier, heaviest*	*fast, faster, fastest*	*pleasant, more pleasant, most pleasant*

Classswork: ✦✦ Read **Graveyard #25** and **#37**, Thesauros pp. 230 and 231.

ἔργα   ~Practice writing out the Middle paradigm. Reach the point where you can write it in less than twenty minutes.
            ~Read and translate "The Gift of Gold" (Part 3). Learn the vocabulary. Parse verbs in bold print.

ὁ δὲ βασιλεὺς εἶπε τάδε· "εἴθε μὴ πένητες ἦτε. λέγε μοι τόδε· εἰ
μεταπέμψαιτο ὑμᾶς ὁ βασιλεύς, ἀκούσας περὶ ταύτης τῆς
εὐδαιμονίας, καὶ εἰ ἐθελήσειε δῶρα διδόναι ὑμῖν, **δέξαισθε** ἄν;"
ὁ δὲ ἀνὴρ **ἀπεκρίνατο**· "ναί, δεχοίμεθα ἄν ἅττα ἄν ὁ βασιλεὺς
διδῷ (subjunctive of δίδωμι). χρὴ γὰρ πάντας **δέξασθαι** ἅττα ἄν ὁ
θεὸς διδῷ." "εὖγε" εἶπεν ὁ βασιλεύς· "**δέχοισθε** δῶρα παρὰ τοῦ
βασιλέως." 2

οἱ δὲ τέτταρες **διελέγοντο** πολὺν χρόνον καὶ τέλος ὁ βασιλεὺς 8
καὶ ὁ σύμβουλος εἶπον χαίρειν τῷ ἀνδρί. καὶ λιπὼν τὴν οἰκίαν
εἶπεν ὁ βασιλεὺς τῷ συμβούλῳ τάδε· "ἀλλὰ τοῦτο ἀληθῶς ἐστι
θαυμαστόν --ἀνθρώπους τοσοῦτον χαίρειν τῷ βίῳ. καὶ εἰ νῦν
χαίρουσι πένητες ὄντες, ἔχεις εἰκάζειν (guess) ἐφ' ὁπόσον χαίροιεν 12
ἄν εἰ δῶρα λάβοιεν παρὰ τοῦ βασιλέως;" καὶ οἱ δύο κατῆλθον
εἰς τὴν οἰκίαν τὴν βασιλικήν.

καὶ τῇ ὑστεραίᾳ **μετεπέμψατο** ὁ βασιλεὺς τὸν ἄνδρα καὶ τὴν
γυναῖκα. καὶ **καθιζόμενος** ἐπὶ τοῦ θρόνου τοῦ βασιλικοῦ εἶπεν
αὐτοῖς· "ἤγγειλέ τις μοι ὑμᾶς ὄντας πένητας. νῦν βούλομαι
διδόναι ὑμῖν τάδε τὰ δῶρα. χαίροιτε." καὶ ἔδωκεν αὐτοῖς σάκκον 18
μεστὸν (full of) χρυσοῦ καὶ δύο ἱμάτια καλὰ ὧν τὰ νήματα
(threads) ἦν ἐξ ἀργύρου τε καὶ χρυσοῦ. 20

ὁ δὲ ἀνὴρ καὶ ἡ γυνὴ κατῆλθον εἰς τὴν οἰκίαν φοροῦντες τὰ νέα
ἱμάτια. καὶ ἐν ταύτῃ τῇ νυκτὶ εἶπεν τάδε ἡ γυνὴ τῷ ἀνδρί· "ὦ
φίλε ἄνερ, **κρούου** (clap) τὰς χεῖρας καὶ **ἄρξαι** ᾄδειν, καὶ ἐγὼ
ἔσομαι ἑτοίμη **ὀρχεῖσθαι**." τοῦ δὲ ἀνδρὸς ταῦτα ποιοῦντος ἡ
γυνὴ ἤρχετο ὀρχεῖσθαι. 25~

ἀλλ' ἐξαίφνης (suddenly) **ἐπαύσατο** ἡ γυνὴ ὀρχουμένη καὶ
ἔστενεν. καὶ τῷ ἀνδρὶ εἶπε τάδε· "ὦ φίλε ἄνερ, τὸ ἱμάτιον τοῦτο
βαρύ ἐστι φορεῖν. ἰδού· οὐ μέλει μοι ὀρχεῖσθαι φορούσῃ αὐτό." 28
ὁ δὲ ἀνὴρ ὧδε ἀπεκρίνατο· "εἰ γὰρ μὴ **ἐδεξάμεθα** τὰ δῶρα τοῦ
βασιλέως."

καὶ οἱ δύο ἐξέδυν (took off) τὰ νέα ἱμάτια. ἡ δὲ γυνὴ τὸ φαῦλον
ἱμάτιον ἐνέδυ (put on) καὶ αὐτὸ φοροῦσα **ἤρξατο** ὀρχεῖσθαι
αὖθις. "νῦν δύναμαι ὀρχεῖσθαι ὥσπερ ὄρνις" εἶπε τῷ ἀνδρί.

ἀλλὰ ὀρχουμένη ἐν τῇ οἰκίᾳ ἐξαίφνης **ᾔσθετο** ἡ γυνὴ τοῦ 34
σάκκου. "ὦ ἄνερ" εἶπεν, τοῦ σάκκου ἁπτομένη· "κρυψώμεθα
τοῦτον αὐτίκα. εἰ γὰρ μή, κλέπται ἄν λάβοιεν τὸν χρυσὸν τὸν
ἡμέτερον."

εἴθε + imperf. in present impossible wishes, + aorist in past (p. 182) - if only
2 μεταπέμπομαι - summon, send for (The active, μεταπέμπω = send after, is rarely used.)
12 ἐφ' = ἐπί + acc. - to (Translate *to what an extent*)
20 ὁ ἄργυρος - silver --> argent (in heraldry) --> Argentina (via Latin)
25~ ἤρχετο could be imperfect of ἔρχομαι or ἄρχομαι. Context tells you which.
(Also see note on ἔρχομαι on Principal Parts Page, p. 249.)
28 βαρύς, εῖα, ύ - heavy --> baritone, barometer
(βαρὺ φορεῖν *too heavy to wear*. Compare p. 162, 16 ὀρθία ἀναβῆναι *too steep to climb*.)
εἰ γὰρ + past tense - if only (for impossible wishes, p. 182)
34 ἐξαίφνης (adverb) - suddenly
αὐτίκα (adverb) - at the very moment, immediately

Lesson 46. The Middle: All Forms

MIDDLE

λείπομαι = *I leave my . . .*

CONTINUOUS		FUTURE		AORIST		PERFECT	
INDICATIVE							
λείπομαι	λειπόμεθα	λείψομαι	λειψόμεθα	ἐλιπόμην	ἐλιπόμεθα	λέλειμμαι	λελείμμεθα
λείπῃ	λείπεσθε	λείψῃ*	λείψεσθε	ἐλίπου	ἐλίπεσθε	λέλειψαι	λέλειφθε
λείπεται	λείπονται	λείψεται	λείψονται	ἐλίπετο	ἐλίποντο	λέλειπται	λελειμμένοι εἰσί(ν)
ἐλειπόμην	ἐλειπόμεθα					ἐλελείμμην	ἐλελείμμεθα
ἐλείπου	ἐλείπεσθε					ἐλέλειψο	ἐλέλειφθε
ἐλείπετο	ἐλείποντο					ἐλέλειπτο	λελειμμένοι ἦσαν
SUBJUNCTIVE							
λείπωμαι	λειπώμεθα	--		λίπωμαι	λιπώμεθα	λελειμμένος,η,ον ὦ	
λείπῃ	λείπησθε			λίπῃ	λίπησθε	etc.	
λείπηται	λείπωνται			λίπηται	λίπωνται		
OPTATIVE							
λειποίμην	λειποίμεθα	λειψοίμην	λειψοίμεθα	λιποίμην	λιποίμεθα	λελειμμένος,η,ον εἴην	
λείποιο	λείποισθε	λείψοιο	λείψοισθε	λίποιο	λίποισθε	etc.	
λείποιτο	λείποιντο	λείψοιτο	λείψοιντο	λίποιτο	λίποιντο		
IMPERATIVE							
λείπου	λείπεσθε	--		λιποῦ	λίπεσθε	λελειμμένος ἴσθι	
λειπέσθω	λειπέσθων			λιπέσθω	λιπέσθων	etc.	
INFINITIVE							
λείπεσθαι		λείψεσθαι		λιπέσθαι		λελεῖφθαι	
PARTICIPLE							
λειπόμενος, η, ον		λειψόμενος, η, ον		λιπόμενος, η, ον		λελείμμενος,η,ον	

☝☝ **Ambiguity Alert:** λείπῃ: The "you" (sing.) present indicative Middle has the same form as the "he, she, it" continuous subjunctive Active.

Above are all the forms of the Middle. What is new are the subjunctive and optative forms. They are exactly as you would expect. Notice that the sigma drops out in all *you* (sing.) forms. This gives ‾οιο in the optative.

Review all the rules for making Middle forms. Now try to write out the entire Middle paradigm for λείπω, excluding the pluperfect. Keep practicing until you can do it in twenty minutes or under.

▶ **Exercise α:** Move your finger to the spot on the paradigm where the following forms are located. Use two fingers if need be.

1. λιπέσθαι 2. ἐλέλειψο 3. ἐλείποντο 4. λείψῃ 5. λειπέσθω 6. λείψοισθε 7. λελείμμεθα 8. λείπῃ

Now try to apply what you know in writing the Middle paradigm for παύω, with its ‾σα aorist. You will need four of the first five principal parts:

παύω, παύσω, ἔπαυσα, πέπαυκα, πέπαυμαι

Try to write the entire Middle paradigm of παύω. Then turn the page to check what you have written.

παύομαι* *I stop my . . .*   (often used as a Reflexive Middle, *I stop [myself]*, as in *I stop shouting*)

CONTINUOUS		FUTURE		AORIST		PERFECT	
INDICATIVE							
παύομαι	παυόμεθα	παύσομαι	παυσόμεθα	ἐπαυσάμην	ἐπαυσάμεθα	πέπαυμαι	πεπαύμεθα
παύῃ*	παύεσθε	**παύσῃ***	παύσεσθε	ἐπαύσω	ἐπαύσασθε	πέπαυσαι	πέπαυσθε
παύεται	παύονται	παύσεται	παύσονται	ἐπαύσατο	ἐπαύσαντο	πέπαυται	πέπαυνται*
ἐπαυόμην	ἐπαυόμεθα					ἐπεπαύμην	ἐπεπαύμεθα
ἐπαύου	ἐπαύεσθε					ἐπέπαυσο	ἐπέπαυσθε
ἐπαύετο	ἐπαύοντο					ἐπέπαυτο	ἐπέπαυντο*
SUBJUNCTIVE							
παύωμαι	παυώμεθα	- -		παύσωμαι	παυσώμεθα	πεπαυμένος ὦ	
παύῃ*	παύησθε			**παύσῃ***	παύσησθε	etc.	
παύηται	παύωνται			παύσηται	παύσωνται		
OPTATIVE							
παυοίμην	παυοίμεθα	παυσοίμην	παυσοίμεθα	παυσαίμην	παυσαίμεθα	πεπαυμένος εἴην	
παύοιο	παύοισθε	παύσοιο	παύσοισθε	παύσαιο	παύσαισθε	etc.	
παύοιτο	παύοιντο	παύσοιτο	παύσοιντο	παύσαιτο	παύσαιντο		
IMPERATIVE							
παύου	παύεσθε	- -		**παῦσαι***	παύσασθε	πεπαυμένος ἴσθι	
παυέσθω	παυέσθων			παυσάτω	παυσάσθων	etc.	
INFINITIVE							
παύεσθαι		παύσεσθαι		παύσασθαι		πεπαῦσθαι	
PARTICIPLE							
παυόμενος, η, ον		παυσόμενος, η, ον		παυσάμενος, η, ον		πεπαυμένος, η, ον	

☙☙ **Ambiguity Alert:**   παύῃ: The "you" (sing.) present indicative Middle has the same form as the "*you*" (sing.) continuous subjunctive Middle and as the "*he, she, it*" continuous subjunctive. Active

παύσῃ: The "you" (sing.) future indicative Middle has the same form as the "*you*" (sing.) aorist subjunctive Middle and as the "*he, she, it*" aorist subjunctive Active.

παῦσαι: The "you" (sing.) imperative Middle may have the same form as the aorist infinitive Active (for παῦσαι or θάψαι pattern) and as the aorist optative Active "*you*" (sing.) (for the θάψαι pattern).

▶ **Exercise β:** Move your finger to the spot on the paradigm where the following forms are located. Use two fingers if need be.

1. παύσασθαι
2. ἐπέπαυντο
3. ἐπαύοντο
4. παύσῃ
5. παυέσθω
6. παύσοισθε
7. ἐπέπαυτο
8. παύῃ

NOTE: There is a nonperiphrastic **perfect Middle imperative**. These forms are not common and can be recognized on sight. You need only to know they exist.

Be in the state of having stopped your . . .
Let him/her/it be in the state of having stopped his / her / its . . .

πέπαυσο	πέπαυσθε
πεπαύσθω	πεπαύσθων

Be in the state of having stopped your . . .
Let them be in the state of having stopped their . . .

Classwork: ✦✦ Read **Heraclitus #23** and **Graveyard #38**, Thesauros pp. 225 and 231.

ἔργα   ~Read and translate the conclusion of "The Gift of Gold." Learn the vocabulary.

* OR perfect πεπαυμένοι εἰσί(ν), pluperfect πεπαυμένοι ἦσαν

οἱ δύο πολὺν χρόνον ἐνόμιζον ὅπου τὸν σάκκον κρύψαιντο.   1~
τέλος δὲ τρῆμα (hole) ποιησάμενοι ἐν τῷ τείχει, ἐνταῦθα
ἐκρύψαντο τὸν σάκκον. καὶ οὐκέτι ἦν αὐτοῖς εἰρήνη. ἀεὶ γὰρ
αἰσθανόμενοί τινος ἐν τῇ ὁδῷ--κυνὸς κράζοντος (bark) ἢ ἀνδρὸς
πταίροντος (sneeze)--ἐφοβοῦντο μὴ κλέπται εἰσέλθοιεν. καὶ
οὕτως ἐλυποῦντο ὥστε μηκέτι βούλεσθαι ὀρχεῖσθαι. καὶ ἀεὶ   6
ἔλεγον ἀλλήλοις · "εἰ γὰρ μὴ ἐδεξάμεθα τὰ τοῦ βασιλέως δῶρα."

Μετὰ δὲ τέτταρας ἡμέρας ἦλθεν ὁ βασιλεὺς μετὰ τοῦ συμβούλου
βουλόμενος εὑρεῖν εἰ χαίροιεν οἱ δύο πένητες τοῖς νέοις δώροις.
ἀλλὰ προσερχόμενοι πρὸς τὴν οἰκίαν οὐκ εἶδον φῶς. "τοῦτο
ἄτοπόν τι" εἶπεν ὁ βασιλεὺς τῷ συμβούλῳ· "τί νομίζεις; ἴσως τῷ   11
χρυσῷ ᾧ ἔδωκα (I gave) οἰκίαν νέαν κεκτημένοι ἂν εἶεν." καὶ   12~
ἔκρουσεν τὴν θύραν.

"μὴ λέγε μηδέν" εἶπεν ἡ γυνὴ τῷ ἀνδρί· "κλέπται ἂν εἶεν." οἱ δὲ   14
δύο ἐσίγων. καὶ αὖθις ἔκρουον ὅ τε βασιλεὺς καὶ ὁ σύμβουλος
ὥστε τέλος ἐκάλεσαν οἱ δύο ἅμα "τίνες ἐστέ;" ὁ δὲ βασιλεὺς
ἀπεκρίνατο "δύο ἄνδρες πορευόμενοι οἳ βουλόμεθα ἀναπαύεσθαι."
"ἄπιτε" εἶπεν ὁ ἀνήρ· "οὔκ ἔστι καθίζεσθαι ἐν ταύτῃ τῇ οἰκίᾳ   18
διότι οὐκ ἔχομεν θρόνους." ὁ δὲ βασιλεὺς ἀπεκρίνατο τάδε·
"ἀλλὰ ἐπιθυμοῦμεν πίνειν. ἔχετε ὕδωρ διδόναι ἡμῖν;" ἡ δὲ γυνὴ
"ὕδωρ ἂν εὕροιτε" ἔφη "εἰ πορεύοισθε πόρρω (further) κατὰ τὴν
ὁδόν."

τοῦτο δὲ τῷ βασιλεῖ ἔδοξε μάλα ἄτοπον ἀνθρώπους ἐν τῷ πρὶν   23
ὄντας φίλους νῦν κελεύειν ἀπιέναι ὥσπερ ἐχθρούς. καὶ εἶπεν
αὐτοῖς τάδε· "βούλομαι εἰσελθεῖν καὶ διαλέγεσθαι ὑμῖν. ἐγώ εἰμι
ὁ βασιλεύς. γιγνώσκετέ με." ὁ δὲ ἀνὴρ εἶπεν· "ἀλλὰ μώρους
νομίζεις ἡμᾶς; διὰ τί ὁ βασιλεὺς ἂν ἔρχοιτο ἐν ταῖς νυξὶν εἰς
φαύλας οἰκίας; κλέπται ἐστέ. ἄπιτε νῦν. εἰ γὰρ μὴ ἤλθετ'   28
ἐνταῦθα." ὁ δὲ εἶπεν· "ἀλλ' ἀκούετε τὴν ἐμὴν φωνήν. οὐ τὴν
φωνὴν γιγνώσκετε τοῦ βασιλέως ὃς ἔδωκε ὑμῖν τὰ ὑμέτερα
δῶρα;" καὶ τῷ ἀνδρὶ καὶ τῇ γυναικὶ ἀκούουσιν ἡ φωνὴ ἐδόκει
ἀληθῶς εἶναι τοῦ βασιλέως. τέλος δὲ τὴν θύραν ἀνέῳξαν.   32

(continue on the next page)

1~   Why no ἄν with κρύψαιντο? Would κρύψοιντο be good Greek too?
     ἡ εἰρήνη - peace   (Irene)
6   λυπέω - distress, cause pain; λυπέομαι - be distressed
11   ἴσως - perhaps (literally "equally," from ἴσος,η,ον = equal) -->isometric, isosceles
12~ Can you explain ᾧ? (Look up Pronoun, Relative in the Index if all else fails.)
23   πρίν - used to modify χρόνῳ (understood): *in former time, in time before*
     ἐχθρός,α,ον -hateful, hostile; as noun - enemy

---

32   ### Genitive of Possession as Predicate

A genitive of possession may act as a predicate.

✦ ἔργα νέων, βουλαὶ δὲ μέσων, εὐχαὶ δὲ γερόντων.
   Deeds belong to the young, plans to the middle-aged, and prayers to the old.   Hesiod

ὁ δὲ βασιλεὺς εἰσελθὼν ἠρώτησεν αὐτούς "ἀλλὰ διὰ τί νῦν οὐ
χαίρετε; διὰ τί νῦν οὔτε ᾄδετε οὔτε ὀρχεῖσθε;" ὁ δὲ ἀνὴρ
ἀπεκρίνατο· "διότι φοβούμεθα." "τί φοβεῖσθε;" ἠρώτησεν ὁ
βασιλεύς. "ἔχοντες πλοῦτον φοβούμεθα μή τις κλέπτῃ. οὐκέτι
ἡμῖν ἐστιν εἰρήνη."   36

ὁ δὲ βασιλεὺς οὐδὲν εἶπεν ἀλλ' ἐσίγα. ᾔδει γὰρ ὅτι οἱ δύο
εὐδαιμονέστεροι οὐκ ἐγένοντο διὰ τὸν πλοῦτον, μᾶλλον δὲ τὸ
ἐναντίον. καὶ ἐνενόει το περὶ τοῦδε· πότερον τὸ δῶρον τοῦ
χρυσοῦ φέροι τοῖς ἀνθρώποις εὐδαιμονίαν ἢ οὔ. τοῦτο ἦν
αἴνιγμα ὃ οὐκ ἐδύνατο εἰδέναι.   42

τρία μῆλα (apples) ἔπεσεν ἐκ τῶν οὐρανῶν, ἓν τῷ τὸν μῦθον
λέγοντι, ἓν τῷ ἀκούοντι, καὶ ἓν πᾶσι τοῖς ἀνθρώποις τοῖς ἐπὶ
γῆς. (A traditional Armenian ending)

36   ὁ πλοῦτος - wealth   --> plutocrat
42   τὸ αἴνιγμα - riddle   (εἰδέναι αἴνιγμα = solve a riddle)   --> enigma

Lesson 47. The Passive System; ὑπό + Genitive;
Verbal Adjectives Ending in -τός,ή,όν

λείπομαι * = *I am being left...*

CONTINUOUS		FUTURE		AORIST	PERFECT	
INDICATIVE						
λείπομαι	λειπόμεθα	λειφθήσομαι	λειφθησόμεθα	ἐλείφθην	λέλειμμαι	λελείμμεθα
λείπῃ	λείπεσθε	λειφθήσῃ	λειφθήσεσθε	to be learned	λέλειψαι	λέλειφθε
λείπεται	λείπονται	λειφθήσεται	λειφθήσοται		λέλειπται	λελειμμένοι εἰσί(ν)
ἐλειπόμην	ἐλειπόμεθα				ἐλελείμμην	ἐλελείμμεθα
ἐλείπου	ἐλείπεσθε				ἐλέλειψο	ἐλέλειφθε
ἐλείπετο	ἐλείποντο				ἐλέλειπτο	λελειμμένοι ἦσαν
SUBJUNCTIVE						
λείπωμαι	λειπώμεθα	- -		λειφθῶ	λελειμμένος,η,ον	
λείπῃ	λείπησθε			t.b.l.	ὦ	
λείπηται	λείπωνται				etc.	
OPTATIVE						
λειποίμην	λειποίμεθα	λειφθησοίμην	λειφθησοίμεθα	λειφθείην	λελειμμένος,η,ον	
λείποιο	λείποισθε	λειφθήσοιο	λειφθήσοισθε	t.b.l.	εἴην	
λείποιτο	λείποιντο	λειφθήσοιτο	λειφθήσονται		etc.	
IMPERATIVE						
λείπου	λείπεσθε	- -		λείφθητι	λελειμμένος	
λειπέσθω	λειπέσθων			t.b.l.	ἴσθι etc.	
INFINITIVE						
λείπεσθαι		λειφθήσεσθαι		t.b.l.	λελεῖφθαι	
PARTICIPLE						
λειπόμενος, η, ον		λειφθησόμενος, η, ον		t.b.l.	λελείμμενος,η,ον	

☽☽ Ambiguity Alert: λείπῃ: The "you" (sing.) present indicative Mddle/Passive has the same form as the "*you*" (sing.) continuous subjunctive Middle and as the "*he,she, it*" continuous subjunctive Active.

Continuous and perfect forms of the Passive are identical with Middle forms. If you see these in context, try to figure out whether the meaning is Middle or Passive. If you see them in isolation (in an exercise), call them **M-P** (Middle-Passive), for example:

λείπεσθαι - continuous M-P infinitive

The **Aorist Passive** is the only stem of the Passive that has totally distinct forms (and hence is capitalized). It will be learned in the next chapter. Forms of the future Passive are predictable once you know the stem, which is based on the Aorist Passive.

✍✍ In English the Passive voice has periphrastic forms made with the verb *to be: I am being left, I was being left, I will be left, I was left, I have been left*, and so on. Turn to the chart at the bottom of p. 171. Can you convert every active translation to its corresponding passive?

❱ Exercise α: Transform all the verbs in the following passage into the Passive voice.

An oracle warned Laius, the king of Thebes, that he should not allow his son to grow up. Laius gave the baby to a herdsman so that he might kill the baby. The herdsman, however, pitied the child and brought him for adoption to the king of Corinth. Many years afterwards the child, now an adult, unintentionally killed Laius.

*For Passive forms in larger print see Paradigm, p. 243.

ὁ παῖς ἐλείπετο.	*The child was being left.*
ἡ γυνὴ ἔλειπε τὸν παῖδα.	*The woman was leaving the child.*
ὁ παῖς ἐλείπετο **ὑπὸ τῆς γυναικός.**	*The child was being left **by the woman.***

Using the Passive voice allows you to show that something was done without saying by whom or by what.

Notice that the second and third statements above give exactly the same information; the *focus* is different. The second statement indicates that we are interested in the woman: what did she do? The third shows that we are interested in the child: what happened to him?

If you do say by whom, you usually use **ὑπό + genitive** to indicate the **agent**. In English you use the word "*by*."

▶ **Exercise β**: Translate, using the Passive and ὑπό + the genitive when needed. ὁ στρατηγός = general
1. They are being stopped by the general.
2. They were being stopped by the general.
3. Being stopped (repeatedly) by him is not pleasant.
   (ὑπό --> ὑπ' before a vowel)
4. If ever they are being stopped, tell me.
5. If (ever) they were being stopped, they used to cry.
6. May the horses not be (repeatedly) stopped by him!
7. Let the horses be (repeatedly) stopped by him!

VERBAL ADJECTIVES ENDING in -τός,ή,όν

Verbal adjectives ending in -τός,ή,όν may be made from a verb stem. (The stem is often but not always Aorist Passive.) The meaning is passive: either *X'd* or *Xable* (able to be X'd). Some verbal adjectives have both meanings, some only one or the other.

-τός word	Meaning(s) of -τός word	"*I X*" form	Aor. Passive
φιλητός,ή,όν-	*loved, lovable*	φιλέω *love*	(ἐ-φιλή-θην)
διδακτός,ή, όν	*taught / teachable*	διδάσκω *teach*	(ἐ-διδάχ-θην)
εὑρετός,ή,όν	*findable*	εὑρίσκω *find*	(εὑρέ-θην)
θαυμαστός	*wonderful* (to be marveled at)	θαυμάζω *wonder, marvel*	(ἐ-θαυμάσ-θην)
κρυπτός,ή,όν	*hidden*	κρύπτω *hide*	(ἐ-κρύφ-θην)
αἰνικτός,ή,όν	*expressed in riddles*	αἰνίττω *speak in riddles*	(ἠνίχ-θην)

▶ **Exercise γ**: Translate, using the above

1. οἱ παῖδες φιλητοί. (2 ways)
2. τὰ ποιήματα αἰνικτά.
3. νομίζω τὰ βιβλία θαυμαστά.
4. τὸ ἀργύριον οὐκ ἔστι εὑρετόν.
5. τὰ πολλὰ διδακτά. (best guess)
6. πολλοὶ οὐ διδακτοί. (best guess)

NOTE: When there is a preposition prefixed to a -τός word, the accent stays on the last syllable if the meaning is *Xable*, but goes all the way back if the meaning is *X'd*:

      ἐξαιρετός *removable* vs. ἐξαίρετος *removed*   (from ἐξαιρέω *take out*)

Classwork: ✦✦Read **Famous Sayings #13-14** and **Graveyard #31-32, #39**, Thesauros pp. 233, and 230, 231.

ἔργα   ~Read "Did the Tailor Have a Nightmare?" (Part 1), a Yiddish tale. Learn the vocabulary. Find the True Passives. (See p. 174 top.)

ἐν τῇ γῇ τῇ Ῥυσσικῇ (Russian) ᾤκει ποτε ἀνὴρ πένης, ῥάπτης, ὃς
καίπερ πένης ὢν ἔχαιρε τῷ βίῳ. ᾤετο γὰρ εἶναι εὐδαίμων. πῶς
γὰρ οὔ; πάντα ἐν τῷ βίῳ ἀγαθὰ ἐφάνη· ἐφιλεῖτο ὑπὸ τῆς   3
γυναικὸς καὶ τῶν παίδων καὶ ἐφίλει αὐτούς. καὶ σῖτος ἦν αὐτοῖς
εἰ μὴ πλείων ἢ τοῖς ἄλλοις ἀνθρώποις, ἀλλ' ἱκανός. καὶ οἰκία ἦν
αὐτοῖς εἰ μὴ μείζων ἢ τοῖς ἄλλοις ἀνθρώποις, ἀλλ' ἱκανή. καὶ
ᾤετο ὁ ῥάπτης πάντας τοὺς ἐν τῇ πόλει εὐδαίμονας. πολέμου
γὰρ εἰσαγομένου εἰς τὴν γῆν τὴν Ῥυσσικὴν ὑπὸ τῶν
στρατιωτῶν τῶν Γαλλικῶν (French) καὶ τοῦ στρατηγοῦ αὐτῶν   9
Ναπολέοντος, οὔποτε ἦν μάχη ἐν ταύτῃ τῇ πόλει. ἴσως ἐνομίζετο
εἶναι μικρὰ περιμάχεσθαι (to fight over).

καὶ νῦν ἐλέγετο ὁ Ναπολέων οὐ νικήσας μέλλειν λείψειν τὴν γῆν   12
τὴν Ῥυσσικήν. "εὖγε" εἶπεν ὁ ῥάπτης ἑαυτῷ· "ἀπελθέτω. οἶδα
ὅτι τοῦ Ναπολέοντος ἀπελθόντος μεγάλη ἡ χαρὰ (joy) ἔσται τοῖς
Ῥυσσικοῖς." καὶ τοῦ ῥάπτου περὶ τοιούτων ἐννοουμένου ἐξαίφνης   15
ἐφάνη ἐπὶ τῇ θύρᾳ ἀνήρ τις μικρὸς ὃν ἔγνω Γαλλικὸν (French)
ὄντα διὰ τὸ ἱμάτιον. "φεύγω" ἔφη ὁ ἀνὴρ μεγάλῳ φόβῳ·
"βούλονταί μ' ἀποκτεῖναι. ταχέως· κρύψον με ἢ ἀπόλωλα."   18

ὁ δὲ ῥάπτης ἐπείθετο. ἄνδρα γὰρ ἐν κινδύνῳ ὄντα χρὴ σῴζειν.   19
καὶ ἐκέλευσε τὸν ἄνδρα κεῖσθαι ἐν τῇ κλίνῃ ἵνα κρυπτὸς εἴη.
καὶ ἐπὶ τῷ ἀνδρὶ κειμένῳ ἐν τῇ κλίνῃ ἔθηκε (he put) μίαν, δύο,
τρεῖς χλαίνας (blankets) πτερύγων. τούτου δὲ πραττομένου
ἔκρουον στρατιῶται Ῥυσσικοί. ὁ δὲ ἠρώτησεν· "τί βούλεσθε;" οἱ
δὲ ἀπεκρίναντο· "ζητοῦμεν ἄνδρα μάλα μικρὸν καὶ φοροῦντα
ἱμάτιον Γαλλικόν (French). ἑώρακας τοιοῦτον; ἔστιν ἐνταῦθα;"   25
ὁ δὲ ῥάπτης ἐθέλων τὰ ψευδῆ φυγεῖν εἶπε μόνον τάδε· "πῶς
ἐνταῦθα; τίνες ἂν εἰσέρχοιντο εἰς τὴν ἐμὴν οἰκίαν πλὴν τῶν
βουλομένων ἱμάτια νέα ποιήσασθαι;"

ὁ ῥάπτης - tailor (from ῥάπτω - stitch --> rhapsode, rhapsody)
οἴομαι, imperfect ᾤμην, οἰήσομαι, ᾠήθην - think
3   φαίνομαι, φανοῦμαι, **ἐφάνην** - appear, seem   --> fantasy, epiphany
   ὑπό + gen. with a passive verb - by (gives agent)
9   ὁ στρατηγός - general (ὁ στρατός *army* + ἄγω *lead*)   --> strategy, strategic
12   ἐλέγετο Notice personal construction "*he was being said*," where we would have
       impersonal "*It was being said that he . . .*"
   νικάω - win a victory (ἡ νίκη)
18   ἀπόλωλα - from ἀπόλλυμι, intransitive perfect as present: *I am destroyed, I have perished*
19   πείθομαι + dat. (middle and passive) - listen to someone, obey, believe in, trust in
   ἡ κλίνη - bed   (from κλίνω - cause to lean or recline)
   κρυπτός,ή,όν - hidden

*This story is freely adapted from "Did the Tailor Have a Nightmare?" from *Let's Steal the Moon*, by Blanche L. Serwer, © 1970; used with permission of Little, Brown, and Company.

Lesson 48. The Aorist Passive; Passive Deponents; Dative of Agent with Perfect Passive

The Aorist Passive is distinctive and must be learned. It has a new stem--the sixth and last, which you need to be able to recognize. This is usually, but not always, formed by adding θη/θε to the verb stem:

παύω, παύσω, ἔπαυσα, πέπαυκα, πέπαυμαι,	**ἐπαύθην**	*stop*
λείπω, λείψω, ἔλιπον, λέλοιπα, λέλειμμαι,	**ἐλείφθην**	*leave*
πλήττω, -πλήξω, -ἔπληξα, πέπληγα, πέπληγμαι,	**ἐπλήγην**	*strike*

AORIST PASSIVE

ἐπαύθην *I was stopped*   **ἐπλήγην** *I was struck*

INDICATIVE

ἐπαύθην	ἐπαύθημεν
ἐπαύθης	ἐπαύθητε
ἐπαύθη	ἐπαύθησαν

SUBJUNCTIVE

παυθῶ	παυθῶμεν
παυθῇς	παυθῆτε
παυθῇ	παυθῶσι(ν)

OPTATIVE

παυθείην	παυθεῖμεν
παυθείης	παυθεῖτε
παυθείη	παυθεῖεν

IMPERATIVE

παύθητι	παύθητε
παυθήτω	παυθέντων

INFINITIVE

παυθῆναι

PARTICIPLE

παυθείς, εῖσα, έν
gen. -έντος, είσης, έντος

INDICATIVE

ἐπλήγην	ἐπλήγημεν
ἐπλήγης	ἐπλήγητε
ἐπλήγη	ἐπλήγησαν

SUBJUNCTIVE

πληγῶ	πληγῶμεν
πληγῇς	πληγῆτε
πληγῇ	πληγῶσι(ν)

OPTATIVE

πληγείην	πληγεῖμεν
πληγείης	πληγεῖτε
πληγείη	πληγεῖεν

IMPERATIVE

πλήγηθι	πλήγητε
πληγήτω	πληγέντων

INFINITIVE

πληγῆναι

PARTICIPLE

πληγείς, εῖσα, έν

▶ **Exercise α:**
Translate :

1. παυθείς
2. ἐπαύθητε
3. παύθητε
4. παυθῆτε
5. παυθῆναι
6. παυθεῖεν
7. λειφθείη
8. λειφθῶ
9. ἐλείφθησαν
10. λειφθῶσι
11. λειφθείσαις
12. λειφθέντων (2)
13. πλήγηθι
14. πληγῶ

-θι is the original "*you*" (sing.) imperative ending of the Aorist Passive.

(We have seen it in ἴσθι, ἴθι, βῆθι, στῆθι, and γνῶθι.)

The -θι changes to -τι in παύθητι because the Greeks avoided two aspirated syllables in a row.

When an Aorist Passive θ meets with a consonant in the verb stem, there will be the same sort of changes we saw in the perfect Middle:

π and β	--> φ	λείπω,	ἐλείφθην	* ττ representing an original palatal sound --> χ
κ and γ	--> χ	λέγω,	ἐλέχθην	φυλάττω, ἐφυλάχθην
τ, δ, θ, and ζ	--> σ	νομίζω,	ἐνομίσθην	ἀλλάττω, ἠλλάχθην (*change*)
		πείθω,	ἐπείσθην	

Just as there were κ-less Perfects, there are **θ-less Aorist Passives**. With these, there may be a vowel change in the verb stem. Or there may be no change at all except for the final ε/η.

κλέπτω, Aorist Passive **ἐκλάπην**
γράφω, Aorist Passive **ἐγράφην**

Note: ἐφάνην is technically a θ-less Aorist Passive with an **intransitive meaning**.

▶ Exercise β: Translate. (Refer to the list of principal parts on pages 249-250 if necessary.)

1. ἐπλήγησαν	3. πληγῆναι	5. κλήθητε	7. ἤχθης	9. ἐπράχθη	11. βληθεῖσα
2. πληγεῖσαι	4. πληγέντι	6. πεμφθέντες	8. ἀχθῆναι	10. ἐκλάπης	12. ἐγράφη

PASSIVE DEPONENTS

Some deponent verbs have a Passive rather than Middle aorist. These are called Passive Deponents. There is no way to predict which deponents will be Middle and which Passive.

Passive Deponents	Passive Deponents or True Passives?
βούλομαι, βουλήσομαι, **ἐβουλήθην** διαλέγομαι, διαλέξομαι, **διελέχθην** δύναμαι, δυνήσομαι, **ἐδυνήθην** οἴομαι, οἰήσομαι, **ᾠήθην** ἐπίσταμαι, ἐπιστήσομαι, ἠπιστήθην ἐννοέομαι, ἐννοήσομαι, **ἐνενοήθην**	ὀργίζομαι, ὀργιοῦμαι, **ὠργίσθην** *be angry, be angered* πορεύομαι, πορεύσομαι, **ἐπορεύθην** *travel, be conveyed* φοβέομαι, φοβήσομαι, **ἐφοβήθην** *be afraid, be frightened* ὀργίζω = *to anger* and φοβέω = *to frighten*. Does this mean that ὀργίζομαι and φοβέομαι are felt as passive? Unlikely, since they take direct objects. πορεύω = *to convey*. What about πορεύομαι?

Note that a Middle Deponent may have a True Passive:

εἰσεδεξάμην τὸν ξένον εἰς τὴν οἰκίαν. *I received* the guest into my house. (Middle Deponent)
ἐδέχθη ὁ ξένος εἰς τὴν οἰκίαν. *The guest **was received*** into my house.   (True Passive)

▶ Exercise γ: Translate as many ways as possible. εἰσδέχομαι *admit, receive into a place*

1. οὐκ ἐδυνήθης ἐλθεῖν.	3. οὐκ εἰσεδέχθην.	5. ἐκρύψασθε.	7. πολλὰ πράττεται.
2. οὐκ ὤφθη ὑπὸ τοῦ ἰατροῦ.	4. οὐκ εἰσεδεχόμην.	6. αἰσθάνεται.	8. ὠργίσθης.

DATIVE OF AGENT WITH PERFECT PASSIVE

ὑπό + **the genitive** shows the personal agent for all Passive verbs except the perfect. A **dative of agent** is used with the **perfect Passive**. (This may be considered a dative of interest, the interested party naturally being the one who has done the act.)

λείπομαι **ὑπὸ τοῦ γεωργοῦ.**   *I am being left by the farmer* vs.
λέλειμμαι **τῷ γεωργῷ.**   *I have been left by the farmer.*

Note: If the agent is not a person, a dative of means is normal.
    ὑπό + genitive can be used even with active verbs to mean "*under the influence of.*"
        This could be considered a personification, as if with a genitive of agent.

τείρομαι τῇ νόσῳ.   *I am being worn out by the illness.*
μαίνεται ὑπὸ τῆς νόσου.   *He is raving under the influence of the sickness.*
                        Ie., the sickness makes him rave (agency).

▶ Exercise δ: Translate. (Consult the Principal Parts list on pp. 249-250.)
    1. I am being seen by the doctor.   3. He has been persuaded by gifts.
    2. I was seen by the doctor.   4. He had been persuaded by gifts.

Classwork: ✦✦ Read **Graveyard #41**, **Famous Sayings #15**, and **Diogenes #11** and **#18**, Thesauros pp. 231, 233, and 235.

ἔργα   ~Read "Did the Tailor Have a Nightmare?" (Part 2), which is particularly challenging. Learn the vocabulary.   Find the Aorist Passive forms. Which are True Passives?

ἀλλ' οἱ στρατιῶται, οὐ τῷ ῥάπτῃ πεποιθότες, ἀπεκρίναντο·
"κρυπτὸς ἂν εἴη." καὶ ἐν παντὶ τόπῳ ἐζήτουν. εἷς δὲ αὐτῶν τὸν
ἄνδρα ηὑρίσκεν ἐν τῇ κλίνῃ, τετραίνων τὰς χλαίνας (piercing the   3~
blankets) τῇ λόγχῃ (spear tip). ἡ δὲ λόγχη διῆλθε διὰ τῆς πρώτης,
διὰ τῆς δευτέρας, ἀλλ' οὐ διὰ τῆς τρίτης. καὶ οὕτως ἐφθάρησαν   5
μὲν αἱ χλαῖναι (blankets), ἐσώθη δὲ ὁ ἀνὴρ ὁ κρυπτός.

τέλος δὲ τῶν στρατιωτῶν ἀπελθόντων ἀνέστη ὁ ἀνήρ. τὸ μὲν
πρόσωπον αὐτοῦ λευκὸν ἐφάνη ὑπὸ φόβου, αἱ δὲ τρίχες (hair)   8
λευκαὶ ἐφάνησαν διὰ τὰς πτέρυγας. ἐξαιρούμενος δὲ πτέρυγα
ἐκ τῶν τριχῶν (hair) "πάντα" ἔφη "δηλώσω. λέλυκάς με θανάτου.   10~
ἐγὼ ὁ σεσωσμένος σοι Ναπολέων εἰμι, ὁ βασιλεὺς-βασιλέων.
χάριν οἶδα. καὶ βούλομαι χάριν ἀποδιδόναι. λέγε μοι ἐννοηθεὶς   12
τρία ὧν ἂν ἐπιθυμῇς. ἀλλὰ ταχέως, αἴτει· τίνων ἂν ἐπιθυμοίης;"

ὁ δὲ ῥάπτης ὡς μάλιστα ἐθαύμασεν, οὐδ' ᾔδειν ὅ τι ἀποκρίναιτο.   14~
μικρὸν δὲ χρόνον ἐσίγα καὶ τέλος εἶπε τῷ βασιλεῖ-βασιλέων τάδε·
"ὅταν ὕῃ (ὕω = rain), ὦ βασιλεῦ, εἰσέρχεται τὸ ὕδωρ εἰς τὴν
οἰκίαν πίπτον διὰ τῆς ὀροφῆς (roof). εἰ ἄνθρωπος πεμφθείη ὃς
δυνήσοιτο ποιεῖν ὀροφὴν (roof) νέαν ἡμῖν, χάριν ἂν εἰδείην." ὁ δὲ   18~
ἀκούσας ἐγέλασεν. αἴτημα γὰρ οὕτω μικρὸν ᾔτει ὁ ῥάπτης. καὶ
εἶπε ὁ Ναπολέων· "τοῦτο πράξομαι. καὶ τίνος ἄλλου χρῄζεις;"   20~

αὖθις ἐνεννοεῖτο ὁ ῥάπτης. χαλεπὸν γὰρ ἔδοξεν ἀποκρίνασθαι
πάντων ἱκανῶν ὄντων. τί χρὴ αἰτῆσαι; τέλος εἶπε τάδε·
"τριάκοντα (30) ἔτη νῦν συνοικοῦμεν ἥ τε γυνὴ καὶ ἐγώ, καὶ   23~
οὔποτε ἐδέξατο ἡ γυνὴ νέον ἱμάτιον. νῦν, ὦ βασιλεῦ, πεμφθείη
ἂν αὐτῇ ἱμάτιον νέον;"

πέποιθα + dat. - intransitive perfect as present - trust, trust in (acts as perfect of πείθομαι)
3~   ηὑρίσκεν   What kind of imperfect is this?
διά + gen. - through (in spatial sense)
φθείρω - destroy, ruin, corrupt, Aorist Passive ἐφθάρην
λευκός,ή,όν - white   --> (leukemia, leukocyte)
8   ὑπό + genitive - can be used to show cause or influence: *under the influence, from*
ἐξαιρέω - to take out (ἐκ + αἱρέω = take)
10~   δηλόω - to make clear (δῆλος) Can you punt this form?
λύω - loosen, release, solve   --> analysis, dialysis
12   ἡ χάρις - grace, favor, thanks   --> charismatic
χάριν ἀποδίδωμι - give back thanks, i.e. return a favor
χάριν εἰδέναι - to be grateful (literally, "to know thanks")
For ᾔδειν, see the paradigm of οἶδα, p. 159.
14~   ἀποκρίναιτο. What was the original question? What if it were ἀπορίνοιτο ἄν?
18~   δυνήσοιτο from δύναμαι. Can you punt this? There are enough clues. Explain.
ἂν εἰδείην - optative of οἶδα. (Stem is ειδ-, p. 159.)
        (For once the perfect optative Active is not periphrastic.)
τὸ αἴτημα - request (αἰτέω)
20~   What use of the Middle is this? (See p. 174.)
23~   συνοικέω - dwell together. We would say, "*We have been living together thirty years.*"
     The Greeks say, "*We are living together* thirty years." This use of the present was first seen
     in "The Doctor Comes," pp. 17-18. Can you find it?

Lesson 49. The Passive Voice: All Forms

PASSIVE

λείπομαι = *I am being left . . .*

CONTINUOUS		FUTURE		AORIST		PERFECT	
INDICATIVE							
λείπομαι	λειπόμεθα	λειφθήσομαι	λειιθησόμεθα	ἐλείφθην	ἐλείφθημεν	λέλειμμαι	λελείμμεθα
λείπῃ	λείπεσθε	λειφθήσῃ	λειφθήσεσθε	ἐλείφθης	ἐλείφθητε	λέλειψαι	λέλειφθε
λείπεται	λείπονται	λειφθήσεται	λειφθήσνοται	ἐλείφθη	ἐλείφθησαν	λέλειπται	λελειμμένοι εἰσί(ν)
ἐλειπόμην	ἐλειπόμεθα					ἐλελείμμην	ἐλελείμμεθα
ἐλείπου	ἐλείπεσθε					ἐλέλειψο	ἐλέλειφθε
ἐλείπετο	ἐλείποντο					ἐλέλειπτο	λελειμμένοι ἦσαν
SUBJUNCTIVE							
λείπωμαι	λειπώμεθα	- -		λειφθῶ	λειφθῶμεν	λελειμμένος,η,ον	
λείπῃ	λείπησθε			λειφθῇς	λειφθῆτε	ὦ	
λείπηται	λείπωνται			λειφθῇ	λειφθῶσι(ν)	etc.	
OPTATIVE							
λειποίμην	λειποίμεθα	λειφθησοίμην	λειφθησοίμεθα	λειφθείην	λειφθεῖμεν	λελειμμένος,η,ον	
λείποιο	λείποισθε	λειφθήσοιο	λειφθήσοισθε	λειφθείης	λειφθεῖτε	εἴην	
λείποιτο	λείποιντο	λειφθήσοιτο	λειφθήσοιντο	λειφθείη	λειφθεῖεν	etc.	
IMPERATIVE							
λείπου	λείπεσθε	- -		λείφθητι	λείφθητε	λελειμμένος	
λειπέσθω	λειπέσθων			λειφθήτω	λειφθέντων	ἴσθι etc.	
INFINITIVE							
λείπεσθαι		λειφθήσεσθαι		λειφθῆναι		λελεῖφθαι	
PARTICIPLE							
λειπόμενος, η, ον		λειφθησόμενος, η, ον		λειφθείς,εῖσα,έν -έντος,είσης,έντος		λελειμμένος,η,ον	

⚥⚥ **Ambiguity Alert:** λείπῃ: The "you" (sing.) present indicative M/P has the same form as the "*you*" (sing.) continuous subjunctive Middle and as the "*he, she, it*" continuous subjunctive.Active

Technically the future Passive is made on a separate stem. But since that stem is, reliably, the Aorist Passive stem + σ, it need not be learned. You can easily punt these forms.

The future Middle is sometimes used with a **passive** sense: ἀδικήσομαι. *I will be wronged.*

There is a nonperiphrastic **perfect imperative Passive**, the same as for the Middle. (p. 186)

There is a future perfect Passive, also easily punted. You need only to know that it exists:

πραχθήσεται	*it will be done* (once)	future Passive
πεπράξεται	*it will be (in the state of having been) done*	future perfect Passive

The future perfect serves as it future to a perfect as present. You have seen this in Graveyard #8:

♦♦ κουρὴ **κεκλήσομαι** ἀεί *I shall always be called a maiden.* (κέκλημαι *I am called*)

▶ **Exercise α:** Translate as passive:
1. ἐπαυόμεθα   2. ἐπαύθης   3. παυθησόμενοι   4. πέπαυται   5. παυθέντος   6. ἐπαύθησαν   7. ἐπαύου

▶ **Exercise β:** Parse and translate the following. Include the possibilities of all three voices.

1. παύω	3. πέπαυται	5. παυθεῖεν	7. παύθει	9. παυθέντα	11. πεπαῦσθαι	13. παυθῶ
2. ἐπαύθη	4. παυθῇ	6. παύσῃ	8. παυώμεθα	10. παυθέντων	12. παύῃ	14. πεπαύσθων

* To see the forms of the Passive in larger print, see παύομαι passive, p. 243.

A Note on Translation

The perfect Passive may be translated "*I have been X'd*" OR "*I am X'd.*" (For example, "*I have been washed*" OR "*I am washed.*") The pluperfect Passive may be translated, "*I had been X'd*" or "*I was X'd.*" The English "*I was X'd*" may, then, represent a pluperfect or an Aorist Passive.

Consider the difference between **burnt** and **burned** and you will understand the distinction.

"*My toast was burnt.*" (pluperfect Passive: was in the state of having been burnt)
"*Joan of Arc was burned at the stake.*" (Aorist Passive: an action occurred)

With burnt / burned we have two forms. Usually there is only a single form:
"*My car was washed, but yours was dirty.*"   (pluperfect Passive)
"*My car was washed by me at 2:00 this morning.*" (Aorist Passive)

❱ **Exercise γ:** Translate, using a verb (not a -τός word).
1. It was hidden. (2 ways)
2. It had been hidden. (2 ways. See top box on p. 125.)
3. It was hidden by women. (2 ways for the verb, two ways for *by*; see p. 196)

Classwork or ἔργα:
Assume that the following forms are passive.
Point to their space on the paradigm chart.

PASSIVE VOICE

	INDICATIVE		
⦀	⦀	⦀	⦀
⦀			⦀
	SUBJUNCTIVE		
⦀	- -	⦀	+ + +
	OPTATIVE		
⦀	⦀	⦀	+ + +
	IMPERATIVE		
⦀	- -	⦀	+ + + +
	INFINITIVE		
⦀	⦀	⦀	⦀
	PARTICIPLE		
⦀	⦀	⦀	⦀

1. ἐγειρόμην
2. ἐγερθείς
3. ἐζήτημαι
4. ἐζητήθημεν
5. τιμηθήσεται
6. τιμηθῆναι
7. ἐτετίμησθε
8. θάπτηται
9. παυθέντων (2)
10. ἦξαι
11. λάβου
12. παυθῶ

Classwork: ✦✦ Read New Testament #11-12, Thesauros p. 223.

ἔργα   ~Write the entire Passive Voice for παύω. Memorize. Keep practicing until you can write the entire Passive Voice in 20 minutes.
~Read and translate "Did the Tailor Have a Nightmare?" (Part 3). Learn the vocabulary.

καὶ αὖθις μειδιῶν (smiling) ὁ Ναπολέων ἀπεκρίνατο· "καὶ τοῦτο
πεπράξεται. ἄττα ἂν αἰτῇς παρέξω. ἀλλὰ νῦν εἰπέ μοι τὸ   2~
τρίτον. τίνος ἄλλου ἐπιθυμεῖς; τί ἄλλο αἰτηθήσεται; ἄμεινον
ἂν εἴη σοι αἰτοῦντι· τίνος ἐπιθυμεῖς;"

ὁ δὲ ῥάπτης οὐκ ἐδυνήθη ἀποκρίνασθαι. ἠρώτησεν δὲ· "ὦ
βασιλεῦ, ἀληθῶς χρή με αἰτῆσαι;" ὁ δὲ εἶπε "ναί, ἀληθῶς χρή
σε αἰτῆσαι. χάριν ἀποδοτέον. τρία εἶπον καὶ τρία ἔσται.   7
τίνος ἐπιθυμεις;" καὶ νῦν ὁ ῥάπτης ἐνενοεῖτο χρόνον πολύν·
πῶς ἂν τοῦτο τὸ ἐρώτημα ἀποκριθείη;   9~

καὶ τέλος τάδε ἔφη· "οὐκ ἔστι τρίτον ὅ τι <u>κεκτῆσθαι</u> βούλομαι
ἀλλ' ἔστι ἕν τι ὃ βούλομαι <u>μαθεῖν</u>· ὦ βασιλεῦ, πῶς εἶχες τότε;" 11
ὁ δὲ βασιλεὺς ἠρώτησεν· " ὁπότε;" ὁ δὲ ἀπεκρίνατο· "τότε, τῶν 12~
στρατιωτῶν ζητούντων σε. ποῖα ἔπαθες; σφόδρα ἐφοβοῦ;"

ταῦτα ἀκούσας ὁ Ναπολέων ὠργίσθη. "τί;" ἀνεβόησεν· "ῥάπτης
τολμᾷ ἐρωτᾶν με τοῦτο; ἆρα τοῦτο ἀνεκτόν; τολμᾷ ῥάπτης   15
ἐρωτᾶν τὸν βασιλέα-βασιλῶν ὁποῖα ἔπαθεν; ὦ μῶρε, οὐκ
ἄξιος δώρων εἶ· ἄξιος εἶ τοῦ ἀποθανεῖν."

καὶ καλέσας στρατιώτας τινὰς Γαλλικούς (French) οἳ
κεκρυμμένοι ἦσαν ἐν τῇ ὕλῃ τῇ πλησία (nearby), ἐκέλευσεν   19
αὐτοὺς ἀπαγαγεῖν τὸν ῥάπτην ἵνα ἀποκτείνωσιν αὐτόν. οἱ δὲ
ἀπήγαγον αὐτὸν εἰς τὴν ὕλην (forest) τῆλε τῆς πόλεως
λέγοντες ὅτι αὔριον ὁ βίος αὐτοῦ τελευτηθήσεται.   22

καὶ πᾶσαν τὴν νύκτα, τῶν στρατιωτῶν φυλαττόντων, ἔπασχεν
ὁ ῥάπτης δεινά, πολλὰ δακρύων καὶ ἐννοούμενος ὡς οὔποτε
ὄψεται αὖθις τὴν γυναῖκα τὴν φιλουμένην οὐδὲ τοὺς παῖδας.

2~   πεπράξεται - What is this form?
        ἀμείνων,ον - better (comparative of ἀγαθός)
7   ἀποδοτέον - one must give back.
9~   ἀποκριθείη - See p. 193 (on middle deponents having a true passive).

-11 | έχω + Adverb |

      ἔχω + an adverb means "to be in a certain condition." The Greek equivalent of "How
      are you?" is πῶς ἔχεις. "How were you?" would represent the imperfect.

12~   πότε / ποτε / ὅτε / ὁπότε / τότε . See p. 163. Why is ὁπότε used here?
15   ἀνεκτός,όν - bearable, endurable (ἀνέχομαι - bear, endure)
19   ἡ ὕλη - forest
        ἀπάγω - lead away (ἀπό ἄγω)
22   τελευτάω - put an end to (τέλος)

Lesson 50. Regular -μι Verbs (δείκνυμι)

There are two kinds of verbs: -ω verbs and -μι **verbs.** -ω verb are called *thematic* because of the theme vowel [ε/ο] on their continuous forms. -μι verbs are called *athematic* because their continuous indicative forms have no theme vowels.

Most -μι verbs have stems ending in -νυ: δείκνυμι, οἴγνυμι, ὄμνυμι, ὄλλυμι *I destroy*; intrans. ὄλλυμαι *I perish* (originally ὄλνυμι). They differ from -ω verbs **only on the continuous stem.**

δείκνυμι is a typical μι-verb, whose pattern can be applied to other normal -μι verbs.

> δείκνυμι, δείξω, ἔδειξα, δέδειχα, δέδειγμαι, ἐδείχθην *show*

CONT. ACTIVE

INDICATIVE
δείκνυμι	δείκνυμεν
δείκνυς	δείκνυτε
δείκνυσι(ν)	δεικνύασι(ν)
ἐδείκνυν	ἐδείκνυμεν
ἐδείκνυς	ἐδείκνυτε
ἐδείκνυ	ἐδείκνυσαν

SUBJUNCTIVE
δεικνύω	δεικνύωμεν
δεικνύῃς	δεικνύητε
δεικνύῃ	δεικνύωσι(ν)

OPTATIVE
δεικνύοιμι	δεικνύοιμεν
δεικνύοις	δεικνύοιτε
δεικνύοι	δεικνύοιεν

IMPERATIVE
δείκνυ	δείκνυτε
δεικνύτω	δεικνύντων

INFINITIVE
δεικνύναι

PARTICIPLE
δεικνύς,ῦσα,ύν
gen. δεικνύντος,ύσης,ύντος**

CONT. MIDDLE-PASSIVE

INDICATIVE
δείκνυμαι	δεικνύμεθα
δείκνυσαι	δείκνυσθε
δείκνυται	δείκνυνται
ἐδεικνύμην	ἐδεικνύμεθα
ἐδείκνυσο	ἐδείκνυσθε
ἐδείκνυτο	ἐδείκνυντο

SUBJUNCTIVE
δεικνύωμαι	δεικνυώμεθα
δεικνύῃ	δεικνύησθε
δεικνύηται	δεικνύωνται

OPTATIVE
δεικνυοίμην	δεικνυοίμεθα
δεικνύοιο	δεικνύοισθε
δεικνύοιτο	δεικνύοιντο

IMPERATIVE
δείκνυσο	δείκνυσθε
δεικνύσθω	δεικνύσθων

INFINITIVE
δείκνυσθαι

PARTICIPLE
δεικνύμενος,η,ον

*Note: δείκνυ (*you* [s.] imperative Active) is stem only, since the ending is zero. Also ἔδεικνυ = ἐ + stem + zero.
**The participle δεικνύς,ῦσα,ύν is a normal 3-A-3 adjective, with dative plural δεικνῦσι(ν).

We have seen "nontheme" aorists. A -μι verb is best thought of as a verb with nontheme continuous forms.

The present (primary) endings are: -μι, -ς, -σι(ν), -μεν, -τε, and -ασι(ν). The imperfect (secondary) endings are: -ν, -ς, -, -μεν, -τε, -σαν. (The "*they*" primary ending was originally -νσι and then became vocalized. So it is the same personal ending we see in λείπουσι [originally λείπ-ο-νσι]. The secondary endings are the endings we have seen in the imperfect and ε/ο aorist.)

▶ **Exercise α:**   Identify and translate the following forms:

1. ἐδείκνυ	3. δείκνυσθε (2)	5. δείκνυσι	7. οἴγνυς	9. οἰγνῦσαι	11. ὄμνυσο	13. ὀλλύν (2)
2. δεικνύτω	4. δεικνύντων (2)	6. δεικνῦσι	8. οἰγνύς	10. οἴγνυσαι	12. ὀμνύασι	14. ὤλλυν

ἔργα   ~Write out the continuous paradigm of δείκνυμι and ὄμνυμι. Be able to recognize all forms.
Be able to write the forms in the double frame. (The rest can be punted.)
~Read and translate the conclusion of "Did the Tailor Have a Nightmare?". Learn the vocabulary.

τῇ δὲ ἡμέρᾳ τῇ ὑστεραίᾳ ἐστάθη πρὸ δένδρου (tree). καὶ ἀντίον 1
(opposite) αὐτοῦ ἀνέστησαν πολλοὶ στρατιῶται ἔχοντες ἀκόντια
(spears). καὶ αὐτοῖς εἶπεν ὁ λοχαγός (captain)· " ἐμοῦ λέγοντος 3
ΈΙΣ, ἀνέχετε τὰ ἀκόντια (spears). ἐμοῦ δὲ λέγοντος ΔΥΟ,
στοχάσασθε (take aim). ἐμοῦ δὲ λέγοντος ΤΡΕΙΣ, βάλετε αὐτόν.
ἆρ' ἕτοιμοί ἐστε;"

ὁ δὲ ῥάπτης ταῦτα ἀκούσας ὡς μάλιστα ἐφοβεῖτο. καὶ ἱδρὼς
(sweat) ἦν ἐπὶ παντὶ τῷ σώματι. καὶ ἐδόκει εἶναι νῦν ψυχρός 8
(cold), νῦν θερμός (hot). πῶς γὰρ ἂν ἔχοις σύ, τοιούτων
γιγνομένων;

καὶ ὁ λοχαγὸς (captain) εἶπεν ΈΙΣ. οἱ δὲ στρατιῶται ἀνέσχον
τὰ ἀκόντια (spears). ΔΥΟ. ἐστοχάσαντο (took aim). ἀλλὰ πρὶν
τὸν λοχαγὸν δύνασθαι ΤΡΕΙΣ λέγειν, ἵππος προσερχόμενος 13
ἠκούσθη. καὶ αὐτίκα (at the very moment) ὤφθη ἄγγελος τοῦ
Ναπολέοντος. "Μὴ ποιήσητε τοῦτο" ἀνεκάλεσεν ὁ ἄγγελος· 15~
"Μὴ βάλητε." 16~

καὶ τῷ ῥάπτῃ εἶπεν τάδε· "ὁ βασιλεὺς-βασιλέων νῦν ἐλευθεροῖ
σε. καὶ ἐκέλευσέ με διδόναι σοι ταύτην τὴν ἐπιστολήν." ὁ δὲ
ῥάπτης λαβὼν τὴν ἐπιστολὴν τάδε ἀνέγνω· "νῦν δέδωκά σοι 19~
πάντα τὰ τρία. ἔπεμψα γὰρ ἄνδρα ὃς ποιήσει ὀροφὴν νέαν. καὶ
τῇ γυναικὶ ἐπεμψάμην νέον ἱμάτιον. καὶ τέλος, ἃ ᾔτησας μαθεῖν,
μεμάθηκας. οἶσθα γὰρ νῦν ὁποῖα ἔπαθον τῶν στρατιωτῶν
ζητούντων με. ταὐτὰ γὰρ δὴ ἔπαθον ἅπερ καὶ σύ." 23

1   ἐστάθη is on the Aorist Passive stem of ἵστημι, a transitive verb - to cause
     someone or something to stand. Note intransitive aorist one line down.
8   ἐπί + dat. - translate "over his body"
15~, 16~ μὴ ποιήσητε, μὴ βάλητε- Explain the construction.
     ἐλευθερόω - set free
19~ δέδωκα is from δίδωμι. Punt.

23
┌───┐
│   ταὐτά = τὰ αὐτά   │
│   This is called **crasis**, the mingling of the vowel sound │
│   at the end of the word with a vowel sound at the beginning │
│   of the next word. An apostrophe is used to indicate that │
│   there has been mingling.   │
└───┘

*Author's note: It was difficult to do without ancient Greek words for "emperor" (Napoleon), "bayonet" (used by
the soldier trying to pierce the blankets), and "guns" (used by the firing squad). It is time to move on to genuine
ancient Greek!

ACTIVE VOICE

	INDICATIVE		
‖‖	‖‖	‖‖	‖‖
‖‖			‖‖
	SUBJUNCTIVE		
‖‖		‖‖	ꞁ ꞁ ꞁ
	OPTATIVE		
‖‖	‖‖	‖‖	+++
	IMPERATIVE		
‖‖	--	‖‖	+++
	INFINITIVE		
‖‖	‖‖	‖‖	‖‖
	PARTICIPLE		
‖‖	‖‖	‖‖	‖‖

MIDDLE VOICE

	INDICATIVE		
‖‖	‖‖	‖‖	‖‖
‖‖			‖‖
	SUBJUNCTIVE		
‖‖	--	‖‖	+++
	OPTATIVE		
‖‖	‖‖	‖‖	+++
	IMPERATIVE		
‖‖	--	‖‖	+++
	INFINITIVE		
‖‖	‖‖	‖‖	‖‖
	PARTICIPLE		
‖‖	‖‖	‖‖	‖‖

PASSIVE VOICE

	INDICATIVE		
‖‖	‖‖	‖‖	‖‖
‖‖			‖‖
	SUBJUNCTIVE		
‖‖	--	‖‖	+++
	OPTATIVE		
‖‖	‖‖	‖‖	+++
	IMPERATIVE		
‖‖	--	‖‖	‖‖
	INFINITIVE		
‖‖	‖‖	‖‖	‖‖
	PARTICIPLE		
‖‖	‖‖	‖‖	‖‖

Now you know all of the basic forms of the Greek verb. If you were given the principal parts of any regular Greek verb, whether an -ω verb or a -μι verb, you should be able to create a paradigm with all of the forms.

Skill in reading Greek is in large measure a matter of being comfortable with the paradigm, of being able to recognize verb forms quickly and securely, the way you recognize most nouns. When you look at a genitive you do not have to puzzle out what it is; you just "know." You are now ready to go for this same sort of "knowing" with verbs--somewhere between intuition and a mental operation.

There are two basic ways to get better at recognizing verb forms. One way is to write the paradigm over and over until it is utterly familiar to you. You should be practicing this now, until you get to the point where you can write out the entire paradigm of a normal verb in less than forty minutes.

The second way is to practice writing and identifying given forms. Parsing and doing synopses can be time-consuming and tedious. You will learn a lot faster by doing the Pointing Exercise. This exercise can be done any time your teacher or a partner provides the forms. Or you can read through stories or Thesauros selections and locate the verbs on the chart.

POINTING EXERCISE

For any form given, look at the chart on this page and point to where it would be found. Try one or two in English first to get the hang of it: (1) *I fear lest <u>they not find</u> the house.* (2) "*<u>Give yourself</u> a good dinner every day.*"

Now for the Greek: Notice that if you are given the form παύομαι, you will need two fingers, one for the Middle "page" and one for the Passive "page." And in some cases, a third hand would help! (See θάψαι p. 182.)

1. γνωσθῆναι	7. ἐγράφου	13. ποιήσω
2. πεπαιδεύκασι	8. κλέψαι	14. κρύψασθε
3. λιπεῖν	9. ποιηθήσεσθε	15. φυλλάξοιεν
4. ἀκούσῃ	10. τεθνηκός	16. ἴδωσι
5. λύουσι	11. δείξειε	17. κλαπείη
6. ἐπεπλήγμην	12. σωθέντων	18. κάλεσον

Now is the time to consolidate what you have learned--so that your recognition of forms is quick and secure. Review the way the verb forms are made. Remember the patterns:

Theme-vowels: ε/ο in the present, imperfect, future and ε/ο aorist Indicative
α in the α-aorist Indicative
(No theme-vowel in Special Aorists or the aorist Passive)

M-P primary endings: μαι, σαι, ται, μεθα, σθε, νται

M-P secondary endings: μην, σο, το, μεθα, σθε, ντο

Remember what happens to σ between vowels:

εσαι -> ῃ   εσο -> ου   ασο -> ω   οισο -> οιο   αισο -> αιο

Remember that the Subjunctive Mood uses primary endings, the Optative Mood secondary.

Remember the Imperatives any way you can!

SOME SIGNALS

σ + ε/ ο = Future σα = Aorist θε /θη = Aorist Pass. θησ + ε/ο = Fut. Pass.	Reduplication = Perfect (Also in continuous stem of the "Big Four" -μι verbs) κ = Perfect (Also there is the "disappearing κ" in ἔδωκα and others of the "Big Four" -μι verbs.)	Lengthened ε/ο vowel = Subjunctive οι / αι / ει diphthong = Optative μένος - Perfect M-P participle

Note: ἐ at beginning signals PAST TENSE (imperfect, aorist, or pluperfect)--unless it is a form of reduplication.

Consider ἐπαύσατε *You (pl.) stopped*   vs.   παύσατε *Stop!*
ἐπαύσω *You stopped your . . .* vs. παύσω *I will stop / Should I stop* (once)

ACTIVE of παύω

1. παύω	2. παύσω	3. ἔπαυσα	4. πέπαυκα	5. πέπαυμαι	6. ἐπαύθην

CONTINUOUS = Stem **1**	FUTURE = Stem **2**	AORIST = Stem **3**	PERFECT = Stem **4**

INDICATIVE

CONTINUOUS		FUTURE		AORIST		PERFECT	
- ω	-ομεν	- ω	-ομεν	ἐ +-ον / -α	-ομεν/-αμεν	-α	-αμεν
- εις	-ετε	- εις	-ετε	-ες / ας	-ετε/-ατε	-ας	-ατε
- ει	-ουσι(ν)	- ει	-ουσι(ν)	-ε(ν)	-ον/-αν	-ε	-ασι(ν)
ἐ + 1 +-ον	-ομεν					ἐ + 4 +-η	εμεν
-ες	-ετε					-ης	ετε
-ε(ν)	-ον					-ει(ν)	εσαν

SUBJUNCTIVE

CONTINUOUS		FUTURE		AORIST		PERFECT	
-ω	-ωμεν	- -		-ω	-ωμεν	Part + ὦ	
-ῃς	-ητε			-ῃς	-ητε		
-ῃ	-ωσι(ν)			-ῃ	-ωσι(ν)		

OPTATIVE

CONTINUOUS		FUTURE		AORIST		PERFECT	
-οιμι	-οιμεν	-οιμι	-οιμεν	-οιμι/αιμι	-οιμεν/αιμεν	Part + εἴην	
-οις	-οιτε	-οις	-οιτε	-οις/ειας	-οιτε/αιτε		
-οι	-οιεν	-οι	-οιεν	-οι/ειε(ν)	-οιεν/ειαν		

IMPERATIVE

CONTINUOUS		FUTURE		AORIST		PERFECT	
-ε	-ετε	- -		-ε /-σον	-ετε/-ατε	Part. + ἴσθι	
-έτω	-όντων			-έτω/-άτω	-όντων/-άντων		

INFINITIVE

CONTINUOUS	FUTURE	AORIST	PERFECT
-ειν	-ειν	-εῖν / -σαι*	-έναι

PARTICIPLE

CONTINUOUS	FUTURE	AORIST	PERFECT
-ων,ουσα,ον	-ων,ουσα,ον	-ών,οῦσα,όν / ας,ασα,αν*	-ώς,υῖα,ός

* Accent on next to last syllable

MIDDLE

CONTINUOUS = Stem **1**		FUTURE = Stem **2**		AORIST = Stem **3**		PERFECT = Stem **5**	

INDICATIVE

- ομαι	-όμεθα	- ομαι	-όμεθα	ἐ+3+όμην/-άμην	-όμεθα/-άμεθα	-μαι	-μεθα
- η	-εσθε	- η	-εσθε	-ου / -ω	-εσθε / -ασθε	-σαι	-σθε
- εται	-ονται	- εται	-ονται	-ετο / ατο	-οντο / -αντο	-ται	-νται
ἐ + 1 + -όμην	-όμεθα					ἐ+5+μην	μεθα
-ου	-εσθε					σο	σθε
-ετο	οντο					το	ντο

SUBJUNCTIVE

-ωμαι	-ώμεθα	- -		-ωμαι	-ώμεθα	Part + ὦ	
-η	-ησθε			-η	-ησθε		
-ηται	-ωνται			-ηται	-ωνται		

OPTATIVE

-οίμην	-οίμεθα	-οίμην	-οίμεθα	-οίμην/-αίμην	οίμεθα/αίμεθα	Part + εἴην	
-οιο	-οισθε	-οιο	-οισθε	-οιο / αιο	οισθε/αισθε		
-οιτο	-οιντο	-οιτο	-οιντο	-οιτο -αιτο	οιντο/αιντο		

IMPERATIVE

-ου	-εσθε	- -		-ου/-αι	-εσθε/-ασθε	Part. + ἴσθι	
-έσθω	-έσθων			-έσθω/-άσθω	-έσθων/-άσθων		

INFINITIVE

-εσθαι	-εσθαι	-έσθαι /-ασθαι	-σθαι *

PARTICIPLE

-όμενος,η,ον	-όμενος,η,ον	-όμενος,η,ον/ -άμενος,η,ον	-μένος,η,ον

* Accent on next to last syllable

PASSIVE

CONTINUOUS = Stem **1**		FUTURE = Stem **7** = 6 + σ		AORIST = Stem **6**		PERFECT = Stem **5**	

INDICATIVE

- ομαι	-όμεθα	- ομαι	-όμεθα	ἐ + 6 + ν	μεν	-μαι	-μεθα
- η	-εσθε	- η	-εσθε	ς	τε	-σαι	-σθε
- εται	-ονται	- εται	-ονται		σαν	-ται	-νται
ἐ +1 + -όμην	-όμεθα					ἐ+5+ μην	μεθα
-ου	-εσθε					σο	σθε
-ετο	-οντο					το	ντο

SUBJUNCTIVE

-ωμαι	-ώμεθα	- -		-ῶ	-ῶμεν	Part. + ὦ	
-η	-ησθε			-ῇς	-ῆτε		
-ηται	-ωνται			-ῇ	-ῶσι(ν)		

OPTATIVE

-οίμην	-οίμεθα	-οίμην	-οίμεθα	-είην	εῖμεν	Part. + εἴην	
-οιο	-οισθε	-οιο	-οισθε	-είης	εῖτε		
-οιτο	-οιντο	-οιτο	-οιντο	-είη	εῖεν		

IMPERATIVE

-ου	-εσθε	- -		-τι / θι	-τε	Part. + ἴσθι	
-έσθω	-έσθων			-έτω	-ντων		

INFINITIVE

-εσθαι	-εσθαι	-ναι *	-σθαι*

PARTICIPLE

-όμενος,η,ον	-όμενος,η,ον	-είς,εῖσα,έν	-μένος,η,ον*

* Accent on next to last syllable
On the aorist Passive the stem is melded into the endings.

KNOW the ambiguities. Be able to find them on the chart.

(1) παύω   *I am stopping / Should I be stopping*

(2) παύετε // παύεσθε // πέπαυσθε *You are stopping / Be stopping! //*
    You are stopping your . . . / Be stopping your . . . // You have been stopped / Be in the state of having been stopped!

(3) παύουσι(ν)   *They are stopping / To them stopping*

(4) παύῃ   *Should he,she,it stop / You stop your... /You are being stopped*

(5) παύσω   *I shall be stopping / Should I be stop (once)*   (With α-aorists)

(6) παύσῃ   *Should he, she, it stop (once) / You will stop your . . .*   (With σα-aorists)

(7) παυόντων // παυσάντων // λιπόντων *Of them stopping / Let them be stopping! //*
    Of them having stopped / Let them stop! (once) // Of them having left / Let them leave (once)

(8) θάψαι   *to bury (once) / May he, she, it bury (once) / Bury (once) your . . .*
    παῦσαι   *to stop (once) / Stop your . . .*

When WRITING Greek aorist forms, always remember to take time-markers off everything except the Indicative.

When READING Greek verb forms, remember to "subtract" in order to guess at the verb or look it up in the dictionary or Principal Parts list: subtract the time marker, adjust for the prefix, and subtract the reduplication.

VERB FORMS

Be able to WRITE OUT: all forms of παύω or λείπω.
all forms of **any normal -ω** verb if you are given the six principal parts.
the Continuous forms of δείκνυμι. (The other forms are like those of παύω.)
all forms of εἰμί.

BE AWARE of **Principal Parts**. Memorize as many as you can. Know how to look up the rest.

VERB SYNTAX

Know the normal meanings of the **VOICES**: Active, Middle, Passive.
Know what is expressed by the **ASPECTS**: Continuous, Aorist, Perfect
Know what is expressed by the **TENSES**: Present, Imperfect, Future, Aorist, Perfect, Pluperfect.

Know how these are used:

CONATIVE IMPERFECT	ηὕρισκον αὐτήν. *I was trying to find her.*
INGRESSIVE AORIST	ἐνόσησα. *I got sick.*
GNOMIC AORIST	μῶρος πάθει ἔμαθεν. *A fool learns by suffering.*
PERFECT AS PRESENT	κέκτηται. *he owns*
PLUPERFECT AS IMPERFECT	ἐκέκτητο. *he owned*
FUTURE PART. OF PURPOSE	ἔρχομαι ζητήσων *I come to seek (a-seeking).*

Know about **DEPONENT VERBS**.   δέχομαι, ἐδεξάμην - *I receive, I received* (Middle Deponent)
βούλομαι, ἐβουλήθην *I want, I wanted* (Passive Deponent)

Know how to make up and how to understand **GENITIVE ABSOLUTES**. ἐλθόντος αὐτοῦ, ἔχαιρον.

Know the USES OF THE SUBJUNCTIVE:
Horatory   ἔλθωμεν
Deliberative   ἔλθωμεν;
Subjunction of Prohibition   μὴ ἔλθῃς
With ἵνα, ὡς, ὅπως (subjunctive of purpose)   ἵνα ἔλθῃ
With μή (subjunctive of fearing)   μὴ ἔλθῃ˙
With Relative Pronoun + ἄν (generalizing subjunctive)   ὃς ἂν μὴ ἔλθῃ
With ὅταν and ἐπειδάν (subjunctive in temporal clauses)   ὅταν ἔλθῃ
In Conditions (present general, future More vivid)   ἐὰν ἔλθῃ

Know the USES OF THE OPTATIVE:
Wish (alone or with εἴθε or εἰ γάρ) εἰ γὰρ ἔλθοι
Potential (optative + ἄν) ἔλθοι ἄν.
In Past or Optative Sequence
εἶπον ὅτι γράψει/γράψοι (all stems; only use of Future Optative)
ἐφοβούμην μὴ γράψῃ / γράψειε
φέροι δῶρα ὧν ἐπιθυμεῖτε / ἐπιθυμοῖτε
δῶρα ὧν ἂν ἐπιθυμῆτε / ὧν ἐπιθυμοῖτε φέροι   (** drop ἄν if subj. --> optative)

In Conditions   (past general)   εἰ λείποι, ἐδάκρυον   vs. ἐὰν λείπῃ, δακρύω
(future less vivid)   εἰ λίποι, δακρύοι ἄν   vs. ἐὰν λείπῃ, δακρύσει

KNOW **ALL THE CONDITIONS** (See Chart on p. 172.)
Be especially aware of **CONTRARY TO FACT** conditions. ἦλθον vs. ἦλθον ἄν.

Know about the εἴθε or εἰ γάρ + Imperfect or Aorist for Impossible Wishes
(a variant on the contrary-to-fact theme)

Know how **INDIRECT DISCOURSE** works.
Construction depends on verb. (ὅτι / ὡς or Infinitive or Participle)
New subject of infinitive or participle is accusative. Nominative if no new subject.
Stem remains the same in all three constructions.
Tense remains the same after ὅτι / ὡς.
An indicative or subjunctive may be made optative when introduced by a past tense verb or by an optative.
The Greek is quite simple; English is complicated.

NOUNS, PRONOUNS, ADJECTIVES, ADVERBS, PREPOSITIONS

Be able to RECOGNIZE all forms of ὅστις.
Be able to RECOGNIZE all forms of πόλις, βασιλεύς, and ἡδύς,εῖα,ύ.
Know how the **ASKING, SHRUGGING, RELATING, POINTING** series works. (Chart p. 163)
Know about ὑπό + **GENITIVE** for AGENT with the Passive or **DATIVE OF AGENT** with perf. Passive.

VOCABULARY

If foreigners told you they knew English but in fact did not know the words for *sky, book, when, do,* and so on,
you would wonder whether they really knew the language, no matter what their mastery of grammar and syntax.
You need to have a starting vocabulary in Greek. You may either look over all of the vocabulary reviews or,
probably better, simply read over the dictionary, which has all the words you have learned and nothing extra.
By now you will have absorbed basic principles of word building. You can see how families of words are built
up, for example τιμάω, τίμιος, τιμή, or δίκη, δίκαιος, δικαστής, ἄδικος. Including words from the Thesauros
you know θνῄσκω, ἀποθνῄσκω, θνητός, θάνατος, θανάσιμος.

REVIEW SENTENCES

These sentences are difficult. Doing them will force you to review much of what you have learned. The aspect is
not always indicated. Sometimes you need to enter a "Greek mind" and think what the best aspect would be.

1. If only they would (always) do noble deeds.
2. Let's dance and rejoice: the city has been saved by the king.
3. After the gifts were stolen (use participle), the king became sick (use a single verb).
4. He (always) wanted to be invited to dinner by the king.
5. Did you somehow perceive the people coming into the city?
6. The king is dead (2 ways) and we fear lest the city should fall.
7. If anyone made a speech, he always agreed with those speaking justly.
8. It was announced that the solders left. (3 constructions, 4 possibilities)
9. If the king had not remained, the city would not have been saved.
10. They guarded the gold so that it (should) not be taken by thieves.
11. What are we to say to the king?
12. The sister thinks she is good. (Two possibilities because English is ambiguous.)
13. No one was so wise as to know everything.
14. Don't let your friends persuade you to hide. (This is **not** a "*you*" command)

LOOKING AHEAD

You will be able to WRITE OUT   the present and imperfect indicative Active of φιλέω and τιμάω.
      to RECOGNIZE   all forms of εἰμί.
                       all forms of φιλέω and τιμάω (or any εω / αω verb).
                       all forms of the Special Aorists ἔβην, ἔστην, ἔγνων.

You will be AWARE of all the forms of όω verbs, so that you may look these up if you encounter them.
You will be AWARE of all the forms of the "Big Four"--ἵημι, ἵστημι, τίθημι and δίδωμι-- so that you
are at least able to look them up if you encounter them. Eventually you should become fluent in your
recognition of these forms. Know about the "disappearing κ" of the aorist indicative singular.

NOUNS

ἡ ----η

ἡ γνώμη
ἡ εἰρήνη
ἡ κλίνη
ἡ ὕλη

ε,ι,ρ

ἡ σοφία

-α

ἡ θάλαττα
ἡ πέτρα

ὁ -της

ὁ εὑρετής
ὁ ῥάπτης

ὁ ---ος

ὁ ἄργυρος
ὁ κίνδυνος
ὁ πέτρος
ὁ πλοῦτος
ὁ πόρος
ὁ σάκκος
ὁ φόβος
ὁ στρατηγός

τὸ πρόσωπον

Third Group

ἡ κύλιξ, gen. κύλικος
ὁ τεκών, gen.τεκόντος
ἡ χάρις gen. χάριτος
  χάριν εἰδέναι
  χάριν ἀποδιδόναι

τὸ αἴνιγμα
τὸ αἴτημα

τὸ γῆρας
τὸ ὄρος

ADJECTIVES

ἄξιος,α,ον
ἐχθρός,ά,όν
λευκός,η,ον

χρυσοῦς,ῆ,οῦν
κάρπιμος, ον

βαρύς,εῖα,ύ

ἀνεκτός,ή,όν
      & ος,ον
κρυπτός,ή,όν

ἀποδοτέον impers.

CONJUNCTIONS

ἵνα, ὡς, ὅπως
μή = lest
εἴθε, εἰ γάρ
ἐάν, ἤν

PREPOSITIONS

διά + gen.
ἐπί + dat.
μετά + gen.
τῆλε + gen.
  (adverb used as prep.)

OTHER

περ
δῆτα
σφόδρα

ἐξαίφνης
αὐτίκα
αὔριον

ἴσως (from ἴσος,η,ον)

ὅστις, ἥτις, ὅ τι

ALSO

ἔχω + adverb - be in
      a certain condition
πῶς ἔχεις;
      how are you?

VERBS

ἄγω
  ἀπάγω
ἀπορέω
βαίνω
βλέπω
  ἀποβλέπω
γιγνώσκω
  συγγιγνώσκω
ἔχω
  παρέχω
θαυμάζω
λαμβάνω
  συλλαμβάνω
λανθάνω
λέγω χαίρειν
λύω
ὀρύττω
πάσχω
φέρω
φεύγω
φθείρω

νικάω
ὁράω
  εἰσοράω
τελευτάω
τολμάω

αἱρέω
  ἐξαιρέω
ἀπειθέω
οἰκέω
  συνοικέω

δηλόω
ἐλευθερόω

ἄρχω vs. ἄρχομαι

παύω vs. παύομαι
  ἀναπαύομαι

πείθω vs. πείθομαι
  intrans. perf. πέποιθα

πέμπω
  μεταπέμπομαι

λυπέω
  λυπέομαι

VERBS (cont.)

ἀπόλλυμι
  intrans. perfect as present
      ἀπόλωλα
οἴγνυμι
  ἀνοίγνυμι

δίδωμι
  aor. ἔδωκα
  ἀποδίδωμι
ἵημι
  ἀφίημι
ἵστημι vs. ἵσταμαι
τίθημι
  aor. ἔθηκα

δέχομαι
ἕπομαι
οἴομαι
φαίνομαι

κτάομαι
  perf. as present κέκτημαι

ἱκνέομαι
  ἀφικνέομαι
ὀρχέομαι

SERIES

τίς, τις, ὅς, ὅστις;
  οὗτος, ὅδε, ἐκεῖνος

πότε, ποτε, ὅτε, ὁπότε;
  τότε

πῶς, πως, ὡς, ὅπως;
  οὕτως, ὧδε, ἐκείνως

ποῦ, που, οὗ, ὅπου;
  ἐνταῦθα, ἐκεῖ

ποῖ, ποι, οἷ, ὅποι;
  ἐνταῦθα, ἐκεῖσε

πόθεν, ποθεν, ὅθεν, ὁπόθεν;
  [ἐντεῦθεν, ἐκεῖθεν]

πόσος, ποσος, ὅσος, ὁπόσος;
  τόσος, τοσοῦτος

ποῖος, ποιος, οἷος, ὁποῖος;
  τοῖος, τοιοῦτος

Lesson 51. Contract Verbs: -έω, -άω, -όω

We have learned the sound patterns and some forms for -έω and -άω verbs. Now it is time to learn the whole system of contract verbs. Like -μι verbs, contract verbs differ from the norm **only on the continuous stem.**

-έω contracts are the most common. Here are the patterns (as seen on p. 126):

ε + ε --> ει
ε + ο --> ου
ε is absorbed into any long vowel or diphthong that follows it.

If the original ε was accented, the contracted syllable has a circumflex. ε + ε --> εῖ

φιλέω, φιλήσω, ἐφίλησα, πεφίληκα, πεφίλημαι, ἐφιλήθην *like / love*

CONT. ACTIVE

INDICATIVE

φιλῶ	φιλοῦμεν
φιλεῖς	**φιλεῖτε**
φιλεῖ	φιλοῦσι(ν)

ἐφίλουν	ἐφιλοῦμεν
ἐφίλεις	ἐφιλεῖτε
ἐφίλει	ἐφίλουν

SUBJUNCTIVE

φιλῶ	φιλῶμεν
φιλῇς	φιλῆτε
φιλῇ	φιλῶσι(ν)

OPTATIVE

φιλοίην	φιλοῖμεν
φιλοίης	φιλοῖτε
φιλοίη	φιλοῖεν

IMPERATIVE

φίλει	**φιλεῖτε**
φιλείτω	**φιλούντων**

INFINITIVE

φιλεῖν

PARTICIPLE

φιλῶν, οῦσα, οῦν
gen. φιλοῦντος, ούσης, οῦντος

CONT. MIDDLE-PASSIVE

INDICATIVE

φιλοῦμαι	φιλούμεθα
φιλῇ	φιλεῖσθε
φιλεῖται	φιλοῦνται

ἐφιλούμην	ἐφιλούμεθα
ἐφιλοῦ	ἐφιλεῖσθε
ἐφιλεῖτο	ἐφιλοῦντο

SUBJUNCTIVE

φιλῶμαι	φιλώμεθα
φιλῇ	φιλῆσθε
φιλῆται	φιλῶνται

OPTATIVE

φιλοίμην	φιλοίμεθα
φιλοῖο	φιλοῖσθε
φιλοῖτο	φιλοῖντο

IMPERATIVE

φιλοῦ	φιλεῖσθε
φιλείσθω	φιλείσθων

INFINITIVE

φιλεῖσθαι

PARTICIPLE

φιλούμενος, η, ον

Learn the principal parts of φιλέω. This gives you the normal -έω pattern. And learn the rules and forms in the boxes with double frames. (The rest can be punted.)

Notice the distinctive optative singular endings for the Active of *all* contract verbs:
-οίην, -οίης, -οίη -- (instead of -οιμι, -οις, -οι).

▶ Exercise α: Translate:

1. ἐφίλουν (2)	4. φιλῇ (2 ways)	7. φιλεῖσθε (2 ways)	10. φιλεῖ	13. γαμούμεθα
2. ἐφιλοῦ	5. ἐφίλει	8. φιλῶ (2 ways)	11. αἱρείσθων	14. ἐκαλχσεῖσθε
3. φιλοῦ	6. φιλούντων (2)	9. φίλει	12. ἐπιθυμοίης	15. ᾕρει

These are the patterns for -άω verbs:

α + ε --> α	α + η --> α	α + ο --> ω	α + οι --> ῳ		If the original α was accented, the contracted syllable has a circumflex. ά + ε --> ᾶ
α + ει --> ᾳ	α + ῃ --> ᾳ	α + ου --> ω	α + ω --> ω		

An α combined with any ε-sound is always long α; an α combined with any o-sound is ω. In other words, an initial α "conquers" any α, ε, or η but "is conquered by" an o-sound.

τιμάω, τιμήσω, ἐτίμησα, τετίμηκα, τετίμημαι, ἐτιμήθην *honor*

CONT. ACTIVE	CONT. MIDDLE-PASSIVE

INDICATIVE

τιμῶ	τιμῶμεν		τιμῶμαι	τιμώμεθα
τιμᾷς	τιμᾶτε		τιμᾷ	τιμᾶσθε
τιμᾷ	τιμῶσι(ν)		τιμᾶται	τιμῶνται

ἐτίμων	ἐτιμῶμεν		ἐτιμώμην	ἐτιμώμεθα
ἐτίμας	ἐτιμᾶτε		ἐτιμῶ	ἐτιμᾶσθε
ἐτίμα	ἐτίμων		ἐτιμᾶτο	ἐτιμῶντο

SUBJUNCTIVE

τιμῶ	τιμῶμεν		τιμῶμαι	τιμώμεθα
τιμᾷς	τιμᾶτε		τιμᾷ	τιμᾶσθε
τιμᾷ	τιμῶσι(ν)		τιμᾶται	τιμῶνται

OPTATIVE

τιμῴην	τιμῷμεν		τιμῴμην	τιμῴμεθα
τιμῴης	τιμῷτε		τιμῷο	τιμῷσθε
τιμῴη	τιμῷεν		τιμῷτο	τιμῷντο

IMPERATIVE

τίμα	τιμᾶτε		τιμῶ	τιμᾶσθε
τιμάτω	τιμώντων		τιμάσθω	τιμάσθων

INFINITIVE

τιμᾶν			τιμᾶσθαι

PARTICIPLE

τιμῶν, ῶσα, ῶν
gen. τιμῶντος, ώσης, ῶντος

τιμώμενος, η, ον

&& **Major Ambiguity Alert:** The present indicative and the continuous subjunctive of -άω verbs have the same forms in all voices.

Learn the principal parts of τιμάω. This gives you the normal -άω pattern. And learn the rules and forms in the boxes with double frames. (The rest can be punted.)

The optative endings have a characteristic ῳ sound (α combining with οι).

▶ **Exercise α:** Translate:

1. τιμᾷ (3 ways)
2. τίμα
3. τιμῶ (3 ways)
4. ἐτίμων
5. τιμῶν
6. τιμώμεθα
7. τιμώμεθα
8. τιμῴην
9. τιμᾶν
10. ἐσιγῶ
11. ὥρα
12. νικῷο
13. τελευτῶνται (2 ways)
14. τολμᾶτε (2 ways)
15. εἰσορῶσα

These are the patterns for -όω verbs:

ο + ε --> ου	ο + η --> ω	ο + ει --> οι
ο + ο --> ου	ο + ω --> ω	ο + η --> οι
ο + ου --> ου		ο + οι --> οι

> If the original ο was accented, the contracted syllable has a circumflex.
> ό + ε --> οῦ

O-contract verbs are the least common type. (There are only two in the Thesauros.) It is enough to be aware of these forms; you need not memorize them. Learn the principal parts pattern. Be familiar enough with -όω forms that you will know to look them up in a paradigm if you come across them in your reading.

-όω verbs are often factitive:

δοῦλος	*slave*	δουλόω	*I enslave*
ἐλεύθερος	*free*	ἐλευθερόω	*I make free*
δῆλος	*clear*	δηλόω	*I make clear*
ὀρθός	*upright*	ὀρθόω	*I set straight*

δηλόω, δηλώσω, ἐδήλωσα, δεδήλωκα, δεδήλωμαι, ἐδηλώθην *make clear*

CONT. ACTIVE

INDICATIVE
δηλῶ	δηλοῦμεν
δηλοῖς	δηλοῖτε
δηλοῖ	δηλοῦσι(ν)
ἐδήλουν	ἐδηλοῦμεν
ἐδήλους	ἐδηλοῦτε
ἐδήλου	ἐδήλουν

SUBJUNCTIVE
δηλῶ	δηλῶμεν
δηλοῖς	δηλῶτε
δηλοῖ	δηλῶσι(ν)

OPTATIVE
δηλῴην	δηλοῖμεν
δηλῴης	δηλοῖτε
δηλῴη	δηλοῖεν

IMPERATIVE
δήλου	δηλοῦτε
δηλούτω	δηλούντων

INFINITIVE
δηλοῦν

PARTICIPLE
δηλῶν, οῦσα, οῦν
gen. δηλοῦντος, ούσης, οῦντος

CONT. MIDDLE-PASSIVE

INDICATIVE
δηλοῦμαι	δηλούμεθα
δηλοῖ	δηλοῦσθε
δηλοῦται	δηλοῦνται
ἐδηλούμην	ἐδηλούμεθα
ἐδηλοῦ	ἐδηλοῦσθε
ἐδηλοῦτο	ἐδηλοῦντο

SUBJUNCTIVE
δηλῶμαι	δηλώμεθα
δηλοῖ	δηλῶσθε
δηλῶται	δηλῶνται

OPTATIVE
δηλοίμην	δηλοίμεθα
δηλοῖο	δηλοῖσθε
δηλοῖτο	δηλοῖντο

IMPERATIVE
δηλοῦ	δηλοῦσθε
δηλούσθω	δηλούσθων

INFINITIVE
δηλοῦσθαι

PARTICIPLE
δηλούμενος, η, ον

Exercise α: Translate: 1. δηλοῖ (4 ways) 2. δήλου 3. δηλοῦ 4. δηλῴη 5. ἐδήλους

Classwork: ✦✦ Read: **Graveyard #33**, Thesauros pp. 230.

ἔργα ~Learn the principal part patterns: φιλέω, τιμάω, δηλόω. Write the paradigms of φιλέω and τιμάω on the continuous stem. Be able to recognize all forms.

~Read the Hippocratic Oath (Part 1). Become so familiar with the oath that it is as if it is in your native tongue. Keep reading and rereading the oath until it is easy, transparent. Read the oath out loud. Can you hear any rhythm in it? Can you imagine taking it?

Ὄμνυμι   Ἀπόλλωνα   ἰατρὸν   καὶ   Ἀσκληπιὸν
ὄμνυμι + acc. swear by   Apollo (god of healing)   Asclepius (legendary first doctor)

καὶ Ὑγίειαν καὶ Πανάκειαν καὶ θεοὺς πάντας τε καὶ πάσας, ἵστορας **ποιούμενος**,
Health   All-cure (panacea)   ὁ ἵστωρ witness --> history

ἐπιτελῆ   **ποιήσειν**   κατὰ   δύναμιν   καὶ   κρίσιν   ἐμὴν   ὅρκον τόνδε
ἐπιτελής,ες fulfilled   ἡ δύναμις power
(having a τέλος)

καὶ   συγγραφὴν   τήνδε·   **ἡγήσεσθαι**   μὲν   τὸν διδάξαντά με   τὴν τέχνην ταύτην
ἡ συγγραφή contract   διδάσκω teach   ἡ τέχνη technique, art
(σύν + γράφω)   --> technique, technical

ἴσα γενέταις ἐμοῖς,   καὶ   βίου **κοινώσεσθαι**,   καὶ   χρεῶν   χρῄζοντι
ὁ γενέτης begettor,   life, living,   κοινόω give a share of   τὸ χρέος money,   χρῄζω have need
ancestor   livelihood   debt   of + gen.

μετάδοσιν   **ποιήσεσθαι**, καὶ γένος τὸ ἐξ αὐτοῦ ἀδελφοῖς   ἴσον   **ἐπικρινεῖν**
share, partial giving   κρίνω, fut. κρινῶ judge

ἄρρεσι,   καὶ   διδάξειν   τὴν   τέχνην   ταύτην,   ἢν χρῄζωσι μανθάνειν,
ἄρρην,εν male   = ἐάν

ἄνευ μισθοῦ καὶ συγγραφῆς,   παραγγελίας τε   καὶ   ἀκροάσεως
salary   contract   precepts   lecture, that which has been heard

καὶ   τῆς   λοιπῆς   ἁπάσης   μαθήσεως   μετάδοσιν   **ποιήσεσθαι**
= πάσης   ἡ μάθησις learning,   partial sharing
                                            education, knowledge

υἱοῖς τε ἐμοῖς   καὶ τοῖς τοῦ ἐμὲ διδάξαντος,   καὶ μαθηταῖς   συγγεγραμμένοις τε
share, partial giving   students   συγγράφω enroll

καὶ   ὡρκισμένοις   νόμῳ   ἰατρικῷ,   ἄλλῳ   δὲ   οὐδενί.
ὁρκίζω put under oath   ἰατρικός,ή,όν pertaining
                                    to medicine, medical

διαιτήμασί   τε   **χρήσομαι**   ἐπ' ὠφελείᾳ   καμνόντων   κατὰ   δύναμιν
ἡ δίαιτα prescribed way of life,   ἡ ὠφέλεια benefit   ἡ δύναμις power
regimen   --> diet

καὶ   κρίσιν   ἐμήν,   ἐπὶ   δηλήσει   δὲ   καὶ   ἀδικίᾳ   εἴρξειν.
                           harm   injustice   εἴργω - bar the way

*The oath is printed here in Attic Greek. It was originally preserved in Ionic.

Lesson 52. Continuous Forms of εἶμι, εἰμί, and φημί; Aorist System of ἔβην, ἔστην, ἔγνων; Verbals ending in -τέος,α,ον

εἶμι *I go*	εἰμί *I am*	φημί *I say*

Present

εἶμι	ἴμεν	εἰμί	ἐσμέν	φημί	φαμέν
εἶ	ἴτε	εἶ	ἐστέ	φῄς	φατέ
εἶσι(ν)	ἴασι(ν)	ἐστί(ν)	εἰσί(ν)	φησί(ν)	φασί(ν)

Imperfect

ᾖα or ᾔειν	ᾖμεν	ἦ (or ἦν)	ἦμεν	ἔφην	ἔφαμεν
ᾔεισθα or ᾔεις	ᾖτε	ἦσθα	ἦτε	ἔφησθα or ἔφης	ἔφατε
ᾔειν or ᾔει	ᾖσαν	ἦν	ἦσαν	ἔφη	ἔφασαν
	or ᾖεσαν				

SUBJUNCTIVE

ἴω	ἴωμεν	ὦ	ὦμεν	φῶ	φῶμεν
ἴῃς	ἴητε	ᾖς	ἦτε	φῇς	φῆτε
ἴῃ	ἴωσι(ν)	ᾖ	ὦσι(ν)	φῇ	φῶσι(ν)

OPTATIVE

ἴοιμι	ἴοιμεν	εἴην	εἶμεν	φαίην	φαῖμεν
ἴοις	ἴοιτε	εἴης	εἶτε	φάιης	φαῖτε
ἴοι	ἴοιεν	εἴη	εἶεν	φάιη	φαῖεν

IMPERATIVE

ἴθι	ἴτε	ἴσθι	ἔστε	φάθι	φάτε
ἴτω	ἰόντων	ἔστω	ἔστων	φάτω	φάντων

INFINITIVE

ἰέναι	εἶναι	φάναι

PARTICIPLE

ἰών, ἰοῦσα, ἰόν	ὤν, οὖσα, ὄν	φάς, φᾶσα, φάν (poetic)
		(φάσκων, ουσα, ον in prose)

Be able to recognize the forms above. (You know εἰμί already. It is included for comparison.)

The forms of εἶμι *I go, will go* and εἰμί *I am* are usually quite different because **their stems are different.** The stem of εἶμι is ι (sometimes visible only as an iota subscript). The stem of εἰμί is εσ (which --> ε when the σ drops). There is **no future for εἶμι** because it is virtually a future itself. Note that in some indicative forms only the accent or an iota subscript enables you to tell whether a verb is εἶμι or εἰμί.

φημί is enclitic. The stem is φη/φα. The future, φήσω, is normal. The form ἔφη is imperfect but it is also **used as aorist.** (It is often translated *he, she, it said* and seems to be used interchangeably with εἶπε.) In fact, apart from the indicative, the whole system of φημί looks just like the aorist systems of ἔβην, ἔστην, and ἔγνων (see below).

▶ **Exercise α:** Distinguish εἰμί from εἶμι in the following forms:

1. εἶμι 2. εἶεν 3. ἰόντων 4. ἦτε 5. ἴσθι 6. ἦσαν 7. ἴητε 8. ᾖς 9. ἴοι 10. ἰόντες

▶ **Exercise β:** Translate:

1. φῇς 2. φασί 3. φᾶσα 4. φησί 5. φάς 6. φῇ 7. ἔφησθα 8. ἔφη 9. φάν 10. φάναι

| ἔβην *I went* | ἔστην *I stood* | ἔγνων *I knew* |

AORIST

INDICATIVE	INDICATIVE	INDICATIVE
ἔβην ἔβημεν	ἔστην ἔστημεν	ἔγνων ἔγνωμεν
ἔβης ἔβητε	ἔστης ἔστητε	ἔγνως ἔγνωτε
ἔβη ἔβησαν	ἔστη ἔστησαν	ἔγνω ἔγνωσαν
SUBJUNCTIVE	**SUBJUNCTIVE**	**SUBJUNCTIVE**
βῶ βῶμεν	στῶ στῶμεν	γνῶ γνῶμεν
βῇς βῆτε	στῇς στῆτε	γνῷς γνῶτε
βῇ βῶσι(ν)	στῇ στῶσι(ν)	γνῷ γνῶσι(ν)
OPTATIVE	**OPTATIVE**	**OPTATIVE**
βαίην βαῖμεν	σταίην σταῖμεν	γνοίην γνοῖμεν
βαίης βαῖτε	σταίης σταῖτε	γνοίης γνοῖτε
βαίη βαῖεν	σταίη σταῖεν	γνοίη γνοῖεν
IMPERATIVE	**IMPERATIVE**	**IMPERATIVE**
βῆθι βῆτε	στῆθι στῆτε	γνῶθι γνῶτε
βήτω βάντων	στήτω στάντων	γνώτω γνόντων
INFINITIVE	**INFINITIVE**	**INFINITIVE**
βῆναι	στῆναι	γνῶναι
PARTICIPLE	**PARTICIPLE**	**PARTICIPLE**
βάς, βᾶσα, βάν	στάς, στᾶσα, στάν	γνούς, γνοῦσα, γνόν
gen. βάντος, βάσης, βάντος	gen. στάντος, στάσης, στάντος	gen. γνόντος, γνούσης, γνόντος

These aorists are athematic in all forms except the subjunctive, with its lengthened ε/ο endings. We have seen the special optative endings (-ιην, -ιη, -ιης, -ιμεν, -ιτε, -ιεν) used for the verb εἰμί, φημί, and also in τεθναίην, a perfect optative on the stem τεθνα-). They are athematic optative endings. There are other athematic aorists, often intransitive:

ἐχάρην - *I rejoiced* (intransitive aorist of χαίρω)
ἔφυν - *I grew, was by nature* (intransitive aorist of φύω = *produce*)
ἔδυν - *I sank, set* (of sun and stars; related to δέδυκε in δέδυκε μὲν ἁ σελάννα); *I put on* (clothes)

▶ **Exercise γ:**
Translate:

1. γνῶθι	4. γνούς	7. ἔγνω	10. βᾶσαι	13. ἔφυς
2. βῶ	5. βάς	8. βήτω	11. στῆθι	14. χαρείς
3. ἔστη	6. στῆτε (2 ways)	9. γνοίη	12. γνῶμεν	15. ἀναγνόν

VERBALS ENDING IN -τέος,α,ον / -τέον

Verbal adjectives in -τέος express **necessity**. They are made by adding -τέος to a verb stem, usually the Aorist Passive stem. The linking verb ἐστί is most often omitted. The agent will be given in the dative. The neuter singular may be used impersonally and may take an object.

σωτέος,α,ον	*to be saved* (ἐ-σω-θήν)	δοτέον,α,ον	*to be given* (ἐ-δό-θην)
ἡ πόλις σωτέα ἡμῖν	*The city must be saved by us.*	χάρις δοτέα.	*Thanks must be given.*
σωτέον τὴν πόλιν	*One must save the city.*	χάριν δοτέον	*One must give thanks.*

✦ **καταβατέον** *One must go down.* Famous statement in Plato's *Republic*, that the philosopher must go back into the cave.

Classwork: ✦✦ Read **Diogenes #19**, and **Famous Sayings #16**, Thesauros p. 235 and 233.

ἔργα   ~Write out the paradigms of ἔβην, ἔστην, ἔγνων. Be able to recognize all forms.
~Write the continuous forms of εἰμι 3x and φημί once. Be able to recognize all forms.
~Read the Hippocratic Oath (Part 2). Keep working at saying it out loud until it feels smooth and comfortable and "native" to you. What connections do you see between this oath and the way medicine is practiced today?

οὐ δώσω δὲ οὐδὲ φάρμακον οὐδενὶ αἰτηθεὶς θανάσιμον, οὐδὲ ὑφηγήσομαι
deadly   lead the way to

συμβουλίαν τοιάνδε· ὁμοίως δὲ οὐδὲ γυναικὶ πεσσὸν φθόριον δώσω.
advice   such as this here   pessary, pebble   destructive

ἁγνῶς δὲ καὶ ὁσίως διατηρήσω βίον τὸν ἐμὸν καὶ τέχνην τὴν ἐμήν.
ἁγνός,ή,όν = pure   keep a close watch on

οὐ τεμῶ δὲ οὐδὲ μήν* λιθιῶντας, ἐκχωρήσω δὲ ἐργάταις ἀνδράσι
those suffering   ἐκχωρέω get out of the   workers,
from stones   way of, yield to   practitioners
          (ἐκ + χώρα = place)

πράξεως τῆσδε. εἰς οἰκίας δὲ ὁπόσας ἂν εἰσίω, εἰσελεύσομαι ἐπ' ὠφελείᾳ
ἡ πρᾶξις deed, work

καμνόντων, ἐκτὸς ὢν πάσης ἀδικίας ἑκουσίας καὶ φθορίας,
ἐκτός -outside of + gen.   ἑκούσιος,α,ον   ἡ φθορία destruction
         willing, voluntary

τῆς τε ἄλλης* καὶ ἀφροδισίων ἔργων ἐπί τε γυναικείων σωμάτων καὶ ἀνδρῴων,
sexual (of Aphrodite)   female   male

ἐλευθέρων τε καὶ δούλων. ἃ δ' ἂν ἐν θεραπείᾳ ἢ ἴδω ἢ ἀκούσω,
ἐλεύθερος,α,ον - free   δοῦλος,η,ον   treatment, therapy
         (as adj.) slave

ἢ καὶ ἄνευ θεραπείας κατὰ βίον ἀνθρώπων ἃ μὴ χρή ποτε ἐκλαλεῖσθαι ἔξω,
blab out   ἔξω (adv.) out,
         outward

σιγήσομαι, ἄρρητα ἡγούμενος εἶναι τὰ τοιαῦτα.
σιγάω - hold in silence   ἄρρητος,ον - not to be spoken of;
        not spoken (ἐρῶ is future of λέγω)

ὅρκον μὲν οὖν μοι τόνδε ἐπιτελῆ ποιοῦντι καὶ μὴ συγχέοντι,
ἐπιτελής,ες   συγχέω pour together, jumble, confuse
fulfilled, having a τέλος   (σύν + χέω = pour)

εἴη ἐπαύρασθαι καὶ βίου καὶ τέχνης δοξαζομένῳ
enjoy the benefits of   δοξάζω have a (good) opinion of, hold in esteem
         (ἡ δόξα opinion, reputation)

παρὰ πᾶσιν ἀνθρώποις εἰς τὸν ἀεὶ χρόνον· παραβαίνοντι δὲ
         παραβαίνω transgress

καὶ ἐπιορκοῦντι τἀναντία τούτων.
ἐπιορκέω swear falsely   = τὰ ἐναντία

*μήν -is a particle used to strengthen assertions - "*I mean it,*" "*verily,*" or "*I swear*"

** This is a Greek idiom. ἄλλος τε comes first; one could say that ἄλλος τε *anticipates* the contrast. Whereas we say in English, "*I read this book and the others,*" a Greek might say, τά τε ἄλλα βιβλία καὶ τοῦτο ἀνέγνων. "*I read both the other books and this.*" So in this passage: "*I will stay away from injustice, both other* [injustice] *and* [the injustice] *of . . .*"

THREE MEDICAL SYMBOLS

Figure 1.

Asclepius, as we have seen in an earlier essay, is both a divine healer and the patron of physicians. His emblem is a staff entwined with a sacred serpent; it represents the healing and rejuvenation that Asclepius brings. The symbol itself occurs in other cultures. For instance, in the book of Numbers of the Bible, Moses places a brass serpent upon a staff as a source of healing. Asclepius' emblem has become one of the major symbols for doctors throughout the world. Asclepius' serpent and staff are often combined, as in Figure 1, with one of the aphorisms of Hippocrates: "Life is short, art is long, the crisis is urgent." This aphorism points to the complexity of the physician's training and the necessity for difficult and prompt medical decisions.

The American Medical Association officially adopted the staff and serpent of Asclepius as its symbol in the 1920s. The World Medical Association followed in 1956. Both groups believed that their former symbol, Hermes' caduceus, was not as appropriate to their role as physicians as is the emblem of Asclepius. The American Medical Association symbol, as shown in figure 2, is a stylized version of Asclepius' staff and serpent. In this graphic, particular attention is given to the staff that represents the flourishing of life.

Figure 2.

Figure 3.

The staff of Hermes, the caduceus, is however still used as a symbol for the healing profession; it is currently the emblem of the U.S. Army Medical Corps. It consists of two snakes facing each other entwined on a winged staff. It has often been confused with the Asclepian staff and serpent, even though that emblem has only a single serpent. The symbolism of the caduceus may also be interpreted as one of rejuvenation, since one of Hermes' functions is to escort souls to and from the underworld. A related function is that of awakening sleepers with his staff – an analog of resurrection. The wings on the caduceus refer to Hermes' ability to transcend realms in a swift flight from heaven to earth to the underworld. However, since Hermes is most commonly a messenger god, the emblem probably developed as a herald's staff. It would originally have been an olive branch entwined with ribbons that allowed safe passage and signified peace. In time the ribbons could have been interpreted as snakes. Even as a traveler's staff, however, the caduceus is still appropriate to ancient physicians. The Hippocratic doctor traveled from city to city. It is from his journeys from *deme* ("district") to *deme* that the word "epidemic" derives.

Lesson 53. τίθημι, ἵημι

Within the group of -μι verbs are the "Big Four": τίθημι, ἵημι, ἵστημι, δίδωμι.
These are important verbs, commonly used, and have unusual aorists as well as athematic forms on the continuous stem.

τίθημι, θήσω, ἔθηκα, τέθηκα, τέθειμαι, ἐτέθην

τίθημι *I put*

ACTIVE CONTINUOUS		ACTIVE AORIST		M-P CONTINUOUS		MIDDLE AORIST	
INDICATIVE				**INDICATIVE**			
τίθημι	τίθεμεν	**ἔθηκα**	ἔθεμεν	τίθεμαι	τιθέμεθα	ἐθέμην	ἐθέμεθα
τίθης	**τίθετε**	**ἔθηκας**	ἔθετε	τίθεσαι	**τίθεσθε**	ἔθου	ἔθεσθε
τίθησι(ν)	τιθέασι(ν)	**ἔθηκε(ν)**	ἔθεσαν	τίθεται	τίθενται	ἔθετο	ἔθεντο
ἐτίθην	ἐτίθεμεν			ἐτιθέμην	ἐτιθέμεθα		
ἐτίθεις	ἐτίθετε			ἐτίθεσο	ἐτίθεσθε		
ἐτίθει	ἐτίθεσαν			ἐτίθετο	ἐτίθεντο		
SUBJUNCTIVE				**SUBJUNCTIVE**			
τιθῶ	τιθῶμεν	θῶ	θῶμεν	τιθῶμαι	τιθώμεθα	θῶμαι	θώμεθα
τιθῇς	τιθῆτε	θῇς	θῆτε	**τιθῇ**	τιθῆσθε	**θῇ**	θῆσθε
τιθῇ	τιθῶσι(ν)	**θῇ**	θῶσι(ν)	τιθῆται	τιθῶνται	θῆται	θῶνται
OPTATIVE				**OPTATIVE**			
τιθείην	τιθεῖμεν	θείην	θεῖμεν	τιθείμην	τιθείμεθα	θείμην	θείμεθα
τιθείης	τιθεῖτε	θείης	θεῖτε	τιθεῖο	τιθεῖσθε	θεῖο	θεῖσθε
τιθείη	τιθεῖεν	θείη	θεῖεν	τιθεῖτο	τιθεῖντο	θεῖτο	θεῖντο
IMPERATIVE				**IMPERATIVE**			
τίθει	**τίθετε**	θές	θέτε	τίθεσο	**τίθεσθε**	θοῦ	θέσθε
τιθέτω	**τιθέντων**	θέτω	θέντων	τιθέσθω	τιθέσθων	θέσθω	θέσθων
INFINITIVE				**INFINITIVE**			
τιθέναι		θεῖναι		τίθεσθαι		θέσθαι	
PARTICIPLE				**PARTICIPLE**			
τιθείς, εῖσα, έν		θείς, θεῖσα, θέν		τιθέμενος, η, ον		θέμενος, η, ον	
gen. τιθέντος, είσης, έντος		gen. θέντος, είσης, έντος					

Stem 3 (aorist Active/Middle) of τίθημι is the shortest stem: simply θε.

Notice the "**disappearing κ**" of the Active aorist singular (ἔθηκα, like ἔδωκα). The κ drops out and is not part of the stem.

Notice the Active optative endings--ίην, ίης, ίη, etc.

▶ **Exercise α:** Translate:
1. ἔθηκας   3. τίθησι   5. θέν   7. θῶνται   9. θῇ (2 ways)   11. θῆσθε
2. θεῖεν   4. τιθῇ (2 ways)   6. ἐτίθει   8. τίθει   10. θεῖντο   12. τιθέντων (2 ways)

When you see a verb ending with -θῶ, -θείην, etc., or a participle ending, or -θείς, θεῖσα, θέν, etc., remember: it may be an Aorist Passive OR it may be the Active aorist of a **compound** of τίθημι. Common compounds include: συντίθημι *put together*, παρατίθημι *put alongside*, κατατίθημι *put down*, μετατίθημι *put differently, change*, προτίθημι *put forth, propose*.

▶ **Exercise β:** Distinguish: 1. σωθείη / συνθείη   2. καταθέν / κριθέν   3. πραχθεῖσα / παραθεῖσα.

ἵημι, ἥσω, ἧκα, εἷκα, εἷμαι, εἵσθην

ἵημι *I release, let go* (*utter* words, *shoot* arrows, etc.)

ACTIVE CONTINUOUS		ACTIVE AORIST		M-P CONTINUOUS		MIDDLE AORIST	
INDICATIVE				**INDICATIVE**			
ἵημι	ἵεμεν	ἧκα	-εἷμεν	ἵεμαι	ἱέμεθα	-εἵμην	-εἵμεθα
ἵης	ἵετε	ἧκας	-εἷτε	ἵεσαι	ἵεσθε	-εἷσο	-εἷσθε
ἵησι(ν)	ἱᾶσι(ν)	ἧκε(ν)	-εἷσαν	ἵεται	ἵενται	-εἷτο	-εἷντο
ἵην	ἵεμεν			ἱέμην	ἱέμεθα		
ἵεις	ἵετε			ἵεσο	ἵεσθε		
ἵει	ἵεσαν			ἵετο	ἵεντο		
SUBJUNCTIVE				**SUBJUNCTIVE**			
ἱῶ	ἱῶμεν	-ῶ	-ῶμεν	ἱῶμαι	ἱώμεθα	-ῶμαι	-ώμεθα
ἱῇς	ἱῆτε	-ῇς	-ῆτε	ἱῇ	ἱῆσθε	-ῇ	-ῆσθε
ἱῇ	ἱῶσι(ν)	-ῇ	-ῶσι(ν)	ἱῆται	ἱῶνται	-ῆται	-ῶνται
OPTATIVE				**OPTATIVE**			
ἱείην	ἱεῖμεν	-εἵην	-εἷμεν	ἱείμην	ἱείμεθα	-εἵμην	-εἵμεθα
ἱείης	ἱεῖτε	-εἵης	-εἷτε	ἱεῖο	ἱεῖσθε	-εἷο	-εἷσθε
ἱείη	ἱεῖεν	-εἵη	-εἷεν	ἱεῖτο	ἱεῖντο	-εἷτο	-εἷντο
IMPERATIVE				**IMPERATIVE**			
ἵει	ἵετε	-ἕς	-ἕτε	ἵεσο	ἵεσθε	-οὗ	-ἕσθε
ἱέτω	ἱέντων	-ἕτω	-ἕντων	ἱέσθω	ἱέσθων	-ἕσθω	-ἕσθων
INFINITIVE				**INFINITIVE**			
ἱέναι		-εἷναι		ἵεσθαι		-ἕσθαι	
PARTICIPLE				**PARTICIPLE**			
ἱείς, εἷσα, ἕν		-εἵς, -εἷσα, -ἕν		ἱέμενος, η, ον		-ἕμενος, η, ον	
gen. ἱέντος, εισης, έντος		gen. -ἕντος, -είσης, -ἕντος					

ἵημι is like τίθημι except that the stem is even briefer. The aorist stem ἑ is seen only in compounds for the most part, and it can seem to disappear in them. Sometimes only the rough breathing is left as a clue.

▶ **Exercise γ:** 1. ἱᾶσι(ν)   3. ἧκα   5. ἱῇ (2 ways) 7. ἱῶ   9. ἵεσαν   11. ἵει
  Translate: 2. ἵεντο   4. ἱέναι   6. ἵεσο (2 ways) 8. ἵεσαι   10. ἱέμενον   12. ἱεῖτο

▶ **Exercise δ:** Distinguish: 1. μεθείς / μεταθείς   2. ἀφιέναι / ἀπιέναι   3. ἱέτω / ἴτω

Classwork: ✦✦ Read: **Graveyard #29**, Thesauros p. 230
    Reread ✦✦ New Testament #1 and Heraclitus #14, Thesauros pp. 221 and 225.
    Learn the opening lines of the *Iliad* below:

✦

Μῆνιν ἄειδε, θεά, Πηληϊάδεω Ἀχιλῆος
οὐλομένην, ἣ μυρί' Ἀχαιοῖς ἄλγε' ἔθηκεν...

Sing to me, goddess, the wrath of Achilles, the baneful wrath which put upon the Greeks pains ten-thousand fold...

ἔργα   ~Write the forms of τίθημι and ἵημι. Be able to recognize them.
    ~Read Hecuba's lament in *The Trojan Women* by Euripides. This has been taken by many
      to be a moving antiwar plea, one that is all too relevant today.

THE TROJAN WOMEN by Euripides

Hecuba grieves over the dead Astyanax and condemns irrational fear.

θέσθ' ἀμφίτορνον ἀσπίδ' Ἕκτορος πέδῳ,
well-rounded   Hector   τὸ πέδον - ground

λυπρὸν θέαμα κοὐ φίλον λεύσσειν ἐμοί.
λεύσσω – ὁράω (a poetic word)

ὦ μεῖζον' ὄγκον δορὸς ἔχοντες ἢ φρενῶν,
ὁ ὄγκος = mass, bulk, weight

τί τόνδ', Ἀχαιοί, παῖδα δείσαντες φόνον
Greeks   δείδω - fear

καινὸν διειργάσασθε; μὴ Τροίαν ποτὲ   1160
διεργάζομαι work out   Troy

πεσοῦσαν ὀρθώσειεν; οὐδὲν ἦτ' ἄρα,

ὅθ' Ἕκτορος μὲν εὐτυχοῦντος ἐς δόρυ
                           = εἰς

διωλλύμεσθα μυρίας τ' ἄλλης χερός,
διόλλυμι - destroy utterly   = χειρός

πόλεως δ' ἁλούσης καὶ Φρυγῶν ἐφθαρμένων
*   having been captured   Phrygians (= Trojans)*

βρέφος τοσόνδ' ἐδείσατ'· οὐκ αἰνῶ φόβον   1165
τὸ βρέφος = embryo   praise
(Hecuba exaggerates for effect)

ὅστις φοβεῖται μὴ διεξελθὼν λόγῳ.

ἡ ἀσπίς, gen. ἀσπίδος - shield

λυπρός,ά,όν - painful, distressful

τὸ θέαμα - sight
    --> theater (θεάομαι)

τὸ δορύ - spear, gen. δόρατος
    or (poetic) δορός   <--> tree
    rel. to δρῦς = oak, --> Druid

ἡ φρήν, gen. φρενός - (usually
    in plural) - heart, mind, wits
    --> frantic, frenzy

ὁ φόνος - murder, bloodshed;
           blood

ὀρθόω - make upright (ὀρθός),
    raise up, restore

ἄρα - then (used to draw a
    conclusion)

εὐτυχέω - flourish, have good
    fortune

μυρίος,α,ον - numberless, countless
    (from μυριάς = 10,000)
    --> myriad

ἑάλων - acts as aorist to
    ἁλίσκομαι = I am captured
    part. ἁλούς,οῦσα,οῦν

τοσόσδε,τοσάδε, τοσόνδε - of
    such size as this here

διεξέρχομαι – go through
                thoroughly

Put the rounded shield of Hektor on the ground,
a painful sight, not dear for me to see.
You Greeks, whose spears swell bigger than your brains,
why this child--why, in fear of him, did you work out
a new way of murder? Lest some day he might lift up
our fallen Troy? Were you nothing then
when by your spear we perished, while Hektor
yet was flourishing and many another strong arm?
But now, the city taken and the Trojans slain,
so small a babe you feared? I do not praise the fear*
that someone fears unreasoning.

---

* The listener first hears "*I do not praise fear*," then amends: "*I do not praise whoever fears a fear*."

Lesson 54. ἵστημι, δίδωμι

ἵστημι, στήσω, ἔστησα - stand, set up *"I set up a gravestone."* (middle: *I set up my...*)
ἵσταμαι, ἐστήξω, ἔστην, ἔστηκα - stand (intransitive) *"I am standing."*
ἵσταμαι, σταθήσομαι or στήσομαι, ἐστάθην - be stood (passive) *"The stone is being stood up."*

ἵστημι *I set up* (intrans. *I stand, I have stood*)

ACTIVE CONTINUOUS	M-P CONTINUOUS	INTRANSITIVE AORIST	INTRANSITIVE PERFECT
I am setting up	*I am setting up my...* (True Middle) *I am being set up* (Passive) *I am standing* (Intransitive)	*I stood*	*I have stood = I am standing*

INDICATIVE / **INDICATIVE** / **INDICATIVE** / **INDICATIVE**

ACTIVE CONTINUOUS		M-P CONTINUOUS		INTRANSITIVE AORIST	INTRANSITIVE PERFECT	
ἵστημι	ἵσταμεν	ἵσταμαι	ἱστάμεθα	ἔστην	ἔστηκα	ἔσταμεν
ἵστης	ἵστατε	ἵστασαι	ἵστασθε	etc.	ἔστηκας	ἔστατε
ἵστησι(ν)	ἱστᾶσι(ν)	ἵσταται	ἵσταντai		ἔστηκε(ν)	ἐστᾶσι(ν)
				(See p. 211)		
ἵστην	ἵσταμεν	ἱστάμην	ἱστάμεθα		εἱστήκη	ἔσταμεν
ἵστης	ἵστατε	ἵστασο	ἵστασθε		εἱστήκης	ἔστατε
ἵστη	ἵστασαν	ἵστατο	ἵσταντο		εἱστήκει	ἔστασαν

SUBJUNCTIVE / **SUBJUNCTIVE** / **SUBJ.** / **SUBJUNCTIVE**

ἱστῶ	ἱστῶμεν	ἱστῶμαι	ἱστώμεθα	στῶ	ἐστῶ	ἐστῶμεν
ἱστῇς	ἱστῆτε	ἱστᾷ	ἱστῆσθε	etc.	ἐστῇς	ἐστῆτε
ἱστᾷ	ἱστῶσι(ν)	ἱστῆται	ἱστῶνται		ἐστῇ	ἐστῶσι(ν)

OPTATIVE / **OPTATIVE** / **OPT.** / **OPTATIVE**

ἱσταίην	ἱσταῖμεν	ἱσταίμην	ἱσταίμεθα	σταίην	ἐσταίην	ἐσταῖμεν
ἱσταίης	ἱσταῖτε	ἱσταῖο	ἱσταῖσθε	etc.	ἐσταίης	ἐσταῖτε
ἱσταίη	ἱσταῖεν	ἱσταῖτο	ἱσταῖντο		ἐσταίη	ἐσταῖεν

IMPERATIVE / **IMPERATIVE** / **IMPER.** / **IMPERATIVE**

ἵστη	ἵστατε	ἵστασο	ἵστασθε	στῆθι	ἔσταθι	ἔστατε
ἱστάτω	ἱστάντων	ἱστάσθω	ἱστάσθων	etc.	ἐστάτω	ἐστάντων

INFINITIVE / **INFINITIVE** / **INFINITIVE** / **INFINITIVE**

ἱστάναι	ἵστασθαι	στῆναι	ἑστάναι

PARTICIPLE / **PARTICIPLE** / **PARTICIPLE** / **PARTICIPLE**

ACTIVE CONTINUOUS	M-P CONTINUOUS	INTRANSITIVE AORIST	INTRANSITIVE PERFECT
ἱστάς, ᾶσα, άν gen. ἱστάντος, άσης, άντος	ἱστάμενος, η, ον	στάς, στᾶσα, στάν	ἑστώς, ῶσα, ός gen. ἑστῶτος, ώσης, ῶτος

ἵστημι has the usual "Big Four" configuration on the continuous stem. Its stem is ἱστα/η and endings are added directly, with the -ίην, -ίης, -ίη optative. It has a disappearing κ, but in the intransitive perfect (a perfect as present) rather than the aorist.

If you see ἱστ/ἱστ, that is a sign of the continuous stem. (There is actually a time-marker; the ι is long in the imperfect, but Greek spelling does not reveal that.) If you see ἑστ/εἱστ/ἔστ, that is a sign of the perfect.

▶ **Exercise α:** Translate:

1. ἱσταίμην	4. ἱσταίην	7. ἵστη (2 ways)	10. ἑστῶσαι	13. στάν
2. σταίην	5. ἵσταμεν	8. ἵστη (2 ways)	11. εἱστήκη	14. ἵστασθαι
3. ἐσταίην	6. ἔσταμεν	9. στῆθι	12. ἱστάντες	15. ἑστάσι

The continuous stems of the "Big Four" are made by reduplicating the short aorist stems:

τίθημι was originally θί-θημι, (but the Greeks did not pronounce two *theta* sounds near each other).
ἵημι was actually yi-yemi, with the same sort of reduplication.
ἵστημι was originally σί-στημι.
δίδωμι has the most obvious reduplication.

δίδωμι, δώσω, ἔδωκα, δέδωκα, δέδομαι, ἐδόθην *give*

δίδωμι *I give*

ACTIVE CONTINUOUS		ACTIVE AORIST		M-P CONTINUOUS		MIDDLE AORIST	
INDICATIVE				**INDICATIVE**			
δίδωμι	δίδομεν	ἔδωκα	ἔδομεν	δίδομαι	διδόμεθα	ἐδόμην	ἐδόμεθα
δίδως	δίδοτε	ἔδωκας	ἔδοτε	δίδοσαι	δίδοσθε	ἔδου	ἔδοσθε
δίδωσι(ν)	διδόασι(ν)	ἔδωκε(ν)	ἔδοσαν	δίδοται	δίδονται	ἔδοτο	ἔδοντο
ἐδίδουν	ἐδίδομεν			ἐδιδόμην	ἐδιδόμεθα		
ἐδίδους	ἐδίδοτε			ἐδίδοσο	ἐδίδοσθε		
ἐδίδου	ἐδίδοσαν			ἐδίδοτο	ἐδίδοντο		
SUBJUNCTIVE				**SUBJUNCTIVE**			
διδῶ	διδῶμεν	δῶ	δῶμεν	διδῶμαι	διδώμεθα	δῶμαι	δώμεθα
διδῷς	διδῶτε	δῷς	δῶτε	διδῷ	διδῶσθε	δῷ	δῶσθε
διδῷ	διδῶσι(ν)	δῷ	δῶσι(ν)	διδῶται	διδῶνται	δῶται	δῶνται
OPTATIVE				**OPTATIVE**			
διδοίην	διδοῖμεν	δοίην	δοῖμεν	διδοίμην	διδοίμεθα	δοίμην	δοίμεθα
διδοίης	διδοῖτε	δοίης	δοῖτε	διδοῖο	διδοῖσθε	δοῖο	δοῖσθε
διδοίη	διδοῖεν	δοίη	δοῖεν	διδοῖτο	διδοῖντο	δοῖτο	δοῖντο
IMPERATIVE				**IMPERATIVE**			
δίδου	δίδοτε	δός	δότε	δίδοσο	δίδοσθε	δοῦ	δόσθε
διδότω	διδόντων	δότω	δόντων	διδόσθω	διδόσθων	δόσθω	δόσθων
INFINITIVE				**INFINITIVE**			
διδόναι		δοῦναι		δίδοσθαι		δόσθαι	
PARTICIPLE				**PARTICIPLE**			
διδούς,οῦσα,όν gen. διδόντος, etc.		δούς,δοῦσα,δόν gen. δόντος, etc.		διδόμενος,η,ον		δόμενος,η,ον	

The stem of δίδωμι ends with o/ω, and many of its forms have endings like those of δηλόω.

▶ **Exercise β:** Translate:
1. ἐδίδου
2. δίδου
3. δοῦ
4. δοῦναι
5. δίδοσθαι
6. δόντες
7. δῷ (2 ways)
8. ἔδωκε(ν)
9. δόν
10. διδοίη

Classwork: ✦✦ Read **Famous Sayings #17**, Thesauros pp. 233. ✦✦ Reread Graveyard #2 and 20, Famous Sayings #7, and Diogenes #5, Thesauros pp. 227, 229, 232, and 234.

ἔργα   ~Write the forms of ἵστημι and δίδωμι. Be able to recognize them.
~Read the exchange between Oedipus and Teiresias by Sophocles. For once, instead of using translationese, make the most beautiful translation you can.

(Read as many translations as you can. You will find that no translator can convey the pith and speed of the dialogue. There are inevitable sacrifices and distortions. After just one year of learning Greek, you can understand why Greek literature needs to be read in the original.)

OEDIPUS TYRANNOS by Sophocles

Oedipus challenges the blind seer Teiresias.

ΟΙΔ· ἦ ταῦτα δῆτ' ἀνεκτὰ πρὸς τούτου κλύειν;
ἦ asks a question (especially beginning a series) = ἀκούειν

οὐκ εἰς ὄλεθρον; οὐχὶ θᾶσσον; οὐ πάλιν 430
destruction = θᾶττον πάλιν back

ἄψορρος οἴκων τῶνδ' ἀποστραφεὶς ἄπει; *
going back

ΤΕΙΡ· οὐδ' ἱκόμην ἔγωγ' ἄν, εἰ σὺ μὴ 'κάλεις. **

ΟΙΔ· οὐ γάρ τί σ' ἤδη μῶρα φωνήσοντ', ἐπεὶ
φωνέω speak since

σχολῇ σ' ἂν οἴκους τοὺς ἐμοὺς ἐστειλάμην.
at leisure--i.e., not soon, hardly at all

ΤΕΙΡ· ἡμεῖς τοιοίδ' ἔφυμεν, ὡς μὲν σοὶ δοκεῖ, 435

μῶροι, γονεῦσι δ', οἵ σ' ἔφυσαν, ἔμφρονες.
ὁ γονεύς begetter ἔμφρων,ον sane,
in one's wits (φρένες)

ΟΙΔ· ποίοισι; μεῖνον. τίς δέ μ' ἐκφύει βροτῶν;
ἐκφύω beget

ΤΕΙΡ· ἥδ' ἡμέρα φύσει σε καὶ διαφθερεῖ.
διαφθείρω ruin utterly

ΟΙΔ· ὡς πάντ' ἄγαν αἰνικτὰ κἀσαφῆ λέγεις.
ἄγαν too much, too

ΤΕΙΡ· οὔκουν σὺ ταῦτ' ἄριστος εὑρίσκειν ἔφυς; 440
from οὐκ + οὖν

ΟΙΔ· τοιαῦτ' ὀνείδιζ' οἷς ἔμ' εὑρήσεις μέγαν.
reproach, blame

ΤΕΙΡ· αὕτη γε μέντοι σ' ἡ τύχη διώλεσεν.
nonetheless

ΟΙΔ· ἀλλ' εἰ πόλιν τήνδ' ἐξέσωσ', οὔ μοι μέλει.
ἐκσῴζω thoroughly save

ἀνεκτός,ή,όν - bearable (ἀνέχομαι)

πρός + gen. - from, at the hands of

στρέφω - turn, twist; mid and passive - turn oneself aorist pass. ἐστράφην --> streptococcus

ἀποστρέφω - turn away

στέλλω - prepare, send; mid and passive - summon

φύω, φύσω, ἔφυσα - bring forth, grow, produce; intr. aorist ἔφυν - I was, grew, came to be; intr. perfect πέφυκα - I am by nature --> physics, physical --> future (via Latin) <--> be

αἰνικτός,ή,όν - expressed in riddles (from αἰνίττομαι - speak in riddles)

ἀσαφής,ές - unclear (σαφής,ές = clear)

γε (postpositive) - at any rate

*One way of giving a command in Greek is to ask a negative question in the future tense: *Will you not do this?* i.e., *Do this!* (And remember εἶμι acts as a future.) You now know three ways of giving a command in Greek: imperative, subjunctive of prohibition, and future negative question. In fact, if you read the continuation of this passage in Sophocles, you will find a fourth way: the infinitive (φάσκειν).

**Without the 99% principle you cannot make sense of this statement. (See p. 130.)

The greater the work, the greater the challenge of translating, it seems. Examine the two translations below. How have the translators caught the pithiness and speed of these exchanges? Where have they succeeded? What have they been unable to render? How different are they? How much does the "style of the times" affect translation?

Look for other translations, too, and compare them. You will realize that in learning Greek, you have given yourself a gift that can be gotten no other way: to be able to read in the original documents of remarkable power, depth, and beauty.

ΟΙΔ   ἦ ταῦτα δῆτ' ἀνεκτὰ πρὸς τούτου κλύειν;
οὐκ εἰς ὄλεθρον; οὐχὶ θᾶσσον; οὐ πάλιν
ἄψορρος οἴκων τῶνδ' ἀποστραφεὶς ἄπει;

ΤΕΙΡ·   οὐδ' ἱκόμην ἔγωγ' ἄν, εἰ σὺ μὴ 'κάλεις.

ΟΙΔ·   οὐ γάρ τί σ' ᾔδη μῶρα φωνήσοντ', ἐπεὶ
σχολῇ σ' ἂν οἴκους τοὺς ἐμοὺς ἐστειλάμην.

ΤΕΙΡ·   ἡμεῖς τοιοίδ' ἔφυμεν, ὡς μὲν σοὶ δοκεῖ,
μῶροι, γονεῦσι δ', οἵ σ' ἔφυσαν, ἔμφρονες.

ΟΙΔ·   ποίοισι; μεῖνον. τίς δέ μ' ἐκφύει βροτῶν;

ΤΕΙΡ·   ἥδ' ἡμέρα φύσει σε καὶ διαφθερεῖ.

ΟΙΔ·   ὡς πάντ' ἄγαν αἰνικτὰ κἀσαφῆ λέγεις.

ΤΕΙΡ·   οὔκουν σὺ ταῦτ' ἄριστος εὑρίσκειν ἔφυς;

ΟΙΔ·   τοιαῦτ' ὀνείδιζ' οἷς ἔμ' εὑρήσεις μέγαν.

ΤΕΙΡ·   αὕτη γε μέντοι σ' ἡ τύχη διώλεσεν.

ΟΙΔ·   ἀλλ' εἰ πόλιν τήνδ' ἐξέσωσ', οὔ μοι μέλει.

Thomas Dale 1824	Dudley Fitts and Robert Fitzgerald 1939*
Oed: Must I then brook such shameless taunts from thee? A curse light on thee, babbler! to thy home Away, and rid us of thy hateful presence.	*Oed: Am I to bear this from him?--Damnation Take you! Out of this place! Out of my sight!*
Teir: But for thy summons, I had never come.	*Teir: I would not have come at all if you had not asked me.*
Oed: I little deemed that thou wouldst prate so weakly Or never had I sought thy presence here.	*Oed: Could I have told that you'd talk nonsense, that You'd come here to make a fool of yourself, and of me?*
Teir: Though to thy better wisdom void of sense We seem, thy parents once esteemed us wise.	*Teir: A fool? Your parents thought me sane enough.*
Oed: Who are they? Stop, and tell who gave me birth.	*Oed: My parents again!--Wait: who were my parents?*
Teir: This day will show thy birth, and seal thy ruin.	*Teir: This day will give you a father, and break your heart.*
Oed: How wild, and how mysterious are thy words!	*Oed: Your infantile riddles! Your damned abracadabra!*
Teir: Art thou not skilled t' unriddle this enigma?	*Teir: You were a great man once at solving riddles.*
Oed: Reproach the path that led me up to greatness.	*Oed: Mock me with that if you like; you will find it true.*
Teir: That very path hath led thee to perdition.	*Teir: It was true enough. It brought about your ruin.*
Oed: I reck not that, so I preserved the state.	*Oed: But if it saved this town?*

*Translation is from SOPHOCLES: THE OEDIPUS CYCLE, AN ENGLISH VERSION by Dudley Fitts and Robert Fitzgerald, copyright © 1949 by Harcourt Brace & Company and renewed 1977 by Cornelia Fitts and Robert Fitzgerald; reprinted by permission of the publisher.

θησαυρός *

NEW TESTAMENT

Lesson

1. τί δὲ βλέπεις τὸ κάρφος τὸ ἐν τῷ ὀφθαλμῷ τοῦ ἀδελφοῦ σου, **τὴν** δὲ ἐν τῷ σῷ   6
    look at   speck, splinter, chip   your

ὀφθαλμῷ **δοκὸν** οὐ κατανοεῖς; ἢ πῶς ἐρεῖς τῷ ἀδελφῷ σου " Ἄφες ἐκβάλω
    beam,   perceive   how will you say   Come on let me throw out,
    roofbeam   get rid of

τὸ κάρφος ἐκ τοῦ ὀφθαλμοῦ σου," καὶ ἰδού **ἡ δοκὸς** ἐν τῷ ὀφθαλμῷ σοῦ;**
    speck   = ἰδοῦ - behold!

ὑποκριτά,*** ἔκβαλε πρῶτον ἐκ τοῦ ὀφθαλμοῦ σοῦ **τὴν δοκόν**, καὶ τότε
vocative of ὑποκριτής   first   then

διαβλέψεις ἐκβαλεῖν τὸ κάρφος ἐκ τοῦ ὀφθαλμοῦ τοῦ ἀδελφοῦ σου.
  you will see clear   speck, splinter, chip   Matthew 7: 3-5

2. ὁ ἀγαθὸς ἄνθρωπος ἐκ τοῦ ἀγαθοῦ θησαυροῦ τῆς καρδίας προφέρει   7
                                                      brings forth

τὸ ἀγαθόν, καὶ ὁ πονηρὸς ἐκ τοῦ πονηροῦ προφέρει **τὸ πονηρόν**.
                  wicked   Luke 6: 45

3. Μὴ θησαυρίζετε ὑμῖν θησαυροὺς ἐπὶ τῆς γῆς, ὅπου σὴς καὶ βρῶσις ἀφανίζει, 8
    store treasure   for you   earth where moth   rust   make disappear,
                                                            destroy, spoil

καὶ ὅπου κλέπται διορύσσουσι καὶ κλέπτουσιν. θησαυρίζετε δὲ ὑμῖν θησαυροὺς
    ὁ κλέπτης = thief   dig through

ἐν οὐρανῷ, ὅπου οὔτε σὴς οὔτε βρῶσις ἀφανίζει, καὶ ὅπου κλέπται οὐ

διορύσσουσιν οὐδὲ κλέπτουσιν. ὅπου γάρ ἐστιν ὁ θησαυρός σου,

ἐκεῖ ἔσται **καὶ** ἡ καρδία σου.
    there will be   Matthew 6: 19-21

---

* The Thesauros contains only selections in genuine ancient or Koine Greek. (The dialect of the New Testament is Koine.) Some passages have been "normalized"--given in Attic Greek. Bold face shows the grammar learned in the Lesson where the reading was assigned. Lesson number is shown to the left.

** Notice difference in accent. σου - yours (unemphatic). σοῦ - <u>yours</u> (emphatic)

*** ὁ ὑποκριτής - hypocrite, originally = actor. In the beginning there were perhaps only choral performances. An actor may have been introduced in performances as one who "replied" (cf. ἀποκρίνομαι) to the chorus or perhaps who "interpreted" or "spoke for" them.

4. ὁ μὴ **ἀγαπῶν** μένει ἐν τῷ θανάτῳ. πᾶς **ὁ μισῶν** τὸν ἀδελφὸν αὐτοῦ   18
μισέω - hate

ἀνθρωποκτόνος ἐστίν, καὶ οἴδατε ὅτι πᾶς ἀνθρωποκτόνος οὐκ ἔχει ζωὴν
killer, manslayer   you (pl.) know

αἰώνιον ἐν αὐτῷ **μένουσαν**. ὃς δ' ἂν ἔχῃ τὸν βίον τοῦ κόσμου καὶ θεωρῇ
eternal   whoever has,   life   world   beholds,
                                 should have   should behold

τὸν ἀδελφὸν αὐτοῦ χρείαν **ἔχοντα** καὶ κλείσῃ   τὰ   σπλάγχνα   αὐτοῦ
need   shuts,   guts as seat of compassion,
should shut   inward parts

ἀπ' αὐτοῦ,   πῶς ἡ ἀγάπη τοῦ θεοῦ μένει ἐν αὐτῷ;
how   love   First Letter of John, 3:15, 17

5. ὁ **λέγων** ἐν τῷ φωτὶ εἶναι καὶ τὸν ἀδελφὸν αὐτοῦ **μισῶν** ἐν τῇ σκοτίᾳ ἐστὶν   18
darkness

ἕως ἄρτι. ὁ **ἀγαπῶν** τὸν ἀδελφὸν αὐτοῦ ἐν τῷ φωτὶ μένει, καὶ σκάνδαλον
up to now   stumbling block,
cause for offence

ἐν αὐτῷ οὐκ ἔστιν. ὁ δὲ **μισῶν** τὸν ἀδελφὸν αὐτοῦ ἐν τῇ σκοτίᾳ ἐστὶν καὶ

ἐν τῇ σκοτίᾳ περιπατεῖ, καὶ οὐκ οἶδε ποῦ ὑπάγει, ὅτι ἡ σκοτία ἐτύφλωσεν
is walking about   where   he is going   blinded

τοὺς ὀφθαλμοὺς αὐτοῦ.   First Letter of John, 2: 9-11

6. μὴ ἀγαπᾶτε τὸν κόσμον μηδὲ τὰ ἐν τῷ κόσμῳ. ἐάν τις ἀγαπᾷ τὸν κόσμον,   19
world   if ever   loves, should love

οὐκ ἔστιν ἡ ἀγάπη τοῦ Πατρὸς ἐν αὐτῷ· ὅτι πᾶν τὸ ἐν τῷ κόσμῳ--ἡ ἐπιθυμία
desire

τῆς σαρκὸς καὶ ἡ ἐπιθυμία τῶν ὀφθαλμῶν καὶ ἡ ἀλαζονεία τοῦ βίου--οὐκ ἔστιν
ἡ σάρξ - flesh   desire   boasting, pretension

ἐκ τοῦ Πατρός, ἀλλὰ ἐκ τοῦ κόσμου ἐστίν. καὶ ὁ κόσμος παράγεται καὶ
goes by

ἡ ἐπιθυμία αὐτοῦ, ὁ δὲ ποιῶν τὸ θέλημα τοῦ Θεοῦ μένει εἰς τὸν αἰῶνα.
desire   will   eternity
First Letter of John 2:15-17

7. Ἠκούσατε ὅτι ἐρρέθη· Ἀγαπήσεις τὸν πλησίον σου καὶ μισήσεις   23
You heard   it was said   Thou shalt love   nearby, i.e., neighbor   thou shalt hate

τὸν ἐχθρόν σου. **ἐγὼ** δὲ λέγω ὑμῖν· ἀγαπᾶτε τοὺς ἐχθροὺς **ὑμῶν** καὶ
enemy

προσεύχεσθε ὑπὲρ τῶν διωκόντων **ὑμᾶς** ὅπως γένησθε υἱοὶ τοῦ Πατρὸς **ὑμῶν**
pray   for   διώκω - pursue, prosecute   so that   you may become

τοῦ ἐν οὐρανοῖς, ὃς τὸν ἥλιον αὐτοῦ ἀνατέλλει ἐπὶ πονηροὺς καὶ ἀγαθοὺς
causes to rise   wicked

καὶ βρέχει ἐπὶ δικαίους καὶ ἀδίκους. ἐὰν γὰρ ἀγαπήσητε τοὺς ἀγαπῶντας
rains   just   if ever   you love, should love

ὑμᾶς, τίνα μισθὸν ἔχετε; οὐχὶ καὶ οἱ τελῶναι τὸ αὐτὸ ποιοῦσιν; καὶ ἐὰν
wage, payment   tax collectors   if ever

ἀσπάσησθε τοὺς ἀδελφοὺς ὑμῶν μόνον, τί περισσὸν ποιεῖτε; οὐχὶ καὶ
you welcome, should welcome   extra
(ἀσπάζομαι = greet lovingly)

οἱ ἐθνικοὶ τὸ αὐτὸ ποιοῦσιν; ἔσεσθε οὖν ὑμεῖς τέλειοι
"of the nation," foreign, gentile   you will be   perfect, complete, fulfilled

ὡς ὁ Πατὴρ ὑμῶν ὁ οὐράνιος τέλειός ἐστιν.
as   perfect, complete, fulfilled   Matthew 5, 43-48

8. Ἠκούσατε ὅτι ἐρρέθη τοῖς ἀρχαίοις· Οὐ **φονεύσεις**· ὃς δ' ἂν φονεύσῃ,   29
it was said   to the ancients   φονεύω - murder   (aorist subjunctive)

ἔνοχος ἔσται τῇ κρίσει. Ἐγὼ δὲ λέγω ὑμῖν ὅτι πᾶς ὁ ὀργιζόμενος τῷ ἀδελφῷ
held in, liable to   judgment

αὐτοῦ ἔνοχος ἔσται τῇ κρίσει. ὃς δ' ἂν εἴπῃ τῷ ἀδελφῷ αὐτοῦ "Ρακά,"
held in, liable to   whoever says, should say   a term of abuse, tr. *"you jerk!"*

ἔνοχος ἔσται τῷ συνεδρίῳ· ὃς δ' ἂν εἴπῃ "Μωρέ," ἔνοχος ἔσται εἰς τὴν γέενναν
held in, liable to   Sanhedrin   = μῶρε   xThe valley of Ge-hinnon is
                                                       the Hebrew equivalent of hell)

τοῦ πυρός.   Matt 5, 21-22

9. Ἠκούσατε ὅτι ἐρρέθη· Οὐ **μοιχεύσεις**. Ἐγὼ δὲ λέγω ὑμῖν ὅτι πᾶς ὁ βλέπων   29
          it was said   μοιχεύω - commit adultery

γυναῖκα πρὸς τὸ ἐπιθυμῆσαι αὐτὴν ἤδη ἐμοίχευσεν αὐτὴν ἐν τῇ καρδίᾳ αὐτοῦ.
                                                         Matthew 5, 27-28

10. ἐάν τις εἴπῃ ὅτι " Ἀγαπῶ τὸν θεόν," καὶ τὸν ἀδελφὸν αὐτοῦ μισῇ,   37
if ever   says, should say

ψεύστης ἐστίν· ὁ γὰρ μὴ ἀγαπῶν τὸν ἀδελφὸν αὐτοῦ ὃν **ἑώρακεν**,
liar   ὁράω

τὸν θεὸν ὃν οὐχ **ἑώρακεν** οὐ δύναται ἀγαπᾶν.   First letter of John 4, 20

11. Μὴ κρίνετε, ἵνα μὴ **κριθῆτε**· ἐν ᾧ γὰρ κρίματι κρίνετε **κριθήσεσθε**,   49
     κρίνω - judge   judgment

καὶ ἐν ᾧ μέτρῳ μετρεῖτε **μετρηθήσεται** ὑμῖν.
     τὸ μέτρον - measure   μετρέω - measure   Matthew 7, 1

12. αἰτεῖτε, καὶ **δοθήσεται** ὑμῖν· ζητεῖτε, καὶ εὑρήσετε· κρούετε, καὶ   49
          δίδωμι

ἀνοιγήσεται ὑμῖν.
as if made from an aorist passive ἀνώγην   (ἀνοίγνυμι- open)   Luke 11, 9

HERACLITUS*

Lesson

FLUX

1. πάντα ῥεῖ.
   ῥέω - flow

   4

2. ποταμοῖς **τοῖς αὐτοῖς** ἐμβαίνομέν τε καὶ οὐκ ἐμβαίνομεν.
   ποταμός - river   we go in

   4

3. δὶς εἰς **τὸν αὐτὸν** ποταμον ουκ αν ἐμβαίης.
   twice   you could not go in

   1

4. ποταμοῖς **τοῖς αὐτοῖς** ἐμβαίνουσιν ἕτερα καὶ ἕτερα ὕδατα ἐπιρρεῖ.
   to those stepping in   other   waters   flow by

   4

OPPOSITES

5. Πόλεμος πάντων μὲν πατήρ ἐστιν, πάντων δὲ βασιλεύς, καὶ **τοὺς μὲν** θεοὺς
   War   father

   ἔδειξε **τοὺς δὲ** ἀνθρώπους, **τοὺς μὲν** δούλους ἐποίησε **τοὺς δὲ** ἐλευθέρους.
   shows   slaves   makes   free

   9

6. Ὁ θεὸς ἡμέρα εὐφρόνη, χειμὼν θέρος, πόλεμος εἰρήνη, κόρος λιμός.
              night   winter summer   war   peace   satiety famine
   lit., "kindly time"

   11

7. νόσος ὑγίειαν ἐποίησεν ἡδὺ καὶ ἀγαθόν, λίμος κόρον, κάματος ἀνάπαυσιν.
   health   makes   sweet, pleasant   famine satiety toil,   pause,
                                                          weariness rest

   11

8. θάλαττα ὕδωρ **καθαρώτατον** καὶ **μιαρώτατον**, ἰχθύσι μὲν πότιμον καὶ
   sea   water καθαρός - pure   μιαρός - foul, polluted for fish drinkable

   σωτήριον, ἀνθρώποις δὲ ἄποτον καὶ ὀλέθρον.
   saving   undrinkable destructive

   11

9. τῷ τόξῳ ὄνομα βίος, ἔργον δὲ θάνατος.   (The bow = βιός in Greek.)
      bow   death

   11

THAT WHICH IS HIDDEN

10. ὁ ἄναξ, **οὗ** τὸ μαντεῖόν ἐστι τὸ ἐν Δελφοῖς, οὔτε λέγει οὔτε κρύπτει
             prophetic seat, oracle   hides

    ἀλλὰ σημαίνει.
    shows by a sign, signifies

    12

11. χρυσὸν οἱ διζήμενοι γῆν πολλὴν ὀρύττουσι καὶ εὑρίσκουσιν ὀλίγον.
    gold   seeking, pursuing   dig   find   little

    12

12. φύσις κρύπτεσθαι φιλεῖ.
    nature to hide

    12

---

*The text of Heraclitus is especially conjectural. Texts come from many sources. Choices were made to favor exposition of grammar.

13. ἁρμονία   ἀφανὴς   φανερᾶς   κρείττων.   21
harmony, lit.   nonapparent   φανερός,ά,όν apparent   better
a "fitting together"

14. οἱ πολλοὶ οὐ συνιᾶσιν ὅπως διαφερόμενον **ἑαυτῷ** ὁμολογεῖ·   23
    συνίημι - understand,   differing from itself,   agrees with
      lit., "throw together"   lit., being brought apart

    παλίντονος ἁρμονία ὅπωσπερ τόξου καὶ λύρας.
    back-stretched   just as   lyre
    (variant: παλίντροπος
        -back-turning)

ONE

15. ὁδὸς ἄνω κάτω **μία** καὶ ἡ αὐτή.   17
      upward downward

16. γναφείῳ ὁδὸς εὐθεῖα καὶ σκολιά· **μία** ἐστι καὶ ἡ αὐτή.   17
     fuller's comb   straight   crooked

17. ξυνὸν ἀρχὴ καὶ πέρας ἐπὶ κύκλου περιφερείας.   17
    common   beginning   end   circle   circumference

18. διδάσκαλος δὲ πλείστων ὁ Ἡσίοδος· τοῦτον ἐπίστανται πλεῖστα εἰδέναι,   32
    teacher   Hesiod   they understand   most   to know

    ὅστις ἡμέραν καὶ εὐφρόνην οὐκ ἐγίγνωσκεν· ἔστι γὰρ **ἕν.**
    someone who   night
        lit., "kindly time,"
         a euphemism

19. πολυμαθία νοῦν ἔχειν οὐ διδάσκει. Ἡσίοδον γὰρ **ἂν ἐδίδαξε** καὶ   32
                            Hesiod

    Πυθαγόρην, αὖθις τε Ξενοφάνη τε καὶ Ἑκαταῖον.
    Pythagoras   Xenophanes   Hecataeus (a geographer)

WISDOM

20. ἦθος ἀνθρώπῳ δαίμων.   33
    character

21. ἦθος ἀνθρώπειον μὲν οὐκ ἔχει γνώμας, θεῖον δὲ ἔχει.   33
                  wise opinions, wisdom   divine

22. ἓν τὸ σοφόν· ἐπίστασθαι γνώμην ἥτις **ἐκυβέρνησε** πάντα διὰ πάντων.   33
       wisdom   κυβερνάω - steer

23. ψυχῆς πείρατα ἰὼν οὐκ ἂν **ἐξεύροιο,** πᾶσαν **ἐπιπορευόμενος** ὁδόν·   46
    soul   boundaries   going   ἐξευρίσκω - find out, discover   = πορευόμενος

    οὕτω βαθὺν λόγον ἔχει.
       deep

XENOPHANES

1. εἷς θεός, ἐν τε θεοῖσι καὶ ἀνθρώποισι μέγιστος   34
      = θεοῖς   = ἀνθρώποις

   οὔτι δέμας θνητοῖσιν ὁμοίιος οὐδὲ νόημα.
   οὐ + τι τὸ δέμας   mortals (subject   similar   τὸ νόημα
             form   to θάνατος)   = ὁμοῖος   thought

2. οὖλος ὁρᾷ, οὖλος δὲ νοεῖ, οὖλος δέ τ' ἀκούει.   34
   = ὅλος   νοέω - perceive,
   whole   think

3. ἀλλ' οἱ βροτοὶ **δοκέουσι γεννᾶσθαι** θεούς   34
                             to be born

   τὴν σφετέρην δ' ἐσθῆτα ἔχειν φωνήν τε δέμας τε.
   their own   clothing   τὸ δέμας form

4. Αἰθίοπές τε θεοὺς σφετέρους σιμοὺς μέλανάς τε   34
   Ethiopians   their own   snub-nosed black

   Θρῆκές τε γλαυκοὺς καὶ πυρροὺς **φασι πέλεσθαι.**
   Thracians   blue-eyed   red-headed   = εἶναι

5. ἀλλ' εἰ χεῖρας ἔχον βόες ἵπποι τ' ἠὲ λέοντες   32
              = εἶχον cows   = ἤ   lions

   ἢ γράψαι χείρεσσι καὶ ἔργα τελεῖν ἅπερ ἄνδρες,
   write, paint   works, statues

   ἵπποι μέν θ' ἵπποισι βόες δέ τε βουσὶν ὁμοίας
   horses   = τε   cows

   καί κε θεῶν ἰδέας ἔγραφον καὶ σώματ' ἐποίουν
   = ἄν   forms   bodies

   τοιαῦθ' οἷόν περ καὐτοὶ δέμας εἶχον ἕκαστοι.
   of such sort as   = καὶ αὐτοὶ τὸ δέμας - form

6. οὔτοι ἀπ' ἀρχῆς πάντα θεοὶ θνητοῖσ' ὑπέδειξαν,   34
         beginning   ὁ θνητός - mortal ὑποδείκνυμι = δείκνυμι - show,
                                                      indicate, mark out

   ἀλλὰ χρόνῳ ζητοῦντες ἐφευρίσκουσιν ἄμεινον.
                ἐφευρίσκω - discover,
                find out, invent

MOTTO FOR LEARNING GREEK!

A WALK THROUGH A GREEK GRAVEYARD*

Lesson

BODY AND SOUL

1. σῶμα σῆμα.
   body   tomb (literally, "sign," tomb as sign of a burial)   Orphic saying   14

2. τὴν ψυχὴν ἀπέδωκεν ἐς ἀέρα, σῶμα δὲ πρὸς γῆν.   14
   soul   he, she, it gave back   = εἰς   ὁ ἀήρ = air   p. 32

3. Ζωσίμη ἡ πρὶν ἐοῦσα μόνῳ τῷ σώματι δούλη   14
   before   = οὖσα being   slave

   καὶ τῷ σώματι νῦν ηὗρον ἐλευθερίαν.
        I found   freedom   p. 305

THE TOMB

4. Μικρὸς οὐ μικρὸν καλύπτω τύμβος ἄνδρα.   p. 227   16
      = κρύπτω   tomb

5. Ἄλλος ἔχει πλοῦτον κἀγὼ τόδε σῆμ' ὁ γεραιὸς . . .   27
      = καὶ ἐγώ

   πάντιμον, πολύευκτον, ὅπερ 'ποίησα προκρίνας
   all-honored,   much prayed-for   = ἐποίησα   προκρίνω - judge before, i.e.,prefer
   highly valued

   μᾶλλον ἔχειν πλούτου, καὶ τεθνεὼς ἄγαμαι.
        I admire   p. 227

THE SORT OF PERSON I WAS

6. τετραετὴς ὢν ἔλιπον ἡλίου τὸ γλυκὺ φέγγος.   p. 162   24
   four years old   light

7. παρθένος οὖσα τέθνηκα Λεοντὼ ὡς νέον ἄνθος...   24
   maiden   I have died, am dead   τὸ ἄνθος - blossom

   καὶ μέλλουσα γάμῳ δ εκαπεντaετὴς μείγνυσθαι
        fifteen years old   μείγνυμι - mix

   ἐν φθιμένοις κεῖμαι ὕπνον ἔχουσα μακρόν.
   those wasting away (the dead)   sleep   p. 192

8. Σῆμα Φρασικλείας· κούρη κεκλήσομαι ἀεί   26
        maiden   I shall have the name, I shall be called

   ἀντὶ γάμου παρὰ θεῶν τοῦτο λαχοῦσ' ὄνομα.
        λαγχάνω - receive as one's share   p. 192

9. οὐ γάμον, οὐχ ὑμέναιον ἰδών, οὐ νύμφια λέκτρα,   44
        wedding song   of a bride or bridegroom   bed(s)

   κεῖμαι ἔρως πολλῶν, ἐσσόμενος πλεόνων.
   sexual love, here = "darling"   = ἐσόμενος   p. 193

* This is a gathering of thoughts about death. Many of them come from *Themes in Greek and Latin Epitaphs*, by Richmond Lattimore, Urbana, 1962, where there is a translation and some commentary. Page numbers refer to Lattimore; bold face shows an inscription (rather than a literary passage). The spelling has been normalized.

10. ταὐτὰ λέγοντες, ταὐτὰ φρονοῦντες, **ἤλθομεν** τὴν ἀμέτρητον ὁδὸν εἰς Ἀίδαν. 26
   = τὰ αὐτά   φρονέω - think   unmeasurable   Hades p. 248

11. Ἐνθάδ' ἐγὼ κεῖμαι Ῥόδιος· τὰ γελοῖα σιωπῶ, 17
    here   from Rhodes   jokes   I keep silent

    καὶ σπαλάκων ὄλεθρον λείπω κατὰ γαῖαν **ἄπασαν**.
      moles   destruction   I leave   the whole (strengthened form of πᾶσαν) p. 287

12. καὶ μὰ Δι' οὐκ εἶδον ἐμαυτοῦ ἀμείνω ὑλοτόμον 21
       by Zeus   ἐμαύτον - myself   woodcutter
    (μά is used instead of νή in oaths with negative statements.) p. 285

13. θνήσκω δὲ ὀγδώκοντα καὶ ἓξ ἐσιδὼν λυκάβαντας 16
    I die   eighty   six   having looked on   years

    καὶ **παῖδας παίδων** λείπω ὑπ' ἡελίῳ . . .
                  I leave   = ἡλίῳ   p. 211

14. πολλὰ **φαγὼν** καὶ πολλὰ **πιὼν** καὶ πολλὰ κακ' **εἰπὼν** 26
                       κακὰ λέγω τινα - say bad things
                       to or of someone (2 acc.)
                       (cf. "badmouth" someone)

    ἀνθρώπους κεῖμαι Τιμοκρέων Ῥόδιος.

FRIENDS AND ENEMIES / LOVE AND HATE

15. αὐτὴ ἡ **γεννήσασα** καὶ **κηδεύσασα ἐπέγραψα** 27
      γεννάω - give birth   κηδεύω - care for

    ἄχθος ἔχουσα κραδίας πένθεος οὐκ ὀλίγου
    burden   = καρδίας   grief   small   p. 180

16. τῷδε τάφῳ κεῖται Χαιρεστράτη ἣν ὁ σύνευνος 27
       grave   husband, bedmate

    ἔστερξε μὲν ζῶσαν, **ἐπένθησεν** δὲ θανοῦσαν.
    στέργω - cherish   πενθέω - mourn   p. 275

17. θνήσκω δ' οἰκτροτάτῳ θανάτῳ διὰ τὴν ἄλοχόν μου 27
       οἰκτρός - pitiful   wife

    κλεψίγαμον μιαρὰν ἣν περὶ Ζεὺς ὀλέσαι.
    marriage-cheating   foul   may Zeus destroy utterly (περιόλλυμι)

    ταύτην γὰρ λάθριος γαμέτης καἰμὸν γένος αἰσχῶν
          secret   husband   =καὶ ἐμὸν   αἰσχέω - shame

    εἷλξέ με κἀφ' ὕψους **δισκοβόλησε** νέον.
    ἕλκω - drag   = καὶ ἀπὸ   τὸ ὕψος - cliff   δισκοβολέω - throw like a discus   p. 118

WHAT MAKES LIFE GOOD?

18. Δύ' ἡμέραι γυναικός εἰσιν ἥδισται, 36

    ὅταν γαμῇ τις **κἀκφέρῃ** τεθνηκυῖαν.
         = καὶ ἐκφέρῃ   dead   Hipponax

19. Μάκαρ Σοφοκλεής, ὃς πολὺν χρόνον **βιοὺς**   28
blessed   βιόω - live, ἐβίων I lived (like ἔγνων)

ἀπέθανεν εὐδαίμων ἀνὴρ καὶ δεξιός,
                          on the right side, i.e., lucky, fortunate; also = clever

πολλὰς ποιήσας καὶ καλὰς τραγῳδίας,

καλῶς δ' ἐτελεύτησεν, οὐδὲν ὑπομείνας κακόν.
          τελευτάω - make an end, die   ὑπομένω - undergo, endure   Phrynichus

20. οὐ πόλεμόν ποτε ἰδών, οὐ χεῖρα φόνοισι μιάνας   42
                          ὁ φόνος - blood, murder   μιαίνω - stain

Χρόνιος ὁ καὶ Ἀρτεμίδωρος Εὐόδιος ἐνθάδε κεῖμαι,

ἑξηκονταέτης, γυναῖκα τε μηδαμοῦ γήμας
60 years old   nowhere = never

μήτε δίκην εἴπας, μήτ' ὅρκον δούς ποτ' ὁμοίῳ.
lawsuit   here = equal

εὐτυχίαν δὲ βίου ταύτην **νόμισον**, παροδεῖτα.
                          passerby   p. 269

NO CHOICE

21. ἐκ γαίης γὰρ πάντα καὶ εἰς γῆν πάντα **τελευτᾷ.**   p. 259   Menander   31
                          end up

22. τοῦτο μόνον θνητοῖς ἶσον πέλει ἐκ Διὸς αἴσης,   32
                  equal   = ἐστι   decree, destiny

πᾶσι θανεῖν καὶ φῶς ἠελίοιο λιπεῖν

εἰ δ' **ἦν** ἀργύριον καὶ χρύσιον αὐτὸ πρίασθαι
                                  buy

οὐδεὶς **ἂν** πλοῦτος εἰς Ἀΐδου **κατέβη.**
          = πλούσιος   Hades   p. 253

THE GREAT EQUALIZER

23. εἰπεῖν τίς δύναται σκῆνος λιπόσαρκον **ἀθρήσας**   27
          τὸ σκῆνος -   which flesh   ἀθρέω - peer at
          hut (= body)   has left

εἴπερ Ὕλας ἢ Θερσείτης ἦν, ὦ παροδεῖτα;
Hylas = a beautiful boy in *Iliad*   passerby   p. 175
Thersites = an ugly man in *Iliad*

24. γῆς **ἐπέβην** γυμνός, γυμνός θ' ὑπὸ γαῖαν ἄπειμι,   28
          naked   = τε

καὶ τί μάτην μοχθῶ, γυμνὸν ὁρῶν τὸ τέλος;
          in vain   I toil   p. 320 (Palladas)

25. Ἄνθρωπος τοῦτ' ἐστί. τίς εἶ βλέπε καὶ τὸ μένον σε. 45

εἰκόνα τήνδ' ἐσορῶν σὸν τὸ τέλος λόγισαι.
ἡ εἰκών - image (icon)   λογίζομαι - reckon   Cf. "As I was so be yee,   p. 256
                                                              As I am ye shall bee."

26. μάνης οὗτος ἀνὴρ ἦν ζῶν ποτέ· νῦν δὲ **τεθνηκὼς** 37
        madman

ἶσον Δαρείῳ τῷ μεγάλῳ δύναται.
        Darius (king of Persia)   Anyte

WHAT IS LIFE? WHAT IS DEATH? CHOICES

27. τὸ μὴ γὰρ εἶναι **κρεῖττον** ἢ τὸ ζῆν κακῶς.   Sophocles, fragment 488   21

28. τὸ φῶς τόδ' ἀνθρώποισιν **ἥδιστον** βλέπειν,   21

τὰ νέρθε δ' οὐδέν. μαίνεται δ' ὃς εὔχεται
    below   rave, be mad   pray

θανεῖν. κακῶς ζῆν **κρεῖττον** ἢ καλῶς θανεῖν.
            to live   p. 46   Euripides *Iph. Aul.* 1250-52

29. σκηνὴ πᾶς ὁ βίος καὶ παίγνιον· ἢ μάθε παίζειν 53
    stage,   plaything, game   play
  because originally a tent was used for the actors to change

τὴν σπουδὴν **μεταθεὶς** ἢ φέρε τὰς ὀδύνας.
    seriousness   having put aside   pains   Palladas

SHALL I PONDER?

30. ἃ ἔφαγον ἔχω, ἃ κατέλιπον ἀπώλεσα. ἀληθῶς εἶπε Φιλιστίων. 40
            καταλείπω - leave behind

ὁ βίος **τοσόνδε.**
    so much, this much   p. 261

31. τίς οἶδεν εἰ τὸ ζῆν μέν ἐστι κατθανεῖν, 47

τὸ κατθανεῖν δὲ ζῆν κάτω **νομίζεται;**
                below   p. 84   Euripides fragment 639

32. τίς οἶδεν εἰ τὸ ζῆν μέν ἐστι κατθανεῖν, 47

τὸ πνεῖν δὲ δειπνεῖν, τὸ δὲ καθεύδειν κώδιον;
    breathe   sheepskin fleece   Aristophanes' spoof, *Frogs* 1477-78

33. τοῦ μὲν θανόντος οὐκ ἂν **ἐνθυμοίμεθα,** 51
            ἐνθυμέομαι - think about, ponder on + gen.

εἴ τι φρονοῖμεν, πλεῖον ἡμέρας μιᾶς.
    φρονέω - be sensible   Semonides

WISHES AND CURSES

34. χαῖρε καὶ εἰν Ἀΐδᾳ· κούφη δέ τε γαῖα **καλύπτοι**.   39
     = ἐν   Hades   light in weight   = κρύπτοι   p. 57 (Meleager)

35. κούφη σοι χθὼν ἐπάνωθε **πέσοι**, γύναι.   39
     light   earth   on from above   p. 65   Euripides *Alcestis*, 463-64

36. νῦν δέ σε μὴ κούφη **κρύπτοι** κόνις, ἀλλὰ βαρεῖα,   39
     light   dust, earth   heavy   (on partridge killed by a cat)

     μὴ τὸ τεὸν 'κείνη λείψανον ἐξερύσῃ
     = σόν   = ἐκείνη   remains   ἐχερύω - drag out
          (the cat)   p. 66, Agathias

37. ἑξηκοντουτὴς Διονύσιος ἐνθάδε κεῖμαι   45
     60 years old   here

     Ταρσεύς, μὴ γήμας. **αἴθε** δὲ μηδ' ὁ πατήρ.
                   = εἴθε   (Anonymous)

38. ὃς ἂν δὲ κακῶς τῷ ἀνδριάντι ποιήσῃ, ὀρφανὰ τέκνα **λίποιτο**, χῆρον βίον,   46
                   statue   children   widowed

     οἶκον ἔρημον, ἐν πυρὶ πάντα δάμοιτο, κακῶν ὑπὸ χεῖρας **ὄλοιτο**.
     empty, desolate   *δαμ=aorist **passive** stem   at the hands of   ὄλλυμι - destroy, lose,
                   be overcome, tamed, destroyed   middle - perish   p. **112**

39. ἔσται δὲ **ἐπικατάρατος** ὁ τοιοῦτος, καὶ ὅσαι ἀραὶ ἐν τῷ Δευτερονομίῳ   47
         accursed   of such sort   curses   biblical reference for short cut!
                i.e., who defiles tomb

     εἰσὶ γεγραμμέναι αὐτῷ τε καὶ τέκνοις καὶ ἐκγόνοις καὶ παντὶ τῷ γένει
                           children   descendants

     αὐτοῦ γένοιντο.   p. 114
          Cf. message on Shakespeare's tomb: "Blest be the man that spares these stones
                                         And cursed be he that moves my bones."

40. πᾶσα γῆ **δακρυσάτω**.   p. **180**   42

41. ἐμοῦ θανόντος γαῖα **μιχθήτω** πυρί.   48
         μείγνυμι - mix

     οὐδὲν μέλει μοι. τἀμὰ γὰρ καλῶς ἔχει.
          = τὰ ἐμά   Anonymous

FAMOUS SAYINGS, OR SAYINGS OF THE FAMOUS

Lesson

1. A lioness: Λέαινα ὀνειδιζομένη ὑπὸ ἀλώπεκος ἐπὶ τὸ διὰ παντὸς ἕνα 19
lioness   being rebuked   by   fox   all the time

τίκτειν, "ἕνα" ἔφη "ἀλλὰ λέοντα."
he, she, it said

2. Aphrodite: Ἡ Κύπρις τὴν Κύπριν ἐνὶ Κνίδῳ εἶπεν ἰδοῦσα 26
Aphrodite (goddess in Cyprus)   Knidos

"Φεῦ, φεῦ· ποῦ γυμνὴν εἶδέ με Πραξιτέλης;"
where?   naked   Praxiteles (a sculptor)

3. Solon: Σόλων ἀποβαλὼν υἱὸν ἔκλαυσεν. Εἰπόντος δέ τινος πρὸς αὐτόν, 28
Solon   ἀποβάλλω - lose   κλαίω, ἔκλαυσα - weep

ὡς οὐδὲν προὔργου ποιεῖ κλαίων, "δι' αὐτὸ γάρ τοι τοῦτο" ἔφη "κλαίω."
of advantage   (y'know)

4. Philip of Macedon: Φίλιππος ἔλεγε κρεῖττον εἶναι στρατόπεδον ἐλάφων 28
camp   ὁ, ἡ ἔλαφος - deer

λέοντος στρατηγοῦντος ἢ λεόντων ἐλάφου στρατηγοῦντος.
ὁ λέων - lion   στρατηγέω - be general

5. Zeno: "διὰ τοῦτο" ἔφη "δύο ὦτα ἔχομεν, στόμα δὲ ἕν, 35
τὸ οὖς   mouth

ἵνα πλείονα μὲν ἀκούωμεν, ἥττονα δὲ λέγωμεν."
πλείων, ον - more   ἥττων, ον - less

6. Alexander the Great: ὁ Ἀλέξανδρος Ἀναξάρχου περὶ κόσμων ἀπειρίας ἀκούων 37
Anaxarchus, a philosopher   worlds, universes   limitlessness

ἐδάκρυεν. καὶ τῶν φίλων ἐρωτησάντων αὐτὸν τί δακρύει, "οὐκ ἄξιον" ἔφη
worthy

"δακρύειν εἰ κόσμων ὄντων ἀπείρων, ἑνὸς οὐδέπω κύριοι γεγόναμεν;"
worlds   limitless   not yet

7. Philip: ἐρωτώμενος οὕστινας μάλιστα φιλεῖ καὶ οὕστινας μάλιστα μισεῖ, 38
being asked

"τοὺς μέλλοντας," ἔφη "προδιδόναι μάλιστα φιλῶ, τοὺς δ' ἤδη προδεδωκότας
προδίδωμι - betray   having betrayed

μάλιστα μισῶ."

8. Socrates: Σωκράτης ἔλεγε τοὺς μὲν ἄλλους ἀνθρώπους ζῆν ἵνα ἐσθίοιεν, 39

αὐτὸς δὲ ἐσθίειν ἵνα ζῴη.
optative of ζάω

9. Gorgias: ἐρωτηθεὶς ποία διαίτη χρώμενος εἰς μακρὸν γῆρας ἦλθεν, 40
having been asked   what (sort of)   way of life, diet   old age

*Most of these sayings and those of Diogenes were taken from *The Greek Reader*, by Frederic Jacobs, New York, 1831.

"οὐδὲν οὐδέποτε" ἔφη "πρὸς ἡδονὴν φαγὼν οὔτε δράσας."

δράω - do (--> δρᾶμα)

10. Themistocles: ἐρωτηθεὶς δὲ πότερον Ἀχιλλεὺς **ἐβούλετ'** ἂν εἶναι ἢ Ὅμηρος

having been asked   Achilles   Homer

Review p.172

"σὺ δὲ αὐτός" ἔφη "πότερον **ἂν ἤθελες** ὁ νικῶν ἐν Ὀλυμπιάσιν ἢ ὁ κηρύσσων

Olympic games   announce

τοὺς νικῶντας εἶναι;"

νικάω - be victorious

11. A Persian soldier, upon hearing that the Greeks, against whom the Persians were about to fight, were competing in the Olympics for the prize of an olive wreath: 43

"παπαί, Μαρδόνιε, ποίους ἐπ' ἄνδρας ἤγαγες **μαχησομένους** ἡμᾶς,

μάχομαι - do battle

οἳ οὐ περὶ χρημάτων τὸν ἀγῶνα **ποιοῦνται** ἀλλὰ περὶ ἀρετῆς."

things, money   contest   excellence

12. Empedocles: τῶν Ἀκραγαντίνων τρυφὴν ἰδών, ἔλεγεν· Ἀκραγαντῖνοι   43

some people in Sicily   luxury

τρυφῶσι μὲν ὡς αὔριον **ἀποθανούμενοι**, οἰκίας δὲ **κατασκευάζονται**

τρυφάω - luxuriate   tomorrow   κατασκευάζω - equip, fit out, build

ὡς πάντα τὸν χρόνον **βιωσόμενοι**."

βιόω - live, future = βιώσομαι

13. A camel: κάμηλος **ἀναγκαζομένη ὑπὸ** τοῦ ἰδίου δεσπότου ὀρχήσασθαι εἶπεν   47

own, private   master   ὀρχέομαι - dance

ἀλλ' οὐ μόνον ὀρχουμένη εἰμὶ ἄσχημος, ἀλλὰ καὶ περιπατοῦσα."

ungraceful   περιπατέ - walk around

14. Phillip. ἐν Χαιρωνείᾳ τοὺς Ἀθηναίους μεγάλῃ νίκῃ ἐνίκησε Φίλιππος.   47

Chaironea   Athenians

Ἐπαρθεὶς δὲ τῇ εὐπραγίᾳ ᾤετο δεῖν αὐτὸν **ὑπομιμνήσκεσθαι**

ἐπαίρω - lift up   success   ὑπομιμνήσκω - remind

ὅτι ἄνθρωπός ἐστιν, καὶ προσέταξέ τινι παιδὶ τοῦτο ἔργον ἔχειν.

προστάττω - appoint   slave

Τρὶς δὲ ἑκάστης ἡμέρας ὁ παῖς ἔλεγεν αὐτῷ· "Φίλιππε, ἄνθρωπος εἶ."

three times

15. Zeno. δοῦλον ἐπὶ κλοπῇ ἐμαστίγου· τοῦ δὲ εἰπόντος "εἵμαρτό μοι κλέψαι"   48

theft   μαστιγόω - whip, flog   it was fated

ἔφη "καὶ **δαρῆναι**."

δέρω - flay, thrash

16. οὐ τὸ ζῆν περὶ πολλοῦ **ποιητέον** ἀλλὰ τὸ εὖ ζῆν.   52

to be made much of

17. Gorgo, the wife of a king of Sparta: τοῦ υἱοῦ αὐτῆς ἐπὶ στρατείαν   54

campaign

πορευομένου, τὴν ἀσπίδα **ἐπιδιδοῦσα**, εἶπεν· "ἢ ταύταν ἢ ἐπὶ ταύτᾳ."

shield   ἐπιδίδωμι - give, bestow   Spartans pronounced "α" rather than "η"

Lesson

DEFINITIONS

1. τὴν φιλαργυρίαν εἶπε μητρόπολιν πάντων τῶν κακῶν.   24
   greed, love of silver   a μητρόπολις sends out colonies (--> metropolis)

2. Ἀναπήρους ἔλεγεν οὐ τοὺς κωφοὺς καὶ τυφλούς, ἀλλὰ τοὺς **μὴ** ἔχοντας πήραν.*   24
   maimed   he used to say   mute   blind   wallet

3. τὸν ἔρωτα ⌊εἶπε⌋ σχολαζόντων ἀσχολίαν.   31
   ὁ ἔρως - love   σχολάζω - be at leisure

4. τοὺς **ἐρῶντας** ἔφη πρὸς ἡδονὴν ἀτυχεῖν.   31
   ἐράω - be in love   be unfortunate, fail to get (= ἀποτυγχάνειν)

SNAPPY ANSWERS

5. ἐρωτηθεὶς τί ποιῶν κύων καλεῖται, ἔφη "τοὺς μὲν διδόντας σαίνων,   24
   having been asked   he is called   participle of δίδωμι   fawning on

   τοὺς δὲ **μὴ** διδόντας ὑλακτῶν, τοὺς δὲ πονηροὺς δάκνων.
                        barking at   good-for-nothing biting
                                                (in N.T. = wicked)

6. **ᾔτει** ποτὲ ἀνδριάντα· ἐρωτηθεὶς δὲ διὰ τί τοῦτο **ποιεῖ**, "μελετῶ"   30
         statue   having been asked   μελετάω - practice

   εἶπεν "ἀποτυγχάνειν."

7. ἐρωτηθεὶς ποῖον οἶνον ἡδέως πίνει, ἔφη "τὸν ἀλλότριον."   36
   having been asked   what sort of   someone else's

8. πρὸς τὸν πυθόμενον ποίᾳ ὥρᾳ δεῖ ἀριστᾶν, "εἰ μὲν πλούσιος" ἔφη " **ὅταν**   36
                           hour   dine

   θέλῃ, εἰ δὲ πένης, **ὅταν ἔχῃ.**"
   = ἐθέλῃ

9. ἐπανήρχετο ἐκ Λακεδαίμονος εἰς Ἀθήνας· πρὸς οὖν τὸν πυθόμενον   40
   ἐπανέρχομαι - set out   Sparta   Athens   πυνθάνομαι - inquire

   "**ποῖ** καὶ **πόθεν**;" "ἐκ τῆς ἀνδρωνίτιδος" εἶπεν "εἰς τὴν γυναικωνῖτιν."
                             men's chamber   women's chamber

10. ἐρωτηθεὶς πόθεν **εἴη** "κοσμοπολίτης" ἔφη.   41

11. ὅτε ἁλοὺς καὶ πωλούμενος **ἠρωτήθη** τί οἶδε ποιεῖν, ἀπεκρίνατο   48
    having been captured   πωλέω - sell

    "ἀνδρῶν ἄρχειν." καὶ πρὸς τὸν κήρυκα "κήρυσσε" ἔφη "εἴ τις ἐθέλει
                                         herald   announce

    δεσπότην αὐτῷ πρίασθαι."
            buy

OUTRAGEOUS WORDS AND DEEDS   35

12. θεασάμενος υἱὸν ἑταίρας λίθον εἰς ὄχλον βάλλοντα "πρόσεχε"
    θεάομαι - behold   prostitute   crowd   = πρόσεχε νοῦν

ἔφη "μὴ τὸν πατέρα πλήξῃς."

13. πρὸς Διδύμωνα τὸν μοιχὸν ἰατρεύοντά ποτε κόρης ὀφθαλμὸν "ὅρα" φησί   35
    Didymon   lecher   maiden   = ὁρά-ε watch out

    "μὴ τὸν ὀφθαλμὸν τῆς παρθένου θεραπεύων τὴν κόρην φθείρῃς."
              maiden   ἡ κόρη = (1) maiden   φθείρω - ruin, corrupt
                                             (2) pupil of eye

14. Μοχθηροῦ τινος ἀνθρώπου ἐπιγράψαντος ἐπὶ τὴν οἰκίαν ΜΗΔΕΝ ΕΙΣΙΤΩ   39
    wicked   let (it) enter

    ΚΑΚΟΝ "ὁ οὖν κύριος τῆς οἰκίας" ἔφη "ποῦ εἰσέλθοι ἄν;"

15. Πλάτωνος ὁρισαμένου, ' " Ἄνθρωπός ἐστι ζῷον δίπουν ἄπτερον "   43
    Πλάτων = Plato   ὁρίζω - divide   two-footed   featherless
              ὁρίζομαι - mark out for oneself, define

    καὶ εὐδοκιμοῦντος, τίλας ἀλεκτρυόνα εἰσήνεγκεν αὐτὸν εἰς τὴν σχολὴν
    enjoy a good reputation   τίλλω - pluck   rooster   school

    καί φησιν, "οὗτός ἐστιν ὁ Πλάτωνος ἄνθρωπος."

16. δύσκολον ᾔτει· τοῦ δὲ εἰπόντος "ἐάν με πείσῃς" ἔφη "εἴ σε ἐδυνάμην πεῖσαι,   43
    grouch

    ἔπεισα ἄν σε ἀπάγξασθαι."
    ἄγχω - strangle

17. θεασάμενός ποτε τοὺς ἱερομνήμονας τῶν ταμιῶν τινα φιάλην ὑφῃρημένον   44
    θεάομαι - behold   temple magistrates   treasurers   bowl   ὑφαιρέω - steal

    ἀπάγοντας ἔφη "οἱ μεγάλοι κλέπται τὸν μικρὸν ἀπάγουσιν."

18. ἰδὼν τοξότην ἀφυῆ παρὰ τὸν σκοπὸν ἐκάθιζεν εἰπὼν "ἵνα μὴ πληγῶ."   48
         archer   untalented   target   ἵζω - sit

19. λύχνον μεθ' ἡμέραν ἄψας περιῄει λέγων "ἄνθρωπον ζητῶ."   52
    portable lamp   by day   ἅπτω = kindle   περίειμι - go around

DIOGENES AND ALEXANDER

20. Ἀλεξάνδρου ποτὲ ἐπιστάντος καὶ εἰπόντος "ἐγώ εἰμι Ἀλέξανδρος   28
                    ἐπί + ἵσταμαι = stand over

    ὁ μέγας βασιλεύς," "καὶ ἐγώ" φησί "Διογένης ὁ κύων."

21. φασὶ δὲ καὶ Ἀλέξανδρον εἰπεῖν ὡς εἴπερ Ἀλέξανδρος μὴ ἐγεγόνειν   37

    "ἠθέλησα ἄν Διογένης γενέσθαι."

22. ἐν τῷ Κρανείῳ ἡλιουμένῳ αὐτῷ Ἀλέξανδρος ἐπιστάς φησιν,   42
              ἡλιόομαι - sun oneself   having stood over

    "αἴτησόν με ὃ θέλεις." καὶ ὅς, " ἀποσκότησόν μου" φησί.
                            ἀποσκοτέω- get one's shadow off

*Irresistible pun: "The truly disabled are the disoboled." (An obol is a Greek penny--the smallest coin.)

PARADIGMS*

A-GROUP NOUNS

	F	F	short α	short α	long α (for η after ε,ι,ρ)		M	M
nom.	φωνή	χελώνη	γλῶττα	θάλαττα	οἰκία	θεά	ποιητής	πολίτης
acc.	φωνήν	χελώνην	γλῶτταν	θάλατταν	οἰκίαν	θεάν	ποιητήν	πολίτην
gen.	φωνῆς	χελώνης	γλώττης	θαλάττης	οἰκίας	θεᾶς	ποιητοῦ	πολίτου
dat.	φωνῇ	χελώνῃ	γλώττῃ	θαλάττῃ	οἰκίᾳ	θεᾷ	ποιητῇ	πολίτῃ
nom.	φωναί	χελῶναι	γλῶτται	θάλατται	οἰκίαι	θεαί	ποιηταί	πολῖται
acc.	φωνάς	χελώνας	γλώττας	θαλάττας	οἰκίας	θεάς	ποιητάς	πολίτας
gen.	φωνῶν	χελωνῶν	γλωττῶν	θαλαττῶν	οἰκιῶν	θεῶν	ποιητῶν	πολιτῶν
dat.	φωναῖς	χελώναις	γλώτταις	θαλάτταις	οἰκίαις	θεαῖς	ποιηταῖς	πολίταις

O-GROUP NOUNS

M	M	M	N	N	F
θεός	μῦθος	ἄνθρωπος	δῶρον	φάρμακον	ὁδός
θεόν	μῦθον	ἄνθρωπον	δῶρον	φάρμακον	ὁδόν
θεοῦ	μύθου	ἀνθρώπου	δώρου	φαρμάκου	ὁδοῦ
θεῷ	μύθῳ	ἀνθρώπῳ	δώρῳ	φαρμάκῳ	ὁδῷ
θεοί	μῦθοι	ἄνθρωποι	δῶρα	φάρμακα	ὁδοί
θεούς	μύθους	ἀνθρώπους	δῶρα	φάρμακα	ὁδούς
θεῶν	μύθων	ἀνθρώπων	δώρων	φαρμάκων	ὁδῶν
θεοῖς	μύθοις	ἀνθρώποις	δώροις	φαρμάκοις	ὁδοῖς

THIRD GROUP NOUNS

M/F	M	F	F	F	F	M
δαίμων	κώνωψ	κύλιξ	ἀσπίς	χάρις	πόλις	βασιλεύς
δαίμονα	κώνωπα	κύλικα	ἀσπίδα	χάριν	πόλιν	βασιλέα
δαίμονος	κώνωπος	κύλικος	ἀσπίδος	χάριτος	πόλεως	βασιλέως
δαίμονι	κώνωπι	κύλικι	ἀσπίδι	χάριτι	πόλει	βασιλεῖ
δαίμονες	κώνωπες	κύλικες	ἀσπίδες	χάριτες	πόλεις	βασιλεῖς
δαίμονας	κώνωπας	κύλικας	ἀσπίδας	χάριτας	πόλεις	βασιλέας
δαιμόνων	κωνώπων	κυλίκων	ἀσπίδων	χαρίτων	πόλεων	βασιλέων
δαίμοσι(ν)	κώνωψι(ν)	κύλιξι(ν)	ἀσπίσι(ν)	χάρισι(ν)	πόλεσι(ν)	βασιλεῦσι(ν)

THIRD GROUP NOUNS

N	N	N	M/F	F	M	F
ὕδωρ	ποίημα	γένος	παῖς	μήτηρ	ἀνήρ	γυνή
ὕδωρ	ποίημα	γένος	παῖδα	μητέρα	ἄνδρα	γυναῖκα
ὕδατος	ποιήματος	γένους	παιδός	μητρός	ἀνδρός	γυναικός
ὕδατι	ποιήματι	γένει	παιδί	μητρί	ἀνδρί	γυναικί
ὕδατα	ποιήματα	γένη	παῖδες	μητέρες	ἄνδρες	γυναῖκες
ὕδατα	ποιήματα	γένη	παῖδας	μητέρας	ἄνδρας	γυναῖκας
ὑδάτων	ποιημάτων	γενῶν	παίδων	μητέρων	ἀνδρῶν	γυναικῶν
ὕδασι(ν)	ποιήμασι(ν)	γένεσι(ν)	παισί(ν)	μητράσι(ν)	ἀνδράσι(ν)	γυναιξί(ν)

* Students may wish to reproduce and staple the Paradigms to have them handy for reading.
    For vocatives and dual of nouns in all groups see p. 240.

ARTICLE

M	F	N
ὁ	ἡ	τό
τόν	τήν	τό
τοῦ	τῆς	τοῦ
τῷ	τῇ	τῷ
οἱ	αἱ	τά
τούς	τάς	τά
τῶν	τῶν	τῶν
τοῖς	ταῖς	τοῖς

O-A-O ADJECTIVE

M	F	N
πρῶτος	πρώτη	πρῶτον
πρῶτον	πρώτην	πρῶτον
πρώτου	πρώτης	πρώτου
πρώτῳ	πρώτῃ	πρώτῳ
πρῶτοι	πρῶται	πρῶτα
πρώτους	πρώτας	πρῶτα
πρώτων	πρώτων	πρώτων
πρώτοις	πρώταις	πρώταις

O-A-O ADJ. with long α

M	F	N
ῥάδιος	ῥαδία	ῥάδιον
ῥάδιον	ῥαδίαν	ῥάδιον
ῥαδίου	ῥαδίας	ῥαδίου
ῥαδίῳ	ῥαδίᾳ	ῥαδίῳ
ῥάδιοι	ῥάδιαι	ῥάδια
ῥαδίους	ῥαδίας	ῥάδια
ῥαδίων	ῥαδίων	ῥαδίων
ῥαδίοις	ῥαδίαις	ῥαδίοις

TWO-ENDING ADJ.

M/F	N
ἄδικος	ἄδικον
ἄδικον	ἄδικον
ἀδίκου	ἀδίκου
ἀδίκῳ	ἀδίκῳ
ἄδικοι	ἄδικα
ἀδίκους	ἄδικα
ἀδίκων	ἀδίκων
ἀδίκοις	ἀδίκοις

μέγας *great, large* (irregular)

M	F	N
μέγας	μεγάλη	μέγα
μέγαν	μεγάλην	μέγα
μεγάλου	μεγάλης	μεγάλου
μεγάλῳ	μεγάλη	μεγάλῳ
μεγάλοι	μεγάλαι	μεγάλα
μεγάλους	μεγάλας	μεγάλα
μεγάλων	μεγάλων	μεγάλων
μεγάλοις	μεγάλαις	μεγάλοις

πολύς *much, many* (irregular)

M	F	N
πολύς	πολλή	πολύ
πολύν	πολλήν	πολύ
πολλοῦ	πολλῆς	πολλοῦ
πολλῷ	πολλῇ	πολλῷ
πολλοί	πολλαί	πολλά
πολλούς	πολλάς	πολλά
πολλῶν	πολλῶν	πολλῶν
πολλοῖς	πολλαῖς	πολλοῖς

U-A-U

M	F	N
ἡδύς	ἡδεῖα	ἡδύ
ἡδύν	ἡδεῖαν	ἡδύ
ἡδέος	ἡδείας	ἡδέος
ἡδεῖ	ἡδείᾳ	ἡδεῖ
ἡδεῖς	ἡδεῖαι	ἡδέα
ἡδεῖς	ἡδείας	ἡδέα
ἡδέων	ἡδειῶν	ἡδέων
ἡδέσι(ν)	ἡδείαις	ἡδέσι(ν)

-εσ STEM

M/F	N
ἀληθής	ἀληθές
ἀληθῆ	ἀληθές
ἀληθοῦς	ἀληθοῦς
ἀληθεῖ	ἀληθεῖ
ἀληθεῖς	ἀληθῆ
ἀληθεῖς	ἀληθῆ
ἀληθῶν	ἀληθῶν
ἀληθέσι(ν)	ἀληθέσι(ν)

THIRD GROUP COMPARATIVE

M/F		N	
ἀμείνων		ἄμεινον	
ἀμείνονα	[ἀμείνω]	ἄμεινον	
ἀμείνονος		ἀμείνονος	
ἀμείνονι		ἀμείνονι	
ἀμείνονες	[ἀμείνους]	ἀμείνονα	[ἀμείνω]
ἀμείνονας	[ἀμείνους]	ἀμείνονα	[ἀμείνω]
ἀμεινόνων		ἀμεινόνων	
ἀμείνοσι(ν)		ἀμείνοσι(ν)	

NUMBERS

M	F	N
εἷς	μία	ἕν
ἕνα	μίαν	ἕν
ἑνός	μιᾶς	ἑνός
ἑνί	μιᾷ	ἑνί

M/F	N
τρεῖς	τρία
τρεῖς	τρία
τριῶν	τριῶν
τρισί(ν)	τρισί(ν)

πᾶς *every, all* (3-A-3)

M	F	N
πᾶς	πᾶσα	πᾶν
πάντα	πᾶσαν	πᾶν
παντός	πάσης	παντός
παντί	πάσῃ	παντί
πάντες	πᾶσαι	πάντα
πάντας	πάσας	πάντα
πάντων	πασῶν	πάντων
πᾶσι(ν)	πάσαις	πᾶσι(ν)

οὐδείς *no one, nothing* (3-A-3)

M	F	N
οὐδείς	οὐδεμία	οὐδέν
οὐδένα	οὐδεμίαν	οὐδέν
οὐδενός	οὐδεμιᾶς	οὐδενός
οὐδενί	οὐδεμιᾷ	οὐδενί
οὐδένες	οὐδεμίαι	οὐδένα
οὐδένας	οὐδεμίας	οὐδένα
οὐδένων	οὐδεμιῶν	οὐδένων
οὐδέσι(ν)	οὐδεμιαῖς	οὐδέσι(ν)

I, me		*you*		*him, her, it**			*him(self), her(self)***	
ἐγώ		σύ		[αὐτός]	[αὐτή]	[αὐτό]	--	
ἐμέ	με	σέ	σε	αὐτόν	αὐτήν	αὐτό	ἕ (νιν)	ἑ (νιν)
ἐμοῦ	μου	σοῦ	σου	αὐτοῦ	αὐτῆς	αὐτοῦ	οὗ	οὗ
ἐμοί	μοι	σοί	σοι	αὐτῷ	αὐτῇ	αὐτῷ	οἷ	οἷ
ἡμεῖς		ὑμεῖς		[αὐτοί]	[αὐταί]	[αὐτά]	σφεῖς	
ἡμᾶς		ὑμᾶς		αὐτούς	αὐτάς	αὐτά	σφᾶς (σφε)	
ἡμῶν		ὑμῶν		αὐτῶν	αὐτῶν	αὐτῶν	σφῶν	
ἡμῖν		ὑμῖν		αὐτοῖς	αὐταῖς	αὐτοῖς	σφίσι(ν)	

this, these			*this here, these here*			*that, those*		
οὗτος	αὕτη	τοῦτο	ὅδε	ἥδε	τόδε	ἐκεῖνος	ἐκείνη	ἐκεῖνο
τοῦτον	ταύτην	τοῦτο	τόνδε	τήνδε	τόδε	ἐκεῖνον	ἐκείνην	ἐκεῖνο
τούτου	ταύτης	τούτου	τοῦδε	τῆσδε	τοῦδε	ἐκείνου	ἐκείνης	ἐκείνου
τούτῳ	ταύτῃ	τούτῳ	τῷδε	τῇδε	τῷδε	ἐκείνῳ	ἐκείνῃ	ἐκείνῳ
οὗτοι	αὗται	ταῦτα	οἵδε	αἵδε	τάδε	ἐκεῖνοι	ἐκεῖναι	ἐκεῖνα
τούτους	ταύτας	ταῦτα	τούσδε	τάσδε	τάδε	ἐκείνους	ἐκείνας	ἐκεῖνα
τούτων	τούτων	τούτων	τῶνδε	τῶνδε	τῶνδε	ἐκείνων	ἐκείνων	ἐκείνων
τούτοις	ταύταις	τούτοις	τοῖσδε	ταῖσδε	τοῖσδε	ἐκείνοις	ἐκείναις	ἐκείνοις

who, which (relative)   *who, which* (interr.)   *whoever, whichever* (indef. relative/indirect interr.)

M	F	N	M/F	N	M		F	N
ὅς	ἥ	ὅ	τίς	τί	ὅστις		ἥτις	ὅ τι
ὅν	ἥν	ὅ	τίνα	τί	ὅντινα		ἥντινα	ὅ τι
οὗ	ἧς	οὗ	τίνος [τοῦ]	τίνος [τοῦ]	οὗτινος	[ὅτου]	ἧστινος	οὗτινος [ὅτου]
ᾧ	ᾗ	ᾧ	τίνι [τῷ]	τίνι [τῷ]	ᾧτινι	[ὅτῳ]	ᾗτινι	ᾧτινι [ὅτῳ]
οἵ	αἵ	ἅ	τίνες	τίνα	οἵτινες		αἵτινες	ἅτινα [ἅττα]
οὕς	ἅς	ἅ	τίνας	τίνα	οὕστινας		ἅστινας	ἅτινα [ἅττα]
ὧν	ὧν	ὧν	τίνων	τίνων	ὧντινων	[ὅτων]	ὧντινων	ὧντινων [ὅτων]
οἷς	αἷς	οἷς	τίσι(ν)	τίσι(ν)	οἷστισι(ν)	[ὅτοις]	αἷστισι(ν)	οἷστισι(ν) [ὅτοις]

myself (reflexive)   *yourself* (reflexive)   *himself, herself, itself* (reflexive)

--	--	--	--	--	--	--
ἐμαυτόν	ἐμαυτήν	σεαυτόν*	σεαυτήν	ἑαυτόν*	ἑαυτήν	ἑαυτό
ἐμαυτοῦ	ἐμαυτῆς	σεαυτοῦ	σεαυτῆς	ἑαυτοῦ	ἑαυτῆς	ἑαυτοῦ
ἐμαυτῷ	ἐμαυτῇ	σεαυτῷ	σεαυτῇ	ἑαυτῷ	ἑαυτῇ	ἑαυτῷ
--	--	--	--	--	--	--
ἡμᾶς αὐτούς	ἡμᾶς αὐτάς	ὑμᾶς αὐτούς	ὑμᾶς αὐτάς	ἑαυτούς	ἑαυτάς	ἑαυτά
ἡμῶν αὐτῶν	ἡμῶν αὐτῶν	ὑμῶν αὐτῶν	ὑμῶν αὐτῶν	ἑαυτῶν	ἑαυτῶν	ἑαυτῶν
ἡμῖν αὐτοῖς	ἡμῖν αὐταῖς	ὑμῖν αὐτοῖς	ὑμῖν αὐταῖς	ἑαυτοῖς	ἑαυταῖς	ἑαυτοῖς

                                   * Also = σαυτόν   * Also = αὑτόν

Him, her, it in all cases except nominative; *same* or *him/her/itself* (emphatic) in all cases.

**This pronoun is sometimes used as an indirect reflexive--to refer back to the subject of the main clause from within another clause. ἑαυτῷ δίδωσι δῶρα - He gives himself gifts. λέγει ὅτι ἡ γυνὴ <u>οἷ</u> δώσει δῶρα - He says the woman will give <u>him(self)</u> gifts.

nom.	χελώνη	πολίτης	ἵππος	δῶρον	δαίμων	βασιλεύς
acc.	χελώνην	πολίτην	ἵππον	δῶρον	δαίμονα	βασιλέα
gen.	χελώνης	πολίτου	ἵππου	δώρου	δαίμονος	βασιλέως
dat.	χελώνῃ	πολίτῃ	ἵππῳ	δώρῳ	δαίμονι	βασιλεῖ
voc.	**χελώνη**	**πολῖτα**	**ἵππε**	**δῶρον**	**δαῖμον**	**βασιλεῦ**

Dual

nom./acc.	χελώνα	πολίτα	ἵππω	δώρω	**δαίμονε**	**βασιλῆ**
gen./dat.	χελώναιν	πολίταιν	ἵπποιν	δώροιν	**δαιμόνοιν**	**βασιλέοιν**

nom.	χελῶναι	πολῖται	ἵπποι	δῶρα	δαίμονες	βασιλεῖς
acc.	χελώνας	πολίτας	ἵππους	δῶρα	δαίμονας	βασιλέας
gen.	χελωνῶν	πολιτῶν	ἵππων	δώρων	δαιμόνων	βασιλέων
dat.	χελώναις	πολίταις	ἵπποις	δώροις	δαίμοσι(ν)	βασιλεῦσι(ν)

All *dual* and *plural* vocatives are the same as their respective nominatives. All *neuter* vocatives, sing.or pl., are the same as their respective nominatives. In Third Group the vocative varies: δαῖμον, κώνωψ, κύλιξ, ἀσπί, χάρι, πόλι, βασιλεῦ.

In the dual there is a single form for both nominative and accusative, and one for both genitive and dative.

3-A-3 PARTICIPLES

Continuous Active

λύων	λύουσα	λῦον
λύοντα	λύουσαν	λῦον
λύοντος	λούσης	λύοντος
λύοντι	λυούσῃ	λύοντι
λύοντες	λύουσαι	λύοντα
λύοντας	λυούσας	λύοντα
λυόντων	λυουσῶν	λυόντων
λύουσι(ν)	λυούσαις	λύουσι(ν)

Aorist Active (ε/ο)

λιπών	λιποῦσα	λιπόν
λιπόντα	λιποῦσαν	λιπόν
λιπόντος	λιπούσης	λιπόντος
λιπόντι	λιπούσῃ	λιπόντι
λιπόντες	λιποῦσαι	λιπόντα
λιπόντας	λιπούσας	λιπόντα
λιπόντων	λιπουσῶν	λιπόντων
λιποῦσι(ν)	λιπούσαις	λιποῦσι(ν)

Aorist Active (σα,λα)

κελεύσας	κελεύσασα	κελεῦσαν
κελεύσαντα	κελεύσασαν	κελεῦσαν
κελεύσαντος	κελευσάσης	κελεύσαντος
κελεύσαντι	κελευσάσῃ	κελεύσαντι
κελεύσαντες	κελεύσασαι	κελεύσαντα
κελεύσαντας	κελευσάσας	κελεύσαντα
κελευσάντων	κελυσασῶν	κελευσάντων
κελεύσασι(ν)	κελευσάσαις	κελεύσασι(ν)

E-Contract

φιλῶν	φιλοῦσα	φιλοῦν
φιλοῦντα	φιλοῦσαν	φιλοῦν
φιλοῦντος	φιλούσης	φιλοῦντος
φιλοῦντι	φιλούσῃ	φιλοῦντι
φιλοῦντες	φιλοῦσαι	φιλοῦντα
φιλοῦντας	φιλούσας	φιλοῦντα
φιλούντων	φιλουσῶν	φιλούντων
φιλοῦσι(ν)	φιλούσαις	φιλοῦσι(ν)

A-Contract

ὁρῶν	ὁρῶσα	ὁρῶν
ὁρῶντα	ὁρῶσαν	ὁρῶν
ὁρῶντος	ὁρώσης	ὁρῶντος
ὁρῶντι	ὁρώσῃ	ὁρῶντι
ὁρῶντες	ὁρῶσαι	ὁρῶντα
ὁρῶντας	ὁρώσας	ὁρῶντα
ὁρώντων	ὁρωσῶν	ὁρώντων
ὁρῶσι(ν)	ὁρώσαις	ὁρῶσι(ν)

O-Contract

δηλῶν	δηλοῦσα	δηλοῦν
δηλοῦντα	δηλοῦσαν	δηλοῦν
δηλοῦντος	δηλούσης	δηλοῦντος
δηλοῦντι	δηλούσῃ	δηλοῦντι
δηλοῦντες	δηλοῦσαι	δηλοῦντα
δηλοῦντας	δηλούσας	δηλοῦντα
δηλούντων	δηλουσῶν	δηλούντων
δηλοῦσι(ν)	δηλούσαις	δηλοῦσι(ν)

Perfect Active

λελυκώς	λελυκυῖα	λελυκός
λελυκότα	λελυκυῖαν	λελυκός
λελυκότος	λελυκυίας	λελυκότος
λελυκότι	λελυκυίᾳ	λελυκότι
λελυκότες	λελυκυῖαι	λελυκότα
λελυκότας	λελυκυίας	λελυκότα
λελυκότων	λελυκυιῶν	λελυκότων
λελυκόσι(ν)	λελυκυίαις	λελυκόσι(ν)

Aorist Passive

λυθείς	λυθεῖσα	λυθέν
λυθέντα	λυθεῖσαν	λυθέν
λυθέντος	λυθείσης	λυθέντος
λυθέντι	λυθείσῃ	λυθέντι
λυθέντες	λυθεῖσαι	λυθέντα
λυθέντας	λυθείσας	λυθέντα
λυθέντων	λυθεισῶν	λυθέντων
λυθεῖσι(ν)	λυθείσαις	λυθεῖσι(ν)

παύω
ACTIVE VOICE

	CONTINUOUS	FUTURE	AORIST	PERFECT
INDICATIVE	παύω παύεις παύει	παύσω παύσεις παύσει	ἔπαυσα ἔπαυσας ἔπαυσε(ν)	πέπαυκα πέπαυκας πέπαυκε(ν)
	παύομεν παύετε παύουσι(ν)	παύσομεν παύσετε παύσουσι(ν)	ἐπαύσαμεν ἐπαύσατε ἔπαυσαν	πεπαύκαμεν πεπαύκατε πεπαύκασι(ν)
	ἔπαυον ἔπαυες ἔπαυε(ν)			ἐπεπαύκη ἐπεπαύκης ἐπεπαύκει(ν)
	ἐπαύομεν ἐπαύετε ἔπαυον			ἐπεπαύκεμεν ἐπεπαύκετε ἐπεπαύκεσαν
SUBJUNCTIVE	παύω παύῃς παύῃ	– –	παύσω παύσῃς παύσῃ	πεπαυκὼς ὦ etc.
	παύωμεν παύητε παύωσι(ν)		παύσωμεν παύσητε παύσωσι(ν)	
OPTATIVE	παύοιμι παύοις παύοι	παύσοιμι παύσοις παύσοι	παύσαιμι παύσειας * παύσειε(ν) *	πεπαυκὼς εἴην etc.
	παύοιμεν παύοιτε παύοιεν	παύσοιμεν παύσοιτε παύσοιεν	παύσαιμεν παύσαιτε παύσειαν *	
IMPERATIVE	παῦε παυέτω	– –	παῦσον παυσάτω	πεπαυκὼς ἴσθι etc.
	παύετε παυόντων		παύσατε παυσάντων	
INFINITIVE	παύειν	παύσειν	παῦσαι	πεπαυκέναι
PARTICIPLE	παύων,ουσα,ον παύοντος,ούσης,οντος	παύσων,ουσα,ον παύσοντος,ούσης,οντος	παύσας,ασα,αν παύσαντος,άσης,άντος	πεπαυκώς,υῖα,ός πεπαυκότος,υίας,ότος

* Also: παύσαιμι, **παύσαις, παῦσαι** / παύσαιμεν, παύσαιτε, **παύσαιεν**

παύω
MIDDLE VOICE

INDICATIVE

	CONTINUOUS	FUTURE	AORIST	PERFECT
	παύομαι	παύσομαι	ἐπαυσάμην	πέπαυμαι
	παύῃ*	παύσῃ*	ἐπαύσω	πέπαυσαι
	παύεται	παύσεται	ἐπαύσατο	πέπαυται
	παυόμεθα	παυσόμεθα	ἐπαυσάμεθα	πεπαύμεθα
	παύεσθε	παύσεσθε	ἐπαύσασθε	πέπαυσθε
	παύονται	παύσονται	ἐπαύσαντο	πέπαυνται
	ἐπαυόμην			ἐπεπαύμην
	ἐπαύου			ἐπέπαυσο
	ἐπαύετο			ἐπέπαυτο
	ἐπαυόμεθα			ἐπεπαύμεθα
	ἐπαύεσθε			ἐπέπαυσθε
	ἐπαύοντο			ἐπέπαυντο

SUBJUNCTIVE

	CONTINUOUS	FUTURE	AORIST	PERFECT
	παύωμαι	--	παύσωμαι	πεπαυμένος ὦ
	παύῃ		παύσῃ	etc.
	παύηται		παύσηται	
	παυώμεθα		παυσώμεθα	
	παύησθε		παύσησθε	
	παύωνται		παύσωνται	

OPTATIVE

	CONTINUOUS	FUTURE	AORIST	PERFECT
	παυοίμην	παυσοίμην	παυσαίμην	πεπαυμένος εἴην
	παύοιο	παύσοιο	παύσαιο	etc.
	παύοιτο	παύσοιτο	παύσαιτο	
	παυοίμεθα	παυσοίμεθα	παυσαίμεθα	
	παύοισθε	παύσοισθε	παύσαισθε	
	παύοιντο	παύσοιντο	παύσαιντο	

IMPERATIVE

	CONTINUOUS	FUTURE	AORIST	PERFECT
	παύου	--	παῦσαι	πέπαυσο **
	παυέσθω		παυσάσθω	πεπαύσθω
	παύεσθε		παύσασθε	τέπαυσθε
	παυέσθων		παυσάσθων	πεπαύσθων

INFINITIVE

CONTINUOUS	FUTURE	AORIST	PERFECT
παύεσθαι	παύσεσθαι	παύσασθαι	πεπαῦσθαι

PARTICIPLE

CONTINUOUS	FUTURE	AORIST	PERFECT
παυόμενος, η, ον	παυσόμενος, η, ον	παυσάμενος, η, ον	πεπαυμένος, η, ον

* or παύε (present), παύσει (future)

** or periphrastic: πεπαυμένος ἴσθι, etc.

παύω
PASSIVE VOICE

	CONTINUOUS		FUTURE		AORIST		PERFECT	
INDICATIVE								
	παύομαι	παυόμεθα	παυθήσομαι	παυθησόμεθα	ἐπαύθην	ἐπαύθημεν	πέπαυμαι	πεπαύμεθα
	παύῃ*	παύεσθε	παυθήσῃ*	παυθήσεσθε	ἐπαύθης	ἐπαύθητε	πέπαυσαι	πέπαυσθε
	παύεται	παύονται	παυθήσεται	παυθήσονται	ἐπαύθη	ἐπαύθησαν	πέπαυται	πέπαυνται
	ἐπαυόμην	ἐπαυόμεθα					ἐπεπαύμην	ἐπεπαύμεθα
	ἐπαύου	ἐπαύεσθε					ἐπέπαυσο	ἐπέπαυσθε
	ἐπαύετο	ἐπαύοντο					ἐπέπαυτο	ἐπέπαυντο
SUBJUNCTIVE								
	παύωμαι	παυώμεθα	--		παυθῶ	παυθῶμεν	πεπαυμένος ὦ	
	παύῃ	παύησθε			παυθῇς	παυθῆτε	etc.	
	παύηται	παύωνται			παυθῇ	παυθῶσι(ν)		
OPTATIVE								
	παυοίμην	παυοίμεθα	παυθησοίμην	παυθησοίμεθα	παυθείην	παυθεῖμεν	πεπαυμένος εἴην	
	παύοιο	παύοισθε	παυθήσοιο	παυθήσοισθε	παυθείης	παυθεῖτε	etc	
	παύοιτο	παύοιντο	παυθήσοιτο	παυθήσοιντο	παυθείη	παυθεῖεν		
IMPERATIVE								
	παύου	παύεσθε	--		παύθητι	παύθητε	πέπαυσο *	πέπαυσθε
	παυέσθω	παυέσθων			παυθήτω	παυθέντων	πεπαύσθω	πεπαύσθων
INFINITIVE								
	παύεσθαι		παυθήσεσθαι		παυθῆναι		πεπαῦσθαι	
PARTICIPLE								
	παυόμενος,η,ον		παυθησόμενος,η,ον		παυθείς,εῖσα,έν		πεπαυμένος,η,ον	
					παυθέντος,είσης,έντος			

* or παύει (present), παυθήσει (future)

** or periphrastic: πεπαυμένος ἴσθι, etc.

STRONG AORIST: ἔλιπον

ACTIVE / MIDDLE-PASSIVE

INDICATIVE

ACTIVE		MIDDLE-PASSIVE	
ἔλιπον	ἐλίπομεν	ἐλιπόμην	ἐλιπόμεθα
ἔλιπες	ἐλίπετε	ἐλίπου	ἐλίπεσθε
ἔλιπε(ν)	ἔλιπον	ἐλίπετο	ἐλίποντο

SUBJUNCTIVE

ACTIVE		MIDDLE-PASSIVE	
λίπω	λίπωμεν	λίπωμαι	λιπώμεθα
λίπῃς	λίπητε	λίπῃ	λίπησθε
λίπῃ	λίπωσι(ν)	λίπηται	λίπωνται

OPTATIVE

ACTIVE		MIDDLE-PASSIVE	
λίποιμι	λίποιμεν	λιποίμην	λιποίμεθα
λίποις	λίποιτε	λίποιο	λίποισθε
λίποι	λίποιεν	λίποιτο	λίποιντο

IMPERATIVE

ACTIVE		MIDDLE-PASSIVE	
λίπε	λίπετε	λιποῦ	λίπεσθε
λιπέτω	λιπόντων	λιπέσθω	λιπέσθων

INFINITIVE

ACTIVE	MIDDLE-PASSIVE
λιπεῖν	λιπέσθαι

PARTICIPLE

ACTIVE	MIDDLE-PASSIVE
λιπών, οῦσα, όν / λιπόντος, οὔσης, όντος	λιπόμενος, η, ον

For the full Middle of λείπω, see p. 185.

εἰμί / εἶμι

ACTIVE

INDICATIVE

εἰμί		εἶμι	
εἰμί	ἐσμέν	εἶμι	ἴμεν
εἶ	ἐστέ	εἶ	ἴτε
ἐστί(ν)	εἰσί(ν)	εἶσι(ν)	ἴασι(ν)
ἦ or ἦν	ἦμεν	ἦα*	ᾖμεν
ἦσθα	ἦτε	ἤεισθα*	ᾖτε
ἦν	ἦσαν	ἤειν*	ᾖσαν*

SUBJUNCTIVE

εἰμί		εἶμι	
ὦ	ὦμεν	ἴω	ἴωμεν
ᾖς	ἦτε	ἴῃς	ἴητε
ᾖ	ὦσι(ν)	ἴῃ	ἴωσι(ν)

OPTATIVE

εἰμί		εἶμι	
εἴην	εἶμεν	ἴοιμι	ἴοιμεν
εἴης	εἶτε	ἴοις	ἴοιτε
εἴη	εἶεν	ἴοι	ἴοιεν

IMPERATIVE

εἰμί		εἶμι	
ἴσθι	ἔστε	ἴθι	ἴτε
ἔστω	ἔστων	ἴτω	ὄντων

INFINITIVE

εἰμί	εἶμι
εἶναι	ἰέναι

PARTICIPLE

εἰμί	εἶμι
ὤν, οὖσα, ὄν / ὄντος, οὔσης, ὄντος	ἰών, ἰοῦσα, ἰόν / ἰόντος, ἰούσης, ἰόντος

For information on εἰμί and εἶμι, see p. 210.

* Or ᾔειν, ᾔεις, ᾔει / ᾔεσαν

CONTINUOUS STEM

φιλέω

	ACTIVE		MIDDLE-PASSIVE	
INDICATIVE				
	φιλῶ	φιλοῦμεν	φιλοῦμαι	φιλούμεθα
	φιλεῖς	φιλεῖτε	φιλῇ / φιλεῖ	φιλεῖσθε
	φιλεῖ	φιλοῦσι(ν)	φιλεῖται	φιλοῦνται
	ἐφίλουν	ἐφιλοῦμεν	ἐφιλούμην	ἐφιλούμεθα
	ἐφίλεις	ἐφιλεῖτε	ἐφιλοῦ	ἐφιλεῖσθε
	ἐφίλει	ἐφίλουν	ἐφιλεῖτο	ἐφιλοῦντο
SUBJUNCTIVE				
	φιλῶ	φιλῶμεν	φιλῶμαι	φιλώμεθα
	φιλῇς	φιλῆτε	φιλῇ	φιλῆσθε
	φιλῇ	φιλῶσι(ν)	φιλῆται	φιλῶνται
OPTATIVE				
	φιλοίην	φιλοῖμεν	φιλοίμην	φιλοίμεθα
	φιλοίης	φιλοῖτε	φιλοῖο	φιλοῖσθε
	φιλοίη	φιλοῖεν	φιλοῖτο	φιλοῖντο
IMPERATIVE				
	φίλει	φιλεῖτε	φιλοῦ	φιλεῖσθε
	φιλείτω	φιλούντων	φιλείσθω	φιλείσθων
INFINITIVE	φιλεῖν		φιλεῖσθαι	
PARTICIPLE	φιλῶν, οὖσα, οῦν / -οῦντος, οὔσης, οῦντος		φιλούμενος, η, ον	

τιμάω

	ACTIVE		MIDDLE-PASSIVE	
INDICATIVE				
	τιμῶ	τιμῶμεν	τιμῶμαι	τιμώμεθα
	τιμᾷς	τιμᾶτε	τιμᾷ	τιμᾶσθε
	τιμᾷ	τιμῶσι(ν)	τιμᾶται	τιμῶνται
	ἐτίμων	ἐτιμῶμεν	ἐτιμώμην	ἐτιμώμεθα
	ἐτίμας	ἐτιμᾶτε	ἐτιμῶ	ἐτιμᾶσθε
	ἐτίμα	ἐτίμων	ἐτιμᾶτο	ἐτιμῶντο
SUBJUNCTIVE				
	τιμῶ	τιμῶμεν	τιμῶμαι	τιμώμεθα
	τιμᾷς	τιμᾶτε	τιμᾷ	τιμᾶσθε
	τιμᾷ	τιμῶσι(ν)	τιμᾶται	τιμῶνται
OPTATIVE				
	τιμῴην	τιμῷμεν	τιμῴμην	τιμῴμεθα
	τιμῴης	τιμῷτε	τιμῷο	τιμῷσθε
	τιμῴη	τιμῷεν	τιμῷτο	τιμῷντο
IMPERATIVE				
	τίμα	τιμᾶτε	τιμῶ	τιμᾶσθε
	τιμάτω	τιμώντων	τιμάσθω	τιμάσθων
INFINITIVE	τιμᾶν		τιμᾶσθαι	
PARTICIPLE	τιμῶν, ῶσα, ῶν, -ῶντος, ώσης, ῶντος		τιμώμενος, η, ον	

δηλόω

	ACTIVE		MIDDLE-PASSIVE	
INDICATIVE				
	δηλῶ	δηλοῦμεν	δηλοῦμαι	δηλούμεθα
	δηλοῖς	δηλοῦτε	δηλοῖ	δηλοῦσθε
	δηλοῖ	δηλοῦσι(ν)	δηλοῦται	δηλοῦνται
	ἐδήλουν	ἐδηλοῦμεν	ἐδηλούμην	ἐδηλούμεθα
	ἐδήλους	ἐδηλοῦτε	ἐδηλοῦ	ἐδηλοῦσθε
	ἐδήλου	ἐδήλουν	ἐδηλοῦτο	ἐδηλοῦντο
SUBJUNCTIVE				
	δηλῶ	δηλῶμεν	δηλῶμαι	δηλώμεθα
	δηλοῖς	δηλῶτε	δηλοῖ	δηλῶσθε
	δηλοῖ	δηλῶσι(ν)	δηλῶται	δηλῶνται
OPTATIVE				
	δηλοίην	δηλοῖμεν	δηλοίμην	δηλοίμεθα
	δηλοίης	δηλοῖτε	δηλοῖο	δηλοῖσθε
	δηλοίη	δηλοῖεν	δηλοῖτο	δηλοῖντο
IMPERATIVE				
	δήλου	δηλοῦτε	δηλοῦ	δηλοῦσθε
	δηλούτω	δηλούντων	δηλούσθω	δηλούσθων
INFINITIVE	δηλοῦν		δηλοῦσθαι	
PARTICIPLE	δηλῶν, οῦσα, οῦν, -οῦντος, οῦσης, οῦντος		δηλούμενος, η, ον	

τίθημι: Continuous

ACTIVE

INDICATIVE

τίθημι	τίθεμεν
τίθης	τίθετε
τίθησι(ν)	τιθέασι(ν)
ἐτίθην	ἐτίθεμεν
ἐτίθεις	ἐτίθετε
ἐτίθει	ἐτίθεσαν

SUBJUNCTIVE

τιθῶ	τιθῶμεν
τιθῇς	τιθῆτε
τιθῇ	τιθῶσι(ν)

OPTATIVE

τιθείην	τιθεῖμεν
τιθείης	τιθεῖτε
τιθείη	τιθεῖεν

IMPERATIVE

τίθει	τίθετε
τιθέτω	τιθέντων

INFINITIVE

τιθέναι

PARTICIPLE

τιθείς, εῖσα, έν
-έντος, -είσης, -έντος

MIDDLE-PASSIVE

INDICATIVE

τίθεμαι	τιθέμεθα
τίθεσαι	τίθεσθε
τίθεται	τίθενται
ἐτιθέμην	ἐτιθέμεθα
ἐτίθεσο	ἐτίθεσθε
ἐτίθετο	ἐτίθεντο

SUBJUNCTIVE

τιθῶμαι	τιθώμεθα
τιθῇ	τιθῆσθε
τιθῆται	τιθῶνται

OPTATIVE

τιθείμην	τιθείμεθα
τιθεῖο	τιθεῖσθε
τιθεῖτο	τιθεῖντο

IMPERATIVE

τίθεσο	τίθεσθε
τιθέσθω	τιθέσθων

INFINITIVE

τίθεσθαι

PARTICIPLE

τιθέμενος, η, ον

τίθημι: Aorist

ACTIVE

INDICATIVE

ἔθηκα	ἔθεμεν
ἔθηκας	ἔθετε
ἔθηκε(ν)	ἔθεσαν

SUBJUNCTIVE

θῶ	θῶμεν
θῇς	θῆτε
θῇ	θῶσι(ν)

OPTATIVE

θείην	θεῖμεν
θείης	θεῖτε
θείη	θεῖεν

IMPERATIVE

θές	θέτε
θέτω	θέντων

INFINITIVE

θεῖναι

PARTICIPLE

θείς, εῖσα, έν
-έντος, -είσης, -έντος

M-P

INDICATIVE

ἐθέμην	ἐθέμεθα
ἔθου	ἔθεσθε
ἔθετο	ἔθεντο

SUBJUNCTIVE

θῶμαι	θώμεθα
θῇ	θῆσθε
θῆται	θῶνται

OPTATIVE

θείμην	θείμεθα
θεῖο	θεῖσθε
θεῖτο	θεῖντο

IMPERATIVE

θοῦ	θέσθε
θέσθω	θέσθων

INFINITIVE

θέσθαι

PARTICIPLE

θέμενος, η, ον

δείκνυμι

ACTIVE

INDICATIVE

δείκνυμι	δείκνυμεν
δείκνυς	δείκνυτε
δείκνυσι(ν)	δεικνύασι(ν)
ἐδείκνυν	ἐδείκνυμεν
ἐδείκνυς	ἐδείκνυτε
ἐδείκνυ	ἐδείκνυσαν

SUBJUNCTIVE

δεικνύω	δεικνύωμεν
δεικνύῃς	δεικνύητε
δεικνύῃ	δεικνύωσι(ν)

OPTATIVE

δεικνύοιμι	δεικνύοιμεν
δεικνύοις	δεικνύοιτε
δεικνύοι	δεικνύοιεν

IMPERATIVE

δείκνυ	δείκνυτε
δεικνύτω	δεικνύντων

INFINITIVE

δεικνύναι

PARTICIPLE

δεικνύς, ῦσα, ύν
-ύντος, -ύσης, -ύντος

MIDDLE-PASSIVE

INDICATIVE

δείκνυμαι	δεικνύμεθα
δείκνυσαι	δείκνυσθε
δείκνυται	δείκνυνται
ἐδεικνύμην	ἐδεικνύμεθα
ἐδείκνυσο	ἐδείκνυσθε
ἐδείκνυτο	ἐδείκνυντο

SUBJUNCTIVE

δεικνύωμαι	δεικνυώμεθα
δεικνύῃ	δεικνύησθε
δεικνύηται	δεικνύωνται

OPTATIVE

δεικνυοίμην	δεικνυοίμεθα
δεικνύοιο	δεικνύοισθε
δεικνύοιτο	δεικνύοιντο

IMPERATIVE

δείκνυσο	δείκνυσθε
δεικνύσθω	δεικνύσθων

INFINITIVE

δείκνυσθαι

PARTICIPLE

δεικνύμενος, η, ον

ἵημι*: Cont. ἵημι*: Aorist φημί: Cont.

φημί: Cont. — ACTIVE

INDICATIVE

φημί	φαμεν
φῄς	φατε
φησί(ν)	φασί(ν)
ἔφην	ἔφαμεν
ἔφης*	ἔφατε
ἔφη	ἔφασαν

SUBJUNCTIVE

φῶ	φῶμεν
φῇς	φῆτε
φῇ	φῶσι(ν)

OPTATIVE

φαίην	φαῖμεν
φαίης	φαῖτε
φαίη	φαῖεν

IMPERATIVE

φάθι**	φάτε
φάτω	φάντων

INFINITIVE

φάναι

PARTICIPLE

φάς, φᾶσα, φάν
φάντος, φάσης, φάντος

* or ἔφησθα
** or φάθι (enclitic)

ἵημι*: Aorist — ACTIVE

INDICATIVE

ἧκα	-εῖμεν
ἧκας	-εῖτε
ἧκε(ν)	-εῖσαν

SUBJUNCTIVE

-ῶ	-ῶμεν
-ῇς	-ῆτε
-ῇ	-ῶσι(ν)

OPTATIVE

-είην	-εῖμεν
-είης	-εῖτε
-είη	-εῖεν

IMPERATIVE

-ές	-έτε
-έτω	-έντων

INFINITIVE

-εῖναι

PARTICIPLE

-είς, -εῖσα, -έν
-έντος, -είσης, -έντος

ἵημι*: Cont. — ACTIVE

INDICATIVE

ἵημι	ἵεμεν
ἵης**	ἵετε
ἵησι(ν)	ἱᾶσι(ν)
ἵην	ἵεμεν
ἵεις	ἵετε
ἵει	ἵεσαν

SUBJUNCTIVE

ἱῶ	ἱῶμεν
ἱῇς	ἱῆτε
ἱῇ	ἱῶσι(ν)

OPTATIVE

ἱείην	ἱεῖμεν
ἱείης	ἱεῖτε
ἱείη	ἱεῖεν

IMPERATIVE

ἵει	ἵετε
ἱέτω	ἱέντων

INFINITIVE

ἱέναι

PARTICIPLE

ἱείς, ἱεῖσα, ἱέν
ἱέντος, ἱείσης, ἱέντος

*The middle forms of ἵημι resemble those of τίθημι
** or ἱεῖς

ἵστημι: Perfect — ACTIVE

INDICATIVE

ἕστηκα	ἕσταμεν
ἕστηκας	ἕστατε
ἕστηκε(ν)	ἑστᾶσι(ν)
εἱστήκη	ἕσταμεν
εἱστήκης	ἕστατε
εἱστήκει(ν)	ἕστασαν

SUBJUNCTIVE

ἑστῶ	ἑστῶμεν
ἑστῇς	ἑστῆτε
ἑστῇ	ἑστῶσι(ν)

OPTATIVE

ἑσταίην	ἑσταῖμεν
ἑσταίης	ἑσταῖτε
ἑσταίη	ἑσταῖεν

IMPERATIVE

ἕσταθι	ἕστατε
ἑστάτω	ἑστάντων

INFINITIVE

ἑστάναι

PARTICIPLE

ἑστώς, ῶσα, ός
ἑστῶτος, ώσης, ῶτος

ἵστημι: Continuous* — MIDDLE-PASSIVE

INDICATIVE

ἵσταμαι	ἱστάμεθα
ἵστασαι	ἵστασθε
ἵσταται	ἵστανται
ἱστάμην	ἱστάμεθα
ἵστασο	ἵστασθε
ἵστατο	ἵσταντο

SUBJUNCTIVE

ἱστῶμαι	ἱστώμεθα
ἱστῇ	ἱστῆσθε
ἱστῆται	ἱστῶνται

OPTATIVE

ἱσταίμην	ἱσταίμεθα
ἱσταῖο	ἱσταῖσθε
ἱσταῖτο	ἱσταῖντο

IMPERATIVE

ἵστασο	ἵστασθε
ἱστάσθω	ἱστάσθων

INFINITIVE

ἵστασθαι

PARTICIPLE

ἱστάμενος, η, ον

ἵστημι: Continuous — ACTIVE

INDICATIVE

ἵστημι	ἵσταμεν
ἵστης	ἵστατε
ἵστησι(ν)	ἱστᾶσι(ν)
ἵστην	ἵσταμεν
ἵστης	ἵστατε
ἵστη	ἵστασαν

SUBJUNCTIVE

ἱστῶ	ἱστῶμεν
ἱστῇς	ἱστῆτε
ἱστῇ	ἱστῶσι(ν)

OPTATIVE

ἱσταίην	ἱσταῖμεν
ἱσταίης	ἱσταῖτε
ἱσταίη	ἱσταῖεν

IMPERATIVE

ἵστη	ἵστατε
ἱστάτω	ἱστάντων

INFINITIVE

ἱστάναι

PARTICIPLE

ἱστάς, ᾶσα, άν
ἱστάντος, άσης, άντος

* For aorist see p. 211.

δίδωμι: Continuous

ACTIVE		MIDDLE-PASSIVE	
INDICATIVE			
δίδωμι	δίδομεν	δίδομαι	διδόμεθα
δίδως	δίδοτε	δίδοσαι	δίδοσθε
δίδωσι(ν)	διδόασι(ν)	δίδοται	δίδονται
ἐδίδουν	ἐδίδομεν	ἐδιδόμην	ἐδιδόμεθα
ἐδίδους	ἐδίδοτε	ἐδίδοσο	ἐδίδοσθε
ἐδίδου	ἐδίδοσαν	ἐδίδοτο	ἐδίδοντο
SUBJUNCTIVE			
διδῶ	διδῶμεν	διδῶμαι	διδώμεθα
διδῷς	διδῶτε	διδῷ	διδῶσθε
διδῷ	διδῶσι(ν)	διδῶται	διδῶνται
OPTATIVE			
διδοίην	διδοῖμεν	διδοίμην	διδοίμεθα
διδοίης	διδοῖτε	διδοῖο	διδοῖσθε
διδοίη	διδοῖεν	διδοῖτο	διδοῖντο
IMPERATIVE			
δίδου	δίδοτε	δίδοσο	δίδοσθε
διδότω	διδόντων	διδόσθω	διδόσθων
INFINITIVE			
διδόναι		δίδοσθαι	
PARTICIPLE			
διδούς,οῦσα,όν		διδόμενος,η,ον	
διδόντος,ούσης,όντος			

δίδωμι: Aorist

ACTIVE		MIDDLE-PASSIVE	
INDICATIVE			
ἔδωκα	ἔδομεν	ἐδόμην	ἐδόμεθα
ἔδωκας	ἔδοτε	ἔδου	ἔδοσθε
ἔδωκε(ν)	ἔδοσαν	ἔδοτο	ἔδοντο
SUBJUNCTIVE			
δῶ	δῶμεν	δῶμαι	δώμεθα
δῷς	δῶτε	δῷ	δῶσθε
δῷ	δῶσι(ν)	δῶται	δῶνται
OPTATIVE			
δοίην	δοῖμεν	δοίμην	δοίμεθα
δοίης	δοῖτε	δοῖο	δοῖσθε
δοίη	δοῖεν	δοῖτο	δοῖντο
IMPERATIVE			
δός	δότε	δοῦ	δόσθε
δότω	δόντων	δόσθω	δόσθων
INFINITIVE			
δοῦναι		δόσθαι	
PARTICIPLE			
δούς,δοῦσα,δόν		δόμενος,η,ον	
δόντος,ούσης,όντος			

οἶδα: PERF. ACTIVE

INDICATIVE	
οἶδα	ἴσμεν
οἶσθα	ἴστε
οἶδε(ν)	ἴσασι(ν)
ᾔδη*	ἴσμεν*
ᾔδησθα*	ἴστε*
ᾔδει(ν)*	ἴσαν*
SUBJUNCTIVE	
εἰδῶ	εἰδῶμεν
εἰδῇς	εἰδῆτε
εἰδῇ	εἰδῶσι(ν)
OPTATIVE	
εἰδείην	εἰδεῖμεν
εἰδείης	εἰδεῖτε
εἰδείη	εἰδεῖεν
IMPERATIVE	
ἴσθι	ἴστε
ἴστω	ἴστων
INFINITIVE	
εἰδέναι	
PARTICIPLE	
εἰδώς,υῖα,ός	
εἰδότος,υἱς,ότος	

*Or ᾔδειν, ᾔδεις, ᾔδει(ν) / ᾔδεμεν, ᾔδετε, ᾔδεσαν

παύω, παύσω, ἔπαυσα, πέπαυκα, πέπαυμαι, ἐπαύθην   (And other regular -ω verbs)*
ποιέω, ποιήσω, ἐποίησα, πεποίηκα, πεποίημαι, ἐποιήθην   (And other regular -έω verbs)
τιμάω, τιμήσω, ἐτίμησα, τετίμηκα, τετίμημαι, ἐτιμήθην   (And other regular -άω verbs)*
δηλόω, δηλώσω, ἐδήλωσα, δεδήλωκα, δεδήλωμαι, ἐδηλώθην   (And other regular -όω verbs)*
δείκνυμι, δείξω, ἔδειξα, δέδειχα, δέδειγμαι, ἐδείχθην

Learn by heart the first three principal parts of the starred verbs below. Be able at least to recognize or look up the rest. Forms for which it would be very hard or impossible to guess the first principal part are in bold print.

Most verbs have some stems that do not follow the normal pattern. (And not all verbs have all principal parts. μεθύω, στένω, and χρήζω have only one stem.) A dash means that a form is found only in compound.

*ἀγγέλλω, ἀγγελῶ, ἤγγειλα, ἤγγελκα, ἤγγελμαι, ἠγγέλθην - announce
*ἄγω, ἄξω, ἤγαγον, **ἦχα, ἦγμαι, ἤχθην** - lead, drive
  ᾄδω, ᾄσομαι, ᾖσα, --, ᾖσμαι, ᾔσθην - sing
*αἱρέω, αἱρήσω, **εἷλον**, ᾕρηκα, ᾕρημαι, ᾑρέθην - take (middle = choose)
*αἰσθάνομαι, αἰσθήσομαι, ᾐσθόμην, ᾔσθημαι - perceive
*ἀκούω, ἀκούσομαι, ἤκουσα, ἀκήκοα, --, ἠκούσθην - hear
  ἅπτω, ἅψω, ἧψα, --, ἧμμαι, ἥφθην - fasten (middle = hold on to, take hold of)
  ἄρχω, ἄρξω, ἦρξα, --, ἦργμαι, ἤρχθην - rule (middle = begin)

*βαίνω, βήσομαι, ἔβην, βέβηκα - go
*βάλλω, βαλῶ, ἔβαλον, βέβληκα, βέβλημαι, ἐβλήθην - throw
  βλέπω, βλέψομαι, ἔβλεψα - see
  βοάω, βοήσομαι, ἐβόησα, -- - shout
*βούλομαι, βουλήσομαι, ἐβουλήθην, βεβούλημαι - will, wish (passive deponent)

  γαμέω, γαμῶ, ἔγημα, γεγάμηκα γεγάμημαι, ἐγαμήθην - marry (active, of a man),
                           to be married (middle or passive, of a woman)
*γελάω, γελάσομαι, ἐγέλασα, ἐγελάσθην - laugh
*γίγνομαι, γενήσομαι, ἐγενόμην, γέγονα, γεγένημαι, ἐγενήθην - become, be
*γιγνώσκω, γνώσομαι, ἔγνων, ἔγνωκα, ἔγνωσμαι, ἐγνώσθην - know
*γράφω, γράψω, ἔγραψα, γέγραφα, γέγραμμαι, ἐγράφην - write

*δέχομαι, δέξομαι, ἐδεξάμην, --, δέδεγμαι, -εδέχθην - receive (middle deponent)
  διαλέγομαι, διαλέξομαι, διαλεξάμην / διελέχθη / διελέγην, διαλεχθήσομαι / διαλεγησομαι - converse
*δίδωμι, δώσω, ἔδωκα, δέδωκα, δέδομαι, ἐδόθην - give
*δοκέω, δόξω, ἔδοξα, --, δέδογμαι, -εδόχθην - seem, think
*δύναμαι, δυνήσομαι, ἐδυνήθην, δεδύνημαι - be able (passive deponent)

*ἐγείρω, ἐγερῶ, ἔγειρα, ἐγρήγορα, ἐγήγερμαι, ἠγέρθην - awaken
*ἐθέλω, ἐθελήσω, ἠθέλησα, ἠθέληκα - wish (also θέλω)
*εἰμί, ἔσομαι - be
*εἶμι - come, go (with future force) For coming/going use ἔρχομαι as present indicative, but -ι (from εἶμι) for
     other moods on the continuous stem and also for the imperfect (ᾖα, etc.). Use εἶμι as future = will come/go
  ἕπομαι, ἕψομαι, ἑσπόμην - follow
*ἔρχομαι, **ἐλεύσομαι, ἦλθον, ἐλήλυθα** - come, go (ἐλευσ- in optative, infinitive, etc.; εἶμι = future indic.)
*ἐσθίω, **ἔδομαι, ἔφαγον, ἐδήδοκα** - eat
*εὑρίσκω, εὑρήσω, ηὗρον (or εὗρον), ηὕρηκα (or εὕρηκα), εὕρημαι, εὑρέθην - find, discover
*ἔχω (imperfect εἶχον), ἕξω or σχήσω, **ἔσχον, ἔσχηκα** - have

  θάπτω, θάψω, ἔθαψα, --, τέθαμμαι, ἐτάφην - bury
  θαυμάζω, θαυμάσομαι, (rest is normal) - wonder
*θνῄσκω, -θανοῦμαι, -έθανον, τέθνηκα - die (usually in compound ἀποθνῄσκω)

*ἵημι, **ἥσω, ἧκα, εἷκα, εἷμαι, εἵθην** - send forth
*ἱκνέομαι, -ἵξομαι, -ἱκόμην (long ι) , ἷγμαι (long ι) - come (usually in compound ἀφικνέομαι)
*ἵστημι, στήσω, ἔστησα, ἔσταμαι, ἐστάθην - stand (transitive), set up
  ἵσταμαι, στήσομαι, **ἔστην, ἕστηκα** (perfect as present) - stand (intransitive)

Other regular verbs that have been learned: βασιλεύω, λύω, παιδεύω, πορεύω. Other regular -έω verbs: ἀδικέω, αἰτέω, ἀπειθέω, γεωργέω, ἐπιθυμέω, ζητέω, κοινωνέω, λυπέω, μετρέω, μισέω, νοσέω, ὁμολογέω, πονέω, ὠφελέω, ὀρχέομαι, φοβέομαι. Other regular -άω verbs: ἐρωτάω, ζάω (regular stems, irregular present), νικάω, σιγάω, τελευτάω, τολμάω. Other regular -όω verb: ἐλευθερόω.

καθαίρω, καθαρῶ, ἐκάθηρα, κεκάθαρμαι, ἐκαθάρθην - purify
καθεύδω (imperfect ἐκάθευδον or καθηῦδον), καθευδήσω, -- - sleep
καθίζω (imperfect. ἐκάθιζον), καθιῶ, ἐκάθισα - seat someone (middle = sit down)
*καλέω, καλῶ, ἐκάλεσα, κέκληκα, κέκλημαι, ἐκλήθην - call
κάμνω, καμοῦμαι, ἔκαμον, κέκμηκα - be sick or weary, toil
κεῖμαι, κείσομαι - to be laid (used as passive of τίθημι); lie, lie down to rest, be situated
*κλέπτω, κλέψω (sometimes κλέψομαι), ἔκλεψα, **κέκλοφα**, κέκλεμμαι, ἐκλάπην - steal
*κρίνω, κρινῶ, ἔκρινα (long ι), κέκρικα, κέκριμαι, ἐκρίθην - discern, judge   (ἀποκρίνομαι is from κρίνω)
*κρύπτω, κρύψω, ἔκρυψα, κέκρυφα, κέκρυμμαι, ἐκρύφθην - hide (normal stems)
*κτάομαι, κτήσομαι, ἐκτησάμην, κέκτημαι, ἐκτήθην - acquire (perf. = possess) (middle deponent)
*κτείνω, κτενῶ, ἔκτεινα, -έκτονα (perfect) - kill   (usually in compound ἀποκτείνω)

*λαμβάνω, **λήψομαι**, ἔλαβον, **εἴληφα, εἴλημμαι, ἐλήφθην** - take
*λανθάνω, **λήσω**, ἔλαθον, λέληθα - escape the notice of (middle = forget)
*λέγω, **ἐρῶ, εἶπον, εἴρηκα**, λέλεγμαι, **ἐρρήθην** - say; also λέξω, ἔλεξα, ἐλέχθην
*λείπω, λείψω, ἔλιπον, λέλοιπα, λέλειμμαι, ἐλείφθην - leave

*μανθάνω, μαθήσομαι, ἔμαθον, μεμάθηκα - learn
*μέλλω, μελλήσω, ἐμέλλησα - be about to
*μένω, μενῶ, ἔμεινα, μεμένηκα - wait

*νομίζω, νομιῶ, ἐνόμισα, νενόμικα, νενόμισμαι, ἐνομίσθην - consider

οἴγνυμι, -οίξω, ἔῳξα, -έῳγα, -έῳγμαι, -εῴχθην - open (usually in compound; ἀνοίγνυμι more common)
οἰκτίρω, οἰκτιρῶ, ᾤκτιρα (long ι) - pity (also οἰκτείρω)
οἰμώζω, οἰμώξομαι, ᾤμωξα - lament
*οἴομαι (also οἶμαι), οἰήσομαι, ᾠήθην - think
*ὄλλυμι, -ολῶ, -ώλεσα, -ολώλεκα - destroy, ruin, lose
ὄλλυμαι, -ολοῦμαι, -ωλόμην, -όλωλα (intransitive perfect as present *I am ruined*) - perish, be ruined or lost
*ὄμνυμι, ὀμοῦμαι, ὤμοσα, ὀμώμοκα, ὀμώμομαι, ὠμόσθην - swear
*ὁράω, **ὄψομαι, εἶδον**, ἑόρακα and ἑώρακα, ἑώραμαι and **ὦμμαι, ὤφθην** - see   (and οἶδα - know)
ὀργίζω, -ὀργιῶ, ὤργισα, --, ὤργισμαι, ὠργίσθην - anger (more frequent as passive = be angered)
ὀρύττω, -ορύξω, ὤρυξα, -ορώρυχα, ὀρώρυγμαι, ὠρύχθην - dig

*πάσχω, **πείσομαι, ἔπαθον, πέπονθα** - suffer, undergo, experience
*πείθω, πείσω, ἔπεισα, πέπεικα, πέπεισμαι, ἐπείσθην - persuade; middle or passive = believe, obey
            πέποιθα (intrans. perfect) = trust
*πέμπω, πέμψω, ἔπεμψα, πέπομφα, πέπεμμαι, ἐπέμφθην - send
πέτομαι, -πτήσομαι, -επτόμην and -επτάμην - fly
*πίνω, πίομαι (or πιοῦμαι), ἔπιον, πέπωκα, -πέπομαι, -επόθην - drink
*πίπτω, πεσοῦμαι, ἔπεσον, πέπτωκα - fall
*πλήττω (also πλήγνυμι), -πλήξω, -έπληξα, πέπληγα, πέπληγμαι, ἐπλήγην (in compound -ἐπλάγην) - strike
*πράττω, πράξα, ἔπραξα, **πέπραχα** and **πέπραγα, πέπραγμαι**, ἐπράχθην- do

*σημαίνω, σημανῶ, ἐσήμηνα, σεσήμασμαι, ἐσημάνθην - signify
*σιγάω, σιγήσομαι, ἐσίγησα, etc. - be silent (forms regular except for future)
*σῴζω, σώσω, ἔσωσα, σέσωκα, σέσωμαι, ἐσώθην - save

*τέμνω, τεμῶ, ἔτεμον, **-τέτμηκα, -τέτμημαι, ἐτμήθην** - cut
*τίθημι, θήσω, ἔθηκα, τέθηκα, τέθειμαι, ἐτέθην - put
*τίκτω, τέξομαι, ἔτεκον, τέτοκα - bring forth, give birth, beget
*τυγχάνω, τεύξομαι, ἔτυχον, τετύχηκα - hit the mark, happen, obtain

ὑπισχνέομαι, ὑποσχήσομαι, ὑπεσχόμην, ὑπέσχημαι - promise

*φαίνω, φανῶ, ἔφηνα, πέφαγκα, πέφασμαι, ἐφάνθη - show (transitive)
   φαίνομαι, φανοῦμαι / φανήσομαι, ἐφάνην, **πέφηνα** - appear (intransitive)
*φέρω, οἴσω, ἤνεγκα and ἤνεγκον, ἐνήνοχα, ἐνήνεγμαι, ἠνέχθην - bear, carry
*φεύγω, φεύξομαι, ἔφυγον, πέφευγα - flee
φημι (imperfect ἔφην), φήσω, ἔφησα - say   (Note: ἔφη is used as aorist - *he, she, it said*)
*φθείρω, φθερῶ, ἔφθειρα, ἔφθαρκα or -έφθορα, ἔφθαρμαι, ἐφθάρην - spoil, corrupt
*φυλάττω, φυλάξω, ἐφύλαξα, πεφύλαχα, πεφύλαγμαι, ἐφυλάχθην - guard

χαίρω, χαιρήσω, ἐχάρην (intransitive aorist), κεχάρηκα - rejoice
*χράομαι, χρήσομαι, ἐχρησάμην, κέχρημαι, ἐχρήσθην - use

This dictionary has all the words used in stories. By subtracting words in parentheses, the dictionary may be used for a final ocabulary review. (Words in parentheses are simple roots of compound verbs or words used in charts or lists but not in conversation or stories.) The coding of information is as follows:

σύ	word in bold print	paradigm of word is given in Paradigm Section pp. 237-248	
βλέπω	underlined word	simple root of verb used only in compound in the readings	
(ἄστυ)	words in parentheses	words from a chart, list, poem, etc. not used in stories or conversation	
19	plain text numeral	page on which word is glossed	
(13)	numeral in parentheses	page on which word is used in script or story (but not glossed)	
92	underlined numeral	page on which word is discussed or included in a box, chart, or list	
80	numeral in bold print	page on which word appears in a paradigm	

When a verb changes meaning in a middle, passive, or intransitive form, those forms are listed separately. For example, λανθάνομαι is glossed separately from λανθάνω because it is encountered first, before the system of Active and Middle has been learned. This dictionary is for use at every stage.

This dictionary gives only those principal parts that are glossed. Consult pp. 249-50 for principal parts.

α

ἀ- / ἀν (alpha privative) - 15, 46

ἀγαθός,ή,όν - good 19

ἀγγεῖον, τό - pot, vessel 140

ἄγγελος, ὁ - messenger 84

ἀγγέλλω - announce, report 70, ἤγγειλα 118

ἀγρός, ὁ - field 38

ἄγω - lead 119

ἀδελφή , ἡ - sister 26, 28

ἀδελφός, ὁ - brother 30, 97

ἀδικέω - do an injustice 122

ἄδικος,ον - unjust 47, 48

ᾄδω - sing 177

ἀεί - always 57

ἀθυμέω - be disheartened 135

αἴνιγμα, τό - riddle 188

αἱρέομαι - choose (mid of αἱρέω) 97

αἱρέω - take, seize 135

αἰσθάνομαι - perceive + acc. or + gen. 140

αἰτέω - request, ask 28, with two accusatives 38, beg 121

αἴτημα, τό - request 194

ἀκούω - hear, listen (13), + gen. person, acc. thing 51, perf. ἀκήκοα 170

ἄκρος,α,ον - at the furthest point: topmost, tipmost, etc. 162

ἀλήθεια, ἡ - truth 128

ἀληθής,ές - true 79, 95

ἀληθῶς - truly (adv.) (2)

ἀλλά - but 19

ἀλλήλους - each other (1)

ἄλλος,η,ο - other (3), 48

ἅμα - at the same time, together (1)

ἀμείνων, ον - better 92, 114, 197

ἀμφισβητέω - dispute 119, 128, imperf. ἠμφισβήτουν 121

ἀμφότεροι,αι,α - both 92, 94

ἄν - contrary-to-fact 133-4, + subjunctive 150 + optative 161

(ἀνά - up [seen in compounds])

ἀναβαίνω - go up 121

ἀναβλέπω - look up 121

ἀναβοάω - shout out 125

ἀναγιγνώσκω - read (9)

ἀναλαμβάνω - take up, pick up 94

ἀναπαύομαι - rest up, rest 181

ἀνεκτός,ή,όν - bearable 197

ἄνεμος, ὁ - wind 111

ἄνευ + gen. - without 81

ἀνέχομαι - endure 131

ἀνέχω - hold up 111

ἀνήρ, ἀνδρός, ὁ - man, male, husband 77, 79

ἀνὴρ πένης - a poor man (redundant ἀνήρ) 89

ἄνθρωπος, ὁ - person, man, human, 28, 34

ἀνίσταμαι - stand up 19

ἀνοίγνυμι - open up 149

ἀντί - instead of + gen. 44

ἄνω - upward 121

ἄξιος,α,ον - worthy, worth or worthy of + gen. 157

ἀπαγγέλλω - report back 70

ἀπάγω - lead away now 197

ἀπειθέω - disobey 149

ἄπειμι - go away, imper. ἄπιθι 89

ἀπέρχομαι - go away (aorist ἀπῆλθον 111)

ἀπῆλθον - see above

ἄπιθι - command of ἄπειμι 89

ἀπό + gen. - away from 38

ἀποβλέπω - look off or away 157

ἀποδίδωμι - give back 140 ἀποδίδωμι χάριν 194

ἀποδοτέον - one must give back 197

ἀποθνῄσκω - die 91, aor. ἀπέθανον 140

ἀποκρίνομαι - reply 29, ἀπεκρίνατο 114, 119, ἀποκριθείη 197

ἀποκτείνω - kill 142

ἀπολαμβάνω - take back 100

ἀπόλλυμαι - (middle) perish, with intrans. perfect ἀπόλωλα 191

ἀπόλλυμι - destroy, lose 128

ἀπορέω - be at a loss 165

ἀποτέμνω - cut off 70

(ἀποτυγχάνω - lose [11])

ἀποφέρω - bring or carry back 84

ἅπτομαι - hold on to + gen. 119

(ἅπτω - fasten [a noose] p. 118)

ἄρα - used to ask questions 125

ἀργύριον, τό - money, silver coin 19, 122

ἄργυρος, ὁ - silver 184

ἄριστος,α,ον - best 92, 94

ἄρχομαι - begin 119

ἄρχω - rule over + gen. 177

(ἄστυ, τό - town 183)

ἄτοπος,ον - strange, odd 97

αὖθις - again (1)

αὔριον - tomorrow 177

αὐτή - fem. pronoun (in all cases but nom.) 36; ἡ αὐτή same 36, 38; αὐτὴ ἡ herself (emphatic) 50, 51

αὕτη - this 67 (fem. of οὗτος)

αὐτῇ - to her (16), <u>36</u>

αὐτήν - her (2), <u>36</u>

αὐτῆς - hers, her, of her (1), <u>36</u>

αὐτίκα - immediately, at the very moment 184

αὐτό - it <u>36</u>, 38, αὐτό τοῦτο <u>70</u>

αὐτόν - him (2), <u>36</u>

αὐτόν = ἑαυτόν <u>96</u>

αὐτόν,ήν,ό - him, her it (except in nom.) <u>36</u>
  ὁ αὐτός, etc. - the same (all cases) <u>36</u>, 38, <u>50</u>
  αὐτὸς ὁ, etc. - him / her / itself (emphatic) <u>50</u>, 51

αὐτοῦ - his, of him (1), **36**

αὐτῷ - to him (16), **36**

ἀφίημι - let go of, release 165

ἀφικνέομαι - arrive 157, aor. ἀφικόμην 181

β

βαίνω - step, go 81, βαίνων **82**, ἔβην **120**, βῆθι 121

βάλλω - throw, hit by throwing 44, aor. ἔβαλον 94

βαρύς,εῖα,ύ - deep, 184

βασιλεύς,έως, ὁ - king 44, **164**

βασιλεύω - be king, rule over + gen. 142

βασιλικός,ή,όν - kingly, royal 119

βῆθι - aorist imperative of βαίνω 121

βιβλίον, τό - book (2), **30**

βίος, ὁ - life 91

<u>βλέπω</u> - look at, look 121 (in ἀναβλέπω and καταβλέπω)

βοάω - shout 119

βουλεύω - plan, deliberate 142

βούλομαι - want, wish (9)

βροτός, ὁ - mortal 114

γ

γαμέω - marry (13)

γάρ (postpositive conjunction) - for 29

γελάω - laugh, aor. ἐγέλασα 119

γελοῖος,α,ον - funny, laughable 119

γένος, τό - race, kind, class 94, **95**

γεραιός,ά,όν - old 131

γέρων, γέροντος, ὁ - old man; as adj. - old **69**, 149

γεωργέω - farm, work the earth 81

γεωργός, ὁ - farmer 81

γλῶττα, ἡ - tongue (2), **26, 37**

γῆ, ἡ - earth, land 64

γῆρας, αος, τό - old age 170

γίγνομαι - come into existence, become, be, arise 89

γίγνωσκω - know (1), 19, aorist ἔγνων **120**, system **211** (ἔγνωκα perfect as present <u>158</u>)

γλυκύς,εῖα,ύ - sweet 70, γλυκύτερος,α,ον - sweeter 70 γλυκύτατος - sweetest 70

γνώμη, ἡ - wisdom 170

γράμμα, τό - letter (of alphabet) (3)

γράφω - write (3)

γυνή, γυναικός, ἡ - woman, wife **77**, 84

δ

δαίμων,ονος, ἡ/ὁ - spirit, divinity **68**, 97

δακρύω - cry 19

δάκτυλος, ὁ - finger 32

δέ (postpositive) - but, and (weakest linking word 12) μέν / δέ <u>38</u>, ὁ δέ 48, <u>48</u> ὁ μέν, ὁ δέ <u>53</u>

δεῖ - it is obligatory, one ought, one should (lit., "it is binding" from δέω - bind) 97

δείκνυμι - show (16), **198**, aor. ἔδειξεν 162

δεινός,ή,όν - awesome, terrible, strange 140

δεῖπνον, τό - meal, dinner (13)

δεσπότης, ὁ - master 131

δεύτερος,α,ον - second 32

δέχομαι - receive, accept 140

δή (postpositive) - emphatic = "underline the word before" 67

δῆλος,η,ον or ος,ον - clear 48

δηλόω - make clear **194**, **208**

δῆτα (postpositive) - more emphatic than δή 170

Δία - Zeus (acc.), "by Zeus" (2)

διά + acc. - through, on account of 48; + gen. through, by (agent), as in by myself 162 + gen. - through (spatial) 194

διαλέγομαι - converse, converse with + dat. 119

δίδωμι - give (16), **218**, future δώσω 125, aorist ἔδωκα 181, perfect δέδωκα 199, aorist command δός give! (16), δός as permit! 122

διέρχομαι - go through 122

δίκαιος,α,ον & ος,ον - just 128

δικαστής, ὁ - judge 81

δίκη, ἡ - justice 128

διότι - since (13), = διά + ὅτι 48

δοκέω - seem, aor. ἔδοξα 119, three uses: seem, seem best, think + acc. + inf. 142

δός - give! (16), permit! 122

δοῦλος, ὁ - slave 135

δρᾶμα, τό - drama (16)

δύναμαι - be able 57, δυνήσοιτο 194

δύο - two 32

δῶρον, τό - gift 44

δώσω - I will give (future of δίδωμι) 125

ε

ἐάν + subj. - if ever <u>150</u>, 157

ἑαυτόν,ή,ό - (reflexive) himself, herself, itself **96**, 97

ἐγείρω, fut. ἐγερῶ - awaken 131

ἐγώ, με, etc. - I, me, etc. (3), <u>96</u>

ἔδωκε - he gave, aor. δίδωμι 181

ἐθέλω - wish, be willing (3)

ἔθηκα - I put, aorist of τίθημι 149

εἰ - if (11)

εἰ γάρ - if only + opt. <u>161</u>, 162, + past tense <u>182</u>, 184

εἶ - "you are" (εἰμι) vs. εἶ = "you go" see p. 25, **210**

εἰδέναι - to know, inf. of οἶδα 142, **159**, εἰδείην 194 εἰδώς,υῖα,ός - knowing (part.) 165; χάριν εἰδέναι - to know thanks, be grateful 194,

εἶδον - I saw (aorist of ὁράω) 51, aor. imper. middle ἰδοῦ 19

εἰδώς,υῖα,ός - knowing, participle of οἶδα 159, 165

εἴθε - if only + opt. 161, 162 + past tense <u>182</u>, 184

εἷλον - I took, seized (aor. of αἱρέω) 135

εἰμί - I am, ἐστί(ν) he, she, it is (1), **210**, εἰσί(ν) they are 19, ἔστι(ν) exists, is possible 54, inf. εἶναι 51, fut. ἔσται 72

εἶμι - I go, will go (used as future of ἔρχομαι) 19, **210**, imperative ἴθι 51

εἶναι - to be 51

εἴπερ - if in fact 121

εἶπον - I said, used as aor. of λέγω 51, 114

εἰρήνη, ἡ - peace 187

(εἴρηκα - I have said: perf. of λέγω 156)

εἰς (ἐς) - into + acc. 29
εἷς, μία, ἕν - one 80, 80, 89
εἰσάγω - lead into 135
εἰσβαίνω - go into 114
εἴσειμι - go in, imper. εἴσιθι 64
εἰσέρχομαι - come or go in 48
εἰσί(ν) - *they are* 19
εἰσοράω - look into 149
ἐκ (ἐξ) - out of + gen. (9), (13),
　44
ἕκαστος,η,ον - each 48
ἑκάτερος,α,ον - either (of two) 93,
　94
ἐκβαίνω - go out 111
ἐκβάλλω - throw out 135
ἐκεῖ - there 131
ἐκεῖνος,η,ο - that 13, 65
ἐκποδών (adverb) - out of the way
　lit., *"out of the feet"* 51
ἔλαβον - aorist of λαμβάνω 111
ἔλαθον - aorist of λανθάνω 165
ἐλευθερόω - set free 199
　(ἐλεύθερός = free)
ἐλέφας,αντος, ὁ - elephant 119
ἐλθεῖν - infinitive of ἦλθον,
　aorist of ἔρχομαι 97
(Ἕλλην, ὁ - Greek (10))
Ἑλληνικός,η,ον - Greek (22)
　(ἐλπίζω - hope 124 + fut. inf.)
ἐμαυτόν,ήν - myself 96, 97
ἐμέ - με (emphatic) 81, 91, 96
ἐμός,ή,όν - my 97, 98
ἐμοῦ - gen. of ἐγώ (emphatic)
　23, 96
ἐν - in + dat. 28
ἐν ᾧ - while
　(= ἐν τῷ χρόνῳ ἐν ᾧ) 91
ἕν - one (neuter) 80
ἐναντίος,α,ον - opposite 128
ἐννοέομαι - reflect on, consider
　(have in one's νοῦς) 128
ἐνταῦθα - here, in this place 142,
　here, to this place 165, 163
ἐντυγχάνω - chance upon + dat.
　94
ἐξαιρέω - take out 194
ἐξαίφνης (adverb) - suddenly,
　instantly 184
ἔξειμι - go out 48
ἐξέρχομαι - come or go out 122
ἔξω - outside, + gen. outside of 142
　(ἐπειδάν + subj. - whenever)
ἔπειτα - then, next 70
ἔπεσον - aorist of πίπτω 111
ἐπί + acc. - to (13), 184
　　+ gen. - on (position above) 48
　　+ dat. - at (13), over (body) 199

ἐπιθυμέω - desire, have a desire for
　　+ gen. 97
ἐπίσταμαι - understand 28
ἐπιστολή, ἡ - letter 28
ἕπομαι - follow + dat. 165
ἔργον, τό - work, deed (6), 79
ἔρχομαι - come 19
ἐρωτάω - ask (1), with two
　accusatives 38
ἐρώτημα, τό - question (3)
ἐσθίω - eat (13)
ἔσται - he, she, it will be (fut. of
　εἰμί) 72
ἐστί(ν) - is (1), with dative of
　possession 29, uses of ἐστι 54
ἔστι(ν) - exists, there exists 38
　(always accented that way at
　beginng of sentence and also
　when it means existence)
ἐστί μοι - I have, literally "is to
　me" 29, 54
ἕτερος,α,ον - other (of two) 93,
　94; other (of many) 93
ἔτι - yet, still 72 (time),
　135 (degree)
-ετο - past tense ending (M-P) 111
ἕτοιμος, - ready 91
ἔτος, τό - year 114
ἔτυχον - aorist of τυγχάνω 125
εὖ - well 71, 72
εὖγε - well done! well said! (1)
εὐδαιμονία, ἡ - good fortune,
　happiness 89
εὐδαίμων,ον - fortunate, happy,
　in good fortune 80, 84
　compar. εὐδαιμονέστερος 181
εὕδω - sleep (in καθεύδω 121)
εὑρέτης, ὁ - discoverer, inventor
　170
εὑρίσκω - find, discover 67, aor.
　ηὗρον, inf. εὑρεῖν 84, 89
ἐφ' = ἐπί - on, over 184
ἔφη - he, she, it said (fr. φημί) 122
　breaks up quote 131
ἐχθρός,ά,όν - hateful, hostile;
　hated, enemy 187
ἐχρῆν - acts as imperfect of χρή
　121
ἔχω - have, hold, possess (2),
　ἔχω + inf. be able; have the
　ability to (9), ἔχω + adverb =
　be in a condition 197, ἔχειν
　ἐν νῷ - have in mind, intend
　121

ζ

ζάω - live 114, 114
ζητέω - 38

ζωή , ἡ - life 72
ζῷον, τό - living thing, creature
　70
ζωός,η,ον - alive 72

η

ἡ - the (fem.) see ὁ, ἡ, τό
ἤ - or (11), than (in comparison)
　56, 57
ἤ . . . ἤ - either . . . or 57
ἦ - I was (OR = a question-asking
　particle 219)
ἡγέομαι - consider 140
ἥδε - this-here (fem.) See ὅδε,
　ἥδε, τόδε
ἤδη - already, now 72
ἥδιστος,η,ον - most pleasant 92,
　183
ἡδύς,εῖα,ύ - pleasant (13), 70,
　183
ἦλθον - aorist of ἔρχομαι 114
　inf. ἐλθεῖν 97
ἥλιος, ὁ - sun 38
ἡμᾶς αὐτούς - ourselves, etc.
　96
ἡμεῖς, ἡμᾶς, ἡμῶν, ἡμῖν -
　we, us, our, to us (1), 96
ἡμέρα, ἡ - day 32
ἡμέτερος, α,ον - our 100
ἤν + subj.= ἐάν if ever 150
ἦν - I was OR he, she, it was 38,
　70, there was 111
ἤνεγκον aorist of φέρω 67, 114
　(also ἤνεγκα)
ηὗρον - aorist of εὑρίσκω 84

θ

θάλαττα, ἡ - sea 34, 157
θάνατος, ὁ - death 79
θάπτω - bury 114
θάττων,ον - faster 92, 114
θαυμάζω - wonder, marvel, be in
　a state of wonderment 177
θαυμαστός,ή,όν - wonderful,
　marvelous 177
θεός, ὁ and θεά, ἡ - god,
　goddess 44 (Note: θεός can be
　used of goddess as well--see
　Hippocratic Oath)
θησαυρός, ὁ - treasure house,
　treasure 37
θήσω - fut. of τίθημι 142
θνῄσκω - die (in ἀποθνῄσκω)
　91, 128, perfect as present
　τέθνηκα 157, optative
　τεθναίην 79, part. τεθνεώς 91
　or τεθνηκώς 157

θρόνος, ὁ - chair 48

θύρα, ἡ - door 64 (pl. for double doors)

ι

ἰατρός, ὁ - doctor 19

ἰδοῦ - See for yourself! See! (aorist middle command) also ἰδού 221

ἱερός,ά,όν or ός,ον - holy 64

ἵημι - 214 let forth, release, let go; also = utter, throw; in ἀφίημι 165

ἴθι - Go! imperative of εἶμι 51, ἴθι ἐκποδών Get out of the way!

ἱκανός,ή,όν - sufficient, enough 135

ἱκνέομαι - come 157 (ἀφικνέομαι)

ἱμάτιον, τό - cloak, piece of clothing 48

ἵνα + subjunctive - so that 148, 149

ἵππος, ὁ - horse 70

ἴσθι - know! imper. of οἶδα 162

ἴσος,η,ον - equal, equal to + dat. 97

(ἵσταμαι - stand, root of ἀνίσταμαι 13)

ἵστημι -set up, stand up (transitive) 217, aor. ἔστησα 140, aorist passive ἐστάθην 199, intr. aor. ἔστην 120, system 211, intr. perfect as present ἕστηκα 158

ἰσχυρός,ά,όν - strong 89

ἴσως - perhaps (adverb from ἴσος) 187

(ἰχθύς - fish 183)

κ

καθ' = κατά before rough breathing

καθαίρω - cleanse, purify 114

καθαρός,ά.όν - pure, clean 114

καθεύδω - sleep, lie down to sleep 121, imperf. ἐκάθευδε 121

καθίζομαι - sit down 44

καί - and (connective) (2), too, also, even (adv.) (11), 50
καί ... καί - both ... and (2)
καὶ δὴ καί and especially 67
οὐ μόνον ἀλλὰ καί 51

καινός,ή,όν - new 135

καίπερ - even though (+ part.) 83, 89

κακίων,ον - worse 92, 131

κάκιστος,η,ον worst 92, 100, 140

κακοδαίμων, ον - unfortunate, unlucky 84

κακός,ή,όν - bad 19

καλέω - call, invite (13), 19

κάλλιστος,η,ον - most καλός 92, 111

(καλλίων,ον - more καλός 92)
καλός,ή,όν - beautiful, fair, noble, fine, good 48

κάμνω - by weary, be sick 19

κάρπιμος,ον - fruitful 149

καρπός, ὁ - fruit, harvest 111

κατά - + acc. down the length or course of 48; according to 91 + gen. down from, against (as in καταγιγνώσκω)

καταβαίνω - go down 121

καταβλέπω - look down 121

καταγιγνώσκω - make accusation against + gen. 79

κατέρχομαι - go down; come or go back, return 44

κεῖμαι - lie down 19, inf. κεῖσθαι

κέκτημαι - possess, perf. of κτάομαι = acquire, perfect as present) 157, 159; κεκτήσεται 197

κελεύω + acc. or dat. + inf. - urge, bid, command someone to do something 70

κίνδυνος, ὁ danger, risk 142

κλέπτης, ὁ - thief 81

κλέπτω - steal 81

κλίνη, ἡ - bed 191

κλοπή, ἡ - theft 128

κοινωνέω - share, share something (gen.) with someone (dat.) 67

(κράτιστος,η,ον - best, strongest 92, a superlative of ἀγαθός)

κρείττων,ον - better, stronger 92, 114, 114 (compar. of ἀγαθός)

κρίνω - judge 91

κρίσις,εως, ἡ - judgment, contest 91, 94

κρούω - knock (on a door), clap (hands) 181

κρυπτός - hidden 191

κρύπτω - hide 114, κρύψαιντο 187

κτάομαι - acquire, come to possess, often in perfect as present κέκτημαι = I possess 157; fut. perf. κεκτήσεται 197

κτείνω - kill, future κτενῶ (in ἀποκτείνω 142)

κύλιξ,ικος, ἡ - cup 69, 157

κύριος,α,ον or ος,ον - in charge of, master of 64

κύων,κυνός, ἡ/ὁ - dog (2), 70, 77

λ

λαμβάνω - take, get, receive (24), aor. ἔλαβον 111, imperative λαβέ 122 (169)

λανθάνομαι + gen. - forget, be forgetful of 64

λανθάνω - escape notice 165

λέαινα, ἡ - lioness 94

λέγω - tell, say (1) say that (ὅτι, ὡς) (11), tell, command 44, three uses 44

λέγω χαίρειν - say goodbye to 157

λείπω - leave 125. ε/ο aorist system is in Paradigm Section. Segments of the paradigm are scattered throughout the book: 109, 112, 113, 123, 147, 155, 160, 169, 175, 179, 182, 185

λευκός,ή,όν - white 194

λίθος, ὁ - stone, rock 142

λόγος, ὁ - word, speech, line of reasoning, rational account 64

λοιπός,ή,όν - remaining 67

λυπέω - cause pain of mind or body, vex, distress 111 middle - be distressed 187

λύπη, ἡ - grief, pain 135

λύω - release 194

μ

μακρός,ά,όν - long, high, tall (11)

μάλα - very (with adjective) 48, 71; with verb very much, indeed 64, 78

μάλιστα - most, exceedingly (with adjective) 71, 72; most, exceedingly (with verbs) 64, 78
ὡς μάλιστα + adj. 71
+ verb 32, 78

μᾶλλον - more (with adjective) 71, more (with verb) 78; rather (with verb) (78), 170
μᾶλλον ἤ rather than 78

μανθάνω - learn (11), aor. ἔμαθον (13)

μάχη - battle (13), 37

με - me (acc.) (2)

μέγας, μεγάλη, μέγα - big, great (13), 54

πάντες - all persons, everyone (1)

πάντα - all things, all, every (3), 64, **80**

παρά - + acc. to (the side of) 81
+ dat. at (the side of) 48
+ gen. from (the side of)

παρέρχομαι - go by 125

παρέχω - provide 149

πᾶς, **πᾶσα, πᾶν,**
gen. παντός, πάσης, παντός ·
every, all **80**, 84

πάσχω - suffer, undergo aor.
ἔπαθον 157, perf. πέπονθα 162

πατήρ, **πατρός, ὁ** - father **77**, 149

παύομαι - (M) stop (oneself) 177

παύω - stop (someone or something else) 91 (M cease 177)

πείθομαι + dat. - obey, believe in 191, intr. perf. πέποιθα 194

πείθω - persuade 122

πεῖνα, ἡ - hunger 84

πεινάω - be hungry 32

πέμπω - send 28

πένης, ητος, ὁ - poor man or used as adjective 84
(redundant πένης ἀνήρ 89)

πέποιθα - I trust (intrans., perf. as present) 158, 194

πέπονθα - perfect of πάσχω 162

περ - indeed, in fact (adds force to preceding word; sometimes is joined to it, as in εἴπερ, καίπερ, ὅσπερ, ὥσπερ) 89

περί + gen. - about (concerning) (13), 79, + acc. about (around) spatial 142

πέτομαι - fly 70

πετρα, ἡ - cliff 162

πέτρος, ὁ - rock 162

πέφυκα - perf. as pres. 158

πίνω - drink (13),

πίπτω - fall 38, aor. ἔπεσον 111
πίπτω εἰς ὕπνον 131

πιστεύω - trust, trust in + dat. 140

πλεῖστος, η, ον - most 92

πλείων, ον - more 92, 149

πλήν - except + gen. 64
as conjunction 142

πλήττω - strike, aor. ἔπληξε 122

πλούσιος, α, ον - wealthy 48

πλοῦτος, ὁ - wealth 188

ποιέω - do, make (3), make (factitive) + two acc. 84

ποίημα, τό - poem (thing made) (11)

ποιητής, ὁ - poet (13)

ποῖος, α, ον - what sort of a? 140

ποιος, α, ον - some sort of a 170

πόλεμος, ὁ - war 84

πόλις, πόλεως, ἡ - city-state 44, **164**

(πολίτης, ὁ - citizen)

πολλά - many (13) See πολύς

πολλῷ - by far (dat. of πολύς) 100

πολύς, πολλή, πολύ much, pl. many (3), 54

πονέω - toil 111

(πονηρός, ά, όν - wicked fr. πόνος 52)

πόνος, ὁ - toil 111

πορεύομαι - travel, journey 29, aor. ἐπορεύσατο 131

πόρος, ὁ - way across a river, solution to a problem 142

πόσος, η, ον - how much? 19, 163

ποταμός, ὁ - river 94

πότε - when? 70, 88, 163

ποτε - once, ever 70, 88, 163

πότερον (adverb) - whether (as question-asker) 72

πότερος, α, ον - which (of 2) 72, 93

ποῦ - where? 88, 89, 163;
ποῦ γῆς - where on earth? 89

που - somewhere 88, 163

πούς, ποδός, ὁ - foot **77**, 79

πράττω - do, fare, act 125, πέπραξεται 197

πρίν - before + inf, until after a negative verb + indic. 130, 170, used adjectivally 187

πρό - in front of, before + gen. (space) 94 (time) 170

προβαίνω - step forth 122

πρός + acc. - to, towards, against 44

προσέρχομαι - come toward 181

προσέχω νοῦν apply the mind to, pay attention 142

προσπίπτω - fall toward 57

πρόσωπον, τό - face (πρός + ὀπ as in ὄψομαι, that which one looks at) 177

πρῶτος, η, ον = first 32, **46**

πτερόν, τό - feather 97

πτέρυξ, υγος, ἡ - wing 97

πῦρ, πυρός, τό - fire **77**, 89

πῶς how? 88, 91, 163

πως - somehow 88, 163

ρ

ῥᾴδιος, α, ον - easy (11), **52**

ῥάπτης, ὁ - tailor 191

ῥᾷστος, η, ον - easiest 92

ῥᾴων, ον - easier 92, 162

σ

σάκκος, ὁ - sack 149

αὑτόν, ήν = σεαυτόν 96

σε (unemphatic) - you (2)

σέ (emphatic) - you 81

σεαυτόν, ήν - yourself **96**

σελήνη, ἡ - moon 37

σῆμα, τό - sign 81

σημαίνω - signify 121

σιγάω - be silent 94

σιγή, ἡ - silence 142

σῖτος, ὁ - grain, food 32

σκέλος, τό - leg 119

σκηνή, ἡ - tent 44; stage (Graveyard # 29)

σκοτία, ἡ - darkness 38

σός, σή, σόν - your 96, 97

σου (unemphatic) - your, of you (1)

σοῦ (emphatic) - your, of you

σοφός, ή, όν - wise 29, clever 79

σοφία - wisdom 162

σπέρμα, τό - seed 111

σπουδή, ἡ - haste 142, also = seriousness, zeal, fuss

σταθμός - weight 142

στένω - moan, sigh, groan 131

στόνος, ὁ - moan, groan 131

στρατηγός, ὁ - general 191

στρατιώτης, ὁ - soldier 44, **45**

σύ, σέ, (σε), etc. - you (sing.) (1) (2), 96

συγγιγνώσκω ἑαυτῷ - be conscious of, acknowledge, confess + (nom) participle 170

συλλαμβάνω - collect, gather 149

συμβουλεύω - advise 142
middle - consult with + dat. 170

σύμβουλος, ὁ - adviser, counselor 142

σύν - with + dat. 97

συνοικέω - dwell with 194

συντίθημι - put together 100

σφόδρα - intensely, strongly 157

σχολή, ἡ - leisure 29

σῴζω - save 125, σεσώσμεθα 177

σῶμα, τό - body 119

τ

τά - the (3)

τάδε - these here things 64, 65, 67

ταῦτα - these (9), 65

τάχιστος, η, ον - fastest 92, 122

ταχύς, εῖα, ύ - fast, quick 94

τε (postpositive, enclitic) - and
τε καί - (both) and 32 (τε καί is
weaker than καί καί but stronger
than καί alone)
τεῖχος, τό - wall 119
τεθναίην - *may I be dead* 79
τεθνεώς,υῖα,ός - dead 91
τέθνηκα, τεθνηκώς - die, dead
(perf. as present)
τεκών, gen. όντος, ὁ - father,
begetter, pl. parents 149
τελευτάω - end 197
τέλος, τό - end (13), **95**, 100, <u>88</u>
<u>τέμνω</u> - cut (in ἀποτέμνω 70)
τέταρτος,η,ον - fourth 119
τέτταρες,α - four 89, **105**
τῆλε + gen. far from 149
τήν - the (13), **31**
τί - what? (1), **87** why? 32, <u>88</u>
τίνα - what? (13), **87**
τίς - who? (3), **87**
τίθημι - put, place 81, **214**
fut. θήσω 142, aor. ἔθηκα 149
τίκτω - give birth, give birth to
+ acc. 84, aor. ἔτεκον 140
τιμάω - honor 131
τιμή, ἡ - honor 131
τίμιος,α,ον or ος,ον - honored,
valued, valuable 142
τίς, τί - who? what? (1) (3) <u>87</u>
τις, τι - (as adjective) some, a
certain (13), (as noun) somebody,
something 67, 79, **87**, 89
τό - this (1), **31**
τόδε - this here (see ὅδε)
τοι - *y'know* 125
τοιοῦτος,η,ον - of such a sort 149,
<u>163</u>
τολμάω - have the heart, dare,
endure to 149, 197
τόξον, τό - bow 94
τόπος, ὁ - place 91
τοσοῦτος,η,ον - so great, so
much, so many 162, <u>163</u>
τότε - then <u>163</u>, 197
τοῦτο - this (3), <u>65</u>
τρεῖς, τρία - three 84, **105**
τρίτος,η,ον - third 119
τυγχάνω - happen; succeed
aor. ἔτυχες 125
τυφλός,ή,όν - blind 119
τύχη, ἡ - fortune, chance 140

υ

ὑγιεινός,ή,όν - healthy 19

ὕδωρ, ὕδατος, τό - water 67,
68
υἱός, ὁ - son 84, <u>**183**</u>
ὕλη - forest 197
ὑμᾶς, αὐτούς, etc. - ourselves
(reflexive) **96**
ὑμεῖς, ὑμᾶς, ὑμῶν, ὑμῖν - you
[pl.] **96**
ὑμέτερος,α,ον - your (pl.) <u>98</u>, 100
ὑπισχνέομαι + fut. inf. - promise
<u>124</u>, 125
ὕπνος, ὁ - sleep 114, πίπτειν εἰς
ὕπνον 131
ὑπό + gen. - by (gives agent with
passive verb) <u>190</u>, 191
by = under the influence of 194
ὑστεραῖος,α,ον - later, next 67,
(often in τῇ ὑστεραίᾳ ἡμέρᾳ
with ἡμέρα omitted)
ὕστερος,α,ον - later; ὕστερον as
adv. - later, afterwards 100

φ

φαίνομαι - appear, seem, aor.
ἐφάνην 191
φάρμακον, τό - drug, medicine
19, 37, poison 79
φαῦλος,η,ον - crummy,
second- rate 48
φέρω - carry, bear, bring; bear,
endure 44, aor. ἤνεγκον - 67, 114
φεῦ - exclamation of grief, anger,
astonishment or admiration 19
φεύγω - flee 142
φημί (with enclitic forms) - say
142, **210**, usually seen as ἔφη
122, breaks up quotations 131
φθείρω - ruin, spoil 194
φιλέω - like, love (1), 32
φίλος, ὁ or φίλη,ἡ - friend (1), 32
φίλος,η,ον - dear 97
φιλῶν (part.) - **82**
φοβέομαι - fear, be afraid of + acc.
19
φόβος, ὁ - fear 142
φοβερός,ά,όν - fearful 142
φορέω - carry around, wear 48
φυλάττω - guard, protect 79
φωνή, ἡ - voice (22)
φῶς, φωτός, τό - light 38, 57

χ

χαίρω - rejoice (1), rejoice in + dat.
64, λέγω χαίρειν - say goodbye
to 157

χαλεπός,ή,όν - difficult, hard (11)
χάρις,ιτος, ἡ - acc. χάριν -
favor, grace, thanks 194 (in
χάριν ἀποδιδόναι, χάριν
εἰδέναι)
χείρ, χειρός, ἡ - hand, arm (2),
77, 79
(χείρων,ον - worse <u>92</u>)
χελώνη, ἡ - turtle (2), 37
χράομαι - make use of + dat. 140
χρή - it is necessary (acts as verb)
(11), 19, imperfect ἐχρῆν 121,
infinitive χρῆναι 149
χρῆναι - see above
χρήζω + gen. - need, have a lack
or want of 140
χρήσιμος,η,ον or ος,ον - useful
57
χρόνος, ὁ - time 19
χρυσός, ὁ - gold 111
χρυσοῦς,ῆ,οῦν - golden, of gold
157

ψ

ψευδής,ές - false 79

ω

ὦ - used with vocative (1)
ᾧ - dat. of ὅς, ὅ 62
ἐν ᾧ - while 91
ὧδε - thus, in this here way
(adv. of ὅδε) 57, <u>66</u>
ὤν,οὖσα,ὄν - being **98**
ὥρα, ἡ - season 111
ὡς - (1) relative - as 64 (ὡς νόμος
ἐστίν)
(2) how! (in exclamations) 94
(3) ὡς = ὅτι how, that 79, <u>138</u>
(4) ὡς + superlative = as . . .
as possible 32, <u>56</u>, <u>71</u>, 78
(5) ὡς + participle - on the
grounds that (gives
assumption) <u>83</u>
(6) ὡς + subjunctive - so
that, in order that <u>148</u>, 157
ὥσπερ - just as 97
ὥστε + inf. - so as to <u>57</u>
+ indic. - so that, and so <u>84</u>
οὕτως ὥστε + inf. 81
οὕτως ὥστε + verb 84
ὠφελέω + acc. - benefit, be of
service to 125

These are the words needed to translate the exercises and sentences assigned in this book. To create your own Greek, look through the Vocabulary Reviews.

a, an - Leave untranslated
  (for *a certain*, use τις,τι)
accept - δέχομαι
afraid, be afraid of - φοβέομαι
                              + acc.
after - can be expressed by use of
  the aorist participle in a
  genitive absolute
agree with - ὁμολογέω + dat.
all - plural of πᾶς, πᾶσα, πᾶν
although - καίπερ + participle
always - ἀεί
(always) - Use continuous
and - καί
announce - ἀγγέλλω + 3
  constructions in Ind. Disc.
anyone - τις, τι
appear - φαίνομαι
apple - τὸ μῆλον
are - εἰσί(ν) (neut. sing + ἐστι)
as... as can be - ὡς μάλιστα . . .
ask - ἐρωτάω
at - Use dative of place where,
  time when, or circumstance;
  for *at night* use gen. of time
  when (νυκτός, lit., within night)
bad - κακός,ή,όν
battle - ἡ μάχη
be, to - εἶναι (inf. of εἰμί)
be about to - μέλλω
bear - φέρω
beautiful - καλός,ή,όν
before - πρίν + inf.
being - ὤν, οὖσα, ὄν (participle
                        of εἰμί)
best - ἄριστος,η,ον, or
  κράτιστος,η,ον (superlatives
  of ἀγαθός)
better - ἀμείνων,ον, κρείττων,ον
  (comparatives of ἀγαθός)
big, great, large - μέγας,
  μεγάλη, μέγα, compar.
  μείζων,ον
bird - ἡ, ὁ ὄρνις, -ιθος
book - τὸ βιβλίον
both ... and - καὶ A καὶ B,
              or A τε καὶ B
bring, carry - φέρω, fut. οἴσω
brother - ὁ ἀδελφός
burst into tears - Use appropriate
  stem of δακρύω

bury - θάπτω
but - ἀλλά. (δέ = a weak *but*)
but he, but she - ὁ δέ, ἡ δέ (if
                      new subject)
but they - οἱ δέ, αἱ δέ (if new
                          subject)
by - dative of means,
  ὑπό + gen. with passive verb
  dative of agent (with perf. pass.)
certain, a - τις, τι
child - ὁ/ἡ παῖς, gen. παιδός
choose - αἱρέομαι
city, city-state - ἡ πόλις,
                    πόλεως
come - εἶμι, ἔρχομαι
consider - νομίζω (+ acc. + inf.)
creature, living - τὸ ζῷον
cry - δακρύω
custom - ὁ νόμος
dance - ὀρχέομαι
day - ἡ ἡμέρα
dead - τεθνεώς,υῖα,όν or
  τεθνηκώς,υῖα,ός. For *be dead*
  use τέθνηκα (perf. as present)
dear - φίλος,η,ον
deed - τὸ ἔργον
die - θνῄσκω, ἀποθνῄσκω
difficult - χαλεπός,ή,όν
dinner - τὸ δεῖπνον
do, make - ποιέω
doctor - ὁ ἰατρός
dog - ὁ, ἡ κύων, κυνός
drink - πίνω
dwell - οἰκέω
each other - ἀλλήλους,ας,α
ear - τὸ οὖς, ὠτός
easy - ῥᾴδιος,α,ον
eat - ἐσθίω
elder - ὁ γέρων, γέροντος
ever - ποτε
every, all - πᾶς,πᾶσα,πᾶν
evil - Use τὸ κακόν
exceedingly - Use superlative or
  μάλιστα
fall - πίπτω
false - ψευδής,ές
father - ὁ πατήρ, gen. πατρός
fear - φοβέομαι
field - ὁ ἀγρός

find - εὑρίσκω + part. or inf.
  in ind. disc.
finger - ὁ δάκτυλος
fire - τὸ πῦρ, πυρός
food - ὁ σῖτος
foolish - μῶρος,α,ον
foot - ὁ πούς, ποδός
for (prep.) - Use dative case
friend - ὁ φίλος, ἡ φίλη
gift - τὸ δῶρον
give - δίδωμι
go - εἶμι, ἔρχομαι, βαίνω
gold - ὁ χρυσός
good - ἀγαθός,ή,όν,
  superl. ἄριστος,η,ον
  or κράτιστος,η,ον
goodness - Use τὸ ἀγαθόν
great - μέγας,μεγάλη, μέγα
Greek - Ἑλληνικός,η,ον
guard - φυλάττω
hand - ἡ χείρ, χειρός
happen to - τυγχάνω + dat.
happiness - ἡ εὐδαιμονία
happy - εὐδαίμων,ον
hate - μισέω
have - ἔχω, OR use ἐστι + dat.
healthy - ὑγιεινός,ή,όν
hear - ἀκούω + 3 constructions
  in ind. disc.
her - αὐτήν, αὐτῆς, αὐτῇ
herself - (reflexive) ἑαυτήν,
  ἑαυτῆς, ἑαυτῇ or αὐτήν,
  αὐτῆς, αὐτῇ OR use Middle
  Voice; (emphatic) αὐτή
hide - κρύπτω (hide oneself
                  κρύπτομαι)
him, his - αὐτόν, αὐτοῦ, αὐτῷ
himself - (reflexive) ἑαυτόν,
  ἑαυτοῦ, ἑαυτῷ or αὐτόν,
  αὐτοῦ, αὐτῷ; (emphatic)
  αὐτός OR use Middle Voice
honor - τιμάω
horse - ὁ ἵππος
house - ἡ οἰκία
hungry, be - πεινάω
I - ἐγώ (only emphatic)
if only - εἴθε or εἰ γάρ + opt.
  or opt. alone in future wishes,
  εἴθε or εἰ γάρ + past in
  impossible wishes (see p. 182)

in - ἐν + dat. (For "in" 5 days use
gen. of time withink which;
for rejoice "in" χαίρω + dat.)

in order that - ἵνα, ὡς, ὅπως

in reality - τῷ ὄντι

in the following way, in this here
way - ὧδε

in this way - οὕτω(ς)

intend - μέλλω + future infinitive

into - εἰς, + acc.

invite - καλέω

is - ἐστί(ν) , from εἰμι

is possible - ἔστι (accented)

it - αὐτό, αὐτοῦ, αὐτῷ

judge - ὁ δικαστής

just - δίκαιος,α,ον

keep silence, be silent - σιγάω

kind - τὸ γένος

king - ὁ βασιλεύς, gen. -έως

know - γιγνώσκω, οἶδα

large - μέγας, μεγάλη, μέγα

laugh - γελάω

law - ὁ νόμος

learn - μανθάνω + ὅτι/ὡς or
part. in Ind. Disc.

leave - λείπω

leisure - ἡ σχολή

lest - μή

let - Use third person imperative

letter -
(correspondence) ἡ ἐπιστολή,
(of alphabet) τὸ γράμμα

life - ἡ ζωή

like - φιλέω

lioness - ἡ λέαινα

listen - ἀκούω

live - ζάω - p. 114

living creature - τὸ ζῷον

long - μακρός,ά,όν

love - φιλέω

majority - οἱ πολλοί

make - ποιέω; make a speech -
λόγον ποιοῦμαι

man (person) - ὁ ἄνθρωπος OR
omit with masculine adjective

man (male, husband) - ὁ ἀνήρ,
gen. ἀνδρός

many - pl. of πολύς,πολλή,πολύ

me - με, ἐμέ, etc.

messenger - ὁ ἄγγελος

money - τὸ ἀργύριον

more (adj.) - πλείων,ον

more (adverb) - μᾶλλον OR use
comparatiave

most (adverb) - μάλιστα OR use
superlative

mother - ἡ μήτηρ, gen. μητρός

much, many - πολύς, πολλή, πολύ

my - μου (emphatic ἐμοῦ),
or ἐμός,ή,όν

myself - (reflexive) ἐμαυτόν,οῦ,ῷ
or ἐμαυτήν,ῆς,ῇ OR use
Middle Voice; (emphatic)
αὐτός, αὐτή

name - τὸ ὄνομα

new - νέος,α,ον

night - ἡ νύξ, gen. νυκτός

no one - οὐδείς, οὐδεμία

noble - καλός,ή,όν

not - οὐ, οὐκ, οὐχ; μή

nothing - οὐδέν

of - Use genitive case

old - παλαιός,ά,όν
(of people - γεραιός,ά,όν)

once - ποτε; (once) - Shows that
aspect is aorist

one - εἷς,μία, ἕν

one / another - Use article (ὁ, ἡ,
τό sing. or pl. in any case)
+ μέν, article + δέ

order someone to do something -
κελεύω + acc. or dat. + inf.

order, in order that (purpose) - ἵνα
or ὡς + subj.

our - ἡμῶν ; ἡμέτερος,α,ον

ourselves - ἡμᾶς αὐτούς or
αὐτάς, ἡμῶν αὐτῶν, ἡμῖν
αὐτοῖς or αὐταῖς

people - plural of ἄνθρωπος
OR omit with masc. plural
adjective

perceive - αἰσθάνομαι + 3
constructions in ind. disc.

person - ὁ ἄνθρωπος OR omit
with masc. singular adjective

persuade - πείθω

poem - τὸ ποίημα, gen.
ποιήματος

poet - ὁ ποιητής

possible, it is - ἔστι + dat. or
acc.+ inf.

promise - ὑπισχνέομαι + future
infinitive

question - ἐρωτάω

read - ἀναγιγνώσκω

reality - τὸ ὄν (p. 98)

receive - λαμβάνω
(also δέχομαι)

rejoice - χαίρω

rejoice in - χαίρω + dat.

remain - μένω

remaining - λοιπός,ή,όν

rich - πλούσιος,α,ον

road - ἡ ὁδός

robe - τὸ ἱμάτιον

save - σῴζω

say - λέγω ὅτι, ὡς or acc. inf.
in ind. disc.
φημί + inf.

see - ὁράω, βλέπω

seek - ζητέω

seem - δοκέω, φαίνομαι

send - πέμπω

share, take or give a share of -
κοινωνέω + gen.

short - μικρός,ά,όν

show - δείκνυμι

sick, be - νοσέω

silence, keep - σιγάω

silent, be - σιγάω

since - ἅτε + participle,
διότι (conjunction)

small - μικρός,ά,όν

so as to - ὥστε + inf.

so . . . as to - οὕτως . . . ὥστε
+inf.

so as for X to - ὥστε + acc. + inf.

so that - ὥστε + indicative verb
(result)
ἵνα, ὡς, ὅπως + subj.
(purpose)

so . . . that - οὕτως . . . ὥστε
+ indicative verb

soldier - ὁ στρατιώτης

some - do not translate OR (= a
certain) use a form of τις,τι

some / others - οἱ μέν, οἱ δέ
or αἱ μέν, αἱ δέ

somehow - πως

someone - τις, τι

something - τι

speak - λέγω

speech - λόγος, ὁ; make a speech
- λόγον ποιοῦμαι

stay - μένω

steal - κλέπτω

step - βαίνω

stop - παύω, stop oneself
παύομαι

story - ὁ μῦθος

stranger, guest-host - ὁ ξένος

strong - ἰσχυρός,ά,όν

suffer - πάσχω

swear - ὄμνυμι + inf. in ind. disc.

sweet - γλυκύς,εῖα,ύ or
ἡδύς,εῖα,ύ

swift - ταχύς,εῖα,ύ,
compar. θάττων,ον

take - λαμβάνω

tell - λέγω; tell someone to -
    λέγω + dat (or acc.) + inf
    OR κελεύω + dat + inf.
tent - ἡ σκηνή
terrible - δεινός,ή,όν
than - Use ἤ + same case or
    gen. of comparison
that - (in indirect discourse) ὅτι
    OR untranslated in indirect
    discourse with infinitive;
    (as demonstrative) ἐκεῖνος,η,ο;
    (as relative) ὅς,ἥ,ὅ
the - ὁ, ἡ, τό
their - αὐτῶν
their own - αὐτῶν, ἑαυτῶν
them, their, to/for them - αὐτούς,
    αὐτάς, αὐτά, etc.
themselves - (reflexive)
    ἑαυτούς, ἑαυτάς or αὐτούς,
    αὐτάς OR use Middle Voice;
    (emphatic) αὐτοί, αὐταί, αὐτά
there is, there are (neut. pl.) - ἔστι
these - plural of οὗτος, αὕτη,
             τοῦτο
these the following, these here -
    οἵδε,αἵδε,τάδε
thief - ὁ κλεπτής
thing - Leave untranslated. (Use
    neuter of an adjective.)
think - νομίζω (+ acc. + inf.)
this - οὗτος, αὕτη, τοῦτο
this-here or this-the following -
    ὅδε, ἥδε, τόδε
    in this-here way, in this-the-
    following way - ὧδε
those - plural of ἐκεῖνος,η,ο

three - τρεῖς (declined p. 105)
throw - βάλλω
thus - οὕτω(ς)
time - ὁ χρόνος
to - often shown by use of dat.
    (sometimes πρός, ἐπί, εἰς,
    all with the accus.)
tongue - ἡ γλῶττα
travel - πορεύομαι
true - ἀληθής,ές
turtle - ἡ χελώνη
unjust - ἄδικος,ον
until - πρίν + indic. verb
    with negative main verb
us - ἡμᾶς; to/for us - ἡμῖν
useful - χρήσιμος,η,ν or ος,ον
very - μάλα
victory - ἡ νίκη
voice - ἡ φωνή
want - ἐθέλω, βούλομαι
way, in such a way as to -
    οὕτως ὥστε + inf.
    in such a way that -
    οὕτως ὥστε + indic.
wealthy - πλούσιος,α,ον
wear - φορέω
well - εὖ
were - ἦσθα, ἦν, ἦσαν, etc. (Use
    imperfect of εἰμί)
what? (in direct question) - τί, τίνα
what(ever)? (in indirect question)
    - ὅστις, ἥτις, ὅ τι
whatever (indefinite relative)
    - ὅστις, ἥτις, ὅ τι
which? (in direct question) - τίς, τί;

which(ever)? (in indirect question)
    - ὅστις, ἥτις, ὅ τι
which (relative) - ὅς, ἥ, ὅ
    OR use a participle;
which(ever) (indefinite relative)
    - ὅστις, ἥτις, ὅ τι
who? (in direct question) - τίς,
                τίνες
who(ever)? (in indirect question)
    - ὅστις, οἵτινες
who (relative) - ὅς, ἥ, ὅ
    OR use a participle;
who(ever) (indefinite relative)
    - ὅστις, ἥτις, ὅ τι
why? - τί
willing, be - ἐθέλω
wine - ὁ οἶνος
wing - ἡ πτέρυξ, πτέρυγος
wise - σοφός,ή,όν
wish - ἐθέλω, βούλομαι
with - often shown by dative;
    also μετά + gen.
    (accompaniment)
woman, wife - ἡ γυνή, γυναικός
    OR omit with fem. adjective
worthy - ἄξιος,α,ον + gen.
write - γράφω
you - σύ, σου, etc., ὑμεῖς, etc.
your - σου (emphatic σοῦ);
    σός,ή,όν; ὑμῶν;
    ὑμέτερος,η,ον
your own - ὑμῶν αὐτῶν
yourself, yourselves - (reflexive)
    σεαυτόν,ήν; ὑμᾶς αὐτούς or
    αὐτάς OR use Middle Voice;
    (emphatic) αὐτοί, αὐταί

Greek and English letters are interspersed.
Bold page numbers indicate especially important information.
First use of a grammatical form in conversation may be included.

*See Dictionary for pages where paradigms and key Greek words can be found.

Appendix: Embroidery in Conversation

The following conversation, an expansion of the script for Day # 4, is taken without change from an audiotape of the fourth day of a beginning ancient Greek class I taught at Butler University September 4, 1992. Time of the tape is **2 minutes and 7 seconds**. I speak at nearly normal speed, students far more slowly. Pronunciation is with uncontracted vowels.

During the **two-minute** interchange **155 Greek words** (based on 13 lexical entries) are used by teacher and students, **149** correctly. It is possible to present an extraordinary amount of ancient Greek in a short time by speaking. Imagine how many Greek words could be *read* in two minutes by the fourth day of class. Considerably less!

The conversation is far from boring to students. Speaking ancient Greek is challenging, and the kernel utterances keep changing slightly. The progression goes from (a) ὁράω ταῦτα τὰ γράμματα, (old material), to (b) ἐθέλω γράφειν ταῦτα τὰ γράμματα (more complex old material), to (c) ἔχω γράφειν ταῦτα τὰ γράμματα (new use of ἔχω), to (d) ἔχω λέγειν ταῦτα τὰ γράμματα (new use of ἔχω with new vocabulary word, λέγω).

There is repetition of the old and sequencing of the new. We go from the better known to the less known to the unknown. The first and second person are the most familiar. They are used over and over again before the less familiar third person singular--ἔχει--is slipped in, probably for the second time in the course.

Learning is natural and effortless. In two minutes students have earned a new usage (ἔχω), a new vocabulary word (λέγω), have re-used the infinitive (learned the day before), and have reviewed the hortatory subjunctive (learned on the first day), as well as having heard familiar words over and over. Multiply this by about twenty, and you can imagine *how much* students can learn, and *how well* they can learn it, in a single class period.

By using ancient Greek conversationally, students acquire in two weeks a *working* vocabulary of over 50 words--not precariously, by studying and reading them several times, but naturally and firmly, by repeated use, having heard these words probably 80 times on average.

Mistakes are underlined. Corrections, both self-corrections and corrections by the teacher, are in bold face. We can see a student absorbing correction. Cammie (who will go on to be an A+ student) begins by mispronouncing ἔχω and also ταῦτα. In the end, after being gently corrected a second time, she makes the sound of ἔχω correctly, and without any prompting, pronounces ταῦτα correctly on her second time around. This is learning in action!

No one has been left out. Eric has the most difficulty of all. He is never shamed. He goes at his own slow pace. He learns primarily by visual means and is often uncomfortable without something written in front of him. He has been told that he will be able to "catch up" once the material is learned primarily through reading.

I once suggested sharing a panel on conversational ancient Greek with an expert on Greek pronunciation. He replied with horror, "Oh no, I would never do that--not until I can speak without errors." I was grateful to him for showing me the attitude that has to be forsaken if ancient Greek is ever to be spoken. In the words of John Henry Cardinal Newman:

> *A man would do nothing if he waited until he could do it so well*
> *that no one would find fault with what he has done.*

Skill in embroidery develops over time. (The transcript was made during my fifth year of teaching ancient Greek by conversation.) Please keep in mind that even the most rudimentary conversation will please your students and is highly educational.

Paula Saffire
Butler University 1999

Teacher: ὦ φίλη (looking at Cammie*, pointing to alphabet on blackboard)

ὁράεις ταῦτα τὰ γράμματα;

Cammie: ναί, ὁράοι-- (Cammie pronounces the omega as if it were οι.)

Teacher: (with an intonation of approval, as a prompt not a critiosm) "ὁράω"--

Cammie: τότα--

Teacher: (with the same intonation) "ταῦτα"--

Cammie: τὸ γράμματα.

Teacher: "τὰ γράμματα. "ταῦτα τὰ γράμματα."

καὶ σύ, Eric, ὁράεις ταῦτα τὰ γράμματα;

Eric: ναί, ὁράεις--

Teacher: "ὁράω"-- (pause) "ταῦτα τὰ--"

Eric: ταῦτα τὰ-- (pause)

Teacher: "τὰ γράμματα"--

Eric: τὰ γράμματα.

Teacher: καὶ σύ, ὦ Judy, ἐθέλεις γράφειν ταῦτα τὰ γράμματα;

ἐθέλεις γράφειν ταῦτα τὰ γράμματα;

Judy: ναί, ἐθέλω γράφειν ταῦτα τὰ γράμματα.

Teacher: καὶ-- And you know... If I say ἔχω with one of those "to do" forms, with an

infinitive, it means "are you able to?" It sounds like "do you have to?" but it really

means "do you have the power to?" ἔχεις γράφειν ταῦτα τὰ γράμματα;

ὦ Shelley, ἔχεις γράφειν ταῦτα τὰ γράμματα;

Shelley: ἔχω γράφειν ταῦτα τὰ γράμματα.

*Names have been changed. Gender remains the same.

Teacher: Yes, "ἔχω γράφειν ταῦτα τὰ γράμματα." ἔχεις λέγειν ταῦτα τὰ γράμματα;

λέγειν means "to say." Vera, ἔχεις λέγειν ταῦτα τὰ γράμματα;

Vera: ναί, ἔχω λέγ--?

Teacher: "λέγειν"--

Vera: <u>ταῦταυ</u>? <u>ταῦτο</u>?

Teacher: "ταῦτα"--

Vera: ταῦτα τὰ γράμματα.

Teacher: ὦ Cammie, Vera ἔχει λέγειν ταῦτα τὰ γράμματα; Vera ἔχει λέγειν?

Cammie: ναί, Vera <u>λέχει</u>--

Teacher: (in prompting tone) "ἔχει"--

Cammie: ἔχει λέγειν <u>ταῦτο</u>--**ταῦτα** τὰ γράμματα.

Teacher: καὶ σύ, ἔχεις λέγειν ταῦτα τὰ γράμματα; καὶ σύ (pause), ἔχεις λέγειν;

Cammie: ναί, <u>ἔχοι</u>--

Teacher: "**ἔχω**"--

Cammie: Oh, **ἔχω**. **ἔχω** λέγειν ταῦτα τὰ γράμματα.

Teacher: πάντα τὰ γράμματα; πάντα τὰ γράμματα; All of them?

Cammie: ναί, πάντα τὰ γράμματα. (Cammie laughs at her own confidence.)

Teacher: εὖγε. λέγωμεν--what is λέγωμεν, with that ⁻ωμεν ending?

What is λέγωμεν?

Class (at more or less the same time): "Let's!"

Teacher: "Let's say." λέγωμεν πάντα τὰ γράμματα. πάντες ἄμα.

OK? All together.   (Class proceeds to read the alphabet out loud from the blackboard.)

'Twas brillig, and the slithy toves

Did gyre and gimble in the wabe:

All mimsy were the borogoves,

And the mome raths outgrabe.

from "Jabberwocky" by Lewis Carroll

This is nonsense, but it is controlled nonsense. We can understand the grammar of the verse even if we don't know what the words mean. This is what a passage in ancient Greek should look like to you after the first year. Second-year Greek is for building up vocabulary. First-year Greek is for mastering the grammatical forms so that the structure of a sentence will be clear.

It is not always a trivial matter to unravel grammar. In "Jabberwocky" it is hard to guess that "outgrabe" is the past tense of "outgribe" as "gave" is of "give." So it will be in Greek. Some Greek will be immediately and delightfully clear. At other times, the Greek will be more of a puzzle. It is my hope that this book will give you enough information to make a start on reading, dictionary in hand, whatever Greek you choose.

--χαίρετε, ὦ φίλοι

--χαῖρε, ὦ φίλε

--χαῖρε, ὦ φίλη

Printed by
Libri Plureos GmbH · Friedensallee 273
22763 Hamburg · Germany